The Writer's Presence

A Pool of Essays

The Writer's Presence
A Pool of Essays

EDITED BY

Donald McQuade
University of California, Berkeley

Robert Atwan
Seton Hall University

Bedford Books *of* St. Martin's Press
Boston

For Bedford Books
Publisher: Charles H. Christensen
Associate Publisher/General Manager: Joan E. Feinberg
Managing Editor: Elizabeth M. Schaaf
Developmental Editor: Jane Betz
Production Editor: John Amburg
Copyeditor: Susanna Brougham
Cover Design: Hannus Design Associates
Cover Art: "Today Is" (1966–67), Billy Morrow Jackson. Collection of the Butler Institute of American Art, Youngstown, OH. Through the cooperation of The Jane Haslem Gallery, Washington, D.C.
Cover Photograph: Courtesy of Billy Morrow Jackson.

Library of Congress Catalog Card Number: 92–83848

Manufactured in the United States of America.

8 7 6 5 4
f e d c b a

For information, write: St. Martin's Press, Inc.
175 Fifth Avenue, New York, NY 10010

Editorial Offices: Bedford Books *of* St. Martin's Press
29 Winchester Street, Boston, MA 02116

ISBN: 0–312–08480–3

Acknowledgments

Diane Ackerman, "The Silent Grandeur of the Grand Canyon." Copyright © 1987 by Diane Ackerman. Originally published in *Harvard Magazine*. Reprinted by permission of the author.

Maya Angelou, " 'What's Your Name, Girl?' " From *I Know Why the Caged Bird Sings* by Maya Angelou. Copyright © 1969 by Maya Angelou. Reprinted by permission of Random House, Inc.

Acknowledgments and copyrights are continued at the back of the book on pages 669–672, which constitute an extension of the copyright page.

Preface
for Instructors

The Writer's Presence pools together a generous selection of highly readable essays on a variety of engaging topics. We think the book is unique in its overall design. We wanted an arrangement of selections that would generally accommodate two basic types of writing courses — those that build the syllabus around the familiar forms of nonfiction writing and those that place a premium on instructional flexibility. We therefore divided our selections into the three most commonly taught essay types — personal, expository, and persuasive — but within those three chapters we simply arranged the writers in alphabetical order. This dual organization should appeal both to instructors who prefer to skip around the book unencumbered by a top-heavy design and to other instructors who would rather use the selections to focus on different modes of writing. These two procedures are, of course, extreme examples; we imagine many teachers will appreciate the abundant opportunities here for *both* flexibility and focus.

Each essay in *The Writer's Presence* features the distinctive intellectual "signature" that marks all memorable writing: the presence of a lively individual mind grappling with the challenges that a writer encounters when attempting to establish an identity, to shape information into meaning, or to contend with issues through conversation or debate. In this sense, *The Writer's Presence* is also designed to provide instructors with an inviting "pool" of essays — a wealth of interconnected essays organized to be readily accessible for varying instructional needs and to strengthen the compositional abilities of your students.

DIVERSE ESSAYS WITH A STRONG WRITER'S PRESENCE

Most of us are better trained at recognizing originality in someone else's writing than representing it in our own. That's not surprising, since originality involves the ability both to articulate a fresh view of a subject and to offer that perception in a distinctive, memorable manner. Sustained attention to these compositional matters informs the selections reprinted in *The Writer's Presence*. Each essay exhibits abundant evidence of a strong, independent mind at work — forging a distinct personal presence in many different kinds of writing and for many purposes and audiences. Ranging widely across subjects, methods of development, and stylistic patterns (as well as idiosyncrasies), these essays illustrate the expectations as well as the uncertainties that surface when a writer attempts to create a memorable individual presence in prose. The same prospects and problems often motivate readers to extend their thinking into an enduring written form.

More than half of the seventy-eight selections in *The Writer's Presence* feature the memorable voices of women and minorities, and an even greater proportion of these essays were first published after 1985 — much higher percentages in both categories than in any similar collection. The freshness of the selections creates plentiful teaching and learning opportunities juxtaposing familiar and emerging voices, long-standing and recent issues, while at the same time providing sources for classroom discussion and writing exercises.

FLEXIBLE ORGANIZATION

Organized to emphasize its instructional flexibility, *The Writer's Presence* presents seventy-eight essays in three alphabetical-by-author sections: Establishing an Identity, Shaping Information, and Contending with Issues. This arrangement balances personal, expository, and argumentative writing, yet without imposing an order or specifying an instructional context for working with individual selections. With its organizational, thematic, and stylistic variety and its wealth of pedagogical possibility, *The Writer's Presence* encourages the instructor to experiment with different expressions of his or her distinctive instructional vision concerning the interactions of reading, thinking, and writing.

HELPFUL AND UNOBTRUSIVE APPARATUS

In the spirit of sustaining students' attention to the texture of voices and ideas that constitute *The Writer's Presence*, we have kept the instructional apparatus to a minimum. No section introductions or headnotes predispose students to a particular interpretation before they have had the opportunity to read the selections themselves. We trust that this openness will facilitate a more productive and unencumbered dialogue between writer and reader — as well as between one selection (and section) and another. For contextual purposes, however, we have included an unobtrusive biographical note on each writer at the end of the book.

Yet *The Writer's Presence* doesn't sacrifice focus for the sake of variety. Following each essay are clusters of questions that help guide students through a careful rereading of the essay. Presented to emphasize The Reader's Presence, these questions draw attention to the specific and different ways in which a reader can be present in a piece of writing — either as an implied reader (the reader imagined by the writer) or as an actual reader. The questions following each selection will develop students' abilities to command the respectful attention of those who read their writing.

RESOURCES FOR TEACHING THE WRITER'S PRESENCE

Carefully managing the amount of instructional apparatus in *The Writer's Presence* does not weaken our commitment to provide teachers with a wealth of specific instructional activities. Accompanying *The Writer's Presence* is an unusually extensive spiral-bound instructor's manual. In addition to an annotated table of contents with a distinctive set of Notes to the Instructor introducing each essay, this manual includes a thorough overview of the pedagogical prospects in each essay, specific strategies for teaching compositional aspects of each essay, and a discussion of the questions posed in The Reader's Presence. Each entry in *Resources for Teaching The Writer's Presence* also includes writing assignments for each selection, as well as a discussion of the connections between selections and sections. Rhetorical and thematic tables of contents point to additional teaching possibilities.

ACKNOWLEDGMENTS

The Writer's Presence grew out of extensive discussions over the past two years with the many teachers who worked with *The Winchester Reader* in their composition classes. We learned from these conversations that the majority of these instructors preferred to pick and choose — at their own discretion and with their own instructional purposes — from among the most teachable reading selections we offered in that book. The plan to develop *The Writer's Presence* emerged from those spirited discussions about broadening the range of material presented to students of writing and simplifying its organization.

We have carried over from *The Winchester Reader* the essays that instructors identified as the most engaging and successful in their classes, and we have streamlined the organization of this new collection to make it as flexible and useful as possible. From its inception, *The Writer's Presence* has been a truly collaborative enterprise. We are grateful to the many instructors across the country who generously took the time to tell us about what did — and did not — work well when they used *The Winchester*

Reader in their writing classes: Lisa Altomari, New York University; Maurice H. Barr, Spokane Community College; Gerri Black, Stockton State College; Dolores M. Burton, Boston University; Michael S. Connell, University of Iowa; Chase Crossingham, University of South Carolina; Jessica Deforest, Michigan State University; Mary Devaney, Rutgers University — Newark Campus; Debra DiPiazza, Bernard M. Baruch College (CUNY); Grace Farrell, Butler University; Joan Gabriele, University of Colorado; Christie Anderson Garcia, Spokane Falls Community College; Jane Gatewood, Mary Washington College; Brian Hale, University of South Carolina; Nancy B. Johnson, Pace University; Harriet Malinowitz, Hunter College (CUNY); Denice Martone, New York University; Andrew Mossin, Temple University; Marty Patton, University of Missouri — Columbia; Gary D. Pratt, Brandeis University; Catherine S. Quick, University of Missouri — Columbia; Larry Rodgers, Kansas State University; Lissa Schneider, University of Miami; Constance Fletcher Smith, Mary Washington College; Roger Sorkin, University of Massachusetts — Dartmouth; J. F. Stenerson, Pace University; Steven Strang, Massachusetts Institute of Technology; Pamela Topping, Long Island University — Southampton Campus; Donna M. Turner, University of North Dakota; Sandra Urban, Loyola University of Chicago.

In addition, we are grateful to the instructors in the Expository Writing Program at New York University — Alfred Guy, Lisa Altomari, Karen Boiko, Darlene Forrest, Mary Helen Kolisnyk, Jim Marcall, Denice Martone, and Will McCormack — for taking the time to talk with us and for sharing their ideas.

We would also like to express our appreciation to the professional staff at Bedford Books of St. Martin's Press for their encouragement and for their innumerable contributions to this project. We drew frequently on the intelligence, imagination, and patience of our editor, Jane Betz, throughout the development of *The Writer's Presence*. Her advice and support were indispensible in producing a book aimed at improving student reading and writing. We also benefited from the assistance of Andrea Goldman. John Amburg, the production editor for *The Writer's Presence* and his assistant Heidi Hood guided the project through the complicated process of production decisions and recastings with an admirable professionalism. We are also grateful to Hannus Design Associates for the elegant and inviting look of the book's cover.

As ever, Chuck Christensen, the publisher of Bedford Books, offered us spirited encouragement, first-rate and rigorous advice, as well as seemingly boundless suggestions for improving the project. He never hesitated to urge us to venture with an idea or to explore an instructional feature of the book if it might make our purposes clearer and more useful to teachers and students. And when our conversations with the editorial staff of Bedford Books occasionally headed toward uncertainty, we all relied on the steady editorial presence of associate publisher Joan Feinberg, who invariably helped us convert pedagogical principle into sound instructional practice.

Jack Roberts of Rutgers University and Alix Schwartz of the University of California, Berkeley, contributed their intelligence, accomplishments as teachers, and, most importantly, their sense of pedagogical responsibility in helping us to develop the instructor's manual. Their experience as dedicated and innovative teachers is everywhere evident in the comprehensive instructional guide that accompanies this book, and we are delighted that they participated in exploring the richness of the selections we have reprinted. We thank too David Harris who helped us with research and manuscript preparation. We would also like to acknowledge Soo Meek Hahn's skills as a researcher and her accomplishments as a writer. Her thumbnail biographical sketches at the end of the *The Writer's Presence* are models of succinctness and invitations to further reading.

Finally, we hope that Helene, Gregory, and Emily Atwan, along with Susanne, Christine, and Marc McQuade, will share our satisfaction in seeing this project in print and our pleasure in continuing our productive collaboration.

Donald McQuade
Robert Atwan

Contents

"My longing was wrong in the eyes of my mother, whose hazel eyes were the eyes of the world, and if that longing continued unchecked, the unwieldy shape of my fate would be cast, and I'd be subjected to a lifetime of scorn."

"My first notebook was a Big Five tablet, given to me by my mother with the sensible suggestion that I stop whining and learn to amuse myself by writing down my thoughts."

"The more I read, the more I was led to abhor and detest my enslavers. I could regard them in no other light than a band of successful robbers, who had left their homes, and gone to Africa, and stolen us from our homes, and in a strange land reduced us to slavery. I loathed them as being the meanest as well as the most wicked of men."

"And I knew that no one would every want to marry me. I had no breasts. I would never have breasts."

"I write because in the act of creation there comes that mysterious, abundant sense of being both parent and child; I am giving birth to an Other and simultaneously being reborn as child in the playground of creation."

"Suddenly the whole room broke into a sea of shouting, as they saw me rise. Waves of rejoicing swept the place. Women leaped in the air. My aunt threw her arms around me. The minister took me by the hand and led me to the platform."

"Among the thousand white persons, I am a dark rock surged upon, and overswept, but through it all, I remain myself. When covered by the waters, I am; and the ebb but reveals me again."

"I didn't realize at the time that my flaws were imagined, not real. I felt compelled to measure up to a cultural ideal in a culture that had never asked me what my ideal was."

"Sometimes when I was growing up, my identity seemed to hurtle toward me and paste itself right to my face."

"When I pulled the trigger I did not hear the bang or feel the kick — one never does when a shot goes home — but I heard the devilish roar of glee that went up from the crowd."

"Sometimes I feel I have seen too long from too many disconnected angles: white, Jewish, anti-Semite, racist, anti-racist, once-married, lesbian, middle-class, feminist, exmatriate southerner, *split at the root* — that I will never bring them whole."

"My brother calls. He's always envied me, my woman's body. The same body I live in and have cursed for its softness. He asks me how I feel about myself. He says, "You know, you are really our father's first-born son.""

"The difference between me and these daughters was that they saw me, because of my sex, as destined from birth to become like their fathers, and therefore as an enemy to their desires. But I knew better . . . I was an ally."

"I have a nine-year old's vision of wealth that would save us from ourselves. For weeks I had drunk Kool-Aid and watched morning reruns of *Father Knows Best,* whose family was so uncomplicated in its routine that I very much wanted to imitate it. The first step was to get my brother and sister to wear shoes at dinner."

"She cast back a worried glance. To her, the youngish black man — a broad six feet two inches with a beard and billowing hair, both hands shoved into the pockets of a bulky military jacket — seemed menacingly close. After a few more quick glimpses, she picked up her pace and was soon running in earnest."

"Black though I may be, it is impossible for me to sit in my single-family house with two cars in the driveway and a swing set in the back yard and *not* see the role class has played in my life."

"Lately, I've been giving more thought to the kind of English my mother speaks. Like others, I have described it to people as "broken" or "fractured" English. But I wince when I say that. It has always bothered me that I can think of no way to describe it other than "broken," as if it were damaged and needed to be fixed, as if it lacked a certain wholeness and soundness."

"Where the BB pellet struck there is a glob of whitish scar tissue, a hideous cataract, on my eye. Now when I stare at people — a favorite pastime, up to now — they will stare back. Not at the 'cute' little girl, but at her scar."

"Summertime, oh summertime, pattern of life indelible, the fadeproof lake, the woods unshatterable, the pasture with the sweetfern and the juniper forever and ever, summer without end."

II. SHAPING INFORMATION   *163*

"In the canyon's long soliloquy of rock, parrots of lights move about the grottos, and real swifts loop and dart, white chevrons on each flank. The silence is broken only by the sounds of air whistling through the gorges and insects or bird song."

"What men know and presume about the earth is part of it, passing always back into it, carried on by it into what they do not know. Even their abuses of it, their diminishments and dooms, belong to it."

"Gossip . . . has a leveling effect, in conveying as shallow and ordinary what is unfathomable. It levels, moreover, by talking of all persons in the same terms, so that even the exceptionally gifted, the dissident, and the artist are brought down to the lowest common denominator."

"There is a close nexus between language and self-perception, self-awareness, self-identity, and self-esteem. Just as our thoughts affect our language, so does our language affect our thoughts and eventually our actions and behavior."

"Smiles are associated with joy, relief, and amusement. But smiles are by no means limited to the expression of positive emotions: People of many differ-

ent cultures smile when they are frightened, embarrassed, angry, or miserable."

"C.E.O. whose grip melts into a glove of putty when he shakes the hand of an important client? Would a criminal hire an effeminate lawyer to defend him in court, or the electorate vote for an effeminate candidate in a major election?"

shop to be useful and productive members of our class and society. We shop
to remind ourselves how much is available to us. We shop to remind ourselves how much is to be striven for. We shop to assert our superiority to the
material objects that spread themselves before us."

among the people whose daily bread it is, is one of the things that makes history."

"We are unalterably opposed to the presentation of the female body being stripped, bound, raped, tortured, mutilated, and murdered in the name of commercial entertainment and free speech."

"If anything, an epithet is designed to short-circuit rationality, to inflame feelings, to draw a curtain, the color of boiling blood, across the life of the mind. Further, it is not just the life of the mind that is threatened: behind the word 'nigger' hangs the noose, just as the ovens burn and smoke hovers behind the word 'kike.'"

"Behind this celebration of the American woman's victory, behind the news, cheerfully and endlessly repeated, that the struggle for women's rights is won, another message flashes: you may be free and equal now, but you have never been more miserable."

"Rather, it's time not to amend Article II of the Bill of Rights (and Obligations) but to read it, publicize it, embrace it, and enforce it."

"Only when we confront the realities of sex, race, and class, the ways they divide us, make us different, stand us in opposition, and work to reconcile and resolve these issues will we be able to participate in the making of feminist revolution, in the transformation of the world."

". . . YOU COPS!
WE THE BROTHER AND SISTER OF WILLIE JORDAN, A FELLOW STONY BROOK STUDENT WHO THE BROTHER OF THE DEAD REGGIE JORDAN. REGGIE, LIKE MANY BROTHER AND SISTER, HE A VICTIM OF BRUTAL RACIST POLICE, OCTOBER 25, 1985. . . . WE AIN'T STAYIN' SILENT NO MORE."

"When my teacher had pinned this map up on the blackboard, she said, 'this is England' — and she said it with authority, seriousness, and adoration, and

we all sat up. It was as if she had said, 'This is Jerusalem, the place you will
go to when you die but only if you have been good.'"

The Writer's Presence

A Pool of Essays

Introduction for Students:
The Writer's Presence

Presence is a word — like *charisma* — that we reserve for people who create powerful and memorable impressions. Many public figures and political leaders are said to "have presence" (John F. Kennedy and Martin Luther King Jr. were two superb examples) as well as many athletes, dancers, and musicians. In fact, the quality of presence is found abundantly in the performing arts; think of Michael Jackson or Madonna, two entertainers who have self-consciously fashioned — through style, costume, and gesture — an instantly recognizable public presence. Clearly, people with presence are able to command our attention. How do they do it?

Presence is far easier to identify than it is to define. We recognize it when we see it, but how do we capture it in words? Virtually everyone would agree, for example, that when Charles Barkley steps onto a basketball court or when Ross Perot steps up to a podium, each displays an exceptional degree of presence; we acknowledge this whether or not we are Chicago Bulls fans or disgruntled with traditional two-party politics. But what is it about such individuals that commands our attention? How can be begin to understand this elusive characteristic known as presence?

On one level, *presence* simply means "being present." But the word is more complex than that; it suggests much more than the mere fact of being physically present. Most dictionaries define *presence* as an ability to project a sense of self-assurance, poise, ease, or dignity. We thus speak of someone's "stage presence" or "presence of mind." But the word is also used today to suggest an impressive personality, an individual who can make his or her presence felt. As every college student knows, to be present in a classroom is not the same thing as *having a presence* there. We may be present in body, but not in spirit. In that sense, presence is also a matter of individual energy and exertion, of getting something of ourselves into whatever it is we do.

1

Presence is especially important in writing, which is what this book is about. Just as we notice individual presence in sports, or music, or conversation, so too we discover it in good writing. If what we read seems dreary, dull, or dead, it's usually because the writer forgot to include an important ingredient: *personal presence*. That doesn't mean that your essays should be written *in* the first-person singular (this book contains many exceptional essays that aren't), but that your essays should be written *by* the first-person singular — by *you*. Interesting essays are produced by a real and distinct person, not an automaton following a set of mechanical rules and abstract principles.

PRESENCE IN WRITING

How can someone be present in writing? How can you project yourself into an essay so that it seems that you're personally there, even though all your reader sees are words on a piece of paper?

The Writer's Presence shows you how this is done. It shows how a wide variety of talented writers establish a distinct presence in many different kinds of writing and for many different purposes and audiences. Though the book offers numerous examples of how presence is compositionally established, there are several methods that nearly all experienced writers observe and that are worth pointing out at the start. Let's examine four of the chief ways a writer can be present in an essay.

1. Personal Experience. One of the most straightforward ways of making your presence felt in an essay is to include appropriate personal experiences. Of course, many assignments may call for a personal essay, and in those cases you will naturally be putting episodes from your own life at the center of your writing. But writers also find ways to build their personal experiences into essays that are basically informative or argumentative, essays on topics other than the self. They do this to show their close connection with a subject, to offer testimony, or to establish their personal authority on a subject. Many of the essays in this collection offer clear illustrations of how writers incorporate personal experience into an essay on a specific topic or issue.

Look, for example, at the essay by Amy Cunningham, "Why Women Smile" (p. 196). This essay is primarily an explanation of a cultural phenomenon — the way women are socially conditioned to maintain a smiling attitude. But note that Cunningham begins the essay not with a general observation but with a personal anecdote: "After smiling brilliantly for nearly four decades, I now find myself trying to quit." Though her essay is not "personal," her opening sentence, besides establishing her own connection with the topic, provides readers with a personal motive for her writing.

One of the first places to look for the writer's presence is in the motive, the purpose, for putting pen to paper. Virginia Woolf calls this a "fierce attachment to an idea." The extent of our success in making clear our motive for writing will largely depend on our interest both in our subject as well as in our idea about the subject. It will prove extremely difficult for any writer to establish a presence when he or she is either bored with — or simply uninterested in — the subject at hand. Investing in a clearly articulated purpose will yield an attractive return in reader attention.

2. *Voice.* Another way a writer makes his or her presence felt is through the creation of a distinctive and identifiable *voice*. All words are composed of sounds, and language itself is something nearly all of us originally learned through *hearing*. Any piece of writing can be read aloud, though many readers have developed such ingrained habits of silent reading that they no longer *hear* the writing. Good writers, however, want their words to be heard. They want their sentences to have rhythm, cadence, and balance. Experienced authors revise a great deal of their writing just to make sure the sentences *sound* right. They're writing for the reader's ear as well as the reader's mind.

In many respects, voice is the writer's "signature," what finally distinguishes the work of one writer from another. Consider how quickly we recognize voice. We only *hear* the opening lines of a humorous sketch on television, yet we instantly recognize the comedian. So, too, whenever we read a piece of writing, we ought to think of it as an experience similar to listening to someone speak aloud. Doing so adds drama to writing and reading. Here is what the poet Robert Frost had to say on the subject:

> Everything written is as good as it is dramatic. . . . A dramatic necessity goes deep into the nature of the sentence. Sentences are not different enough to hold the attention unless they are dramatic. No ingenuity of varying structure will do. All that can save them is the speaking tone of voice somehow entangled in the words and fastened to the page for the ear of the imagination. That is all that can save poetry from singing, all that can save prose from itself. (Preface to *A Way Out*, 1)

Frost spent a good portion of his celebrated public life encouraging people to cultivate what he called "the hearing imagination."

A writer's voice is usually fairly consistent from essay to essay and can be detected quickly by an experienced reader who pays attention to "the hearing imagination." To be distinctive and effective, a writer's voice need not be strange, artificial, or self-consciously literary. Many essayists develop a casual, familiar, flexible tone of voice that allows them to range easily from the intimate to the intellectual. Sentence rhythm and word choice play a large part in determining a writer's tone of voice. Observe how Raymond Carver begins an essay about his father (p. 18):

> My dad's name was Clevie Raymond Carver. His family called him Raymond and friends called him C.R. I was named Raymond Clevie Carver, Jr. I hated the "Junior" part. When I was little my dad called me Frog, which was okay. . . .

Carver's voice here is casual and almost childlike, a quality he is striving for in an essay intended to be candid, intimate, and low-key. Throughout the essay, for example, he rarely uses the word *father* but always the more colloquial *dad*. If you read this passage aloud, you will get the feeling that someone is speaking directly to you.

A more specific dimension of voice is *tone,* which refers not only to the implied social relationship of the writer to the reader, but also the manner the writer adopts in addressing the reader. When considering tone as a feature of the writer's presence, it is useful to remember that tone addresses the ways in which writers convey attitudes. In this respect, tone does not speak to the attitudes themselves but to the manner in which those attitudes are revealed. In either projecting or analyzing the writer's tone, writers and readers ought to consider its intensity, the force with which the writer's attitudes are expressed. The strength of the writer's tone depends on such factors as the seriousness of the situation, the nature and extent of the writer's involvement in the situation, and the control the writer exercises over expression. In practical terms, tone is usually a matter of diction and individual word choice.

3. Point of View. Another sure way to establish presence is in the point of view we adopt toward a subject. In this sense, point of view comprises the "whereness" of the writer's presence. Sometimes a point of view can be a literal reality, an actual place or situation in which we physically locate ourselves as writers. This occurs most frequently in autobiographical essays in which the writer is present both as the narrator and as a character. For example, in "A Clack of Tiny Sparks: Remembrances of a Gay Boyhood" (p. 40), Bernard Cooper is always meticulous about telling us his actual location at any given moment in his writing. The essay begins: "Theresa Sanchez sat behind me in ninth-grade algebra."

Note, too, how extremely important point of view is to another essayist in the volume, Brent Staples, in "Just Walk on By: A Black Man Ponders His Power to Alter Public Space" (p. 130). Here is how Staples opens his essay:

> My first victim was a woman — white, well dressed, probably in her early twenties. I came upon her late one evening on a deserted street in Hyde Park, a relatively affluent neighborhood in an otherwise mean, impoverished section of Chicago. As I swung onto the avenue behind her, there seemed to be a discreet, uninflammatory distance between us. Not so. She cast back a worried glance. To her, the youngish black man — a broad six feet two inches with a beard and billowing hair, both hands shoved into the pockets of a bulky military jacket — seemed menacingly close. After a few more quick glimpses, she picked up her pace and was soon running in earnest. Within seconds she disappeared into a cross street.

Point of view in this essay is crucial to Staples, since, in order to see why he frightens people, he needs to see himself in the stereotypical ways that others see him. Thus, by the middle of this opening paragraph (in the sentence beginning "To her"), he literally switches the point of view from his own perspective to that of the young and terrified white woman, describing his appearance as she would perceive it.

Point of view is not always a matter of a specific location or position. Writers are not always present in their essays as dramatic characters. In many reflective, informative, or argumentative essays, the point of view is determined more by a writer's intellectual attitude or opinions — an angle of vision — than by a precise physical perspective. As an example of how a writer establishes a personal perspective without introducing a first-person narrator or a characterized self, note the following passage from Judith Martin's essay on etiquette, "The Pursuit of Politeness" (p. 309):

> The idea that people can behave "naturally," without resorting to an artificial code tacitly agreed upon by their own society, is as silly as the idea that they can communicate by a spoken language without commonly accepted semantic and grammatical rules. Like language, a code of manners can be used with more or with less skill, for laudable or for evil purposes, to express a great variety of ideas and emotions. Like language, manners continually undergo slow changes and adaptations, but these changes have to be global, not atomic. For if everyone improvises his own manners, no one will understand the meaning of anyone else's behavior, and the result will be social chaos, or about what we have now.

There is no first person singular here, nor a dramatically rendered self. Yet this passage conveys a very distinct point of view. Only from a specific intellectual perspective could a writer regard an idea as "silly," and only from such a perspective could someone assume that today's public behavior approximates "social chaos." Clearly, this is a writer with a definite opinion about what constitutes proper behavior in our time.

4. *Patterns.* A writer can also be present in an essay as a *writer* — that is, a person consciously crafting and shaping his or her work. This artistic presence is not always obvious. Yet when we begin to detect in our reading certain kinds of repeated elements — a metaphor or an image, a twist on an earlier episode, a conclusion that echoes the opening — we become aware that someone is deliberately shaping experience or ideas in a special manner. We often find this type of presence in imaginative literature — especially in novels and poems — as well as in essays that possess a distinct literary flavor.

As an example of creating a presence through patterns, look at the opening paragraph of E. B. White's now classic essay, "Once More to the Lake" (p. 156).

> One summer, along about 1904, my father rented a camp on a lake in Maine and took us all there for the month of August. We all got ringworm from some kittens and had to rub Pond's Extract on our arms and legs night and morning, and my father rolled over in a canoe with all his clothes on; but outside of that the vacation was a success and from then on none of us ever thought there was any place in the world like that lake in Maine. We returned summer after summer — always on August 1st for one month. I have since become a salt-water man, but sometimes in summer there are days when the restlessness of the tides and the fearful cold

of the sea water and the incessant wind that blows across the afternoon and into the evening make me wish for the placidity of a lake in the woods. A few weeks ago this feeling got so strong I bought myself a couple of bass hooks and a spinner and returned to the lake where we used to go, for a week's fishing and to revisit old haunts.

If in rereading this opening, you circle every use of the word *and,* you will clearly see a pattern of repetition. *And,* of course, is a very unobtrusive word, and you may not notice right off how White keeps it present throughout the passage. This repetition alone may strike you at first as of no special importance, but as you read through the essay and see how much of White's central theme depends on the idea of return and repetition, you will get a better sense of why the little word *and* — a word that subtly reinforces the idea of repetition itself — is so significant.

E. B. White is present in his essay in more obvious ways — he is both telling us the story and he appears in it as a character. But he is also present to us as a writer, someone consciously shaping the language and form of his essay. We are thus dealing here with three levels of presence (which might also be described as three levels of "I"). If this sounds confusing, just think of a movie in which a single person directs the film, writes the script, and plays a leading role. It's not that uncommon. If you watch the 1987 film *Hannah and Her Sisters,* for example, you can observe the three presences of Woody Allen. Allen is not only visibly present in the film as one of the chief characters, but we also can detect his creative and shaping presence as the author of the screenplay (for which he won an Oscar) and as the director. The audience can directly see him on the screen as an actor; but the audience can also infer his presence as a scriptwriter and especially as a director — presences that, though less directly observable, are still original and powerful.

THE ESSAYS IN THIS BOOK

The writer's presence, then, can be felt both directly and indirectly. In some of the essays in this book you will encounter the first-person point of view directly. These essays appear mostly in the opening part, "Establishing an Identity." In many of these essays, the writer will appear as both narrator and character, and the writer's presence will be quite observable.

But not all essays are about the self. In fact, autobiography and memoir occupy only a small part of the nonfiction writing that regularly appears in magazines and newspapers. Many essays are written on specific topics and deal with specific issues. Most of the essays appearing in America's dominant periodicals, for example, are either intended to be informative or persuasive; the author wants to convey information about a particular subject (a Civil War battle) or wants to express an opinion about a particular issue (how to deal with the homeless). The book's second and third chapters, "Shaping Information" and "Contending with Issues," contain a large number of selections that illustrate writing intended to inform, argue, and persuade.

You'll notice, however, a strong writer's presence in many of the informative and persuasive essays. This is deliberate. To write informatively or persuasively about subjects other than yourself doesn't mean that you have to disappear as a writer. Sometimes you will want to insert your own experiences and testimony into an argumentative essay; at other times you will want to assume a distinct viewpoint concerning a piece of information; and at still other times — though you may not introduce the first-person singular — you will make your presence strongly felt in your tone of voice or simply in the way you arrange your facts and juxtapose details. At the heart of the word *information* is *form*. Writers don't passively receive facts and information in a totally finished format; they need to shape their information, to give it form. This shaping or patterning is something the writer *contributes*. A large part of the instructional purpose of this collection is to encourage you to pay more attention to the different ways writers are present in their work.

THE READER'S PRESENCE

Since almost all writing (and *all* published writing) is intended to be read, we can't dismiss the importance of the reader. Just as we find different levels of a writer's presence in a given piece of writing, so too can we detect different ways in which a reader can be present.

An author writes a short essay offering an opinion about gun control. The author herself has been the victim of a shooting, and her piece, though it includes her personal experiences, is largely made up of a concrete plan to eliminate all guns — even hunting rifles — from American life. She would like lawmakers to adopt her plan. Yet, in writing her essay, she imagines a great deal of resistance to her argument. In other words, she imagines a reader who will most likely disagree with her and who needs to be won over. Let's imagine she gets her essay published in *Newsweek*.

Now imagine three people in a dentist's office who within the same afternoon pick up this issue of *Newsweek* and read the essay. One of them has also been victimized by guns (her son was accidentally wounded by a hunter), and she reads the essay with great sympathy and conviction. She understands perfectly what this woman has gone through and believes in her plan completely. The next reader, a man who has never once in his life committed a crime and has no tolerance for criminals, is outraged by the essay. He was practically brought up in the woods and loves to hunt. He could never adopt a gun control plan that would in effect criminalize hunting. He's ready to fire off a letter attacking this woman's plan. The third reader also enjoys hunting and has always felt that hunting rifles should be exempt from any government regulation of firearms. But he finds the woman's plan convincing and feasible. He spends the rest of the day trying to think of counterarguments.

Obviously, these are only three of many possibilities. But you should be able to see from this example the differences between the reader imagined by the writer and some actual readers. The one person who totally agreed with the writer was not the kind of reader the author had originally imagined or was trying to persuade; she was already persuaded. And though the other two readers were part of her intended audience, one of them could never be persuaded to her point of view, whereas the other one might.

The differences briefly outlined here are distinctions between what can be called implied readers and actual readers. The implied reader is the reader imagined by the writer for a particular piece of writing. In constructing arguments, for example, it is usually effective to imagine readers we are *trying* to win over to our views. Otherwise, we are simply asking people who already agree with us to agree with us — what's commonly known as "preaching to the converted."

In informative or critical essays, a writer also needs to be careful about the implied reader; for example, it's always important to ask how much your intended audience may already know about your subject. Here's a practical illustration. If you were asked to write a review of a recent film for your college newspaper, you would assume your readers had not yet seen it (or else you might annoy them by giving away some surprises). On the other hand, if you were asked to write a critical essay about the same movie for a film course, you could assume your readers had seen it. It's the same movie, and you have the same opinions about it, but your two essays had two different purposes, and in the process of writing them you imagined readers with two different levels of knowledge about the film.

Actual readers, of course, differ from implied readers in that they are real people who read the writing — not readers intended or imagined by the writer. As you read the essays in this collection, you should be aware of at least two readers — (1) the reader you think the writer imagines for the essay, and (2) the reader you are in actuality. Sometimes you will seem very close to the kind of reader the writer is imagining. In those cases, you might say that you "identify" with a particular writer, essay, or point of view. At other times, however, you will notice a great deal of distance between the reader the author imagines and you as an actual reader. For example, you may feel excluded by the author on the basis of race, gender, class, or expected education. Or you may feel you know more than the author does about a particular topic.

To help you get accustomed to your role as a reader, each selection in the book is followed by a set of questions, "The Reader's Presence." These questions are designed to orient you to the various levels of reading suggested by the selection. Some of the questions will ask you to identify the kind of reader you think the author imagines; other questions will prompt you to think about specific ways you may differ from the author's intended reader. In general, the questions are intended to make you more deeply aware of your *presence* as a reader. In this brief introduction, we covered only two levels of readers (imagined and actual), but some literary essays demand more complex consideration. Whenever we think more than these two types of readers need to be identified in an essay, we will introduce this information in the questions.

We hope you will find *The Writer's Presence* a stimulating book to read and think about. To make our presence felt as writers is as much a matter of self-empowerment as it is of faith. It requires the confidence that we can affect others, or determine a course of action, or even surprise ourselves by new ideas or by acquiring new powers of articulation. Part of the enduring pleasure of writing is precisely that element of surprise, of originality — that lifelong pleasure of discovering new resources of language, finding new means of knowing ourselves, and inventing new ways to be present in the world.

Part I

Establishing an Identity

1

Maya Angelou

"What's Your Name, Girl?"

Recently a white woman from Texas, who would quickly describe herself as a liberal, asked me about my hometown. When I told her that in Stamps[1] my grandmother had owned the only Negro general merchandise store since the turn of the century, she exclaimed, "Why, you were a debutante." Ridiculous and even ludicrous. But Negro girls in small Southern towns, whether poverty-stricken or just munching along on a few of life's necessities, were given as extensive and irrelevant preparations for adulthood as rich white girls shown in magazines. Admittedly the training was not the same. While white girls learned to waltz and sit gracefully with a teacup balanced on their knees, we were lagging behind, learning the mid-Victorian values with very little money to indulge them. (Come and see Edna Lomax spending the money she made picking cotton on five balls of ecru tatting thread. Her fingers are bound to snag the work and she'll have to repeat the stitches time and time again. But she knows that when she buys the thread.)

We were required to embroider and I had trunkfuls of colorful dishtowels, pillowcases, runners, and handkerchiefs to my credit. I mastered the art of crocheting and tatting, and there was a lifetime's supply of dainty doilies that would never be used in sacheted dresser drawers. It went without saying that all girls could iron and wash, but the finer touches around the home, like setting a table with real silver, baking roasts, and cooking vegetables without meat, had to be learned elsewhere. Usually at the source of those habits. During my tenth year, a white woman's kitchen became my finishing school.

Mrs. Viola Cullinan was a plump woman who lived in a three-bedroom house somewhere behind the post office. She was singularly un-

---

For biographical information on Maya Angelou, see p. 641.
[1]*Stamps:* A town in southwestern Arkansas. — EDS.

attractive until she smiled, and then the lines around her eyes and mouth which made her look perpetually dirty disappeared, and her face looked like the mask of an impish elf. She usually rested her smile until late afternoon when her women friends dropped in and Miss Glory, the cook, served them cold drinks on the closed-in porch.

The exactness of her house was inhuman. This glass went here and only here. That cup had its place and it was an act of impudent rebellion to place it anywhere else. At twelve o'clock the table was set. At 12:15 Mrs. Cullinan sat down to dinner (whether her husband had arrived or not). At 12:16 Miss Glory brought out the food.

It took me a week to learn the difference between a salad plate, a bread   5
plate, and a dessert plate.

Mrs. Cullinan kept up the tradition of her wealthy parents. She was from Virginia. Miss Glory, who was a descendant of slaves that had worked for the Cullinans, told me her history. She had married beneath her (according to Miss Glory). Her husband's family hadn't had their money very long and what they had "didn't 'mount to much."

As ugly as she was, I thought privately, she was lucky to get a husband above or beneath her station. But Miss Glory wouldn't let me say a thing against her mistress. She was very patient with me, however, over the housework. She explained the dishware, silverware, and servants' bells.

The large round bowl in which soup was served wasn't a soup bowl, it was a tureen. There were goblets, sherbet glasses, ice-cream glasses, wine glasses, green glass coffee cups with matching saucers, and water glasses. I had a glass to drink from, and it sat with Miss Glory's on a separate shelf from the others. Soup spoons, gravy boat, butter knives, salad forks, and carving platter were additions to my vocabulary and in fact almost represented a new language. I was fascinated with the novelty, with the fluttering Mrs. Cullinan and her Alice-in-Wonderland house.

Her husband remains, in my memory, undefined. I lumped him with all the other white men that I had ever seen and tried not to see.

On our way home one evening, Miss Glory told me that Mrs. Cullinan   10
couldn't have children. She said that she was too delicate-boned. It was hard to imagine bones at all under those layers of fat. Miss Glory went on to say that the doctor had taken out all her lady organs. I reasoned that a pig's organs included the lungs, heart, and liver, so if Mrs. Cullinan was walking around without these essentials, it explained why she drank alcohol out of unmarked bottles. She was keeping herself embalmed.

When I spoke to Bailey[2] about it, he agreed that I was right, but he also informed me that Mr. Cullinan had two daughters by a colored lady and that I knew them very well. He added that the girls were the spitting image of their father. I was unable to remember what he looked like, although I had just left him a few hours before, but I thought of the Coleman girls.

[2]*Bailey:* Her brother. — EDS.

They were very light-skinned and certainly didn't look very much like their mother (no one ever mentioned Mr. Coleman).

My pity for Mrs. Cullinan preceded me the next morning like the Cheshire cat's smile. Those girls, who could have been her daughters, were beautiful. They didn't have to straighten their hair. Even when they were caught in the rain, their braids still hung down straight like tamed snakes. Their mouths were pouty little cupid's bows. Mrs. Cullinan didn't know what she missed. Or maybe she did. Poor Mrs. Cullinan.

For weeks after, I arrived early, left late, and tried very hard to make up for her barrenness. If she had had her own children, she wouldn't have had to ask me to run a thousand errands from her back door to the back door of her friends. Poor old Mrs. Cullinan.

Then one evening Miss Glory told me to serve the ladies on the porch. After I set the tray down and turned toward the kitchen, one of the women asked, "What's your name, girl?" It was the speckled-face one. Mrs. Cullinan said, "She doesn't talk much. Her name's Margaret."

"Is she dumb?"

"No. As I understand it, she can talk when she wants to but she's usually quiet as a little mouse. Aren't you, Margaret?"

I smiled at her. Poor thing. No organs and couldn't even pronounce my name correctly.

"She's a sweet little thing, though."

"Well, that may be, but the name's too long. I'd never bother myself. I'd call her Mary if I was you."

I fumed into the kitchen. That horrible woman would never have the chance to call me Mary because if I was starving I'd never work for her. I decided I wouldn't pee on her if her heart was on fire. Giggles drifted in off the porch and into Miss Glory's pots. I wondered what they could be laughing about.

Whitefolks were so strange. Could they be talking about me? Everybody knew that they stuck together better than the Negroes did. It was possible that Mrs. Cullinan had friends in St. Louis who heard about a girl from Stamps being in court and wrote to tell her. Maybe she knew about Mr. Freeman.[3]

My lunch was in my mouth a second time and I went outside and relieved myself on the bed of four-o'clocks. Miss Glory thought I might be coming down with something and told me to go on home, that Momma would give me some herb tea, and she'd explain to her mistress.

I realized how foolish I was being before I reached the pond. Of course Mrs. Cullinan didn't know. Otherwise she wouldn't have given me the two nice dresses that Momma cut down, and she certainly wouldn't have called me a "sweet little thing." My stomach felt fine, and I didn't mention anything to Momma.

---

[3]*Mr. Freeman:* A friend of Angelou's mother; he was convicted of raping Angelou when she was a child. — Eds.

That evening I decided to write a poem on being white, fat, old, and without children. It was going to be a tragic ballad. I would have to watch her carefully to capture the essence of her loneliness and pain.

The very next day, she called me by the wrong name. Miss Glory and   25
I were washing up the lunch dishes when Mrs. Cullinan came to the doorway. "Mary?"

Miss Glory asked, "Who?"

Mrs. Cullinan, sagging a little, knew and I knew. "I want Mary to go down to Mrs. Randall's and take her some soup. She's not been feeling well for a few days."

Miss Glory's face was a wonder to see. "You mean Margaret, ma'am. Her name's Margaret."

"That's too long. She's Mary from now on. Heat that soup from last night and put it in the china tureen and, Mary, I want you to carry it carefully."

Every person I knew had a hellish horror of being "called out of his   30
name." It was a dangerous practice to call a Negro anything that could be loosely construed as insulting because of the centuries of their having been called niggers, jigs, dinges, blackbirds, crows, boots, and spooks.

Miss Glory had a fleeting second of feeling sorry for me. Then as she handed me the hot tureen she said, "Don't mind, don't pay that no mind. Sticks and stones may break your bones, but words . . . You know, I been working for her for twenty years."

She held the back door open for me. "Twenty years; I wasn't much older than you. My name used to be Hallelujah. That's what Ma named me, but my mistress give me 'Glory,' and it stuck. I likes it better too."

I was in the little path that ran behind the houses when Miss Glory shouted. "It's shorter too."

For a few seconds it was a tossup over whether I would laugh (imagine being named Hallelujah) or cry (imagine letting some white woman rename you for her convenience). My anger saved me from either outburst. I had to quit the job, but the problem was going to be how to do it. Momma wouldn't allow me to quit for just any reason.

"She's a peach. That woman is a real peach." Mrs. Randall's maid was   35
talking as she took the soup from me, and I wondered what her name used to be and what she answered to now.

For a week I looked into Mrs. Cullinan's face as she called me Mary. She ignored my coming late and leaving early. Miss Glory was a little annoyed because I had begun to leave egg yolk on the dishes and wasn't putting much heart in polishing the silver. I hoped that she would complain to our boss, but she didn't.

Then Bailey solved my dilemma. He had me describe the contents of the cupboard and the particular plates she liked best. Her favorite piece was a casserole shaped like a fish and the green glass coffee cups. I kept his instructions in mind, so on the next day when Miss Glory was hanging out clothes and I had again been told to serve the old biddies on the porch, I dropped the empty serving tray. When I heard Mrs. Cullinan scream, "Mary!" I picked up the casserole and two of the green glass cups in readiness. As she rounded the kitchen door I let them fall on the tiled floor.

I could never absolutely describe to Bailey what happened next, because each time I got to the part where she fell on the floor and screwed up her ugly face to cry, we burst out laughing. She actually wobbled around on the floor and picked up shards of the cups and cried, "Oh, Momma. Oh, dear Gawd. It's Momma's china from Virginia. Oh, Momma, I sorry."

Miss Glory came running in from the yard and the women from the porch crowded around. Miss Glory was almost as broken up as her mistress. "You mean to say she broke our Virginia dishes? What we gone do?"

Mrs. Cullinan cried louder. "That clumsy nigger. Clumsy little black   40 nigger."

Old speckled-face leaned down and asked, "Who did it, Viola? Was it Mary? Who did it?"

Everything was happening so fast I can't remember whether her action preceded her words, but I know that Mrs. Cullinan said, "Her name's Margaret, goddamn it, her name's Margaret!" And she threw a wedge of the broken plate at me. It could have been the hysteria which put her aim off, but the flying crockery caught Miss Glory right over her ear and she started screaming.

I left the front door wide open so all the neighbors could hear.

Mrs. Cullinan was right about one thing. My name wasn't Mary.

1969

The Reader's Presence

1. At the center of this autobiographical episode is the importance of people's names in African-American culture. Where does Angelou make this point clear? If she hadn't explained the problem of names directly, how might your interpretation of the episode be different? To what extent do the names of things also play an important role in the essay?

2. After rereading the essay, try to describe the emotional attitudes of the characters to one another. What, for example, is Margaret's attitude toward Mrs. Cullinan? Do you feel pity or sympathy at any point for Mrs. Cullinan? How does Margaret's attitude toward her fluctuate throughout the episode? With whom do you sympathize most in the final scene, and why? For which character do you have the least sympathy?

3. Consider Margaret's final act very carefully. Why does she re-

spond by deliberately destroying Mrs. Cullinan's china? What else could she have done? Why was that act especially appropriate? What does the china represent? In what way is the china associated with Mrs. Cullinan? In what way is it associated with the theme of names and language?

2

Raymond Carver

My Father's Life

My dad's name was Clevie Raymond Carver. His family called him Raymond and friends called him C. R. I was named Raymond Clevie Carver, Jr. I hated the "Junior" part. When I was little my dad called me Frog, which was okay. But later, like everybody else in the family, he began calling me Junior. He went on calling me this until I was thirteen or fourteen and announced that I wouldn't answer to that name any longer. So he began calling me Doc. From then until his death, on June 17, 1967, he called me Doc, or else Son.

When he died, my mother telephoned my wife with the news. I was away from my family at the time, between lives, trying to enroll in the School of Library Science at the University of Iowa. When my wife answered the phone, my mother blurted out, "Raymond's dead!" For a moment, my wife thought my mother was telling her that I was dead. Then my mother made it clear *which* Raymond she was talking about and my wife said, "Thank God. I thought you meant *my* Raymond."

My dad walked, hitched rides, and rode in empty boxcars when he went from Arkansas to Washington State in 1934, looking for work. I don't know whether he was pursuing a dream when he went out to Washington. I doubt it. I don't think he dreamed much. I believe he was simply looking for steady work at decent pay. Steady work was meaningful work. He picked apples for a time and then landed a construction laborer's job on the Grand Coulee Dam. After he'd put aside a little money, he bought a car and drove back to Arkansas to help his folks, my grandparents, pack up for the move west. He said later that they were about to starve down there, and this wasn't meant as a figure of speech. It was during that short while in Arkansas, in a town called Leola, that my mother met my dad on the sidewalk as he came out of a tavern.

For biographical information on Raymond Carver, see p. 644.

"He was drunk," she said. "I don't know why I let him talk to me. His eyes were glittery. I wish I'd had a crystal ball." They'd met once, a year or so before, at a dance. He'd had girlfriends before her, my mother told me. "Your dad always had a girlfriend, even after we married. He was my first and last. I never had another man. But I didn't miss anything."

They were married by a justice of the peace on the day they left for   5 Washington, this big, tall country girl and a farmhand-turned-construction worker. My mother spent her wedding night with my dad and his folks, all of them camped beside the road in Arkansas.

In Omak, Washington, my dad and mother lived in a little place not much bigger than a cabin. My grandparents lived next door. My dad was still working on the dam, and later, with the huge turbines producing electricity and the water backed up for a hundred miles into Canada, he stood in the crowd and heard Franklin D. Roosevelt when he spoke at the construction site. "He never mentioned those guys who died building that dam," my dad said. Some of his friends had died there, men from Arkansas, Oklahoma, and Missouri.

He then took a job in a sawmill in Clatskanie, Oregon, a little town alongside the Columbia River. I was born there, and my mother has a picture of my dad standing in front of the gate to the mill, proudly holding me up to face the camera. My bonnet is on crooked and about to come untied. His hat is pushed back on his forehead, and he's wearing a big grin. Was he going in to work or just finishing his shift? It doesn't matter. In either case, he had a job and a family. These were his salad days.

In 1941 we moved to Yakima, Washington, where my dad went to work as a saw filer, a skilled trade he'd learned in Clatskanie. When war broke out, he was given a deferment because his work was considered necessary to the war effort. Finished lumber was in demand by the armed services, and he kept his saws so sharp they could shave the hair off your arm.

After my dad had moved us to Yakima, he moved his folks into the same neighborhood. By the mid-1940s the rest of my dad's family — his brother, his sister, and her husband, as well as uncles, cousins, nephews, and most of their extended family and friends — had come out from Arkansas. All because my dad came out first. The men went to work at Boise Cascade, where my dad worked, and the women packed apples in the canneries. And in just a little while, it seemed — according to my mother — everybody was better off than my dad. "Your dad couldn't keep money," my mother said. "Money burned a hole in his pocket. He was always doing for others."

The first house I clearly remember living in, at 1515 South Fifteenth   10 Street, in Yakima, had an outdoor toilet. On Halloween night, or just any night, for the hell of it, neighbor kids, kids in their early teens, would carry our toilet away and leave it next to the road. My dad would have to get somebody to help him bring it home. Or these kids would take the toilet and stand it in somebody else's backyard. Once they actually set it on fire. But ours wasn't the only house that had an outdoor toilet. When I was old enough to know what I was doing, I threw rocks at the other toilets when I'd see someone go inside. This was called bombing the toilets. After a while, though, everyone went to indoor plumbing until, suddenly, our toilet was the last outdoor one in the neighborhood. I remember the shame I felt when my third-grade teacher, Mr. Wise, drove me home from school one day. I asked him to stop at the house just before ours, claiming I lived there.

I can recall what happened one night when my dad came home late to find that my mother had locked all the doors on him from the inside. He was drunk, and we could feel the house shudder as he rattled the door. When he'd managed to force open a window, she hit him between the eyes with a colander and knocked him out. We could see him down there on the grass. For years afterward, I used to pick up this colander — it was as heavy as a rolling pin — and imagine what it would feel like to be hit in the head with something like that.

It was during this period that I remember my dad taking me into the bedroom, sitting me down on the bed, and telling me that I might have to go live with my Aunt LaVon for a while. I couldn't understand what I'd done that meant I'd have to go away from home to live. But this, too — whatever prompted it — must have blown over, more or less, anyway, because we stayed together, and I didn't have to go live with her or anyone else.

I remember my mother pouring his whiskey down the sink. Sometimes she'd pour it all out and sometimes, if she was afraid of getting caught, she'd only pour half of it out and then add water to the rest. I tasted some of his whiskey once myself. It was terrible stuff, and I don't see how anybody could drink it.

After a long time without one, we finally got a car, in 1949 or 1950, a 1938 Ford. But it threw a rod the first week we had it, and my dad had to have the motor rebuilt.

"We drove the oldest car in town," my mother said. "We could have had a Cadillac for all he spent on car repairs." One time she found someone else's tube of lipstick on the floorboard, along with a lacy handkerchief. "See this?" she said to me. "Some floozy left this in the car."   15

Once I saw her take a pan of warm water into the bedroom where my dad was sleeping. She took his hand from under the covers and held it in the water. I stood in the doorway and watched. I wanted to know what was going on. This would make him talk in his sleep, she told me. There were things she needed to know, things she was sure he was keeping from her.

Every year or so, when I was little, we would take the North Coast Limited across the Cascade Range from Yakima to Seattle and stay in the Vance Hotel and eat, I remember, at a place called the Dinner Bell Cafe. Once we went to Ivar's Acres of Clams and drank glasses of warm clam broth.

In 1956, the year I was to graduate from high school, my dad quit his job at the mill in Yakima and took a job in Chester, a little sawmill town in northern California. The reasons given at the time for his taking the job had to do with a higher hourly wage and the vague promise that he might, in a few years' time, succeed to the job of head filer in this new mill. But I think, in the main, that my dad had grown restless and simply wanted to try his luck elsewhere. Things had gotten a little too predictable for him in Yakima. Also, the year before, there had been the deaths, within six months of each other, of both his parents.

But just a few days after graduation, when my mother and I were packed to move to Chester, my dad penciled a letter to say he'd been sick for a while. He didn't want us to worry, he said, but he'd cut himself on a saw. Maybe he'd got a tiny sliver of steel in his blood. Anyway, something had happened and he'd had to miss work, he said. In the same mail was an unsigned postcard from somebody down there telling my mother that my dad was about to die and that he was drinking "raw whiskey."

When we arrived in Chester, my dad was living in a trailer that be- 20 longed to the company. I didn't recognize him immediately. I guess for a moment I didn't want to recognize him. He was skinny and pale and looked bewildered. His pants wouldn't stay up. He didn't look like my dad. My mother began to cry. My dad put his arm around her and patted her shoulder vaguely, like he didn't know what this was all about, either. The three of us took up life together in the trailer, and we looked after him as best we could. But my dad was sick, and he couldn't get any better. I worked with him in the mill that summer and part of the fall. We'd get up in the mornings and eat eggs and toast while we listened to the radio, and then go out the door with our lunch pails. We'd pass through the gate together at eight in the morning, and I wouldn't see him again until quitting time. In November I went back to Yakima to be closer to my girlfriend, the girl I'd made up my mind I was going to marry.

He worked at the mill in Chester until the following February, when he collapsed on the job and was taken to the hospital. My mother asked if I would come down there and help. I caught a bus from Yakima to Chester, intending to drive them back to Yakima. But now, in addition to being physically sick, my dad was in the midst of a nervous breakdown, though none of us knew to call it that at the time. During the entire trip back to Yakima, he didn't speak, not even when asked a direct question. ("How do you feel, Raymond?" "You okay, Dad?") He'd communicate, if he communicated at all, by moving his head or by turning his palms up as if to say he didn't know or care. The only time he said anything on the trip, and for nearly a month afterward, was when I was speeding down a gravel road in Oregon and the car muffler came loose. "You were going too fast," he said.

Back in Yakima a doctor saw to it that my dad went to a psychiatrist. My mother and dad had to go on relief, as it was called, and the county paid for the psychiatrist. The psychiatrist asked my dad, "Who is the President?" He'd had a question put to him that he could answer. "Ike," my dad said. Nevertheless, they put him on the fifth floor of Valley Memorial Hospital and began giving him electroshock treatment. I was married by then and about to start my own family. My dad was still locked up when my wife went into this same hospital, just one floor down, to have our first baby. After she had delivered, I went upstairs to give my dad the news. They let me in through a steel door and showed me where I could find him. He was sitting on a couch with a blanket over his lap. *Hey,* I thought. *What in hell is happening to my dad?* I sat down next to him and told him he was a grandfather. He waited a minute and then he said, "I feel like a grandfather." That's all he said. He didn't smile or move. He was in a big room with a lot of other people. Then I hugged him, and he began to cry.

Somehow he got out of there. But now came the years when he couldn't work and just sat around the house trying to figure what next and what he'd done wrong in his life that he'd wound up like this. My mother went from job to crummy job. Much later she referred to that time he was in the hospital, and those years just afterward, as "when Raymond was sick." The word *sick* was never the same for me again.

In 1964, through the help of a friend, he was lucky enough to be hired on at a mill in Klamath, California. He moved down there by himself to see if he could hack it. He lived not far from the mill, in a one-room cabin not much different from the place he and my mother had started out living in when they went west. He scrawled letters to my mother, and if I called she'd read them aloud to me over the phone. In the letters, he said it was touch and go. Every day that he went to work, he felt like it was the most important day of his life. But every day, he told her, made the next day that much easier. He said for her to tell me he said hello. If he couldn't sleep at night, he said, he thought about me and the good times we used to have. Finally, after a couple of months, he regained some of his confidence. He could do the work and didn't think he had to worry that he'd let anybody down ever again. When he was sure, he sent for my mother.

He'd been off from work for six years and had lost everything in that time — home, car, furniture, and appliances, including the big freezer that had been my mother's pride and joy. He'd lost his good name too — Raymond Carver was someone who couldn't pay his bills — and his self-respect was gone. He'd even lost his virility. My mother told my wife, "All during that time Raymond was sick we slept together in the same bed, but we didn't have relations. He wanted to a few times, but nothing happened. I didn't miss it, but I think he wanted to, you know." 25

During those years I was trying to raise my own family and earn a living. But, one thing and another, we found ourselves having to move a lot. I couldn't keep track of what was going down in my dad's life. But I did have a chance one Christmas to tell him I wanted to be a writer. I might as well have told him I wanted to become a plastic surgeon. "What are you going to write about?" he wanted to know. Then, as if to help me out, he said, "Write about stuff you know about. Write about some of those fishing trips we took." I said I would, but I knew I wouldn't. "Send me what you write," he said. I said I'd do that, but then I didn't. I wasn't writing anything about fishing, and I didn't think he'd particularly care about, or even necessarily understand, what I was writing in those days. Besides, he wasn't a reader. Not the sort, anyway, I imagined I was writing for.

Then he died. I was a long way off, in Iowa City, with things still to say to him. I didn't have the chance to tell him goodbye, or that I thought he was doing great at his new job. That I was proud of him for making a comeback.

My mother said he came in from work that night and ate a big supper. Then he sat at the table by himself and finished what was left of a bottle of whiskey, a bottle she found hidden in the bottom of the garbage under some coffee grounds a day or so later. Then he got up and went to bed, where my mother joined him a little later. But in the night she had to get up and make a bed for herself on the couch. "He was snoring so loud I couldn't sleep," she said. The next morning when she looked in on him, he was on his back with his mouth open, his cheeks caved in. *Graylooking*, she said. She knew he was dead — she didn't need a doctor to tell her that. But she called one anyway, and then she called my wife.

Among the pictures my mother kept of my dad and herself during those early days in Washington was a photograph of him standing in front of a car, holding a beer and a stringer of fish. In the photograph he is wearing his hat back on his forehead and has this awkward grin on his face. I asked her for it and she gave it to me, along with some others. I put it up on my wall, and each time we moved, I took the picture along and put it up on another wall. I looked at it carefully from time to time, trying to figure out some things about my dad, and maybe myself in the process. But I couldn't. My dad just kept moving further and further away from me and back into time. Finally, in the course of another move, I lost the photograph. It was then that I tried to recall it, and at the same time make an attempt to say something about my dad, and how I thought that in some important ways we might be alike. I wrote the poem when I was living in an apartment house in an urban area south of San Francisco, at a time when I found myself, like my dad, having trouble with alcohol. The poem was a way of trying to connect up with him.

PHOTOGRAPH OF MY FATHER IN HIS TWENTY-SECOND YEAR

October. Here in this dank, unfamiliar kitchen
I study my father's embarrassed young man's face.
Sheepish grin, he holds in one hand a string
of spiny yellow perch, in the other
a bottle of Carlsberg beer.

In jeans and flannel shirt, he leans
against the front fender of a 1934 Ford.
He would like to pose brave and hearty for his posterity,
wear his old hat cocked over his ear.
All his life my father wanted to be bold.

> But the eyes give him away, and the hands
> that limply offer the string of dead perch
> and the bottle of beer. Father, I love you,
> yet how can I say thank you, I who can't hold my liquor either
> and don't even know the places to fish.

The poem is true in its particulars, except that my dad died in June and   30
not October, as the first word of the poem says. I wanted a word with more
than one syllable to it to make it linger a little. But more than that, I wanted
a month appropriate to what I felt at the time I wrote the poem — a month
of short days and failing light, smoke in the air, things perishing. June was
summer nights and days, graduations, my wedding anniversary, the birthday of one of my children. June wasn't a month your father died in.

After the service at the funeral home, after we had moved outside, a
woman I didn't know came over to me and said, "He's happier where he is
now." I stared at this woman until she moved away. I still remember the
little knob of a hat she was wearing. Then one of my dad's cousins — I
didn't know the man's name — reached out and took my hand. "We all
miss him," he said, and I knew he wasn't saying it just to be polite.

I began to weep for the first time since receiving the news. I hadn't
been able to before. I hadn't had the time, for one thing. Now, suddenly, I
couldn't stop. I held my wife and wept while she said and did what she
could do to comfort me there in the middle of that summer afternoon.

I listened to people say consoling things to my mother, and I was glad
that my dad's family had turned up, had come to where he was. I thought
I'd remember everything that was said and done that day and maybe find
a way to tell it sometime. But I didn't. I forgot it all, or nearly. What I do
remember is that I heard our name used a lot that afternoon, my dad's
name and mine. But I knew they were talking about my dad. *Raymond*,
these people kept saying in their beautiful voices out of my childhood.
Raymond.

                                                                    1984

The Reader's Presence

1. You may have noticed that Carver begins and ends his essay with
   a reference to his and his father's name. Of what importance is
   this information at the opening? What do we learn about his relationship with his father through their names? How do names matter in the final paragraph?
2. Though the essay is titled "My Father's Life," Carver throughout
   uses the word *dad*. Why do you think he chose to do this? What
   difference does it make? Why do you think Carver used *father* instead of *dad* in the poem he wrote years earlier?

3. Try rereading the essay with particular attention to the conversations between father and son. How many reported conversations can you find? What do the conversations sound like? Can you find any pattern to them? To what extent do these conversations help you understand Carver's relationship with his father?

3

Sucheng Chan

You're Short, Besides!

When asked to write about being a physically handicapped Asian American woman, I considered it an insult. After all, my accomplishments are many, yet I was not asked to write about any of them. Is being handicapped the most salient feature about me? The fact that it might be in the eyes of others made me decide to write the essay as requested. I realized that the way I think about myself may differ considerably from the way others perceive me. And maybe that's what being physically handicapped is all about.

I was stricken simultaneously with pneumonia and polio at the age of four. Uncertain whether I had polio of the lungs, seven of the eight doctors who attended me — all practitioners of Western medicine — told my parents they should not feel optimistic about my survival. A Chinese fortune-teller my mother consulted also gave a grim prognosis, but for an entirely different reason: I had been stricken because my name was offensive to the gods. My grandmother had named me "grandchild of wisdom," a name that the fortune-teller said was too presumptuous for a girl. So he advised my parents to change my name to "chaste virgin." All these pessimistic predictions notwithstanding, I hung on to life, if only by a thread. For three years, my body was periodically pierced with electric shocks as the muscles of my legs atrophied. Before my illness, I had been an active, rambunctious, precocious, and very curious child. Being confined to bed was thus a mental agony as great as my physical pain. Living in war-torn China, I received little medical attention; physical therapy was unheard of. But I was determined to walk. So one day, when I was six or seven, I instructed my mother to set up two rows of chairs to face each other so that I could use them as I would parallel bars. I attempted to walk by holding my body up and moving it forward with my arms while dragging my legs along behind.

For biographical information on Sucheng Chan, see p. 645.

Each time I fell, my mother gasped, but I badgered her until she let me try again. After four nonambulatory years, I finally walked once more by pressing my hands against my thighs so my knees wouldn't buckle.

My father had been away from home during most of those years because of the war. When he returned, I had to confront the guilt he felt about my condition. In many East Asian cultures, there is a strong folk belief that a person's physical state in this life is a reflection of how morally or sinfully he or she lived in previous lives. Furthermore, because of the tendency to view the family as a single unit, it is believed that the fate of one member can be caused by the behavior of another. Some of my father's relatives told him that my illness had doubtless been caused by the wild carousing he did in his youth. A well-meaning but somewhat simple man, my father believed them.

Throughout my childhood, he sometimes apologized to me for having to suffer retribution for his former bad behavior. This upset me; it was bad enough that I had to deal with the anguish of not being able to walk, but to have to assuage his guilt as well was a real burden! In other ways, my father was very good to me. He took me out often, carrying me on his shoulders or back, to give me fresh air and sunshine. He did this until I was too large and heavy for him to carry. And ever since I can remember, he has told me that I am pretty.

After getting over her anxieties about my constant falls, my mother   5
decided to send me to school. I had already learned to read some words of Chinese at the age of three by asking my parents to teach me the sounds and meaning of various characters in the daily newspaper. But between the ages of four and eight, I received no education since just staying alive was a full-time job. Much to her chagrin, my mother found no school in Shanghai, where we lived at the time, which would accept me as a student. Finally, as a last resort, she approached the American School which agreed to enroll me only if my family kept an *amah* (a servant who takes care of children) by my side at all times. The tuition at the school was twenty U.S. dollars per month — a huge sum of money during those years of runaway inflation in China — and payable only in U.S. dollars. My family afforded the high cost of tuition and the expense of employing a full-time *amah* for less than a year.

We left China as the Communist forces swept across the country in victory. We found an apartment in Hong Kong across the street from a school run by Seventh-Day Adventists.[1] By that time I could walk a little, so the principal was persuaded to accept me. An *amah* now had to take care of me only during recess when my classmates might easily knock me over as they ran about the playground.

After a year and a half in Hong Kong, we moved to Malaysia, where my father's family had lived for four generations. There I learned to swim in the lovely warm waters of the tropics and fell in love with the sea. On

---

[1] *Seventh-Day Adventists:* A Protestant sect. — EDS.

land I was a cripple; in the ocean I could move with the grace of a fish. I liked the freedom of being in the water so much that many years later, when I was a graduate student in Hawaii, I became greatly enamored with a man just because he called me a "Polynesian water nymph."

As my overall health improved, my mother became less anxious about all aspects of my life. She did everything possible to enable me to lead as normal a life as possible. I remember how once some of her colleagues in the high school where she taught criticized her for letting me wear short skirts. They felt my legs should not be exposed to public view. My mother's response was, "All girls her age wear short skirts, so why shouldn't she?"

The years in Malaysia were the happiest of my childhood, even though I was constantly fending off children who ran after me calling, "*Baikah! Baikah!*" ("Cripple! Cripple!" in the Hokkien dialect commonly spoken in Malaysia). The taunts of children mattered little because I was a star pupil. I won one award after another for general scholarship as well as for art and public speaking. Whenever the school had important visitors my teacher always called on me to recite in front of the class.

A significant event that marked me indelibly occurred when I was   10
twelve. That year my school held a music recital and I was one of the students chosen to play the piano. I managed to get up the steps to the stage without any problem, but as I walked across the stage, I fell. Out of the audience, a voice said loudly and clearly, "Ayah! A *baikah* shouldn't be allowed to perform in public." I got up before anyone could get on stage to help me and, with tears streaming uncontrollably down my face, I rushed to the piano and began to play. Beethoven's "Für Elise" had never been played so fiendishly fast before or since, but I managed to finish the whole piece. That I managed to do so made me feel really strong. I never again feared ridicule.

In later years I was reminded of this experience from time to time. During my fourth year as an assistant professor at the University of California at Berkeley, I won a distinguished teaching award. Some weeks later I ran into a former professor who congratulated me enthusiastically. But I said to him, "You know what? I became a distinguished teacher by *limping* across the stage of Dwinelle 155!" (Dwinelle 155 is a large, cold classroom that most colleagues of mine hate to teach in.) I was rude not because I lacked graciousness but because this man, who had told me that my dissertation was the finest piece of work he had read in fifteen years, had nevertheless advised me to eschew a teaching career.

"Why?" I asked.

"Your leg . . . " he responded.

"What about my leg?" I said, puzzled.

"Well, how would you feel standing in front of a large lecture class?"   15

"If it makes any difference, I want you to know I've won a number of speech contests in my life, and I am not the least bit self-conscious about speaking in front of large audiences. . . . Look, why don't you write me a letter of recommendation to tell people how brilliant I am, and let *me* worry about my leg!"

This incident is worth recounting only because it illustrates a dilemma that handicapped persons face frequently: Those who care about us sometimes get so protective that they unwittingly limit our growth. This former professor of mine had been one of my greatest supporters for two decades. Time after time, he had written glowing letters of recommendation on my behalf. He had spoken as he did because he thought he had my best interests at heart; he thought that if I got a desk job rather than one that required me to be a visible, public person, I would be spared the misery of being stared at.

Americans, for the most part, do not believe as Asians do that physically handicapped persons are morally flawed. But they are equally inept at interacting with those of us who are not able-bodied. Cultural differences in the perception and treatment of handicapped people are most clearly expressed by adults. Children, regardless of where they are, tend to be openly curious about people who do not look "normal." Adults in Asia have no hesitation in asking visibly handicapped people what is wrong with them, often expressing their sympathy with looks of pity, whereas adults in the United States try desperately to be polite by pretending not to notice.

One interesting response I often elicited from people in Asia but have never encountered in America is the attempt to link my physical condition to the state of my soul. Many a time while living and traveling in Asia people would ask me what religion I belonged to. I would tell them that my mother is a devout Buddhist, that my father was baptized a Catholic but has never practiced Catholicism, and that I am an agnostic. Upon hearing this, people would try strenuously to convert me to their religion so that whichever God they believed in could bless me. If I would only attend this church or that temple regularly, they urged, I would surely get cured. Catholics and Buddhists alike have pressed religious medallions into my palm, telling me if I would wear these, the relevant deity or saint would make me well. Once while visiting the tomb of Muhammad Ali Jinnah[2] in Karachi, Pakistan, an old Muslim, after finishing his evening prayers, spotted me, gestured toward my legs, raised his arms heavenward, and began a new round of prayers, apparently on my behalf.

In the United States adults who try to act "civilized" toward handi-   20
capped people by pretending they don't notice anything unusual sometimes end up ignoring handicapped people completely. In the first few months I lived in this country, I was struck by the fact that whenever children asked me what was the matter with my leg, their adult companions would hurriedly shush them up, furtively look at me, mumble apologies, and rush their children away. After a few months of such encounters, I decided it

---

[2]***Muhammad Ali Jinnah:*** Indian Leader (1876–1948) who supported an independent Muslim state. — EDS.

was my responsibility to educate these people. So I would say to the flustered adults, "It's okay, let the kid ask." Turning to the child, I would say, "When I was a little girl, no bigger than you are, I became sick with something called polio. The muscles of my leg shrank up and I couldn't walk very well. You're much luckier than I am because now you can get a vaccine to make sure you never get my disease. So don't cry when your mommy takes you to get a polio vaccine, okay?" Some adults and their little companions I talked to this way were glad to be rescued from embarrassment; others thought I was strange.

Americans have another way of covering up their uneasiness: They become jovially patronizing. Sometimes when people spot my crutch, they ask if I've had a skiing accident. When I answer that unfortunately it is something less glamorous than that, they say, "I bet you *could* ski if you put your mind to it!" Alternately, at parties where people dance, men who ask me to dance with them get almost belligerent when I decline their invitation. They say, "Of course you can dance if you *want* to!" Some have given me pep talks about how if I would only develop the right mental attitude, I would have more fun in life.

Different cultural attitudes toward handicapped persons came out clearly during my wedding. My father-in-law, as solid a representative of middle America as could be found, had no qualms about objecting to the marriage on racial grounds, but he could bring himself to comment on my handicap only indirectly. He wondered why his son, who had dated numerous high school and college beauty queens, couldn't marry one of them instead of me. My mother-in-law, a devout Christian, did not share her husband's prejudices, but she worried aloud about whether I could have children. Some Chinese friends of my parents, on the other hand, said that I was lucky to have found such a noble man, one who would marry me despite my handicap. I, for my part, appeared in church in a white lace wedding dress I had designed and made myself — a miniskirt!

How Asian Americans treat me with respect to my handicap tells me a great deal about their degree of acculturation. Recent immigrants behave just like Asians in Asia; those who have been here longer or who grew up in the United States behave more like their white counterparts. I have not encountered any distinctly Asian American pattern of response. What makes the experience of Asian American handicapped people unique is the duality of responses we elicit.

Regardless of racial or cultural background, most handicapped people have to learn to find a balance between the desire to attain physical independence and the need to take care of ourselves by not overtaxing our bodies. In my case, I've had to learn to accept the fact that leading an active life has its price. Between the ages of eight and eighteen, I walked without using crutches or braces but the effort caused my right leg to become badly misaligned. Soon after I came to the United States, I had a series of operations to straighten out the bones of my right leg; afterwards though my leg looked straighter and presumably better, I could no longer walk on my own. Initially my doctors fitted me with a brace, but I found wearing one cumbersome and soon gave it up. I could move around much more easily — and more important, faster — by using one crutch. One orthopedist after another warned me that using a single crutch was a bad practice. They were right. Over the years my spine developed a double-S curve and for the last twenty years I have suffered from severe, chronic back pains, which neither conventional physical therapy nor a lighter work load can eliminate.

The only thing that helps my backaches is a good massage, but the   25
soothing effect lasts no more than a day or two. Massages are expensive, especially when one needs them three times a week. So I found a job that pays better, but at which I have to work longer hours, consequently increasing the physical strain on my body — a sort of vicious circle. When I was in my thirties, my doctors told me that if I kept leading the strenuous life I did, I would be in a wheelchair by the time I was forty. They were right on target: I bought myself a wheelchair when I was forty-one. But being the incorrigible character that I am, I use it only when I am *not* in a hurry!

It is a good thing, however, that I am too busy to think much about my handicap or my backaches because pain can physically debilitate as well as cause depression. And there are days when my spirits get rather low. What has helped me is realizing that being handicapped is akin to growing old at an accelerated rate. The contradiction I experience is that often my mind races along as though I'm only twenty while my body feels about sixty. But fifteen or twenty years hence, unlike my peers who will have to cope with aging for the first time, I shall be full of cheer because I will have already fought, and I hope won, that battle long ago.

Beyond learning how to be physically independent and, for some of us, living with chronic pain or other kinds of discomfort, the most difficult thing a handicapped person has to deal with, especially during puberty and early adulthood, is relating to potential sexual partners. Because American culture places so much emphasis on physical attractiveness, a person with a shriveled limb, or a tilt to the head, or the inability to speak clearly, experiences great uncertainty — indeed trauma — when interacting with someone to whom he or she is attracted. My problem was that I was not only physically handicapped, small, and short, but worse, I also wore glasses and was smarter than all the boys I knew! Alas, an insurmountable combination. Yet somehow I have managed to have intimate relationships, all of them with extraordinary men. Not surprisingly, there have also been countless men who broke my heart — men who enjoyed my company "as a friend," but who never found the courage to date or make love with me, although I am sure my experience in this regard is no different from that of many able-bodied persons.

The day came when my backaches got in the way of having an active sex life. Surprisingly that development was liberating because I stopped worrying about being attractive to men. No matter how headstrong I had been, I, like most women of my generation, had had the desire to be alluring to men ingrained into me. And that longing had always worked like a brake on my behavior. When what men think of me ceased to be compelling, I gained greater freedom to be myself.

I've often wondered if I would have been a different person had I not been physically handicapped. I really don't know, though there is no question that being handicapped has marked me. But at the same time I usually do not *feel* handicapped — and consequently, I do not *act* handicapped. People are therefore less likely to treat me as a handicapped person. There is no doubt, however, that the lives of my parents, sister, husband, other family members, and some close friends have been affected by my physical condition. They have had to learn not to hide me away at home, not to feel embarrassed by how I look or react to people who say silly things to me, and not to resent me for the extra demands my condition makes on them. Perhaps the hardest thing for those who live with handicapped people is to know when and how to offer help. There are no guidelines applicable to all situations. My advice is, when in doubt, ask, but ask in a way that does not smack of pity or embarrassment. Most important, please don't talk to us as though we are children.

So, has being physically handicapped been a handicap? It all depends 30 on one's attitude. Some years ago, I told a friend that I had once said to an affirmative action compliance officer (somewhat sardonically since I do not believe in the head count approach to affirmative action) that the institution which employs me is triply lucky because it can count me as nonwhite, female, and handicapped. He responded, "Why don't you tell them to count you four times? . . . Remember, you're short, besides!"

1989

The Reader's Presence

1. Some essays — such as those you write for class — are occasioned by specific assignments. Why is Sucheng Chan writing this essay? What seems to have been the assignment? What is her immediate reaction to that assignment? How is that reaction borne out by the substance of her remarks?

2. In comparing one culture with another, writers often tend to show one as superior and the other as inferior. In what ways does Sucheng Chan avoid this common oversimplification? Why do you think she is able to avoid it?

3. Insults play a large role in this essay. While rereading the essay, identify as many kinds of insults as you can. Which insults strike you as the most hurtful? Consider the title. In what sense is it an

insulting remark? Why do you think the author chose this expression for her title? Where does it come from in the essay, and how do you think it was intended to be taken — first by the person who said it, and then by the author who repeated it?

4

Judith Ortiz Cofer

Silent Dancing

We have a home movie of this party. Several times my mother and I have watched it together, and I have asked questions about the silent revelers coming in and out of focus. It is grainy and of short duration, but it's a great visual aid to my memory of life at that time. And it is in color — the only complete scene in color I can recall from those years.

We lived in Puerto Rico until my brother was born in 1954. Soon after, because of economic pressures on our growing family, my father joined the United States Navy. He was assigned to duty on a ship in Brooklyn Yard — a place of cement and steel that was to be his home base in the States until his retirement more than twenty years later. He left the Island first, alone, going to New York City and tracking down his uncle who lived with his family across the Hudson River in Paterson, New Jersey. There my father found a tiny apartment in a huge tenement that had once housed Jewish families but was just being taken over and transformed by Puerto Ricans, overflowing from New York City. In 1955 he sent for us. My mother was only twenty years old, I was not quite three, and my brother was a toddler when we arrived at *El Building,* as the place had been christened by its newest residents.

My memories of life in Paterson during those first few years are all in shades of gray. Maybe I was too young to absorb vivid colors and details, or to discriminate between the slate blue of the winter sky and the darker hues of the snow-bearing clouds, but that single color washes over the whole period. The building we lived in was gray, as were the streets, filled with slush the first few months of my life there. The coat my father had bought for me was similar in color and too big; it sat heavily on my thin frame.

For biographical information on Judith Ortiz Cofer, see p. 645.

I do remember the way the heater pipes banged and rattled, startling all of us out of sleep until we got so used to the sound that we automatically shut it out or raised our voices above the racket. The hiss from the valve punctuated my sleep (which has always been fitful) like a nonhuman presence in the room — a dragon sleeping at the entrance of my childhood. But the pipes were also a connection to all the other lives being lived around us. Having come from a house designed for a single family back in Puerto Rico — my mother's extended-family home — it was curious to know that strangers lived under our floor and above our heads, and that the heater pipe went through everyone's apartments. (My first spanking in Paterson came as a result of playing tunes on the pipes in my room to see if there would be an answer.) My mother was as new to this concept of beehive life as I was, but she had been given strict orders by my father to keep the doors locked, the noise down, ourselves to ourselves.

It seems that Father had learned some painful lessons about prejudice   5 while searching for an apartment in Paterson. Not until years later did I hear how much resistance he had encountered with landlords who were panicking at the influx of Latinos into a neighborhood that had been Jewish for a couple of generations. It made no difference that it was the American phenomenon of ethnic turnover which was changing the urban core of Paterson, and that the human flood could not be held back with an accusing finger.

"You Cuban?" one man had asked my father, pointing at his name tag on the Navy uniform — even though my father had the fair skin and light-brown hair of his northern Spanish background, and the name Ortiz is as common in Puerto Rico as Johnson is in the United States.

"No," my father had answered, looking past the finger into his adversary's angry eyes. "I'm Puerto Rican."

"Same shit." And the door closed.

My father could have passed as European, but we couldn't. My brother and I both have our mother's black hair and olive skin, and so we lived in El Building and visited our great-uncle and his fair children on the next block. It was their private joke that they were the German branch of the family. Not many years later that area too would be mainly Puerto Rican. It was as if the heart of the city map were being gradually colored brown — *café con leche*[1] brown. Our color.

The movie opens with a sweep of the living room. It is "typical" immi-   10 *grant Puerto Rican decor for the time: The sofa and chairs are square and hard-looking, upholstered in bright colors (blue and yellow in this instance), and covered with the transparent plastic that furniture salesmen then were so adept at convincing women to buy. The linoleum on the floor is light blue; if it had been subjected to spike heels (as it was in most places),*

---

[1]*café con leche:* Coffee with cream. In Puerto Rico it is sometimes prepared with boiled milk. — COFER'S NOTE.

there were dime-sized indentations all over it that cannot be seen in this movie. The room is full of people dressed up: dark suits for the men, red dresses for the women. When I have asked my mother why most of the women are in red that night, she has shrugged, "I don't remember. Just a coincidence." She doesn't have my obsession for assigning symbolism to everything.

The three women in red sitting on the couch are my mother, my eighteen-year-old cousin, and her brother's girlfriend. The novia *is just up from the Island, which is apparent in her body language. She sits up formally, her dress pulled over her knees. She is a pretty girl, but her posture makes her look insecure, lost in her full-skirted dress, which she has carefully tucked around her to make room for my gorgeous cousin, her future sister-in-law. My cousin has grown up in Paterson and is in her last year of high school. She doesn't have a trace of what Puerto Ricans call* la mancha *(literally, the stain: the mark of the new immigrant — something about the posture, the voice, or the humble demeanor that makes it obvious to everyone the person has just arrived on the mainland). My cousin is wearing a tight, sequined, cocktail dress. He brown hair has been lightened with peroxide around the bangs, and she is holding a cigarette expertly between her fingers, bringing it up to her mouth in a sensuous arc of her arm as she talks animatedly. My mother, who has come up to sit between the two women, both only a few years younger then herself, is somewhere between the poles they represent in our culture.*

It became my father's obsession to get out of the barrio, and thus we were never permitted to form bonds with the place or with the people who lived there. Yet El Building was a comfort to my mother, who never got over yearning for *la isla*. She felt surrounded by her language: The walls were thin, and voices speaking and arguing in Spanish could be heard all day. *Salsas* blasted out of radios, turned on early in the morning and left on for company. Women seemed to cook rice and beans perpetually — the strong aroma of boiling red kidney beans permeated the hallways.

Though Father preferred that we do our grocery shopping at the supermarket when he came home on weekend leaves, my mother insisted that she could cook only with products whose labels she could read. Consequently, during the week I accompanied her and my little brother to *La Bodega* — a hold-in-the-wall grocery store across the street from El Building. There we squeezed down three narrow aisles jammed with various products. Goya's and Libby's — those were the trademarks that were trusted by *her mamá,* so my mother bought many cans of Goya beans, soups, and condiments, as well as little cans of Libby's fruit juices for us. And she also bought Colgate toothpaste and Palmolive soap. (The final *e* is pronounced in both these products in Spanish, so for many years I believed that they were manufactured on the Island. I remember my surprise at first hearing a commercial on television in which Colgate rhymed with "ate.") We always lingered at La Bodega, for it was there that Mother breathed best, taking in the familiar aromas of the foods she knew from Mamá's kitchen. It was also there that she got to speak to the other women of El Building without violating outright Father's dictates against fraternizing with our neighbors.

Yet Father did his best to make our "assimilation" painless. I can still see him carrying a real Christmas tree up several flights of stairs to our apartment, leaving a trail of aromatic pine. He carried it formally, as if it were a flag in a parade. We were the only ones in El Building that I knew of who got presents on both Christmas day AND *dia de Reyes,* the day when the Three Kings brought gifts to Christ and to Hispanic children.

Our supreme luxury in El Building was having our own television set. 15 It must have been a result of Father's guilt feelings over the isolation he had imposed on us, but we were among the first in the barrio to have one. My brother quickly became an avid watcher of Captain Kangaroo and Jungle Jim, while I loved all the series showing families. By the time I started first grade, I could have drawn a map of Middle America as exemplified by the lives of characters in "Father Knows Best," "The Donna Reed Show," "Leave It to Beaver," "My Three Sons," and (my favorite) "Bachelor Father," where John Forsythe treated his adopted teenage daughter like a princess because he was rich and had a Chinese houseboy to do everything for him. In truth, compared to our neighbors in El Building, *we* were rich. My father's Navy check provided us with financial security and a standard of life that the factory workers envied. The only thing his money could not buy us was a place to live away from the barrio — his greatest wish, Mother's greatest fear.

In the home movie the men are shown next, sitting around a card table set up in one corner of the living room, playing dominoes. The clack of the ivory pieces was a familiar sound. I heard it in many houses on the Island and in many apartments in Paterson. In "Leave It to Beaver," the Cleavers played bridge in every other episode; in my childhood, the men started every social occasion with a hotly debated round of dominoes. The women would sit around and watch, but they never participated in the games.

Here and there you can see a small child. Children were always brought to parties and, whenever they got sleepy, were put to bed in the host's bedroom. Babysitting was a concept unrecognized by the Puerto Rican women I knew: A responsible mother did not leave her children with any stranger. And in a culture where children are not considered intrusive, there was no need to leave the children at home. We went where our mother went.

Of my preschool years I have only impressions: the sharp bite of the wind in December as we walked with our parents toward the brightly lit stores downtown; how I felt like a stuffed doll in my heavy coat, boots, and mittens; how good it was to walk into the five-and-dime and sit at the counter drinking hot chocolate. On Saturdays our whole family would walk downtown to shop at the big department stores on Broadway. Mother bought all our clothes at Penney's and Sears, and she liked to buy her dresses at the women's specialty shops like Lerner's and Diana's. At some point we'd go into Woodworth's and sit at the soda fountain to eat.

We never ran into other Latinos at these stores or when eating out, and it became clear to me only years later that the women from El Building shopped mainly in other places — stores owned by other Puerto Ricans or by Jewish merchants who had philosophically accepted our presence in the city and decided to make us their good customers, if not real neighbors and friends. These establishments were located not downtown but in the blocks around our street, and they were referred to generically as *La Tienda, El Bazar, La Bodega, La Botánica.* Everyone knew what was meant. These were the stores where your face did not turn a clerk to stone, where your money was as green as anyone else's.

One New Year's Eve we were dressed up like child models in the Sears   20 catalogue: my brother in a miniature man's suit and bow tie, and I in black patent-leather shoes and a frilly dress with several layers of crinoline underneath. My mother wore a bright red dress that night, I remember, and spike heels; her long black hair hung to her waist. Father, who usually wore his Navy uniform during his short visits home, had put on a dark civilian suit for the occasion: We had been invited to his uncle's house for a big celebration. Everyone was excited because my mother's brother Hernan — a bachelor who could indulge himself with luxuries — had bought a home movie camera, which he would be trying out that night.

Even the home movie cannot fill in the sensory details such a gathering left imprinted in a child's brain. The thick sweetness of women's perfumes mixing with the ever-present smells of food cooking in the kitchen: meat and plantain *pasteles,* as well as the ubiquitous rice dish made special with pigeon peas — *gandules* — and seasoned with precious *sofrito*[2] sent up from the Island by somebody's mother or smuggled in by a recent traveler. *Sofrito* was one of the items that women hoarded, since it was hardly ever in stock at La Bodega. It was the flavor of Puerto Rico.

The men drank Palo Viejo rum, and some of the younger ones got weepy. The first time I saw a grown man cry was at a New Year's Eve party: He had been reminded of his mother by the smells in the kitchen. But what I remember most were the boiled *pasteles* — plantain or yucca rectangles stuffed with corned beef or other meats, olives, and many other savory ingredients, all wrapped in banana leaves. Everybody had to fish one out with a fork. There was always a "trick" pastel — one without stuffing — and whoever got that one was the "New Year's Fool."

There was also the music. Long-playing albums were treated like precious china in these homes. Mexican recordings were popular, but the

---

[2]*sofrito:* A cooked condiment. A sauce composed of a mixture of fatback, ham, tomatoes, and many island spices and herbs. It is added to many typical Puerto Rican dishes for a distinctive flavor. — COFER'S NOTE.

songs that brought tears to my mother's eyes were sung by the melancholy Daniel Santos, whose life as a drug addict was the stuff of legend. Felipe Rodríguez was a particular favorite of couples, since he sang about faithless women and brokenhearted men. There is a snatch of one lyric that has stuck in my mind like a needle on a worn groove: *De piedra ha de ser mi cama, de piedra la cabezera . . . la mujer que a mi me quiera . . . ha de quererme de veras. Ay, Ay, Ay, corazón, porque no amas.*[3] . . . I must have heard it a thousand times since the idea of a bed made of stone, and its connection to love, first troubled me with its disturbing images.

The five-minute home movie ends with people dancing in a circle — the creative filmmaker must have set it up, so that all of them could file past him. It is both comical and sad to watch silent dancing. Since there is no justification for the absurd movements that music provides for some of us, people appear frantic, their faces embarrassingly intense. It's as if you were watching sex. Yet for years I've had dreams in the form of this home movie. In a recurring scene, familiar faces push themselves forward into my mind's eyes, plastering their features into distorted close-ups. And I'm asking them: "Who is *she*? Who is the old woman I don't recognize? Is she an aunt? Somebody's wife? Tell me who she is."

"See the beauty mark on her cheek as big as a hill on the lunar landscape of her face — well, that runs in the family. The women on your father's side of the family wrinkle early; it's the price they pay for that fair skin. The young girl with the green stain on her wedding dress is *La Novia* — just up from the Island. See, she lowers her eyes when she approaches the camera, as she's supposed to. Decent girls never look at you directly in the face. *Humilde,* humble, a girl should express humility in all her actions. She will make a good wife for your cousin. He should consider himself lucky to have met her only weeks after she arrived here. If he marries her quickly, she will make him a good Puerto Rican–style wife; but if he waits too long, she will be corrupted by the city — just like your cousin there."

"She means me. I do what I want. This is not some primitive island I live on. Do they expect me to wear a black mantilla on my head and go to mass every day? Not me. I'm an American woman, and I will do as I please. I can type faster than anyone in my senior class at Central High, and I'm going to be a secretary to a lawyer when I graduate. I can pass for an American girl anywhere — I've tried it. At least for Italian, anyway — I never speak Spanish in public. I hate these parties, but I wanted the dress. I look better than any of these *humildes* here. *My* life is going to be different. I have an American boyfriend. He is older and has a car. My parents don't know it, but I sneak out of the house late at night sometimes to be

---

[3] *De piedra ha de ser . . . amas:* Lyrics from a popular romantic ballad (called a *bolero* in Puerto Rico). Freely translated: "My bed will be made of stone, of stone also my headrest (or pillow), the woman who (dares to) loves me, will have to love me for real. Ay, Ay, Ay, my heart, why can't you (let me) love. . . . " — COFER'S NOTE.

with him. If I marry him, even my name will be American. I hate rice and beans — that's what makes these women fat."

"Your *prima*[4] is pregnant by that man she's been sneaking around with. Would I lie to you? I'm your *Tía Política*,[5] your great-uncle's common-law wife — the one he abandoned on the Island to go marry your cousin's mother. *I* was not invited to this party, of course, but I came anyway. I came to tell you that story about your cousin that you've always wanted to hear. Do you remember the comment your mother made to a neighbor that has always haunted you? The only thing you heard was your cousin's name, and then you saw your mother pick up your doll from the couch and say: 'It was as big as this doll when they flushed it down the toilet.' This image has bothered you for years, hasn't it? You had nightmares about babies being flushed down the toilet, and you wondered why anyone would do such a horrible thing. You didn't dare ask your mother about it. She would only tell you that you had not heard her right, and yell at you for listening to adult conversations. But later, when you were old enough to know about abortions, you suspected.

"I am here to tell you that you were right. Your cousin was growing an *Americanito* in her belly when this movie was made. Soon after she put something long and pointy into her pretty self, thinking maybe she could get rid of the problem before breakfast and still make it to her first class at the high school. Well, *Niña*,[6] her screams could be heard downtown. Your aunt, her mamá, who had been a midwife on the Island, managed to pull the little thing out. Yes, they probably flushed it down the toilet. What else could they do with it — give it a Christian burial in a little white casket with blue bows and ribbons? Nobody wanted that baby — least of all the father, a teacher at her school with a house in West Paterson that he was filling with real children, and a wife who was a natural blonde.

"Girl, the scandal sent your uncle back to the bottle. And guess where your cousin ended up? Irony of ironies. She was sent to a village in Puerto Rico to live with a relative on her mother's side: a place so far away from civilization that you have to ride a mule to reach it. A real change in scenery. She found a man there — women like that cannot live without male company — but believe me, the men in Puerto Rico know how a put a saddle on a woman like her. *La Gringa*,[7] they call her. Ha, ha, ha. *La Gringa* is what she always wanted to be. . . . "

The old woman's mouth becomes a cavernous black hole I fall into. And as I fall, I can feel the reverberations of her laughter. I hear the echoes of her last mocking words: *La Gringa, La Gringa!* And the conga line keeps moving silently past me. There is no music in my dream for the dancers.

When Odysseus visits Hades to see the spirit of his mother, he makes   25
an offering of sacrificial blood, but since all the souls crave an audience with the living, he has to listen to many of them before he can ask questions. I, too, have to hear the dead and the forgotten speak in my dream.

---

[4]*prima:* Female cousin. — COFER'S NOTE.
[5]*Tía Política:* Aunt by marriage. — COFER'S NOTE.
[6]*Niña:* Girl. — COFER'S NOTE.
[7]*La Gringa:* Derogatory epithet used here to ridicule a Puerto Rican girl who wants to look like a blonde North American. — COFER'S NOTE.

Those who are still part of my life remain silent, going around and around in their dance. The others keep pressing their faces forward to say things about the past.

My father's uncle is last in line. He is dying of alcoholism, shrunken and shriveled like a monkey, his face a mass of wrinkles and broken arteries. As he comes closer I realize that in his features I can see my whole family. If you were to stretch that rubbery flesh, you could find my father's face, and deep within *that* face — my own. I don't want to look into those eyes ringed in purple. In a few years he will retreat into silence, and take a long, long time to die. *Move back, Tio*, I tell him. *I don't want to hear what you have to say. Give the dancers room to move. Soon it will be midnight. Who is the New Year's Fool this time?*

1990

The Reader's Presence

1. "Silent Dancing" explores the personal, familial, and communal transformations that resulted from moving in the 1950s to Paterson, New Jersey — to "a huge tenement that had once housed Jewish families," and to a new community that emerged from the sprawling barrio that Puerto Ricans "overflowing from New York City" called home. Reread the essay carefully and summarize the transformations that occurred in the life of the narrator, her family, and their larger Puerto Rican community.

2. Judith Ortiz Cofer uses an account of a home movie to create a structure for her essay. Comment on the specific advantages and disadvantages of this strategy. How, for example, does the home movie serve as "a great visual aid" to recounting life in the barrio of Paterson, New Jersey? What effect does the fact that the home movie is in color have on what she notices? on how she writes?

3. Because Cofer's essay is built around the occasion of watching a home movie, the narrator assumes the position of an observer of the scenes and people she describes. What specific strategies as a writer does Cofer use to establish a presence for herself in this narrative and descriptive account of growing up?

5

Bernard Cooper

A Clack of Tiny Sparks: Remembrances of a Gay Boyhood

Theresa Sanchez sat behind me in ninth-grade algebra. When Mr. Hubbley faced the blackboard, I'd turn around to see what she was reading; each week a new book was wedged inside her copy of *Today's Equations*. The deception worked; from Mr. Hubbley's point of view, Theresa was engrossed in the value of *X*, but I knew otherwise. One week she perused *The Wisdom of the Orient,* and I could tell from Theresa's contemplative expression that the book contained exotic thoughts, guidelines handed down from high. Another week it was a paperback novel whose title, *Let Me Live My Life,* appeared in bold print atop every page, and whose cover, a gauzy photograph of a woman biting a strand of pearls, head thrown back in an attitude of ecstasy, confirmed my suspicion that Theresa Sanchez was mature beyond her years. She was the tallest girl in school. Her bouffant hairdo, streaked with blond, was higher than the flaccid bouffants of other girls. Her smooth skin, plucked eyebrows, and painted fingernails suggested hours of pampering, a worldly and sensual vanity that placed her within the domain of adults. Smiling dimly, steeped in daydreams, Theresa moved through the crowded halls with a languid, self-satisfied indifference to those around her. "You are merely children," her posture seemed to say. "I can't be bothered." The week Theresa hid *101 Ways to Cook Hamburger* behind her algebra book, I could stand it no longer and, after the bell rang, ventured a question.

"Because I'm having a dinner party," said Theresa. "Just a couple of intimate friends."

No fourteen-year-old I knew had ever given a dinner party, let alone

For biographical information on Bernard Cooper, see p. 646.

used the word "intimate" in conversation. "Don't you have a mother?" I asked.

Theresa sighed a weary sigh, suffered my strange inquiry. "Don't be so naive," she said. "Everyone has a mother." She waved her hand to indicate the brick school buildings outside the window. "A higher education should have taught you that." Theresa draped an angora sweater over her shoulders, scooped her books from the graffiti-covered desk, and just as she was about to walk away, she turned and asked me, "Are you a fag?"

There wasn't the slightest hint of rancor or condescension in her voice.   5
The tone was direct, casual. Still I was stunned, giving a sidelong glance to make sure no one had heard. "No," I said. Blurted really, with too much defensiveness, too much transparent fear in my response. Octaves lower than usual, I tried a "Why?"

Theresa shrugged. "Oh, I don't know. I have lots of friends who are fags. You remind me of them." Seeing me bristle, Theresa added, "It was just a guess." I watched her erect, angora back as she sauntered out the classroom door.

She had made an incisive and timely guess. Only days before, I'd invited Grady Rogers to my house after school to go swimming. The instant Grady shot from the pool, shaking water from his orange hair, freckled shoulders shining, my attraction to members of my own sex became a matter I could no longer suppress or rationalize. Sturdy and boisterous and gap-toothed, Grady was an inveterate backslapper, a formidable arm wrestler, a wizard at basketball. Grady was a boy at home in his body.

My body was a marvel I hadn't gotten used to; my arms and legs would sometimes act of their own accord, knocking over a glass at dinner or flinching at an oncoming pitch. I was never singled out as a sissy, but I could have been just as easily as Bobby Keagan, a gentle, intelligent, and introverted boy reviled by my classmates. And although I had always been aware of a tacit rapport with Bobby, a suspicion that I might find with him a rich friendship, I stayed away. Instead, I emulated Grady in the belief that being seen with him, being like him, would somehow vanquish my self-doubt, would make me normal by association.

Apart from his athletic prowess, Grady had been gifted with all the trappings of what I imagined to be a charmed life: a fastidious, aproned mother who radiated calm, maternal concern; a ruddy, stoic father with a knack for home repairs. Even the Rogerses' small suburban house in Hollywood, with its spindly Colonial furniture and chintz curtains, was a testament to normalcy.

Grady and his family bore little resemblance to my clan of Eastern   10
European Jews, a dark and vociferous people who ate with abandon — matzo and halvah and gefilte fish; foods the goyim couldn't pronounce — who cajoled one another during endless games of canasta, making the simplest remark about the weather into a lengthy philosophical discourse on the sun and the seasons and the passage of time. My mother was a chain-smoker, a dervish in a frowsy housedress. She showed her love in the most peculiar

and obsessive ways, like spending hours extracting every seed from a watermelon before she served it in perfectly bite-sized, geometric pieces. Preoccupied and perpetually frantic, my mother succumbed to bouts of absentmindedness so profound she'd forget what she was saying midsentence, smile and blush and walk away. A divorce attorney, my father wore roomy, iridescent suits, and the intricacies, the deceits inherent in his profession, had the effect of making him forever tense and vigilant. He was "all wound up," as my mother put it. But when he relaxed, his laughter was explosive, his disposition prankish: "Walk this way," a waitress would say, leading us to our table, and my father would mimic the way she walked, arms akimbo, hips liquid, while my mother and I were wracked with laughter. Buoyant or brooding, my parents' moods were unpredictable, and in a household fraught with extravagant emotion it was odd and awful to keep my longing secret.

One day I made the mistake of asking my mother what a "fag" was. I knew exactly what Theresa had meant but hoped against hope it was not what I thought; maybe "fag" was some French word, a harmless term like "naive." My mother turned from the stove, flew at me, and grabbed me by the shoulders. "Did someone call you that?" she cried.

"Not me," I said. "Bobby Keagan."

"Oh," she said, loosening her grip. She was visibly relieved. And didn't answer. The answer was unthinkable.

For weeks after, I shook with the reverberations from that afternoon in the kitchen with my mother, pained by the memory of her shocked expression and, most of all, her silence. My longing was wrong in the eyes of my mother, whose hazel eyes were the eyes of the world, and if that longing continued unchecked, the unwieldy shape of my fate would be cast, and I'd be subjected to a lifetime of scorn.

During the remainder of the semester, I became the scientist of my own 15 desire, plotting ways to change my yearning for boys into a yearning for girls. I had enough evidence to believe that any habit, regardless of how compulsive, how deeply ingrained, could be broken once and for all: The plastic cigarette my mother purchased at the Thrifty pharmacy — one end was red to approximate an ember, the other tan like a filtered tip — was designed to wean her from the real thing. To change a behavior required self-analysis, cold resolve, and the substitution of one thing for another: plastic, say, for tobacco. Could I also find a substitute for Grady? What I needed to do, I figured, was kiss a girl and learn to like it.

This conclusion was affirmed one Sunday morning when my father, seeing me wrinkle my nose at the pink slabs of lox he layered on a bagel, tried to convince me of its salty appeal. "You should try some," he said. "You don't know what you're missing."

"It's loaded with protein," added my mother, slapping a platter of sliced onions onto the dinette table. She hovered above us, cinching her housedress, eyes wet from onion fumes, the mock cigarette dangling from her lips.

My father sat there chomping with gusto, emitting a couple of hearty grunts to dramatize his satisfaction. And still I was not convinced. After a loud and labored swallow, he told me I may not be fond of lox today, but sooner or later I'd learn to like it. One's tastes, he assured me, are destined to change.

"Live," shouted my mother over the rumble of the Mixmaster. "Expand your horizons. Try new things." And the room grew fragrant with the batter of a spice cake.

The opportunity to put their advice into practice, and try out my plan to adapt to girls, came the following week when Debbie Coburn, a member of Mr. Hubbley's algebra class, invited me to a party. She cornered me in the hall, furtive as a spy, telling me her parents would be gone for the evening and slipping into my palm a wrinkled sheet of notebook paper. On it were her address and telephone number, the lavender ink in a tidy cursive. "Wear cologne," she advised, wary eyes darting back and forth. "It's a make-out party. Anything can happen."

The Santa Ana wind blew relentlessly the night of Debbie's party, careening down the slopes of the Hollywood hills, shaking the road signs and stoplights in its path. As I walked down Beachwood Avenue, trees thrashed, surrendered their leaves, and carob pods bombarded the pavement. The sky was a deep but luminous blue, the air hot, abrasive, electric. I had to squint in order to check the number of the Coburns' apartment, a three-story building with glitter embedded in its stucco walls. Above the honeycombed balconies was a sign that read BEACHWOOD TERRACE in lavender script resembling Debbie's.

From down the hall, I could hear the plaintive strains of Little Anthony's "I Think I'm Going Out of My Head." Debbie answered the door bedecked in an Empire dress, the bodice blue and orange polka dots, the rest a sheath of black and white stripes. "Op art," proclaimed Debbie. She turned in a circle, then proudly announced that she'd rolled her hair in orange juice cans. She patted the huge unmoving curls and dragged me inside. Reflections from the swimming pool in the courtyard, its surface ruffled by wind, shuddered over the ceiling and walls. A dozen of my classmates were seated on the sofa or huddled together in corners, their whispers full of excited imminence, their bodies barely discernible in the dim light. Drapes flanking the sliding glass doors bowed out with every gust of wind, and it seemed that the room might lurch from its foundations and sail with its cargo of silhouettes into the hot October night.

Grady was the last to arrive. He tossed a six-pack of beer into Debbie's arms, barreled toward me, and slapped my back. His hair was slicked back with Vitalis, lacquered furrows left by the comb. The wind hadn't shifted a single hair. "Ya ready?" he asked, flashing the gap between his front teeth and leering into the darkened room. "You bet," I lied.

Once the beers had been passed around, Debbie provoked everyone's attention by flicking on the overhead light. "Okay," she called. "Find a partner." This was the blunt command of a hostess determined to have her guests aroused in an orderly fashion. Everyone blinked, shuffled about, and

grabbed a member of the opposite sex. Sheila Garabedian landed beside me
— entirely at random, though I wanted to believe she was driven by passion — her timid smile giving way to plain fear as the light went out. Nothing for a moment but the heave of the wind and the distant banter of dogs.
I caught a whiff of Sheila's perfume, tangy and sweet as Hawaiian Punch.
I probed her face with my own, grazing the small scallop of an ear, a vel-
vety temple, and though Sheila's trembling made me want to stop, I persisted with my mission until I found her lips, tightly sealed as a private
letter. I held my mouth over hers and gathered her shoulders closer, resigned to the possibility that, no matter how long we stood there, Sheila
would be too scared to kiss me back. Still, she exhaled through her nose,
and I listened to the squeak of every breath as though it were a sigh of
inordinate pleasure. Diving within myself, I monitored my heartbeat and
respiration, trying to will stimulation into being, and all the while an image
intruded, an image of Grady erupting from our pool, rivulets of water sliding down his chest. "Change," shouted Debbie, switching on the light.
Sheila thanked me, pulled away, and continued her routine of gracious terror with every boy throughout the evening. It didn't matter whom I held —
Margaret Sims, Betty Vernon, Elizabeth Lee — my experiment was a failure; I continued to picture Grady's wet chest, and Debbie would bellow
"change" with such fervor, it could have been my own voice, my own incessant reprimand.

Our hostess commandeered the light switch for nearly half an hour.   25
Whenever the light came on, I watched Grady pivot his head toward the
newest prospect, his eyebrows arched in expectation, his neck blooming
with hickeys, his hair, at last, in disarray. All that shuffling across the carpet charged everyone's arms and lips with static, and eventually, between
low moans and soft osculations, I could hear the clack of tiny sparks and
see them flare here and there in the dark like meager, short-lived stars.

I saw Theresa, sultry and aloof as ever, read three more books —
North American Reptiles, Bonjour Tristesse, and *MGM: A Pictorial History* — before she vanished early in December. Rumors of her fate
abounded. Debbie Coburn swore that Theresa had been "knocked up" by
an older man, a traffic cop, she thought, or a grocer. Nearly quivering with
relish, Debbie told me and Grady about the home for unwed mothers in the
San Fernando Valley, a compound teeming with pregnant girls who had
nothing to do but touch their stomachs and contemplate their mistake.
Even Bobby Keagan, who took Theresa's place behind me in algebra, had
a theory regarding her disappearance colored by his own wish for escape;
he imagined that Theresa, disillusioned with society, booked passage to a
tropical island, there to live out the rest of her days without restrictions or
ridicule. "No wonder she flunked out of school," I overheard Mr. Hubbley
tell a fellow teacher one afternoon. "Her head was always in a book."

Along with Theresa went my secret, or at least the dread that she might
divulge it, and I felt, for a while, exempt from suspicion. I was, however, to

run across Theresa one last time. It happened during a period of torrential rain that, according to reports on the six o'clock news, washed houses from the hillsides and flooded the downtown streets. The halls of Joseph Le Conte Junior High were festooned with Christmas decorations: crepe-paper garlands, wreaths studded with plastic berries, and one requisite Star of David twirling above the attendance desk. In Arts and Crafts, our teacher, Gerald (he was the only teacher who allowed us — *required* us — to call him by his first name), handed out blocks of balsa wood and instructed us to carve them into bugs. We would paint eyes and antennae with tempera and hang them on a Christmas tree he'd made the previous night. "Voilà," he crooned, unveiling his creation from a burlap sack. Before us sat a tortured scrub, a wardrobe-worth of wire hangers that were bent like branches and soldered together. Gerald credited his inspiration to a Charles Addams cartoon he's seen in which Morticia, grimly preparing for the holidays, hangs vampire bats on a withered pine. "All that red and green," said Gerald. "So predictable. So *boring*."

As I chiseled a beetle and listened to rain pummel the earth, Gerald handed me an envelope and asked me to take it to Mr. Kendrick, the drama teacher. I would have thought nothing of his request if I hadn't seen Theresa on my way down the hall. She was cleaning out her locker, blithely dropping the sum of its contents — pens and textbooks and mimeographs — into a trash can. "Have a nice life," she sang as I passed. I mustered the courage to ask her what had happened. We stood alone in the silent hall, the reflections of wreaths and garlands submerged in brown linoleum.

"I transferred to another school. They don't have grades or bells, and you get to study whatever you want." Theresa was quick to sense my incredulity. "Honest," she said. "The school is progressive." She gazed into a glass cabinet that held the trophies of track meets and intramural spelling bees. "God," she sighed, "this place is so . . . barbaric." I was still trying to decide whether or not to believe her story when she asked me where I was headed. "Dear," she said, her exclamation pooling in the silence, "that's no ordinary note, if you catch my drift." The envelope was blank and white; I looked up at Theresa, baffled. "Don't be so naive," she muttered, tossing an empty bottle of nail polish into the trash can. It struck bottom with a resolute thud. "Well," she said, closing her locker and breathing deeply, "bon voyage." Theresa swept through the double doors and in seconds her figure was obscured by rain.

As I walked toward Mr. Kendrick's room, I could feel Theresa's insinuation burrow in. I stood for a moment and watched Mr. Kendrick through the pane in the door. He paced intently in front of the class, handsome in his shirt and tie, reading from a thick book. Chalked on the blackboard behind him was THE ODYSSEY BY HOMER. I have no recollection of how Mr. Kendrick reacted to the note, whether he accepted it with pleasure or embarrassment, slipped it into his desk drawer or the pocket of his shirt. I have scavenged that day in retrospect, trying to see Mr. Kendrick's expression, wondering if he acknowledged me in any way as his liaison. All

I recall is the sight of his mime through a pane of glass, a lone man mouthing an epic, his gestures ardent in empty air.

Had I delivered a declaration of love? I was haunted by the need to know. In fantasy, a kettle shot steam, the glue released its grip, and I read the letter with impunity. But how would such a letter begin? Did the common endearments apply? This was a message between two men, a message for which I had no precedent, and when I tried to envision the contents, apart from a hasty, impassioned scrawl, my imagination faltered.

Once or twice I witnessed Gerald and Mr. Kendrick walk together into the faculty lounge or say hello at the water fountain, but there was nothing especially clandestine or flirtatious in their manner. Besides, no matter how acute my scrutiny, I wasn't sure, short of a kiss, exactly what to look for — what semaphore of gesture, what encoded word. I suspected there were signs, covert signs that would give them away, just as I'd unwittingly given myself away to Theresa.

In the school library, a *Webster's* unabridged dictionary lay on a wooden podium, and I padded toward it with apprehension; along with clues to the bond between my teachers, I risked discovering information that might incriminate me as well. I had decided to consult the dictionary during lunch period, when most of the students would be on the playground. I clutched my notebook, moving in such a way as to appear both studious and nonchalant, actually believing that, unless I took precautions, someone would see me and guess what I was up to. The closer I came to the podium, the more obvious, I thought, was my endeavor; I felt like the model of The Visible Man in our science class, my heart's undulations, my overwrought nerves legible through transparent skin. A couple of kids riffled through the card catalogue. The librarian, a skinny woman whose perpetual whisper and rubber-soled shoes caused her to drift through the room like a phantom, didn't seem to register my presence. Though I'd looked up dozens of words before, the pages felt strange beneath my fingers. *Homer* was the first word I saw. *Hominid. Homogenize.* I feigned interest and skirted other words before I found the word I was after. Under the heading HO·MO·SEX·U·AL was the terse definition: *adj. Pertaining to, characteristic of, or exhibiting homosexuality. — n. A homosexual person.* I read the definition again and again, hoping the words would yield more than they could. I shut the dictionary, swallowed hard, and, none the wiser, hurried away.

As for Gerald and Mr. Kendrick, I never discovered evidence to prove or dispute Theresa's claim. By the following summer, however, I had overheard from my peers a confounding amount about homosexuals: They wore green on Thursday, couldn't whistle, hypnotized boys with a piercing glance. To this lore, Grady added a surefire test to ferret them out.

"A test?" I said.   35

"You ask a guy to look at his fingernails, and if he looks at them like this" — Grady closed his fingers into a fist and examined his nails with manly detachment — "then he's okay. But if he does this" — he held out his hands at arm's length, splayed his fingers, and coyly cocked his head — "you'd better watch out." Once he'd completed his demonstration, Grady peeled off his shirt and plunged into our pool. I dove in after. It was early June, the sky immense, glassy, placid. My father was cooking spareribs on the barbecue, an artist with a basting brush. His apron bore the caricature of a frazzled French chef. Mother curled on a chaise longue, plumes of smoke wafting from her nostrils. In a stupor of contentment she took another drag, closed her eyes, and arched her face toward the sun.

Grady dog-paddled through the deep end, spouting a fountain of chlorinated water. Despite shame and confusion, my longing for him hadn't diminished; it continued to thrive without air and light, like a luminous fish in the dregs of the sea. In the name of play, I swam up behind him, encircled his shoulders, astonished by his taut flesh. The two of us flailed, pretended to drown. Beneath the heavy press of water, Grady's orange hair wavered, a flame that couldn't be doused.

I've lived with a man for seven years. Some nights, when I'm half-asleep and the room is suffused with blue light, I reach out to touch the expanse of his back, and it seems as if my fingers sink into his skin, and I feel the pleasure a diver feels the instant he enters a body of water.

I have few regrets. But one is that I hadn't said to Theresa, "Of course I'm a fag." Maybe I'd have met her friends. Or become friends with her. Imagine the meals we might have concocted: hamburger Stroganoff, Swedish meatballs in a sweet translucent sauce, steaming slabs of Salisbury steak.

1991

The Reader's Presence

1. Cooper's essay begins and ends with references to a sophisticated classmate, Theresa Sanchez. Of what importance is she to the essay? Why does Cooper like her? What information does she provide the reader?
2. Cooper's first stirrings of attraction for his friend Grady occur in a swimming pool. What importance does swimming play in Cooper's essay? How does it provide him with a cluster of images for sexual experience?
3. Why does Cooper attend the "make-out party"? What does he hope will happen? Why do you think he ends his description of the party with the observation of the "clack of tiny sparks"? Why do you think he used that image for his title? What does it suggest about Cooper's ideas about sexuality?

6

Joan Didion

On Keeping a Notebook

" 'That woman Estelle,' " the note reads, " 'is partly the reason why George Sharp and I are separated today.' *Dirty crepe-de-Chine wrapper, hotel bar, Wilmington RR, 9:45 a.m. August Monday morning.*"

Since the note is in my notebook, it presumably has some meaning to me. I study it for a long while. At first I have only the most general notion of what I was doing on an August Monday morning in the bar of the hotel across from the Pennsylvania Railroad station in Wilmington, Delaware (waiting for a train? missing one? 1960? 1961? why Wilmington?), but I do remember being there. The woman in the dirty crepe-de-Chine wrapper had come down from her room for a beer, and the bartender had heard before the reason why George Sharp and she were separated today. "Sure," he said, and went on mopping the floor. "You told me." At the other end of the bar is a girl. She is talking, pointedly, not to the man beside her but to a cat lying in the triangle of sunlight cast through the open door. She is wearing a plaid silk dress from Peck & Peck, and the hem is coming down.

Here is what it is: The girl has been on the Eastern Shore, and now she is going back to the city, leaving the man beside her, and all she can see ahead are the viscous summer sidewalks and the 3 A.M. long-distance calls that will make her lie awake and then sleep drugged through all the steaming mornings left in August (1960? 1961?). Because she must go directly from the train to lunch in New York, she wishes that she had a safety pin for the hem of the plaid silk dress, and she also wishes that she could forget about the hem and the lunch and stay in the cool bar that smells of disinfectant and malt and make friends with the woman in the crepe-de-Chine wrapper. She is afflicted by a little self-pity, and she wants to compare Estelles. That is what that was all about.

For biographical information on Joan Didion, see p. 646.

Why did I write it down? In order to remember, of course, but exactly what was it I wanted to remember? How much of it actually happened? Did any of it? Why do I keep a notebook at all? It is easy to deceive oneself on all those scores. The impulse to write things down is a peculiarly compulsive one, inexplicable to those who do not share it, useful only accidentally, only secondarily, in the way that any compulsion tries to justify itself. I suppose that it begins or does not begin in the cradle. Although I have felt compelled to write things down since I was five years old, I doubt that my daughter ever will, for she is a singularly blessed and accepting child, delighted with life exactly as life presents itself to her, unafraid to go to sleep and unafraid to wake up. Keepers of private notebooks are a different breed altogether, lonely and resistant rearrangers of things, anxious malcontents, children afflicted apparently at birth with some presentiment of loss.

My first notebook was a Big Five tablet, given to me by my mother   5 with the sensible suggestion that I stop whining and learn to amuse myself by writing down my thoughts. She returned the tablet to me a few years ago; the first entry is an account of a woman who believed herself to be freezing to death in the Arctic night, only to find, when day broke, that she had stumbled onto the Sahara Desert, where she would die of the heat before lunch. I have no idea what turn of a five-year-old's mind could have prompted so insistently "ironic" and exotic a story, but it does reveal a certain predilection for the extreme which has dogged me into adult life; perhaps if I were analytically inclined I would find it a truer story than any I might have told about Donald Johnson's birthday party or the day my cousin Brenda put Kitty Litter in the aquarium.

So the point of my keeping a notebook has never been, nor is it now, to have an accurate factual record of what I have been doing or thinking. That would be a different impulse entirely, an instinct for reality which I sometimes envy but do not possess. At no point have I ever been able successfully to keep a diary; my approach to daily life ranges from the grossly negligent to the merely absent, and on those few occasions when I have tried dutifully to record a day's events, boredom has so overcome me that the results are mysterious at best. What is this business about "shopping, typing piece, dinner with E, depressed"? Shopping for what? Typing what piece? Who is E? Was this "E" depressed, or was I depressed? Who cares?

In fact I have abandoned altogether that kind of pointless entry; instead I tell what some would call lies. "That's simply not true," the members of my family frequently tell me when they come up against my memory of a shared event. "The party was *not* for you, the spider was *not* a black widow, *it wasn't that way at all.*" Very likely they are right, for not only have I always had trouble distinguishing between what happened and what merely might have happened, but I remain unconvinced that the distinction, for my purposes, matters. The cracked crab that I recall having for lunch the day my father came home from Detroit in 1945 must certainly be embroidery, worked into the day's pattern to lend verisimilitude; I was ten years old and would not now remember the cracked crab. The day's events did not turn on cracked crab. And yet it is precisely that fictitious crab that makes me see the afternoon all over again, a home movie run all too often, the father bearing gifts, the child weeping, an exercise in family love and guilt. Or that is what it was to me. Similarly, perhaps it never did snow that August in Vermont; perhaps there never were flurries in the night wind, and maybe no one else felt the ground hardening and summer already dead even as we pretended to bask in it, but that was how it felt to me, and it might as well have snowed, could have snowed, did snow.

How it felt to me: that is getting closer to the truth about a notebook. I sometimes delude myself about why I keep a notebook, imagine that some thrifty virtue derives from preserving everything observed. See enough and write it down, I tell myself, and then some morning when the world seems drained of wonder, some day when I am only going through the motions of doing what I am supposed to do, which is write — on that bankrupt morning I will simply open my notebook and there it will all be, a forgotten account with accumulated interest, paid passage back to the world out there: diaglogue overheard in hotels and elevators and at the hatcheck counter in Pavillon (one middle-aged man shows his hat check to another and says, "That's my old football number"); impressions of Bettina Aptheker and Benjamin Sonnenberg and Teddy ("Mr. Acapulco") Stauffer; careful *aperçus*[1] about tennis bums and failed fashion models and Greek shipping heiresses, one of whom taught me a significant lesson (a lesson I could have learned from F. Scott Fitzgerald, but perhaps we all must meet the very rich for ourselves) by asking, when I arrived to interview her in her orchid-filled sitting room on the second day of a paralyzing New York blizzard, whether it was snowing outside.

I imagine, in other words, that the notebook is about other people. But of course it is not. I have no real business with what one stranger said to another at the hatcheck counter in Pavillon; in fact I suspect that the line "That's my old football number" touched not my own imagination at all, but merely some memory of something once read, probably "The Eighty-Yard Run."[2] Nor is my concern with a woman in a dirty crepe-de-Chine wrapper in a Wilmington bar. My stake is always, of course, in the unmentioned girl in the plaid silk dress. *Remember what it was to be me:* that is always the point.

It is a difficult point to admit. We are brought up in the ethic that   10
others, any others, all others, are by definition more interesting than ourselves; taught to be diffident, just this side of self-effacing. ("You're the

---

[1]*aperçus:* Summarizing glimpse or insight (French). — EDS.
[2]*"The Eighty-Yard Run"*: Popular short story by Irwin Shaw. — EDS.

least important person in the room and don't forget it," Jessica Mitford's[3] governess would hiss in her ear on the advent of any social occasion; I copied that into my notebook because it is only recently that I have been able to enter a room without hearing some such phrase in my inner ear.) Only the very young and the very old may recount their dreams at breakfast, dwell upon self, interrupt with memories of beach picnics and favorite Liberty lawn dresses and the rainbow trout in a creek near Colorado Springs. The rest of us are expected, rightly, to affect absorption in other people's favorite dresses, other people's trout.

And so we do. But our notebooks give us away, for however dutifully we record what we see around us, the common denominator of all we see is always, transparently, shamelessly, the implacable "I." We are not talking here about the kind of notebook that is patently for public consumption, a structural conceit for binding together a series of graceful *pensées;*[4] we are talking about something private, about bits of the mind's string too short to use, an indiscriminate and erratic assemblage with meaning only for its maker.

And sometimes even the maker has difficulty with the meaning. There does not seem to be, for example, any point in my knowing for the rest of my life that, during 1964, 720 tons of soot fell on every square mile of New York City, yet there it is in my notebook, labeled "FACT." Nor do I really need to remember that Ambrose Bierce liked to spell Leland Stanford's[5] name "£eland $tanford" or that "smart women almost always wear black in Cuba," a fashion hint without much potential for practical application. And does not the relevance of these notes seem marginal at best?:

> In the basement museum of the Inyo County Courthouse in Independence, California, sign pinned to a mandarin coat: "This MANDARIN COAT was often worn by Mrs. Minnie S. Brooks when giving lectures on her TEAPOT COLLECTION."

> Redhead getting out of car in front of Beverly Wilshire Hotel, chinchilla stole, Vuitton bags with tags reading:
> MRS LOU FOX
> HOTEL SAHARA
> VEGAS

Well, perhaps not entirely marginal. As a matter of fact, Mrs. Minnie S. Brooks and her MANDARIN COAT pull me back into my own childhood, for although I never knew Mrs. Brooks and did not visit Inyo County until I was thirty, I grew up in just such a world, in houses cluttered with Indian relics and bits of gold ore and ambergris and the souvenirs my Aunt Mercy

---

[3]*Jessica Mitford* (b. 1917): British satirical writer and essayist. — EDS.
[4]*pensées:* Thoughts or reflections (French) — EDS.
[5]*Bierce . . . Stanford's:* Ambrose Bierce (1842–1914?), American journalist and short story writer known for his savage wit; Leland Stanford (1824–1893), wealthy railroad builder who was a governor of California and the founder of Stanford University. — EDS.

Farnsworth brought back from the Orient. It is a long way from that world to Mrs. Lou Fox's world, where we all live now, and is it not just as well to remember that? Might not Mrs. Minnie S. Brooks help me to remember what I am? Might not Mrs. Lou Fox help me to remember what I am not?

But sometimes the point is harder to discern. What exactly did I have in mind when I noted down that it cost the father of someone I know $650 a month to light the place on the Hudson in which he lived before the Crash? What use was I planning to make of this line by Jimmy Hoffa[6]: "I may have my faults, but being wrong ain't one of them"? And although I think it interesting to know where the girls who travel with the Syndicate have their hair done when they find themselves on the West Coast, will I ever make suitable use of it? Might I not be better off just passing it on to John O'Hara?[7] What is a recipe for sauerkraut doing in my notebook? What kind of magpie keeps this notebook? *"He was born the night the Titanic went down."* That seems a nice enough line, and I even recall who said it, but is it not really a better line in life than it could ever be in fiction?

But of course that is exactly it: not that I should ever use the line, but   15
that I should remember the woman who said it and the afternoon I heard it. We were on her terrace by the sea, and we were finishing the wine left from lunch, trying to get what sun there was, a California winter sun. The woman whose husband was born the night the *Titanic* went down wanted to rent her house, wanted to go back to her children in Paris. I remember wishing that I could afford the house, which cost $1,000 a month. "Someday you will," she said lazily. "Someday it all comes." There in the sun on her terrace it seemed easy to believe in someday, but later I had a low-grade afternoon hangover and ran over a black snake on the way to the supermarket and was flooded with inexplicable fear when I heard the checkout clerk explaining to the man ahead of me why she was finally divorcing her husband. "He left me no choice," she said over and over as she punched the register. "He has a little seven-month-old baby by her, he left me no choice." I would like to believe that my dread then was for the human condition, but of course it was for me, because I wanted a baby and did not then have one and because I wanted to own the house that cost $1,000 a month to rent and because I had a hangover.

It all comes back. Perhaps it is difficult to see the value in having one's self back in that kind of mood, but I do see it; I think we are well advised to keep on nodding terms with the people we used to be whether we find them attractive company or not. Otherwise they turn up unannounced and surprise us, come hammering on the mind's door at 4 A.M. of a bad night and demand to know who deserted them, who betrayed them, who is going

---

[6]*Jimmy Hoffa* (1913–1975?): Controversial leader of the Teamsters Union who disappeared in the mid-seventies. — EDS.
    [7]*John O'Hara* (1905–1970): American novelist who wrote several books about gangsters. — EDS.

to make amends. We forget all too soon the things we thought we could never forget. We forget the loves and the betrayals alike, forget what we whispered and what we screamed, forget who we were. I have already lost touch with a couple of people I used to be; one of them, a seventeen-year-old, presents little threat, although it would be of some interest to me to know again what it feels like to sit on a river levee drinking vodka-and-orange-juice and listening to Les Paul and Mary Ford[8] and their echoes sing "How High the Moon" on the car radio. (You see I still have the scenes, but I no longer perceive myself among those present, no longer could even improvise the dialogue.) The other one, a twenty-three-year-old, bothers me more. She was always a good deal of trouble, and I suspect she will reappear when I least want to see her, skirts too long, shy to the point of aggravation, always the injured party, full of recriminations and little hurts and stories I do not want to hear again, at once saddening me and angering me with her vulnerability and ignorance, an apparition all the more insistent for being so long banished.

It is a good idea, then, to keep in touch, and I suppose that keeping in touch is what notebooks are all about. And we are all on our own when it comes to keeping those lines open to ourselves: your notebook will never help me, nor mine you. "*So what's new in the whiskey business?*" What could that possibly mean to you? To me it means a blonde in a Pucci bathing suit sitting with a couple of fat men by the pool at the Beverly Hills Hotel. Another man approaches, and they all regard one another in silence for a while. "So what's new in the whiskey business?" one of the fat men finally says by way of welcome, and the blonde stands up, arches one foot and dips it in the pool, looking all the while at the cabaña where Baby Pignatari is talking on the telephone. That is all there is to that, except that several years later I saw the blonde coming out of Saks Fifth Avenue in New York with her California complexion and a voluminous mink coat. In the harsh wind that day she looked old and irrevocably tired to me, and even the skins in the mink coat were not worked the way they were doing them that year, not the way she would have wanted them done, and there is the point of the story. For a while after that I did not like to look in the mirror, and my eyes would skim the newspapers and pick out only the deaths, the cancer victims, the premature coronaries, the suicides, and I stopped riding the Lexington Avenue IRT because I noticed for the first time that all the strangers I had seen for years — the man with the seeing-eye dog, the spinster who read the classified pages every day, the fat girl who always got off with me at Grand Central — looked older than they once had.

It all comes back. Even that recipe for sauerkraut: even that brings it back. I was on Fire Island when I first made that sauerkraut, and it was raining, and we drank a lot of bourbon and ate the sauerkraut and went to bed at ten, and I listened to the rain and the Atlantic and felt safe. I made

---

[8]*Les Paul and Mary Ford:* Husband-and-wife musical team of the forties and fifties who had many hit records. — Eds.

the sauerkraut again last night and it did not make me feel any safer, but that is, as they say, another story.

1966

The Reader's Presence

1. Notice that Didion begins her essay not with a general comment about notebooks but with an actual notebook entry. What does the entry sound like at first? Why is it disorienting? What effect do you think Didion wants it to have on you as a reader?
2. Consider the comparison Didion makes in paragraph 6 between a notebook and a diary. How do they differ? Why is she fond of one and not the other? How does her example of a diary entry support her distinction?
3. Didion's notebook entries were never intended to have an audience. How is that apparent from the entries themselves? In what sense is Didion now the audience for her own writing? Where do you fit in as a reader? How has she now created a public audience for her private writing?

7 _____

Frederick Douglass

Learning to Read and Write

I lived in Master Hugh's family about seven years. During this time, I succeeded in learning to read and write. In accomplishing this, I was compelled to resort to various stratagems. I had no regular teacher. My mistress, who had kindly commenced to instruct me, had, in compliance with the advice and direction of her husband, not only ceased to instruct, but had set her face against my being instructed by anyone else. It is due, however, to my mistress to say of her, that she did not adopt this course of treatment immediately. She at first lacked the depravity indispensable to shutting me up in mental darkness. It was at least necessary for her to have some training in the exercise of irresponsible power, to make her equal to the task of treating me as though I were a brute.

For biographical information on Frederick Douglass, see p. 647.

My mistress was, as I have said, a kind and tender-hearted woman; and in the simplicity of her soul she commenced, when I first went to live with her, to treat me as she supposed one human being ought to treat another. In entering upon the duties of a slaveholder, she did not seem to perceive that I sustained to her the relation of a mere chattel, and that for her to treat me as a human being was not only wrong, but dangerously so. Slavery proved as injurious to her as it did to me. When I went there, she was a pious, warm, and tender-hearted woman. There was no sorrow or suffering for which she had not a tear. She had bread for the hungry, clothes for the naked, and comfort for every mourner that came within her reach. Slavery soon proved its ability to divest her of these heavenly qualities. Under its influence, the tender heart became stone, and the lamb-like disposition gave way to one of tiger-like fierceness. The first step in her downward course was in her ceasing to instruct me. She now commenced to practice her husband's precepts. She finally became even more violent in her opposition than her husband himself. She was not satisfied with simply doing as well as he had commanded; she seemed anxious to do better. Nothing seemed to make her more angry than to see me with a newspaper. She seemed to think that here lay the danger. I have had her rush at me with a face made all up of fury, and snatch from me a newspaper, in a manner that fully revealed her apprehension. She was an apt woman; and a little experience soon demonstrated, to her satisfaction, that education and slavery were incompatible with each other.

From this time I was most narrowly watched. If I was in a separate room any considerable length of time, I was sure to be suspected of having a book, and was at once called to give an account of myself. All this, however, was too late. The first step had been taken. Mistress, in teaching me the alphabet, had given me the *inch,* and no precaution could prevent me from taking the *ell.*

The plan which I adopted, and the one by which I was most successful, was that of making friends of all the little white boys whom I met in the street. As many of these as I could, I converted into teachers. With their kindly aid, obtained at different times and in different places, I finally succeeded in learning to read. When I was sent to errands, I always took my book with me, and by going one part of my errand quickly, I found time to get a lesson before my return. I used also to carry bread with me, enough of which was always in the house, and to which I was always welcome; for I was much better off in this regard than many of the poor white children in our neighborhood. This bread I used to bestow upon the hungry little urchins, who, in return, would give me that more valuable bread of knowledge. I am strongly tempted to give the names of two or three of those little boys, as a testimonial of the gratitude and affection I bear them; but prudence forbids — not that it would injure me, but it might embarrass them; for it is almost an unpardonable offense to teach slaves to read in this Christian country. It is enough to say of the dear little fellows, that they lived on Philpot Street, very near Durgin and Bailey's ship-yard. I used to talk this matter of slavery over with them. I would sometimes say to them, I wished I could be as free as they would be when they got to be men. "You will be free as soon as you are twenty-one, *but I am a slave for life!* Have not I as good a right to be free as you have?" These words used to trouble them; they would express for me the liveliest sympathy, and console me with the hope that something would occur by which I might be free.

I was now about twelve-years-old, and the thought of being *a slave for life* began to bear heavily upon my heart. Just about this time, I got hold of a book entitled "The Columbian Orator." Every opportunity I got, I used to read this book. Among much of other interesting matter, I found in it a dialogue between a master and his slave. The slave was represented as having run away from his master three times. The dialogue represented the conversation which took place between them, when the slave was retaken the third time. In this dialogue, the whole argument in behalf of slavery was brought forward by the master, all of which was disposed of by the slave. The slave was made to say some very smart as well as impressive things in reply to his master — things which had the desired though unexpected effect; for the conversation resulted in the voluntary emancipation of the slave on the part of the master.

In the same book, I met with one of Sheridan's[1] mighty speeches on and in behalf of Catholic emancipation. These were choice documents to me. I read them over and over again with unabated interest. They gave tongue to interesting thoughts of my own soul, which had frequently flashed through my mind, and died away for want of utterance. The moral which I gained from the dialogue was the power of truth over the conscience of even a slaveholder. What I got from Sheridan was a bold denunciation of slavery, and a powerful vindication of human rights. The reading of these documents enabled me to utter my thoughts, and to meet the arguments brought forward to sustain slavery; but while they relieved me of one difficulty, they brought on another even more painful than the one of which I was relieved. The more I read, the more I was led to abhor and detest my enslavers. I could regard them in no other light than a band of successful robbers, who had left their homes, and gone to Africa, and stolen us from our homes, and in a strange land reduced us to slavery. I loathed them as being the meanest as well as the most wicked of men. As I read and contemplated the subject, behold! that very discontentment which Master Hugh had predicted would follow my learning to read had already come, to torment and sting my soul to unutterable anguish. As I writhed under it, I would at times feel that learning to read had been a curse rather than a blessing. It had given me a view of my wretched condition, without the remedy. It opened my eyes to the horrible pit, but to no ladder upon which to get out. In moments of agony, I envied my fellow-

5

---

[1]*Sheridan's:* Richard Brinsley Butler Sheridan (1751–1816), Irish dramatist and orator. — EDS.

slaves for their stupidity. I have often wished myself a beast. I preferred the condition of the meanest reptile to my own. Anything, no matter what, to get rid of thinking! It was this everlasting thinking of my condition that tormented me. There was no getting rid of it. It was pressed upon me by every object within sight or hearing, animate or inanimate. The silver trump of freedom had roused my soul to eternal wakefulness. Freedom now appeared, to disappear no more forever. It was heard in every sound, and seen in every thing. It was ever present to torment me with a sense of my wretched condition. I saw nothing without seeing it, I heard nothing without hearing it, and felt nothing without feeling it. It looked from every star, it smiled in every calm, breathed in every wind, and moved in every storm.

I often found myself regretting my own existence, and wishing myself dead; and but for the hope of being free, I have no doubt but that I should have killed myself, or done something for which I should have been killed. While in this state of mind, I was eager to hear anyone speak of slavery. I was a ready listener. Every little while, I could hear something about the abolitionists. It was some time before I found what the word meant. It was always used in such connections as to make it an interesting word to me. If a slave ran away and succeeded in getting clear, or if a slave killed his master, set fire to a barn, or did anything very wrong in the mind of a slaveholder, it was spoken of as the fruit of *abolition.* Hearing the word in this connection very often, I set about learning what it meant. The dictionary afforded me little or no help. I found it was "the act of abolishing"; but then I did not know what was to be abolished. Here I was perplexed. I did not dare to ask anyone about its meaning, for I was satisfied that it was something they wanted me to know very little about. After a patient waiting, I got one of our city papers, containing an account of the number of petitions from the North, praying for the abolition of slavery in the District of Columbia, and of the slave trade between the States. From this time I understood the words *abolition* and *abolitionist,* and always drew near when that word was spoken, expecting to hear something of importance to myself and fellow-slaves. The light broke in upon me by degrees. I went one day down on the wharf of Mr. Waters; and seeing two Irishmen unloading a scow of stone, I went, unasked, and helped them. When we had finished, one of them came to me and asked me if I were a slave. I told him I was. He asked, "Are ye a slave for life?" I told him that I was. The good Irishman seemed to be deeply affected by the statement. He said to the other that it was a pity so fine a little fellow as myself should be a slave for life. He said it was a shame to hold me. They both advised me to run away to the North; that I should find friends there, and that I should be free. I pretended not to be interested in what they said, and treated them as if I did not understand them; for I feared they might be treacherous. White men have been known to encourage slaves to escape, and then, to get the reward, catch them and return them to their masters. I was afraid that these seemingly good men might use me so; but I nevertheless remembered their advice, and from that time I resolved to run away. I looked forward to a time at which it would be safe for me to escape. I was too young to think of doing so immediately; besides, I wished to learn how to write, as I might have occasion to write my own pass. I consoled myself with the hope that I should one day find a good chance. Meanwhile, I would learn to write.

The idea as to how I might learn to write was suggested to me by being in Durgin and Bailey's shipyard, and frequently seeing the ship carpenters, after hewing, and getting a piece of timber ready for use, write on the timber the name of that part of the ship for which it was intended. When a piece of timber was intended for the larboard side, it would be marked thus — "L." When a piece was for the starboard side, it would be marked thus — "S." A piece for the larboard side forward, would be marked thus — "L.F." When a piece was for starboard side forward, it would be marked thus — "S.F." For larboard aft, it would be marked thus — "L.A." For starboard aft, it would be marked thus — "S.A." I soon learned the names of these letters, and for what they were intended when placed upon a piece of timber in the shipyard. I immediately commenced copying them, and in a short time was able to make the four letters named. After that, when I met with any boy who I knew could write, I would tell him I could write as well as he. The next word would be, "I don't believe you. Let me see you try it." I would then make the letters which I had been so fortunate as to learn, and ask him to beat that. In this way I got a good many lessons in writing, which it is quite possible I should never have gotten in any other way. During this time, my copy-book was the board fence, brick wall, and pavement; my pen and ink was a lump of chalk. With these, I learned mainly how to write. I then commenced and continued copying the Italics in *Webster's Spelling Book,* until I could make them all without looking on the book. By this time, my little Master Thomas had gone to school, and learned how to write, and had written over a number of copy-books. These had been brought home, and shown to some of our near neighbors, and then laid aside. My mistress used to go to class meeting at the Wilk Street meeting-house every Monday afternoon, and leave me to take care of the house. When left thus, I used to spend the time in writing in the spaces left in master Thomas's copy-book, copying what he had written. I continued to do this until I could write a hand very similar to that of Master Thomas. Thus, after a long, tedious effort for years, I finally succeeded in learning how to write.

1845

The Reader's Presence

1. What sort of audience does Douglass anticipate for his reminiscence? How much does he assume his readers know about the conditions of slavery?

2. What kind of book seems to interest Douglass the most? What les-

sons does he learn from his reading? Why does he say that learning to read was more of a curse than a blessing? In general, what
are his motives for wanting to read and write? In what ways are
his motives connected to slavery?

3. Notice that Douglass learns to read *before* he learns to write. Is
that the way you learned? What other ways are possible? What
method seems best to you? While rereading the essay, try making
a chart of Douglass's educational progress. Having already
learned to read, why does he need the letters used by ship carpenters in order to learn how to write?

8

Nora Ephron

A Few Words about Breasts

I have to begin with a few words about androgyny. In grammar school,
in the fifth and sixth grades, we were all tyrannized by a rigid set of rules
that supposedly determined whether we were boys or girls. The episode in
Huckleberry Finn where Huck is disguised as a girl and gives himself away
by the way he threads a needle and catches a ball — that kind of thing. We
learned that the way you sat, crossed your legs, held a cigarette, and looked
at your nails — the way you did these things instinctively was absolute
proof of your sex. Now obviously most children did not take this literally,
but I did. I thought that just one slip, just one incorrect cross of my legs or
flick of an imaginary cigarette ash would turn me from whatever I was into
the other thing; that would be all it took, really. Even though I was out-
wardly a girl and had many of the trappings generally associated with girl-
dom — a girl's name, for example, and dresses, my own telephone, an autograph book — I spent the early years of my adolescence absolutely
certain that I might at any point gum it up. I did not feel at all like a girl. I
was boyish. I was athletic, ambitious, outspoken, competitive, noisy, rambunctious. I had scabs on my knees and my socks slid into my loafers and
I could throw a football. I wanted desperately not to be that way, not to be
a mixture of both things, but instead just one, a girl, a definite indisputable
girl. As soft and as pink as a nursery. And nothing would do that for me, I
felt, but breasts.

For biographical information on Nora Ephron, see p. 648.

I was about six months younger than everyone else in my class, and so for about six months after it began, for six months after my friends had begun to develop (that was the word we used, develop), I was not particularly worried. I would sit in the bathtub and look down at my breasts and know that any day now, any second now, they would start growing like everyone else's. They didn't. "I want to buy a bra," I said to my mother one night. "What for?" she said. My mother was really hateful about bras, and by the time my third sister had gotten to the point where she was ready to want one, my mother had worked the whole business into a comedy routine. "Why not use a Band-Aid instead?" she would say. It was a source of great pride to my mother that she had never even had to wear a brassiere until she had her fourth child, and then only because her gynecologist made her. It was incomprehensible to me that anyone could ever be proud of something like that. It was the 1950s, for God's sake. Jane Russell. Cashmere sweaters. Couldn't my mother see that? "*I am too old to wear an undershirt.*" Screaming. Weeping. Shouting. "Then don't wear an undershirt," said my mother. "But I want to buy a bra." "What for?"

I suppose that for most girls, breasts, brassieres, that entire thing, has more trauma, more to do with the coming of adolescence, with becoming a woman, than anything else. Certainly more than getting your period, although that, too, was traumatic, symbolic. But you could see breasts; they were there; they were visible. Whereas a girl could claim to have her period for months before she actually got it and nobody would ever know the difference. Which is exactly what I did. All you had to do was make a great fuss over having enough nickels for the Kotex machine and walk around clutching your stomach and moaning for three to five days a month about The Curse and you could convince anybody. There is a school of thought somewhere in the women's lib/women's mag/gynecology establishment that claims that menstrual cramps are purely psychological, and I lean toward it. Not that I didn't have them finally. Agonizing cramps, heating-pad cramps, go-down-to-the-school-nurse-and-lie-on-the-cot cramps. But unlike any pain I had ever suffered, I adored the pain of cramps, welcomed it, wallowed in it, bragged about it. "I can't go. I have cramps." "I can't do that. I have cramps." And most of all, gigglingly, blushingly: "I can't swim. I have cramps." Nobody ever used the hard-core word. Menstruation. God, what an awful word. Never that. "I have cramps."

The morning I first got my period, I went into my mother's bedroom to tell her. And my mother, my utterly-hateful-about-bras mother, burst into tears. It was really a lovely moment, and I remember it so clearly not just because it was one of the two times I ever saw my mother cry on my account (the other was when I was caught being a six-year-old kleptomaniac), but also because the incident did not mean to me what it meant to her. Her little girl, her firstborn, had finally become a woman. That was what she was crying about. My reaction to the event, however, was that I might well be a woman in some scientific, textbook sense (and could at least stop faking every month and stop wasting all those nickels). But in another sense — in a visible sense — I was as androgynous and as liable to tip over into boyhood as ever.

I started with a 28 AA bra. I don't think they made them any smaller   5 in those days, although I gather that now you can buy bras for five-year-olds that don't have any cups whatsoever in them; trainer bras they are called. My first brassiere came from Robinson's Department Store in Beverly Hills. I went there alone, shaking, positive they would look me over and smile and tell me to come back next year. An actual fitter took me into the dressing room and stood over me while I took off my blouse and tried the first one on. The little puffs stood out on my chest. "Lean over," said the fitter. (To this day, I am not sure what fitters in bra departments do except to tell you to lean over.) I leaned over, with the fleeting hope that my breasts would miraculously fall out of my body and into the puffs. Nothing.

"Don't worry about it," said my friend Libby some months later, when things had not improved. "You'll get them after you're married."

"What are you talking about?" I said.

"When you get married," Libby explained, "your husband will touch your breasts and rub them and kiss them and they'll grow."

That was the killer. Necking I could deal with. Intercourse I could deal with. But it had never crossed by mind that a man was going to touch my breasts, that breasts had something to do with all that, petting, my God, they never mentioned petting in my little sex manual about the fertilization of the ovum. I became dizzy. For I knew instantly — as naïve as I had been only a moment before — that only part of what she was saying was true: the touching, rubbing, kissing part, not the growing part. And I knew that no one would ever want to marry me. I had no breasts. I would never have breasts.

My best friend in school was Diana Raskob. She lived a block from me   10 in a house full of wonders. Engligh muffins, for instance. The Raskobs were the first people in Beverly Hills to have English muffins for breakfast. They also had an apricot tree in the back, and a badminton court, and a subscription to *Seventeen* magazine, and hundreds of games, like Sorry and Parcheesi and Treasure Hunt and Anagrams. Diana and I spent three or four afternoons a week in their den reading and playing and eating. Diana's mother's kitchen was full of the most colossal assortment of junk food I have ever been exposed to. My house was full of apples and peaches and milk and homemade chocolate-chip cookies — which were nice, and good for you, but-not-right-before-dinner-or-you'll-spoil-your-appetite. Diana's house had nothing in it that was good for you, and what's more, you could stuff it in right up until dinner and nobody cared. Bar-B-Q potato chips (they were the first in them, too), giant bottles of ginger ale, fresh popcorn with melted butter, hot fudge sauce on Baskin-Robbins jamoca ice cream, powdered-sugar doughnuts from Van de Kamp's. Diana and I had been best friends since we were seven; we were about equally popular in school (which is to say, not particularly), we had about the same success with boys (extremely intermittent), and we looked much the same. Dark. Tall. Gangly.

It is September, just before school begins. I am eleven years old, about to enter the seventh grade, and Diana and I have not seen each other all summer. I have been to camp and she has been somewhere like Banff with her parents. We are meeting, as we often do, on the street midway between our two houses, and we will walk back to Diana's and eat junk and talk about what has happened to each of us that summer. I an walking down Walden Drive in my jeans and my father's shirt hanging out and my old red loafers with the socks falling into them and coming toward me is . . . I take a deep breath . . . a young woman. Diana. Her hair is curled and she has a waist and hips and a bust and she is wearing a straight skirt, an article of clothing I have been repeatedly told I will be unable to wear until I have the hips to hold it up. My jaw drops, and suddenly I am crying, crying hysterically, can't catch my breath sobbing. My best friend has betrayed me. She has gone ahead without me and done it. She has shaped up.

Here are some things I did to help:
Bought a Mark Eden Bust Developer.
Slept on my back for four years.
Splashed cold water on them every night because some French actress   15
said in *Life* magazine that that was what *she* did for her perfect bustline.
Ultimately, I resigned myself to a bad toss and began to wear padded bras. I think about them now, think about all those years in high school and I went around in them, my three padded bras, every single one of them with different-sized breasts. Each time I changed bras I changed sizes: one week nice perky but not too obtrusive breasts, the next medium-sized slightly pointy ones, the next week knockers, true knockers; all the time, whatever size I was, carrying around this rubberized appendage on my chest that occasionally crashed into a wall and was poked inward and had to be poked outward — I think about all that and wonder how anyone kept a straight face through it. My parents, who normally had no restraints about needling me — why did they say nothing as they watched my chest go up and down? My friends, who would periodically inspect my breasts for signs of growth and reassure me — why didn't they at least counsel consistency?

And the bathing suits. I die when I think about the bathing suits. That was the era when you could lay an uninhabited bathing suit on the beach and someone would make a pass at it. I would put one on, an absurd swimsuit with its enormous bust built into it, the bones from the suit stabbing me in the rib cage and leaving little red welts on my body, and there I would be, my chest plunging straight downward absolutely vertically from my collarbone to the top of my suit and then suddenly, wham, out came all that padding and material and wiring absolutely horizontally.

Buster Klepper was the first boy who ever touched them. He was my boyfriend my senior year of high school. There is a picture of him in my high-school yearbook that makes him look quite attractive in a Jewish, horn-rimmed-glasses sort of way, but the picture does not show the pimples, which were air-brushed out, or the dumbness. Well, that isn't really fair. He wasn't dumb. He just wasn't terribly bright. His mother refused to accept it, refused to accept the relentlessly average report cards, refused to deal with her son's inevitable destiny in some junior college or other. "He was tested," she would say to me, apropos of nothing, "and it came out a hundred and forty-five. That's near-genius." Had the word "under-achiever" been coined, she probably would have lobbed that one at me, too. Anyway, Buster was really very sweet — which is, I know, damning with faint praise, but there it is. I was the editor of the front page of the high-school newspaper and he was editor of the back page; we had to work together, side by side, in the print shop, and that was how it started. On our first date, we went to see *April Love,* starring Pat Boone. Then we started going together. Buster had a green coupe, a 1950 Ford with an engine he had hand-chromed until it shone, dazzled, reflected the image of anyone who looked into it, anyone usually being Buster polishing it or the gas-station attendants he constantly asked to check the oil in order for them to be overwhelmed by the sparkle on the valves. The car also had a boot stretched over the back seat for reasons I never understood; hanging from the rearview mirror, as was the custom, was a pair of angora dice. A previous girlfriend named Solange, who was famous throughout Beverly Hills High School for having no pigment in her right eyebrow, had knitted them for him. Buster and I would ride around town, the two of us seated to the left of the steering wheel. I would shift gears. It was nice.

There was necking. Terrific necking. First in the car, overlooking Los Angeles from what is now the Trousdale Estates. Then on the bed of his parents' cabana at Ocean House. Incredibly wonderful, frustrating necking, I loved it, really, but no further than necking, please don't, please, because there I was absolutely terrified of the general implications of going-a-step-further with a near-dummy and also terrified of his finding out there was next to nothing there (which he knew, of course; he wasn't that dumb).

I broke up with him at one point. I think we were apart for about   20
two weeks. At the end of that time, I drove down to see a friend at a boarding school in Palos Verdes Estates and a disc jockey played "April Love" on the radio four times during the trip. I took it as a sign. I drove straight back to Griffith Park to a golf tournament Buster was playing in (he was the sixth-seeded teenage golf player in southern California) and presented myself back to him on the green of the eighteenth hole. It was all very dramatic. That night we went to a drive-in and I let him get his hand under my protuberances and onto my breasts. He really didn't seem to mind at all.

"Do you want to marry my son?" the woman asked me.

"Yes," I said.

I was nineteen years old, a virgin, going with this woman's son, this big strange woman who was married to a Lutheran minister in New Hampshire and pretended she was gentile and had this son, by her first husband, this total fool of a son who ran the hero-sandwich concession at Harvard Business School and whom for one moment one December in New Hampshire I said — as much out of politeness as anything else — that I wanted to marry.

"Fine," she said. "Now, here's what you do. Always make sure you're on top of him so you won't seem so small. My bust is very large, you see, so I always lie on my back to make it look smaller, but you'll have to be on top most of the time."

I nodded. "Thank you," I said.

"I have a book for you to read," she went on. "Take it with you when you leave. Keep it." She went to the bookshelf, found it, and gave it to me. It was a book on frigidity.

"Thank you," I said.

That is a true story. Everything in this article is a true story, but I feel I have to point out that that story in particular is true. It happened on December 30, 1960. I think about it often. When it first happened, I naturally assumed that the woman's son, my boyfriend, was responsible. I invented a scenario where he had had a little heart-to-heart with his mother and had confessed that his only objection to me was that my breasts were small; his mother then took it upon herself to help out. Now I think I was wrong about the incident. The mother was acting on her own, I think: That was her way of being cruel and competitive under the guise of being helpful and maternal. You have small breasts, she was saying; therefore you will never make him as happy as I have. Or you have small breasts; therefore you will doubtless have sexual problems. Or you have small breasts; therefore you are less woman than I am. She was, as it happens, only the first of what seems to me to be a never-ending string of women who have made competitive remarks to me about breast size. "I would love to wear a dress like that," my friend Emily says to me, "but my bust is too big." Like that. Why do women say these things to me? Do I attract these remarks the way other women attract married men or alcoholics or homosexuals? This summer, for example. I am at a party in East Hampton and I am introduced to a woman from Washington. She is a minor celebrity, very pretty and Southern and blond and outspoken, and I am flattered because she has read something I have written. We are talking animatedly, we have been talking no more than five minutes, when a man comes up to join us. "Look at the two of us," the woman says to the man, indicating me and her. "The two of us together couldn't fill an A cup." Why does she say that? It isn't even true, dammit, so why? Is she even more addled than I am on this subject? Does she honestly believe there is something wrong with her size breasts, which, it seems to me, now that I look hard at them, are just right? Do I unconsciously bring out competitiveness in women? In that form? What did I do to deserve it?

As for men.

There were men who minded and let me know that they minded. There were men who did not mind. In any case, *I* always minded.

And even now, now that I have been countlessly reassured that my figure is a good one, now that I am grown-up enough to understand that most of my feelings have very little to do with the reality of my shape, I am nonetheless obsessed by breasts. I cannot help it. I grew up in the terrible fifties — with rigid stereotypical sex roles, the insistence that men be men and dress like men and women be women and dress like women, the intolerance of androgyny — and I cannot shake it, cannot shake my feelings of inadequacy. Well, that time is gone, right? All those exaggerated examples of breast worship are gone, right? Those women were freaks, right? I know all that. And yet here I am, stuck with the psychological remains of it all, stuck with my own peculiar version of breast worship. You probably think I am crazy to go on like this: Here I have set out to write a confession that is meant to hit you with the shock of recognition, and instead you are sitting there thinking I am thoroughly warped. Well, what can I tell you? If I had had them, I would have been a completely different person. I honestly believe that.

After I went into therapy, a process that made it possible for me to tell   25 total strangers at cocktail parties that breasts were the hang-up of my life, I was often told that I was insane to have been bothered by my condition. I was also frequently told, by close friends, that I was extremely boring on the subject. And my girlfriends, the ones with nice big breasts, would go on endlessly about how their lives had been far more miserable than mine. Their bra straps were snapped in class. They couldn't sleep on their stomachs. They were stared at whenever the word "mountain" cropped up in geography. And *Evangeline,* good God what they went through every time someone had to stand up and recite the Prologue to Longfellow's *Evangeline:* " . . . stand like druids of eld . . . / With beards that rest on their bosoms." It was much worse for them, they tell me. They had a terrible time of it, they assure me. I don't know how lucky I was, they say.

I have thought about their remarks, tried to put myself in their place, considered their point of view. I think they are full of shit.

1972

The Reader's Presence

1. How does Ephron make small breasts a matter of identity as well as appearance? Do you agree with her? Do you think her reasons for this are well founded? Are they based only on her personal experience?

2. "That is a true story. Everything in this article is a true story, . . . " Ephron maintains in paragraph 21. Why does she feel she must say this? What attitude does she anticipate in her reader? Why might she think her readers would doubt her story? Do you?

3. In paragraph 24, Ephron addresses her readers directly: "You probably think I am crazy to go on like this: Here I have set out to write a confession that is meant to hit you with the shock of recognition, and instead you are sitting there thinking I am thoroughly warped." What are her assumptions about her readers at this point? What does she seem worried about? What is your response as a reader? How closely do you fit into the role she is assigning for her readers?

9

Francine du Plessix Gray

I Write for Revenge against Reality

A nightmare recurs since childhood:

Facing a friend, I struggle for words and emit no sound. I have an urgent message to share but am struck dumb, my jaw is clamped shut as in a metal vise, I gasp for breath and cannot set my tongue free. At the dream's end my friend has fled and I am locked into the solitude of silence.

The severe stutter I had as a child, my father's impatience and swiftness of tongue, his constant interruption of me when I tried to speak?

Or perhaps another incident which also has to do with the threat of the Father and the general quirkiness of my French education: One day when I was 9 I was assigned my first free composition. From infancy I had been tutored at home in Paris by a tyrannical governess, the two of us traveling once a week to a correspondence school whose Gallically rigid assignments (memorization of Asian capitals and Latin verbs, codifying of sentence parts) were hardly conducive to a fertile imagination. "Write a Story About Anything You Wish," Central Bureau suddenly ordered. Filled with excitement and terror by this freedom, I began as a severe minimalist:

"The little girl was forbidden by her parents to walk alone to the lake at the other end of the long lawn. But she wished to visit a luminous green-eyed frog who would offer her the key to freedom. One day she disobeyed her parents and walked to the lake and immediately drowned." (The End)   5

"Pathetic dribble!" the Father stormed on his daily visit to my study room. "You dare call that a story! What will become of you if you can't ever finish anything!"

For biographical information on Francine du Plessix Gray, see p. 650.

It was a warm May evening of 1939, the year before he died in the Resistance. The love of my life (my father was himself an occasional scribbler) was warning me that I should never write again. I still remember the hours I spent honing those meager sentences, the square white china inkwell into which I squeezed the rubber filler of a Waterman pen, the awkwardness of ink-stained fingers as I struggled to shape my letters (I was born left-handed and had been forced to use my right), the tears, the sense that my writing was doomed to be sloppy, abortive, good for naught.

So it may have begun, the central torment of my life, my simultaneous need to commit fantasies to paper and the terror that accompanies that need, the leaden slowness of the words' arrival, my struggle with the clamped metal jaws of mouth and mind. An affliction deepened by that infatuation with the written word that possesses most solitary children. For books had been the only companions of my childhood prison, particularly such stirring tales of naval adventure as *Captains Courageous* or *Two Years Before the Mast,* which fueled dreams of running away to sea and never being seen again.

Then came the war, the flight to America, the need to learn a new language. English was learned as a means of survival and became a lover to be seduced and conquered as swiftly as possible, to be caressed and rolled on the tongue in a continuous ecstasy of union. English words, from the time I was 11 on, were my medium of joy and liberation. I fondled them by memorizing twenty lines of Blake when ten had been assigned; I wooed them so assiduously that I won the Lower School Spelling Bee within 10 months of having come to the the United States. (I was the only foreign scholarship student at the Spence School; shortly after the contest a delegation of Spence parents descended on my mother, who was supporting us by designing hats at Henri Bendel's, to verify that we were true emigrés and not usurpers from Brooklyn.)

I continued to court my new tongue by struggling for A's in English, by 10 being elected editor of the school paper, which a predecessor had artfully named Il Spenceroso. Omens of a "literary gift" continued to accrete — a prize in Bryn Mawr's Freshman Essay Contest, the Creative Writing Award at Barnard for three stories of a strictly autobiographical nature. Such portents brought no security. I fled from myself by being a compulsive talker, a bureaucrat, polemicist, hack journalist. I had taken no more than two courses in literature beyond Freshman English, thinking I was smartass enough to learn it for myself. One of the other courses had been a creative writing class that earned me a C — for first-person fictions about situations I knew nothing about — I seemed always to be a middle-aged alcoholic actor seeking salvation in a Bowery church. After that fiasco I had sought refuge in rigor and formalism — physics, philosophy, medieval history. There was a curious furtiveness about the way I continued to carry on my love affair with literature. I copied entire paragraphs from Henry James or T. S. Eliot into private notebooks out of sheer delectation in the texture of their prose. In a stretch of a few solitary vacation weeks I would memorize two hundred lines of Marvell for the pleasure of speaking them to myself during nights of insomnia. Why all this reluctance and covertness?

"You're writing pure junk," Charles Olson[1] had stormed at me during a summer workshop at Black Mountain when I'd handed him my prize-winning college stories. "If you want to be a writer keep it to a journal." The giant walrus rising from his chair, 6 feet 7 inches of him towering. ". . . AND ABOVE ALL DON'T TRY TO PUBLISH ANYTHING FOR TEN YEARS!" Another paternal figure had censored me into silence, perhaps this time for the best.

I followed Big Charles's advice. I kept my journal in New Orleans where I dallied as if I had 10 lives to squander, drinking half a bottle of gin a night as I followed a jazz clarinetist on the rounds of Bourbon Street. I remained faithful to my secret vice in the dawns of New York when I worked the night shift at United Press, writing World in Briefs about Elks' Meetings and watermelon-eating contests in Alabama. I remained loyal to my journal through a myriad of failed aspirations while flirting with the thought of entering Harvard's Department of Architecture, of going to Union Theological Seminary for a degree in divinity. I persevered with it when I moved to Paris to earn my living as a fashion reporter, dallying with a succession of consummate narcissists to whom I eventually gave their literary due. I continued to write it when I fulfilled one of my life's earliest dreams and spent five years as a painter of meticulously naturalistic landscapes and still lifes.

By then I was married and had two children. And since I lived in deep country and in relative solitude, encompassed by domestic duties, the journal became increasingly voluminous, angry, introspective. The nomad, denied flight and forced to turn inward, was beginning to explode. One day when I was thirty-three, after I'd cooked and smiled for a bevy of weekend guests whom I never wished to see again, I felt an immense void, great powerlessness, the deepest loneliness I'd ever known. I wept for some hours, took out a notebook, started rewriting one of the three stories that had won me my Barnard prize. It was the one about my governess. It was published a short time later in *The New Yorker*, one year past the deadline Charles Olson had set me. It was to become, 12 years and two books of nonfiction later, the first chapter of *Lovers and Tyrants*. The process of finishing that book was as complex and lengthy as it was painful. It entailed a solid and delicate psychoanalysis which forced me to accept my father's death. Epiphany achieved, I was able to write the novel's three last chapters — my first genuine at-

---

[1]*Olson:* Charles Olson (1910–1970), the influential American poet who taught at the experimental Black Mountain College. — EDS.

tempt at fiction — in a mere six months. I may have had to bury my father to set my tongue free.

And yet what kind of writer have I become, six years and two novels later? Few scribblers I know have struggled so hard for so little. I am too many things I do not wish to be — a Jane of all trades shuttling back and forth between scant fiction, voluminous reporting, innumerable and un- memorable literary essays. I feel honored but yet undeserving of the appel- lation "novelist." I am merely a craftsperson, a cabinetmaker of texts and occasionally, I hope, a witness to our times. My terror of fictional inven- tion has denied me that activity which from childhood on has been the most furtively longed for, which has proved to be (when I finally began to tackle it) the most deeply satisfying.

Might I remain brainwashed, along with many of my generation, by   15 the notion that fiction is the noblest, the most "creative" of all genres of prose? No avocation has better clarified that issue or my identity as a writer than the business of teaching. I stress to young colleagues that some of the greatest masterpieces of our time have been works of non- fiction or hybrid forms which defy classification — James Agee's *Let Us Now Praise Famous Men*, Edmund Wilson's criticism, Peter Handke's *A Sorrow Beyond Dreams*, all of Roland Barthes's work. I urge them to shake loose from the peculiarly American fixation on novel-writing. I tell them that the obsession to write The Great American Novel might have done more harm to generations of Americans than all the marijuana in Mexico. The syllabus for the course I taught at Yale last fall sums it all up:

THE WRITING OF THE TEXT: This is a seminar in the reading and writing of literature which I hope can remain untainted by the word "cre- ative." It is dedicated to the premise that a distinction between "fiction" and "nonfiction" is potentially harmful to many aspiring writers who will progress more fruitfully if they are encouraged to think of their writing as pure "text" without worrying about what "form" or "genre" it will fall into.

Reading Assignments: F. Scott Fitzgerald's *Crack-Up*, Max Frisch's *Sketchbooks*, Flaubert's *Dictionary of Accepted Ideas*, Elizabeth Hardwick's *Sleepless Nights*, Boris Pasternak's *Safe Conduct*, William Gass's *On Being Blue*, Maureen Howard's *Facts of Life*.

The first thing we must do when we set out to write, I also tell my classes, is to shed all narcissism. My own decades of fear came from my anxiety that my early drafts were ugly, sloppy, not promising enough. We must persevere and scrawl atrocities; persevere dreadful draft after dread- ful draft in an unhindered stream of consciousness, persevere, if need be, in Breton's[2] technique of automatic writing, of mindless trance. And within

---

[2]**Breton:** André Breton (1896–1966), French surrealist poet and literary theorist. — EDS.

that morass of words there may be an ironic turn of phrase, a dislocation that gives us a key to the voice, the tone, the structure we're struggling to find. I am a witness to the lateness of my own vocation, the hesitation and terrors that still haunt all my beginnings, the painful slowness with which I proceed through a minimum of four drafts in both fiction and nonfiction.

Question:

Why do I go on writing, seeing the continuing anguish of the act, the   20 dissatisfaction I feel toward most results?

Flannery O'Connor[3] said it best: "I write because I don't know what I think until I read what I say."

I write out of a desire for revenge against reality, to destroy forever the stuttering powerless child I once was, to gain the love and attention that silenced child never had, to allay the dissatisfaction I still have with myself, to be something other than what I am. I write out of hate, out of a desire for revenge against all the men who have oppressed and humiliated me.

I also write out of love and gratitude for a mother and stepfather who made me feel worthy by hoarding every scrap of correspondence I ever sent them; love and gratitude for a husband of exquisite severity who still edits every final draft that leaves my typewriter. I write out of an infantile dread of ever disappointing them again.

I write because in the act of creation there comes that mysterious, abundant sense of being both parent and child; I am giving birth to an Other and simultaneously being reborn as child in the playground of creation.

I write on while continuing to despair that I can't ever achieve the   25 inventiveness, irreverence, complexity of my favorite contemporary authors — Milan Kundera, Italo Calvino, Günter Grass, Salman Rushdie, to name only the foreign ones. They are certain enough of their readers' love (or indifferent enough to it, since the great Indifferents are the great Seducers) to indulge in that shrewd teasing and misguiding of the reader, that ironic obliqueness which is the marrow of the best modernist work. It is not only my lesser gift that is at fault. Behind my impulsive cataloguing, my Slavic unleashing of emotion, my Quaker earnestness to inform my readers guilelessly of all I know, there still lurks the lonely, stuttering child too terrified of losing the reader's love to take the necessary risks.

Yet, I remain sustained by a definition of faith once offered me by Ivan Illich: "Faith is a readiness for the Surprise." I write because I have faith in the possibility that I can eventually surprise myself. I am still

---

[3]*Flannery O'Connor* (1925–1964): American short story writer and novelist. — EDS.

occasionally plagued by that recurring nightmare of my jaw being clamped shut, my mouth frozen in silence. But I wake up from it with less dread, with the hope that some day my tongue will loosen and emit a surprising new sound which even I, at first, shall not be able to understand.

1982

The Reader's Presence

1. What do you think the author means by her title? In what sense can writing be considered an act of vengeance? Why does she take her revenge against "reality"? Why isn't she more specific? What did reality do to her?

2. In what ways does Gray portray herself as a victim? By whom was she victimized? By what institutions? As a reader, do you feel that she is inviting your sympathy? Are there any aspects of her background and career that you might find enviable? If so, how as a reader do you reconcile the feelings of empathy and envy?

3. The author quotes the American writer Flannery O'Connor as saying: "I write because I don't know what I think until I read what I say." Examine that statement carefully. What does it presuppose about the relationship between thinking and writing? Do you think O'Connor's comment supports or contradicts Gray's motive for writing as defined in her essay?

10 —————————————————————

Langston Hughes

Salvation

I was saved from sin when I was going on thirteen. But not really saved. It happened like this. There was a big revival at my Auntie Reed's church. Every night for weeks there had been much preaching, singing, praying, and shouting, and some very hardened sinners had been brought to Christ, and the membership of the church had grown by leaps and bounds. Then just before the revival ended, they held a special meeting for children, "to bring the young lambs to the fold." My aunt spoke of it for days ahead. That night I was escorted to the front row and placed on the mourners' bench with all the other young sinners, who had not yet been brought to Jesus.

My aunt told me that when you were saved you saw a light, and something happened to you inside! And Jesus came into your life! And God was with you from then on! She said you could see and hear and feel Jesus in your soul. I believed her. I had heard a great many old people say the same thing and it seemed to me they ought to know. So I sat there calmly in the hot, crowded church, waiting for Jesus to come to me.

The preacher preached a wonderful rhythmical sermon, all moans and shouts and lonely cries and dire pictures of hell, and then he sang a song about the ninety and nine safe in the fold, but one little lamb was left out in the cold. Then he said: "Won't you come? Won't you come to Jesus? Young lambs, won't you come?" And he held out his arms to all us young sinners there on the mourners' bench. And the little girls cried. And some of them jumped up and went to Jesus right away. But most of us just sat there.

A great many old people came and knelt around us and prayed, old women with jet-black faces and braided hair, old men with work-gnarled hands. And the church sang a song about the lower lights are burning,

For biographical information on Langston Hughes, see p. 652.

some poor sinners to be saved. And the whole building rocked with prayer and song.

Still I kept waiting to *see* Jesus.   5

Finally all the young people had gone to the altar and were saved, but one boy and me. He was a rounder's son named Westley. Westley and I were surrounded by sisters and deacons praying. It was very hot in the church, and getting late now. Finally Westley said to me in a whisper: "God damn! I'm tired o' sitting here. Let's get up and be saved." So he got up and was saved.

Then I was left all alone on the mourners' bench. My aunt came and knelt at my knees and cried, while prayers and song swirled all around me in the little church. The whole congregation prayed for me alone, in a mighty wail of moans and voices. And I kept waiting serenely for Jesus, waiting, waiting — but he didn't come. I wanted to see him, but nothing happened to me. Nothing! I wanted something to happen to me, but nothing happened.

I heard the songs and the minister saying: "Why don't you come? My dear child, why don't you come to Jesus? Jesus is waiting for you. He wants you. Why don't you come? Sister Reed, what is this child's name?"

"Langston," my aunt sobbed.

"Langston, why don't you come? Why don't you come and be saved?   10 Oh, Lamb of God! Why don't you come?"

Now it was really getting late. I began to be ashamed of myself, holding everything up so long. I began to wonder what God thought about Westley, who certainly hadn't seen Jesus eitner, but who was now sitting proudly on the platform, swinging his knickerbockered legs and grinning down at me, surrounded by deacons and old women on their knees praying. God had not struck Westley dead for taking his name in vain or for lying in the temple. So I decided that maybe to save further trouble, I'd better lie, too, and say that Jesus had come, and get up and be saved.

So I got up.

Suddenly the whole room broke into a sea of shouting, as they saw me rise. Waves of rejoicing swept the place. Women leaped in the air. My aunt threw her arms around me. The minister took me by the hand and led me to the platform.

When things quieted down, in a hushed silence, punctuated by a few ecstatic "Amens," all the new young lambs were blessed in the name of God. Then joyous singing filled the room.

That night, for the first time in my life but one — for I was a big boy   15 twelve years old — I cried. I cried, in bed alone, and couldn't stop. I buried my head under the quilts, but my aunt heard me. She woke up and told my uncle I was crying because the Holy Ghost had come into my life, and because I had seen Jesus. But I was really crying because I couldn't bear to tell her that I had lied, that I had deceived everybody in the church, that I hadn't seen Jesus, and that now I didn't believe there was a Jesus anymore, since he didn't come to help me.

                                                                    1940

The Reader's Presence

1. Pay close attention to Hughes's two opening sentences. How would you describe their tone? How do they suggest the underlying pattern of the essay? How do they introduce the idea of deception right from the start? Who is being deceived in the essay? Is it the congregation? God? Hughes's aunt? the reader?

2. Consider the character of Westley. Why is he important to Hughes's narrative? What would happen to the essay if Westley were not introduced and described?

3. In many ways this is an essay about belief. What is it that Hughes has been asked to believe? What does he expect to see? Reread the essay and consider the word *come*. Hughes waits for Jesus to come to him. Yet the preacher invites the children to come to Jesus. How does an awareness of this difference affect your reading of the essay?

11

Zora Neale Hurston

How It Feels to Be Colored Me

I am colored but I offer nothing in the way of extenuating circumstances except the fact that I am the only Negro in the United States whose grandfather on the mother's side was *not* an Indian chief.

I remember the very day that I became colored. Up to my thirteenth year I lived in the little Negro town of Eatonville, Florida. It is exclusively a colored town. The only white people I knew passed through the town going to or coming from Orlando. The native whites rode dusty horses, the Northern tourists chugged down the sandy village road in automobiles. The town knew the Southerners and never stopped cane chewing[1] when they passed. But the Northerners were something else again. They were peered at cautiously from behind curtains by the timid. The more venturesome would come out on the porch to watch them go past and got just as much pleasure out of the tourists as the tourists got out of the village.

The front porch might seem a daring place for the rest of the town,

---

For biographical information on Zora Neale Hurston, see p. 652.
[1] *cane chewing:* Chewing on sugar cane. — EDS.

but it was a gallery seat for me. My favorite place was atop the gate-post. Proscenium box for a born first-nighter. Not only did I enjoy the show, but I didn't mind the actors knowing that I liked it. I usually spoke to them in passing. I'd wave at them and when they returned my salute, I would say something like this: "Howdy-do-well-I-thank-you-where-you-goin'?" Usually automobile or the horse paused at this, and after a queer exchange of compliments, I would probably "go a piece of the way" with them, as we say in farthest Florida. If one of my family happened to come to the front in time to see me, of course negotiations would be rudely broken off. But even so, it is clear that I was the first "welcome-to-our-state" Floridian, and I hope the Miami Chamber of Commerce will please take notice.

During this period, white people differed from colored to me only in that they rode through town and never lived there. They liked to hear me "speak pieces" and sing and wanted to see me dance the parse-me-la,[2] and gave me generously of their small silver for doing these things, which seemed strange to me for I wanted to do them so much that I needed bribing to stop. Only they didn't know it. The colored people gave no dimes. They deplored any joyful tendencies in me, but I was their Zora nevertheless. I belonged to them, to the nearby hotels, to the county — everybody's Zora.

But changes came in the family when I was thirteen, and I was sent to   5 school in Jacksonville. I left Eatonville, the town of the oleanders, as Zora. When I disembarked from the river-boat at Jacksonville, she was no more. It seemed that I had suffered a sea change. I was not Zora of Orange County any more, I was now a little colored girl. I found it out in certain ways. In my heart as well as in the mirror, I became a fast brown — warranted not to rub nor run.

But I am not tragically colored. There is no great sorrow dammed up in my soul, nor lurking behind my eyes. I do not mind at all. I do not belong to the sobbing school of Negrohood who hold that nature somehow has given them a lowdown dirty deal and whose feelings are all hurt about it. Even in the helter-skelter skirmish that is my life, I have seen that the world is to the strong regardless of a little pigmentation more or less. No, I do not weep at the world — I am too busy sharpening my oyster knife.

Someone is always at my elbow reminding me that I am the granddaughter of slaves. It fails to register depression with me. Slavery is sixty years in the past. The operation was successful and the patient is doing well, thank you. The terrible struggle that made me an American out of a potential slave said "On the line!" The Reconstruction[3] said "Get set!"; and the generation before said "Go!" I am off to a flying start and I must

[2]*parse-me-la:* Probably an old dance song. — EDS.
[3]*Reconstruction:* The period of rebuilding and reorganizing immediately following the Civil War. — EDS.

not halt in the stretch to look behind and weep. Slavery is the price I paid for civilization, and the choice was not with me. It is a bully adventure and worth all that I have paid through my ancestors for it. No one on earth ever had a greater chance for glory. The world to be won and nothing to be lost. It is thrilling to think — to know that for any act of mine, I shall get twice as much praise or twice as much blame. It is quite exciting to hold the center of the national stage, with the spectators not knowing whether to laugh or to weep.

The position of my white neighbor is much more difficult. No brown specter pulls up a chair beside me when I sit down to eat. No dark ghost thrusts its leg against mine in bed. The game of keeping what one has is never so exciting as the game of getting.

I do not always feel colored. Even now I often achieve the unconscious Zora of Eatonville before the Hegira.[4] I feel most colored when I am thrown against a sharp white background.

For instance at Barnard. "Beside the waters of the Hudson" I feel my   10 race. Among the thousand white persons, I am a dark rock surged upon, and overswept, but through it all, I remain myself. When covered by the waters, I am; and the ebb but reveals me again.

Sometimes it is the other way around. A white person is set down in our midst, but the contrast is just as sharp for me. For instance, when I sit in the drafty basement that is The New World Cabaret with a white person, my color comes. We enter chatting about any little nothing that we have in common and are seated by the jazz waiters. In the abrupt way that jazz orchestras have, this one plunges into a number. It loses no time in circumlocutions, but gets right down to business. It constricts the thorax and splits the heart with its tempo and narcotic harmonies. This orchestra grows rambunctious, rears on its hind legs and attacks the tonal veil with primitive fury, rending it, clawing it until it breaks through to the jungle beyond. I follow those heathen — follow them exultingly. I dance wildly inside myself; I yell within, I whoop; I shake my assegai[5] above my head, I hurl it true to the mark *yeeeeoooww!* I am in the jungle and living in the jungle way. My face is painted red and yellow and my body is painted blue. My pulse is throbbing like a war drum. I want to slaughter something — give pain, give death to what, I do not know. But the piece ends. The men of the orchestra wipe their lips and rest their fingers. I creep back slowly to the veneer we call civilization with the last tone and find the white friend sitting motionless in his seat, smoking calmly.

"Good music they have here," he remarks, drumming the table with his fingertips.

[4]*Hegira:* A journey to safety. Historically it refers to Mohammed's flight from Mecca in 622 A.D. — EDS.
    [5]*assegai:* A hunting spear. — EDS.

Music. The great blobs of purple and red emotion have not touched him. He has only heard what I felt. He is far away and I see him but dimly across the ocean and the continent that have fallen between us. He is so pale with his whiteness then and I am *so* colored.

At certain times I have no race, I am *me*. When I set my hat at a certain angle and saunter down Seventh Avenue, Harlem City, feeling as snooty as the lions in front of the Forty-Second Street Library, for instance. So far as my feelings are concerned, Peggy Hopkins Joyce[6] on the Boule Mich[7] with her gorgeous raiment, stately carriage, knees knocking together in a most aristocratic manner, has nothing on me. The cosmic Zora emerges. I belong to no race nor time. I am the eternal feminine with its string of beads.

I have no separate feeling about being an American citizen and colored. I am merely a fragment of the Great Soul that surges within the boundaries. My country, right or wrong.

Sometimes, I feel discriminated against, but it does not make me angry. It merely astonishes me. How *can* any deny themselves the pleasure of my company? It's beyond me.

But in the main, I feel like a brown bag of miscellany propped against a wall. Against a wall in company with other bags, white, red, and yellow. Pour out the contents, and there is discovered a jumble of small things priceless and worthless. A first-water diamond, an empty spool, bits of broken glass, lengths of string, a key to a door long since crumbled away, a rusty knife-blade, old shoes saved for a road that never was and never will be, a nail bent under the weight of things too heavy for any nail, a dried flower or two still a little fragrant. In your hand is the brown bag. On the ground before you is the jumble it held — so much like the jumble in the bags, could they be emptied, that all might be dumped in a single heap and the bags refilled without altering the content of any greatly. A bit of colored glass more or less would not matter. Perhaps that is how the Great Stuffer of Bags filled them in the first place — who knows?

1928

The Reader's Presence

1. Hurston's essay is divided into four sections. Do you find this division significant? What relationships can you detect among the separate parts?

[6]*Peggy Hopkins Joyce:* A fashionable American who was a celebrity in the 1920s. — EDS.

[7]*Boul Mich:* The Boulevard Saint-Michel in Paris. — EDS.

2. How much does being "colored" inform Hurston's identity? Does it seem to matter throughout the essay? At what points does color seem deeply important to Hurston? When does it seem less important? What do you think the reasons are for these differences?

3. Consider Hurston's startling image in the final paragraph: "But in the main, I feel like a brown bag of miscellany propped against a wall." Try rereading the essay with this image in mind. In what ways does it help you understand Hurston's sense of personal identity? In what ways can it be said to describe the form and style of the essay itself?

12 _____

Edward Iwata

Race without Face

I would soon discover I was different from white people.

A cosmetic surgeon was about to cut into my face that gray winter morning. Hot lights glared as I lay on the operating table. Surgical tools clattered in containers, sharp metal against metal. I felt like a lamb awaiting a shearing of its wool.

Shivering from the air-conditioned chill, I wondered if I'd made a mistake. Had my hatred of Oriental facial features, fanned by my desire to do well in a white world, blinded me so easily?

An instant before the anesthetic numbed my brain cells, I felt the urge to cry out. I imagined ripping off my gown and sprinting to freedom. But at that point, even wetting my cracked lips was hard to do.

"I trust you implicitly," I said, as a supplicant might beseech a priest.   5

Oddly, I imagined seeing, as if peering through a bloody gauze, the contours of two faces rushing toward me. One face was twisted into sadness. The other glowed with a look akin to pride. One white, one yellow; one white, one yellow. I did not know which was which.

For biographical information on Edward Iwata, see p. 653.

A month earlier in her Beverly Hills medical office, the surgeon said she planned to taper the thick, round tip of my nose. She also wanted to build up my flat bridge with strips of cartilage.

"Oriental noses have no definition," she said, waving a clipboard like an inspector on an auto assembly line.

While she was at it, she suggested, why not work on the eyes, also? They looked dark and tired, even though I was twenty years old then. A simple slash along my eyelids would remove the fat cells that kept my eyes from springing into full, double-lidded glory.

Why not? I had thought. Didn't I want to distance myself from the 10 faceless, Asian masses? I hated the pale image in the mirror. I hated the slurs hurled at me that I couldn't shut out. I hated being a gook, a Nip.

It's a taboo subject, but true: Many people of color have, at some point in their youths, imagined themselves as Caucasian, the Nordic or Western European ideal. Hop Sing meets Rock Hudson. Michael Jackson magically transformed into Robert Redford.

For myself, an eye and nose job — or *blepharoplasty* and *rhinoplasty* in surgeons' tongue — would bring me the gift of acceptance. The flick of a scalpel would buy me respect.

To make the decision easier, a close friend loaned me $1500. I didn't tell my parents or anyone else about it.

The surgery was quick and painless. My friend drove me at dawn to the medical clinic. At 7 A.M. sharp, the surgeon, a brusque Hispanic woman, swept into the office and rushed passed us.

The next time I saw her, she was peering down at me and penciling 15 lines on my face to guide her scalpel. A surgeon's mask and cap hid her own face; I saw only a large pair of eyes plotting the attack on my epidermis and cartilage. While I shivered, a nurse and an anesthesiologist laughed and gossiped.

"You have beautiful eyelashes, Edward," the surgeon said. It seemed like an odd thing to notice at that moment.

I tumbled into darkness. My last memory was a deep desire to yell or strike out, to stab the surgeon and her conspirators with their knives.

The surgeon went for my eyes first. Gently, she cut and scooped out the fat cells that lined my upper eyelid. That created a small furrow, which popped open my eyes a bit and created double-lids, every Asian model's dream.

Ignoring the blood, she then slit the upper inside of my nostril. Like a shortorder cook trimming a steak, she carved the cartilage and snipped off bits of bone and tissue. Soon she was done. After a coffee break or lunch, she would move on to the next patient.

Later that day, I was wheeled out of a bright recovery room. My head 20 and limbs felt dull and heavy, as if buried in mud. A draft swept up my surgical gown and chilled my legs. Although my face was bound in bandages, I felt naked. Without warning, a sharp sense of loss engulfed me, a child away from home who is not sure why he aches so.

"Eddie, what did you do?" asked my mother when I next saw her. Then, her voice shaking, "Why did you do this? Were you ashamed of yourself?" As if struck by a lance, my legs weakened, my body cleaved. I was lost, flailing away in shadows, but I shrugged off her question and said something lame. I didn't sense at the time that whatever had compelled me to scar my face could also drive me further from home.

One week passed before I was brave enough to take my first look in the mirror. I stood in the bathroom, staring at my reflection until my feet got sore.

Stitch marks scarred my face like tracks on a drug addict's arm. My haggard eyes were rounder; my nose smaller and puggy. In the glare of the bathroom light, my skin seemed pale and washed out, a claylike shade of light brown. I looked like a medical illustration from a century ago, when doctors would have measured my facial angle and cranium size for racial intelligence.

I wanted to claw my new face.

The image I pictured in the mirror was an idealized Anglo man, an   25 abstraction. I didn't realize at the time that my flaws were imagined, not real. I felt compelled to measure up to a cultural ideal in a culture that had never asked me what my ideal was.

Indeed, to many Anglos, the males of our culture are a mystery. Most whites know us only through the neutered images: Japanese salarymen. Sumo wrestlers. Sushi chefs. We're judged by our slant of eye and color of skin. We're seen only as eunuchs, as timid dentists and engineers. Books and movies portray us as ugly and demonic. We're truly a race of Invisible Men.

Clearly, Asian-American men have been psychologically castrated in this country. Our history is one of emasculation and accommodation. Japanese-Americans, for the most part, filed quietly into the internment camps. Proud Cantonese immigrants were trapped in their Chinatown ghettoes and bachelor societies by poverty and discrimination.

In the corporate arena, Asian-American men find their cultural values and strengths overshadowed by ego-driven, back-slapping, hyper-competitive whites. And, while socially we may be more "acceptable" than blacks and Hispanics, we are not acceptable enough to run legislatures, schools, corporations. Our women may be marriage material for whites, but our men are still seen as gooks. On the street, we're cursed or spat upon — even killed — because of our looks.

It cannot be denied, either, that we're regarded as kowtowing wimps not only by whites, but by a lot of Asian-American women — even those with racial and ethnic pride. Privately, they confess they see a lack of strong Asian-American men who fit an ideal of manhood: virile and sensitive, intelligent and intuitive, articulate and confident.

Of course, we must share part of the blame. Many of us grow up   30 swallowing the stereotypes, accepting the role white society imposes on us. And aside from a handful of us in politics, law, the media, education, and the arts, the rest of us are too reserved and opinionless in the white world.

Simone de Beauvoir wrote that a woman "insinuates herself into a world that has doomed her to passivity." The same could have been said of too many Asian-American men, including myself.

I recall an episode four years ago when a former boss and I lunched at a Thai restaurant. I thought I deserved a promotion — new status, new duties, a bigger paycheck — real fast. He disagreed. Between bites of curry chicken, I was startled to hear this executive label me in words used for "docile" Asian men and "uppity" blacks.

"You're a quiet, reserved kind of guy," he said, waving his hands in the air. A few bites later, he veered the other way and portrayed me as a "cocky, arrogant young reporter . . . with a chip on your shoulder."

I was confused. Was I an obedient employee, or a hard-charging militant? And how could I be both? I ate my rice and said little. My face flushed with anger. Later that day, I left work early, fantasizing about a bloody, *ninja*-style revenge.

Why didn't I fight back? Instead of sitting silently, why didn't I challenge his superficial view of me? 35

Part of it was cultural. Our Eastern values are living, breathing elements in our lives, not topics we study in Zen Buddhism class. Regardless of how assimilated we may be, these values rise to claim our attention at unpredictable moments. So while I fancied myself a strong-minded journalist, I still felt shackled by cultural bonds, afraid of arguing back. It was the whole *deference* thing, this Asian habit of respecting authority to a fault.

I yearned for my boss' acceptance. I was blinded by my desire to fit in as a man, a journalist, a corporate player. In Japan, this could be called *ittaikan,* a longing for oneness with a person or a group. Readers of the Japanese psychiatrist Takeo Doi might think of it as *amae,* a passive dependency on another's love or kindness.

And so, by others and by ourselves, we're rendered impotent. I wasn't a limp lover. But outside my home or bedroom, I often felt powerless — desexed like a baby chick. It was as if I didn't exist. Employers didn't acknowledge my work. Professors in college rebuffed my remarks in the classroom. *Maître d*'s ignored my presence in restaurants. I felt voiceless, faceless.

A friend of mine, a San Francisco lawyer in her thirties, was thrilled to meet a liberal Japanese man from Tokyo after years of dating Asian-Americans. Several of her boyfriends had been bright and sensitive, but they lacked what she called "male energy" — a strength of purpose and destiny, a vision of one's goals in life.

"It's almost a *samurai* spirit that Asian-American men somehow lost in 40 white society, as if they'd been neutered," she said. "Even though I'm a career woman, sometimes I want a man to take the lead, while I play the mothering role. . . . Reconnecting with a strong, decisive Asian male has been an eye-opener."

My friend's opinion is not unusual. Unfortunately some Asian-American men, scared of the nerd label, charge blindly in the opposite direction, aping Western notions of kick-ass masculinity: Rambo. Mike Tyson. Michael Milken. They become obsessed with the art of war, obsessed with competition. It's yet another stereotype, and equally damaging.

One example, a hot item in our community, is an all-male calendar, featuring pin-ups of Asian-American hunks. While the men photographed are all respected, the beefcake images they project are caricatures of the white physical ideal: the well-oiled, muscular body, the chiseled face, the hint of male power and violence. They're like minorities in beauty pageants who look more like the blond Miss America prototype than their own race.

"How warped that sense of manhood and beauty is," observes King-Kok Cheung, a literary scholar at UCLA. "In some ways, our internal oppression as Asians is greater than white oppression. We need to understand that anyone who is comfortable with himself is attractive."

Probably the biggest blow to my young psyche occurred at my predominantly white high school. My advanced English class boasted students who were versed in Petrarchan sonnets before I had learned to read baseball box scores. Even so, as a teenager I saw myself as a maverick writer in the manner of Jack Kerouac or Jack London. Mrs. Worthy, our strict teacher, showed me otherwise.

"Mr. Iwata, I'd like you to work on 'A Book Is Like a Frigate' by Emily   45
Dickinson," she said, assigning homework. "That shouldn't be too difficult to handle, even for you."

I still get chills when I recall my classmates shifting in their seats, their blue and green eyes staring at me. To Mrs. Worthy, I was the slow, quiet Asian boy who sat by the window, waiting for the school bus to dump me back in the inner-city.

Outside the classroom, media images confused me even more. Nowhere — from racist children's books to great literature to movies with evil Jap soldiers — did I see my true reflection in the larger world. Unlike students today, I had no Asian or Asian-American heroes, no cultural icons, to lead the way.

In sociological jargon, I was an Assimilationist, a Marginal Man, a Stranger. Like many Asian-Americans, I craved admiration and acceptance, mostly from whites. I worshipped Anglo models of success, the middle-class ethos carried to extremes.

But contrary to our shining image as model minorities, I learned I had *not* arrived. All the hard work and schooling and cosmetic surgery in the world couldn't change the way I looked, or the way I was perceived. I could not erase my skin color, no matter how hard I tried. My status in the white professional world was illusory; it did not transcend the harsh realities of race and class.

In my search for acceptance, I modeled myself after whites, especially 50
in college — in speech and diction, style and dress, body language and eye
contact. I thought I was a failure when no white coeds danced with me at
a frat party. At beer busts, I avoided Asian-American women because they
looked like the girls in my old neighborhood, with their moon faces and
daikon (white radish) legs.

Before that, I used to hang with Hispanic buddies from East L.A. I was
a *vato,* an *esé,* a buddha brother. And before that, I played basketball and
dodged gangs in Crenshaw, a black and Asian neighborhood in Los Angeles. I wasn't cool, but I could fake it. When black classmates called me
"nigger" or "homes" (short for "homeboy"), I smiled inside. Another
mask.

At the same time, I fought the tug of family and culture. Seeking a
place beyond my ken, I left Crenshaw to live on campus as a college freshman. I saw my new world as a stage ripe for rebellion.

My courses — journalism, literature, history — disappointed my
parents. They hoped I would study medicine or business, like all good
Japanese-American kids.

I was studying, all right: the science of interviewing accident victims
for newspaper stories. Themes of Dionysian abandon, from Blake to Lord
Byron. My literary hero was James Joyce, whose modernist art promised to
transport me to Arabys unknown. I had not yet begun to study myself.

My bid for a cultural identity, a sense of manhood, quickened as my 55
mother and father retired, and as Dad's health worsened. Clearly, a strong
impulse pushed me to step up and fill their vacuum, to carry on a family
legacy in some way.

My parents, Phillip and Midori, and sixteen relatives spent the years
during World War II at Manzanar, the internment camp eight miles from
the town of Independence in the Mojave Desert. When I was a kid, Mom
never talked about Manzanar. Instead, she wove harmless tales for my
brother, my sister, and me. The stories protected us from the truth.

Dad, a strong silent type, claimed he never cared about the political
quest for redress — the twenty thousand dollars due each Japanese-
American interned during the war. Interviewing him for the first story I
did on Manzanar was not easy. "You don't have to write about this,
do you?" he asked. Speaking to him the next time was even harder. "I told
you I'm not a good person to interview," he snapped. "Talk to Mom
again."

His reticence was understandable. Conservative Japanese-Americans
hide their private faces in public. *Nomen no yo,* their ancestors said. The
face is like a Noh mask. My mother and father calmly accepted their fates.

Like many Japanese-Americans, my parents veiled the past and whitewashed their memories. They believed the government line that Uncle Sam
sent them to the concentration camps for their own good, for their safety.
The camps also gave them postwar opportunities by spreading them across
the great land, they were told.

In truth, the internment was a horror for families, a civil rights disas- 60
ter, the death of the old Japanese-American culture. For the men, the sense
of powerlessness must have been devastating.

In my parents' desire to hide the past, I sensed a reflection of my own
self-hate. Like most *sansei* (third generation), I ignored or never sought out the
tragic facts of that era. As a student, I never read about the camps. As a young
journalist, I picked up shards of history, but never the whole dark tale.

But after much cajoling, I persuaded my folks to join me on a pilgrimage to Manzanar in 1988. Only tumbleweeds, stone ruins, and barbed wire
remained at the windy, desolate site. Nonetheless, the pilgrimage was a
glimpse into a forgotten world, a gateway to the past. The ghosts were
powerful. But I found no neat, easy answers.

There was no stopping now. The next spring, we flew to Japan. While
trade wars dominated the news in Tokyo, my parents and I journeyed into
the rural heart of our ancestral homeland.

For the first time, we met the Iwata and Kunitomi clans, who still live
on the rice farms in Wakayama and Okayama that our families have
owned since the eighteenth century. Among other revelations, I learned
that the head of the Iwata family, my father's cousin, shared my Japanese
name, Masao ("righteous boy").

Seated on a *tatami* floor at the Iwata homestead, we enjoyed *sukiyaki* 65
and country-style vegetables we hadn't eaten since my grandmothers died
several years ago. The *gohan* (steamed rice) was the lightest and sweetest
we had ever tasted. Masao smiled broadly as he served the hot food, its
steam rising toward the small family altar in the corner of the dining room.

At one point, I noticed Masao staring at Dad. His steady gaze was rude
by Japanese standards. But apparently struck by the family resemblance,
Masao couldn't avert his eyes from Dad's face. With their wavy hair and
thick eyebrows, their dark skin and rakish grins, they could have been
brothers.

I'm not a misty-eyed romantic longing for an ancestral past. Peering
for gods in mountain shrines and temple ruins is not my idea of good journalism. Still, this was my flesh and blood seated in an old farmhouse on
that warm spring night. I thought of a line from *No-No Boy*, a novel of
WWII by John Okada: "If he was to find his way back to that point of
wholeness and belonging, he must do so in the place where he had begun
to lose it." Here was my point of origin, where my family began. As we
scooped bowlfuls of rice into our hungry selves, a light rain wet the furrows of black soil in the field outside.

For me, Japan brought to the surface cultural conflicts and competing
values. Even though I was as American as teriyaki chicken, the old Buddhist and Confucian values reached me in Southern California. *Giri* (obligation). *Omoiyari* (empathy). *Oyakoko* (filial piety). The Japanese, in fact,
have a phrase unique to them: "*Jibun ga nai*," or "to have no self." They
rarely use the first-person pronoun when they speak. Loyal *samurai*
who followed their feudal barons to the grave had little over some
Japanese-American kids.

Those values gave me strength — and also confused the hell out of me. The issue of personal independence and family ties was the most painful. How was I to pursue my goals, forge an identity, yet honor my parents without question? And if I chose filial piety, how was I to keep the bond strong without sacrificing my hard-won, American-style autonomy?

A Zen koan[1] asks, "What was your face like before you were born?" I   70 cannot know for sure how deeply the culture of my ancestors touches me, but I know I will never again see myself as a scarred, hollow man lost in the shadows, beating back death.

Japan freed my spirit and gave rise to an atavistic pride I had never known. The past, I realized, could be cradled like an heirloom found in an old trunk in the attic. I was a player in a family history that spanned the reigns of emperors, from feudal Japan to the modern Heisei Era, Year One — the year of my first visit to Japan. And my story would add a few scenes to that unfolding narrative.

After Manzanar and Japan, I began to see my surgery in a new slant of light. Like the victims of internment, I started coming to terms with my real and emotional scars.

Obviously, the surgery had been a rebellion against my "Japaneseness" and the traditional values of my parents. It was psychic surgery, an act of mutilation, a symbolic suicide. It was my self-hatred finding a stage.

Like many Asian Americans, I'm searching for a new cultural character and destiny.

Certainly, we need to change many of our past goals. While much is   75 known of our drive toward the American dream, little is written of our worship of materialism, our narcissism, our obsession with showing that we've *arrived*. We're brilliant students of what historian Richard Hofstadter called "status politics," the effort to enhance one's social standing.

Somewhere between Asia and an "A+" in Achievement, we lost our way. The trappings of style and success — a fancy degree, a prestigious job, a Mercedes in every garage — have become more important than the accomplishments. Instead, the images we impress upon white society and other Asian-Americans are paramount. We have become the "racial bourgeoisie," a term coined by legal scholar Mari Matsuda. The hard work may bring "success," but this kind of success will not set us free.

The numbers reflect the reality. They tell a sad story, especially in education, supposedly our stronghold. Asian-Americans held 3.1 percent of administrative and management jobs in California colleges and universities, according to an analysis of 1980 census data by Amado Cabezas and Gary Kawaguchi of UC Berkeley's Ethnic Studies Department. Even more startling were the income figures. Asian-American faculty and staff were paid salaries *40 to 70 percent* of the mean annual income of white men. And this is only in one field.

[1]*koan:* A paradoxical question used for Zen Buddhist meditation. — EDS.

A century ago, sugar plantation owners in Hawaii counted Asian laborers as part of their business supplies. Today, we're still regarded similarly: as bodies to fill affirmative-action goals, as background in movies. Even worse, we gladly accept what society imposes on us, so anxious are we to measure up to its standards of "success."

There is so much cultural brainwashing to undo, and so much to learn about our place in this country.

Many of us will not tolerate the status quo anymore. The *Miss Saigon*   80
controversy reflects our rising anger. It's *our* March on Washington, *our* Stonewall gay riot, *our* Jackson, Mississippi. In other recent shows of strength, we've rallied around the racial killings of Asian-Americans. Our congressional and community leaders won redress payments for the internment of Japanese-Americans. And more Asian-Americans are filling seats in public office.

But where do we go next? And how do we define our community, if at all?

Clearly, we need new visions, new models. Elaine Kim, a UC Berkeley dean and ethnic studies scholar, says our community defies easy branding. The boundaries of Asian America are changing, fusing, changing again. "We're much more than white versus nonwhite, suburbanites versus urban people of color, East versus West, tradition versus modernity," she argues. "We're creating our culture every day."

Slowly and surely, a strong Asian-American culture is coming of age. It's a bold culture, unashamed and true to itself. It's a culture with a common destiny, *a community of the mind and soul.* And it's taking many forms — in plays and films, in literature and journalism, in history and the social sciences, in professional groups and political caucuses. We can certainly start by realizing we don't need to parrot anyone else's notions of success and beauty. "We're not slaves to culture, but agents of culture, agents of change," says King-Kok Cheung. Instead of conforming to prefabricated images and stereotypes, we must define our own successes, our own personalities, our own images.

We must not vanish completely into the suburbs, nor must we isolate ourselves in our close-knit but ethnocentric Asian communities. Instead, we must find a new common ethos, a new aesthetic, a new psychology.

This new Asian America must transcend, yet embrace, our differences.   85
It must value collective ethnic pride, yet respect individualism. It must honor equality of race and gender, and bury our hypocritical racism, sexism, and homophobia. And it must not hide behind moral self-righteousness or ideological rigidity, which poisons the radical left and fundamentalist right.

Our artists and scholars and educators, for the most part, create positive images, but we need many more; we cannot wait for Hollywood. Role models in all fields are important. Parents must teach their kids inner strength, not outer conformity. We must build more bridges with whites and others in a meaningful sense, not merely for show.

And as for Asian-American manhood? For Buddha's sake, let's use our imagination. The Lone Ranger and Bruce Lee are dead. We don't need to out-gun or measure up to anyone. We can return to the original meaning of compete, which comes from the Latin word *competere*, "to come together." Manhood now is a destructive, stereotyped, behavioral trap. Asian-Americans must recast our concept of masculinity, sculpting it into a larger definition of humanity.

For our role models, we can look to the past. The Japanese *bushido* ethic, the *samurai* spiritual and martial philosophy, is one. The scholarly Sage-King and Superior Man of Confucian thought is another, as is the Greek concept of *areté* — virtue in thought and action. All prized a male beauty and an ethos of strength and serenity, action and calmness, *yin* and *yang*.

To be sure, more Asian-American men are refusing to lock themselves into narrow roles and models. Rick Yuen, for example, a dean at Stanford, often finds himself caring for his two children and deferring to his wife, SF Community College board member Mabel Teng, on many family and career decisions. "I start with the basic assumption that we're men and women of equal standing," he says simply.

In the literary arts, playwrights David Henry Hwang and Philip 90 Gotanda and poet David Mura explore themes of ethnic manhood and sexuality. In the social arena, gay Asians are starting to emerge, attacking the layer upon layer of racism and homophobia they face in the straight and gay worlds.

On a recent trip to Los Angeles, I stumbled across an irresistible metaphor for our culture. A journalist friend, Brenda Sunoo of the *Korea Times,* had invited me to join her family at a concert of young Asian-American musicians, all amateurs.

The concert was a romp in culture-bending and blending. There were Korean rappers. A Japanese folksinger. A Filipino multimedia artist. When the rap dancers blew a tricky move and fell to the ground, drawing laughs, they hid their faces in their hands in embarrassment. Another singer, his set delayed by technical problems, repeatedly thanked the audience for its patience.

The performers seemed much like Asian America: shy but daring; apologetic but confident; imitative yet novel. "There's no blueprint for us," said Brenda. "Our history is being written now. Our individual choices will make us unique."

We've barely started to explore the beauty of our culture. With a little luck, the new Asian America will be a choral celebration, not an aria sung to an elite few. This will keep us from fading into white society as admired but bleached Americans.

We're trying to change the cultural paradigm, image by image. We 95 have to. For it is how we see each other that will ultimately transform the world. How we see each other, and how we see ourselves.

So where does this all lead me? Do I feel more whole in my newfound identity? Have I tossed the masks slapped on me by society, my family, myself? Do I know why I cut off my nose to spite my race?

Yes, to all of the above. Now I see my image and others in a less harsh light. I know one's slant of eye and color of skin are bogus issues. For beyond acculturation, beyond racial identity, is the larger question of *kokoro* — Japanese for heart and soul. Make no mistake: I've learned I *am* different from white people. Not better, not worse, but distinct. The faces rushing toward me in my pre-surgical daze were neither white nor yellow. They were mine.

1991

The Reader's Presence

1. What does Iwata believe are the common assumptions whites make about Asian men? Does he imply that you (the reader) personally make these assumptions? Did you see yourself as inside or outside of his intended audience?

2. What image of himself does Iwata create for his readers? What does he say to establish his presence in the essay as an independent, tough-minded thinker? Why do you think he wants to project that image of himself?

3. Iwata discusses the importance of "cultural brainwashing" on his decision. Who is responsible for that brainwashing? Why was he unable at first to resist it? Do you or do you not believe his surgery has transformed him intellectually?

13

Kesaya E. Noda

Growing Up Asian in America

Sometimes when I was growing up, my identity seemed to hurtle toward me and paste itself right to my face. I felt that way, encountering the stereotypes of my race perpetuated by non-Japanese people (primarily white) who may or may not have had contact with other Japanese in America. "You don't like cheese, do you?" someone would ask. "I know your people don't like cheese." Sometimes questions came making allusions to history. That was another aspect of the identity. Events that had happened quite apart from the me who stood silent in that moment connected my face with an incomprehensible past. "Your parents were in California? Were they in those camps during the war?" And sometimes there were phrases or nicknames: "Lotus Blossom." I was sometimes addressed or referred to as racially Japanese, sometimes as Japanese-American, and sometimes as an Asian woman. Confusions and distortions abounded.

How is one to know and define oneself? From the inside — within a context that is self-defined, from a grounding in community and a connection with culture and history that are comfortably accepted? Or from the outside — in terms of messages received from the media and people who are often ignorant? Even as an adult I can still see two sides of my face and past. I can see from the inside out, in freedom. And I can see from the outside in, driven by the old voices of childhood and lost in anger and fear.

I AM RACIALLY JAPANESE

A voice from my childhood says: "You are other. You are less than. You are unalterably alien." This voice has its own history. We have indeed been seen as other and alien since the early years of our arrival in the

For biographical information on Kesaya E. Noda, see p. 658.

United States. The very first immigrants were welcomed and sought as laborers to replace the dwindling numbers of Chinese, whose influx had been cut off by the Chinese Exclusion Act of 1882. The Japanese fell natural heir to the same anti-Asian prejudice that had arisen against the Chinese. As soon as they began striking for better wages, they were no longer welcomed.

I can see myself today as a person historically defined by law and custom as being forever alien. Being neither "free white," nor "African," our people in California were deemed "aliens, ineligible for citizenship," no matter how long they intended to stay here. Aliens ineligible for citizenship were prohibited from owning, buying, or leasing land. They did not and could not belong here. The voice in me remembers that I am always a *Japanese*-American in the eyes of many. A third-generation German-American is an American. A third-generation Japanese-American is a Japanese-American. Being Japanese means being a danger to the country during the war and knowing how to use chopsticks. I wear this history on my face.

I move to the other side. I see a different light and claim a different   5
context. My race is a line that stretches across ocean and time to link me to the shrine where my grandmother was raised. Two high, white banners lift in the wind at the top of the stone steps leading to the shrine. It is time for the summer festival. Black characters are written against the sky as boldly as the clouds, as lightly as kites, as sharply as the big black crows I used to see above the fields in New Hampshire. At festival time there is liquor and food, ritual, discipline, and abandonment. There is music and drunkenness and invocation. There is hope. Another season has come. Another season has gone.

I am racially Japanese. I have a certain claim to this crazy place where the prayers intoned by a neighboring Shinto priest (standing in for my grandmother's nephew who is sick) are drowned out by the rehearsals for the pop singing contest in which most of the villagers will compete later that night. The village elders, the priest, and I stand respectfully upon the immaculate, shining wooden floor of the outer shrine, bowing our heads before the hidden powers. During the patchy intervals when I can hear him, I notice the priest has a stutter. His voice flutters up to my ears only occasionally because two men and a women are singing gustily into a microphone in the compound, testing the sound system. A prerecorded tape of guitars, samisens,[1] and drums accompanies them. Rock music and Shinto prayers. That night, to loud applause and cheers, a young man is given the award for the most *netsuretsu* — passionate, burning — rendition of a song. We roar our approval of the reward. Never mind that his voice had wandered and slid, now slightly above, now slightly below the given line of the melody. Netsuretsu. Netsuretsu.

In the morning, my grandmother's sister kneels at the foot of the stone stairs to offer her morning prayers. She is too crippled to climb the stairs,

---

[1]*samisen:* A guitar-like instrument with a long neck and three strings. — EDS.

so each morning she kneels here upon the path. She shuts her eyes for a few seconds, her motions as matter of fact as when she washes rice. I linger longer than she does, so reluctant to leave, savoring the connection I feel with my grandmother in America, the past, and the power that lives and shines in the morning sun.

Our family has served this shrine for generations. The family's need to protect this claim to identity and place outweighs any individual claim to any individual hope. I am Japanese.

I AM A JAPANESE-AMERICAN

"Weak." I hear the voice from my childhood years. "Passive," I hear. Our parents and grandparents were the ones who were put into those camps. They went without resistance; they offered cooperation as proof of loyalty to America. "Victim," I hear. And, "Silent."

Our parents are painted as hard workers who were socially uncomfort-　10 able and had difficulty expressing even the smallest opinion. Clean, quiet, motivated, and determined to match the American way; that is us, and that is the story of our time here.

"Why did you go into those camps?" I raged at my parents, frightened by my own inner silence and timidity. "Why didn't you do anything to resist? Why didn't you name it the injustice it was?" Couldn't our parents even think? Couldn't they? Why were we so passive?

I shift my vision and my stance. I am in California. My uncle is in the midst of the sweet potato harvest. He is pressed, trying to get the harvesting crews onto the field as quickly as possible, worried about the flow of equipment and people. His big pickup is pulled off to the side, motor running, door ajar. I see two tractors in the yard in front of an old shed; the flatbed harvesting platform on which the workers will stand has already been brought over from the other field. It's early morning. The workers stand loosely grouped and at ease, but my uncle looks as harried and tense as a police officer trying to unsnarl a New York City traffic jam. Driving toward the shed, I pull my car off the road to make way for an approaching tractor. The front wheels of the car sink luxuriously into the soft, white sand by the roadside and the car slides to a dreamy halt, tail still on the road. I try to move forward. I try to move back. The front bites contentedly into the sand, the back lifts itself at a jaunty angle. My uncle sees me and storms down the road, running. He is shouting before he is even near me.

"What's the matter with you?" he screams. "What the hell are you doing?" In his frenzy, he grabs his hat off his head and slashes it through the air across his knee. He is beside himself. "Don't you know how to drive in sand? What's the matter with you? You've blocked the whole roadway. How am I supposed to get my tractors out of here?

Can't you use your head? You've cut off the whole roadway, and we've got to get out of here."

I stand on the road before him helplessly thinking, "No, I don't know how to drive in sand. I've never driven in sand."

"I'm sorry, uncle," I say, burying a smile beneath a look of sincere 15
apology. I notice my deep amusement and my affection for him with great curiosity. I am usually devastated by anger. Not this time.

During the several years that follow I learn about the people and the place, and much more about what has happened in this California village where my parents grew up. The issei, our grandparents, made this settlement in the desert. Their first crops were eaten by rabbits and ravaged by insects. The land was so barren that men walking from house to house sometimes got lost. Women came here too. They bore children in 114-degree heat, then carried the babies with them into the fields to nurse when they reached the end of each row of grapes or other truck-farm crops.

I had had no idea what it meant to buy this kind of land and make it grow green. Or how, when the war came, there was no space at all for the subtlety of being who we were — Japanese-Americans. Either/or was the way. I hadn't understood that people were literally afraid for their lives then, that their money had been frozen in banks; that there was a five-mile travel limit; that when the early evening curfew came and they were inside their houses, some of them watched helplessly as people they knew went into their barns to steal their belongings. The police were patrolling the road, interested only in violators of curfew. There was no help for them in the face of thievery. I had not been able to imagine before what it must have felt like to be an American — to know absolutely that one is an American — and yet to have almost everyone else deny it. Not only deny it, but challenge that identity with machine guns and troops of white American soldiers. In those circumstances it was difficult to say, "I'm a Japanese-American." "American" had to do.

But now I can say that I am a Japanese-American. It means I have a place here in this country, too. I have a place here on the East Coast, where our neighbor is so much a part of our family that my mother never passes her house at night without glancing at the lights to see if she is home and safe; where my parents have hauled hundreds of pounds of rocks from fields and arduously planted Christmas trees and blueberries, lilacs, asparagus, and crab apples; where my father still dreams of angling a stream to a new bed so that he can dig a pond in the field and fill it with water and fish. "The neighbors already came for their Christmas tree?" he asks in December. "Did they like it? Did they like it?"

I have a place on the West Coast where my relatives still farm, where I heard the stories of feuds and backbiting, and where I saw that people survived and flourished because fundamentally they trusted and relied upon one another. A death in the family is not just a death in a family; it is a death in the community. I saw people help each other with money, materials, labor, attention, and time. I saw men gather once a year, without fail, to clean the grounds of a ninety-year-old woman who had helped the community before, during, and after the war. I saw her remembering them with birthday cards sent to each of their children.

I come from a people with a long memory and a distinctive grace. We   20
live our thanks. And we are Americans. Japanese-Americans.

I AM A JAPANESE-AMERICAN WOMAN

Woman. The last piece of my identity. It has been easier by far for me to know myself in Japan and to see my place in America than it has been to accept my line of connection with my own mother. She was my dark self, a figure in whom I thought I saw all that I feared most in myself. Growing into womanhood and looking for some model of strength, I turned away from her. Of course, I could not find what I sought. I was looking for a black feminist or a white feminist. My mother is neither white nor black.

My mother is a woman who speaks with her life as much as with her tongue. I think of her with her own mother. Grandmother had Parkinson's disease and it had frozen her gait and set her fingers, tongue, and feet jerking and trembling in a terrible dance. My aunts and uncles wanted her to be able to live in her own home. They fed her, bathed her, dressed her, awoke at midnight to take her for one last trip to the bathroom. My aunts (her daughters-in-law) did most of the care, but my mother went from New Hampshire to California each summer to spend a month living with Grandmother, because she wanted to and because she wanted to give my aunts at least a small rest. During those hot summer days, mother lay on the couch watching the television or reading, cooking foods that Grandmother liked, and speaking little. Grandmother thrived under her care.

The time finally came when it was too dangerous for Grandmother to live alone. My relatives kept finding her on the floor beside her bed when they went to wake her in the mornings. My mother flew to California to help clean the house and make arrangements for Grandmother to enter a local nursing home. On her last day at home, while Grandmother was sitting in her big, overstuffed armchair, hair combed and wearing a green summer dress, my mother went to her and knelt at her feet. "Here, Mamma," she said. "I've polished your shoes." She lifted Grandmother's legs and helped her into the shiny black shoes. My Grandmother looked down and smiled slightly. She left her house walking, supported by her children, carrying her pocket book, and wearing her polished black shoes. "Look, Mamma," my mom had said, kneeling. "I've polished your shoes."

Just the other day, my mother came to Boston to visit. She had recently lost a loft of weight and was pleased with her new shape and her feeling of good health. "Look at me, Kes," she exclaimed, turning toward me, front and back, as naked as the day she was born. I saw her small breasts and the wide, brown scar, belly button to pubic hair, that marked her because my brother and I were both born by Caesarean section. Her hips were small. I was not a large baby, but there was so little room for me in her that when she was carrying me she could not even begin to bend over toward the floor. She hated it, she said.

"Don't I look good? Don't you think I look good?"   25

I looked at my mother, smiling and as happy as she, thinking of all the times I have seen her naked. I have seen both my parents naked throughout my life, as they have seen me. From childhood through adulthood we've had our naked moments, sharing baths, idle conversations picked up as we moved between showers and closets, hurried moments at the beginning of days, quiet moments at the end of days.

I know this to be Japanese, this ease with the physical, and it makes me think of an old Japanese folk song. A young nursemaid, a fifteen-year-old girl, is singing a lullaby to a baby who is strapped to her back. The nursemaid has been sent as a servant to a place far from her own home. "We're the beggars," she says, "and they are the nice people. Nice people wear fine sashes. Nice clothes."

> If I should drop dead,
> bury me by the roadside!
> I'll give a flower
> to everyone who passes.

> What kind of flower?
> The cam-cam-camellia [tsun-tsun-tsubaki]
> watered by Heaven:
> alms water.

The nursemaid is the intersection of heaven and earth, the intersection of the human, the natural world, the body, and the soul. In this song, with clear eyes, she looks steadily at life, which is sometimes so very terrible and sad. I think of her while looking at my mother, who is standing on the red and purple carpet before me, laughing, without any clothes.

I am my mother's daughter. And I am myself.

I am a Japanese-American woman.   30

EPILOGUE

I recently heard a man from West Africa share some memories of his childhood. He was raised Muslim, but when he was a young man, he found himself deeply drawn to Christianity. He struggled against his inner impulse for years, trying to avoid the church yet feeling pushed to return to it again and again. "I would have done *anything* to avoid the change," he said. At last, he became Christian. Afterwards he was afraid to go home, fearing that he would not be accepted. The fear was groundless, he discovered, when at last he returned — he had separated himself, but his family and friends (all Muslim) had not separated themselves from him.

The man, who is now a professor of religion, said that in the Africa he knew as a child and a young man, pluralism was embraced rather than feared. There was "a kind of tolerance that did not deny your particularity," he said. He alluded to zestful, spontaneous debates that would sometimes loudly erupt between Muslims and Christians in the village's public spaces. His memories of an atheist who harangued the villagers when he came to visit them once a week moved me deeply. Perhaps the man was an agricultural advisor or inspector. He harassed the women. He would say: "Don't go to the fields! Don't even bother to go to the fields. Let God take care of you. He'll send you the food. If you believe in God, why do you need to work? You don't need to work! Let God put the seeds in the ground. Stay home."

The professor said, "The women laughed, you know? They just laughed. Their attitude was, 'Here is a child of God. When will he come home?'"

The storyteller, the professor of religion, smiled a most fantastic tender smile as he told this story. "In my country, there is a deep affirmation of the oneness of God," he said. "The atheist and the women were having quite different experiences in their encounter, though the atheist did not know this. He saw himself as quite separate from the women. But the women did not see themselves as being separate from him. 'Here is a child of God,' they said. 'When will he come home?'"

1989

The Reader's Presence

1. Throughout the essay, Noda cites various voices of prejudice and discrimination. Where do these voices come from? To what extent do they represent those of the reader? How do these voices affect Noda's sense of identity?

2. In what other ways do voices surface in Noda's essay? Where, for example, do more positive voices come from? From what groups? To what extent are these voices internal or external? In what ways do these positive voices resemble Noda's own voice — the one we hear throughout the essay?

3. In rereading the essay, take note of Noda's method of organization. You might attempt to make up the outline you think she used. What problems do you encounter in your reconstructed outline?

14 _____

George Orwell

Shooting an Elephant

In Moulmein, in Lower Burma, I was hated by large numbers of people — the only time in my life that I have been important enough for this to happen to me. I was subdivisional police officer of the town, and in an aimless, petty kind of way anti-European feeling was very bitter. No one had the guts to raise a riot, but if a European woman went through the bazaars alone somebody would probably spit betel juice over her dress. As a police officer I was an obvious target and was baited whenever it seemed safe to do so. When a nimble Burman tripped me up on the football field and the referee (another Burman) looked the other way, the crowd yelled with hideous laughter. This happened more than once. In the end the sneering yellow faces of young men that met me everywhere, the insults hooted after me when I was at a safe distance, got badly on my nerves. The young Buddhist priests were the worst of all. There were several thousands of them in the town and none of them seemed to have anything to do except stand on street corners and jeer at Europeans.

All this was perplexing and upsetting. For at that time I had already made up my mind that imperialism was an evil thing and the sooner I chucked up my job and got out of it the better. Theoretically — and secretly, of course — I was all for the Burmese and all against the oppressors, the British. As for the job I was doing, I hated it more bitterly than I can perhaps make clear. In a job like that you see the dirty work of Empire at close quarters. The wretched prisoners huddling in the stinking cages of the lockups, the grey, cowed faces of the long-term convicts, the scarred buttocks of the men who had been flogged with bamboos — all these oppressed me with an intolerable sense of guilt. But I could get nothing into perspective. I was young and ill-educated and I had had to think out my problems in the utter silence that is imposed on every Englishman in the East. I did not even know that the British Empire is dying, still less did I

For biographical information on George Orwell, see p. 659.

know that it is a great deal better than the younger empires that are going
to supplant it. All I knew was that I was stuck between my hatred of the
empire I served and my rage against the evil-spirited little beasts who tried
to make my job impossible. With one part of my mind I thought of the
British Raj[1] as an unbreakable tyranny, as something clamped down, in
saecula saeculorum,[2] upon the will of prostrate peoples; with another part
I thought that the greatest joy in the world would be to drive a bayonet into
a Buddhist priest's guts. Feelings like these are the normal by-products
of imperialism; ask any Anglo-Indian official, if you can catch him off
duty.

One day something happened which in a roundabout way was enlightening. It was a tiny incident in itself, but it gave me a better glimpse than I
had had before the real nature of imperialism — the real motives for which
despotic governments act. Early one morning the subinspector at a police
station the other end of town rang me up on the phone and said that an
elephant was ravaging the bazaar. Would I please come and do something
about it? I did not know what I could do, but I wanted to see what was
happening and I got on to a pony and started out. I took my rifle, an old
.44 Winchester and much too small to kill an elephant, but I thought the
noise might be useful *in terrorem.*[3] Various Burmans stopped me on the
way and told me about the elephant's doings. It was not, of course, a wild
elephant, but a tame one which had gone "must."[4] It had been chained up,
as tame elephants always are when their attack of "must" is due, but on the
previous night it had broken its chain and escaped. Its mahout,[5] the only
person who could manage it when it was in that state, had set out in pursuit, but had taken the wrong direction and was now twelve hours' journey
away, and in the morning the elephant had suddenly reappeared in the
town. The Burmese population had no weapons and were quite helpless
against it. It had already destroyed somebody's bamboo hut, killed a cow,
and raided some fruit stalls and devoured the stock; also it had met the
municipal rubbish van and, when the driver jumped out and took to his
heels, had turned the van over and inflicted violences upon it.

The Burmese subinspector and some Indian constables were waiting
for me in the quarter where the elephant had been seen. It was a very poor
quarter, a labyrinth of squalid bamboo huts, thatched with palmleaf, winding all over a steep hillside. I remember that it was a cloudy, stuffy morning
at the beginning of the rains. We began questioning the people as to where
the elephant had gone and, as usual, failed to get any definite information.
That is invariably the case in the East; a story always sounds clear enough
at a distance, but the nearer you get to the scene of events the vaguer it
becomes. Some of the people said that the elephant had gone in one direc-

---

[1] *Raj:* The British administration. — EDS.
[2] *saecula saeculorum:* Forever and ever (Latin). — EDS.
[3] *in terrorem:* As a warning (Latin). — EDS.
[4] *"must":* Sexual arousal. — EDS.
[5] *mahout:* Keeper (Hindi). — EDS.

tion, some said that he had gone in another, some professed not even to have heard of any elephant. I had almost made up my mind that the whole story was a pack of lies, when we heard yells a little distance away. There was a loud, scandalized cry of "Go away, child! Go away this instant!" and an old woman with a switch in her hand came round the corner of a hut, violently shooing away a crowd of naked children. Some more women followed, clicking their tongues and exclaiming; evidently there was something that the children ought not to have seen. I rounded the hut and saw a man's dead body sprawling in the mud. He was an Indian, a black Dravidian[6] coolie, almost naked, and he could not have been dead many minutes. The people said that the elephant had come suddenly upon him round the corner of the hut, caught him with its trunk, put its foot on his back, and ground him into the earth. This was the rainy season and the ground was soft, and his face had scored a trench a foot deep and a couple of yards long. He was lying on his belly with arms crucified and head sharply twisted to one side. His face was coated with mud, the eyes wide open, the teeth bared and grinning with an expression of unendurable agony. (Never tell me, by the way, that the dead look peaceful. Most of the corpses I have seen looked devilish.) The friction of the great beast's foot had stripped the skin from his back as neatly as one skins a rabbit. As soon as I saw the dead man I sent an orderly to a friend's house nearby to borrow an elephant rifle. I had already sent back the pony, not wanting it to go mad with fright and throw me if it smelled the elephant.

The orderly came back in a few minutes with a rifle and five cartridges,   5 and meanwhile some Burmans had arrived and told us that the elephant was in the paddy fields below, only a few hundred yards away. As I started forward practically the whole population of the quarter flocked out of the houses and followed me. They had seen the rifle and were all shouting excitedly that I was going to shoot the elephant. They had not shown much interest in the elephant when he was merely ravaging their homes, but it was different now that he was going to be shot. It was a bit of fun to them, as it would be to an English crowd; besides they wanted the meat. It made me vaguely uneasy. I had no intention of shooting the elephant — I had merely sent for the rifle to defend myself if necessary — and it is always unnerving to have a crowd following you. I marched down the hill, looking and feeling a fool, with the rifle over my shoulder and an ever-growing army of people jostling at my heels. At the bottom, when you got away from the huts, there was a metalled road and beyond that a miry waste of paddy fields a thousand yards across, not yet ploughed but soggy from the first rains and dotted with coarse grass. The elephant was standing eight yards from the road, his left side towards us. He took not the slightest notice of the crowd's approach. He was tearing up bunches of

[6]*Dravidian:* A populous Indian group. — EDS.

grass, beating them against his knees to clean them and stuffing them into his mouth.

I had halted on the road. As soon as I saw the elephant I knew with perfect certainty that I ought not to shoot him. It is a serious matter to shoot a working elephant — it is comparable to destroying a huge and costly piece of machinery — and obviously one ought not to do it if it can possibly be avoided. And at that distance, peacefully eating, the elephant looked no more dangerous than a cow. I thought then and I think now that his attack of "must" was already passing off; in which case he would merely wander harmlessly about until the mahout came back and caught him. Moreover, I did not in the least want to shoot him. I decided that I would watch him for a little while to make sure that he did not turn savage again, and then go home.

But at that moment, I glanced round at the crowd that had followed me. It was an immense crowd, two thousand at the least and growing every minute. It blocked the road for a long distance on either side. I looked at the sea of yellow faces above the garish clothes — faces all happy and ex-cited over this bit of fun, all certain that the elephant was going to be shot. They were watching me as they would watch a conjuror about to perform a trick. They did not like me, but with the magical rifle in my hands I was momentarily worth watching. And suddenly I realized that I should have to shoot the elephant after all: The people expected it of me and I had got to do it; I could feel their two thousand wills pressing me forward, irresistibly. And it was at this moment, as I stood there with the rifle in my hands, that I first grasped the hollowness, the futility of the white man's dominion in the East. Here was I, the white man with his gun, standing in front of the unarmed native crowd — seemingly the leading actor of the piece; but in reality I was only an absurd puppet pushed to and fro by the will of those yellow faces behind. I perceived in this moment that when the white man turns tyrant it is his own freedom that he destroys. He becomes a sort of hollow, posing dummy, the conventionalized figure of a sahib. For it is the condition of his rule that he shall spend his life in trying to impress the "natives," and so in every crisis he has got to do what the "natives" expect of him. He wears a mask, and his face grows to fit it. I had got to shoot the elephant. I had committed myself to doing it when I sent for the rifle. A sahib has got to act like a sahib; he has got to appear resolute, to know his own mind and do definite things. To come all that way, rifle in hand, with two thousand people marching at my heels, and then to trail feebly away, having done nothing — no, that was impossible. The crowd would laugh at me. And my whole life, every white man's life in the East, was one long struggle not to be laughed at.

But I did not want to shoot the elephant. I watched him beating his bunch of grass against his knees, with that preoccupied grandmotherly air that elephants have. It seemed to me that it would be murder to shoot him. At that age I was not squeamish about killing animals, but I had never shot an elephant and never wanted to. (Somehow it always seems worse to kill a *large* animal.) Besides, there was the beast's owner to be considered. Alive, the elephant was worth at least a hundred pounds; dead, he would only be worth the value of his tusks, five pounds, possibly. But I had got to act quickly. I turned to some experienced-looking Burmans who had been there when we arrived, and asked them how the elephant had been behaving. They all said the same thing: He took no notice of you if you left him alone, but he might charge if you went too close to him.

It was perfectly clear to me what I ought to do. I ought to walk up to within, say, twenty-five yards of the elephant and test his behavior. If he charged, I could shoot; if he took no notice of me, it would be safe to leave him until the mahout came back. But also I knew that I was going to do no such thing. I was a poor shot with a rifle and the ground was soft mud into which one would sink at every step. If the elephant charged and I missed him, I should have about as much chance as a toad under a steamroller. But even then I was not thinking particularly of my own skin, only of the watchful yellow faces behind. For at that moment, with the crowd watching me, I was not afraid in the ordinary sense, as I would have been if I had been alone. A white man mustn't be frightened in front of "natives"; and so, in general, he isn't frightened. The sole thought in my mind was that if anything went wrong those two thousand Burmans would see me pursued, caught, trampled on, and reduced to a grinning corpse like that Indian up the hill. And if that happened it was quite probable that some of them would laugh. That would never do. There was only one alternative. I shoved the cartridges into the magazine and lay down on the road to get a better aim.

The crowd grew very still, and a deep, low, happy sigh, as of people   10
who see the theatre curtain go up at last, breathed from innumerable throats. They were going to have their bit of fun after all. The rifle was a beautiful German thing with cross-hair sights. I did not then know that in shooting an elephant one would shoot to cut an imaginary bar running from ear-hole to ear-hole. I ought, therefore, as the elephant was sideways on, to have aimed straight at his ear-hole; actually I aimed several inches in front of this, thinking the brain would be further forward.

When I pulled the trigger I did not hear the bang or feel the kick — one never does when a shot goes home — but I heard the devilish roar of glee that went up from the crowd. In that instant, in too short a time, one would have thought, even for the bullet to get there, a mysterious, terrible change had come over the elephant. He neither stirred nor fell, but every line of his body had altered. He looked suddenly stricken, shrunken, immensely old, as though the frightful impact of the bullet had paralyzed him without knocking him down. At last, after what seemed a long time — it might have been five seconds, I dare say — he sagged flabbily to his knees. His mouth slobbered. An enormous senility seemed to have settled upon him. One could have imagined him thousands of years old. I fired again into the same spot. At the second shot he did not collapse but climbed with desperate slowness to his feet and stood weakly upright, with legs sagging and head drooping. I fired a third time. That was the shot that did for him. You could see the agony of it jolt his whole body and knock the last remnant of strength from his legs. But in falling he seemed for a moment to rise, for as his hind legs collapsed beneath him he seemed to tower upward like a huge rock toppling, his trunk reaching skywards like a tree. He trumpeted, for the first and only time. And then down he came, his belly towards me, with a crash that seemed to shake the ground even where I lay.

I got up. The Burmans were already racing past me across the mud. It was obvious that the elephant would never rise again, but he was not dead. He was breathing very rhythmically with long rattling gasps, his great mound of a side painfully rising and falling. His mouth was wide open. I could see far down into caverns of pale pink throat. I waited a long time for him to die, but his breathing did not weaken. Finally, I fired my two remaining shots into the spot where I thought his heart must be. The thick blood welled out of him like red velvet, but still he did not die. His body did not even jerk when the shots hit him, the tortured breathing continued without a pause. He was dying, very slowly and in great agony, but in some world remote from me where not even a bullet could damage him further. I felt I had got to put an end to that dreadful noise. It seemed dreadful to see the great beast lying there, powerless to move and yet powerless to die, and not even to be able to finish him. I sent back for my small rifle and poured shot after shot into his heart, and down his throat. They seemed to make no impression. The tortured gasps continued as steadily as the ticking of a clock.

In the end I could not stand it any longer and went away. I heard later that it took him half an hour to die. Burmans were bringing dahs[7] and baskets even before I left, and I was told they had stripped his body almost to the bones by the afternoon.

Afterwards, of course, there were endless discussions about the shooting of the elephant. The owner was furious, but he was only an Indian and could do nothing. Besides, legally I had done the right thing, for a mad elephant has to be killed, like a mad dog, if its owner fails to control it. Among the Europeans opinion was divided. The older men said I was right, the younger men said it was a damn shame to shoot an elephant for killing a coolie, because the elephant was worth more than any damn Coringhee coolie. And afterwards I was very glad that the coolie had been killed; it put me legally in the right and it gave me sufficient pretext for shooting the elephant. I often wondered whether any of the others grasped that I had done it solely to avoid looking a fool.

1936

---

[7]*dahs:* Large knives. — EDS.

The Reader's Presence

1. Discuss Orwell's dilemma. How would you react in his situation? Is he recommending that readers see his behavior as a model of what to do in such a conflict?

2. Do you find Orwell's final sentence believable? Do you think that Orwell shot the elephant solely to avoid looking like a fool? In what sense would he have looked like a fool if he refused to kill the creature? Why do you think he makes this claim, and how does it affect your reading of the entire essay?

3. Some literary critics doubt that Orwell really did shoot an elephant in Burma. No external historical documentation has ever been found to corroborate Orwell's account. Yet what *internal* elements in the essay — what details or features — help persuade you that the episode is fact and not fiction? In other words, what makes you think that you are reading an essay and not a short story?

15 _____

Adrienne Rich

Split at the Root: An Essay on Jewish Identity

For about fifteen minutes I have been sitting chin in hand in front of the typewriter, staring out at the snow. Trying to be honest with myself, trying to figure out why writing this seems to be so dangerous an act, filled with fear and shame, and why it seems so necessary. It comes to me that in order to write this I have to be willing to do two things: I have to claim my father, for I have my Jewishness from him and not from my gentile mother, and I have to break his silence, his taboos; in order to claim him I have in a sense to expose him.

And there is, of course, the third thing: I have to face the sources and the flickering presence of my own ambivalence as a Jew; the daily, mundane anti-Semitisms of my entire life.

For biographical information on Adrienne Rich, see p. 660.

These are stories I have never tried to tell before. Why now? Why, I asked myself sometime last year, does this question of Jewish identity float so impalpably, so ungraspably around me, a cloud I can't quite see the outlines of, which feels to me to be without definition?

And yet I've been on the track of this longer than I think.

In a long poem written in 1960, when I was thirty-one years old, I   5 described myself as "Split at the root, neither Gentile nor Jew, / Yankee nor Rebel."[1] I was still trying to have it both ways: to be neither/nor, trying to live (with my Jewish husband and three children more Jewish in ancestry than I) in the predominantly gentile Yankee academic world of Cambridge, Massachusetts.

But this begins, for me, in Baltimore, where I was born in my father's workplace, a hospital in the black ghetto, whose lobby contained an immense white marble statue of Christ.

My father was then a young teacher and researcher in the department of pathology at the Johns Hopkins Medical School, one of the very few Jews to attend or teach at that institution. He was from Birmingham, Alabama; his father, Samuel, was Ashkenazic,[2] an immigrant from Austria-Hungary and his mother, Hattie Rice, a Sephardic[3] Jew from Vicksburg, Mississippi. My grandfather had had a shoe store in Birmingham, which did well enough to allow him to retire comfortably and to leave my grandmother income on his death. The only souvenirs of my grandfather, Samuel Rich, were his ivory flute, which lay on our living-room mantel and was not to be played with; his thin gold pocket watch, which my father wore; and his Hebrew prayer book, which I discovered among my father's books in the course of reading my way through his library. In this prayer book there was a newspaper clipping about my grandparents' wedding, which took place in a synagogue.

My father, Arnold, was sent in adolescence to a military school in the North Carolina mountains, a place for training white southern Christian gentlemen. I suspect that there were few, if any, other Jewish boys at Colonel Bingham's, or at "Mr. Jefferson's university" in Charlottesville, where he studied as an undergraduate. With whatever conscious forethought, Samuel and Hattie sent their son into the dominant southern WASP culture to become an "exception," to enter the professional class. Never, in describing these experiences, did he speak of having suffered — from loneli-

---

[1]Adrienne Rich, "Readings of History," in *Snapshots of a Daughter-in-Law* (New York: W. W. Norton, 1967), pp. 36–40. — RICH'S NOTE.

[2]*Ashkenazic:* Descendants of the Jews, generally Yiddish-speaking, who settled in middle and northern Europe. — EDS.

[3]*Sephardic:* Descendants of the Jews who settled for the most part in Spain, Portugal, and northern Africa. — EDS.

ness, cultural alienation, or outsiderhood. Never did I hear him use the word *anti-Semitism*.

It was only in college, when I read a poem by Karl Shapiro beginning "To hate the Negro and avoid the Jew / is the curriculum," that it flashed on me that there was an untold side to my father's story of his student years. He looked recognizably Jewish, was short and slender in build with dark wiry hair and deep-set eyes, high forehead, and curved nose.

My mother is a gentile. In Jewish law I cannot count myself a Jew. If it is true that "we think back through our mothers if we are women" (Virginia Woolf) — and I myself have affirmed this — then even according to lesbian theory, I cannot (or need not?) count myself a Jew.   10

The white southern Protestant woman, the gentile, has always been there for me to peel back into. That's a whole piece of history in itself, for my gentile grandmother and my mother were also frustrated artists and intellectuals, a lost writer and a lost composer between them. Readers and annotators of books, note takers, my mother a good pianist still, in her eighties. But there was also the obsession with ancestry, with "background," the southern talk of family, not as people you would necessarily know and depend on, but as heritage, the guarantee of "good breeding." There was the inveterate romantic heterosexual fantasy, the mother telling the daughter how to attract men (my mother often used the word "fascinate"); the assumption that relations between the sexes could only be romantic, that it was in the woman's interest to cultivate "mystery," conceal her actual feelings. Survival tactics of a kind, I think today, knowing what I know about the white woman's sexual role in the southern racist scenario. Heterosexuality as protection, but also drawing white women deeper into collusion with white men.

It would be easy to push away and deny the gentile in me — that white southern woman, that social christian. At different times in my life I have wanted to push away one or the other burden of inheritance, to say merely *I am a woman; I am a lesbian.* If I call myself a Jewish lesbian, do I thereby try to shed some of my southern gentile white woman's culpability? If I call myself only through my mother, is it because I pass more easily through a world where being a lesbian often seems like outsiderhood enough?

According to Nazi logic, my two Jewish grandparents would have made me a *Mischling, first-degree* — nonexempt from the Final Solution.[4]

The social world in which I grew up was christian virtually without needing to say so — christian imagery, music, language, symbols, assumptions everywhere. It was also a genteel, white, middle-class world in which "common" was a term of deep opprobrium. "Common" white people might speak of "niggers"; *we* were taught never to use that word — *we*

---

[4]***Final Solution:*** The Nazi plan to exterminate all members of the Jewish race. — Eds.

said "Negroes" (even as we accepted segregation, the eating taboo, the assumption that black people were simply of a separate species). Our language was more polite, distinguishing us from the "rednecks" or the lynch-mob mentality. But so charged with negative meaning was even the word "Negro" that as children we were taught never to use it in front of black people. We were taught that any mention of skin color in the presence of colored people was treacherous, forbidden ground. In a parallel way, the word *Jew* was not used by polite gentiles. I sometimes heard my best friend's father, a Presbyterian minister, allude to "the Hebrew people" or "people of the Jewish faith." The world of acceptable folk was white, gentile (christian, really), and had "ideals" (which colored people, white "common" people, were not supposed to have). "Ideals" and "manners" included not hurting someone's feelings by calling her or him a Negro or a Jew — naming the hated identity. This is the mental framework of the 1930s and 1940s in which I was raised.

(Writing this, I feel dimly like the betrayer: of my father, who did not speak the word; of my mother, who must have trained me in the messages; of my caste and class; of my whiteness itself.)

Two memories: I am in a play reading at school of *The Merchant of Venice.* Whatever Jewish law says, I am quite sure I was *seen* as Jewish (with a reassuringly gentile mother) in that double vision that bigotry allows. I am the only Jewish girl in the class, and I am playing Portia. As always, I read my part aloud for my father the night before, and he tells me to convey, with my voice, more scorn and contempt with the word *Jew:* "Therefore, Jew . . . " I have to say the word out, and say it loudly. I was encouraged to pretend to be a non-Jewish child acting a non-Jewish character who has to speak the word *Jew* emphatically. Such a child would not have had trouble with the part. But *I* must have had trouble with the part, if only because the word itself was really taboo. I can see that there was a kind of terrible, bitter bravado about my father's way of handling this. And who would not dissociate from Shylock in order to identify with Portia? As a Jewish child who was also a female, I loved Portia — and, like every other Shakespearean heroine, she proved a treacherous role model.

A year or so later I am in another play, *The School for Scandal,* in which a notorious spendthrift is described as having "many excellent friends . . . among the Jews." In neither case was anything explained, either to me or to the class at large, about this scorn for Jews and the disgust surrounding Jews and money. Money, when Jews wanted it, had it, or lent it to others, seemed to take on a peculiar nastiness; Jews and money had some peculiar and unspeakable relation.

At the same school — in which we had Episcopalian hymns and prayers, and read aloud through the Bible morning after morning — I gained the impression that Jews were in the Bible and mentioned in English literature, that they had been persecuted centuries ago by the wicked Inquisition, but that they seemed not to exist in everyday life. These were the 1940s, and we were told a great deal about the Battle of Britain, the noble French

15

Resistance fighters, the brave, starving Dutch — but I did not learn of the resistance of the Warsaw ghetto until I left home.

I was sent to the Episcopal church, baptized and confirmed, and attended it for about five years, though without belief. That religion seemed to have little to do with belief or commitment; it was liturgy that mattered, not spiritual passion. Neither of my parents ever entered that church, and my father would not enter *any* church for any reason — wedding or funeral. Nor did I enter a synagogue until I left Baltimore. When I came home from church, for a while, my father insisted on reading aloud to me from Thomas Paine's *The Age of Reason* — a diatribe against institutional religion. Thus, he explained, I would have a balanced view of these things, a choice. He — they — did not give me the choice to be a Jew. My mother explained to me when I was filling out forms for college that if any question was asked about "religion," I should put down "Episcopalian" rather than "none" — to seem to have no religion was, she implied, dangerous.

But it was white social christianity, rather than any particular christian   20
sect, that the world was founded on. The very word *Christian* was used as a synonym for virtuous, just, peace-loving, generous, etc., etc.[5] The norm was christian: "Religion: none" was indeed not acceptable. Anti-Semitism was so intrinsic as not to have a name. I don't recall exactly being taught that the Jews killed Jesus — "Christ killer" seems too strong a term for the bland Episcopal vocabulary — but certainly we got the impression that the Jews had been caught out in a terrible mistake, failing to recognize the true Messiah, and were thereby less advanced in moral and spiritual sensibility. The Jews had actually allowed *moneylenders in the Temple* (again, the unexplained obsession with Jews and money). They were of the past, archaic, primitive, as older (and darker) cultures are supposed to be primitive; christianity was lightness, fairness, peace on earth, and combined the feminine appeal of "The meek shall inherit the earth" with the masculine stride of "Onward, Christian Soldiers."

Sometime in 1946, while still in high school, I read in the newspaper that a theater in Baltimore was showing films of the Allied liberation of the Nazi concentration camps. Alone, I went downtown after school one afternoon and watched the stark, blurry, but unmistakable newsreels. When I try to go back and touch the pulse of that girl of sixteen, growing up in many ways so precocious and so ignorant, I am overwhelmed by a memory of despair, a sense of inevitability more enveloping than any I had ever known. Anne Frank's diary and many other personal narratives of the Holocaust were still unknown or unwritten. But it came to me that every one of those piles of corpses, mountains of shoes and clothing had contained, simply, individuals, who had believed, as I now believed of myself, that

---

[5]In a similar way the phrase *That's white of you* implied that you were behaving with the superior decency and morality expected of white but not of black people. — RICH'S NOTE.

they were intended to live out a life of some kind of meaning, that the world possessed some kind of sense and order; yet *this* had happened to them. And I, who believed my life was intended to be so interesting and meaningful, was connected to those dead by something — not just mortality but a taboo name, a hated identity. Or was I — did I really have to be? Writing this now, I feel belated rage that I was so impoverished by the family and social worlds I lived in, that I had to try to figure out by myself what this did indeed mean for me. That I had never been taught about resistance, only about passing. That I had no language for anti-Semitism itself.

When I went home and told my parents where I had been, they were not pleased. I felt accused of being morbidly curious, not healthy, sniffing around death for the thrill of it. And since, at sixteen, I was often not sure of the sources of my feelings or of my motives for doing what I did, I probably accused myself as well. One thing was clear: There was nobody in my world with whom I could discuss those films. Probably at the same time, I was reading accounts of the camps in magazines and newspapers; what I remember were the films and having questions that I could not even phrase, such as *Are those men and women "them" or "us"?*

To be able to ask even the child's astonished question *Why do they hate us so?* means knowing how to say "we." The guilt of not knowing, the guilt of perhaps having betrayed my parents or even those victims, those survivors, through mere curiosity — these also froze in me for years the impulse to find out more about the Holocaust.

1947: I left Baltimore to go to college in Cambridge, Massachusetts, left (I thought) the backward, enervating South for the intellectual, vital North. New England also had for me some vibration of higher moral rectitude, of moral passion even, with its seventeenth-century Puritan self-scrutiny, its nineteenth-century literary "flowering," its abolitionist righteousness, Colonel Shaw and his black Civil War regiment depicted in granite on Boston Common. At the same time, I found myself, at Radcliffe, among Jewish women. I used to sit for hours over coffee with what I thought of as the "real" Jewish students, who told me about middle-class Jewish culture in America. I described my background — for the first time to strangers — and they took me on, some with amusement at my illiteracy, some arguing that I could never marry into a strict Jewish family, some convinced I didn't "look Jewish," others that I did. I learned the names of holidays and foods, which surnames are Jewish and which are "changed names"; about girls who had had their noses "fixed," their hair straightened. For these young Jewish women, students in the late 1940s, it was acceptable, perhaps even necessary, to strive to look as gentile as possible; but they stuck proudly to being Jewish, expected to marry a Jew, have children, keep the holidays, carry on the culture.

I felt I was testing a forbidden current, that there was danger in these 25 revelations. I bought a reproduction of a Chagall portrait of a rabbi in striped prayer shawl and hung it on the wall of my room. I was admittedly young and trying to educate myself, but I was also doing something that *is* dangerous: I was flirting with identity.

One day that year I was in a small shop where I had bought a dress with a too-long skirt. The shop employed a seamstress who did alterations, and she came in to pin up the skirt on me. I am sure that she was a recent immigrant, a survivor. I remember a short, dark woman wearing heavy glasses, with an accent so foreign I could not understand her words. Something about her presence was very powerful and disturbing to me. After marking and pinning up the skirt, she sat back on her knees, looked up at me, and asked in a hurried whisper: "You Jewish?" Eighteen years of training in assimilation sprang into the reflex by which I shook my head, rejecting her, and muttered, "No."

What was I actually saying "no" to? She was poor, older, struggling with a foreign tongue, anxious; she had escaped the death that had been intended for her, but I had no imagination of her possible courage and foresight, her resistance — I did not see in her a heroine who had perhaps saved many lives, including her own. I saw the frightened immigrant, the seamstress hemming the skirts of college girls, the wandering Jew. But I was an American college girl having her skirt hemmed. And I was frightened myself, I think, because she had recognized me ("It takes one to know one," my friend Edie at Radcliffe had said) even if I refused to recognize myself or her, even if her recognition was sharpened by loneliness or the need to feel safe with me.

But why should she have felt safe with me? I myself was living with a false sense of safety.

There are betrayals in my life that I have known at the very moment were betrayals: this was one of them. There are other betrayals committed so repeatedly, so mundanely, that they leave no memory trace behind, only a growing residue of misery, of dull, accreted self-hatred. Often these take the form not of words but of silence. Silence before the joke at which everyone is laughing: the anti-woman joke, the racist joke, the anti-Semitic joke. Silence and then amnesia. Blocking it out when the oppressor's language starts coming from the lips of one we admire, whose courage and eloquence have touched us: *She didn't really mean that; he didn't really say that.* But the accretions build up out of sight, like scale inside a kettle.

1948: I come home from my freshman year at college, flaming with   30 new insights, new information. I am the daughter who has gone out into the world, to the pinnacle of intellectual prestige, Harvard, fulfilling my father's hopes for me, but also exposed to dangerous influences. I have already been reproved for attending a rally for Henry Wallace[6] and the

---

[6]*Henry Wallace* (1888–1965): American journalist, agriculturist, and politician. Was the 1948 Progressive party's candidate for the presidency. — EDS.

Progressive party. I challenge my father: "Why haven't you told me that I am Jewish? Why do you never talk about being a Jew?" He answers measuredly, "You know that I have never denied that I am a Jew. But it's not important to me. I am a scientist, a deist. I have no use for organized religion. I choose to live in a world of many kinds of people. There are Jews I admire and others whom I despise. I am a person, not simply a Jew." The words are as I remember them, not perhaps exactly as spoken. But that was the message. And it contained enough truth — as all denial drugs itself on partial truth — so that it remained for the time being unanswerable, leaving me high and dry, split at the root, gasping for clarity, for air.

At that time Arnold Rich was living in suspension, waiting to be appointed to the professorship of pathology at Johns Hopkins. The appointment was delayed for years, no Jew ever having held a professional chair in that medical school. And he wanted it badly. It must have been a very bitter time for him, since he had believed so greatly in the redeeming power of excellence, of being the most brilliant, inspired man for the job. With enough excellence, you could presumably make it stop mattering that you were Jewish; you could become the *only* Jew in the gentile world, a Jew so "civilized," so far from "common," so attractively combining southern gentility with European cultural values that no one would ever confuse you with the raw, "pushy" Jews of New York, the "loud, hysterical" refugees from eastern Europe, the "overdressed" Jews of the urban South.

We — my sister, mother, and I — were constantly urged to speak quietly in public, to dress without ostentation, to repress all vividness or spontaneity, to assimilate with a world which might see us as too flamboyant. I suppose that my mother, pure gentile though she was, could be seen as acting "common" or "Jewish" if she laughed too loudly or spoke aggressively. My father's mother, who lived with us half the year, was a model of circumspect behavior, dressed in dark blue or lavender, retiring in company, ladylike to an extreme, wearing no jewelry except a good gold chain, a narrow brooch, or a string of pearls. A few times, within the family, I saw her anger flare, felt the passion she was repressing. But when Arnold took us out to a restaurant or on a trip, the Rich women were always tuned down to some WASP level my father believed, surely, would protect us all — maybe also make us unrecognizable to the "real Jews" who wanted to seize us, drag us back to the *shtetl*, the ghetto, in its many manifestations.

For, yes, that *was* a message — that some Jews would be after you, once they "knew," to rejoin them, to re-enter a world that was messy, noisy, unpredictable, maybe poor — "even though," as my mother once wrote me, criticizing my largely Jewish choice of friends in college, "some of them will be the most brilliant, fascinating people you'll ever meet." I wonder if that isn't one message of assimilation — of America — that the unlucky or the unachieving want to pull you backward, that to identify with them is to court downward mobility, lose the precious chance of passing, of token existence. There was always within this sense of Jewish identity a strong class discrimination. Jews might be "fascinating" as individuals but came with huge unruly families who "poured chicken soup over everyone's head" (in the phrase of a white southern male poet). Anti-Semitism could thus be justified by the bad behavior of certain Jews; and if you did not effectively deny family and community, there would always be a remote cousin claiming kinship with you who was the "wrong kind" of Jew.

I have always believed his attitude toward other Jews depended on who they were. . . . It was my impression that Jews of this background looked down on Eastern European Jews, including Polish Jews and Russian Jews, who generally were not as well educated. This from a letter written to me recently by a gentile who had worked in my father's department, whom I had asked about anti-Semitism there and in particular regarding my father. This informant also wrote me that it was hard to perceive anti-Semitism in Baltimore because the racism made so much more intense an impression: *I would almost have to think that blacks went to a different heaven than the whites, because the bodies were kept in a separate morgue, and some white persons did not even want blood transfusions from black donors.* My father's mind was predictably racist and misogynist; yet as a medical student he noted in his journal that southern male chivalry stopped at the point of any white man in a streetcar giving his seat to an old, weary black woman standing in the aisle. Was this a Jewish insight — an outsider's insight, even though the outsider was striving to be on the inside?

Because what isn't named is often more permeating than what is, I   35
believe that my father's Jewishness profoundly shaped my own identity and our family existence. They were shaped both by external anti-Semitism and my father's self-hatred, and by his Jewish pride. What Arnold did, I think, was call his Jewish pride something else: achievement, aspiration, genius, idealism. Whatever was unacceptable got left back under the rubric of Jewishness or the "wrong kind" of Jews — uneducated, aggressive, loud. The message I got was that we were really superior: Nobody else's father had collected so many books, had traveled so far, knew so many languages. Baltimore was a musical city, but for the most part, in the families of my school friends, culture was for women. My father was an amateur musician, read poetry, adored encyclopedic knowledge. He prowled and pounced over my school papers, insisting I use "grown-up" sources; he criticized my poems for faulty technique and gave me books on rhyme and meter and form. His investment in my intellect and talent was egotistical, tyrannical, opinionated, and terribly wearing. He taught me, nevertheless, to believe in hard work, to mistrust easy inspiration, to write and rewrite; to feel that I *was* a person of the book, even though a woman; to take ideas seriously. He made me feel, at a very young age, the power of language and that I could share it.

The Riches were proud, but we also had to be very careful. Our behavior had to be more impeccable than other people's. Strangers were not to be trusted, nor even friends; family issues must never go beyond the family; the world was full of potential slanderers, betrayers, *people who could not understand.* Even within the family, I realize that I never in my whole life knew what my father was really feeling. Yet he spoke — monologued — with driving intensity. You could grow up in such a house mesmerized by the local electricity, the crucial meanings assumed by the merest things. This used to seem to me a sign that we were all living on some high emotional plane. It was a difficult force field for a favored daughter to disengage from.

Easy to call that intensity Jewish; and I have no doubt that passion is one of the qualities required for survival over generations of persecution. But what happens when passion is rent from its original base, when the white gentile world is softly saying "Be more like us and you can be almost one of us"? What happens when survival seems to mean closing off one emotional artery after another? His forebears in Europe had been forbidden to travel or expelled from one country after another, had special taxes levied on them if they left the city walls, had been forced to wear special clothes and badges, restricted to the poorest neighborhoods. He had wanted to be a "free spirit," to travel widely, among "all kinds of people." Yet in his prime of life he lived in an increasingly withdrawn world, in his house up on a hill in a neighborhood where Jews were not supposed to be able to buy property, depending almost exclusively on interactions with his wife and daughters to provide emotional connectedness. In his home, he created a private defense system so elaborate that even as he was dying, my mother felt unable to talk freely with his colleagues or others who might have helped her. Of course, she acquiesced in this.

The loneliness of the "only," the token, often doesn't feel like loneliness but like a kind of dead echo chamber. Certain things that ought to don't resonate. Somewhere Beverly Smith writes of women of color "inspiring the behavior" in each other. When there's nobody to "inspire the behavior," act out of the culture, there is an atrophy, a dwindling, which is partly invisible.

Sometimes I feel I have seen too long from too many disconnected angles: white, Jewish, anti-Semite, racist, anti-racist, once-married, lesbian, middle-class, feminist, exmatriate southerner, *split at the root* — that I will never bring them whole. I would have liked, in this essay, to bring together the meanings of anti-Semitism and racism as I have experienced them and as I believe they intersect in the world beyond my life. But I'm not able to do this yet. I feel the tension as I think, make notes: *If you really look at the one reality, the other will waver and disperse.* Trying in one week to read Angela Davis and Lucy Davidowicz,[7] trying to hold throughout to a femi-

---

[7]Angela Y. Davis, *Women, Race and Class* (New York: Random House, 1981): Lucy S. Davidowicz, *The War against the Jews 1933–1945* (1975) (New York: Bantam, 1979). — RICH'S NOTE.

nist, a lesbian, perspective — what does this mean? Nothing has trained me for this. And sometimes I feel inadequate to make any statement as a Jew; I feel the history of denial within me like an injury, a scar. For assimilation has affected *my* perceptions; those early lapses in meaning, those blanks, are with me still. My ignorance can be dangerous to me and to others.

Yet we can't wait for the undamaged to make our connections for us;   40
we can't wait to speak until we are perfectly clear and righteous. There is no purity and, in our lifetimes, no end to this process.

This essay, then, has no conclusions: It is another beginning for me. Not just a way of saying, in 1982 Right Wing America, *I, too, will wear the yellow star.* It's a moving into accountability, enlarging the range of accountability. I know that in the rest of my life, the next half century or so, every aspect of my identity will have to be engaged. The middle-class white girl taught to trade obedience for privilege. The Jewish lesbian raised to be a heterosexual gentile. The woman who first heard oppression named and analyzed in the black Civil Rights struggle. The woman with three sons, the feminist who hates male violence. The woman limping with a cane, the woman who has stopped bleeding are also accountable. The poet who knows that beautiful language can lie, that the oppressor's language sometimes sounds beautiful. The woman trying, as part of her resistance, to clean up her act.

1986

The Reader's Presence

1. Why does Rich feel she needs to "claim" her father in order to come to terms with her identity? What does she mean by "claim"? How do we make such claims? Why is her father so closely tied to her sense of identity?

2. Rich doesn't begin with a statement about her personal history but with a reference to her act of writing at the moment. What is the effect of beginning this way? How does writing figure throughout the essay? What connection can you see between writing and identity?

3. In rereading Rich's essay, pay close attention to her use of time. Try to construct a chronology for the essay. How does she organize that chronology in the essay itself? Can you think of some explanations for why Rich does not proceed in an orderly and straightforward manner? Can you discover any patterns in the procedure she chose to follow?

16 _____

Judy Ruiz

Oranges and Sweet Sister Boy

I am sleeping, hard, when the telephone rings. It's my brother, and he's calling to say that he is now my sister. I feel something fry a little, deep behind my eyes. Knowing how sometimes dreams get mixed up with not-dreams, I decide to do a reality test at once. "Let me get a cigarette," I say, knowing that if I reach for a Marlboro and it turns into a trombone or a snake or anything else on the way to my lips that I'm still out in the large world of dreams.

The cigarette stays a cigarette. I light it. I ask my brother to run that stuff by me again.

It is the Texas Zephyr[1] at midnight — the woman in a white suit, the man in a blue uniform; she carries flowers — I know they are flowers. The petals spill and spill into the aisle, and a child goes past this couple who have just come from their own wedding — goes past them and past them, going always to the toilet but really just going past them; and the child could be a horse or she could be the police and they'd not notice her any more than they do, which is not at all — the man's hands high up on the woman's legs, her skirt up, her stockings and garters, the petals and finally all the flowers spilling out into the aisle and his mouth open on her. My mother. My father. I am conceived near Dallas in the dark while a child passes, a young girl who knows and doesn't know, who witnesses, in glimpses, the creation of the universe, who feels an odd hurt as her own mother, fat and empty, snores with her mouth open, her false teeth slipping down, snores and snores just two seats behind the Creators.

News can make a person stupid. It can make you think you can do something. So I ask The Blade question, thinking that if he hasn't had the

For biographical information on Judy Ruiz, see p. 661.
[1]*Texas Zephyr:* A passenger train. — EDS.

operation yet that I can fly to him, rent a cabin out on Puget Sound. That we can talk. That I can get him to touch base with reality.

"Begin with an orange," I would tell him. "Because oranges are mildly intrusive by nature, put the orange somewhere so that it will not bother you — in the cupboard, in a drawer, even a pocket or a handbag will do. The orange, being a patient fruit, will wait for you much longer than say a banana or a peach."

I would hold an orange out to him. I would say, "This is the one that   5 will save your life." And I would tell him about the woman I saw in a bus station who bit right into her orange like it was an apple. She was wild looking, as if she'd been outside for too long in a wind that blew the same way all the time. One of the dregs of humanity, our mother would have called her, the same mother who never brought fruit into the house except in cans. My children used to ask me to "start" their oranges for them. That meant to make a hole in the orange so they could peel the rind away, and their small hands weren't equipped with fingernails that were long enough or strong enough to do the job. Sometimes they would suck the juice out of the hole my thumbnail had made, leaving the orange flat and sad.

> The earrings are as big as dessert plates, filigree gold-plated with thin dangles hanging down that touch her bare shoulders. She stands in front of the Alamo while a bald man takes her picture. The sun is absorbed by the earrings so quickly that by the time she feels the heat, it is too late. The hanging dangles make small blisters on her shoulders, as if a centipede had traveled there. She takes the famous river walk in spiked heels, rides in a boat, eats some Italian noodles, returns to the motel room, soaks her feet, and applies small band-aids to her toes. She is briefly concerned about the gun on the nightstand. The toilet flushes. She pretends to be sleeping. The gun is just large and heavy. A .45? A .357 magnum? She's never been good with names. She hopes he doesn't try to. Or that if he does, that it's not loaded. But he'll say it's loaded just for fun. Or he'll pull the trigger and the bullet will lodge in her medulla oblongata, ripping through her womb first, taking everything else vital on the way.

In the magazine articles, you don't see this: "Well, yes. The testicles have to come out. And yes. The penis is cut off." What you get is tonsils. So-and-so has had a "sex change" operation. A sex change operation. How precious. How benign. Doctor, just what do you people do with those penises?

News can make a person a little crazy also. News like, "We regret to inform you that you have failed your sanity hearing."

The bracelet on my wrist bears the necessary information about me, but there is one small error. The receptionist typing the information asked me my religious preference. I said, "None." She typed, "Neon."

> Pearl doesn't have any teeth and her tongue looks weird. She says "Pumpkin pie." That's all she says. Sometimes she runs her hands over my bed sheets and says pumpkin pie. Sometimes I am under the sheets. Mar-

sha got stabbed in the chest, but she tells everyone she fell on a knife. Elizabeth — she's the one who thinks her shoe is a baby — hit me in the back with a tray right after one of the cooks gave me extra toast. There's a note on the bulletin board about a class for the nurses: "How Putting A Towel On Someone's Face Makes Them Stop Banging Their Spoon/OR Reduction of Disruptive Mealtime Behavior By Facial Screening — 7 P.M. — Conference Room." Another note announces the topic for remotivation class: "COWS." All the paranoid schizophrenics will be there.

Here, in the place for the permanently bewildered, I fit right in. Not because I stood at the window that first night and listened to the trains. Not because I imagined those trains were bracelets, the jewelry of earth. Not even because I imagined that one of those bracelets was on my own arm and was the Texas Zephyr where a young couple made love and conceived me. I am eighteen and beautiful and committed to the state hospital by a district court judge for a period of one day to life. Because I am a paranoid schizophrenic.

I will learn about cows.

So I'm being very quiet in the back of the classroom, and I'm peeling an orange. It's the smell that makes the others begin to turn around, that mildly intrusive nature. The course is called "Women and Modern Literature," and the diaries of Virginia Woolf are up for discussion except nobody has anything to say. I, of course, am making a mess with the orange; and I'm wanting to say that my brother is now my sister.

Later, with my hands still orangey, I wander in to leave something on   10
a desk in a professor's office, and he's reading so I'm being very quiet, and then he says, sort of out of nowhere, "Emily Dickinson up there in her room making poems while her brother was making love to her best friend right downstairs on the dining room table. A regular thing. Think of it. And Walt Whitman out sniffing around the boys. Our two great American poets." And I want to grab this professor's arm and say, "Listen. My brother called me and now he's my sister, and I'm having trouble making sense out of my life right now, so would you mind not telling me any more stuff about sex." And I want my knuckles to turn white while the pressure of my fingers leaves imprints right through his jacket, little indentations he can interpret as urgent. But I don't say anything. And I don't grab his arm. I go read a magazine. I find this:

> "I've never found an explanation for why the human race has so many languages. When the brain became a language brain, it obviously needed to develop an intense degree of plasticity. Such plasticity allows languages to be logical, coherent systems and yet be extremely variable. The same brain that thinks in words and symbols is also a brain that has to be freed up with regard to sexual turn-on and partnering. God knows why sex attitudes have been subject to the corresponding degrees of modification and variety as language. I suspect there's a close parallel between the two. The brain doesn't seem incredibly efficient with regard to sex."

John Money said that. The same John Money who, with surgeon Howard

W. Jones, performed the first sex change operation in the United States in 1965 at Johns Hopkins University and Hospital in Baltimore.

Money also tells about the *hijra* of India who disgrace their families because they are too effeminate: "The ultimate stage of the *hijra* is to get up the courage to go through the amputation of penis and testicles. They had no anesthetic." Money also answers anyone who might think that "heartless members of the medical profession are forcing these poor darlings to go and get themselves cut up and mutilated," or who think the medical profession should leave them alone. "You'd have lots of patients willing to get a gun and blow off their own genitals if you don't do it. I've had several who got knives and cut themselves trying to get rid of their sex organs. That's their obsession!"

Perhaps better than all else, I understand obsession. It is of the mind. And it is language-bound. Sex is of the body. It has no words. I am stunned to learn that someone with an obsession of the mind can have parts of the body surgically removed. This is my brother I speak of. This is not some lunatic named Carl who becomes Carlene. This is my brother.

So while we're out in that cabin on Puget Sound, I'll tell him about LuAnn. She is the sort of woman who orders the in-season fruit and a little cottage cheese. I am the sort of woman who orders a double cheeseburger and fries. LuAnn and I are sitting in her car. She has a huge orange, and she peels it so the peel falls off in one neat strip. I have a sack of oranges, the small ones. The peel of my orange comes off in hunks about the size of a baby's nail. "Oh, you bought the *juice* oranges," LuAnn says to me. Her emphasis on the word "juice" makes me want to die or something. I lack the courage to admit my ignorance, so I smile and breathe "yes," as if I know some secret, when I'm wanting to scream at her about how my mother didn't teach me about fruit and my own blood pounds in my head wanting out, out.

> There is a pattern to this thought as there is a pattern for a jumpsuit. Sew the sleeve to the leg, sew the leg to the collar. Put the garment on. Sew the mouth shut. This is how I tell about being quiet because I am bad, and because I cannot stand it when he beats me or my brother.

"The first time I got caught in your clothes was when I was four years old and you were over at Sarah what's-her-name's babysitting. Dad beat me so hard I thought I was going to die. I really thought I was going to die. That was the day I made up my mind I would *never* get caught again. And I never got caught again." My brother goes on to say he continued to go through my things until I was hospitalized. A mystery is solved.

He wore my clothes. He played in my makeup. I kept saying, back then, that someone was going through my stuff. I kept saying it and saying it. I told the counselor at school. "Someone goes in my room when I'm not there, and I *know* it — goes in there and wears my clothes and goes

15

through my stuff." I was assured by the counselor that this was not so. I was assured by my mother that this was not so. I thought my mother was doing it, snooping around for clues like mothers do. It made me a little crazy, so I started deliberately leaving things in a certain order so that I would be able to prove to myself that someone, indeed, was going through my belongings. No one, not one person, ever believed that my room was being ransacked; I was accused of just making it up. A paranoid fixation.

And all the time it was old Goldilocks.

So I tell my brother to promise me he'll see someone who counsels adult children from dysfunctional families. I tell him he needs to deal with the fact that he was physically abused on a daily basis. He tells me he doesn't remember being beaten except on three occasions. He wants me to get into a support group for families of people who are having a sex change. Support groups are people who are in the same boat. Except no one has any oars in the water.

I tell him I know how it feels to think you are in the wrong body. I tell him how I wanted my boyfriend to put a gun up inside me and blow the woman out, how I thought wearing spiked heels and low-cut dresses would somehow help my crisis, that putting on an ultrafeminine outside would mask the maleness I felt needed hiding. I tell him it's the rule, rather than the exception, that people from families like ours have very spooky sexual identity problems. He tells me that his sexuality is a birth defect. I recognize the lingo. It's support-group-for-transsexuals lingo. He tells me he sits down to pee. He told his therapist that he used to wet all over the floor. His therapist said, "You can't aim the bullets if you don't touch the gun." Lingo. My brother is hell-bent for castration, the castration that started before he had language: the castration of abuse. He will simply finish what was set in motion long ago.

I will tell my brother about the time I took ten sacks of oranges into a school so that I could teach metaphor. The school was for special students — those who were socially or intellectually impaired. I had planned to have them peel the oranges as I spoke about how much the world is like the orange. I handed out the oranges. The students refused to peel them, not because they wanted to make life difficult for me — they were enchanted with the gift. One child asked if he could have an orange to take home to his little brother. Another said he would bring me ten dollars the next day if I would give him a sack of oranges. And I knew I was at home, that these children and I shared something that *makes* the leap of mind the metaphor attempts. And something in me healed.

A neighbor of mine takes pantyhose and cuts them up and sews them   20
up after stuffing them. Then she puts these things into Mason jars and sells

them, you know, to put out on the mantel for conversation. They are little penises and little scrotums, complete with hair. She calls them "Pickled Peters."

A friend of mine had a sister who had a sex change operation. This young woman had her breasts removed and ran around the house with no shirt on before the stitches were taken out. She answered the door one evening. A young man had come to call on my friend. The sex-changed sister invited him in and offered him some black bean soup as if she were perfectly normal with her red surgical wounds and her black stitches. The young man left and never went back. A couple years later, my friend's sister/brother died when s/he ran a car into a concrete bridge railing. I hope for a happier ending. For my brother, for myself, for all of us.

My brother calls. He's done his toenails: Shimmering Cinnamon. And he's left his wife and children and purchased some nightgowns at a yard sale. His hair is getting longer. He wears a special bra. Most of the people he works with know about the changes in his life. His voice is not the same voice I've heard for years; he sounds happy.

My brother calls. He's always envied me, my woman's body. The same body I live in and have cursed for its softness. He asks me how I feel about myself. He says, "You know, you are really our father's first-born son." He tells me he used to want to be me because I was the only person our father almost loved.

The drama of life. After I saw that woman in the bus station eat an orange as if it were an apple, I went out into the street and smoked a joint with some guy I'd met on the bus. Then I hailed a cab and went to a tattoo parlor. The tattoo artist tried to talk me into getting a nice bird or butterfly design; I had chosen a design on his wall that appealed to me — a symbol I didn't know the meaning of. It is the Yin-Yang, and it's tattooed above my right ankle bone. I supposed my drugged, crazed consciousness knew more than I knew: that yin combines with yang to produce all that comes to be. I am drawn to androgyny.

Of course there is the nagging possibility that my brother's dilemma is   25 genetic. Our father used to dress in drag on Halloween, and he made a beautiful woman. One year, the year my mother cut my brother's blond curls off, my father taped those curls to his own head and tied a silk scarf over the tape. Even his close friends didn't know it was him. And my youngest daughter was a body builder for a while, her lean body as muscular as a man's. And my sons are beautiful, not handsome: they look androgynous.

Then there's my grandson. I saw him when he was less than an hour old. He was naked and had hiccups. I watched as he had his first bath, and I heard him cry. He had not been named yet, but his little crib had a blue card affixed to it with tape. And on the card were the words "Baby Boy." There was no doubt in me that the words were true.

When my brother was born, my father was off flying jets in Korea. I went to the hospital with my grandfather to get my mother and this new brother. I remember how I wanted a sister, and I remember looking at him as my mother held him in the front seat of the car. I was certain he was a sister, certain that my mother was joking. She removed his diaper to show me that he was a boy. I still didn't believe her. Considering what has happened lately, I wonder if my child-skewed consciousness knew more than the anatomical proof suggested.

I try to make peace with myself. I try to understand his decision to alter himself. I try to think of him as her. I write his woman name, and I feel like I'm betraying myself. I try to be open-minded, but something in me shuts down. I think we humans are in big trouble, that many of us don't really have a clue as to what acceptable human behavior is. Something in me says no to all this, that this surgery business is the ultimate betrayal of the self. And yet, I want my brother to be happy.

It was in the city of San Antonio that my father had his surgery. I rode the bus from Kansas to Texas, and arrived at the hospital two days after the operation to find my father sitting in the solarium playing solitaire. He had a type of cancer that particularly thrived on testosterone. And so he was castrated in order to ease his pain and to stop the growth of tumors. He died six months later.

Back in the sleep of the large world of dreams, I have done surgeries 30 under water in which I float my father's testicles back into him, and he — the brutal man he was — emerges from the pool a tan and smiling man, parting the surface of the water with his perfect head. He loves all the grief away.

I will tell my brother all I know of oranges, that if you squeeze the orange peel into a flame, small fires happen because of the volatile oil in the peel. Also, if you squeeze the peel and it gets into your cat's eyes, the cat will blink and blink. I will tell him there is no perfect rhyme for the word "orange," and that if we can just make up a good word we can be immortal. We will become obsessed with finding the right word, and I will be joyous at our legitimate pursuit.

I have purchased a black camisole with lace to send to my new sister. And a card. On the outside of the card there's a drawing of a woman sitting by a pond and a zebra is off to the left. Inside are these words: "The past is ended. Be happy." And I have asked my companions to hold me and I have cried. My self is wet and small. But it is not dark. Sometimes, if no one touches me, I will die.

Sister, you are the best craziness of the family. Brother, love what you love.

1988

The Reader's Presence

1. The essay opens with the author asleep. How do sleep and dreams figure throughout the essay? How might they help account for the odd jumps and connections that sometimes make the essay hard to follow?

2. Note the moments in the essay where Ruiz inserts paragraphs in smaller type. What are these moments? What have they to do with the main body of the essay? What do those moments have in common? How are you intended to read them?

3. In rereading the essay make a note of all references to the body. In what ways is the human body present? According to Ruiz, how does the body differ from the mind? (See paragraph 12.) How is that difference dramatized by the essay itself?

17 _____

Scott Russell Sanders

The Men We Carry in Our Minds

"This must be a hard time for women," I say to my friend Anneke. "They have so many paths to choose from, and so many voices calling them."

"I think it's a lot harder for men," she replies.

"How do you figure that?"

"The women I know feel excited, innocent, like crusaders in a just cause. The men I know are eaten up with guilt."

We are sitting at the kitchen table drinking sassafras tea, our hands 5 wrapped around the mugs because this April morning is cool and drizzly. "Like a Dutch morning," Anneke told me earlier. She is Dutch herself, a writer and midwife and peacemaker, with the round face and sad eyes of a woman in a Vermeer painting who might be waiting for the rain to stop, for a door to open. She leans over to sniff a sprig of lilac, pale lavender, that rises from a vase of cobalt blue.

"Women feel such pressure to be everything, do everything," I say. "Career, kids, art, politics. Have their babies and get back to the office a week later. It's as if they're trying to overcome a million years' worth of evolution in one lifetime."

For biographical information on Scott Russell Sanders, see p. 662.

"But we help one another. We don't try to lumber on alone, like so many wounded grizzly bears, the way men do." Anneke sips her tea. I gave her the mug with the owls on it, for wisdom. "And we have this deep-down sense that we're in the *right* — we've been held back, passed over, used — while men feel they're in the wrong. Men are the ones who've been discredited, who have to search their souls."

I search my soul. I discover guilty feelings aplenty — toward the poor, the Vietnamese, Native Americans, the whales, an endless list of debts — a guilt in each case that is as bright and unambiguous as a neon sign. But toward women I feel something more confused, a snarl of shame, envy, wary tenderness, and amazement. This muddle troubles me. To hide my unease I say, "You're right, it's tough being a man these days."

"Don't laugh." Anneke frowns at me, mournful-eyed, through the sassafras steam. "I wouldn't be a man for anything. It's much easier being the victim. All the victim has to do is break free. The persecutor has to live with his past."

How deep is that past? I find myself wondering after Anneke has left. ⟨10⟩ How much of an inheritance do I have to throw off? Is it just the beliefs I breathed in as a child? Do I have to scour memory back through father and grandfather? Through St. Paul? Beyond Stonehenge and into the twilit caves? I'm convinced the past we must contend with is deeper even than speech. When I think back on my childhood, on how I learned to see men and women, I have a sense of ancient, dizzying depths. The back roads of Tennessee and Ohio where I grew up were probably closer, in their sexual patterns, to the campsites of Stone Age hunters than to the genderless cities of the future into which we are rushing.

The first men, besides my father, I remember seeing were black convicts and white guards, in the cottonfield across the road from our farm on the outskirts of Memphis. I must have been three or four. The prisoners wore dingy gray-and-black zebra suits, heavy as canvas, sodden with sweat. Hatless, stooped, they chopped weeds in the fierce heat, row after row, breathing the acrid dust of boll-weevil poison. The overseers wore dazzling white shirts and broad shadowy hats. The oiled barrels of their shotguns flashed in the sunlight. Their faces in memory are utterly blank. Of course those men, white and black, have become for me an emblem of racial hatred. But they have also come to stand for the twin poles of my early vision of manhood — the brute toiling animal and the boss.

When I was a boy, the men I knew labored with their bodies. They were marginal farmers, just scraping by, or welders, steelworkers, carpenters; they swept floors, dug ditches, mined coal, or drove trucks, their forearms ropy with muscle; they trained horses, stoked furnaces, built tires, stood on assembly lines wrestling parts onto cars and refrigerators. They got up before light, worked all day long whatever the weather, and when they came home at night they looked as though somebody had been whipping them. In the evenings and on weekends they worked on their own places, tilling gardens that were lumpy with clay, fixing broken-down cars, hammering on houses that were always too drafty, too leaky, too small.

The bodies of the men I knew were twisted and maimed in ways visible and invisible. The nails of their hands were black and split, the hands tattooed with scars. Some had lost fingers. Heavy lifting had given many of them finicky backs and guts weak from hernias. Racing against conveyor belts had given them ulcers. Their ankles and knees ached from years of standing on concrete. Anyone who had worked for long around machines was hard of hearing. They squinted, and the skin of their faces was creased like the leather of old work gloves. There were times, studying them, when I dreaded growing up. Most of them coughed, from dust or cigarettes, and most of them drank cheap wine or whiskey, so their eyes looked bloodshot and bruised. The fathers of my friends always seemed older than the mothers. Men wore out sooner. Only women lived into old age.

As a boy I also knew another sort of men, who did not sweat and break down like mules. They were soldiers, and so far as I could tell they scarcely worked at all. During my early school years we lived on a military base, an arsenal in Ohio, and every day I saw GIs in the guardshacks, on the stoops of barracks, at the wheels of olive drab Chevrolets. The chief fact of their lives was boredom. Long after I left the Arsenal I came to recognize the sour smell the soldiers gave off as that of souls in limbo. They were all waiting — for wars, for transfers, for leaves, for promotions, for the end of their hitch — like so many braves waiting for the hunt to begin. Unlike the warriors of older tribes, however, they would have no say about when the battle would start or how it would be waged. Their waiting was broken only when they practiced for war. They fired guns at targets, drove tanks across the churned-up fields of the military reservation, set off bombs in the wrecks of old fighter planes. I knew this was all play. But I also felt certain that when the hour for killing arrived, they would kill. When the real shooting started, many of them would die. This was what soldiers were *for*, just as a hammer was for driving nails.

Warriors and toilers: those seemed, in my boyhood vision, to be the 15
chief destinies for men. They weren't the only destinies, as I learned from having a few male teachers, from reading books, and from watching television. But the men on television — the politicians, the astronauts, the generals, the savvy lawyers, the philosophical doctors, the bosses who gave orders to both soldiers and laborers — seemed as remote and unreal to me as the figures in tapestries. I could no more imagine growing up to become one of these cool, potent creatures than I could imagine becoming a prince.

A nearer and more hopeful example was that of my father, who had escaped from a red-dirt farm to a tire factory, and from the assembly line to the front office. Eventually he dressed in a white shirt and tie. He carried himself as if he had been born to work with his mind. But his body, remembering the earlier years of slogging work, began to give out on him in his fifties, and it quit on him entirely before he turned sixty-five. Even such a partial escape from man's fate as he had accomplished did not seem possible for most of the boys I knew. They joined the army, stood in line for jobs in the smoky plants, helped build highways. They were bound to work as their fathers had worked, killing themselves or preparing to kill others.

A scholarship enabled me not only to attend college, a rare enough feat in my circle, but even to study in a university meant for the children of the rich. Here I met for the first time young men who had assumed from birth that they would lead lives of comfort and power. And for the first time I met women who told me that men were guilty of having kept all the joys and privileges of the earth for themselves. I was baffled. What privileges? What joys? I thought about the maimed, dismal lives of most of the men back home. What had they stolen from their wives and daughters? The right to go five days a week, twelve months a year, for thirty or forty years to a steel mill or a coal mine? The right to drop bombs and die in war? The right to feel every leak in the roof, every gap in the fence, every cough in the engine, as a wound they must mend? The right to feel, when the lay-off comes or the plant shuts down, not only afraid but ashamed?

I was slow to understand the deep grievances of women. This was because, as a boy, I had envied them. Before college, the only people I had ever known who were interested in art or music or literature, the only ones who read books, the only ones who ever seemed to enjoy a sense of ease and grace were the mothers and daughters. Like the menfolk, they fretted about money, they scrimped and made-do. But, when the pay stopped coming in, they were not the ones who had failed. Nor did they have to go to war, and that seemed to me a blessed fact. By comparison with the narrow, ironclad days of fathers, there was an expansiveness, I thought, in the days of mothers. They went to see neighbors, to shop in town, to run errands at school, at the library, at church. No doubt, had I looked harder at their lives, I would have envied them less. It was not my fate to become a woman, so it was easier for me to see the graces. Few of them held jobs outside the home, and those who did filled thankless roles as clerks and waitresses. I didn't see, then, what a prison a house could be, since houses seemed to me brighter, handsomer places than any factory. I did not realize — because such things were never spoken of — how often women suffered from men's bullying. I did learn about the wretchedness of abandoned wives, single mothers, widows; but I also learned about the wretchedness of lone men. Even then I could see how exhausting it was for a mother to cater all day to the needs of young children. But if I had been asked, as a boy, to choose between tending a baby and tending a machine, I think I would have chosen the baby. (Having now tended both, I know I would choose the baby.)

So I was baffled when the women at college accused me and my sex of having cornered the world's pleasures. I think something like my bafflement has been felt by other boys (and by girls as well) who grew up in dirt-poor farm country, in mining country, in black ghettos, in Hispanic barrios, in the shadows of factories, in Third World nations — any place where the fate of men is as grim and bleak as the fate of women. Toilers and warriors. I realize now how ancient these identities are, how deep the tug they exert on men, the undertow of a thousand generations. The miseries I saw, as a boy, in the lives of nearly all men I continue to see in the lives of many — the body-breaking toil, the tedium, the call to be tough, the humiliating powerlessness, the battle for a living and for territory.

When the women I met at college thought about the joys and privileges 20 of men, they did not carry in their minds the sort of men I had known in my childhood. They thought of their fathers, who were bankers, physicians, architects, stockbrokers, the big wheels of the big cities. These fathers rode the train to work or drove cars that cost more than any of my childhood houses. They were attended from morning to night by female helpers, wives, and nurses and secretaries. They were never laid off, never short of cash at month's end, never lined up for welfare. These fathers made decisions that mattered. They ran the world.

The daughters of such men wanted to share in this power, this glory. So did I. They yearned for a say over their future, for jobs worthy of their abilities, for the right to live at peace, unmolested, whole. Yes, I thought, yes yes. The difference between me and these daughters was that they saw me, because of my sex, as destined from birth to become like their fathers, and therefore as an enemy to their desires. But I knew better. I wasn't an enemy, in fact or in feeling. I was an ally. If I had known, then, how to tell them so, would they have believed me? Would they now?

1974

The Reader's Presence

1. Consider the title of the essay. Why does Sanders use the word *carry?* What image does the word convey? How is that image reinforced throughout the essay?

2. Sanders begins the essay by jumping directly into a conversation. What effect does this conversation have on the reader? What does Sanders want you to think of him during that conversation? (See paragraphs 1–9.) Do your first impressions of Sanders remain the same throughout your reading?

3. Why did Sanders once envy women? What did women possess that men didn't? Has his impression of women's lives changed, or does he still envy them? If not, why not? If so, have his reasons changed?

18

Gary Soto

Looking for Work

One July, while killing ants on the kitchen sink with a rolled newspaper, I had a nine-year-old's vision of wealth that would save us from ourselves. For weeks I had drunk Kool-Aid and watched morning reruns of *Father Knows Best,* whose family was so uncomplicated in its routine that I very much wanted to imitate it. The first step was to get my brother and sister to wear shoes at dinner.

"Come on, Rick — come on, Deb," I whined. But Rick mimicked me and the same day that I asked him to wear shoes he came to the dinner table in only his swim trunks. My mother didn't notice, nor did my sister, as we sat to eat our beans and tortillas in the stifling heat of our kitchen. We all gleamed like cellophane, wiping the sweat from our brows with the backs of our hands as we talked about the day: Frankie our neighbor was beat up by Faustino; the swimming pool at the playground would be closed for a day because the pump was broken.

Such was our life. So that morning, while doing-in the train of ants which arrived each day, I decided to become wealthy, and right away! After downing a bowl of cereal, I took a rake from the garage and started up the block to look for work.

We lived on an ordinary block of mostly working class people: warehousemen, egg candlers,[1] welders, mechanics, and a union plumber. And there were many retired people who kept their lawns green and the gutters uncluttered of the chewing gum wrappers we dropped as we rode by on our bikes. They bent down to gather our litter, muttering at our evilness.

At the corner house I rapped the screen door and a very large woman 5 in a muu-muu answered. She sized me up and then asked what I could do.

"Rake leaves," I answered smiling.

"It's summer, and there ain't no leaves," she countered. Her face was

---

For biographical information on Gary Soto, see p. 663.
[1]*egg candlers:* Inspectors of eggs. — EDS.

pinched with lines; fat jiggled under her chin. She pointed to the lawn, then the flower bed, and said: "You see any leaves there — or there?" I followed her pointing arm, stupidly. But she had a job for me and that was to get her a Coke at the liquor store. She gave me twenty cents, and after ditching my rake in a bush, off I ran. I returned with an unbagged Pepsi, for which she thanked me and gave me a nickel from her apron.

I skipped off her porch, fetched my rake, and crossed the street to the next block where Mrs. Moore, mother of Earl the retarded man, let me weed a flower bed. She handed me a trowel and for a good part of the morning my fingers dipped into the moist dirt, ripping up runners of Bermuda grass. Worms surfaced in my search for deep roots, and I cut them in halves, tossing them to Mrs. Moore's cat who pawed them playfully as they dried in the sun. I made out Earl whose face was pressed to the back window of the house, and although he was calling to me I couldn't understand what he was trying to say. Embarrassed, I worked without looking up, but I imagined his contorted mouth and the ring of keys attached to his belt — keys that jingled with each palsied step. He scared me and I worked quickly to finish the flower bed. When I did finish Mrs. Moore gave me a quarter and two peaches from her tree, which I washed there but ate in the alley behind my house.

I was sucking on the second one, a bit of juice staining the front of my T-shirt, when Little John, my best friend, came walking down the alley with a baseball bat over his shoulder, knocking over trash cans as he made his way toward me.

Little John and I went to St. John's Catholic School, where we sat   10 among the "stupids." Miss Marino, our teacher, alternated the rows of good students with the bad, hoping that by sitting side-by-side with the bright students the stupids might become more intelligent, as though intelligence were contagious. But we didn't progress as she had hoped. She grew frustrated when one day, while dismissing class for recess, Little John couldn't get up because his arms were stuck in the slats of the chair's backrest. She scolded us with a shaking finger when we knocked over the globe, denting the already troubled Africa. She muttered curses when Leroy White, a real stupid but a great softball player with the gift to hit to all fields, openly chewed his host[2] when he made his First Communion; his hands swung at his sides as he returned to the pew looking around with a big smile.

Little John asked what I was doing, and I told him that I was taking a break from work, as I sat comfortably among high weeds. He wanted to join me, but I reminded him that the last time he'd gone door-to-door asking for work his mother had whipped him. I was with him when his mother, a New Jersey Italian who could rise up in anger one moment and love the next, told me in a polite but matter-of-fact voice that I had to leave

[2]*host:* The Catholic Communion wafer. — EDS.

because she was going to beat her son. She gave me a homemade popsicle, ushered me to the door, and said that I could see Little John the next day. But it was sooner than that. I went around to his bedroom window to suck my popsicle and watch Little John dodge his mother's blows, a few hitting their mark but many whirring air.

It was midday when Little John and I converged in the alley, the sun blazing in the high nineties, and he suggested that we go to Roosevelt High School to swim. He needed five cents to make fifteen, the cost of admission, and I lent him a nickel. We ran home for my bike and when my sister found out that we were going swimming, she started to cry because she didn't have the fifteen cents but only an empty Coke bottle. I waved for her to come and three of us mounted the bike — Debra on the cross bar, Little John on the handle bars and holding the Coke bottle which we would cash for a nickel and make up the difference that would allow all of us to get in, and me pumping up the crooked streets, dodging cars and pot holes. We spent the day swimming under the afternoon sun, so that when we got home our mom asked us what was darker, the floor or us? She feigned a stern posture, her hands on her hips and her mouth puckered. We played along. Looking down, Debbie and I said in unison, "Us."

That evening at dinner we all sat down in our bathing suits to eat our beans, laughing and chewing loudly. Our mom was in a good mood, so I took a risk and asked her if sometime we could have turtle soup. A few days before I had watched a television program in which a Polynesian tribe killed a large turtle, gutted it, and then stewed it over an open fire. The turtle, basted in a sugary sauce, looked delicious as I ate an afternoon bowl of cereal, but my sister, who was watching the program with a glass of Kool-Aid between her knees, said, "Caca."

My mother looked at me in bewilderment. "Boy, are you a crazy Mexican. Where did you get the idea that people eat turtles?"

"On television," I said, explaining the program. Then I took it a step further. "Mom, do you think we could get dressed up for dinner one of these days? David King does." 15

"*Ay, Dios,*" my mother laughed. She started collecting the dinner plates, but my brother wouldn't let go of his. He was still drawing a picture in the bean sauce. Giggling, he said it was me, but I didn't want to listen because I wanted to answer from Mom. This was the summer when I spent the mornings in front of the television that showed the comfortable lives of white kids. There were no beatings, no rifts in the family. They wore bright clothes; toys tumbled from their closets. They hopped into bed with kisses and woke to glasses of fresh orange juice, and to a father sitting before his morning coffee while the mother buttered his toast. They hurried through the day making friends and gobs of money, returning home to a warmly lit living room, and then dinner. *Leave It to Beaver* was the program I replayed in my mind:

"May I have the mashed potatoes?" asks Beaver with a smile.

"Sure, Beav," replies Wally as he taps the corners of his mouth with a starched napkin.

The father looks on in his suit. The mother, decked out in earrings and a pearl necklace, cuts into her steak and blushes. Their conversation is politely clipped.

"Swell," says Beaver, his cheeks puffed with food.   20

Our own talk at dinner was loud with belly laughs and marked by our pointing forks at one another. The subjects were commonplace.

"Gary, let's go to the ditch tomorrow," my brother suggests. He explains that he has made a life preserver out of four empty detergent bottles strung together with twine and that he will make me one if I can find more bottles. "No way are we going to drown."

"Yeah, then we could have a dirt clod fight," I reply, so happy to be alive.

Whereas the Beaver's family enjoyed dessert in dishes at the table, our mom sent us outside, and more often than not I went into the alley to peek over the neighbor's fences and spy out fruit, apricot or peaches.

I had asked my mom and again she laughed that I was a crazy   25
chavalo[3] as she stood in front of the sink, her arms rising and falling with suds, facing glistening from the heat. She sent me outside where my brother and sister were sitting in the shade that the fence threw out like a blanket. They were talking about me when I plopped down next to them. They looked at one another and then Debbie, my eight-year-old sister, started in.

"What's this crap about getting dressed up?"

She had entered her *profanity* stage. A year later she would give up such words and slip into her Catholic uniform, and into squealing on my brother and me when we "cussed this" and "cussed that."

I tried to convince them that if we improved the way we looked we might get along better in life. White people would like us more. They might invite us to places, like their homes or front yards. They might not hate us so much.

My sister called me a "craphead," and got up to leave with a stalk of grass dangling from her mouth. "They'll never like us."

My brother's mood lightened as he talked about the ditch — the white   30
water, the broken pieces of glass, and the rusted car fenders that awaited our knees. There would be toads, and rocks to smash them.

David King, the only person we knew who resembled the middle class, called from over the fence. David was Catholic, of Armenian and French descent, and his closet was filled with toys. A bear-shaped cookie jar, like the ones on television, sat on the kitchen counter. His mother was remarkably kind while she put up with the racket we made on the street. Evenings, she often watered the front yard and it must have upset her to see us — my brother and I and others — jump from trees laughing, the unkillable kids

---

[3]*chavalo:* Kid. — EDS.

of the very poor, who got up unshaken, brushed off, and climbed into another one to try again.

David called again. Rick got up and slapped grass from his pants.
When I asked if I could come along he said no. David said no. They were
two years older so their affairs were different from mine. They greeted one
another with foul names and took off down the alley to look for trouble.

I went inside the house, turned on the television, and was about to sit
down with a glass of Kool-Aid when Mom shooed me outside.

"It's still light," she said. "Later you'll bug me to let you stay out
longer. So go on."

I downed my Kool-Aid and went outside to the front yard. No one was   35
around. The day had cooled and a breeze rustled the trees. Mr. Jackson,
the plumber, was watering his lawn and when he saw me he turned away
to wash off his front steps. There was more than an hour of light left, so I
took advantage of it and decided to look for work. I felt suddenly alive as
I skipped down the block in search of an overgrown flower bed and the
dime that would end the day right.

1985

The Reader's Presence

1. Why does the author want to become "wealthy"? What connection does he establish between his desire for wealth and his obsession with television? What details in the two opening paragraphs
   reveal — without Soto's saying it directly — how far from wealth
   he is?
2. In what particular ways does Soto's family life differ from the
   family lives he sees on television? For example, what contrasts
   can you find between his own family experiences and what he
   sees on television? What kind of audience is Soto himself? What
   aspect of television family life does Soto focus on in the essay?
   Why is that aspect important to him?
3. Does Soto's family as he describes it seem especially unhappy?
   Does he seem unhappy? What emotional response do you think
   Soto wants his readers to have toward his childhood experiences?
   Does he expect his readers to be saddened? sympathetic? amused?
   surprised?

19 _____

Brent Staples

Just Walk on By:
A Black Man Ponders His Power
to Alter Public Space

My first victim was a woman — white, well dressed, probably in her early twenties. I came upon her late one evening on a deserted street in Hyde Park, a relatively affluent neighborhood in an otherwise mean, impoverished section of Chicago. As I swung onto the avenue behind her, there seemed to be a discreet, uninflammatory distance between us. Not so. She cast back a worried glance. To her, the youngish black man — a broad six feet two inches with a beard and billowing hair, both hands shoved into the pockets of a bulky military jacket — seemed menacingly close. After a few more quick glimpses, she picked up her pace and was soon running in earnest. Within seconds she disappeared into a cross street.

That was more than a decade ago. I was twenty-two years old, a graduate student newly arrived at the University of Chicago. It was in the echo of that terrified woman's footfalls that I first began to know the unwieldy inheritance I'd come into — the ability to alter public space in ugly ways. It was clear that she thought herself the quarry of a mugger, a rapist, or worse. Suffering a bout of insomnia, however, I was stalking sleep, not defenseless wayfarers. As a softy who is scarcely able to take a knife to a raw chicken — let alone hold it to a person's throat — I was surprised, embarrassed, and dismayed all at once. Her flight made me feel like an accomplice in tyranny. It also made it clear that I was indistinguishable from the muggers who occasionally seeped into the area from the surrounding ghetto. That first encounter, and those that followed, signified that a vast, unnerving gulf lay between nighttime pedestrians — particularly women — and me. And I soon gathered that being perceived as dan-

For biographical information on Brent Staples, see p. 664.

gerous is a hazard in itself. I only needed to turn a corner into a dicey situation, or crowd some frightened, armed person in a foyer somewhere, or make an errant move after being pulled over by a policeman. Where fear and weapons meet — and they often do in urban America — there is always the possibility of death.

In that first year, my first away from my hometown, I was to become thoroughly familiar with the language of fear. At dark, shadowy intersections in Chicago, I could cross in front of a car stopped at a traffic light and elicit the *thunk, thunk, thunk, thunk* of the driver — black, white, male, or female — hammering down the door locks. On less traveled streets after dark, I grew accustomed to but never comfortable with people who crossed to the other side of the street rather than pass me. Then there were the standard unpleasantries with police, doormen, bouncers, cabdrivers, and others whose business is to screen out troublesome individuals *before* there is any nastiness.

I moved to New York nearly two years ago and I have remained an avid night walker. In central Manhattan, the near-constant crowd cover minimizes tense one-on-one street encounters. Elsewhere — visiting friends in SoHo,[1] where sidewalks are narrow and tightly spaced buildings shut out the sky — things can get very taut indeed.

Black men have a firm place in New York mugging literature. Norman 5 Podhoretz[2] in his famed (or infamous) 1963 essay, "My Negro Problem — And Ours," recalls growing up in terror of black males; they "were tougher than we were, more ruthless," he writes — and as an adult on the Upper West Side of Manhattan, he continues, he cannot constrain his nervousness when he meets black men on certain streets. Similarly, a decade later, the essayist and novelist Edward Hoagland extols a New York where once "Negro bitterness bore down mainly on other Negroes." Where some see mere panhandlers, Hoagland sees "a mugger who is clearly screwing up his nerve to do more than just *ask* for money." But Hoagland has "the New Yorker's quick-hunch posture for broken-field maneuvering," and the bad guy swerves away.

I often witness that "hunch posture," from women after dark on the warrenlike streets of Brooklyn where I live. They seem to set their faces on neutral and, with their purse straps strung across their chests bandolier style, they forge ahead as though bracing themselves against being tackled. I understand, of course, that the danger they perceive is not a hallucination. Women are particularly vulnerable to street violence, and young black males are drastically overrepresented among the perpetrators of that violence. Yet these truths are no solace against the kind of alienation that

---

[1] *Soho:* A district of lower Manhattan known for its art galleries. — EDS.
[2] *Norman Podhoretz:* A well-known literary critic and editor of *Commentary* magazine. — EDS.

comes of being ever the suspect, against being set apart, a fearsome entity with whom pedestrians avoid making eye contact.

It is not altogether clear to me how I reached the ripe old age of twenty-two without being conscious of the lethality nighttime pedestrians attributed to me. Perhaps it was because in Chester, Pennsylvania, the small, angry industrial town where I came of age in the 1960s, I was scarcely noticeable against a backdrop of gang warfare, street knifings, and murders. I grew up one of the good boys, had perhaps a half-dozen fist-fights. In retrospect, my shyness of combat has clear sources.

Many things go into the making of a young thug. One of those things is the consummation of the male romance with the power to intimidate. An infant discovers that random flailings send the baby bottle flying out of the crib and crashing to the floor. Delighted, the joyful babe repeats those mo-tions again and again, seeking to duplicate the feat. Just so, I recall the points at which some of my boyhood friends were finally seduced by the perception of themselves as tough guys. When a mark cowered and surren-dered his money without resistance, myth and reality merged — and paid off. It is, after all, only manly to embrace the power to frighten and intim-idate. We, as men, are not supposed to give an inch of our lane on the highway; we are to seize the fighter's edge in work and in play and even in love; we are to be valiant in the face of hostile forces.

Unfortunately, poor and powerless young men seem to take all this nonsense literally. As a boy, I saw countless tough guys locked away; I have since buried several, too. They were babies, really — a teenage cousin, a brother of twenty-two, a childhood friend in his midtwenties — all gone down in episodes of bravado played out in the streets. I came to doubt the virtues of intimidation early on. I chose, perhaps even unconsciously, to remain a shadow — timid, but a survivor.

The fearsomeness mistakenly attributed to me in public places often 10 has a perilous flavor. The most frightening of these confusions occurred in the late 1970s and early 1980s when I worked as a journalist in Chicago. One day, rushing into the office of a magazine I was writing for with a deadline story in hand, I was mistaken for a burglar. The office manager called security and, with an ad hoc posse, pursued me through the labyrin-thine halls, nearly to my editor's door. I had no way of proving who I was. I could only move briskly toward the company of someone who knew me.

Another time I was on assignment for a local paper and killing time before an interview. I entered a jewelry store on the city's affluent Near North Side. The proprietor excused herself and returned with an enormous red Doberman pinscher straining at the end of a leash. She stood, the dog extended toward me, silent to my questions, her eyes bulging nearly out of her head. I took a cursory look around, nodded, and bade her good night. Relatively speaking, however, I never fared as badly as another black male journalist. He went to nearby Waukegan, Illinois, a couple of summers ago to work on a story about a murderer who was born there. Mistaking the reporter for the killer, police hauled him from his car at gunpoint and but for his press credentials would probably have tried to book him. Such episodes are not uncommon. Black men trade tales like this all the time.

In "My Negro Problem — And Ours," Podhoretz writes that the hatred he feels for blacks makes itself known to him through a variety of avenues — one being his discomfort with that "special brand of paranoid touchiness" to which he says blacks are prone. No doubt he is speaking here of black men. In time, I learned to smother the rage I felt at so often being taken for a criminal. Not to do so would surely have led to madness — via that special "paranoid touchiness" that so annoyed Podhoretz at the time he wrote the essay.

I began to take precautions to make myself less threatening. I move about with care, particularly late in the evening. I give a wide berth to nervous people on subway platforms during the wee hours, particularly when I have exchanged business clothes for jeans. If I happen to be entering a building behind some people who appear skittish, I may walk by, letting them clear the lobby before I return, so as not to seem to be following them. I have been calm and extremely congenial on those rare occasions when I've been pulled over by the police.

And on late-evening constitutionals along streets less traveled by, I employ what has proved to be an excellent tension-reducing measure: I whistle melodies from Beethoven and Vivaldi and the more popular classical composers. Even steely New Yorkers hunching toward nighttime destinations seem to relax, and occasionally they even join in the tune. Virtually everybody seems to sense that a mugger wouldn't be warbling bright, sunny selections from Vivaldi's *Four Seasons*. It is my equivalent of the cowbell that hikers wear when they know they are in bear country.

1986

The Reader's Presence

1. Why does Staples use the word *victim* in his opening sentence? In what sense is the white woman a "victim"? How is he using the term? As readers, how might we interpret the opening sentence upon first reading? How does the meaning of the term change in rereading?

2. Does Staples blame the woman for being afraid of him? How does he deal with her anxiety? How does Staples behave on the street? How has he "altered" his own public behavior? In what ways is his behavior on the street similar to his "behavior" as a writer?

3. In rereading the essay, pay close attention to the way Staples handles point of view. When does he shift viewpoints or perspectives? What is his purpose in doing so? What are some of the connections Staples makes in this essay between the point of view one chooses and one's identity?

20

Shelby Steele

On Being Black and Middle Class

Not long ago a friend of mine, black like myself, said to me that the term "black middle class" was actually a contradiction in terms. Race, he insisted, blurred class distinctions among blacks. If you were black, you were just black and that was that. When I argued, he let his eyes roll at my naiveté. Then he went on. For us, as black professionals, it was an exercise in self-flattery, a pathetic pretention, to give meaning to such a distinction. Worse, the very idea of class threatened the unity that was vital to the black community as a whole. After all, since when had white America taken note of anything but color when it came to blacks? He then reminded me of an old Malcolm X line that had been popular in the sixties. Question: What is a black man with a Ph.D.? Answer: A nigger.

For many years I had been on my friend's side of this argument. Much of my conscious thinking on the old conundrum of race and class was shaped during my high school and college years in the race-charged sixties, when the fact of my race took on an almost religious significance. Progressively, from the mid-sixties on, more and more aspects of my life found their explanation, their justification, and their motivation in race. My youthful concerns about career, romance, money, values, and even styles of dress became a subject to consultation with various oracular sources of racial wisdom. And these ranged from a figure as ennobling as Martin Luther King, Jr., to the underworld elegance of dress I found in jazz clubs on the South Side of Chicago. Everywhere there were signals, and in those days I considered myself so blessed with clarity and direction that I pitied my white classmates who found more embarrassment than guidance in the face of *their* race. In 1968, inflated by my new power, I took a mischievous delight in calling them culturally disadvantaged.

But now, hearing my friend's comment was like hearing a priest from a church I'd grown disenchanted with. I understood him, but my faith was

For biographical information on Shelby Steele, see p. 664.

weak. What had sustained me in the sixties sounded monotonous and off the mark in the eighties. For me, race had lost much of its juju, its singular capacity to conjure meaning. And today, when I honestly look at my life and the lives of many other middle-class blacks I know, I can see that race never fully explained our situation in American society. Black though I may be, it is impossible for me to sit in my single-family house with two cars in the driveway and a swing set in the back yard and *not* see the role class has played in my life. And how can my friend, similarly raised and similarly situated, not see it?

Yet despite my certainty I felt a sharp tug of guilt as I tried to explain myself over my friend's skepticism. He is a man of many comedic facial expressions and, as I spoke, his brow lifted in extreme moral alarm as if I were uttering the unspeakable. His clear implication was that I was being elitist and possibly (dare he suggest?) antiblack — crimes for which there might well be no redemption. He pretended to fear for me. I chuckled along with him, but inwardly I did wonder at myself. Though I never doubted the validity of what I was saying, I felt guilty saying it. Why?

After he left (to retrieve his daughter from a dance lesson) I realized   5 that the trap I felt myself in had a tiresome familiarity and, in a sort of slow-motion epiphany, I began to see its outline. It was like the suddenly sharp vision one has at the end of a burdensome marriage when all the long-repressed incompatibilities come undeniably to light.

What became clear to me is that people like myself, my friend, and middle-class blacks generally are caught in a very specific double bind that keeps two equally powerful elements of our identity at odds with each other. The middle-class values by which we were raised — the work ethic, the importance of education, the value of property ownership, of respect-ability, of "getting ahead," of stable family life, of initiative, of self-reliance, etc. — are, in themselves, raceless and even assimilationist. They urge us toward participation in the American mainstream, toward integra-tion, toward a strong identification with the society — and toward the en-tire constellation of qualities that are implied in the word "individualism." These values are almost rules for how to prosper in a democratic, free-enterprise society that admires and rewards individual effort. They tell us to work hard for ourselves and our families and to seek our opportunities whenever they appear, inside or outside the confines of whatever ethnic group we may belong to.

But the particular pattern of racial identification that emerged in the sixties and that still prevails today urges middle-class blacks (and all blacks) in the opposite direction. This pattern asks us to see ourselves as an embattled minority, and it urges an adversarial stance toward the main-stream, an emphasis on ethnic consciousness over individualism. It is or-ganized around an implied separatism.

The opposing thrust of these two parts of our identity results in the double bind of middle-class blacks. There is no forward movement on ei-ther plane that does not constitute backward movement on the other. This was the familiar trap I felt myself in while talking with my friend. As I spoke about class, his eyes reminded me that I was betraying race. Clearly, the two indispensable parts of my identity were a threat to each other.

Of course when you think about it, class and race are both similar in some ways and also naturally opposed. They are two forms of collective identity with boundaries that intersect. But whether they clash or peacefully coexist has much to do with how they are defined. Being both black and middle class becomes a double bind when class and race are defined in sharply antagonistic terms, so that one must be repressed to appease the other.

But what is the "substance" of these two identities, and how does each   10
establish itself in an individual's overall identity? It seems to me that when we identify with any collective we are basically identifying with images that tell us what it means to be a member of that collective. Identity is not the same thing as the fact of membership in a collective; it is, rather, a form of self-definition, facilitated by images of what we wish our membership in the collective to mean. In this sense, the images we identify with may reflect the aspirations of the collective more than they reflect reality, and their content can vary with shifts in those aspirations.

But the process of identification is usually dialectical. It is just as necessary to say what we are *not* as it is to say what we are — so that finally identification comes about by embracing a polarity of positive and negative images. To identify as middle class, for example, I must have both positive and negative images of what being middle class entails; then I will know what I should and should not be doing in order to be middle class. The same goes for racial identity.

In the racially turbulent sixties the polarity of images that came to define racial identification was very antagonistic to the polarity that defined middle-class identification. One might say that the positive images of one lined up with the negative images of the other, so that to identify with both required either a contortionist's flexibility or a dangerous splitting of the self. The double bind of the black middle class was in place.

The black middle class has always defined its class identity by means of positive images gleaned from middle- and upper-class white society, and by means of negative images of lower-class blacks. This habit goes back to the institution of slavery itself, when "house" slaves both mimicked the whites they served and held themselves above the "field" slaves. But in the sixties the old bourgeois impulse to dissociate from the lower classes (the "we-they" distinction) backfired when racial identity suddenly called for the celebration of this same black lower class. One of the qualities of a double bind is that one feels it more than sees it, and I distinctly remember the tension and strange sense of dishonesty I felt in those days as I moved back and forth like a bigamist between the demands of class and race.

Though my father was born poor, he achieved middle-class standing through much hard work and sacrifice (one of his favorite words) and by identifying fully with solid middle-class values — mainly hard work, family life, property ownership, and education for his children (all four of whom have advanced degrees). In his mind these were not so much values as laws of nature. People who embodied them made up the positive images in his class polarity. The negative images came largely from the blacks he had left behind because they were "going nowhere."

No one in my family remembers how it happened, but as time went on, 15 the negative images congealed into an imaginary character named Sam, who, from the extensive service we put him to, quickly grew to mythic proportions. In our family lore he was sometimes a trickster, sometimes a boob, but always possessed of a catalogue of sly faults that gave up graphic images of everything we should not be. On sacrifice: "Sam never thinks about tomorrow. He wants it now or he doesn't care about it." On work: "Sam doesn't favor it too much." On children: "Sam likes to have them but not to raise them." On money: "Sam drinks it up and pisses it out." On fidelity: "Sam has to have two or three women." On clothes: "Sam features loud clothes. He likes to see and be seen." And so on. Sam's persona amounted to a negative instruction manual in class identity.

I don't think that any of us believed Sam's faults were accurate representations of lower-class black life. He was an instrument of self-definition, not of sociological accuracy. It never occurred to us that he looked very much like the white racist stereotype of blacks, or that he might have been a manifestation of our own racial self-hatred. He simply gave us a counterpoint against which to express our aspirations. If self-hatred was a factor, it was not, for us, a matter of hating lower-class blacks but of hating what we did not want to be.

Still, hate or love aside, it is fundamentally true that my middle-class identity involved a dissociation from images of lower-class black life and a corresponding identification with values and patterns of responsibility that are common to the middle class everywhere. These values sent me a clear message: Be both an individual and a responsible citizen; understand that the quality of your life will approximately reflect the quality of effort you put into it; know that individual responsibility is the basis of freedom and that the limitations imposed by fate (whether fair or unfair) are no excuse for passivity.

Whether I live up to these values or not, I know that my acceptance of them is the result of lifelong conditioning. I know also that I share this conditioning with middle-class people of all races and that I can no more easily be free of it than I can be free of my race. Whether all this got started because the black middle class modeled itself on the white middle class is no longer relevant. For the middle-class black, conditioned by these values from birth, the sense of meaning they provide is as immutable as the color of his skin.

I started the sixties in high school feeling that my class-conditioning was the surest way to overcome racial barriers. My racial identity was pretty much taken for granted. After all, it was obvious to the world that I was black. Yet I ended the sixties in graduate school a little embarrassed by my class background and with an almost desperate need to be "black." The tables had turned. I knew very clearly (though I struggled to repress it) that my aspirations and my sense of how to operate in the world came from my class background, yet "being black" required certain attitudes and stances that made me feel secretly a little duplicitous. The inner compatibility of class and race I had known in 1960 was gone.

For blacks, the decade between 1960 and 1969 saw racial identifica- 20 tion undergo the same sort of transformation that national identity undergoes in times of war. It became more self-conscious, more narrowly focused, more prescribed, less tolerant of opposition. It spawned an implicit party line, which tended to disallow competing forms of identity. Race-as-identity was lifted from the relative slumber it knew in the fifties and pressed into service in a social and political war against oppression. It was redefined along sharp adversarial lines and directed toward the goal of mobilizing the great mass of black Americans in this warlike effort. It was imbued with a strong moral authority, useful for denouncing those who opposed it and for celebrating those who honored it as a positive achievement rather than as a mere birthright.

The form of racial identification that quickly evolved to meet this challenge presented blacks as a racial monolith, a singular people with a common experience of oppression. Differences within the race, no matter how ineradicable, had to be minimized. Class distinctions were one of the first such differences to be sacrificed, since they not only threatened racial unity but also seemed to stand in contradiction to the principle of equality which was the announced goal of the movement for racial progress. The discomfort I felt in 1969, the vague but relentless sense of duplicity, was the result of a historical necessity that put my race and class at odds, that was asking me to cast aside the distinction of my class and identify with a monolithic view of my race.

If the form of this racial identity was the monolith, its substance was victimization. The civil rights movement and the more radical splinter groups of the late sixties were all dedicated to ending racial victimization, and the form of black identity that emerged to facilitate this goal made blackness and victimization virtually synonymous. Since it was our victimization more than any other variable that identified and unified us, moreover, it followed logically that the purest black was the poor black. It was images of him that clustered around the positive pole of the race polarity; all other blacks were, in effect, required to identify with him in order to confirm their own blackness.

Certainly there were more dimensions to the black experience than victimization, but no other had the same capacity to fire the indignation needed for war. So, again out of historical necessity, victimization became the overriding focus of racial identity. But this only deepened the double bind for middle-class blacks like me. When it came to class we were accustomed to defining ourselves against lower-class blacks and identifying with at least the values of middle-class whites; when it came to race we were now being asked to identify with images of lower-class blacks and to see whites, middle class or otherwise, as victimizers. Negative lining up with positive, we were called upon to reject what we had previously embraced and to embrace what we had previously rejected. To put it still more personally, the Sam figure I had been raised to define myself against had now become the "real" black I was expected to identify with.

The fact that the poor black's new status was only passively earned by the condition of his victimization, not by assertive, positive action made little difference. Status was status apart from the means by which it was achieved, and along with it came a certain power — the power to define the terms of access to that status, to say who was black and who was not. If a lower-class black said you were not really "black" — a sellout, an Uncle Tom — the judgment was all the more devastating because it carried the authority of his status. And this judgment soon enough came to be accepted by many whites as well.

In graduate school I was once told by a white professor, "Well, but . . .   25 you're not really black. I mean, you're not disadvantaged." In his mind my lack of victim status disqualified me from the race itself. More recently I was complimented by a black student for speaking reasonably correct English, "proper" English as he put it. "But I don't know if I really want to talk like that," he went on. "Why not?" I asked. "Because then I wouldn't be black no more," he replied without a pause.

To overcome his marginal status, the middle-class black had to identify with a degree of victimization that was beyond his actual experience. In college (and well beyond) we used to play a game called "nap matching." It was a game of one-upmanship, in which we sat around outdoing each other with stories of racial victimization, symbolically measured by the naps of our hair. Most of us were middle class and so had few personal stories to relate, but if we could not match naps with our own biographies, we would move on to those legendary tales of victimization that came to us from the public domain.

The single story that sat atop the pinnacle of racial victimization for us was that of Emmett Till, the Northern black teenager who, on a visit to the South in 1955, was killed and grotesquely mutilated for supposedly looking at or whistling at (we were never sure which, though we argued the point endlessly) a white woman. Oh, how we probed his story, finding in his youth and Northern upbringing the quintessential embodiment of black innocence, brought down by a white evil so portentous and apocalyptic, so gnarled and hideous, that it left us with a feeling not far from awe. By telling his story and others like it, we came to *feel* the immutability of our victimization, its utter indigenousness, as a thing on this earth like dirt or sand or water.

Of course, these sessions were a ritual of group identification, a means by which we, as middle-class blacks, could be at one with our race. But why were we, who had only a moderate experience of victimization (and that offset by opportunities our parents never had), so intent on assimilating or appropriating an identity that in so many ways contradicted our own? Because, I think, the sense of innocence that is always entailed in feeling victimized filled us with a corresponding feeling of entitlement, or even license, that helped us endure our vulnerability on a largely white college campus.

In my junior year in college I rode to a debate tournament with three white students and our faculty coach, an elderly English professor. The experience of being the lone black in a group of whites was so familiar to me that I thought nothing of it as our trip began. But when halfway through the trip the professor casually turned to me and, in an isn't-the-world-funny sort of tone, said that he had just refused to rent an apartment in a house he owned to a "very nice" black couple because their color would "offend" the white couple who lived downstairs. His eyebrows lifted helplessly over his hawkish nose, suggesting that he too, like me, was a victim of America's racial farce. His look assumed a kind of comradeship: he and I were above this grimy business of race, though for expediency we had occasionally to concede the world its madness.

My vulnerability in this situation came not so much from the   30
professor's blindness to his own racism as from his assumption that I would participate in it, that I would conspire with him against my own race so that he might remain comfortably blind. Why did he think I would be amenable to this? I can only guess that he assumed my middle-class identity was so complete and all-encompassing that I would see his action as nothing more than a trifling concession to the folkways of our land, that I would in fact applaud his decision not to disturb propriety. Blind to both his own racism and to me — one blindness serving the other — he could not recognize that he was asking me to betray my race in the name of my class.

His blindness made me feel vulnerable because it threatened to expose my own repressed ambivalence. His comment pressured me to choose between my class identification, which had contributed to my being a college student and a member of the debating team, and my desperate desire to be "black." I could have one but not both; I was double-bound.

Because double binds are repressed there is always an element of terror in them: the terror of bringing to the conscious mind the buried duplicity, self-deception, and pretense involved in serving two masters. This terror is the stuff of vulnerability, and since vulnerability is one of the least tolerable of all human feelings, we usually transform it into an emotion that seems to restore the control of which it has robbed us; most often, that emotion is anger. And so, before the professor had even finished his little story, I had become a furnace of rage. The year was 1967, and I had been primed by endless hours of nap-matching to feel, at least consciously, completely at one with the victim-focused black identity. This identity gave me the license, and the impunity, to unleash upon this professor one of those volcanic eruptions of racial indignation familiar to us from the novels of Richard Wright. Like Cross Damon in *Outsider,* who kills in perfectly righteous anger, I tried to annihilate the man. I punished him not according to the measure of his crime but according to the measure of my vulnerability, a measure set by the cumulative tension of years of repressed terror. Soon I saw that terror in *his* face, as he stared hollow-eyed at the road ahead. My white friends in the back seat, knowing no conflict between their own class and race, were astonished that someone they had taken to be so much like themselves could harbor a rage that for all the world looked murderous.

Though my rage was triggered by the professor's comment, it was deepened and sustained by a complex of need, conflict, and repression in myself of which I had been wholly unaware. Out of my racial vulnerability I had developed the strong need of an identity with which to defend myself. The only such identity available was that of me as victim, him as victimizer. Once in the grip of this paradigm, I began to do far more damage to myself than he had done.

Seeing myself as a victim meant that I clung all the harder to my racial identity, which, in turn, meant that I suppressed my class identity. This cut me off from all the resources my class values might have offered me. In those values, for instance, I might have found the means to a more dispassionate response, the response less of a victim attacked by a victimizer than of an individual offended by a foolish old man. As an individual I might have reported this professor to the college dean. Or I might have calmly tried to reveal his blindness to him, and possibly won a convert. (The flagrancy of his remark suggested a hidden guilt and even self-recognition on which I might have capitalized. Doesn't confession usually signal a willingness to face oneself?) Or I might have simply chuckled and then let my silence serve as an answer to his provocation. Would not my composure, in any form it might take, deflect into his own heart the arrow he'd shot at me?

Instead, my anger, itself the hair-trigger expression of a long-repressed   35 double bind, not only cut me off from the best of my own resources, it also distorted the nature of my true racial problem. The righteousness of this anger and the easy catharsis it brought buoyed the delusion of my victimization and left me as blind as the professor himself.

As a middle-class black I have often felt myself *contriving* to be "black." And I have noticed this same contrivance in others — a certain stretching away from the natural flow of one's life to align oneself with a victim-focused black identity. Our particular needs are out of sync with the form of identity available to meet those needs. Middle-class blacks need to identify racially; it is better to think of ourselves as black and victimized than not black at all; so we contrive (more unconsciously than consciously) to fit ourselves into an identity that denies our class and fails to address the true source of our vulnerability

For me this once meant spending inordinate amounts of time at black faculty meetings, though these meetings had little to do with my real racial anxieties or my professional life. I was new to the university, one of two blacks in an English department of over seventy, and I felt a little isolated and vulnerable, though I did not admit it to myself. But at these meetings we discussed the problems of black faculty and students within a framework of victimization. The real vulnerability we felt was covered over by all the adversarial drama the victim/victimized polarity inspired, and hence went unseen and unassuaged. And this, I think, explains our rather chronic ineffectiveness as a group. Since victimization was not our primary problem — the university had long ago opened its doors to us — we had to contrive to make it so, and there is not much energy in contrivance. What I got at these meetings was ultimately an object lesson in how fruitless struggle can be when it is not grounded in actual need.

At our black faculty meetings, the old equation of blackness with victimization was ever present — to be black was to be a victim; therefore, not to be a victim was not to be black. As we contrived to meet the terms of this formula there was an inevitable distortion of both ourselves and the larger university. Through the prism of victimization the university seemed more impenetrable than it actually was, and we more limited in our powers. We fell prey to the victim's myopia, making the university an institution from which we could seek redress but which we could never fully join. And this mind-set often led us to look more for compensations for our supposed victimization than for opportunities we could pursue as individuals.

The discomfort and vulnerability felt by middle-class blacks in the sixties, it could be argued, was a worthwhile price to pay considering the progress achieved during that time of racial confrontation. But what may have been tolerable then is intolerable now. Though changes in American society have made it an anachronism, the monolithic form of racial identification that came out of the sixties is still very much with us. It may be more loosely held, and its power to punish heretics has probably diminished, but it continues to catch middle-class blacks in a double bind, thus impeding not only their own advancement but even, I would contend, that of blacks as a group.

The victim-focused black identity encourages the individual to feel that   40
his advancement depends almost entirely on that of the group. Thus he loses sight not only of his own possibilities but of the inextricable connection between individual effort and individual advancement. This is a profound encumbrance today, when there is more opportunity for blacks than ever before, for it reimposes limitations that can have the same oppressive effect as those the society has only recently begun to remove.

It was the emphasis on mass action in the sixties that made the victim-focused black identity a necessity. But in the eighties and beyond, when racial advancement will come only through a multitude of individual advancements, this form of identity inadvertently adds itself to the forces that hold us back. Hard work, education, individual initiative, stable family life, property ownership — these have always been the means by which ethnic groups have moved ahead in America. Regardless of past or present victimization, these "laws" of advancement apply absolutely to black Americans also. There is no getting around this. What we need is a form of racial identity that energizes the individual by putting him in touch with both his possibilities and his responsibilities.

It has always annoyed me to hear from the mouths of certain arbiters of blackness that middle-class blacks should "reach back" and pull up those blacks less fortunate than they — as though middle-class status were an unearned and essentially passive condition in which one needed a large measure of noblesse oblige to occupy one's time. My own image is of reaching back from a moving train to lift on board those who have no tickets. A noble enough sentiment — but might it not be wiser to show them the entire structure of principles, efforts, and sacrifice that puts one in a position to buy a ticket any time one likes? This, I think, is something members of the black middle class can realistically offer to other blacks. Their example is not only a testament to possibility but also a lesson in method. But they cannot lead by example until they are released from a black identity that regards that example as suspect, that sees them as "marginally" black, indeed that holds *them* back by catching them in a double bind.

To move beyond the victim-focused black identity we must learn to make a difficult but crucial distinction: between actual victimization, which we must resist with every resource, and identification with the victim's status. Until we do this we will continue to wrestle more with ourselves than with the new opportunities which so many paid so dearly to win.

1988

The Reader's Presence

1. Steele introduces his topic by means of a reported conversation he had with a friend. What effect does this have on the reader? If you rewrote his opening paragraph and eliminated the conversational context, how would you then introduce the main topic? Try it and see how it works.

2. Why does Steele's friend maintain that class and race are antagonistic terms? Do you agree? Would his argument apply to all races and historical periods, or is it dependent only on present history? What personal experiences would you offer either to confirm or contradict Steele's friend's opening remark?

3. Steele's feeling of being in a "double bind" is seen exclusively in the context of being middle class. How does Steel define *middle*

class? Would blacks from other economic groups feel differently? For example, does Steele imply that blue-collar, working-class black people feel greater racial solidarity? On the other hand, would very wealthy blacks feel a greater conflict than Steele's? Can you infer answers to these questions from Steele's essay?

21

Amy Tan

Mother Tongue

I am not a scholar of English or literature. I cannot give you much more than personal opinions on the English language and its variations in this country or others.

I am a writer. And by that definition, I am someone who has always loved language. I am fascinated by language in daily life. I spend a great deal of my time thinking about the power of language — the way it can evoke an emotion, a visual image, a complex idea, or a simple truth. Language is the tool of my trade. And I use them all — all the Englishes I grew up with.

Recently, I was made keenly aware of the different Englishes I do use. I was giving a talk to a large group of people, the same talk I had already given to half a dozen other groups. The nature of the talk was about my writing, my life, and my book, *The Joy Luck Club.* The talk was going along well enough, until I remembered one major difference that made the whole talk sound wrong. My mother was in the room. And it was perhaps the first time she had heard me give a lengthy speech, using the kind of English I have never used with her. I was saying things like "The intersection of memory upon imagination" and "There is an aspect of my fiction that relates to thus-and-thus" — a speech filled with carefully wrought grammatical phrases, burdened, it suddenly seemed to me, with nominalized forms, past perfect tenses, conditional phrases, all the forms of standard English that I had learned in school and through books, the forms of English I did not use at home with my mother.

Just last week, I was walking down the street with my mother, and I again found myself conscious of the English I was using, the English I do use with her. We were talking about the price of new and used furniture and I heard myself saying this: "Not waste money that way." My husband

For biographical information on Amy Tan, see p. 665.

was with us as well, and he didn't notice any switch in my English. And then I realized why. It's because over the twenty years we've been together I've often used that same kind of English with him, and sometimes he even uses it with me. It has become our language of intimacy, a different sort of English that relates to family talk, the language I grew up with.

So you'll have some idea of what this family talk I heard sounds like, 5 I'll quote what my mother said during a recent conversation which I video-taped and then transcribed. During this conversation, my mother was talking about a political gangster in Shanghai who had the same last name as her family's, Du, and how the gangster in his early years wanted to be adopted by her family, which was rich by comparison. Later, the gangster became more powerful, far richer than my mother's family, and one day showed up at my mother's wedding to pay his respects. Here's what she said in part:

"Du Yusong having business like fruit stand. Like off the street kind. He is Du like Du Zong — but not Tsung-ming Island people. The local people call putong, the river east side, he belong to that side local people. That man want to ask Du Zong father take him in like become own family. Du Zong father wasn't look down on him, but didn't take seriously, until that man big like become a mafia. Now important person, very hard to inviting him. Chinese way, came only to show respect, don't stay for dinner. Respect for making big celebration, he shows up. Mean gives lots of respect. Chinese custom. Chinese social life that way. If too important won't have to stay too long. He come to my wedding. I didn't see, I heard it. I gone to boy's side, they have YMCA dinner. Chinese age I was nineteen."

You should know that my mother's expressive command of English belies how much she actually understands. She reads the *Forbes* report, listens to *Wall Street Week*, converses daily with her stockbroker, reads all of Shirley MacLaine's books with ease — all kinds of things I can't begin to understand. Yet some of my friends tell me they understand 50 percent of what my mother says. Some say they understand 80 to 90 percent. Some say they understand none of it, as if she were speaking pure Chinese. But to me, my mother's English is perfectly clear, perfectly natural. It's my mother tongue. Her language, as I hear it, is vivid, direct, full of observation and imagery. That was the language that helped shape the way I saw things, expressed things, made sense of the world.

Lately, I've been giving more thought to the kind of English my mother speaks. Like others, I have described it to people as "broken" or "fractured" English. But I wince when I say that. It has always bothered me that I can think of no other way to describe it other than "broken," as if it were damaged and needed to be fixed, as if it lacked a certain wholeness and soundness. I've heard other terms used, "limited English," for example. But they seem just as bad, as if everything is limited, including people's perceptions of the limited English speaker.

I know this for a fact, because when I was growing up, my mother's "limited" English limited *my* perception of her. I was ashamed of her English. I believed that her English reflected the quality of what she had to say. That is, because she expressed them imperfectly her thoughts were imperfect. And I had plenty of empirical evidence to support me: the fact that people in department stores, at banks, and at restaurants did not take her seriously, did not give her good service, pretended not to understand her, or even acted as if they did not hear her.

My mother has long realized the limitations of her English as well.   10
When I was fifteen, she used to have me call people on the phone to pretend I was she. In this guise, I was forced to ask for information or even to complain and yell at people who had been rude to her. One time it was a call to her stockbroker in New York. She had cashed out her small portfolio and it just so happened we were going to go to New York the next week, our very first trip outside California. I had to get on the phone and say in an adolescent voice that was not very convincing, "This is Mrs. Tan."

And my mother was standing in the back whispering loudly, "Why he don't send me check, already two weeks late. So mad he lie to me, losing me money."

And then I said in perfect English, "Yes, I'm getting rather concerned. You had agreed to send the check two weeks ago, but it hasn't arrived."

Then she began to talk more loudly. "What he want, I come to New York tell him front of his boss, you cheating me?" And I was trying to calm her down, make her be quiet, while telling the stockbroker, "I can't tolerate any more excuses. If I don't receive the check immediately, I am going to have to speak to your manager when I'm in New York next week." And sure enough, the following week there we were in front of this astonished stockbroker, and I was sitting there red-faced and quiet, and my mother, the real Mrs. Tan, was shouting at his boss in her impeccable broken English.

We used a similar routine just five days ago, for a situation that was far less humorous. My mother had gone to the hospital for an appointment, to find out about a benign brain tumor a CAT scan had revealed a month ago. She said she had spoken very good English, her best English, no mistakes. Still, she said, the hospital did not apologize when they said they had lost the CAT scan and she had come for nothing. She said they did not seem to have any sympathy when she told them she was anxious to know the exact diagnosis, since her husband and son had both died of brain tumors. She said they would not give her any more information until the next time and she would have to make another appointment for that. So she said she would not leave until the doctor called her daughter. She wouldn't budge. And when the doctor finally called her daughter, me, who spoke in perfect English — lo and behold — we had assurances the CAT scan would be found, promises that a conference call on Monday would be held, and apologies for any suffering my mother had gone through for a most regrettable mistake.

I think my mother's English almost had an effect on limiting my possi-   15
bilities in life as well. Sociologists and linguists probably will tell you that

a person's developing language skills are more influenced by peers. But I do think that the language spoken in the family, especially in immigrant families which are more insular, plays a large role in shaping the language of the child. And I believe that it affected my results on achievement tests, IQ tests, and the SAT. While my English skills were never judged as poor, compared to math, English could not be considered my strong suit. In grade school I did moderately well, getting perhaps B's, sometimes B-pluses, in English and scoring perhaps in the sixtieth or seventieth percentile on achievement tests. But those scores were not good enough to override the opinion that my true abilities lay in math and science, because in those areas I achieved A's and scored in the ninetieth percentile or higher.

This was understandable. Math is precise; there is only one correct answer. Whereas, for me at least, the answers on English tests were always a judgment call, a matter of opinion and personal experience. Those tests were constructed around items like fill-in-the-blank sentence completion, such as "Even though Tom was _____, Mary thought he was _____." And the correct answer always seemed to be the most bland combinations of thoughts, for example, "Even though Tom was shy, Mary thought he was charming," with the grammatical structure "even though" limiting the correct answer to some sort of semantic opposites, so you wouldn't get answers like, "Even though Tom was foolish, Mary thought he was ridiculous." Well, according to my mother, there were very few limitations as to what Tom could have been and what Mary might have thought of him. So I never did well on tests like that.

The same was true with word analogies, pairs of words in which you were supposed to find some sort of logical, semantic relationship — for example, "*Sunset* is to *nightfall* as _____ is to _____." And here you would be presented with a list of four possible pairs, one of which showed the same kind of relationship: *red* is to *stoplight*, *bus* is to *arrival*, *chills* is to *fever*, *yawn* is to *boring*. Well, I could never think that way. I knew what the tests were asking, but I could not block out of my mind the images already created by the first pair, "*sunset* is to *nightfall*" — and I would see a burst of colors against a darkening sky, the moon rising, the lowering of a curtain of stars. And all the other pairs of words — red, bus, stoplight, boring — just threw up a mass of confusing images, making it impossible for me to sort out something as logical as saying: "A sunset precedes nightfall" is the same as "a chill precedes a fever." The only way I would have gotten that answer right would have been to imagine an associative situation, for example, my being disobedient and staying out past sunset, catching a chill at night, which turns into feverish pneumonia as punishment, which indeed did happen to me.

I have been thinking about all this lately, about my mother's English, about achievement tests. Because lately I've been asked, as a writer, why there are not more Asian Americans represented in American literature. Why are there few Asian Americans enrolled in creative writing programs? Why do so many Chinese students go into engineering? Well, these are broad sociological questions I can't begin to answer. But I have noticed in surveys — in fact, just last week — that Asian students, as a whole, always do significantly better on math achievement tests than in English. And this makes me think that there are other Asian-American students whose English spoken in the home might also be described as "broken" or "limited." And perhaps they also have teachers who are steering them away from writing and into math and science, which is what happened to me.

Fortunately, I happen to be rebellious in nature and enjoy the challenge of disproving assumptions made about me. I became an English major my first year in college, after being enrolled as pre-med. I started writing nonfiction as a freelancer the week after I was told by my former boss that writing was my worst skill and I should hone my talents toward account management.

But it wasn't until 1985 that I finally began to write fiction. And at first 20 I wrote using what I thought to be wittily crafted sentences, sentences that would finally prove I had mastery over the English language. Here's an example from the first draft of a story that later made its way into *The Joy Luck Club*, but without this line: "That was my mental quandary in its nascent state." A terrible line, which I can barely pronounce.

Fortunately, for reasons I won't get into today, I later decided I should envision a reader for the stories I would write. And the reader I decided upon was my mother, because these were stories about mothers. So with this reader in mind — and in fact she did read my early drafts — I began to write stories using all the Englishes I grew up with: the English I spoke to my mother, which for lack of a better term might be described as "simple": the English she used with me, which for lack of a better term might be described as "broken"; my translation of her Chinese, which could certainly be described as "watered down"; and what I imagined to be her translation of her Chinese if she could speak in perfect English, her internal language, and for that I sought to preserve the essence, but neither an English nor a Chinese structure. I wanted to capture what language ability tests can never reveal: her intent, her passion, her imagery, the rhythms of her speech, and the nature of her thoughts.

Apart from what any critic had to say about my writing, I knew I had succeeded where it counted when my mother finished reading my book and gave me her verdict: "So easy to read."

1990

The Reader's Presence

1. In her second paragraph, Amy Tan mentions "all the Englishes" she grew up with. What were those "Englishes"? What is odd about the term? How does the oddity of the word reinforce the point of her essay?

2. What exactly is Tan's "mother tongue"? What does the phrase

usually mean? How is Tan using it? How would you describe this language? Would you call it "broken English"? What does that phrase imply?

3. In paragraph 20, Tan gives an example of a sentence that she once thought showed her "mastery" of English. What does she now find wrong with that sentence? What do you think of it? What would her mother have thought of it? What sort of reader does that sentence anticipate?

22

Alice Walker

Beauty: When the Other Dancer Is the Self

It is a bright summer day in 1947. My father, a fat, funny man with beautiful eyes and a subversive wit, is trying to decide which of his eight children he will take with him to the county fair. My mother, of course, will not go. She is knocked out from getting most of us ready: I hold my neck stiff against the pressure of her knuckles as she hastily completes the braiding and the beribboning of my hair.

My father is the driver for the rich old white lady up the road. Her name is Miss Mey. She owns all the land for miles around, as well as the house in which we live. All I remember about her is that she once offered to pay my mother thirty-five cents for cleaning her house, raking up piles of her magnolia leaves, and washing her family's clothes, and that my mother — she of no money, eight children, and a chronic earache — refused it. But I do not think of this in 1947. I am two-and-a-half years old. I want to go everywhere my daddy goes. I am excited at the prospect of riding in a car. Someone has told me fairs are fun. That there is room in the car for only three of us doesn't faze me at all. Whirling happily in my starchy frock, showing off my biscuit-polished patent-leather shoes and lavender socks, tossing my head in a way that makes my ribbons bounce, I stand, hands on hips, before my father. "Take me, Daddy," I say with assurance; "I'm the prettiest!"

Later, it does not surprise me to find myself in Miss Mey's shiny black car, sharing the back seat with the other lucky ones. Does not surprise me

For biographical information on Alice Walker, see p. 666.

that I thoroughly enjoy the fair. At home that night I tell the unlucky ones all I can remember about the merry-go-round, the man who eats live chickens, and the teddy bears, until they say: that's enough, baby Alice. Shut up now, and go to sleep.

It is Easter Sunday, 1950. I am dressed in a green, flocked, scalloped-hem dress (handmade by my adoring sister, Ruth) that has its own smooth satin petticoat and tiny hot-pink roses tucked into each scallop. My shoes, new T-strap patent leather, again highly biscuit-polished. I am six years old and have learned one of the longest Easter speeches to be heard that day, totally unlike the speech I said when I was two: "Easter lilies / pure and white / blossom in / the morning light." When I rise to give my speech I do so on a great wave of love and pride and expectation. People in the church stop rustling their new crinolines. They seem to hold their breath. I can tell they admire my dress, but it is my spirit, bordering on sassiness (womanishness), they secretly applaud.

"That girl's a little *mess*," they whisper to each other, pleased.   5

Naturally I say my speech without stammer or pause, unlike those who stutter, stammer, or, worst of all, forget. This is before the word "beautiful" exists in people's vocabulary, but "Oh, isn't she the *cutest* thing!" frequently floats my way. "And got so much sense!" they gratefully add . . . for which thoughtful addition I thank them to this day.

It was great fun being cute. But then, one day, it ended.

I am eight years old and a tomboy. I have a cowboy hat, cowboy boots, checkered shirt and pants, all red. My playmates are my brothers, two and four years older than I. Their colors are black and green, the only difference in the way we are dressed. On Saturday nights we all go to the picture show, even my mother; Westerns are her favorite kind of movie. Back home, "on the ranch," we pretend we are Tom Mix, Hopalong Cassidy, Lash LaRue (we've even named one of our dogs Lash LaRue); we chase each other for hours rustling cattle, being outlaws, delivering damsels from distress. Then my parents decide to buy my brothers guns. These are not "real" guns. They shoot BBs, copper pellets my brothers say will kill birds. Because I am a girl, I do not get a gun. Instantly I am relegated to the position of Indian. Now there appears a great distance between us. They shoot and shoot at everything with their new guns. I try to keep up with my bow and arrows.

One day while I am standing on top of our makeshift "garage" — pieces of tin nailed across some poles — holding my bow and arrow and looking out toward the fields, I feel an incredible blow in my right eye. I look down just in time to see my brother lower his gun.

Both brothers rush to my side. My eye stings, and I cover it with my   10 hand. "If you tell," they say, "we will get a whipping. You don't want that to happen, do you?" I do not. "Here is a piece of wire," says the older brother, picking it up from the roof; "say you stepped on one end of it and the other flew up and hit you." The pain is beginning to start. "Yes," I say. "Yes, I will say that is what happened." If I do not say this is what happened, I know my brothers will find ways to make me wish I had. But now I will say anything that gets me to my mother.

Confronted by our parents we stick to the lie agreed upon. They place me on a bench on the porch and I close my left eye while they examine the right. There is a tree growing from underneath the porch that climbs past the railing to the roof. It is the last thing my right eye sees. I watch as its trunk, its branches, and then its leaves are blotted out by the rising blood.

I am in shock. First there is intense fever, which my father tries to break using lily leaves bound around my head. Then there are chills: my mother tries to get me to eat soup. Eventually, I do not know how, my parents learn what has happened. A week after the "accident" they take me to see a doctor. "Why did you wait so long to come?" he asks, looking into my eye and shaking his head. "Eyes are sympathetic," he ways. "If one is blind, the other will likely become blind to."

This comment of the doctor's terrifies me. But it is really how I look that bothers me most. Where the BB pellet struck there is a glob of whitish scar tissue, a hideous cataract, on my eye. Now when I stare at people — a favorite pastime, up to now — they will stare back. Not at the "cute" little girl, but at her scar. For six years I do not stare at anyone, because I do not raise my head.

Years later, in the throes of a mid-life crisis, I ask my mother and sister whether I changed after the "accident." "No," they say, puzzled. "What do you mean?"

What do I mean?   15

I am eight, and, for the first time, doing poorly in school, where I have been something of a whiz since I was four. We have just moved to the place where the "accident" occurred. We do not know any of the people around us because this is a different county. The only time I see the friends I knew is when we go back to our old church. The new school is the former state penitentiary. It is a large stone building, cold and drafty, crammed to overflowing with boisterous, ill-disciplined children. On the third floor there is a huge circular imprint of some partition that has been torn out.

"What used to be here?" I ask a sullen girl next to me on our way past it to lunch.

"The electric chair," says she.

At night I have nightmares about the electric chair, and about all the people reputedly "fried" in it. I am afraid of the school, where all the students seem to be budding criminals.

"What's the matter with your eye?" they ask, critically.   20

When I don't answer (I cannot decide whether it was an "accident" or not), they shove me, insist on a fight.

My brother, the one who created the story about the wire, comes to my rescue. But then brags so much about "protecting" me, I become sick.

After months of torture at the school, my parents decide to send me back to our old community, to my old school. I live with my grandparents and the teacher they board. But there is no room for Phoebe, my cat. By the time my grandparents decide there *is* room, and I ask for my cat, she cannot be found. Miss Yarborough, the boarding teacher, takes me under her wing, and begins to teach me to play the piano. But soon she marries an African — a "prince," she says — and is whisked away to his continent.

At my old school there is at least one teacher who loves me. She is the teacher who "knew me before I was born" and bought my first baby clothes. It is she who makes life bearable. It is her presence that finally helps me turn on the one child at the school who continually calls me "one-eyed bitch." One day I simply grab him by his coat and beat him until I am satisfied. It is my teacher who tells me my mother is ill.

My mother is lying in bed in the middle of the day, something I have   25
never seen. She is in too much pain to speak. She has an abscess in her ear. I stand looking down on her, knowing that if she dies, I cannot live. She is being treated with warm oils and hot bricks held against her cheek. Finally a doctor comes. But I must go back to my grandparents' house. The weeks pass but I am hardly aware of it. All I know is that my mother might die, my father is not so jolly, my brothers still have their guns, and I am the one sent away from home.

"You did not change," they say.

Did I imagine the anguish of never looking up?

I am twelve. When relatives come to visit I hide in my room. My cousin Brenda, just my age, whose father works in the post office and whose mother is a nurse, comes to find me. "Hello," she says. And then she asks, looking at my recent school picture, which I did not want taken, and on which the "glob," as I think of it, is clearly visible, "You still can't see out of that eye?"

"No," I say, and flop back on the bed over my book.

That night, as I do almost every night, I abuse my eye. I rant and rave   30
at it, in front of the mirror. I plead with it to clear up before morning. I tell it I hate and despise it. I do not pray for sight. I pray for beauty.

"You did not change," they say.

I am fourteen and baby-sitting for my brother Bill, who lives in Boston. He is my favorite brother and there is a strong bond between us. Understanding my feelings of shame and ugliness he and his wife take me to a local hospital, where the "glob" is removed by a doctor named O. Henry. There is still a small bluish crater where the scar tissue was, but the ugly white stuff is gone. Almost immediately I become a different person from the girl who does not raise her head. Or so I think. Now that I've raised my head I win the boyfriend of my dreams. Now that I've raised my head I have plenty of friends. Now that I've raised my head classwork comes from my lips as faultlessly as Easter speeches did, and I leave high school as valedictorian, most popular student, and *queen*, hardly believing my luck. Ironically, the girl who was voted most beautiful in our class (and was) was later shot twice through the chest by a male companion, using a "real" gun, while she was pregnant. But that's another story in itself. Or is it?

"You did not change," they say.

It is now thirty years since the "accident." A beautiful journalist comes to visit and to interview me. She is going to write a cover story for her magazine that focuses on my latest book. "Decide how you want to look on the cover," she says. "Glamorous, or whatever."

Never mind "glamorous," it is the "whatever" that I hear. Suddenly all   35
I can think of is whether I will get enough sleep the night before the photography session: If I don't, my eye will be tired and wander, as blind eyes will.

At night in bed with my lover I think up reasons why I should not appear on the cover of a magazine. "My meanest critics will say I've sold out," I say. "My family will now realize I write scandalous books."

"But what's the real reason you don't want to do this?" he asks.

"Because in all probability," I say in a rush, "my eye won't be straight."

"It will be straight enough," he says. Then, "Besides, I thought you'd made your peace with that."

And I suddenly remember that I have.   40

I remember:

I am talking to my brother Jimmy, asking if he remembers anything unusual about the day I was shot. He does not know I consider that day the last time my father, with his sweet home remedy of cool lily leaves, chose me, and that I suffered and raged inside because of this. "Well," he says, "all I remember is standing by the side of the highway with Daddy, trying to flag down a car. A white man stopped, but when Daddy said he needed somebody to take his little girl to the doctor, he drove off."

I remember:

I am in the desert for the first time. I fall totally in love with it. I am so overwhelmed by its beauty, I confront for the first time, consciously, the meaning of the doctor's words years ago: "Eyes are sympathetic. If one is blind, the other will likely become blind too." I realize I have dashed about the world madly, looking at this, looking at that, storing up images against the fading of the light. *But I might have missed seeing the desert!* The shock of that possibility — and gratitude for over twenty-five years of sight — sends me literally to my knees. Poem after poem comes — which is perhaps how poets pray.

ON SIGHT

I am so thankful I have seen
The Desert
And the creatures in the desert
And the desert Itself.

The desert has its own moon
Which I have seen
With my own eye.
There is no flag on it.

Trees of the desert have arms
All of which are always up
That is because the moon is up
The sun is up
Also the sky
The Stars
Clouds
None with flags.

If there were flags, I doubt
the trees would point.
Would you?

But mostly, I remember this: 45

I am twenty-seven, and my baby daughter is almost three. Since her birth I have worried about her discovery that her mother's eyes are different from other people's. Will she be embarrassed? I think. What will she say? Every day she watches a television program called *Big Blue Marble*. It begins with a picture of the earth as it appears from the moon. It is bluish, a little battered-looking, but full of light, with whitish clouds swirling around it. Every time I see it I weep with love, as if it is a picture of Grandma's house. One day when I am putting Rebecca down for her nap, she suddenly focuses on my eye. Something inside me cringes, gets ready to try to protect myself. All children are cruel about physical differences, I know from experience, and that they don't always mean to be is another matter. I assume Rebecca will be the same.

But no-o-o-o. She studies my face intently as we stand, her inside and me outside her crib. She even holds my face maternally between her dimpled little hands. Then, looking every bit as serious and lawyerlike as her father, she says, as if it may just possibly have slipped my attention: "Mommy, there's a *world* in your eye." (As in, "Don't be alarmed, or do anything crazy.") And then, gently, but with great interest: "Mommy, where did you *get* that world in your eye?"

For the most part, the pain left then. (So what, if my brothers grew up to buy even more powerful pellet guns for their sons and to carry real guns themselves. So what, if a young "Morehouse[1] man" once nearly fell off the

---

[1]***Morehouse:*** Morehouse College, a black men's college in Atlanta, Georgia. — EDS.

steps of Trevor Arnett Library because he thought my eyes were blue.) Crying and laughing I ran to the bathroom, while Rebecca mumbled and sang herself to sleep. Yes indeed, I realized, looking into the mirror. There *was* a world in my eye. And I saw that it was possible to love it: that in fact, for all it had taught me of shame and anger and inner vision, I *did* love it. Even to see it drifting out of orbit in boredom, or rolling up out of fatigue, not to mention floating back at attention in excitement (bearing witness, a friend has called it), deeply suitable to my personality, and even characteristic of me.

That night I dream I am dancing to Stevie Wonder's song "Always" (the name of the song is really "As," but I hear it as "Always"). As I dance, whirling and joyous, happier than I've ever been in my life, another bright-faced dancer joins me. We dance and kiss each other and hold each other through the night. The other dancer has obviously come through all right, as I have done. She is beautiful, whole, and free. And she is also me.

1983

The Reader's Presence

1. In her opening paragraph, Walker refers to her father's "beautiful eyes." How does that phrase take on more significance in rereading? Can you find other words, phrases, or images that do the same? For example, why might Walker have mentioned the pain of having her hair combed?

2. Note that Walker uses the present tense throughout the essay. Why might this be unusual, given her subject? What effect does it have for both writer and reader? Try rewriting the opening paragraph in the past tense. What difference do you think it makes?

3. What is the meaning of Walker's occasional italicized comments? What do they have in common? Whose comments are they? To whom do they seem addressed? What time frame do they seem to be in? What purpose do you think they serve?

23 _____

E. B. White

Once More to the Lake

One summer, along about 1904, my father rented a camp on a lake in Maine and took us all there for the month of August. We all got ringworm from some kittens and had to rub Pond's Extract on our arms and legs night and morning, and my father rolled over in a canoe with all his clothes on; but outside of that the vacation was a success and from then on none of us ever thought there was any place in the world like that lake in Maine. We returned summer after summer — always on August 1st for one month. I have since become a salt-water man, but sometimes in summer there are days when the restlessness of the tides and the fearful cold of the sea water and the incessant wind that blows across the afternoon and into the evening make me wish for the placidity of a lake in the woods. A few weeks ago this feeling got so strong I bought myself a couple of bass hooks and a spinner and returned to the lake where we used to go, for a week's fishing and to revisit old haunts.

I took along my son, who had never had any fresh water up his nose and who had seen lily pads only from train windows. On the journey over to the lake I began to wonder what it would be like. I wondered how time would have marred this unique, this holy spot — the coves and streams, the hills that the sun set behind, the camps and the paths behind the camps. I was sure that the tarred road would have found it out and I wondered in what other ways it would be desolated. It is strange how much you can remember about places like that once you allow your mind to return into the grooves that lead back. You remember one thing, and that suddenly reminds you of another thing. I guess I remembered clearest of all the early mornings, when the lake was cool and motionless, remembered how the bedroom smelled of the lumber it was made of and the wet woods whose scent entered through the screen. The partitions in the camp were thin and did not extend clear to the top of the rooms, and as I was always the first

For biographical information on E. B. White, see p. 667.

up I would dress softly so as not to wake the others, and sneak out into the sweet outdoors and start out in the canoe, keeping close along the shore in the long shadows of the pines. I remembered being very careful never to rub my paddle against the gunwale for fear of disturbing the stillness of the cathedral.

The lake had never been what you would call a wild lake. There were cottages sprinkled about the shores, and it was in farming country although the shores of the lake were quite heavily wooded. Some of the cottages were owned by nearby farmers, and you would live at the shore and eat your meals at the farmhouse. That's what our family did. But although it wasn't wild, it was a fairly large and undisturbed lake and there were places in it which, to a child at least, seemed infinitely remote and primeval.

I was right about the tar: It led to within half a mile of the shore. But when I got back there, with my boy, and we settled into a camp near a farmhouse and into the kind of summertime I had known, I could tell that it was going to be pretty much the same as it had been before — I knew it, lying in bed the first morning, smelling the bedroom, and hearing the boy sneak quietly out and go off along the shore in a boat. I began to sustain the illusion that he was I, and therefore, by simple transposition, that I was my father. This sensation persisted, kept cropping up all the time we were there. It was not an entirely new feeling, but in this setting it grew much stronger. I seemed to be living a dual existence. I would be in the middle of some simple act, I would be picking up a bait box or laying down a table fork, or I would be saying something, and suddenly it would be not I but my father who was saying the words or making the gesture. It gave me a creepy sensation.

We went fishing the first morning. I felt the same damp moss covering the worms in the bait can, and saw the dragonfly alight on the tip of my rod as it hovered a few inches from the surface of the water. It was the arrival of this fly that convinced me beyond any doubt that everything was as it always had been, that the years were a mirage and there had been no years. The small waves were the same, chucking the rowboat under the chin as we fished at anchor, and the boat was the same boat, the same color green and the ribs broken in the same places, and under the floor-boards the same fresh-water leavings and debris — the dead hellgrammite, the wisps of moss, the rusty discarded fishhook, the dried blood from yesterday's catch. We stared silently at the tips of our rods, at the dragonflies that came and went. I lowered the tip of mine into the water, tentatively, pensively dislodging the fly, which darted two feet away, poised, darted two feet back, and came to rest again a little farther up the rod. There had been no years between the ducking of this dragonfly and the other one — the one that was part of memory. I looked at the boy, who was silently watching his fly, and it was my hands that held his rod, my eyes watching. I felt dizzy and didn't know which rod I was at the end of.

We caught two bass, hauling them in briskly as though they were mackerel, pulling them over the side of the boat in a businesslike manner without any landing net, and stunning them with a blow on the back of the head. When we got back for a swim before lunch, the lake was exactly where we had left it, the same number of inches from the dock, and there was only the merest suggestion of a breeze. This seemed an utterly enchanted sea, this lake you could leave to its own devices for a few hours and come back to, and find that it had not stirred, this constant and trustworthy body of water. In the shallows, the dark, watersoaked sticks and twigs, smooth and old, were undulating in clusters on the bottom against the clean ribbed sand, and the track of the mussel was plain. A school of minnows swam by, each minnow with its small individual shadow, doubling the attendance, so clear and sharp in the sunlight. Some of the other campers were in swimming, along the shore, one of them with a cake of soap, and the water felt thin and clear and unsubstantial. Over the years there had been this person with the cake of soap, this cultist, and here he was. There had been no years.

Up to the farmhouse to dinner through the teeming, dusty field, the road under our sneakers was only a two-track road. The middle track was missing, the one with the marks of the hooves and splotches of dried, flaky manure. There had always been three tracks to choose from in choosing which track to walk in; now the choice was narrowed down to two. For a moment I missed terribly the middle alternative. But the way led past the tennis court, and something about the way it lay there in the sun reassured me; the tape had loosened along the backline, the alleys were green with plantains and other weeds, and the net (installed in June and removed in September) sagged in the dry noon, and the whole place steamed with midday heat and hunger and emptiness. There was a choice of pie for dessert, and one was blueberry and one was apple, and the waitresses were the same country girls, there having been no passage of time, only the illusion of it as in a dropped curtain — the waitresses were still fifteen; their hair had been washed, that was the only difference — they had been to the movies and seen the pretty girls with the clean hair.

Summertime, oh summertime, pattern of life indelible, the fade-proof lake, the woods unshatterable, the pasture with the sweetfern and the juniper forever and ever, summer without end; this was the background, and the life along the shore was the design, the cottages with their innocent and tranquil design, their tiny docks with the flagpole and the American flag floating against the white clouds in the blue sky, the little paths over the roots of the trees leading from camp to camp and the paths leading back to the outhouses and the can of lime for sprinkling, and at the souvenir counters at the store the miniature birch-bark canoes and the post cards that showed things looking a little better than they looked. This was the American family at play, escaping the city heat, wondering whether the newcomers in the camp at the head of the cove were "common" or "nice," wondering whether it was true that the people who drove up for Sunday dinner at the farmhouse were turned away because there wasn't enough chicken.

It seemed to me, as I kept remembering all this, that those times and those summers had been infinitely precious and worth saving. There had been jollity and peace and goodness. The arriving (at the beginning of August) had been so big a business in itself, at the railway station the farm wagon drawn up, the first smell of the pine-laden air, the first glimpse of the smiling farmer, and the great importance of the trunks and your father's enormous authority in such matters, and the feel of the wagon under you for the long ten-mile haul, and at the top of the last long hill catching the first view of the lake after eleven months of not seeing this cherished body of water. The shouts and cries of the other campers when they saw you, and the trunks to be unpacked, to give up their rich burden. (Arriving was less exciting nowadays, when you sneaked up in your car and parked it under a tree near the camp and took out the bags and in five minutes it was all over, no fuss, no loud wonderful fuss about trunks).

Peace and goodness and jollity. The only thing that was wrong now, really, was the sound of the place, an unfamiliar nervous sound of the outboard motors. This was the note that jarred, the one thing that would sometimes break the illusion and set the years moving. In those other summertimes all motors were inboard; and when they were at a little distance, the noise they made was a sedative, an ingredient of summer sleep. They were one-cylinder and two-cylinder engines, and some were make-and-break and some were jump-spark, but they all made a sleepy sound across the lake. The one-lungers throbbed and fluttered, and the twin-cylinder ones purred and purred, and that was a quiet sound too. But now the campers all had outboards. In the daytime, in the hot mornings, these motors made a petulant, irritable sound; at night, in the still evening when the afterglow lit the water, they whined about one's ears like mosquitoes. My boy loved our rented outboard, and his great desire was to achieve singlehanded mastery over it, and authority, and he soon learned the trick of choking it a little (but not too much), and the adjustment of the needle valve. Watching him I would remember the things you could do with the old one-cylinder engines with the heavy flywheel, how you could have it eating out of your hand if you got really close to it spiritually. Motor boats in those days didn't have clutches, and you would make a landing by shutting off the motor at the proper time and coasting in with a dead rudder. But there was a way of reversing them, if you learned the trick, by cutting the switch and putting it on again exactly on the final dying revolution of the flywheel, so that it would kick back against compression and begin reversing. Approaching a dock in a strong following breeze, it was difficult to slow up sufficiently by the ordinary coasting method, and if a boy felt he had complete mastery over his motor, he was tempted to keep it running beyond its time and then reverse it a few feet from the dock. It took a cool nerve, because if you threw the switch a twentieth of a second too soon you could catch the flywheel when it still had speed enough to go up past center, and the boat would leap ahead, charging bull-fashion at the dock.

We had a good week at the camp. The bass were biting well and the sun shone endlessly, day after day. We would be tired at night and lie down in the accumulated heat of the little bedrooms after the long hot day and the breeze would stir almost imperceptibly outside and the smell of the swamp drift in through the rusty screens. Sleep would come easily and in the morning the red squirrel would be on the roof, tapping out his gay routine. I kept remembering everything, lying in bed in the mornings — the small steamboat that had a long rounded stern like the lip of a Ubangi, and how quietly she ran on the moonlight sails, when the older boys played their mandolins and the girls sang and we ate doughnuts dipped in sugar, and how sweet the music was on the water in the shining night, and what it had felt like to think about girls then. After breakfast we would go up to the store and the things were in the same place — the minnows in a bottle, the plugs and spinners disarranged and pawed over by the youngsters from the boys' camp, the Fig Newtons and the Beeman's gum. Outside, the road was tarred and cars stood in front of the store. Inside, all was just as it had always been, except there was more Coca-Cola and not so much Moxie and root beer and birch beer and sarsaparilla. We would walk out with a bottle of pop apiece and sometimes the pop would backfire up our noses and hurt. We explored the streams, quietly, where the turtles slid off the sunny logs and dug their way into the soft bottom; and we lay on the town wharf and fed worms to the tame bass. Everywhere we went I had trouble making out which was I, the one walking at my side, the one walking in my pants.

One afternoon while we were there at that lake a thunderstorm came up. It was like the revival of an old melodrama that I had seen long ago with childish awe. The second-act climax of the drama of the electrical disturbance over a lake in America had not changed in any important respect. This was the big scene, still the big scene. The whole thing was so familiar, the first feeling of oppression and heat and a general air around camp of not wanting to go very far away. In midafternoon (it was all the same) a curious darkening of the sky, and a lull in everything that had made life tick; and then the way the boats suddenly swung the other way at their moorings with the coming of a breeze out of the new quarter, and the premonitory rumble. Then the kettle drum, then the snare, then the bass drum and cymbals, then crackling light against the dark, and the gods grinning and licking their chops in the hills. Afterward the calm, the rain steadily rustling in the calm lake, the return of light and hope and spirits, and the campers running out in joy and relief to go swimming in the rain, their bright cries perpetuating the deathless joke about how they were getting simply drenched, and the children screaming with delight at the new sensation of bathing in the rain, and the joke about getting drenched linking the generations in a strong indestructible chain. And the comedian who waded in carrying an umbrella.

When the others went swimming my son said he was going in too. He pulled his dripping trunks from the line where they had hung all through the shower, and wrung them out. Languidly, and with no thought of going in, I watched him, his hard little body, skinny and bare, saw him wince slightly as he pulled up around his vitals the small, soggy, icy garment. As he buckled the swollen belt suddenly my groin felt the chill of death.

1941

The Reader's Presence

1. In this essay, almost every word is deliberately chosen and intended to contribute to the meaning. Even the little words are important. For example, in paragraph 5, why does White say "*the* dragonfly" rather than "*a* dragonfly"? What difference does this word choice make?

2. In paragraph 4, White refers to a "creepy sensation." What is the basis of that sensation? Why is it "creepy"? In rereading the essay, pay close attention to other examples of fear and anxiety. What connection do these have to White's main theme?

3. Go through the essay and identify words and images having to do with the sensory details of seeing, hearing, touching, and so on. How do these details contribute to the overall effect of the essay? How do they anticipate White's final paragraph?

Part II

Shaping Information

24

Diane Ackerman

The Silent Grandeur of the Grand Canyon

Nothing prepares you for the visual thrill of sailing over the rim, from a state of flatland predictability suddenly into one of limitless depth, change, and color. All at once we are down in its jungles of rock, plunging toward sheer crevices, skimming limestone jags by only a few yards, then swooping down even farther to trace the winding path of the Colorado River, rocketing up toward a large butte, wing left, wing right, as we twist along the unraveling alleyways of rock, part of a spectacle both dainty and massive. Who could measure it, when we are the only object of certain size moving through the mazes? Off one wing tip, a knob of limestone curves into arrowhead edges and disappears at the base of a half-shattered tree, whose open roots catch the sunlight in a cage of iridescence.

When we land, we begin to explore the Grand Canyon on foot from lookouts and trails along the rim. Hypnotized by the intricate vastness, I hike from one triangulation station to another, finding two of the ninety bronze survey disks that were installed fifteen years ago by the Boston Museum of Science–*National Geographic* expedition. Sitting alone on a plinth jutting far out over the emptiness, I listen to the monumental silence and find my mind roaming over the notion of wonder. The canyon is, in part, a touchstone to other wonders, revealing the uncanny work of erosion, a great builder of landscapes. Five geologic eras are here piled one on top of the other like Berber rugs, the evolution of life viewable in a fossil record. Gigantic as the canyon is (217 miles long), it is the world in miniature: seven environments (from Sonoran to Arctic Circle), desert barrenness to spring lushness. It is certainly the grandest American cliché, explored by many but an enigma nonetheless. No response to it seems robust enough.

In a world governed by proportion — in which the eye frames a mo-

---

For biographical information on Diane Ackerman, see p. 641.

ment, digests it, frames another — scale is lost: visual scale, mental scale, emotional scale. If your lips form a silent *wow* at the sight of Niagara Falls, what is suitable here, where your heart explores some of its oldest dwellings? How can you explain an emptiness so vast and intricate, an emptiness so rare on this planet? Not the sprawling, flat, oddly clean emptiness of a desert or arctic region, but an emptiness with depth. There are no yardsticks, unless one is lucky enough to catch sight of a dark speck moving along the canyon floor, which is a mule and rider. But that is part of the puzzle of this labyrinth, a maze both of direction and of proportion, a maze in three dimensions.

It's easy to forget how ugly nature often seemed to people before Romanticism reexplored the unevenness of natural beauty. Early-nineteenth-century writers found the canyon grotesque — not just dangerous and obstructive and rife with bloodthirsty Indians, but actually a vision of evil. C. B. Spencer described it as "Horror! Tragedy! Silence! Death! Chaos! . . . a delirium of Nature," while another writer called it "the grave of the world." After two World Wars and assorted smaller ones, with all the atrocities attendant to them, it's no longer possible to find works of nature horrible, tragic, deadly, chaotic; mankind has personalized those traits forever. Now the canyon is just the opposite: a sanctuary, an emblem of serenity, a view of innocence.

The Cárdenas expedition of 1540 discovered the canyon for the Caucasian world but felt no need to name it. For three hundred years it was too overwhelming to report except in whole phrases and sentences. And then in the 1850s and 1860s, "Big Cañon" and "Grand Cañon of the Colorado" came into use, as if it were *one* of anything. For it is not one but thousands of canyons, thousands of gorges and buttes, interflowing, mute, radiant, changing, all with a single river among them, as if joined by a common thought. 5

In the canyon's long soliloquy of rock, parrots of light move about the grottoes, and real swifts loop and dart, white chevrons on each flank. The silence is broken only by the sounds of air whistling through the gorges and insect or bird song. Now and then one hears the sound of a furnace whumping on: a bird taking flight.

There is no way to catalog the endless dialects and languages and body types of the tourists encountered at the rim. With binoculars as various as they are, visitors search the canyon for trails, mules, signs of other people. The need to humanize the marvel is obsessive, obvious, and universal. With glass lenses extending real eyes, canyon visitors become part of the evolution on show. If we cannot go backward in time, we can at least creep into it, above desert floors and red-rock mesas and ponderosa pine, then suddenly slip over the rim of dreams and down through the layers of geological time.

What is *grandeur* that the word should form rapidly in the mind when one first sees the Grand Canyon? Why do we attach that concept to this spectacle? Is it merely the puniness of human beings compared with the gigantic structures of rock? The moon, the biggest rock most of us know, has been domesticated in literature and song, but the canyon has resisted great literature. Like the universe and the workings of nature, there is no way to summarize it. The ultimate model of a labyrinth, it is gargantuan and cryptic, full of blind alleys and culs-de-sac. We are compulsive architects; to see engineering as complete, colossal, and inimitable as this — still far beyond our abilities — is humbling indeed. As John Muir said in 1896, upon first viewing the canyon, "Man seeks the finest marbles for sculptures; Nature takes cinders, ashes, sediments, and makes all divine in fineness of beauty — turrets, towers, pyramids, battlemented castles, rising in glowing beauty from the depths of this canyon of canyons noiselessly hewn from the smooth mass of the featureless plateau."

Most of all, the canyon is so vastly uninvolved with us, with mercy or pity. Even the criminal mind is more explicable than this — a quiddity we cannot enter, a consciousness that does not include us. We pass through much of our world as voyeurs, and yet we are driven, from sheer loneliness, I suppose, to attribute consciousness to all sorts of nonconscious things — dolls, cars, computers. We still call one another totemic names by way of endearment: We would like to keep the world as animate as it was for our ancestors. But that is difficult when facing a vision as rigidly dead as the Grand Canyon. It is beautiful and instructive and calming, but it cannot be anything other than it is: the absolute, intractable "other" that human beings face from birth to death.

In between consciousness and the Grand Canyon, matter has odd fits   10 and whims: lymph, feathers, Astro Turf, brass. Cactus strikes me as a very odd predicament for matter to get into. But perhaps it is no stranger than the comb of an iris, or the way flowers present their sex organs to the world, or the milky sap that often oozes from inedible plants. There is something about the poignant senselessness of all that rock, wave after wave of blunt, endless rock, that reminds us, as nothing else could so dramatically, what a bit of luck *we* are, what a natural wonder.

At the south rim, brass sighting tubes make arbitrary sense out of the vista. Lay the lensless tube into a slot marked Battleship, and there will be a facsimile in rock. The other sites are mainly temples: Vishnu Temple, Wotan's Throne, Zoroaster Temple, Brahma Temple, Buddha Temple, Tower of Ra, Cheops Pyramid, Osiris Temple, Shiva Temple, Isis Temple, and so on. One of the most dramatic, tall, and precarious buttes is referred to as Snoopy, because, they say, it resembles the cartoon dog lying on his doghouse. All this taming of the spectacle appalls me. Why define a site with another site that is smaller and in some cases trivial? Nothing can compare with the Grand Canyon, and that is part of its marvel and appeal.

It was John Wesley Powell who, in 1860, gave the salient buttes their temple names. Now that the gods who instructed us are remote, we are quite obsessed with temples. We have moved our gods farther and farther away, off the planet, into the Solar System, beyond the Milky Way, beyond the Big Bang. But once upon a time, when time was seasonal, the gods were neighbors who lived just across the valley on a proscribed mountain. Their deeds and desires were tangible; they were intimates.

Today on the Hopi mesas close to the Grand Canyon, in rituals older than memory, men still dress as kachinas — garish, expressionist recreations of the essences in their world. There is a kachina of meteors, and one of maize, and one of water vapor. In the winter months the kachinas dwell on the twelve-thousand-foot slopes of Humphreys Peak, and in the growing season they come down to move among men. The Hopi have traditionally traveled down into the canyon to perform some of their rituals, and there is a spot on the bank of the Little Colorado where they believe humans may first have entered the world.

Indeed, the whole area around the Grand Canyon is full of lore and natural wonders. The volcanic field just north of Flagstaff is the largest in the United States, and flying over it you can see where the black paws of lava stopped cold. The aerial turbulence at midday evokes the early turbulence from which the canyon was partially formed, and long before that the chaos of the Big Bang. At the Lowell Observatory, in Flagstaff, Pluto was first sighted. In half a dozen other observatories, astronomers cast their gaze upward while, close by, a million tourists cast theirs down into the canyon.

There would be no canyon as we perceive it — subtle, mazy, unrepeat-   15
ing — without the intricate habits of light. For the canyon traps light, rehearses all the ways a thing can be lit: the picadors of light jabbing the horned spray of the Colorado River; light like caramel syrup pouring over the dusky buttes; the light almost fluorescent in the hot green leaves of seedlings. In places the canyon is so steep that sunlight only enters it, briefly, at noon; the rest is darkness.

It is hard to assimilate such a mix of intensities; it is too close to the experience of being alive. Instead, we order it with names that are cozy, trendy, or ancient. Available, viewable, definable, reducible to strata of limestone and fossil, they are still mysterious crevices, still unknowable, still overwhelming, still ample and unearthly, still the earth at its earthiest.

The Douglas fir crop out, under, around, between, through every place one looks; they survive the rock. Many of their twisted, lightning-licked limbs are still in leaf. The cottonwoods, growing over a hundred feet tall, can use more than fifty gallons of water each day. There are a thousand kinds of flower and species of squirrel and bird indigenous to the canyon (some nearly extinct). And endless otters, skunks, beavers, ring-tailed cats, deer, porcupines, shrews, chipmunks, rats, and wild burros. In the low, common desert of the inner canyon depths, only the prickly-pear cactus survives well the high temperatures and rare precipitation. It is not erosion on a large scale that has formed the canyon but small, daily acts of erosion by tiny plants and streams, reminding us what the merest trickle over limestone can achieve. From rim to floor, the canyon reveals the last two billion years of biological and geological history and thus typifies the processes of evolution and decay in which we all take part.

But mainly there is the steep persuasion of something devastatingly fixed, something durable in a world too quick to behold, a world of fast, slippery perceptions where it can sometimes seem that there is nothing to cling to. By contrast the canyon is solid and forever; going nowhere, it will wait for you to formulate your thoughts. The part of us that yearns for the supernaturalism we sprang from yearns for this august view of nature.

At nightfall, when we reboard the plane for our flight back to Phoenix, there is no canyon anywhere, just starry blackness above and moorish blackness below. Like a hallucination, the canyon has vanished, completely hidden now by the absence of light. Hidden, as it was from human eyes for millennia, it makes you wonder what other secrets lie in the shade of our perception. Bobbing through the usual turbulence over the desert, we pick our way home from one cluster of town lights to another, aware from this height of the patterns of human habitation. Seven skirts of light around a mountain reveal how people settled in waves. Some roads curve to avoid, others to arrive. Except for the lights running parallel along the ridges, people seem desperate to clump and bunch, swarming all over each other in towns while most of the land lies empty. The thick, dark rush of the desert below, in which there is not one human light for miles, drugs me. Looking up drowsily after a spell, I'm startled to see the horizon glittering like Oz: Phoenix and its suburbs. That, or one long, sprawling marquee.

1987

The Reader's Presence

1. Reread the opening paragraph of Diane Ackerman's essay. From what point of view — what physical location — does she describe the grandeur of the Grand Canyon? When — and in what specific ways — does that point of view change as the essay proceeds? With what effect? What compositional techniques does Ackerman use to re-create the powerful immediacy of the scene she encounters?

2. Near the end of the first paragraph, Ackerman raises a crucial question for her readers to ponder and an important challenge for herself as a writer: "Who could measure it, when we are the only object of certain size moving through the maze?" Ackerman's struggle in this essay is to find adequate language to describe her sense of grandeur at viewing the Grand Canyon. What specific strategies (such as the use of diction and metaphor) does Ackerman employ to convey what she calls "the intricate vastness" (paragraph 2) of the Grand Canyon's complexity and scope?

How does she satisfy what she identifies as the "need to humanize the marvel"?
3. Ackerman characterizes the Grand Canyon, in the wake of world
   wars and countless human atrocities, as "a sanctuary, an emblem
   of serenity, a view of innocence" (paragraph 4). Explain how this
   judgment shapes the way she presents historical information
   about the Grand Canyon, the sense of natural mystery it conveys,
   and the conviction that the Grand Canyon remains "something
   durable in a world too quick to behold, a world of fast, slippery
   perceptions where it can sometimes seem that there is nothing to
   cling to" (paragraph 18).

25

Wendell Berry

The Journey's End

Early in 1968 the state's newspapers were taking note of the discovery,
in one of the rock houses in the Gorge, of a crude hut built of short split
planks overlaying a framework of poles. The hut was hardly bigger than a
pup tent, barely large enough, I would say, to accommodate one man and
a small stone fireplace. One of its planks bore the carved name: "D. boon."
There was some controversy over whether or not it really was built by
Daniel Boone. Perhaps it does not matter. But the news of the discovery
and of the controversy over it had given the place a certain fame.

The find interested me, for I never cease to regret the scarcity of knowledge of the first explorations of the continent. Some hint, such as the
"Boone hut" might provide, of the experience of the Long Hunters would
be invaluable. And so one of my earliest visits to the Gorge included a trip
to see the hut.

The head of the trail was not yet marked, but once I found the path
leading down through the woods it was clear to me that I had already had
numerous predecessors. And I had not gone far before I knew their species:
scattered more and more thickly along the trail the nearer I got to the site
of the hut was the trash that has come to be more characteristic than
shoeprints of the race that produced (as I am a little encouraged to remember) such a man as D. boon. And when I came to the rock house itself I
found the mouth of it entirely closed, from the ground to the overhanging
rock some twenty-five feet above, by a chain-link fence. Outside the fence

For biographical information on Wendell Berry, see p. 642.

the ground was littered with Polaroid negatives, film spools, film boxes, food wrappers, cigarette butts, a paper plate, a Coke bottle.

And inside the fence, which I peered through like a prisoner, was the hut, a forlorn relic overpowered by what had been done to protect it from collectors of mementos, who would perhaps not even know what it was supposed to remind them of. There it was, perhaps a vital clue to our history and our inheritance, turned into a curio. Whether because of the ignorant enthusiasm of souvenir hunters, or because of the strenuous measures necessary to protect it from them, Boone's hut had become a doodad — as had Boone's name, which now stood for a mendacious TV show and a brand of fried chicken.

I did not go back to that place again, not wanting to be associated with   5
the crowd whose vandalism had been so accurately foreseen and so overwhelmingly thwarted. But I did not forget it either, and the memory of it seems to me to bear, both for the Gorge and for ourselves, a heavy premonition of ruin. For are those who propose damming the Gorge, arguing *convenience,* not the same as these who can go no place, not even a few hundred steps to see the hut of D. boon, without the trash of convenience? Are they not the same who will use the proposed lake as a means of transporting the same trash into every isolated cranny that the shoreline will penetrate? I have a vision (I don't know if it is nightmare or foresight) of a time when our children will go to the Gorge and find there a webwork of paved, heavily littered trails passing through tunnels of steel mesh. When people are so ignorant and destructive that they must be divided by a fence from what is vital to them, whether it is their history or their world, they are imprisoned.

On a cold drizzly day in the middle of October I walk down the side of a badly overgrazed ridge into a deep, steep hollow where there remains the only tiny grove of virgin timber still standing in all the Red River country. It is a journey backward through time, from the freeway droning both directions through 1969, across the old ridge denuded by the agricultural policies and practices of the white man's era, and down into such a woods as the Shawnees knew before they knew white men.

Going down, the sense that it is a virgin place comes over you slowly. First you notice what would be the great difficulty of getting in and out, were it not for such improvements as bridges and stairways in the trail. It is this difficulty that preserved the trees, and that even now gives the hollow a feeling of austerity and remoteness. And then you realize that you are passing among poplars and hemlocks of a startling girth and height, the bark of their trunks deeply grooved and moss-grown. And finally it comes to you where you are; the virginity, the uninterrupted wildness, of the place comes to you in a clear strong dose like the first breath of a wind. Here the world is in its pure state, and such men as have been here have all been here in their pure state, for they have destroyed nothing. It has lived whole into our lifetime out of the ages. Its life is a vivid link between us and Boone and the Long Hunters and their predecessors, the Indians. It stands, brooding upon its continuance, in a strangely moving perfection, from the tops of the immense trees down to the leaves of the partridge berries on the ground. Standing and looking, moving on and looking again, I suddenly realize what is missing from nearly all the Kentucky woodlands I have known: the summit, the grandeur of these old trunks that lead the eyes up through the foliage of the lesser trees toward the sky.

At the foot of the climb, over the stone floor of the hollow, the stream is mottled with the gold leaves of the beeches. The water has taken on a vegetable taste from the leaves steeping in it. It has become a kind of weak tea, infused with the essence of the crown of the forest. By spring the fallen leaves on the stream bed will all have been swept away, and the water, filtered once again through the air and the ground, will take back the clear taste of the rock. I drink the cool brew of the autumn.

And then I wander some more among the trees. There is a thought repeating itself in my mind: This is a great Work, this is a great Work. It occurs to me that my head has gone to talking religion, that it is going ahead more or less on its own, assenting to the Creation, finding it good, in the spirit of the first chapters of Genesis. For no matter the age or the hour, I am celebrating the morning of the seventh day. I assent to my mind's assent. It *is* a great Work. It is a *great* Work — begun in the beginning, carried on until now, to be carried on, not by such processes as men make or understand, but by "the kind of intelligence that enables grass seed to grow grass; the cherry stone to make cherries."

Here is the place to remember D. boon's hut. Lay aside all questions of   10 its age and ownership — whether or not he built it, he undoubtedly built others like it in similar places. Imagine it in a cave in a cliff overlooking such a place as this. Imagine it separated by several hundred miles from the nearest white men and by two hundred years from the drone, audible even here, of the parkway traffic. Imagine that the great trees surrounding it are part of a virgin wilderness still nearly as large as the continent, vast rich unspoiled distances quietly peopled by scattered Indiana tribes, its ways still followed by buffalo and bear and panther and wolf. Imagine a cold gray winter evening, the wind loud in the branches above the protected hollows. Imagine a man dressed in skins coming silently down off the ridge and along the cliff face into the shelter of the rock house. Imagine his silence that is unbroken as he enters, crawling, a small hut that is only a negligible detail among the stone rubble of the cave floor, as unobtrusive there as the nest of an animal or bird, and as he livens the banked embers of a fire on the stone hearth, adding wood, and holds out his chilled hands before the blaze. Imagine him roasting his supper meat on a stick over the fire while the night falls and the darkness and the wind enclose the hollow. Imagine him sitting on there, miles and months from words, staring into the fire, letting its warmth deepen in him until finally he sleeps. Imagine his sleep.

When I return again it is the middle of December, getting on toward the final shortening, the first lengthening of the days. The year is ending, and my trip too has a conclusive feeling about it. The ends are gathering. The things I have learned about the Gorge, my thoughts and feelings about it, have begun to have a sequence, a pattern. From the start of the morning, because of this sense of the imminence of connections and conclusions, the day has both an excitement and a comfort about it.

As I drive in I see small lots staked off and a road newly graveled in one of the creek bottoms. And I can hear chain saws running in the vicinity of another development on Tunnel Ridge. This work is being done in antici-pation of the lake, but I know that it has been hastened by the publicity surrounding the effort to keep the Gorge unspoiled. I consider the ironic possibility that what I will write for love of it may also contribute to its destruction, enlarging the hearsay of it, bringing in more people to drive the roads and crowd the "points of interest" until they become exactly as interesting as a busy street. And yet I might as well leave the place anony-mous, for what I have learned here could be learned from any woods and any free-running river.

I pull off the road near the mouth of a hollow I have not yet been in. The day is warm and overcast, but it seems unlikely to rain. Taking only a notebook and a map, I turn away from the road and start out. The woods closes me in. Within a few minutes I have put the road, and where it came from and is going, out of mind. There comes to be a wonderful friendliness, a sort of sweetness I have not known here before, about this day and this solitary walk — as if, having finally understood this country well enough to accept it on its terms, I am in turn accepted. It is as though, in this year of men's arrival on the moon, I have completed my own journey at last, and have arrived, an exultant traveler, here on the earth.

I come around a big rock in the stream and two grouse flush in the open not ten steps away. I walk on more quietly, full of the sense of ending and beginning. At any moment, I think, the forest may reveal itself to you in a new way. Some intimate insight, that all you have known has been secretly adding up to, may suddenly open into the clear — like a grouse, that one moment seemed only a part of the forest floor, the next moment rising in flight. Also it may not.

Where I am going I have never been before. And since I have no desti-   15
nation that I know, where I am going is always where I am. When I come to good resting places, I rest. I rest whether I am tired or not because the places are good. Each one is an arrival. I am where I have been going. At a narrow place in the stream I sit on one side and prop my feet on the other. For a while I content myself to be a bridge. The water of heaven and earth is flowing beneath me. While I rest a piece of the world's work is continu-ing here without my help.

Since I was here last the leaves have fallen. The forest has been at work, dying to renew itself, covering the tracks of those of us who were here,

burying the paths and the old campsites and the refuse. It is showing us
what to hope for. And that we can hope. And *how* to hope. It will always
be a new world, if we will let it be.

The place as it was is gone, and we are gone as we were. We will never
be in that place again. Rejoice that it is dead, for having received that
death, the place of next year, a new place, is lying potent in the ground like
a deep dream.

Somewhere, somewhere behind me that I will not go back to, I have
lost my map. At first I am sorry, for on these trips I have always kept it
with me. I brood over the thought of it, the map of this place rotting into it
along with its leaves and its fallen wood. The image takes hold of me, and
I suddenly realize that it is the culmination, the final insight, that I have felt
impending all through the day. It is the symbol of what I have learned here,
and of the process: the gradual relinquishment of maps, the yielding of
knowledge before the new facts and the mysteries of growth and renewal
and change. What men know and presume about the earth is part of it,
passing always back into it, carried on by it into what they do not know.
Even their abuses of it, their diminishments and dooms, belong to it. The
tragedy is only ours, who have little time to be here, not the world's whose
creation bears triumphantly on and on from the fulfillment of catastrophe
to the fulfillment of hepatica blossoms. The thought of the lost map, the
map fallen and decaying like a leaf among the leaves, grows in my mind to
the force of a cleansing vision. As though freed of a heavy weight, I am
light and exultant here in the end and the beginning.

1971

The Reader's Presence

1. In what sense is the title of Berry's essay a description of both its
   purpose and its structure? For example, what does he mean when
   he says: "It is as though, in this year of men's arrival on the moon,
   I have completed my own journey at last, and have arrived, an
   exultant traveler, here on the earth" (paragraph 13)? Where does
   his journey begin? Where does it end? What new knowledge —
   about nature, other people, and himself — does he gain through
   this journey?

2. Does Berry seem to be more interested in gaining new knowledge
   about the natural world or in preserving its mysteries? In this respect, what do you make of his repetition of the word *imagine* in
   paragraph 10? Point to other passages to support and clarify your
   response. How does Berry establish an effective contrast between
   the state of nature before and after a human presence is asserted
   in it? What specific examples does he use to create this contrast?
   What element of surprise does he embed in each example? What

presence as a writer does Berry establish for himself at these moments? How does he identify himself with — and distinguish himself from — the attitudes displayed in this human presence?

3. At the beginning of paragraph 9, Berry tells his readers: "And then I wander some more among the trees." In what specific ways might this sentence describe the structure of Berry's essay? Later, in paragraph 15, Berry tells us: "At a narrow place in the stream I sit on one side and prop my feet on the other. For a while I content myself to be a bridge." Comment on the ways in which this metaphor characterizes Berry's own presence — and purpose — in this essay. In a similar sense, how does his losing the map symbolize what he has learned during the course of his journey in nature?

26

Sissela Bok

Gossip

DEFINITIONS

Round the samovar and the hostess the conversation had been meanwhile vacillating . . . between three inevitable topics: the latest piece of public news, the theater, and scandal. It, too, came finally to rest on the last topic, that is, ill-natured gossip. . . . and the conversation crackled merrily like a burning fagot-stick.

Tolstoy's group portrait from *Anna Karenina* brings to mind many a cluster of malicious gossips, delighting in every new morsel of intimate information about others, the more scandalous the better.[1] So well do we recognize this temptation, and so often do we see it indulged, that it is easy to think of all gossip as petty, ill-willed, too often unfounded — as either trivial and thus demeaning to those whose lives it rakes over, or else as outright malicious. In either case, gossip seems inherently questionable from a moral point of view.

Dictionary definitions reinforce the view of gossip as trivial. Thus the *American Heritage Dictionary* defines it as "trifling, often groundless rumor, usually of a personal, sensational, or intimate nature; idle talk."[2]

For biographical information on Sissela Bok, see p. 643.

Thinkers who adopt a normative point of view often stress the more negative evaluation of gossip. Aristotle wrote of that tantalizing and yet strangely limited "great-souled man," who "claims much and deserves much," that he is no gossip *[anthropologos]*,

> for he will not talk either about himself or about another, as he neither wants to receive compliments nor to hear other people run down . . . ; and so he is not given to speaking evil himself, even of his enemies, except when he deliberately intends to give offense.[3]

Thomas Aquinas distinguished "talebearers" from "backbiters": both speak evil of their neighbors, but a talebearer differs from a backbiter "since he intends, not to speak ill as such, but to say anything that may stir one man against another," in order to sever friendship.[4]

Kierkegaard abhorred gossip. He spoke out against its superficiality   5
and its false fellow-feeling. Gossip and chatter, he wrote, "obliterate the vital distinction between what is private and what is public" and thereby trivialize all that is inward and inherently inexpressible. He castigated his own age as one in which the expanding press offered snide and leveling gossip to a garrulous, news-hungry public.[5] Heidegger likewise, in pages echoing those of Kierkegaard, deplored idle talk as "something which any-one can rake up." He held that it perverts genuine efforts at understanding by making people think they already know everything.[6] And in their 1890 article on the right to privacy, Samuel Warren and Louis Brandeis spoke of gossip with similar distaste, assailing in particular its spread in the expand-ing yellow press: "Gossip is no longer the resource of the idle and vicious but has become a trade which is pursued with industry as well as effron-tery."[7]

Cheap, superficial, intrusive, unfounded, even vicious: surely gossip can be all that. Yet to define it in these ways is to overlook the whole network of human exchanges of information, the need to inquire and to learn from the experience of others, and the importance of not taking ev-erything at face value. The desire for such knowledge leads people to go beneath the surface of what is said and shown, and to try to unravel con-flicting clues and seemingly false leads. In order to do so, information has to be shared with others, obtained from them, stored in memory for future use, tested and evaluated in discussion, and used at times to encourage, to entertain, or to warn.

Everyone has a special interest in personal information about others. If we knew about people only what they wished to reveal, we would be sub-jected to ceaseless manipulation; and we would be deprived of the pleasure and suspense that comes from trying to understand them. Gossip helps to absorb and to evaluate intimations about other lives, as do letters, novels, biography, and chronicles of all kinds. In order to live in both the inner and the shared worlds, the exchange of views about each — in spite of all the difficulties of perception and communication — is indispensable.[8]

Thanks to the illuminating studies of gossip by anthropologists and others — in villages around the world as in offices, working teams, schools, or conventions — we now have a livelier and clearer documentation of the role it actually plays.[9] These studies have disproved the traditional stereotype of women as more garrulous and prone to gossip than men, and have shown how such forms of communication spring up in every group, regardless of sex.[10] By tracing the intricate variations of gossip, these writings have led to a subtler understanding of how it channels, tests, and often reinforces judgments about human nature.

Before considering the moral problems that some forms of gossip clearly raise, we must therefore define it in a less dismissive way than those mentioned at the beginning of this chapter. We shall then be able to ask what makes it more or less problematic from a moral point of view, and weigh more carefully the dangers that Kierkegaard, Heidegger, and others have signaled.

I shall define gossip as informal personal communication about other people who are absent or treated as absent. It is informal, first of all, unlike communication in court proceedings or lectures or hospital records or biographies, in that it lacks formal rules setting forth who may speak and in what manner, and with what limitations from the point of view of accuracy and reliability. It is informal, too, in that it takes place more spontaneously and relies more on humor and guesswork, and in what it is casual with respect to who ends up receiving the information, in spite of the frequent promises not to repeat it that are ritualistically exacted along its path. (In each of these respects, gossip nevertheless has standards as well, though usually unspoken, as all who have tried to take part in gossip and been rebuffed have learned.) And the formal modes of discourse may themselves slip into more or less gossipy variations.

Secrecy is one of the factors that make gossip take the place of more formal communication about persons. Gossip increases whenever information is both scarce and desirable — whenever people want to find out more about others than they are able to. It is rampant, for instance, in speculations about the selection of prize-winners, or the marriage plans of celebrities, or the favors of a capricious boss. Gossip is more likely, too, when formal modes of discourse, though possible, have drawbacks for the participants. Thus hospital and school personnel gossip about their charges rather than entering the information on institutional records. And those who have the power to retaliate should they learn that their personal affairs are discussed are criticized in gossip rather than to their faces.

The seventeenth- and eighteenth-century New England Puritans illustrate in their writings the intensity with which human lives may be raked over, both in personal soul-searching and in talking about the lives of others. They labored with the strongest fears of not being among those who would turn out to be saved in the life to come; but they had no evidence for who was and who was not saved, and recognized no way to influence their fate, believing that it had been decided for them before birth. Might they nevertheless discern traces of such evidence in their own lives and in those of others? Might behavior and demeanor not hold some clues? Speculating about imperceptible yet all-important differences between persons took on an urgency rarely exceeded before or since. Hypocrisy naturally abounded. One of the foremost tasks of thinkers such as Thomas Shepard and Jonathan Edwards became the effort to separate the hypocrites from the sincere, and above all, to discern in self and others what they called the "inner hypocrisy" or self-deception that masked one's sins and doubts even from oneself.[11]

The second element in my definition of gossip is personal communication. The original source of what is said may be hidden or forgotten, but each time, gossip is communicated by one or more persons to others, most often in personal encounters, but also by telephone, by letter, or, in the last few centuries, in the mass media. This personal element, combined with the third — that the information is also *about* persons — makes gossip a prime vehicle for moral evaluation. Part of the universal attraction of gossip is the occasion it affords for comparing oneself with others, usually silently, while seeming to be speaking strictly about someone else. Few activities tempt so much to moralizing, through stereotyped judgments and the head-shaking, seemingly all-knowing distancing of those speaking from those spoken about. The result is hypocrisy — judging the lives of others as one would hardly wish one's own judged. As one student of the anthropology of gossip has said:

> If I suggest that gossip and scandal are socially virtuous and valuable, this does not mean that I always approve of them. Indeed, in practice I find that when I am gossiping about my friends as well as my enemies I am deeply conscious of performing a social duty; but that when I hear they gossip viciously about me, I am rightfully filled with righteous indignation.[12]

Because gossip is primarily about persons, it is not identical with the larger category of rumor; there can be rumors of war or rumors of an imminent stock-market collapse, but hardly gossip.[13] And there can be stories, but not gossip, about the foibles and escapades of animals, so long as humans are not part of the plot, or the animals taken to represent individual persons or endowed with human characteristics.

Gossip, finally, is not only about persons but about persons absent, 15 isolated, or excluded, rather than about the participants themselves. The subjects of gossip, while usually physically absent, can also be treated as if they were absent should they be part of the group engaging in gossip. While the conversation is directed past them and around them, they are then its targets, and are meant to overhear it. Least of all can people gossip about themselves, unless they manage to treat themselves as if they were absent, and as subjects of scandal or concern. Though it is hard to gossip about oneself, one can lay oneself open to gossip, or talk about one's doings that include others in such a way as to arouse gossip. Compare, from this point of view, the rumored divorce and the announced one, or the gossip about a young girl's pregnancy and her acknowledgment of it.

These four elements of gossip — that it is (1) informal (2) personal communication (3) about persons who (4) are absent or excluded — are clearly not morally problematic in their own right. Consider the many harmless or supportive uses of gossip: the talk about who might marry, have a baby, move to another town, be in need of work or too ill to ask for help, and the speculations about underlying reasons, possible new developments, and opportunities for advice or help. Some may find such talk uninteresting, even tedious, or too time-consuming, but they can hardly condemn it on moral grounds.

On the other hand, it is equally easy to conceive of occasions when the four elements do present moral problems. The informality and the speculative nature of what is said may be inappropriate, as it would be if gossip were the basis for firing people from their jobs. The communication about other persons may be of a degrading or invasive nature that renders it inappropriate, whether in gossip or in other discourse. And the talk about persons in their absence — behind their backs — is sometimes of such a nature as to require that it either be spoken to their faces or not spoken at all. Pirandello's play *Right You Are! (If You Think So)* shows how irresistibly such gossip can build up among men and women in a small town, and the havoc it can wreak.[14]

For an example of gossip that is offensive on all such grounds, and as a contrast to the many forms of harmless gossip mentioned earlier, consider the alleged leak by an FBI official to a Hollywood columnist about the private life of the actress Jean Seberg. The leak indicated that she had engaged in extramarital relations with a member of the Black Panther Party, who was said to have fathered her unborn child.[15] It was meant to cast suspicion on her support of black nationalist causes. Reprinted by *Newsweek*, it was disseminated, as intended, throughout the world. Such uses of gossip have not been rare. They injure most directly the person whose reputation they are meant to call in question. But they debilitate as well those who take part in manufacturing and spreading the rumor, and their superiors who are responsible for permitting such a scheme to go ahead; and thus they endanger still others who may be the targets of similar attacks. Such acts, with all their ramifications, overstep all bounds of discretion and of respect for persons. They are especially reprehensible and dangerous when undertaken in secrecy by a government agency in the name of the public's best interest.

In between these extremes of innocuousness and harm lie most forms of gossip: the savoring of salacious rumors, the passing on of unverified suspicions, the churning over seemingly self-inflicted burdens in the lives of acquaintances, and the consequent self-righteousness and frequent hypocrisy of those passing judgment in gossip. No testing ground for the exercise of discretion and indiscretion is more common than such everyday probing and trading of personal matters. Just as all of us play the roles of host and guest at different times, so all of us gossip and are gossiped about. Gossip brings into play intuitive responses to the tensions of insider and outsider,

and forces us to choose between concealing and revealing, between inquisitiveness and restraint. Each of us develops some standards, however inarticulate, however often honored in the breach, for amounts and kinds of
gossip we relish, tolerate, or reject. Can these standards be made more explicit? If so, how might we weigh them?

REPREHENSIBLE GOSSIP

> Why is gossip like a three-pronged tongue? Because it destroys three
> people: the person who says it, the person who listens to it, and the
> person about whom it is told.
>
> – THE BABYLONIAN TALMUD

Not all gossip, as I have defined it, is injurious or otherwise to be   20
avoided. But when it is, it can harm all who take part in it, as the Babylonian Talmud warned.[16] Out of respect for oneself as much as for others,
therefore, it matters to discern such cases. Three categories of gossip
should be singled out as especially reprehensible: gossip in breach of confidence, gossip the speaker knows to be false, and unduly invasive gossip.

It is wrong, first of all, to reveal in gossip what one has promised to
keep secret. This is why the gossip of doctors at staff meetings and cocktail
parties about the intimate revelations of their patients is so inexcusable.
True, pledges of confidentiality must at times be broken — to save the life of
an adolescent who confides plans of suicide, for example. But such legitimate
breaches could hardly be carried out through gossip, because of its lack of
discrimination with respect to who ends up hearing it. Such information
should, rather, be disclosed only to those who have a particular need to know,
and with the utmost respect for the privacy of the individual concerned.

Must we then bar all gossip conveyed in spite of a pledge of silence?
And would we then not exclude *most* gossip? After all, few pieces of information are more rapidly disseminated than those preceded by a "promise
not to tell." At times such a promise is worthless, a mere empty gesture,
and both parties know it; one can hardly call the subsequent repeating of
the "secret" a breach of confidence. Sometimes the person who asks for the
promise before sharing his bits of gossip may believe it to be more binding
than it turns out to be. But, as La Rochefoucauld asked, why should we
imagine that others will keep the secret we have ourselves been unable to
keep?[17] At still other times, a promise may have been sincere, but should
never have been made to begin with. Many promises of secrecy are exacted
with the aggressive intent of burdening someone, or of creating a gulf between that individual and others. The best policy is to be quite sparing in
one's promises of secrecy about any information, but scrupulous, once
having given such a promise, in respecting it.

Second, gossip is unjustifiable whenever those who convey it know
that it is false and intend to deceive their listeners (unlike someone who
makes it clear that he exaggerates or speaks in jest). Whether they spread

false gossip just to tell a good story, or to influence reputations, perhaps even as a weapon — as when newly separated spouses sometimes overstate each other's misdeeds and weaknesses in speaking to friends — they are exceeding the bounds of what they owe to their listeners and to those whose doings they misrepresent. The same is true of the false gossip that can spring up in the competition for favor, as in office politics or in academic backbiting, and of collective strategies for deceit. Thus in the reelection campaign of President Nixon in 1972, some individuals had been assigned the task of spreading false rumors about his opponents. Conspiratorial groups and secret police have employed such methods through the ages. Whatever the reason, there can be no excuse for such dissemination of false gossip.

Might there not be exceptional circumstances that render false gossip excusable?* I argued, in *Lying,* that certain lies might be excusable, such as those that offer the only way to deflect someone bent on violence. But whatever lies one might tell such an assailant, false gossip about third parties would hardly provide the requisite help at such a time of crisis; and if by any chance the assailant could be stalled simply by talking about other persons, there would be no need to use falsehood in so doing.

Are there forms of false gossip that correspond to innocent white lies? 25 Gossip to please someone on his deathbed, for instance, who has always enjoyed hearing about the seedy and salacious doings of his friends, by a wife who can think of nothing truthful that is sufficiently titillating? Should she then invent stories about neighbors or friends, thinking that no harm could come thereof, since her husband would not live to spread the stories further? Such a way out would be demeaning for both, even if it injured no one else: demeaning to the dying man in the unspoken judgment about what would most please him, and in the supposition that lying to him would therefore be acceptable; and demeaning to his wife, as she reflected back on her inability to muster alternative modes of silence and speech at such a time. No matter how well meant, falsehoods about the lives of others bear little resemblance to harmless white lies.

Much of the time, of course, those who convey false gossip do not know it to be false. It may rest on hearsay, or be unverified, or be pure speculation. Often the facts cannot easily *be* verified, or not without serious intrusion. Thus to spread rumors that a person is a secret alcoholic is made more serious because of the difficulty that listeners have in ascertaining the basis of the allegation. At times such gossip cannot be known to be true by the speakers, nor credibly denied by the subjects. This was one reason why the dissemination of the rumor about Jean Seberg's unborn

---

*One could imagine a club dedicated to false gossip, in which members vied with one another for who could tell the most outrageous stories about fellow human beings. So long as all knew the tales were false, and the stories went no farther, the practice would not be a deceptive one, and more allied to storytelling and fiction than to the intentional misleading about the lives of others that is what renders false gossip inexcusable. Such a club, however, would be likely to have but few members; for gossip loses its interest when it is *known* to be false. — BOK'S NOTE.

baby was so insidious. She had no way before the baby's birth to demonstrate the falsity of the rumor.

In the third place, gossip may be reprehensible, even if one has given no pledge of silence and believes one's information correct, simply because it is unduly invasive. On this ground, too, planting the rumor about Jean Seberg's sexual life and the identity of the father of her unborn child was unjustifiable, regardless of whether the FBI thought the story accurate or not.

Is any gossip, then, unduly invasive whenever it concerns what is private, perhaps stigmatizing, often secret? If so, much of the gossip about the personal lives of neighbors, co-workers, and public figures would have to be judged inexcusable. But such a judgment seems unreasonable. It would dismiss many harmless or unavoidable exchanges about human foibles. To such strictures, the perspective of Mr. Bennett in Jane Austen's *Pride and Prejudice* should give pause: "For what do we live," he asked, "but to make sport for our neighbors and to laugh at them in turn?"[18]

How then might we sort out what is unduly invasive from all the gossip about private and secret lives? To begin with, there is reason to stop to consider whether gossip is thus invasive whenever those whose doings are being discussed claim to feel intruded upon. But these claims must obviously not be taken at face value: They are often claims to ownership of information about oneself. While such claims should give gossipers pause, they are not always legitimate. People cannot be said, for instance, to own aspects of their lives that are clearly evident to others and thus in fact public, such as a nasty temper or a manipulative manner, nor can they reasonably argue that others have no right to discuss them. Least of all can they suppress references to what may be an "open secret," known to all, and half-suspected even by themselves — a topic treated in innumerable comedies about marital infidelity. Similarly, more concealed aspects of their lives may be of legitimate interest to others — their mistreatment of their children, for example, or their past employment record. And the information that government leaders often try to withhold through claims to executive privilege is often such that the public has every right to acquire it. At such times, gossip may be an indispensable channel for public information.

Merely to *say* that gossip about oneself is unduly invasive, therefore, does not make it so. I would argue that additional factors must be present to render gossip unduly invasive: The information must be about matters legitimately considered private; and it must hurt the individuals talked about.* They may be aware of the spreading or of the harm; or else they

30

---

*For this reason, gossip should give pause whenever the speaker believes it may reach someone in a position to injure the person spoken of. If the listener is a judge, for instance, or an executive having the power to make decisions over someone's employment, the gossiper must weigh his words with care. Even when the listener is not in an official position, gossip directed to him is problematic if he is given to injurious responses: if he is malicious, slanderous, indiscreet, profiteering, or in any way likely to put the information to inappropriate use. Gossip is problematic, too, if the listener is a poor intermediary: perhaps one who exaggerates gossip in conveying it further, or who is likely to misunderstand it and spread it in false garb, or is unable to discriminate in turn between listeners, so that he conveys the gossip to one who is incompetent or dangerous. — BOK'S NOTE.

may be injured by invasive gossip without ever knowing why — fail to keep their jobs, perhaps, because of rumors about their unspoken political dissent. But the speculations in bars or sewing circles concerning even the most intimate aspects of the married life of public figures is not intrusive so long as it does not reach them or affect their lives in any way. Such talk may diminish the speakers, but does not intrude on the persons spoken about.

While the three categories of reprehensible gossip — gossip in breach of confidence, gossip that is known to be false, and gossip that is clearly invasive — should be avoided, each one has somewhat uncertain boundaries and borderline regions. One cannot always be sure whether one owes someone silence, whether one is conveying false gossip, or whether what is said of an intimate nature about people will find its way back to them or otherwise hurt them. In weighing such questions, discretion is required; and, given the capacity of gossip to spread, it is best to resolve doubts in favor of silence.

Extra caution is needed under certain circumstances, when the temptation to indulge in any of the three forms may be heightened. At such times, the borderline cases carry an even stronger presumption against taking part in gossip. Discretion is then needed more than ever to prevent gossip from blending with one or more of the kinds earlier ruled out. The desire to have an effect, first of all, to impress people, perhaps to deal a blow, easily leads to greater pressure to breach secrecy or exaggerate in gossip or to speak intrusively about others. As soon as a speaker gains in any way from passing on gossip, these pressures arise. Prestige, power, affection, intimacy, even income (as for gossip columnists): Such are the gains that gossipers envisage. It cannot be wrong to gain from gossip in its own right, since in one sense most gossip aims at a gain of some sort — if nothing else, in closeness to the listener, or in the status of someone who seems to be "in the know." But the prospect of such gain increases the likelihood that promises will be broken, unverified rumors passed on, privacy invaded. The misfortunes of another may then be used in such a way as to traffic in them. This is in part why the inside gossip of the former employee or the divorced spouse is more troubling when it is published for financial gain or as revenge.

A desire for gain of a different kind motivates those who take special pleasure in passing on discreditable gossip. Maimonides, like Aquinas and many others, distinguished the talebearer from the person who speaks to denigrate: the scandalmonger, or, as Maimonides expressed it, "the evil tongue."[19] He spoke, too, of "the dust of the evil tongue": the insinuations that sow suspicion without shedding light either on the implied offense or on the evidence concerning it. Before scandalmongers and insinuators are known as such, they can destroy trust among friends or in entire communities; in consequence they have been more distasteful to commentators than all others. And yet, all disparaging or discreditable personal information cannot be avoided. On the contrary, it must sometimes be conveyed, as when the deceitful or the aggressive or, indeed, the indiscreet are pointed out to put newcomers on their guard. Consider, as an illustration of such cautioning remarks, the following exchange in a Mexican village:

> Down the path someone spotted a young man named Xun, whose reputation as a drunkard made everyone anxious to be on his way.
> "If you meet him drunk on the path, he has no mercy. He won't listen to what you say, that Xun."
> "He doesn't understand what you say; you're right. If he's just a bit tight when you meet him on the path — puta, 'Let's go, let's go,' he'll say. You will be forced to drink."
> "But doesn't he get angry?"
> "No, no. He'll just say, 'Let's go have a little soft drink.'"
> "He's good-natured."
> "But he doesn't bother to ask if you're in a hurry to get someplace . . . "
> "No, he's good-hearted . . . "
> "If you find yourself in a hurry to get somewhere and you see him coming the best thing to do is hide . . . "
> " . . . or run away."
> And with that, the various men went on about their business.[20]

TRIVIALIZING GOSSIP

Beyond such questions of avoiding reprehensible and harmful gossip lies a larger one: that of the tone gossip can lend to discourse about human lives. It is this tone that Kierkegaard and Heidegger aimed at, in arguing that gossip streamlines and demeans what is spoken. What is utterly private and inward, Kierkegaard held, cannot be expressed; as a result, talking about it must necessarily distort and trivialize. Gossip therefore has a leveling effect, in conveying as shallow and ordinary what is unfathomable. It levels, moreover, by talking of all persons in the same terms, so that even the exceptionally gifted, the dissident, and the artist are brought down to the lowest common denominator. Finally, it erases and levels the differences between the different modes of talking, so that all is glossed over in the same superficial and informal chatter.

According to such a view, the informality with which we talk about the weather or the latest price rises can only trivialize what we say about human beings. And this informality of gossip can combine with the special liberties taken in the absence of those spoken about so as to permit the speaker to indulge in a familiarity disrespectful of their humanity and in turn of his own. It was this reflection that gossip casts on so many who convey it that made George Eliot compare it to smoke from dirty tobacco pipes: "It proves nothing but the bad taste of the smoker."[21]

Gossip can also trivialize and demean when it substitutes personal anecdote for a careful exploration of ideas. Someone incapable of taking up political or literary questions without dwelling endlessly on personalities can do justice neither to the ideas nor to the persons under debate.

Such gossip can be an intoxicating surrogate for genuine efforts to understand. It can be the vehicle for stereotypes — of class, for instance, or race or sex. It turns easily into a habit, and for some a necessity. They may then become unable to think of other human beings in other than trivial ways. If they cannot attribute scope and depth and complexity to others, moreover, it is unlikely that they will perceive these dimensions in themselves. All news may strike them as reducible to certain trite formulas about human behavior; all riddles seem transparent.

Many do not merely gossip but are known *as* gossips. They may serve an important group function; but such a role should cause concern to the individuals thus labeled. It is far more likely to tempt to breaches of confidence, to falsehoods, to invasive gossiping — and thus to a general loss of discernment about reasons to avoid gossip and persons to shield from it. At the extreme of this spectrum is the pathological gossip, whose life revolves around prying into the personal affairs of others and talking about them.

Plutarch wrote of the garrulous that they deny themselves the greatest benefits of silence: hearing and being heard. In their haste to speak, they listen but poorly; others, in turn, pay little heed to their words.[22] And Heidegger expounded on the strange way in which gossip and all facile discourse, so seemingly open and free-ranging, turns out instead to inhibit understanding: "By its very nature, idle talk is a closing-off, since to go back to the ground of what is talked about is something which it *leaves undone.*"[23] Those whose casual talk stops at no boundaries, leaves no secret untouched, may thereby shut themselves off from the understanding they seem to seek. Gossip can be the means whereby they distance themselves from all those about whom they speak with such seeming familiarity, and they may achieve but spurious intimacy with those *with whom* they speak. In this way gossip can deny full meaning and depth to human beings, much like some forms of confession: gossip, through such trivializing and distancing; confession, through molding those who confess and overcoming their independence.

These warnings go to the heart of the meaning of discernment concerning human beings, including oneself, and of its links with the capacity to deal with openness and secrecy. Quite apart from the obvious problems with false or invasive gossip discussed earlier, all gossip can become trivializing in tone, or turn into garrulity.   40

Yet gossip need not deny meaning and debilitate thus. Those who warn against it often fail to consider its extraordinary variety. They ignore the attention it can bring to human complexity, and are unaware of its role in conveying information without which neither groups nor societies could function.[24] The view of all gossip as trivializing human lives is itself belittling if applied indiscriminately. When Kierkegaard and Heidegger speak out against idle talk, gossip, and chatter, and against "the public" and the "average understanding" taken in by such discourse, they erase differences and deny meaning in their own way.[25] One cannot read their strictures without sensing their need to stand aloof, to maintain distance, to hold common practices vulgar. In these passages, they stereotype social intercourse and deny it depth and diversity, just as much as gossip can deny those of individuals. When moral judgment takes such stereotyped form, it turns into moralizing: one more way in which moral language can be used to avoid a fuller understanding of human beings and of their efforts to make sense of their lives.

1984

NOTES

1. Leo Tolstoy, *Anna Karenina,* trans. Constance Garnett (New York: Random House, Modern Library, 1950), p. 158.
2. *The American Heritage Dictionary* (Boston: Houghton Mifflin & Co., 1969).
3. Aristotle, *Nicomachean Ethics,* bk. 4, chap. 3, 31. Aristotle contrasted the "great-souled man" with the "small-souled man," on the one hand, who claims less than he deserves, and with the "vain man" on the other, who claims more than he deserves. I have used the traditional translation of Aristotle's *anthropos megalopsuchos,* as "great-souled man"; it must, needless to say, not be thought to refer to males only.
4. Thomas Aquinas, *Summa Theologica* II-II. Ques. 73–74, trans. Fathers of the English Dominican Province (New York: Benziger Brothers, 1918), pp. 290–303.
5. Søren Kierkegaard, *Two Ages* (1846), trans. Howard V. and Edna H. Hong (Princeton, N.J.: Princeton University Press, 1978). See esp. pp. 97–102.
6. Martin Heidegger, *Being and Time* (New York: Harper & Row, 1962), p. 213. See p. 212 for Heidegger's view of the role of gossip and "scribbling" in "idle talk."
7. Warren and Brandeis, "The Right to Privacy," pp. 193–220. For a discussion of this article and of the authors' distaste for gossip, see Dorothy J. Glancy, "The Invention of the Right to Privacy," *Arizona Law Review* 21 (1979): 1–39.
8. For the central role of gossip for information storage and retrieval in a society, see John M. Roberts, "The Self-Management of Cultures," in Ward H. Goodenough, *Explorations in Cultural Anthropology* (New York: McGraw-Hill Book Co., 1964), p. 441. And for an economic interpretation of information management through secrecy and gossip, see Richard A. Posner, "The Right to Privacy," *Georgia Law Review* 12 (Spring 1978): 398–422.
9. See, among others, Max Gluckman, "Gossip and Scandal," *Current Anthropology* 4 (1963):307–16; Don Handelman, "Gossip in Encounters: The Transmission of Information in a Bounded Social Setting," *Man,* n.s. 8 (1973): 210–27; Robert Paine,

"What is Gossip About? An Alternative Hypothesis," *Man,* n.s. 2(1967): 278–85; Ralph L. Rosnow and Gary A. Fine, *Rumor and Gossip: The Social Psychology of Hearsay* (New York: Elsevier, 1976); John Beard Haviland, *Gossip, Reputation, and Knowledge in Zinacantan* (Chicago: University of Chicago Press, 1977).

10. We need not go back to Aesop, Plutarch, or the eighteenth-century moralists for vivid examples of such distinctions based on sex. Carl Fullerton Sulzberger permitted himself the following tortuous speculation, put forth as self-evident fact, in "Why It Is Hard to Keep Secrets," p. 42: "As we all know, most women habitually indulge in acquiring secrets only to give them away with celebrity and obvious enjoyment. . . . When I once asked a patient why she was so eager to acquire and then spread secret rumors, her first association was 'it is like adorning myself with borrowed feathers.' . . . the greater readiness of women to disseminate secrets entrusted to them is directly related to the working of the castration complex."

11. Michael McGiffert, ed., *God's Plot: The Paradoxes of Puritan Piety, Being the Autobiography and Journal of Thomas Shepard* (Amherst: University of Massachusetts Press, 1972); Jonathan Edwards, *Religious Affections* (Edinburgh: W. Laing & J. Matthews, 1789). See also Perry Miller, *The New England Mind: The Seventeenth Century* (New York: Macmillan Co., 1939).

12. Gluckman, "Gossip and Scandal," p. 315.

13. See Gordon W. Allport and Leo Postman, *The Psychology of Rumor* (New York: Henry Holt & Co., 1947), and articles cited in note 9 above.

14. Luigi Pirandello, *Right You Are! (If You Think So),* in Montrose J. Moses, ed., *Dramas of Modernism and their Forerunners* (Boston: Little, Brown & Co., 1931), pp. 239–75.

15. "FBI Admits It Spread Lies About Actress Jean Seberg," *Los Angeles Times,* September 15, 1979, p. 1, and editorial, September 19.

16. The Babylonian Talmud, cited in Francine Klagsbrun, *Voices of Wisdom: Jewish Ideals and Ethics for Everyday Living* (New York: Pantheon Books, 1980), p. 74.

17. La Rochefoucauld, *Maximes et réflexions diverses* (1664; Paris: Gallimard, 1976), p. 143.

18. Jane Austen, *Pride and Prejudice* (New York: E. P. Dutton & Co., 1976), p. 384.

19. Maimonides, *Code,* "Laws Concerning Moral Dispositions and Ethical Conduct," chap. 7, secs. 1–4, quoted in Klagsbrun, *Voices of Wisdom,* p. 75.

20. Haviland, *Gossip, Reputation, and Knowledge in Zinacantan,* p. 15.

21. George Eliot, *Daniel Deronda,* Standard Edition, *The Works of George Eliot* (Edinburgh & London: William Blackwood & Sons, 1897), 1:207.
22. Plutarch, "Concerning Talkativeness," *Moralia,* 6:399.
23. Heidegger, *Being and Time,* p. 213.
24. See Elizabeth Drew, *The Literature of Gossip: Nine English Letter-Writers* (New York: W. W. Norton & Co., 1964), p. 26, for examples of gossipers who can "inspire the commonplace with an uncommon flavor, and transform trivialities by some original grace or sympathy or humor or affection."
25. See, for example, Kierkegaard, *Two Ages,* p. 100, and Heidegger, *Being and Time,* p. 212.

The Reader's Presence

1. Based on your reading of this selection, what would you identify as Bok's principal purpose in writing about gossip? Is it, for example, to identify the major features of gossip? its origins and consequences? the moral issues it raises? some combination of these? Explain, and then support your reading by examining specific passages.

2. Identify the major characteristics of gossip as defined by Sissela Bok. In what social circumstances does gossip flourish? On what specific occasions is gossip permissible and perhaps even to be encouraged? What does Bok explain to be the advantages of gossip? Who benefits from gossip? In what sense — and in which circumstances — is gossip "indispensable"? How does she distinguish gossip from such terms as *rumor, hypocrisy,* and *inquisitiveness?* What standards does Bok establish for assessing the nature — and the moral complexities — of gossip?

3. What specific compositional strategies does Bok draw on to assert her own intellectual and moral presence in her definition of gossip and her account of its complexity? What personal "stake" does she establish in her discussion of this fascinating subject? What patterns do you notice in Bok's use of historical evidence, especially from literature and philosophy? Which do you find most effective? Why?

27

Haig A. Bosmajian

The Language of Oppression

"Sticks and stones may break my bones, but words can never hurt me." To accept this adage as valid is sheer folly. "What's in a name? that which we call a rose by any other name would smell as sweet." The answer to Juliet's question is "Plenty!" and to her own response to the question we can only say that this is by no means invariably true. The importance, significance, and ramifications of naming and defining people cannot be overemphasized. From *Genesis* and beyond, to the present time, the power which comes from naming and defining people has had positive as well as negative effects on entire populations.

The magic of words and names has always been an integral part of both "primitive" and "civilized" societies. As Margaret Schlauch has observed, "from time immemorial men have thought there is some mysterious essential connection between a thing and the spoken name for it. You could use the name of your enemy, not only to designate him either passionately or dispassionately, but also to exercise a baleful influence."[1]

Biblical passages abound in which names and naming are endowed with great power; from the very outset, in *Genesis,* naming and defining are attributed a significant potency: "And out of the ground the Lord God formed every beast of the field and every fowl of the air; and brought them unto Adam to see what he would call them: and whatsoever Adam called every living creature, that was the name thereof."[2] Amidst the admonitions in *Leviticus* against theft, lying, and fraud is the warning: "And ye shall not swear my name falsely, neither shalt thou profane the name of thy God: I am the Lord."[3] So important is the name that it must not be blasphemed; those who curse and blaspheme shall be stoned "and he that blasphemeth

---

For biographical information on Haig A. Bosmajian, see p. 643.

[1]Margaret Schlauch, *The Gift of Language* (New York: Dover, 1955), p. 13 — BOSMAJIAN'S NOTE.

[2]*Genesis,* 2:19. — BOSMAJIAN'S NOTE.

[3]*Leviticus,* 19:12. — BOSMAJIAN'S NOTE.

the name of the Lord, he shall surely be put to death, and all the congregation shall certainly stone him."[4] So important is the name that the denial of it is considered a form of punishment: "But ye are they that forsake the Lord, that forget my holy mountain. . . . Therefore will I number you to the sword, and ye shall all bow down to the slaughter: because when I called, ye did not answer; when I spake, ye did not hear. . . . Therefore thus saith the Lord God, behold, my servants shall eat, but ye shall be hungry. . . . And ye shall leave your name for a curse unto my chosen: for the Lord God shall slay thee, and call his servants by another name."[5]

To be unnamed is to be unknown, to have no identity. William Saroyan has observed that "the word nameless, especially in poetry and in much prose, signifies an alien, unknown, and almost unwelcome condition, as when, for instance, a writer speaks of 'a nameless sorrow.'" "Human beings," continues Saroyan, "are for the fact of being named at all, however meaninglessly, lifted out of an area of mystery, doubt, or undesirability into an area in which belonging to everybody else is taken for granted, so that one of the first questions asked by new people, two-year-olds even, whether they are speaking to other new people or to people who have been around for a great many years, is 'What is your name?'"[6]

To receive a name is to be elevated to the status of a human being; without a name one's identity is questionable. In stressing the importance of a name and the significance of having none, Joyce Hertzler has said that "among both primitives and moderns, an individual has no definition, no validity for himself, without a name. His name is his badge of individuality, the means whereby he identifies himself and enters upon a truly subjective existence. My own name, for example, stands for me, a person. Divesting me of it reduces me to a meaningless, even pathological, nonentity."[7]

In his book *What Is in a Name?* Farhang Zabeeh reminds us that "the Roman slaves originally were without names. Only after being sold they took their master's praenomen in the genitive case followed by the suffix — 'por' (boy), e.g., 'Marcipor,' which indicates that some men, so long as they were regarded by others as cattle, did not need a name. However, as soon as they became servants some designation was called forth."[8] To this day one of the forms of punishment meted out to wrongdoers who are imprisoned is to take away their names and to give them numbers. In an increasingly computerized age people are becoming mere numbers — credit card numbers, insurance numbers, bank account numbers, student numbers, et cetera. Identification of human beings by numbers is a negation of their humanity and their existence.

[4]*Leviticus*, 25:16. — BOSMAJIAN'S NOTE.

[5]*Isaiah*, 66:11–12. — BOSMAJIAN'S NOTE.

[6]William Saroyan, "Random Notes on the Names of People," *Names*, 1 (December 1953), p. 239. — BOSMAJIAN'S NOTE.

[7]Joyce Hertzler, *A Sociology of Language* (New York: Random House, 1965), p. 271. — BOSMAJIAN'S NOTE.

[8]Farhang Zabeeh, *What Is in a Name?* (The Hague: Martinus Nijhoff, 1968), p. 66. — BOSMAJIAN'S NOTE.

Philologist Max Muller has pointed out that "if we examine the most ancient word for 'name,' we find it is *naman* in Sanskrit, *nomen* in Latin, *namo* in Gothic. This *naman* stands for gnaman and is derived from the root, *gna*, to know, and meant originally that by which we know a thing."[9] In the course of the evolution of human society, R. P. Masani tells us, the early need for names "appears to have been felt almost simultaneously with the origin of speech . . . personality and the rights and obligations connected with it would not exist without the name."[10] In his classic work *The Golden Bough* James Frazer devotes several pages to tabooed names and words in ancient societies, taboos reflecting the power and magic people saw in names and words. Frazer notes, for example, that "the North American Indian regards his name, not as a mere label, but as a distinct part of his personality, just as much as are his eyes or his teeth, and believes that injury will result as surely from the malicious handling of his name as from a wound inflicted on any part of his physical organism."[11]

A name can be used as a curse. A name can be blasphemed. Namecalling is so serious a matter that statutes and court decisions prohibit "fighting words" to be uttered. In 1942 the United States Supreme Court upheld the conviction of a person who had addressed a police officer as "a God damned racketeer" and "a damned Fascist" (*Chaplinsky v. New Hampshire*, 315 U.S. 568). Such namecalling, such epithets, said the Court, are not protected speech. So important is one's "good name" that the law prohibits libel.

History abounds with instances in which the mere utterance of a name was prohibited. In ancient Greece, according to Frazer, "the names of the priests and other high officials who had to do with the performance of the Eleusinian mysteries might not be uttered in their lifetime. To pronounce them was a legal offense."[12] Jörgen Ruud reports in *Taboo: A Study of Malagasy Customs and Beliefs* that among the Antandroy people the father has absolute authority in his household and that "children are forbidden to mention the name of their father. They must call him father, daddy. . . . The children may not mention his house or the parts of his body by their ordinary names, but must use other terms, i.e., euphemisms."[13]

It was Iago who said in *Othello*:   10

Who steals my purse steals trash; 'tis something nothing;
'Twas mine, 'tis his, and has been slave to thousands;
But he that filches from me my good name
Robs me of that which not enriches him
And makes me poor indeed.

[9]Cited in Elsdon Smith, *Treasury of Name Lore* (New York: Harper and Row, 1967), p. vii. — BOSMAJIAN'S NOTE.
[10]R. P. Masani, *Folk Culture Reflected in Names* (Bombay: Popular Prakashan, 1966), p. 6. — BOSMAJIAN'S NOTE.
[11]James Frazer, *The Golden Bough* (New York: Macmillan, 1951), p. 284. — BOSMAJIAN'S NOTE.
[12]*Ibid.*, p. 302. — BOSMAJIAN'S NOTE.
[13]Jörgen Ruud, *Taboo: A Study of Malagasy Customs and Beliefs* (Oslo: Oslo University Press, 1960), p. 15. — BOSMAJIAN'S NOTE.

Alice, in Lewis Carroll's *Through the Looking Glass,* had trepidations about entering the woods where things were nameless: "This must be the wood," she said thoughtfully to herself, "where things have no names. I wonder what'll become of *my* name when I go in? I shouldn't like to lose it at all — because they'd have to give me another, and it would almost be certain to be an ugly one."

A Nazi decree of August 17, 1938, stipulated that "Jews may receive only those first names which are listed in the directives of the Ministry of the Interior concerning the use of first names." Further, the decree provided: "If Jews should bear first names other than those permitted . . . they must . . . adopt an additional name. For males, that name shall be Israel, for females Sara." Another Nazi decree forbade Jews in Germany "to show themselves in public without a Jew's star. . . . [consisting] of a six-pointed star of yellow cloth with black borders, equivalent in size to the palm of the hand. The inscription is to read 'JEW' in black letters. It is to be sewn to the left breast of the garment, and to be worn visibly."

The power which comes from names and naming is related directly to the power to define others — individuals, races, sexes, ethnic groups. Our identities, who and what we are, how others see us, are greatly affected by the names we are called and the words with which we are labeled. The names, labels, and phrases employed to "identify" a people may in the end determine their survival. The word "define" comes from the Latin *definire,* meaning to limit. Through definition we restrict, we set boundaries, we name.

"When I use a word," said Humpty Dumpty in *Through the Looking Glass,* "it means just what I choose it to mean — neither more nor less." "The question is," said Alice, "whether you can make words mean so many different things." "The question is," said Humpty Dumpty, "which is to be master — that's all."

During his days as a civil rights–black power activist, Stokely Carmichael accurately asserted: "It [definition] is very, very important because I believe that people who can define are masters."[14] Self-determination must include self-definition, the ability and right to name oneself; the master-subject relationship is based partly on the master's power to name and define the subject.

While names, words, and language can be and are used to inspire us, to motivate us to humane acts, to liberate us, they can also be used to dehumanize human beings and to "justify" their suppression and even their extermination. It is not a great step from the coercive suppression of dissent to the extermination of dissenters (as the United States Supreme Court declared in its 1943 compulsory flag salute opinion in *West Virginia State Board of Education v. Barnette*); nor is it a large step from defining a

15

---

[14]Stokely Carmichael, speech delivered in Seattle, Washington, April 19, 1967. — BOSMAJIAN'S NOTE.

people as non-human or sub-human to their subjugation or annihilation. One of the first acts of an oppressor is to redefine the "enemy" so they will be looked upon as creatures warranting separation, suppression, and even eradication.

The Nazis redefined Jews as "bacilli," "parasites," "disease," "demon," and "plague." In his essay "The Hollow Miracle," George Steiner informs us that the Germans "who poured quicklime down the openings of the sewers in Warsaw to kill the living and stifle the stink of the dead wrote about it. They spoke of having to 'liquidate vermin.' . . . Gradually, words lost their original meaning and acquired nightmarish definitions. *Jude, Pole, Russe* came to mean two-legged lice, putrid vermin which good Aryans must squash, as a [Nazi] Party manual said, 'like roaches on a dirty wall.' 'Final solution,' *endgültige Lösung,* came to signify the death of six million human beings in gas ovens."[15]

The language of white racism has for centuries been used to "keep the nigger in his place." Our sexist language has allowed men to define who and what a woman is and must be. Labels like "traitors," "saboteurs," "queers," and "obscene degenerates" were applied indiscriminately to students who protested the war in Vietnam or denounced injustices in the United States. Are such people to be listened to? Consulted? Argued with? Obviously not! One does not listen to, much less talk to, traitors and outlaws, sensualists and queers. One only punishes them or, as Spiro Agnew suggested in one of his 1970 speeches, there are some dissenters who should be separated "from our society with no more regret than we should feel over discarding rotten apples."[16]

What does it mean to separate people? When the Japanese-Americans were rounded up in 1942 and sent off to "relocation camps" they were "separated." The Jews in Nazi Germany were "separated." The Indians of the United States, the occupants of the New World before Columbus "discovered" it, have been systematically "separated." As "chattels" and slaves, the blacks in the United States were "separated"; legally a black person was a piece of property, although human enough to be counted as three-fifths of a person in computing the number of people represented by white legislators.

How is the forcible isolation of human beings from society at large 20 justified? To make the separation process more palatable to the populace, what must the oppressor first do? How does he make the populace accept the separation of the "creatures," or, if not accept it, at least not protest it? Consideration of such questions is not an academic exercise without practical implications. There is a close nexus between language and self-perception, self-awareness, self-identity, and self-esteem. Just as our thoughts affect our language, so does our language affect our thoughts and eventually

---

[15]George Steiner, *Language and Silence* (New York: Atheneum, 1970), p. 100. — BOSMAJIAN'S NOTE.
[16]*The New York Times,* October 31, 1969, p. 25. — BOSMAJIAN'S NOTE.

our actions and behavior. As Edward Sapir has observed, we are all "at the mercy of the particular language which has become the medium of expression" in our society. The "real world," he points out, "is to a large extent unconsciously built up on the language habits of the group. . . . We see and hear and otherwise experience very largely as we do because the language habits of our community predispose certain choices of interpretation."[17]

George Orwell has written in his famous essay "Politics and the English Language": "A man may take to drink because he feels himself to be a failure, and then fail all the more completely because he drinks. It is rather the same thing that is happening to the English language. It becomes ugly and inaccurate because our thoughts are foolish, but the slovenliness of our language makes it easier for us to have foolish thoughts."[18] Orwell maintains that "the decadence in our language is probably curable" and that "silly words and expressions have often disappeared, not through any evolutionary process but owing to the conscious action of a minority."[19] Wilma Scott Heide, speaking as president of the National Organization for Women several years ago, indicated that feminists were undertaking this conscious action: "In any social movement, when changes are effected, the language sooner or later reflects the change. Our approach is different. Instead of passively noting the change, we are changing language patterns to actively effect the changes, a significant part of which is the conceptual tool of thought, our language."[20]

This then is our task — to identify the decadence in our language, the inhumane uses of language, the "silly words and expressions" which have been used to justify the unjustifiable, to make palatable the unpalatable, to make reasonable the unreasonable, to make decent the indecent. Hitler's "Final Solution" appeared reasonable once the Jews were successfully labeled by the Nazis as sub-humans, as "parasites," "vermin," and "bacilli." The segregation and suppression of blacks in the United States was justified once they were considered "chattels" and "inferiors." The subjugation of the "American Indians" was defensible since they were defined as "barbarians" and "savages." As Peter Farb has said, "cannibalism, torture, scalping, mutilation, adultery , incest, sodomy, rape, filth, drunkenness — such a catalogue of accusations against a people is an indication not so much of their depravity as that their land is up for grabs."[21] As long as adult women are "chicks," "girls," "dolls," "babes," and "ladies," their status in society

[17]Cited in John Carroll (ed.), *Language, Thought and Reality: Selected Writings of Benjamin Lee Whorf* (Cambridge, Mass.: The M.I.T. Press, 1956), p. 134. — BOSMAJIAN'S NOTE.

[18]George Orwell, "Politics and the English Language," in C. Muscatine and M. Griffith, *The Borzoi College Reader,* 2nd ed. (New York: Alfred A. Knopf, 1971), p. 88. — BOSMAJIAN'S NOTE.

[19]*Ibid.* — BOSMAJIAN'S NOTE.

[20]Wilma Scott Heide, "Feminism: The *sine qua non* for a Just Society," *Vital Speeches,* 38 (1971–72), p. 402. — BOSMAJIAN'S NOTE.

[21]Peter Farb, "Indian Corn," *The New York Review,* 17 (December 16, 1971), p. 36. — BOSMAJIAN'S NOTE.

will remain "inferior"; they will go on being treated as subjects in the subject-master relationship as long as the language of the law places them into the same class as children, minors, and the insane.

It is my hope that an examination of the language of oppression will result in a conscious effort by the reader to help cure this decadence in our language, especially that language which leads to dehumanization of the human being. One way for us to curtail the use of the language of oppression is for those who find themselves being defined into subjugation to rebel against such linguistic suppression. It isn't strange that those persons who insist on defining themselves, who insist on this elemental privilege of self-naming, self-definition, and self-identity encounter vigorous resistance. Predictably, the resistance usually comes from the oppressor or would-be oppressor and is a result of the fact that he or she does not want to relinquish the power which comes from the ability to define others.

1974

The Reader's Presence

1. Early in the first paragraph of "The Language of Oppression," Haig A. Bosmajian announces: "The importance, significance, and ramifications of naming and defining people cannot be over-emphasized." Bosmajian creates here the expectation that his essay will have a three-part structure. As you reread the essay, demonstrate when and how he does (or does not) fulfill these expectations. What distinctions can you draw between the words *importance* and *significance*? Explain why these distinctions are important (and/or significant) to the ramifications of his essay.

2. Bosmajian offers a series of illustrations for each of the definitions and points he articulates. One measure of his — and any other writer's — interest in a subject is the number of examples he provides to support each of his points. Given this criterion, does Bosmajian seem more interested in what he calls "the language of white racism" or in "our sexist language"? Consider, too, the sequence in which he presents his examples. What are the implications of the order he creates in the sequence of examples in paragraph 9? What more general point about being "separated" does he make through using these examples?

3. What would you identify to be Bosmajian's overall purpose in writing this essay? Where does he announce that purpose most clearly and succinctly? What plan or course of action does he propose that his readers adopt, as he says, "to help cure this decadence in our language, especially that language which leads to dehumanization of the human being" (paragraph 23)? In this respect, how would you characterize the tone of his appeal? Of his essay more generally?

28 ⎯⎯⎯⎯⎯⎯⎯⎯⎯⎯⎯⎯⎯⎯⎯⎯⎯

Amy Cunningham

Why Women Smile

After smiling brilliantly for nearly four decades, I now find myself trying to quit. Or, at the very least, seeking to lower the wattage a bit.

Not everyone I know is keen on this. My smile has gleamed like a cheap plastic night-light so long and so reliably that certain friends and relatives worry that my mood will darken the moment my smile dims. "Gee," one says, "I associate you with your smile. It's the essence of you. I should think you'd want to smile more!" But the people who love me best agree that my smile — which springs forth no matter where I am or how I feel — hasn't been serving me well. Said my husband recently, "Your smiling face and unthreatening demeanor make people like you in a fuzzy way, but that doesn't seem to be what you're after these days."

Smiles are not the small and innocuous things they appear to be: Too many of us smile in lieu of showing what's really on our minds. Indeed, the success of the women's movement might be measured by the sincerity — and lack of it — in our smiles. Despite all the work we American women have done to get and maintain full legal control of our bodies, not to mention our destinies, we still don't seem to be fully in charge of a couple of small muscle groups in our faces.

We smile so often and so promiscuously — when we're angry, when we're tense, when we're with children, when we're being photographed, when we're interviewing for a job, when we're meeting candidates to employ — that the Smiling Woman has become a peculiarly American archetype. This isn't entirely a bad thing, of course. A smile lightens the load, diffuses unpleasantness, redistributes nervous tension. Women doctors smile more than their male counterparts, studies show, and are better liked by their patients.

Oscar Wilde's old saw that "a woman's face is her work of fiction" is 5

For biographical information on Amy Cunningham, see p. 646.

often quoted to remind us that what's on the surface may have little connection to what we're feeling. What is it in our culture that keeps our smiles on automatic pilot? The behavior seems to be an equal blend of nature and nurture. Research has demonstrated that since females often mature earlier than males and are less irritable, girls smile more than boys from the very beginning. But by adolescence, the differences in the smiling rates of boys and girls are so robust that it's clear the culture has done more than its share of the dirty work. Just think of the mothers who painstakingly embroidered the words ENTER SMILING on little samplers, and then hung their handiwork on doors by golden chains. Translation: "Your real emotions aren't welcome here."

Clearly, our instincts are another factor. Our smiles have their roots in the greetings of monkeys, who pull their lips up and back to show their fear of attack, as well as their reluctance to vie for a position of dominance. And like the opossum caught in the light by the clattering garbage cans, we, too, flash toothy grimaces when we make major mistakes. By declaring ourselves nonthreatening, our smiles provide an extremely versatile means of protection.

Our earliest baby smiles are involuntary reflexes having only the vaguest connection to contentment or comfort. In short, we're genetically wired to pull on our parents' heartstrings. As Desmond Morris explains in *Babywatching,* this is our way of attaching ourselves to our caretakers, as truly as baby chimps clench their mothers' fur. Even as babies we're capable of projecting onto others (in this case, our parents) the feelings we know we need to get back in return.

Bona fide social smiles occur at two-and-a-half to three months of age, usually a few weeks after we first start gazing with intense interest into the faces of our parents. By the time we are six months old, we are smiling and laughing regularly in reaction to tickling, feedings, blown raspberries, hugs, and peekaboo games. Even babies who are born blind intuitively know how to react to pleasurable changes with a smile, though their first smiles start later than those of sighted children.

Psychologists and psychiatrists have noted that babies also smile and laugh with relief when they realize that something they thought might be dangerous is not dangerous after all. Kids begin to invite their parents to indulge them with "scary" approach-avoidance games; they love to be chased or tossed up into the air. (It's interesting to note that as adults, we go through the same gosh-that's-shocking-and-dangerous-but-it's-okay-to-laugh-and-smile cycles when we listen to raunchy stand-up comics.)

From the wilds of New Guinea to the sidewalks of New York, smiles   10 are associated with joy, relief, and amusement. But smiles are by no means limited to the expression of positive emotions: People of many different cultures smile when they are frightened, embarrassed, angry, or miserable. In Japan, for instance, a smile is often used to hide pain or sorrow.

Psychologist Paul Ekman, the head of the University of California's

Human Interaction Lab in San Francisco, has identified 18 distinct types of smiles, including those that show misery, compliance, fear, and contempt. The smile of true merriment, which Dr. Ekman calls the Duchenne Smile, after the 19th century French doctor who first studied it, is characterized by heightened circulation, a feeling of exhilaration, and the employment of two major facial muscles: the zygomaticus major of the lower face, and the orbicularis oculi, which crinkles the skin around the eyes. But since the average American woman's smile often has less to do with her actual state of happiness than it does with the social pressure to smile no matter what, her baseline social smile isn't apt to be a felt expression that engages the eyes like this. Ekman insists that if people learned to read smiles, they could see the sadness, misery, or pain lurking there, plain as day.

Evidently, a woman's happy, willing deference is something the world wants visibly demonstrated. Woe to the waitress, the personal assistant or receptionist, the flight attendant, or any other woman in the line of public service whose smile is not offered up to the boss or client as proof that there are no storm clouds — no kids to support, no sleep that's been missed — rolling into the sunny workplace landscape. Women are expected to smile no matter where they line up on the social, cultural, or economic ladder: College professors are criticized for not smiling, political spouses are pilloried for being too serious, and women's roles in films have historically been smiling ones. It's little wonder that men on the street still call out, "Hey, baby, smile! Life's not *that* bad, is it?" to women passing by, lost in thought.

A friend remembers being pulled aside by a teacher after class and asked, "What is wrong, dear? You sat there for the whole hour looking so sad!" "All I could figure," my friends says now, "is that I wasn't smiling. And the fact that *she* felt sorry for me for looking normal made me feel horrible."

Ironically, the social laws that govern our smiles have completely reversed themselves over the last 2,000 years. Women weren't always expected to seem animated and responsive; in fact, immoderate laughter was once considered one of the more conspicuous vices a woman could have, and mirth was downright sinful. Women were kept apart, in some cultures even veiled, so that they couldn't perpetuate Eve's seductive, evil work. The only smile deemed appropriate on a privileged woman's face was the serene, inward smile of the Virgin Mary at Christ's birth, and even that expression was best directed exclusively at young children. Cackling laughter and wicked glee were the kinds of sounds heard only in hell.

What we know of women's facial expressions in other centuries comes 15 mostly from religious writings, codes of etiquette, and portrait paintings. In 15th century Italy, it was customary for artists to paint lovely, blank-faced women in profile. A viewer could stare endlessly at such a woman, but she could not gaze back. By the Renaissance, male artists were taking some pleasure in depicting women with a semblance of complexity, Leonardo da

Vinci's Mona Lisa, with her veiled enigmatic smile, being the most famous example.

The Golden Age of the Dutch Republic marks a fascinating period for studying women's facial expressions. While we might expect the drunken young whores of Amsterdam to smile devilishly (unbridled sexuality and lasciviousness were *supposed* to addle the brain), it's the faces of the Dutch women from fine families that surprise us. Considered socially more free, these women demonstrate a fuller range of facial expressions than their European sisters. Frans Hals's 1622 portrait of Stephanus Geraerdt and Isabella Coymans, a married couple, is remarkable not just for the full, friendly smiles on each face, but for the frank and mutual pleasure the couple take in each other.

In the 1800s, sprightly, pretty women began appearing in advertisements for everything from beverages to those newfangled Kodak Land cameras. Women's faces were no longer impassive, and their willingness to bestow status, to offer, proffer, and yield, was most definitely promoted by their smiling images. The culture appeared to have turned the smile, originally a bond shared between intimates, into a socially required display that sold capitalist ideology as well as kitchen appliances. And female viewers soon began to emulate these highly idealized pictures. Many longed to be more like her, that perpetually smiling female. She seemed so beautiful. So content. So whole.

By the middle of the 19th century, the bulk of America's smile burden was falling primarily to women and African-American slaves, providing a very portable means of protection, a way of saying, "I'm harmless. I won't assert myself here." It reassured those in power to see signs of gratitude and contentment in the faces of subordinates. As long ago as 1963, adman David Ogilvy declared the image of a woman smiling approvingly at a product clichéd, but we've yet to get the message. Cheerful Americans still appear in ads today, smiling somewhat less disingenuously than they smiled during the middle of the century, but smiling broadly nonetheless.

Other countries have been somewhat reluctant to import our "Don't worry, be happy" American smiles. When McDonald's opened in Moscow not long ago and when EuroDisney debuted in France last year, the Americans involved in both business ventures complained that they couldn't get the natives they'd employed to smile worth a damn.

Europeans visiting the United States for the first time are often surprised at just how often Americans smile. But when you look at our history, the relentless good humor (or, at any rate, the pretense of it) falls into perspective. The American wilderness was developed on the assumption that this country had a shortage of people in relation to its possibilities. In countries with a more rigid class structure or caste system, fewer people are as captivated by the idea of quickly winning friends and influencing people. Here in the States, however, every stranger is a potential associate. Our smiles bring new people on board. The American smile is a democratic version of a curtsy or doffed hat, since, in this land of free equals, we're not especially formal about the ways we greet social superiors.

The civil rights movement never addressed the smile burden by name, but activists worked on their own to set new facial norms. African-American males stopped smiling on the streets in the 1960s, happily aware of the unsettling effect this action had on the white population. The image of the simpleminded, smiling, white-toothed black was rejected as blatantly racist, and it gradually retreated into the distance. However, like the women of Sparta and the wives of samurai, who were expected to look happy upon learning their sons or husbands had died in battle, contemporary American women have yet to unilaterally declare their faces their own property.

For instance, imagine a woman at a morning business meeting being asked if she could make a spontaneous and concise summation of a complicated project she's been struggling to get under control for months. She might draw the end of her mouth back and clench her teeth — *Eek!* — in a protective response, a polite, restrained expression of her surprise, not unlike the expression of a conscientious young schoolgirl being told to get out paper and pencil for a pop quiz. At the same time, the woman might be feeling resentful of the supervisor who sprang the request, but she fears taking that person on. So she holds back a comment. The whole performance resolves in a weird grin collapsing into a nervous smile that conveys discomfort and unpreparedness. A pointed remark by way of explanation or self-defense might've worked better for her — but her mouth was otherwise engaged.

We'd do well to realize just how much our smiles misrepresent us, and swear off for good the self-deprecating grins and ritual displays of deference. Real smiles have beneficial physiological effects, according to Paul Ekman. False ones do nothing for us at all.

"Smiles are as important as sound bites on television," insists producer and media coach Heidi Berenson, who has worked with many of Washington's most famous faces. "And women have always been better at understanding this than men. But the smile I'm talking about is not a cutesy smile. It's an authoritative smile. A genuine smile. Properly timed, it's tremendously powerful."

To limit a woman to one expression is like editing down an orchestra 25
to one instrument. And the search for more authentic means of expression isn't easy in a culture in which women are still expected to be magnanimous smilers, helpmates in crisis, and curators of everybody else's morale. But change is already floating in the high winds. We see a boon in assertive female comedians who are proving that women can *dish out* smiles, not just wear them. Actress Demi Moore has stated that she doesn't like to take smiling roles. Nike is running ads that show unsmiling women athletes sweating, reaching, pushing themselves. These women aren't overly concerned with issues of rapport; they're not being "nice" girls — they're working out.

If a woman's smile were truly her own, to be smiled or not, according to how the *woman* felt, rather than according to what someone else needed, she would smile more spontaneously, without ulterior, hidden motives. As Rainer Maria Rilke wrote in *The Journal of My Other Self,* "Her smile was not meant to be seen by anyone and served its whole purpose in being smiled."

That smile is my long-term aim. In the meantime, I hope to stabilize on the smile continuum somewhere between the eliciting grin of Farrah Fawcett and the haughty smirk of Jeane Kirkpatrick.

1993

The Reader's Presence

1. Amy Cunningham presents an informative precis of the causes and effects of smiling in Western culture. Consider the points of view from which she addresses this subject. Summarize and evaluate her treatment of smiling from a psychological, physiological, sociological, and historical point of view. Which do you find most incisive? Why? What other points of view does she introduce into her discussion of smiling? What effects do they create? What does she identify as the benefits (and the disadvantages) of smiling?

2. At what point in this essay does Cunningham address the issue of gender? Characterize the language she uses to introduce this issue. She proceeds to draw a series of distinctions between the different patterns — and the consequences — of men and women who smile. Summarize these differences and assess the nature and the extent of the evidence she provides to validate each of her points. What more general distinctions does she make about various kinds of smiles? What are their different purposes and degrees of intensity? What information does she provide about smiling as an issue of nationality and race? What is the overall purpose of this essay? Where — and how — does Cunningham create and sustain a sense of her own presence in this essay? What does she set as her personal goal in relation to smiling?

3. Cunningham presents an explanation of the causes of an activity that few of her readers think of in either scientific or historical terms. How does her audience's knowledgeability affect the nature of the metaphors and diction she uses? Point to specific words and phrases to support and develop your point. What principles of organization does she rely on to create a sequence and structure for her essay? Comment on her use of the element of surprise in her essay — in terms of the structure, metaphors, and diction she uses to make her points.

29

Annie Dillard

Seeing

When I was six or seven years old, growing up in Pittsburgh, I used to take a precious penny of my own and hide it for someone else to find. It was a curious compulsion; sadly, I've never been seized by it since. For some reason I always "hid" the penny along the same stretch of sidewalk up the street. I would cradle it at the roots of a sycamore, say, or in a hole left by a chipped-off piece of sidewalk. Then I would take a piece of chalk, and, starting at either end of the block, draw huge arrows leading up to the penny from both directions. After I learned to write I labeled the arrows: SURPRISE AHEAD or MONEY THIS WAY. I was greatly excited, during all this arrow-drawing, at the thought of the first lucky passer-by who would receive in this way, regardless of merit, a free gift from the universe. But I never lurked about. I would go straight home and not give the matter another thought, until, some months later, I would be gripped again by the impulse to hide another penny.

It is still the first week in January, and I've got great plans. I've been thinking about seeing. There are lots of things to see, unwrapped gifts and free surprises. The world is fairly studded and strewn with pennies cast broadside from a generous hand. But — and this is the point — who gets excited by a mere penny? If you follow one arrow, if you crouch motionless on a bank to watch a tremulous ripple thrill on the water and are rewarded by the sight of a muskrat kit paddling from its den, will you count that sight a chip of copper only, and go your rueful way? It is dire poverty indeed when a man is so malnourished and fatigued that he won't stoop to pick up a penny. But if you cultivate a healthy poverty and simplicity, so that finding a penny will literally make your day, then, since the world is in fact planted in pennies, you have with your poverty bought a lifetime of days. It is that simple. What you see is what you get.

For biographical information on Annie Dillard, see p. 646.

I used to be able to see flying insects in the air. I'd look ahead and see, not the row of hemlocks across the road, but the air in front of it. My eyes would focus along that column of air, picking out flying insects. But I lost interest, I guess, for I dropped the habit. Now I can see birds. Probably some people can look at the grass at their feet and discover all the crawling creatures. I would like to know grasses and sedges — and care. Then my least journey into the world would be a field trip, a series of happy recognitions. Thoreau, in an expansive mood, exulted, "What a rich book might be made about buds, including, perhaps, sprouts!" It would be nice to think so. I cherish mental images I have of three perfectly happy people. One collects stones. Another — an Englishman, say — watches clouds. The third lives on a coast and collects drops of seawater which he examines microscopically and mounts. But I don't see what the specialist sees, and so I cut myself off, not only from the total picture, but from the various forms of happiness.

Unfortunately, nature is very much a now-you-see-it, now-you-don't affair. A fish flashes, then dissolves in the water before my eyes like so much salt. Deer apparently ascend bodily into heaven; the brightest oriole fades into leaves. These disappearances stun me into stillness and concentration; they say of nature that it conceals with a grand nonchalance, and they say of vision that it is a deliberate gift, the revelation of a dancer who for my eyes only flings away her seven veils. For nature does reveal as well as conceal: now-you-don't-see-it, now-you-do. For a week last September migrating red-winged blackbirds were feeding heavily down by the creek at the back of the house. One day I went out to investigate the racket; I walked up to a tree, an Osage orange, and a hundred birds flew away. They simply materialized out of the tree. I saw a tree, then a whisk of color, then a tree again. I walked closer and another hundred blackbirds took flight. Not a branch, not a twig budged: The birds were apparently weightless as well as invisible. Or, it was as if the leaves of the Osage orange had been freed from a spell in the form of red-winged blackbirds; they flew from the tree, caught my eye in the sky, and vanished. When I looked again at the tree the leaves had reassembled as if nothing had happened. Finally I walked directly to the trunk of the tree and a final hundred, the real diehards, appeared, spread, and vanished. How could so many hide in the tree without my seeing them? The Osage orange, unruffled, looked just as it had looked from the house, when three hundred red-winged blackbirds cried from its crown. I looked downstream where they flew, and they were gone. Searching, I couldn't spot one. I wandered downstream to force them to play their hand, but they'd crossed the creek and scattered. One show to a customer. These appearances catch at my throat; they are the free gifts, the bright coppers at the roots of trees.

It's all a matter of keeping my eyes open. Nature is like one of those 5 line drawings of a tree that are puzzles for children: Can you find hidden in the leaves a duck, a house, a boy, a bucket, a zebra, and a boot? Specialists can find the most incredibly well-hidden things. A book I read when I was young recommended an easy way to find caterpillars to rear: You simply find some fresh caterpillar droppings, look up, and there's your caterpillar. More recently an author advised me to set my mind at ease about those piles of cut stems on the ground in grassy fields. Field mice make them; they cut the grass down by degrees to reach the seeds at the head. It seems that when the grass is tightly packed, as in a field of ripe grain, the blade won't topple at a single cut through the stem; instead, the cut stem simply drops vertically, held in the crush of grain. The mouse severs the bottom again and again, the stem keeps dropping an inch at a time, and finally the head is low enough for the mouse to reach the seeds. Meanwhile, the mouse is positively littering the field with its little piles of cut stems into which, presumably, the author of the book is constantly stumbling.

If I can't see these minutiae, I still try to keep my eyes open. I'm always on the lookout for antlion traps in sandy soil, monarch pupae near milkweed, skipper larvae in locust leaves. These things are utterly common, and I've not seen one. I bang on hollow trees near water, but so far no flying squirrels have appeared. In flat country I watch every sunset in hopes of seeing the green ray. The green ray is a seldom-seen streak of light that rises from the sun like a spurting fountain at the moment of sunset; it throbs into the sky for two seconds and disappears. One more reason to keep my eyes open. A photography professor at the University of Florida just happened to see a bird die in midflight; it jerked, died, dropped, and smashed on the ground. I squint at the wind because I read Stewart Edward White: "I have always maintained that if you looked closely enough you could *see* the wind — the dim, hardly-made-out, fine débris fleeing high in the air." White was an excellent observer, and devoted an entire chapter of *The Mountains* to the subject of seeing deer: "As soon as you can forget the naturally obvious and construct an artificial obvious, then you too will see deer."

But the artificial obvious is hard to see. My eyes account for less than one percent of the weight of my head; I'm bony and dense; I see what I expect. I once spent a full three minutes looking at a bullfrog that was so unexpectedly large I couldn't see it even though a dozen enthusiastic campers were shouting directions. Finally I asked, "What color am I looking for?" and a fellow said, "Green." When at last I picked out the frog, I saw what painters are up against: The thing wasn't green at all, but the color of wet hickory bark.

The lover can see, and the knowledgeable. I visited an aunt and uncle at a quarter-horse ranch in Cody, Wyoming. I couldn't do much of anything useful, but I could, I thought, draw. So, as we all sat around the kitchen table after supper, I produced a sheet of paper and drew a horse. "That's one lame horse," my aunt volunteered. The rest of the family joined in: "Only place to saddle that one is his neck"; "Looks like we better shoot the poor thing, on account of those terrible growths." Meekly, I slid the pencil and paper down the table. Everyone in that family, including my three young cousins, could draw a horse. Beautifully. When the paper came back it looked as though five shining, real quarter horses had been corralled by mistake with a papier-mâché moose; the real horses seemed to gaze at the monster with a steady, puzzled air. I stay away from horses now, but I can do a creditable goldfish. The point is that I just don't know what the lover knows; I just can't see the artificial obvious that those in the know construct. The herpetologist asks the native, "Are there snakes in that ravine?" "Nosir." And the herpetologist comes home with, yessir, three bags full. Are there butterflies on that mountain? Are the bluets in bloom, are there arrowheads here, or fossil shells in the shale?

Peeping through my keyhole I see within the range of only about thirty percent of the light that comes from the sun; the rest is infrared and some little ultraviolet, perfectly apparent to many animals, but invisible to me. A nightmare network of ganglia, charged and firing without my knowledge, cuts and splices what I do see, editing it for my brain. Donald E. Carr points out that the sense impressions of one-celled animals are *not* edited for the brain: "This is philosophically interesting in a rather mournful way, since it means that only the simplest animals perceive the universe as it is."

A fog that won't burn away drifts and flows across my field of vision.   10 When you see fog move against a backdrop of deep pines, you don't see the fog itself, but streaks of clearness floating across the air in dark shreds. So I see only tatters of clearness through a pervading obscurity. I can't distinguish the fog from the overcast sky; I can't be sure if the light is direct or reflected. Everywhere darkness and the presence of the unseen appalls. We estimate now that only one atom dances alone in every cubic meter of intergalactic space. I blink and squint. What planet or power yanks Halley's Comet out of orbit? We haven't seen that force yet; it's a question of distance, density, and the pallor of reflected light. We rock, cradled in the swaddling band of darkness. Even the simple darkness of night whispers suggestions to the mind. Last summer, in August, I stayed at the creek too late.

Where Tinker Creek flows under the sycamore log bridge to the tear-shaped island, it is slow and shallow, fringed thinly in cattail marsh. At this spot an astonishing bloom of life supports vast breeding populations of insects, fish, reptiles, birds, and mammals. On windless summer evenings I stalk along the creek bank or straddle the sycamore log in absolute stillness, watching for muskrats. The night I stayed too late I was hunched on the log staring spellbound at spreading, reflected stains of lilac on the water. A cloud in the sky suddenly lighted as if turned on by a switch; its reflection just as suddenly materialized on the water upstream, flat and floating, so that I couldn't see the creek bottom, or life in the water under the cloud. Downstream, away from the cloud on the water, water turtles smooth as beans were gliding down with the current in a series of easy, weightless push-offs, as men bound on the moon. I didn't know whether to trace the progress of one turtle I was sure of, risking sticking my face in one of the bridge's spider webs made invisibly by the gathering dark, or take a chance on seeing the carp, or scan the mudbank in hope of seeing a muskrat, or follow the last of the swallows who caught at my heart and trailed it after them like streamers as they appeared from directly below, under the log, flying upstream with the tails forked, so fast.

But the shadows spread, and deepened, and stayed. After thousands of years we're still strangers to darkness, fearful aliens in an enemy camp with our arms crossed over our chests. I stirred. A land turtle on the bank, startled, hissed the air from its lungs and withdrew into its shell. An uneasy pink here, an unfathomable blue there, gave great suggestion of lurking beings. Things were going on. I couldn't see whether that sere rustle I heard was a distant rattlesnake, slit-eyed, or a nearby sparrow kicking in the dry flood debris slung at the foot of a willow. Tremendous action roiled the water everywhere I looked, big action, inexplicable. A tremor welled up beside a gaping muskrat burrow in the bank and I caught my breath, but no muskrat appeared. The ripples continued to fan upstream with a steady, powerful thrust. Night was knitting over my face an eyeless mask, and I still sat transfixed. A distant airplane, a delta wing out of nightmare, made a gliding shadow on the creek's bottom that looked like a stingray cruising upstream. At once a black fin slit the pink cloud on the water, shearing it in two. The two halves merged together and seemed to dissolve before my eyes. Darkness pooled in the cleft of the creek and rose, as water collects in a well. Untamed, dreaming lights flickered over the sky. I saw hints of hulking underwater shadows, two pale splashes out of the water, and round ripples rolling close together from a blackened center.

At last I stared upstream where only the deepest violet remained of the cloud, a cloud so high its underbelly still glowed feeble color reflected from a hidden sky lighted in turn by a sun halfway to China. And out of that violet, a sudden enormous black body arced over the water. I saw only a cylindrical sleekness. Head and tail, if there was a head and tail, were both submerged in cloud. I saw only one ebony fling, a headlong dive to darkness; then the waters closed, and the lights went out.

I walked home in a shivering daze, up hill and down. Later I lay open-mouthed in bed, my arms flung wide at my sides to steady the whirling darkness. At this latitude I'm spinning 836 miles an hour round the earth's axis; I often fancy I feel my sweeping fall as a breakneck arc like the dive of dolphins, and the hollow rushing of wind raises hair on my neck and the side of my face. In orbit around the sun I'm moving 64,800 miles an hour. The solar system as a whole, like a merry-go-round unhinged, spins, bobs, and blinks at the speed of 43,200 miles an hour along a course set east of Hercules. Someone has piped, and we are dancing a tarantella until the sweat pours. I open my eyes and I see dark, muscled forms curl out of water, with flapping gills and flattened eyes. I close my eyes and I see stars, deep stars giving way to deeper stars, deeper stars bowing to deepest stars at the crown of an infinite cone.

"Still," wrote van Gogh in a letter, "a great deal of light falls on every-   15
thing." If we are blinded by darkness, we are also blinded by light. When too much light falls on everything, a special terror results. Peter Freuchen describes the notorious kayak sickness to which Greenland Eskimos are

prone. "The Greenland fjords are peculiar for the spells of completely quiet weather, when there is not enough wind to blow out a match and the water is like a sheet of glass. The kayak hunter must sit in his boat without stirring a finger so as not to scare the shy seals away. . . . The sun, low in the sky, sends a glare into his eyes, and the landscape around moves into the realm of the unreal. The reflex from the mirror-like water hypnotizes him, he seems to be unable to move, and all of a sudden it is as if he were floating in a bottomless void, sinking, sinking, and sinking. . . . Horror-stricken, he tries to stir, to cry out, but he cannot, he is completely paralyzed, he just falls and falls." Some hunters are especially cursed with this panic, and bring ruin and sometimes starvation to their families.

Sometimes here in Virginia at sunset low clouds on the southern or northern horizon are completely invisible in the lighted sky. I only know one is there because I can see its reflection in still water. The first time I discovered this mystery I looked from cloud to no-cloud in bewilderment, checking my bearings over and over, thinking maybe the ark of the covenant was just passing by south of Dead Man Mountain. Only much later did I read the explanation: Polarized light from the sky is very much weakened by reflection, but the light in clouds isn't polarized. So invisible clouds pass among visible clouds, till all slide over the mountains; so a greater light extinguishes a lesser as though it didn't exist.

In the great meteor shower of August, the Perseid, I wail all day for the shooting stars I miss. They're out there showering down, committing hara-kiri in a flame of fatal attraction, and hissing perhaps at last into the ocean. But at dawn what looks like a blue dome clamps down over me like a lid on a pot. The stars and planets could smash and I'd never know. Only a piece of ashen moon occasionally climbs up or down the inside of the dome, and our local star without surcease explodes on our heads. We have really only that one light, one source for all power, and yet we must turn away from it by universal decree. Nobody here on the planet seems aware of this strange, powerful taboo, that we all walk about carefully averting our faces, this way and that, lest our eyes be blasted forever.

Darkness appalls and light dazzles; the scrap of visible light that doesn't hurt my eyes hurts my brain. What I see sets me swaying. Size and distance and the sudden swelling of meanings confuse me, bowl me over. I straddle the sycamore log bridge over Tinker Creek in the summer. I look at the lighted creek bottom: Snail tracks tunnel the mud in quavering curves. A crayfish jerks, but by the time I absorb what has happened, he's gone in a billowing smokescreen of silt. I look at the water: minnows and shiners. If I'm thinking minnows, a carp will fill my brain till I scream. I look at the water's surface: skaters, bubbles, and leaves sliding down. Suddenly, my own face, reflected, startles me witless. Those snails have been tracking my face! Finally, with a shuddering wrench of the will, I see clouds, cirrus clouds. I'm dizzy, I fall in. This looking business is risky.

Once I stood on a humped rock on nearby Purgatory Mountain, watching through binoculars the great autumn hawk migration below, until I discovered that I was in danger of joining the hawks on a vertical migration of my own. I was used to binoculars, but not, apparently, to balancing on humped rocks while looking through them. I staggered. Everything advanced and receded by turns; the world was full of unexplained foreshortenings and depths. A distant huge tan object, a hawk the size of an elephant, turned out to be the browned bough of a nearby loblolly pine. I followed a sharp-shinned hawk against a featureless sky, rotating my head unawares as it flew, and when I lowered the glass a glimpse of my own looming shoulder sent me staggering. What prevents the men on Palomar from falling, voiceless and blinded, from their tiny, vaulted chairs?

I reel in confusion; I don't understand what I see. With the naked eye I   20 can see two million light-years to the Andromeda galaxy. Often I slop some creek water in a jar and when I get home I dump it in a white china bowl. After the silt settles I return and see tracings of minute snails on the bottom, a planarian or two winding round the rim of water, roundworms shimmying frantically, and finally, when my eyes have adjusted to these dimensions, amoebae. At first the amoebae look like muscae volitantes, those curled moving spots you seem to see in your eyes when you stare at a distant wall. Then I see the amoebae as drops of water congealed, bluish, translucent, like chips of sky in the bowl. At length I choose one individual and give myself over to its idea of an evening. I see it dribble a grainy foot before it on its wet, unfathomable way. Do its unedited sense impressions include the fierce focus of my eyes? Shall I take it outside and show it Andromeda, and blow its little endoplasm? I stir the water with a finger, in case it's running out of oxygen. Maybe I should get a tropical aquarium with motorized bubblers and lights, and keep this one for a pet. Yes, it would tell its fissioned descendants, the universe is two feet by five, and if you listen closely you can hear the buzzing music of the spheres.

Oh, it's mysterious lamplit evenings, here in the galaxy, one after the other. It's one of those nights when I wander from window to window, looking for a sign. But I can't see. Terror and a beauty insoluble are a ribband of blue woven into the fringes of garments of things both great and small. No culture explains, no bivouac offers real haven or rest. But it could be that we are not seeing something. Galileo thought comets were an optical illusion. This is fertile ground: Since we are certain that they're not, we can look at what our scientists have been saying with fresh hope. What if there are *really* gleaming, castellated cities hung upside-down over the desert sand? What limpid lakes and cool date palms have our caravans always passed untried? Until, one by one, by the blindest of leaps, we light on the road to these places, we must stumble in darkness and hunger. I turn from the window. I'm blind as a bat, sensing only from every direction the echo of my own thin cries.

I chanced on a wonderful book by Marius von Senden, called *Space and Light.* When Western surgeons discovered how to perform safe cataract operations, they ranged across Europe and America operating on dozens of men and women of all ages who had been blinded by cataracts since

birth. Von Senden collected accounts of such cases; the histories are fascinating. Many doctors had tested their patients' sense perceptions and ideas
of space both before and after the operations. The vast majority of patients,
of both sexes and all ages, had, in von Senden's opinion, no idea of space
whatsoever. Form, distance, and size were so many meaningless syllables.
A patient "had no idea of depth, confusing it with roundness." Before the
operation a doctor would give a blind patient a cube and a sphere; the
patient would tongue it or feel it with his hands, and name it correctly.
After the operation the doctor would show the same objects to the patient
without letting him touch them; now he had no clue whatsoever what he
was seeing. One patient called lemonade "square" because it pricked on his
tongue as a square shape pricked on the touch of his hands. Of another
postoperative patient, the doctor writes, "I have found in her no notion of
size, for example, not even within the narrow limits which she might have
encompassed with the aid of touch. Thus when I asked her to show me
how big her mother was, she did not stretch out her hands, but set her two
index-fingers a few inches apart." Other doctors reported their patients'
own statements to similar effect. "The room he was in . . . he knew to be
but part of the house, yet he could not conceive that the whole house could
look bigger"; "Those who are blind from birth . . . have no real conception
of height or distance. A house that is a mile away is thought of as nearby,
but requiring the taking of a lot of steps. . . . The elevator that whizzes him
up and down gives no more sense of vertical distance than does the train of
horizontal."

For the newly sighted, vision is pure sensation unencumbered by meaning: "The girl went through the experience that we all go through and forget, the moment we are born. She saw, but it did not mean anything but a
lot of different kinds of brightness." Again, "I asked the patient what he
could see; he answered that he saw an extensive field of light, in which
everything appeared dull, confused, and in motion. He could not distinguish objects." Another patient saw "nothing but a confusion of forms and
colours." When a newly sighted girl saw photographs and paintings, she
asked, " 'Why do they put those dark marks all over them?' 'Those aren't
dark marks,' her mother explained, 'those are shadows. That is one of the
ways the eye knows that things have shape. If it were not for shadows
many things would look flat.' 'Well, that's how things do look,' Joan answered, 'Everything looks flat with dark patches.' "

But it is the patients' concepts of space that are most revealing. One
patient, according to his doctor, "practiced his vision in a strange fashion;
thus he takes off one of his boots, throws it some way off in front of him,
and then attempts to gauge the distance at which it lies; he takes a few steps
toward the boot and tries to grasp it; on failing to reach it, he moves on a
step or two and gropes for the boot until he finally gets hold of it." "But
even at this stage, after three weeks' experience of seeing," von Senden goes
on, " 'space,' as he conceives it, ends with visual space, i.e., with color-
patches that happen to bound his view. He does not yet have the notion

that a larger object (a chair) can mask a smaller one (a dog), or that the latter can still be present even though it is not directly seen."

In general the newly sighted see the world as a dazzle of color-patches. 25 They are pleased by the sensation of color, and learn quickly to name the colors, but the rest of seeing is tormentingly difficult. Soon after his operation a patient "generally bumps into one of these color-patches and observes them to be substantial, since they resist him as tactual objects do. In walking about it also strikes him — or can if he pays attention — that he is continually passing in between the colors he sees, that he can go past a visual object, that a part of it then steadily disappears from view; and that in spite of this, however he twists and turns — whether entering the room from the door, for example, or returning back to it — he always has a visual space in front of him. Thus he gradually comes to realize that there is also a space behind him, which he does not see."

The mental effort involved in these reasonings proves overwhelming for many patients. It oppresses them to realize, if they ever do at all, the tremendous size of the world, which they had previously conceived of as something touchingly manageable. It oppresses them to realize that they have been visible to people all along, perhaps unattractively so, without their knowledge or consent. A disheartening number of them refuse to use their new vision, continuing to go over objects with their tongues, and lapsing into apathy and despair. "The child can see, but will not make use of his sight. Only when pressed can he with difficulty be brought to look at objects in his neighborhood; but more than a foot away it is impossible to bestir him to the necessary effort." Of a twenty-one-year-old girl, the doctor relates, "Her unfortunate father, who had hoped for so much from this operation, wrote that his daughter carefully shuts her eyes whenever she wishes to go about the house, especially when she comes to a staircase, and that she is never happier or more at ease than when, by closing her eyelids, she relapses into her former state of total blindness." A fifteen-year-old boy, who was also in love with a girl at the asylum for the blind, finally blurted out, "No, really, I can't stand it any more; I want to be sent back to the asylum again. If things aren't altered, I'll tear my eyes out."

Some do learn to see, especially the young ones. But it changes their lives. One doctor comments on "the rapid and complete loss of that striking and wonderful serenity which is characteristic only of those who have never yet seen." A blind man who learns to see is ashamed of his old habits. He dresses up, grooms himself, and tries to make a good impression. While he was blind he was indifferent to objects unless they were edible; now, "a sifting of values sets in . . . his thoughts and wishes are mightily stirred and some few of the patients are thereby led into dissimulation, envy, theft and fraud."

On the other hand, many newly sighted people speak well of the world, and teach us how dull is our own vision. To one patient, a human hand, unrecognized, is "something bright and then holes." Shown a bunch of grapes, a boy calls out, "It is dark, blue and shiny. . . . It isn't smooth, it

has bumps and hollows." A little girl visits a garden. "She is greatly astonished, and can scarcely be persuaded to answer, stands speechless in front
of the tree, which she only names on taking hold of it, and then as 'the tree
with the lights in it.'" Some delight in their sight and give themselves over
to the visual world. Of a patient just after her bandages were removed, her
doctor writes, "The first things to attract her attention were her own
hands; she looked at them very closely, moved them repeatedly to and fro,
bent and stretched the fingers, and seemed greatly astonished at the sight."
One girl was eager to tell her blind friend that "men do not really look like
trees at all," and astounded to discover that her every visitor had an utterly
different face. Finally, a twenty-two-year-old girl was dazzled by the
world's brightness and kept her eyes shut for two weeks. When at the end
of that time she opened her eyes again, she did not recognize any objects, but,
"the more she now directed her gaze upon everything about her, the more it
could be seen how an expression of gratification and astonishment overspread
her features; she repeatedly exclaimed: 'Oh God! How beautiful!'"

I saw color-patches for weeks after I read this wonderful book. It was
summer; the peaches were ripe in the valley orchards. When I woke in the
morning, color-patches wrapped round my eyes, intricately, leaving not
one unfilled spot. All day long I walked among shifting color-patches that
parted before me like the Red Sea and closed again in silence, transfigured,
wherever I looked back. Some patches swelled and loomed, while others
vanished utterly, and dark marks flitted at random over the whole dazzling
sweep. But I couldn't sustain the illusion of flatness. I've been around for
too long. Form is condemned to an eternal danse macabre with meaning: I
couldn't unpeach the peaches. Nor can I remember ever having seen without understanding; the color-patches of infancy are lost. My brain then
must have been smooth as any balloon. I'm told I reached for the moon;
many babies do. But the color-patches of infancy swelled as meaning filled
them; they arrayed themselves in solemn ranks down distance which un-
rolled and stretched before me like a plain. The moon rocketed away. I live
now in a world of shadows that shape and distance color, a world where
space makes a kind of terrible sense. What gnosticism is this, and what
physics? The fluttering patch I saw in my nursery window — silver and
green and shape-shifting blue — is gone; a row of Lombardy poplars takes
its place, mute, across the distant lawn. That humming oblong creature
pale as light that stole along the walls of my room at night, stretching ex-
hilaratingly around the corners, is gone, too, gone the night I ate of the
bittersweet fruit, put two and two together and puckered forever my brain.
Martin Buber tells this tale: "Rabbi Mendel once boasted to his teacher
Rabbi Elimelekh that evenings he saw the angel who rolls away the light
before the darkness, and mornings the angel who rolls away the darkness
before the light. 'Yes,' said Rabbi Elimelekh, 'in my youth I saw that too.
Later on you don't see these things any more.'"

Why didn't someone hand those newly sighted people paints and 30 brushes from the start, when they still didn't know what anything was? Then maybe we all could see color-patches too, the world unraveled from reason. Eden before Adam gave names. The scales would drop from my eyes; I'd see trees like men walking; I'd run down the road against all orders, hallooing and leaping.

Seeing is of course very much a matter of verbalization. Unless I call my attention to what passes before my eyes, I simply won't see it. It is, as Ruskin says, "not merely unnoticed, but in the full, clear sense of the word, unseen." My eyes alone can't solve analogy tests using figures, the ones which show, with increasing elaborations, a big square, then a small square in a big square, then a big triangle, and expect me to find a small triangle in a big triangle. I have to say the words, describe what I'm seeing. If Tinker Mountain erupted, I'd be likely to notice. But if I want to notice the lesser cataclysms of valley life, I have to maintain in my head a running description of the present. It's not that I'm observant; it's just that I talk too much. Otherwise, especially in a strange place, I'll never know what's happening. Like a blind man at the ball game, I need a radio.

When I see this way I analyze and pry. I hurl over logs and roll away stones; I study the bank a square foot at a time, probing and tilting my head. Some days when a mist covers the mountains, when the muskrats won't show and the microscope's mirror shatters, I want to climb up the blank blue dome as a man would storm the inside of a circus tent, wildly, dangling, and with a steel knife claw a rent in the top, peep, and, if I must, fall.

But there is another kind of seeing that involves a letting go. When I see this way I sway transfixed and emptied. The difference between the two ways of seeing is the difference between walking with and without a camera. When I walk with a camera I walk from shot to shot, reading the light on a calibrated meter. When I walk without a camera, my own shutter opens, and the moment's light prints on my own silver gut. When I see this second way I am above all an unscrupulous observer.

It was sunny one evening last summer at Tinker Creek; the sun was low in the sky, upstream. I was sitting on the sycamore log bridge with the sunset at my back, watching the shiners the size of minnows who were feeding over the muddy sand in skittery schools. Again and again, one fish, then another, turned for a split second across the current and flash! the sun shot out from its silver side. I couldn't watch for it. It was always just happening somewhere else, and it drew my vision just as it disappeared: flash, like a sudden dazzle of the thinnest blade, a sparking over a dun and olive ground at chance intervals from every direction. Then I noticed white specks, some sort of pale petals, small, floating from under my feet on the creek's surface, very slow and steady. So I blurred my eyes and gazed toward the brim of my hat and saw a new world. I saw the pale white circles roll up, roll up, like the world's turning, mute and perfect, and I saw the linear flashes, gleaming silver, like stars being born at random down a rolling scroll of time. Something broke and something opened. I filled up like a new wineskin. I breathed an air like light; I saw a light like water. I was the lip of a fountain the creek filled forever; I was ether, the leaf in the zephyr; I was flesh-flake, feather, bone.

When I see this way I see truly. As Thoreau says, I return to my senses. 35
I am the man who watches the baseball game in silence in an empty stadium. I see the game purely; I'm abstracted and dazed. When it's all over and the white-suited players lope off the green field to their shadowed dugouts, I leap to my feet; I cheer and cheer.

But I can't go out and try to see this way. I'll fail, I'll go mad. All I can do is try to gag the commentator, to hush the noise of useless interior babble that keeps me from seeing just as surely as a newspaper dangled before my eyes. The effort is really a discipline requiring a lifetime of dedicated struggle; it marks the literature of saints and monks of every order East and West, under every rule and no rule, discalced and shod. The world's spiritual geniuses seem to discover universally that the mind's muddy river, this ceaseless flow of trivia and trash, cannot be dammed, and that trying to dam it is a waste of effort that might lead to madness. Instead you must allow the muddy river to flow unheeded in the dim channels of consciousness; you raise your sights; you look along it, mildly, acknowledging its presence without interest and gazing beyond it into the realm of the real where subjects and objects act and rest purely, without utterance. "Launch into the deep," says Jacques Ellul, "and you shall see."

The secret of seeing is, then, the pearl of great price. If I thought he could teach me to find it and keep it forever I would stagger barefoot across a hundred deserts after any lunatic at all. But although the pearl may be found, it may not be sought. The literature of illumination reveals this above all: Although it comes to those who wait for it, it is always, even to the most practiced and adept, a gift and a total surprise. I return from one walk knowing where the killdeer nests in the field by the creek and the hour the laurel blooms. I return from the same walk a day later scarcely knowing my own name. Litanies hum in my ears; my tongue flaps in my mouth Ailinon, alleluia! I cannot cause light; the most I can do is try to put myself in the path of its beam. It is possible, in deep space, to sail on solar wind. Light, be it particle or wave, has force: you rig a giant sail and go. The secret of seeing is to sail on solar wind. Hone and spread your spirit till you yourself are a sail, whetted, translucent, broadside to the merest puff.

When her doctor took her bandages off and led her into the garden, the girl who was no longer blind saw "the tree with the lights in it." It was for this tree I searched through the peach orchards of summer, in the forests of fall and down winter and spring for years. Then one day I was walking along Tinker Creek thinking of nothing at all and I saw the tree with the lights in it. I saw the backyard cedar where the mourning doves roost charged and transfigured, each cell buzzing with flame. I stood on the grass with the lights in it, grass that was wholly fire, utterly focused and utterly dreamed. It was less like seeing than like being for the first time seen, knocked breathless by a powerful glance. The flood of fire abated, but I'm still spending the power. Gradually the lights went out in the cedar, the colors died, the cells unflamed and disappeared. I was still ringing. I had been my whole life a bell, and never knew it until at that moment I was lifted and struck. I have since only very rarely seen the tree with the lights in it. The vision comes and goes, mostly goes, but I live for it, for the moment when the mountains open and a new light roars in spate through the crack, and the mountains slam.

1974

The Reader's Presence

1. In addition to providing a fascinating view of some overlooked aspects of nature, Annie Dillard's essay constitutes a primer on the principles and practices of observation and inference — on seeing and coming to terms with the natural world around us. What principles about how we ought to see the world can you infer from reading this essay? Summarize the information Dillard provides about each of these principles, and show how she puts each principle into practice in her essay. What distinction, for example, does she draw between "seeing" and "observing"? between "the naturally obvious" and "the artificial obvious"? For example, what does she mean when she says: "When I see this way I see truly" (paragraph 35)?

2. Dillard is quite conscious of her readers' presence. How does this interest serve as a commentary on her statement: "Seeing is of course very much a matter of verbalization" (paragraph 31)? What does she mean here? Explain why this principle remains so important to her purpose in writing this essay. How is this statement complicated by what she says later in that same paragraph: "It's not that I'm observant; it's just that I talk too much"? In what specific ways does this sentence characterize the relationship she establishes with her readers and what she would like to see her readers learn from her essay?

3. Much of Dillard's essay is written in the form of first-person narrative. Yet Dillard also manages to convey a great deal of information about seeing and about the natural world. What advantages and disadvantages can you identify that result from this choice? What specific strategies does Dillard use to work in so much information — especially from secondary sources — about seeing and the natural world?

30

Gerald Early

Life with Daughters: Watching the Miss America Pageant

> The theater is an expression of our dream life — of our unconscious aspirations.
>
> — DAVID MAMET, "A Tradition of the Theater as Art,"
> WRITING IN RESTAURANTS

> Aunt Hester went out one night, — where or for what I do not know, — and happened to be absent when my master desired her presence.
>
> — FREDERICK DOUGLASS, NARRATIVE OF THE LIFE OF FREDERICK DOUGLASS

> Adults, older girls, shops, magazines, newspapers, window signs — all the world had agreed that a blue-eyed, yellow-haired, pink-skinned doll was what every girl child treasured.
>
> — TONI MORRISON, THE BLUEST EYE

It is now fast become a tradition, if one can use that word to describe a habit about which I still feel a certain amount of shame-facedness, for our household to watch the Miss America contest on television every year. The source of my embarrassment is that this program remains, despite its attempts in recent years to modernize its frightfully antique quality of "women on parade," a kind of maddeningly barbarous example of the persistent hard, crass urge to sell: from the plugs for the sponsor that are made a part of the script (that being an antique of fifties and sixties television; the show does not remember its history as much as it seems bent on repeating it) to the constant references to the success of some of the previous contes-

For biographical information on Gerald Early, see p. 647.

tants and the reminders that this is some sort of scholarship competition; the program has all the cheap earnestness of a social uplift project being played as a musical revue in Las Vegas. Paradoxically, it wishes to convince the public that it is a common entertainment while simultaneously wishing to convey that it is more than mere entertainment. The Miss America pageant is the worst sort of "Americanism," the soft smile of sex and the hard sell of toothpaste and hair dye ads wrapped in the dreamy ideological gauze of "making it through one's own effort." In a perverse way, I like the show; it is the only live television left other than sports, news broadcasts, performing arts awards programs, and speeches by the president. I miss live TV. It was the closest thing to theater for the masses. And the Miss America contest is, as it has been for some time, the most perfectly rendered theater in our culture, for it so perfectly captures what we yearn for: a low-class ritual, a polished restatement of vulgarity, that wants to open the door to high-class respectability by way of plain middle-class anxiety and ambition. Am I doing all right? the contestants seem to ask in a kind of reassuring, if numbed, way. The contest brings together all the American classes in a showbiz spectacle of classlessness and tastelessness.

My wife has been interested in the Miss America contest since childhood, and so I ascribe her uninterrupted engagement with America's cultural passage into fall (Miss America, like college and pro football, signifies for us as a nation, the end of summer; the contest was invented, back in 1921, by Atlantic City merchants to prolong the summer season past Labor Day) as something mystically and uniquely female. She, as a black woman, had a long-standing quarrel with the contest until Vanessa Williams was chosen the first black Miss America, in September 1983. Somehow she felt vindicated by Williams for all those years as a black girl in Dallas, Texas, watching white women win the crown and thumb their noses at her, at her blackness, at her straightened hair, her thick lips, her wide nose. She played with white Barbie dolls as a little girl and had, I suppose, a "natural" or at least an understandable and predictable interest in seeing the National White Barbie Doll chosen every year because for such a long time, of course, the Miss America contest, with few exceptions, was a totemic preoccupation with and representation of a particularly stilted form of patriarchal white supremacy. In short, it was a national white doll contest. And well we know that every black girl growing up in the fifties and early sixties had her peculiar love-hate affair with white dolls, with mythicized white femininity. I am reminded of this historical instance: Everyone knows that in the Brown versus Topeka Board of Education case (the case that resulted in the Supreme Court decision to integrate public schools) part of the sociological evidence used by the plaintiffs to show the psychological damage suffered by blacks because of Jim Crow was an account by Kenneth Clarke of how, when offered a choice between a black doll and a white doll, little black girls invariably chose the white doll because they thought it "prettier."

On the front page of the January 6, 1962, *Pittsburgh Courier,* a black weekly, is a picture of a hospitalized black girl named Connie Smith holding a white doll sent to her by Attorney General Robert Kennedy. Something had occurred between 1954, when the Supreme Court made its decision, and 1962 which made it impossible for Kennedy to send the girl a black doll, and this impossibility was to signal, ironically, that the terms of segregation and the terms of racial integration, the very icon of them, were to be exactly the same. Kennedy could not send the girl a black doll as it would have implied, in the age of integration, that he was, in effect, sending her a Jim Crow toy, a toy that would emphasize the girl's race. In the early sixties such a gesture would have been considered condescending. To give the black girl a white doll in the early sixties was to mainstream the black girl into the culture, to say that she was worthy of the same kind of doll that a white girl would have. But how can it be that conservatism and liberalism, segregation and integration could produce, fantastically, the same results, the identical iconography: a black girl hugging a white doll because everyone thinks it is best for her to have it? How can it be that at one time the white doll is the sign of the black girl's rejection and inferiority and fewer than ten years later it is the sign of her acceptance and redemption? Those who are knowledgeable about certain aspects of the black mind or the collective black consciousness realize, of course, that the issues of segregation and integration, of conservatism and liberalism, of acceptance and rejection, of redemption and inferiority, are all restatements of the same immovable and relentless reality of the meaning of American blackness; that this is all a matter of the harrowing and compelling intensity that is called, quaintly, race pride. And in this context, the issue of white dolls, this fetishization of young white feminine beauty, and the complexity of black girlhood becomes an unresolved theme stated in a strident key. Blacks have preached for a long time about how to heal their daughters of whiteness: In the November 1908 issue of *The Colored American Magazine,* E. A. Johnson wrote an article entitled "Negro Dolls for Negro Babies," in which he said, "I am convinced that one of the best ways to teach Negro children to respect their own color would be to see to it that the children be given colored dolls to play with. . . . To give a Negro child a white doll means to create in it a prejudice against its own color, which will cling to it through life" (583). Lots of black people believed this and, for all I know, probably still do, as race pride, or the lack thereof, burns and crackles like a current through most African-American public and private discourse. Besides, it is no easy matter to wish white dolls away.

A few years ago I was thumbing through an album of old family photographs and saw one of me and my oldest sister taken when I was four and she was nine. It struck me, transfixed me really, as it was a color photo and most of the old family pictures taken when I was a boy were black and white because my mother could not afford to have color pictures developed. We, my sister and I, are sitting on an old stuffed blue chair and she is holding a white doll in her hand, displaying it for the picture. I remember the occasion very well as my sister was to be confirmed in our small, all-black Episcopal church that day and she was, naturally, proud of the moment and wanted to share it with her favorite toy. That, I remembered, was why these were color pictures. It was a very special day for the family, a day my mother wanted to celebrate by taking very special pictures. My mother is a very dark woman who has a great deal of race pride and often speaks about my sisters having black dolls. I was surprised, in looking at the picture recently, that they ever owned a white one, that, indeed, a white one had been a favorite.

My wife grew up, enjoyed the primary years of black girlhood, so to   5 speak, during the years 1954 through 1962; she was about five or six years younger than my oldest sister. She lived in a southern state or a state that was a reasonable facsimile of a southern state. She remembers that signs for colored and white bathrooms and water fountains persisted well into the mid-sixties in Texas. She remembers also Phyllis George, the Miss America from Denton, Texas, who went on to become a television personality for several years. She has always been very interested in George's career and she has always disliked her. "She sounds just like a white girl from Texas," my wife likes to say, always reminding me that while both blacks and whites in Texas have accents, they do not sound alike. George won the contest in 1971, my wife's freshman year at the University of Pennsylvania and around the time she began to wear an Afro, a popular hairstyle for young black women in the days of "our terrible blackness" or "our black terribleness." It was a year fraught with complex passages into black womanhood for her. To think that a white woman from Texas should win the Miss America title that year! For my wife, the years of watching the Miss America contest were nothing more, in some sense continue to be nothing more, than an expression of anger made all the worse by the very unconscious or semi-conscious nature of it. But if the anger has been persistent, so has her enormous capacity to "take it"; for in all these years it has never occurred to her to refuse because, like the black girl being offered the white doll, like all black folk being offered white gifts, she has absolutely no idea how that is done and she is not naive enough to think that a simple refusal would be an act of empowerment. Empowerment comes only through making demands of our bogeymen, not by trying to convince ourselves we are not tormented. Yet, paradoxically, among blacks there is the bitter hope that a simplistic race pride will save us, a creed that masks its complex contradictions beneath lapping waves of bourgeois optimism and bourgeois anguish; for race pride clings to the opposing notions that the great hope (but secret fear) of an African-American future is, first, that blacks will always remain black and, second, that the great fear (but secret hope) of an African-American future is that blacks will not always remain black but evolve into something else. Race pride, which at its most insistent, argues that blackness is everything, becomes, in its attempt to be the psychological quest for sanity, a form of dementia that exists as a response to that form of white dementia that says blackness is nothing. Existing as it does as a reactive force battling against a white preemptive presumption, race pride begins to take on the vices of an unthinking dogma and the virtues of a disciplined religious faith, all in the same instance. With so much at stake, race pride becomes both the act of making a virtue of a necessity and making a necessity of a virtue and, finally, making a profound and touching absurdity of both virtue and necessity. In some ways my wife learned her lessons well in her youth: She never buys our daughters white dolls.

My daughters, Linnet, age ten, and Rosalind, age seven, have become staunch fans of beauty contests in the last three years. In that time they have watched, in their entirety, several Miss America pageants, one Miss Black America contest, and one Miss USA. At first, I ascribed this to the same impulse that made my wife interested in such events when she was little: something secretly female just as an interest in professional sports might be ascribed to something peculiarly male. Probably it is a sort of resentment that black girls harbor toward these contests. But that could not really be the case with my daughters. After all they have seen several black contestants in these contests and have even seen black winners. They also have black dolls.

Back in the fall of 1983 when Vanessa Williams became Miss America, we, as a family, had our picture taken with her when she visited Saint Louis. We went, my wife and I, to celebrate the grand moment when white American popular culture decided to embrace black women as something other than sexual subversives or as fat, kindly maids cleaning up and caring for white families. We had our own, well, royalty, and royal origins mean a great deal to people who have been denied their myths and their right to human blood. White women reformers may be ready to scrap the Miss America contest. (And the contest has certainly responded to the criticism it has been subjected to in recent years by muting some of the fleshier aspects of the program while, in its attempts to be even more the anxiety-ridden middle-class dream-wish, emphasizing more and more the magic of education and scholarly attainments.) It is now the contest that signifies the quest for professionalism among bourgeois women, and the first achievement of the professional career is to win something in a competition. But if there is a movement afoot to bring down the curtain finally on Miss America, my wife wants no part of it: "Whites always want to reform and end things when black people start getting on the gravy train they've been enjoying for years. What harm does the Miss America contest do?" None, I suppose, especially since black women have been winning lately.

Linnet and Rosalind were too young when we met Vanessa Williams to recall anything about the pictures, but they are amazed to see themselves in a bright, color Polaroid picture with a famous person, being part of an event which does not strike a chord in their consciousness, because they cannot remember being alive when it happened. I often wonder if they attach any significance to the pictures at all. They think Vanessa is very pretty, prettier than their mother, but they attach no significance to being pretty, that is to say, no real value; they would not admire someone simply because he or she was good-looking. They think Williams is beautiful, but they do not wish that she was their mother. And this issue of being beautiful is not to be taken lightly in the life of a black girl. About two years ago Linnet started coming home from school wishing aloud that her hair was long and blond so that she could fling it about, the way she saw many of her white classmates doing. As she attends a school that is more than 90 percent white, it seemed inevitable to my wife that one of our daughters would become sensitive about her appearance. At this time Linnet's hair was not straightened and she wore it in braids. Oddly, despite the fact that she wanted a different hairstyle that would permit her hair to "blow in the wind," so to speak, she vehemently opposed having it straightened, although my wife has straightened hair, after having worn an Afro for several years. I am not sure why Linnet did not want her hair straightened; perhaps, after seeing her teenage cousin have her hair straightened on several occasions, the process of hair straightening seemed distasteful or disheartening or frightening. Actually, I do not think Linnet wanted to change her hair to be beautiful; she wanted to be like everyone else. But perhaps this is simply wishful thinking here or playing with words because Linnet must have felt her difference as being a kind of ugliness. Yet she is not a girl who is subject to illusion. Once, about a year earlier, when she had had a particularly rough day in school, I told her, in a father's patronizing way with a daughter, that I thought she was the most beautiful girl in the world. She looked at me strangely when I said that and then replied matter-of-factly: "I don't think I'm beautiful at all. I think I'm just ordinary. There is nothing wrong with that, is there, Daddy? Just to be ordinary?" "Are you unhappy to be ordinary?" I asked. She thought for a moment, then said quietly and finally, "No. Are you?"

Hair straightening, therefore, was not an option and would not have been even if Linnet had wanted it, because my wife was opposed to having Linnet's hair straightened at her age. At first, Linnet began going to school with her hair unbraided. Unfortunately, this turned out to be a disastrous hairdo as her hair shrank during the course of a day to a tangled mess. Finally, my wife decided to have both Linnet and Rosalind get short Afro haircuts. Ostensibly, this was to ease the problem of taking swim lessons during the summer. In reality, it was to end Linnet's wishes for a white hairstyle by, in effect, foreclosing any possibility that she could remotely capture such a look. Rosalind's hair was cut so that Linnet would not feel that she was being singled out. (Alas, the trials of being both the second and the younger child!) At first, the haircuts caused many problems in school. Some of the children — both black and white — made fun of them. Brillo heads, they were called, and fungus and Afro heads. One group of black girls at school refused to play with Linnet. "You look so ugly with that short hair," they would say. "Why don't you wear your hair straight like your mom. You mom's hair is so pretty." Then, for the first time, the girls were called niggers by a white child on their school bus, although I think neither the child nor my daughters completely understood the gravity of that obscenity. People in supermarkets would refer to them as boys unless they were wearing dresses. Both girls went through a period when they suffered most acutely from that particularly American disease, that particularly African-American disease, the conjunction of oppression and exhibitionistic desire: self-consciousness. They thought about their hair all the time. My wife called the parents of the children who teased them. The teasing stopped for the most part, although a few of the black girls remained so persistent that the white school counselor suggested that Linnet and Rosalind's hair be straightened. "I'm white," he said, "and maybe I shouldn't get into this, but they might feel more comfortable if they wore a different hairstyle." My wife angrily rejected that bit of advice. She had them wear dresses more often to make them look unmistakably like girls, although she refused out of hand my suggestion of having their ears pierced. She is convinced that pierced ears are just a form of mutilation, primitive tattooing or scarring, passing itself off as something fashionable. Eventually, the girls became used to their hair. Now, after more than a year, they hardly think about it and even if Linnet wears a sweat suit or jeans, no one thinks she is a boy because she is budding breasts. Poor Rosalind still suffers on occasion in supermarkets because she shows no outward signs of sexual maturity. Once, while watching Linnet look at her mother's very long and silken, straight hair, the hair that the other black girls at school admire, always calling it "pretty," I asked her if she would like to have hers straightened.

"Not now," she said. "Maybe when I'm older. It'll be something different."   10

"Do you think you will like it?" I asked.

"Maybe," she said.

And in that "maybe," so calmly and evenly uttered, rests the complex contradictions, the uneasy tentative negotiations of that which cannot be compromised yet can never be realized in this flawed world as an ideal; there is, in that "maybe," the epistemology of race pride for black American women so paradoxically symbolized by their straightened hair. In the February, 1939, issue of the *Atlantic Monthly*, a black woman named Kimbal Goffman (possibly a pseudonym) wrote an essay entitled "Black Pride" in which she accused blacks of being ashamed of their heritage and, even more damningly in some of her barbs obviously aimed at black women, of their looks:

> . . . why are so many manufacturers becoming rich through the manufacture of bleaching preparations? Why are hair-straightening combs found in nearly every Negro home? Why is the following remark made so often to a newborn baby, when grandma or auntie visits it for the first time? "Tell Mother she must pinch your nose every morning. If she doesn't, you're gonna have a sure 'nough darky nose." (236)

According to Goffman, blacks do not exploit what society has given them; they are simply ashamed to have what they have, tainted as it is with being associated with a degraded people, and long to be white or to have possessions that would accrue a kind of white status. In the essay, blacks in general receive their share of criticism but only black women are criticized in a gender-specific way that their neurotic sense of inferiority concerning physical appearance is a particularly dangerous form of reactionism as it stigmatizes each new generation. According to Goffman, it is black women, because they are mothers, who perpetuate their sense of inferiority by passing it on to their children. In this largely DuBoisian argument, Goffman advises, "Originality is the backbone of all progress." And, in this sense, originality means understanding blackness as something uncontrolled or uninfluenced by what whites say it is. This is the idealism of race pride that demands both purity and parity. Exactly one year later, in the February, 1940, issue of *The Brown American Magazine,* a black publication published in Philadelphia, Lillian Franklin McCall wrote an article about the history of black women beauty shop owners and entrepreneurs entitled "Appointment at Seven." The opening paragraph is filled with dollar signs:

> The business of straightening milady's insistent curls tinkles cash registers in the country to the tune of two million and a half dollars a year. And that covers merely the semimonthly session with the hairdresser for the estimated four million of Eve's sepia adult daughters by national census. Today there is a growing trend to top off the regular, "Shampoo and wave," with a facial; and, perhaps, a manicure. New oil treatments and rinses prove a lure, too, so milady finds her beauty budget stepped up from approximately $39 yearly for an average $1.25 or $1.50 "hair-do," to $52.00 per year if she adds a facial to the beauty rite, and $10 more, for the manicure. (9)

In a Booker T. Washington-tone, McCall goes on to describe how the establishment of a black beauty culture serves as a source of empowerment for black women:

> Brown business it is, in all its magnitude for Miss Brown America receives her treatments from the hands of Negro beauticians and her hair preparations and skin creams come, usually from Negro laboratories.

She then tells the reader that leading companies in this field were founded by black women: Madam C. J. Walker, Mrs. Annie Turbo Malone, Madame Sara Spencer Washington. And one is struck by the absences that this essay evokes, not only in comparison to Goffman's piece but also to Elsie Johnson McDougald's major manifesto on black women, "The Task of Negro Womanhood," that appeared in Alain Locke's seminal 1925 anthology of African-American thought, *The New Negro.* In McDougald's piece, which outlines all the economic status and achievements of black women at the time, there is absolutely no mention of black beauty culture, no mention of Madame C. J. Walker, although her newspaper ads were among the biggest in black newspapers nationwide during the twenties. (And why did McDougald not mention black women's beauty workers and business people-culture along with the nurses, domestics, clerks, and teachers she discusses at length? It can scarcely be because she, as a trained and experienced writer on black sociological matters, did not think of it.[1]) It is not simply money or black woman's industry or endeavor that makes the black woman present or a presence; it is beauty culture generally which finally brings her into being, and specifically, her presence is generated by her hair. What, for one black woman writer, Goffman, is an absence and thus a sign of degradation, is for another a presence and a sign of economic possibilities inherent in feminine aesthetics.

What did I see as a boy when I passed the large black beauty shop on Broad and South streets in Philadelphia where the name of its owner, Adele Reese, commanded such respect or provoked such jealousy? What did I see there but a long row of black women dressed immaculately in white tunics, washing and styling the hair of other black women. That was a sign of what culture, of what set of politics? The sheen of those straightened heads, the entire enterprise of the making of black feminine beauty: Was it an enactment of a degradation inspirited by a bitter inferiority or was it a womanly laying on of hands where black women were, in their way, helping themselves to live through and transcend their degradation? As a boy, I used to watch and wonder as my mother straightened my sisters' hair every Saturday night for church on Sunday morning. Under a low flame on the stove, the hot comb would glow dully; from an opened jar of Apex bergamont hair oil or Dixie Peach, my mother would extract blobs and place them on the back of one hand, deftly applying the oil to strands of my sisters' hair with the other. And the strange talk about a "light press" or a "heavy press" or a "close press" to get the edges and the ends; the concern about the hair "going back" if caught in the rain. Going back where, I wondered. To Africa? To the bush? And the constant worry and vigil about burning, getting too close to the scalp. I can remember hearing my sisters' hair sizzle and crackle as the comb passed through with a kind of pungent smell of actually burning hair. And I, like an intentional moth, with lonely narrow arcs, hovered near this flame of femininity with a fascinated impertinence. Had I witnessed the debilitating nullity of absence or was it the affirmation of an inescapable presence? Had I witnessed a mutilation or a rite of devotion? Black women's hair is, I decided even as a boy, unintelligible. And now I wonder, is the acceptance of the reigns of black women as Miss America a sign that black beauty has become part of the mainstream culture? Is the black woman now truly a presence?

We, I and my wife and our daughters, sat together and watched the latest Miss America contest. We did what we usually do. We ate popcorn. We laughed at all the talent numbers, particularly the ones when the contestants were opera singers or dancers. We laughed when the girls tried to

15

answer grand social questions — such as "How can we inspire children to achieve and stay in school?" or "How can we address the problem of mainstreaming physically disadvantaged people?" in thirty seconds. In fact, as Rosalind told me after the show, the main reason my daughters watch the Miss America pageant is that "it's funny." My daughters laugh because they cannot understand why the women are doing what they are doing, why they are trying so hard to please, to be pleasing. This must certainly be a refreshing bit of sanity, as the only proper response for such a contest is simply to dismiss it as hilarious; this grandiose version of an elocution, charm school, dance and music recital, which is not a revelation of talent but a reaffirmation of bourgeois cultural conditioning. And this bit of sanity on my daughters' part may prove hopeful for our future, for our American future, for our African-American future, if black girls are, unlike my wife when she was young, no longer angry. When it was announced that Miss Missouri, Debbye Turner, the third black to be Miss America, was the winner, my children were indifferent. It hardly mattered to them who won, and a black woman's victory meant no more than if any other contestant had prevailed. "She's pretty," Linnet said. She won two dollars in a bet with my wife who did not think it possible that another black Miss America would be chosen. "Vanessa screwed up for the whole race," she told me once. "It's the race burden, the sins of the one become the original sins of us all." Linnet said simply, "She'll win because she is the best." Meritocracy is still a valid concept with the young.

For me, it was almost to be expected that Miss Turner would win. First she received more pre-contest publicity than any other contestant in recent years with the possible exception of the black woman who was chosen Miss Mississippi a few years ago. Second, after the reign of Vanessa Williams, one would think that the Miss America powers-that-be very much wanted to have another black win and have a successful reign so that the contest itself could prove both its good faith (to blacks) and forestall criticism from white feminists and liberals (who are always put in a difficult position when the object of their disapproval is a black woman). As with the selection of Williams, the contest gained a veneer of postmodernist social and political relevance not only by selecting a black again but by having an Asian, a kidney donor, and a hearing impaired woman among the top ten finalists. This all smacks of affirmative action or the let's-play-fair-with-the-underrepresented doctrine which, as Miss Virginia pointed out after the contest, smacks of politics. But the point she missed, of course, is the point that all people who oppose affirmative action miss. The selection process for the Miss America contest has always been political. Back in the days when only white college women, whose main interest in most instances was a degree in MRS, could win, the contest was indeed just as political as it is now, a clear ideological bow to both patriarchal ideals and racism. It is simply a matter of which politics you prefer, and while no politics are perfect, some are clearly better than others. But in America, it must be added, the doctrine of fair play should not even be graced with such a sophisticated term as *political*. It is more our small-town, bourgeois Christian, muscular myth of ethical rectitude, the tremendous need Americans feel to be decent. So Miss Turner is intended to be both the supersession of Vanessa Williams — a religious vet student whose ambitions are properly, well, postmodernist Victorianism, preach do-goodism, evoke the name of God whenever you speak your ambitions, and live with smug humility — and the redemption of the image of black women in American popular culture since the Miss America contest is one of the few vehicles of display and competition for women in popular culture.

And if my daughters have come to one profound penetration of this cultural rite, it is that the contest ought to be laughed at in some ways, as most of the manifestations of popular culture ought to be for being the shoddy illusions that they are. For one always ought to laugh at someone or a group of someones who are trying to convince you that nothing is something — and that is not really the same as someone trying to convince you that you can have something for nothing, because in the popular culture business, the price for nothing is the same as the price for something; this "nothing is something" is, in fact, in most cases, what the merchandising of popular culture is all about. (But as Mother reminded me as a boy: Nothing is nothing and something is something. Accept no substitutes!) For my children, the contest can be laughed at because it is so completely meaningless to them; they know it is an illusion despite its veneer as a competition. And it is that magical word, *competition,* that is used over and over again all night long by the host and hostesses of the Miss America show (a contest, like most others these days, from the SATs to professional sports, that is made up of a series of competitions within the framework of larger competitions in such a pyramid that the entire structure of the outside world, for the bourgeois mind, is a frightful maze, a strangulating skein of competitions) that is the touchstone of reality, the momentous signifier, that the sponsors of the pageant hope will give this extravaganza new significance and new life. For everything that we feel is important now is a matter of competition, beating out someone else for a prize, for some cheap prestige, a moment of notice before descending to cipherhood again; competition ranging from high culture (literary prizes, which seem to be awarded every day in the week, and classical musical competitions for every instrument in a symphony orchestra, because of course for high culture one can never have enough art) to mid-culture (the entire phenomenon of American education, from academic honors to entrance requirements to enter prestigious schools because, of course, for the middle class one can never have enough education or enough professionalism) to low culture (playing the lottery and various forms of gambling because, of course, for the lower class one can never hope enough for money). And the more stringent and compulsively expressed the competition is (and the Miss America contest has reached a new height of hysteria in both the stridency and compulsion of the competition), the more legitimate and noteworthy it is.

Everyone in our culture wants to win a prize. Perhaps that is the grand lesson we have taken with us from kindergarten in the age of the perversions of Dewey-style education: Everyone gets a ribbon, and praise becomes a meaningless narcotic to soothe egoistic distemper. And in our bourgeois coming-of-age, we simply crave more and more ribbons and praise, the attainment of which becomes all the more delightful and satisfying if they are gotten at someone else's expense. Competition, therefore, becomes in the end a kind of laissez-faire psychotherapy that structures and orders our impossible rages of ambition, our rages to be noticed. But competition does not produce better people (a myth we have swallowed whole); it does not even produce better candidates, it simply produces more desperately grasping competitors. The "quality" of the average Miss America contestant is not significantly better now than it was twenty-five years ago, although the desires of today's contestants may meet with our approval (who could possibly disapprove of a black woman who wishes to be a vet in this day of careerism as the expression of independence and political empowerment), but then the women of twenty-five years ago wanted what their audiences approved of as well. That is not necessarily an advance or progress; that is simply a recognition that we are all bound by the mood and temper of our time. So, in this vast competition, this fierce theatrical warfare where all the women are supposed to love their neighbor while they wish to beat her brains out, this warfare so pointedly exposed before the nation, what we have chosen is, not the Royal American Daughter (although the contest's preoccupation with the terminology of aristocracy mirrors the public's need for such a person as the American princess), but rather the Cosmopolitan Girl. As the magazine ad states[2]

> Can a girl be too Busy? I'm taking seventeen units at Princeton, pushing on with my career during vacations and school breaks, study singing and dancing when I can, try never to lose track of my five closest chums, steal the time for Michael Jackson and Thomas Hardy, work for an anti-drug program for kids and, oh yes, I hang out with three horses, three cats, two birds and my dog Jack. My favorite magazine says "too busy" just means you don't want to miss anything . . . I love that magazine. I guess you can say I'm That Cosmopolitan Girl. (8)

When one reads about these women in the Miss America contest, that is precisely what they sound like: The Cosmopolitan Girl who knows how to have serious fun and she has virtually nothing with which to claim our attention except a moralistic bourgeois diligence. To use a twenties term: She sounds "swell." She is an amalgam of both lead characters portrayed by Patty Duke on her old TV show: the studious, serious kid and the "typical" wacky but good-hearted suburban teenager or, to borrow Ann Douglas's concept, she is the Teen Angel: the bourgeois girl who can do everything, is completely self-absorbed with her leisure, and has a heart of gold. Once again, with the Miss America contest, we have America's vehement preoccupation with innocence, with its inability to deal with the darkness of youth, the darkness of its own uselessly expressed ambition, the dark complexity of its own simplistic morality of sunshine and success, the darkness, righteous rage, and bitter depth of its own daughters. Once again, when the new Miss America, victorious and smiling, walks down the runway, we know that runway, that victory march, to be the American catwalk of supreme bourgeois self-consciousness and supreme illusion. We are still being told that nothing is something.

Nonetheless, the fact that Miss Turner won struck both my wife and me as important, as something important for the race. We laughed during the contest, but we did not laugh when she was chosen. We wanted her to win very much; it is impossible to escape that need to see the race uplifted, to thumb your nose at whites in a competition. It is impossible for blacks not to want to see their black daughters elevated to the platforms where white women are. Perhaps this tainted desire, an echoing "Ballad of the Brown Girl" that resounds in the unconscious psyche of all black people, is the unity of feeling which is the only race pride blacks have ever had since they became Americans; for race pride for the African-American, finally, is something that can only be understood as existing on the edge of tragedy and history and is, finally, that which binds both together to make the African-American the darkly and richly compli-cated person he or she is. In the end, both black women magazine writ-ers quoted earlier were right: Race pride is transcending your degrada-tion while learning to live in it and with it. To paraphrase an idea of Dorothy Sayers, race pride must teach blacks that they are not to be saved *from* degradation but saved *in* it.

A few days after the contest I watched both my daughters playing   20 Barbies as they call it. They squat on the floor on their knees moving their dolls around through an imaginary town and in imaginary houses. I de-cided to join them and squatted down too, asking them the rules of their game which they patiently explained as though they did not mind having me, the strange adult, invade their children's world. I told them it was hard for me to squat and asked if I could simply sit down, but they said that one always plays Barbies while squatting. It was a rule that had to be obeyed. As they went along, explaining relationships among their myriad dolls and the several landscapes, as complicated a genealogy as anything Faulkner ever dreamed up, a theater as vast as the entire girlhood of the world, they told me that one particular black Ken doll and one particular black Barbie doll were married and that the dolls had a child. Then Rosalind help up a white doll that someone, probably a grandparent, had given them (my wife is fairly strict on the point of our daughters not having white dolls, but I guess a few have slipped through), explaining that this doll was the daugh-ter of the black Ken and Barbie.

"But," I said, "how could two black dolls have a white daughter?"

"Oh," said Rosalind, looking at me as if I were an object deserving of only her indulgent pity, "we're not racial. That's old-fashioned. Don't you think so, Daddy? Aren't you tired of all that racial stuff?"

Bowing to that wisdom which, it is said, is the only kind that will lead us to Christ and to ourselves, I decided to get up and leave them to their play. My knees had begun to hurt and I realized, painfully, that I was much too old, much too at peace with stiffness and inflexibility, for children's games.

1990

NOTES

[1]Richard Wright tells a story in his 1956 account of the Bandung conference entitled *The Color Curtain* that emphasizes the absence of the black woman. He relates how a white woman journalist knocks upon his hotel room door during the course of the conference and confides the strange behavior of her roommate — a black woman journalist from Boston. Her roommate walks around in the middle of the night and the white woman often covertly spies her in "a dark corner of the room . . . bent over a tiny blue light, a very low and a very blue flame. . . . It seemed like she was combing her hair, but I wasn't sure. Her right arm was moving and now and then she would look over her shoulder toward my bed. . . . " The white woman thinks that the black woman is practicing voodoo. But Wright soon explains that the black woman is simply straightening her hair:

> "But why would she straighten her hair? Her hair seems all right" [the white woman journalist asks].
> "Her hair is all right. But it's not straight. It's kinky. But she does not want you, a white woman, to see her when she straightens her hair. She would feel embarrassed — "
> "Why?"
> "Because you were born with straight hair, and she wants to look as much like you as possible. . . . "
> The woman stared at me, then clapped her hands to her eyes and exclaimed: "Oh!"
> I leaned back and thought: Here is Asia, where everybody was dark, that poor American Negro woman was worried about the hair she was born with. Here, where practically nobody was white, her hair would have been acceptable; no one would have found her "inferior" because her hair was kinky; on the contrary, the Indonesians would perhaps have found her different and charming.

The conversation continues with an account of the black woman's secretive skin lightening treatments. What is revealing in this dialogue which takes on both political and psychoanalytic proportions is the utter absence of the black woman's voice, her presence. She is simply the dark, neurotic ghost that flits in the other room while the black male and the white female, both in the same room, one with dispassionate curtness and the other with sentimentalized guilt, consider the illness that is enacted before them as a kind of bad theater. Once again, the psychopathology of the black American is symbolized by the black woman's straightened hair, by her beauty culture.

[2]Jacques Barzun. "Culture High and Dry." *The Culture We Deserve*. (Middletown, CT: Wesleyan UP, 1989).

The Reader's Presence

1. "Life with Daughters: Watching the Miss America Pageant" is a remarkably informative and incisive essay about individual — and racial — presence and absence. Reread the essay, with special attention to the strategies Gerald Early uses to introduce — and then unravel — the complexities of what he means by presence

and absence in American popular culture. How, for example, does Early manage to work in so much historical information without losing his readers' attention? Consider, too, the different points of view introduced in Early's account of America's obsession with beauty pageants and the nature of the competition they symbolize. Identify each point of view, and characterize Early's summary and attitude toward that perception of the Miss America Pageant.

2. In the opening paragraph, Early expresses his regret that there is so little "live TV," calling it "the closest thing to theater for the masses." In the next sentence, he identifies the Miss America contest as "the most perfectly rendered theater in our culture," noting that the pageant "brings together all the American classes in a showbiz spectacle of classlessness and tastelessness." How does Early explain this point and demonstrate its validity? When does he return to it? With what effect?

3. Reread the beginning and the ending of Early's essay. What element of surprise do these paragraphs share? What is their effect? How does Early structure his essay around explanations and examples of his own "shame-facedness" and "embarrassment"? Comment on the overall structure of the essay — on the pattern of alternating personal experience and exposition, often linked by brief argumentative passages. In what specific sense is this pattern a reflection of the issue of presence and absence?

31

Lars Eighner

On Dumpster Diving

Long before I began Dumpster diving I was impressed with Dumpsters, enough so that I wrote the Merriam-Webster research service to discover what I could about the word "Dumpster." I learned from them that "Dumpster" is a proprietary word belonging to the Dempster Dumpster company.

Since then I have dutifully capitalized the word although it was lower-cased in almost all of the citations Merriam-Webster photocopied for me. Dempster's word is too apt. I have never heard these things called anything but Dumpsters. I do not know anyone who knows the generic name for these objects. From time to time, however, I hear a wino or hobo give some corrupted credit to the original and call them Dipsy Dumpsters.

I began Dumpster diving about a year before I became homeless.

I prefer the term "scavenging" and use the word "scrounging" when I mean to be obscure. I have heard people, evidently meaning to be polite, using the word "foraging,"but I prefer to reserve that word for gathering nuts and berries and such which I do also according to the season and the opportunity. "Dumpster diving" seems to me to be a little too cute and, in my case, inaccurate because I lack the athletic ability to lower myself into the Dumpsters as the true divers do, much to their increased profit.

I like the frankness of the word "scavenging," which I can hardly think 5 of without picturing a big black snail on an aquarium wall. I live from the refuse of others. I am a scavenger. I think it a sound and honorable niche, although if I could I would naturally prefer to live the comfortable con-sumer life, perhaps — and only perhaps — as a slightly less wasteful con-sumer owing to what I have learned as a scavenger.

While my dog Lizbeth and I were still living in the house on Avenue B in Austin, as my savings ran out, I put almost all my sporadic income into rent. The necessities of daily life I began to extract from Dumpsters. Yes,

For biographical information on Lars Eighner, see p. 647.

we ate from Dumpsters. Except for jeans, all my clothes came from Dumpsters. Boom boxes, candles, bedding, toilet paper, medicine, books, a typewriter, a virgin male love doll, change sometimes amounting to many dollars: I acquired many things from the Dumpsters.

I have learned much as a scavenger. I mean to put some of what I have learned down here, beginning with the practical art of Dumpster diving and proceeding to the abstract.

What is safe to eat?

After all, the finding of objects is becoming something of an urban art. Even respectable employed people will sometimes find something tempting sticking out of a Dumpster or standing beside one. Quite a number of people, not all of them of the bohemian type, are willing to brag that they found this or that piece in the trash. But eating from Dumpsters is the thing that separates the dilettanti from the professionals.

Eating safely from the Dumpsters involves three principles: using 10 the senses and common sense to evaluate the condition of the found materials, knowing the Dumpsters of a given area and checking them regularly, and seeking always to answer the question "Why was this discarded?"

Perhaps everyone who has a kitchen and a regular supply of groceries has, at one time or another, made a sandwich and eaten half of it before discovering mold on the bread or got a mouthful of milk before realizing the milk had turned. Nothing of the sort is likely to happen to a Dumpster diver because he is constantly reminded that most food is discarded for a reason. Yet a lot of perfectly good food can be found in Dumpsters.

Canned goods, for example, turn up fairly often in the Dumpsters I frequent. All except the most phobic people would be willing to eat from a can even if it came from a Dumpster. Canned goods are among the safest of foods to be found in Dumpsters, but are not utterly foolproof.

Although very rare with modern canning methods, botulism is a possibility. Most other forms of food poisoning seldom do lasting harm to a healthy person. But botulism is almost certainly fatal and often the first symptom is death. Except for carbonated beverages, all canned goods should contain a slight vacuum and suck air when first punctured. Bulging, rusty, dented cans and cans that spew when punctured should be avoided, especially when the contents are not very acidic or syrupy.

Heat can break down the botulin, but this requires much more cooking than most people do to canned goods. To the extent that botulism occurs at all, of course, it can occur in cans on pantry shelves as well as in cans from Dumpsters. Need I say that home-canned goods found in Dumpsters are simply too risky to be recommended.

From time to time one of my companions, aware of the source of my 15 provisions, will ask, "Do you think these crackers are really safe to eat?" For some reason it is most often the crackers they ask about.

This question always makes me angry. Of course I would not offer my companion anything I had doubts about. But more than that I wonder why he cannot evaluate the condition of the crackers for himself. I have no special knowledge and I have been wrong before. Since he knows where the food comes from, it seems to me he ought to assume some of the responsibility for deciding what he will put in his mouth.

For myself I have few qualms about dry foods such as crackers, cookies, cereal, chips, and pasta if they are free of visible contaminates and still dry and crisp. Most often such things are found in the original packaging, which is not so much a positive sign as it is the absence of a negative one.

Raw fruits and vegetables with intact skins seem perfectly safe to me, excluding of course the obviously rotten. Many are discarded for minor imperfections which can be pared away. Leafy vegetables, grapes, cauliflower, broccoli, and similar things may be contaminated by liquids and may be impractical to wash.

Candy, especially hard candy, is usually safe if it has not drawn ants. Chocolate is often discarded only because it has become discolored as the cocoa butter de-emulsified. Candying after all is one method of food preservation because pathogens do not like very sugary substances.

All of these foods might be found in any Dumpster and can be evaluated with some confidence largely on the basis of appearance. Beyond these are foods which cannot be correctly evaluated without additional information.   20

I began scavenging by pulling pizzas out of the Dumpster behind a pizza delivery shop. In general prepared food requires caution, but in this case I knew when the shop closed and went to the Dumpster as soon as the last of the help left.

Such shops often get prank orders, called "bogus." Because help seldom stays long at these places pizzas are often made with the wrong topping, refused on delivery for being cold, or baked incorrectly. The products to be discarded are boxed up because inventory is kept by counting boxes: A boxed pizza can be written off; an unboxed pizza does not exist.

I never placed a bogus order to increase the supply of pizzas and I believe no one else was scavenging in this Dumpster. But the people in the shop became suspicious and began to retain their garbage in the shop overnight.

While it lasted I had a steady supply of fresh, sometimes warm pizza. Because I knew the Dumpster I knew the source of the pizza, and because I visited the Dumpster regularly I knew what was fresh and what was yesterday's.

The area I frequent is inhabited by many affluent college students. I am   25
not here by chance; the Dumpsters in this area are very rich. Students throw out many good things, including food. In particular they tend to throw everything out when they move at the end of a semester, before and

after breaks, and around midterm when many of them despair of college. So I find it advantageous to keep an eye on the academic calendar.

The students throw food away around the breaks because they do not know whether it has spoiled or will spoil before they return. A typical discard is a half jar of peanut butter. In fact nonorganic peanut butter does not require refrigeration and is unlikely to spoil in any reasonable time. The student does not know that, and since it is Daddy's money, the student decides not to take a chance.

Opened containers require caution and some attention to the question "Why was this discarded?" But in the case of discards from student apartments, the answer may be that the item was discarded through carelessness, ignorance, or wastefulness. This can sometimes be deduced when the item is found with many others, including some that are obviously perfectly good.

Some students, and others, approach defrosting a freezer by chucking out the whole lot. Not only do the circumstances of such a find tell the story, but also the mass of frozen goods stays cold for a long time and items may be found still frozen or freshly thawed.

Yogurt, cheese, and sour cream are items that are often thrown out while they are still good. Occasionally I find a cheese with a spot of mold, which of course I just pare off, and because it is obvious why such a cheese was discarded, I treat it with less suspicion than an apparently perfect cheese found in similar circumstances. Yogurt is often discarded, still sealed, only because the expiration date on the carton had passed. This is one of my favorite finds because yogurt will keep for several days, even in warm weather.

Students throw out canned goods and staples at the end of semesters 30 and when they give up college at midterm. Drugs, pornography, spirits, and the like are often discarded when parents are expected — Dad's day, for example. And spirits also turn up after big party weekends, presumably discarded by the newly reformed. Wine and spirits, of course, keep perfectly well even once opened.

My test for carbonated soft drinks is whether they still fizz vigorously. Many juices or other beverages are too acid or too syrupy to cause much concern provided they are not visibly contaminated. Liquids, however, require some care.

One hot day I found a large jug of Pat O'Brien's Hurricane mix. The jug had been opened, but it was still ice cold. I drank three large glasses before it became apparent to me that someone had added the rum to the mix, and not a little rum. I never tasted the rum and by the time I began to feel the effects I had already ingested a very large quantity of the beverage. Some divers would have considered this a boon, but being suddenly and thoroughly intoxicated in a public place in the early afternoon is not my idea of a good time.

I have heard of people maliciously contaminating discarded food and even handouts, but mostly I have heard of this from people with vivid imaginations who have had no experience with the Dumpsters themselves. Just before the pizza shop stopped discarding its garbage at night, jalapeños began showing up on most of the discarded pizzas. If indeed this was meant to discourage me it was a wasted effort because I am native Texan.

For myself, I avoid game, poultry, pork, and egg-based foods whether I find them raw or cooked. I seldom have the means to cook what I find, but when I do I avail myself of plentiful supplies of beef which is often in very good condition. I suppose fish becomes disagreeable before it becomes dangerous. The dog is happy to have any such thing that is past its prime and, in fact, does not recognize fish as food until it is quite strong.

Home leftovers, as opposed to surpluses from restaurants, are very   35 often bad. Evidently, especially among students, there is a common type of personality that carefully wraps up even the smallest leftover and shoves it into the back of the refrigerator for six months or so before discarding it. Characteristic of this type are the reused jars and margarine tubs which house the remains.

I avoid ethnic foods I am unfamiliar with. If I do not know what it is supposed to look like when it is good, I cannot be certain I will be able to tell if it is bad.

No matter how careful I am I still get dysentery at least once a month, oftener in warm weather. I do not want to paint too romantic a picture. Dumpster diving has serious drawbacks as a way of life.

I learned to scavenge gradually, on my own. Since then I have initiated several companions into the trade. I have learned that there is a predictable series of stages a person goes through in learning to scavenge.

At first the new scavenger is filled with disgust and self-loathing. He is ashamed of being seen and may lurk around, trying to duck behind things, or he may try to dive at night.

(In fact, most people instinctively look away from a scavenger. By   40 skulking around, the novice calls attention to himself and arouses suspicion. Diving at night is ineffective and needlessly messy.)

Every grain of rice seems to be a maggot. Everything seems to stink. He can wipe the egg yolk off the found can, but he cannot erase the stigma of eating garbage out of his mind.

That stage passes with experience. The scavenger finds a pair of running shoes that fit and look and smell brand new. He finds a pocket calculator in perfect working order. He finds pristine ice cream, still frozen, more than he can eat or keep. He begins to understand: People do throw away perfectly good stuff, a lot of perfectly good stuff.

At this stage, Dumpster shyness begins to dissipate. The diver, after all, has the last laugh. He is finding all manner of good things which are his for the taking. Those who disparage his profession are the fools, not he.

He may begin to hang onto some perfectly good things for which he has neither a use nor a market. Then he begins to take note of the things which are not perfectly good but are nearly so. He mates a Walkman with broken earphones and one that is missing a battery cover. He picks up things which he can repair.

At this stage he may become lost and never recover. Dumpsters are full 45 of things of some potential value to someone and also of things which never have much intrinsic value but are interesting. All the Dumpster divers I have known come to the point of trying to acquire everything they touch. Why not take it, they reason, since it is all free.

This is, of course, hopeless. Most divers come to realize that they must restrict themselves to items of relatively immediate utility. But in some cases the diver simply cannot control himself. I have met several of these pack-rat types. Their ideas of the values of various pieces of junk verge on the psychotic. Every bit of glass may be a diamond, they think, and all that glistens, gold.

I tend to gain weight when I am scavenging. Partly this is because I always find far more pizza and doughnuts than water-packed tuna, nonfat yogurt, and fresh vegetables. Also I have not developed much faith in the reliability of Dumpsters as a food source, although it has been proven to me many times. I tend to eat as if I have no idea where my next meal is coming from. But mostly I just hate to see food go to waste and so I eat much more than I should. Something like this drives the obsession to collect junk.

As for collecting objects, I usually restrict myself to collecting one kind of small object at a time, such as pocket calculators, sunglasses, or campaign buttons. To live on the street I must anticipate my needs to a certain extent: I must pick up and save warm bedding I find in August because it will not be found in Dumpsters in November. But even if I had a home with extensive storage space I could not save everything that might be valuable in some contingency.

I have proprietary feelings about my Dumpsters. As I have suggested, it is no accident that I scavenge from Dumpsters where good finds are common. But my limited experience with Dumpsters in other areas suggests to me that it is the population of competitors rather than the affluence of the dumpers that most affects the feasibility of survival by scavenging. The large number of competitors is what puts me off the idea of trying to scavenge in places like Los Angeles.

Curiously, I do not mind my direct competition, other scavengers, so 50 much as I hate the can scroungers.

People scrounge cans because they have to have a little cash. I have tried scrounging cans with an able-bodied companion. Afoot a can scrounger simply cannot make more than a few dollars a day. One can extract the necessities of life from the Dumpsters directly with far less effort than would be required to accumulate the equivalent value in cans.

Can scroungers, then, are people who *must* have small amounts of cash. These are drug addicts and winos, mostly the latter because the amounts of cash are so small.

Spirits and drugs do, like all other commodities, turn up in Dumpsters and the scavenger will from time to time have a half bottle of a rather good wine with his dinner. But the wino cannot survive on these occasional finds; he must have his daily dose to stave off the DTs. All the cans he can carry will buy about three bottles of Wild Irish Rose.

I do not begrudge them the cans, but can scroungers tend to tear up the Dumpsters, mixing the contents and littering the area. They become so specialized that they can see only cans. They earn my contempt by passing up change, canned goods, and readily hockable items.

There are precious few courtesies among scavengers. But it is a com- 55 mon practice to set aside surplus items: pairs of shoes, clothing, canned goods, and such. A true scavenger hates to see good stuff go to waste and what he cannot use he leaves in good condition in plain sight.

Can scroungers lay waste to everything in their path and will stir one of a pair of good shoes to the bottom of a Dumpster, to be lost or ruined in the muck. Can scroungers will even go through individual garbage cans, something I have never seen a scavenger do.

Individual garbage cans are set out on the public easement only on garbage days. On other days going through them requires trespassing close to a dwelling. Going through individual garbage cans without scattering litter is almost impossible. Litter is likely to reduce the public's tolerance of scavenging. Individual garbage cans are simply not as productive as Dumpsters; people in houses and duplexes do not move as often and for some reason do not tend to discard as much useful material. Moreover, the time required to go through one garbage can that serves one household is not much less than the time required to go through a Dumpster that contains the refuse of twenty apartments.

But my strongest reservation about going through individual garbage cans is that this seems to me a very personal kind of invasion to which I would object if I were a householder. Although many things in Dumpsters are obviously meant never to come to light, a Dumpster is somehow less personal.

I avoid trying to draw conclusions about the people who dump in the Dumpsters I frequent. I think it would be unethical to do so, although I know many people will find the idea of scavenger ethics too funny for words.

Dumpsters contain bank statements, bills, correspondence, and other 60 documents, just as anyone might expect. But there are also less obvious sources of information. Pill bottles, for example. The labels on pill bottles contain the name of the patient, the name of the doctor, and the name of the drug. AIDS drugs and antipsychotic medicines, to name but two groups, are specific and are seldom prescribed for any other disorders. The plastic compacts for birth control pills usually have complete label information.

Despite all of this sensitive information, I have had only one apartment resident object to my going through the Dumpster. In that case it turned out the resident was a university athlete who was taking bets and who was afraid I would turn up his wager slips.

Occasionally a find tells a story. I once found a small paper bag containing some unused condoms, several partial tubes of flavored sexual lubricant, a partially used compact of birth control pills, and the torn pieces of a picture of a young man. Clearly she was through with him and planning to give up sex altogether.

Dumpster things are often sad — abandoned teddy bears, shredded wedding books, despaired-of sales kits. I find many pets lying in state in Dumpsters. Although I hope to get off the streets so that Lizbeth can have a long and comfortable old age, I know this hope is not very realistic. So I suppose when her time comes she too will go into a Dumpster. I will have no better place for her. And after all, for most of her life her livelihood has come from the Dumpster. When she finds something I think is safe that has been spilled from the Dumpster I let her have it. She already knows the route around the best Dumpsters. I like to think that if she survives me she will have a chance of evading the dog catcher and of finding her sustenance on the route.

Silly vanities also come to rest in the Dumpsters. I am a rather accomplished needleworker. I get a lot of materials from the Dumpsters. Evidently sorority girls, hoping to impress someone, perhaps themselves, with their mastery of a womanly art, buy a lot of embroider-by-number kits, work a few stitches horribly, and eventually discard the whole mess. I pull out their stitches, turn the canvas over, and work an original design. Do not think I refrain from chuckling as I make original gifts from these kits.

I find diaries and journals. I have often thought of compiling a book of 65 literary found objects. And perhaps I will one day. But what I find is hopelessly commonplace and bad without being, even unconsciously, camp. College students also discard their papers. I am horrified to discover the kind of paper which now merits an A in an undergraduate course. I am grateful, however, for the number of good books and magazines the students throw out.

In the area I know best I have never discovered vermin in the Dumpsters, but there are two kinds of kitty surprise. One is alley cats which I meet as they leap, claws first, out of Dumpsters. This is especially thrilling when I have Lizbeth in tow. The other kind of kitty surprise is a plastic garbage bag filled with some ponderous, amorphous mass. This always proves to be used cat litter.

City bees harvest doughnut glaze and this makes the Dumpster at the doughnut shop more interesting. My faith in the instinctive wisdom of animals is always shaken whenever I see Lizbeth attempt to catch a bee in her mouth, which she does whenever bees are present. Evidently some birds find Dumpsters profitable, for birdie surprise is almost as common as kitty surprise of the first kind. In hunting season all kinds of small game turn up in Dumpsters, some of it, sadly, not entirely dead. Curiously, summer and winter, maggots are uncommon.

The worst of the living and near-living hazards of the Dumpsters are the fire ants. The food that they claim is not much of a loss, but they are vicious and aggressive. It is very easy to brush against some surface of the Dumpster and pick up half a dozen or more fire ants, usually in some sensitive area such as the underarm. One advantage of bringing Lizbeth along as I make Dumpster rounds is that, for obvious reasons, she is very alert to ground-based fire ants. When Lizbeth recognizes the signs of fire ant infestation around our feet she does the Dance of the Zillion Fire Ants. I have learned not to ignore this warning from Lizbeth, whether I perceive the tiny ants or not, but to remove ourselves at Lizbeth's first pas de bourrée.[1] All the more so because the ants are the worst in the months I wear flip-flops, if I have them.

(Perhaps someone will misunderstand the above. Lizbeth does the Dance of the Zillion Fire Ants when she recognizes more fire ants than she cares to eat, not when she is being bitten. Since I have learned to react promptly, she does not get bitten at all. It is the isolated patrol of fire ants that falls in Lizbeth's range that deserves pity. Lizbeth finds them quite tasty.)

By far the best way to go through a Dumpster is to lower yourself into   70
it. Most of the good stuff tends to settle at the bottom because it is usually weightier than the rubbish. My more athletic companions have often demonstrated to me that they can extract much good material from a Dumpster I have already been over.

To those psychologically or physically unprepared to enter a Dumpster, I recommend a stout stick, preferably with some barb or hook at one end. The hook can be used to grab plastic garbage bags. When I find canned goods or other objects loose at the bottom of a Dumpster I usually can roll them into a small bag that I can then hoist up. Much Dumpster diving is a matter of experience for which nothing will do except practice.

Dumpster diving is outdoor work, often surprisingly pleasant. It is not entirely predictable; things of interest turn up every day and some days there are finds of great value. I am always very pleased when I can turn up exactly the thing I most wanted to find. Yet in spite of the element of change, scavenging more than most other pursuits tends to yield returns in some proportion to the effort and intelligence brought to bear. It is very sweet to turn up a few dollars in change from a Dumpster that has just been gone over by a wino.

---

[1]*pas de bourrée:* A transitional ballet step — EDS.

The land is now covered with cities. The cities are full of Dumpsters. I think of scavenging as a modern form of self-reliance. In any event, after ten years of government service, where everything is geared to the lowest common denominator, I find work that rewards initiative and effort refreshing. Certainly I would be happy to have a sinecure again, but I am not heartbroken not to have one anymore.

I find from the experience of scavenging two rather deep lessons. The first is to take what I can use and let the rest go by. I have come to think that there is no value in the abstract. A thing I cannot use or make useful, perhaps by trading, has no value however fine or rare it may be. I mean useful in a broad sense — so, for example, some art I would think useful and valuable, but other art might be otherwise for me.

I was shocked to realize that some things are not worth acquiring, but   75
now I think it is so. Some material things are white elephants that eat up the possessor's substance.

The second lesson is of the transience of material being. This has not quite converted me to a dualist, but it has made some headway in that direction. I do not suppose that ideas are immortal, but certainly mental things are longer-lived than other material things.

Once I was the sort of person who invests material objects with sentimental value. Now I no longer have those things, but I have the sentiments yet.

Many times in my travels I have lost everything but the clothes I was wearing and Lizbeth. The things I find in Dumpsters, the love letters and ragdolls of so many lives, remind me of this lesson. Now I hardly pick up a thing without envisioning the time I will cast it away. This I think is a healthy state of mind. Almost everything I have now has already been cast out at least once, proving that what I own is valueless to someone.

Anyway, I find my desire to grab for the gaudy bauble has been largely sated. I think this is an attitude I share with the very wealthy — we both know there is plenty more where what we have came from. Between us are the rat-race millions who have confounded their selves with the objects they grasp and who nightly scavenge the cable channels looking for they know not what.

I am sorry for them.   80

1991

The Reader's Presence

1. At the center of "On Dumpster Diving" is Lars Eighner's effort to bring out from the shadows of contemporary American life the lore and practices of scavenging, what he calls "a modern form of self-reliance." His essay also provides a compelling account of his

self-education as he took to the streets for "the necessities of life." Outline the stages in this process, and summarize the ethical and moral issues and the questions of decorum that Eighner confronted along the way. Show how this process reflects the structure of his essay, "beginning with the practical art of Dumpster diving and proceeding to the abstract."

2. One of the most remarkable aspects of Eighner's essay is the tone (the attitude) he expresses toward his subject. Select a paragraph from Eighner's essay. Read it aloud. How would you characterize the sound of his voice? Does he sound, for example, tough-minded? polite? strident? experienced? cynical? something else? Consider, for example, paragraph 34, where he notes: "For myself, I avoid game, poultry, pork, and egg-based foods whether I find them raw or cooked." Where have you heard talk like this before? Do you notice any changes as the essay develops, or does Eighner maintain the same tone in discussing his subject? What responses does he elicit from his readers when he speaks of scavenging as a "profession" and a "trade"?

3. Consider Eighner's relationship with his readers. Does he consider himself fundamentally different from or similar to his audience? In what specific ways? Consider, for example, the nature of the information Eighner provides in the essay. Does he expect his readers to be familiar with the information? How does he characterize his own knowledgeability about this often-noticed but rarely discussed activity in urban America? Comment on his use of irony in presenting information about Dumpster diving and in anticipating his readers' responses to the circumstances within which he does the work of his trade.

32

Mary Gordon

More than Just a Shrine: Paying Homage to the Ghosts of Ellis Island

I once sat in a hotel in Bloomsbury trying to have breakfast alone. A Russian with a habit of compulsively licking his lips asked if he could join me. I was afraid to say no; I thought it might be bad for détente. He explained to me that he was a linguist, and that he always liked to talk to Americans to see if he could make any connection between their speech and their ethnic background. When I told him about my mixed ancestry — my mother is Irish and Italian, my father a Lithuanian Jew — he began jumping up and down in his seat, rubbing his hands together, and licking his lips even more frantically.

"Ah," he said, "so you are really somebody who comes from what is called the boiling pot of America." Yes, I told him, yes I was, but I quickly rose to leave. I thought it would be too hard to explain to him the relation of the boiling potters to the main course, and I wanted to get to the British Museum. I told him that the only thing I could think of that united people whose backgrounds, histories, and points of view were utterly diverse was that their people had landed at a place called Ellis Island.

I didn't tell him that Ellis Island was the only American landmark I'd ever visited. How could I describe to him the estrangement I'd always felt from the kind of traveler who visits shrines to America's past greatness, those rebuilt forts with muskets behind glass and sabers mounted on the walls and gift shops selling maple sugar candy in the shape of Indian head-dresses, those reconstructed villages with tables set for fifty and the Paul Revere silver gleaming? All that Americana — Plymouth Rock, Gettys-burg, Mount Vernon, Valley Forge — it all inhabits for me a zone of

For biographical information on Mary Gordon, see p. 650.

blurred abstraction with far less hold on my imagination than the Bastille or Hampton Court. I suppose I've always known that my uninterest in it contains a large component of the willed: I am American, and those places purport to be my history. But they are not mine.

Ellis Island is, though; it's the one place I can be sure my people are connected to. And so I made a journey there to find my history, like any Rotarian traveling in his Winnebago to Antietam to find his. I had become part of that humbling democracy of people looking in some site for a past that has grown unreal. The monument I traveled to was not, however, a tribute to some old glory. The minute I set foot upon the island I could feel all that it stood for: insecurity, obedience, anxiety, dehumanization, the terrified and careful deference of the displaced. I hadn't traveled to the Battery and boarded a ferry across from the Statue of Liberty to raise flags or breathe a richer, more triumphant air. I wanted to do homage to the ghosts.

I felt them everywhere, from the moment I disembarked and saw the   5
building with its high-minded brick, its hopeful little lawn, its ornamental cornices. The place was derelict when I arrived; it had not functioned for more than thirty years — almost as long as the time it had operated at full capacity as a major immigration center. I was surprised to learn what a small part of history Ellis Island had occupied. The main building was constructed in 1892, then rebuilt between 1898 and 1900 after a fire. Most of the immigrants who arrived during the latter half of the nineteenth century, mainly northern and western Europeans, landed not at Ellis Island but on the western tip of the Battery at Castle Garden, which had opened as a receiving center for immigrants in 1855.

By the 1880s the facilities at Castle Garden had grown scandalously inadequate. Officials looked for an island on which to build a new immigration center because they thought that on an island immigrants could be more easily protected from swindlers and quickly transported to railroad terminals in New Jersey. Bedloe's Island was considered, but New Yorkers were aghast at the idea of a "Babel" ruining their beautiful new treasure, "Liberty Enlightening the World." The statue's sculptor, Frédéric Auguste Bartholdi, reacted to the prospect of immigrants landing near his masterpiece in horror; he called it a "monstrous plan." So much for Emma Lazarus.

Ellis Island was finally chosen because the citizens of New Jersey petitioned the federal government to remove from the island an old naval powder magazine that they thought dangerously close to the Jersey shore. The explosives were removed; no one wanted the island for anything. It was the perfect place to build an immigration center.

I thought about the island's history as I walked into the building and made my way to the room that was the center in my imagination of the Ellis Island experience: the Great Hall. It had been made real for me in the stark, accusing photographs of Louis Hine and others who took those pictures to make a point. It was in the Great Hall that everyone had waited — waiting, always, the great vocation of the dispossessed. The room was empty, except for me and a handful of other visitors and the park ranger who showed us around. I felt myself grow insignificant in that room, with its huge semicircular windows, its air, even in dereliction, of solid and official probity.

I walked in the deathlike expansiveness of the room's disuse and tried to think of what it might have been like, filled and swarming. More than sixteen million immigrants came through that room; approximately 250,000 were rejected. Not really a large proportion, but the implications for the rejected were dreadful. For some, there was nothing to go back to, or there was certain death; for others, who left as adventurers, to return would be to adopt in local memory the fool's role, and the failure's. No wonder that the island's history includes reports of three thousand suicides.

Sometimes immigrants could pass through Ellis Island in mere hours,   10 though for some the process took days. The particulars of the experience in the Great Hall were often influenced by the political events and attitudes on the mainland. In the 1890s and the first years of the new century, when cheap labor was needed, the newly built receiving center took in its immigrants with comparatively little question. But as the century progressed, the economy worsened, eugenics became both scientifically respectable and popular, and World War I made American xenophobia seem rooted in fact.

Immigration acts were passed; newcomers had to prove, besides moral correctness and financial solvency, their ability to read. Quota laws came into effect, limiting the number of immigrants from southern and eastern Europe to less than 14 percent of the total quota. Intelligence tests were biased against all non-English-speaking persons and medical examinations became increasingly strict, until the machinery of immigration nearly collapsed under its own weight. The Second Quota Law of 1924 provided that all immigrants be inspected and issued visas at American consular offices in Europe, rendering the center almost obsolete.

On the day of my visit, my mind fastened upon the medical inspections, which had always seemed to me most emblematic of the ignominy and terror the immigrants endured. The medical inspectors, sometimes dressed in uniforms like soldiers, were particularly obsessed with a disease of the eyes called trachoma, which they checked for by flipping back the immigrants' top eyelids with a hook used for buttoning gloves — a method that sometimes resulted in the transmission of the disease to healthy people. Mothers feared that if their children cried too much, their red eyes would be mistaken for a symptom of the disease and the whole family would be sent home. Those immigrants suspected of some physical disability had initials chalked on their coats. I remembered the photographs I'd seen of people standing, dumbstruck and innocent as cattle, with their manifest numbers hung around their necks and initials marked in chalk upon their coats: "E" for eye trouble, "K" for hernia, "L" for lameness, "X" for mental defects, "H" for heart disease.

I thought of my grandparents as I stood in the room; my seventeen-year-old grandmother, coming alone from Ireland in 1896, vouched for by a stranger who had found her a place as a domestic servant to some Irish who had done well. I tried to imagine the assault it all must have been for her; I've been to her hometown, a collection of farms with a main street — smaller than the athletic field of my local public school. She must have watched the New York skyline as the first- and second-class passengers were whisked off the gangplank with the most cursory of inspections while she was made to board a ferry to the new immigration center.

What could she have made of it — this buff-painted wooden structure with its towers and its blue slate roof, a place *Harper's Weekly* described as "a latter-day watering place hotel"? It would have been the first time she'd have heard people speaking something other than English. She would have mingled with people carrying baskets on their heads and eating foods unlike any she had ever seen — dark-eyed people, like the Sicilian she would marry ten years later, who came over with his family, responsible even then for his mother and sister. I don't know what they thought, my grandparents, for they were not expansive people, nor romantic; they didn't like to think of what they called "the hard times," and their trip across the ocean was the single adventurous act of lives devoted after landing to security, respectability, and fitting in.

What is the potency of Ellis Island for someone like me — an American, obviously, but one who has always felt that the country really belonged to the early settlers, that, as J. F. Powers wrote in "Morte D'Urban," it had been "handed down to them by the Pilgrims, George Washington and others, and that they were taking a risk in letting you live in it." I have never been the victim of overt discrimination; nothing I have wanted has been denied me because of the accidents of blood. But I suppose it is part of being an American to be engaged in a somewhat tiresome but always self-absorbing process of national definition. And in this process, I have found in traveling to Ellis Island an important piece of evidence that could remind me I was right to feel my differentness. Something had happened to my people on that island, a result of the eternal wrongheadedness of American protectionism and the predictabilities of simple greed. I came to the island, too, so I could tell the ghosts that I was one of them, and that I honored them — their stoicism, and their innocence, the fear that turned them inward, and their pride. I wanted to tell them that I liked them better than the Americans who made them pass through the Great Hall and stole their names and chalked their weaknesses in public on their clothing. And to tell the ghosts what I have always thought: that American history was a very classy party that was not much fun until they arrived, brought the good food, turned up the music, and taught everyone to dance.

1985

The Reader's Presence

1. Mary Gordon's essay is an engaging exercise in historical observation and inference, and a narrative testament to the responsibility of being an American — to what she calls "a somewhat tiresome but always self-absorbing process of national definition." In what specific ways is this process "self-absorbing"? How is this process reflected in the shape of her essay? If, as she tells us, she is not disposed to visit "shrines to America's past greatness," why then does she decide to "journey" to Ellis Island? How is Ellis Island different from the other shrines she mentions — those which constitute "a zone of blurred abstraction"?

2. Consider the overall structure of this essay. What does Gordon gain (and lose) by beginning her essay with a brief account of her encounter with the Russian linguist? How does Gordon connect that conversation to the issues and themes she unfolds in her observations and inferences about Ellis Island? What do you make of the final lines of the essay? What does she gain (and lose) by concluding her essay with a fragment? In what specific ways does this line summarize her attitude toward immigrants?

3. Consider Gordon's relationship with her readers. What responses does she try to evoke in her readers when she recounts, in detail, the complicated process of selecting a site to process immigrants? What does this account reveal about America's attitudes toward immigrants? How is this point reinforced or challenged by her characterizations of the immigrants? of the "Americans" who processed them? of the procedures used to admit immigrants into the United States? Within this context, comment on the effectiveness of the metaphor of ghosts and the homage paid to them.

33

Stephen Jay Gould

Sex, Drugs, Disasters, and the Extinction of Dinosaurs

Science, in its most fundamental definition, is a fruitful mode of inquiry, not a list of enticing conclusions. The conclusions are the consequence, not the essence.

My greatest unhappiness with most popular presentations of science concerns their failure to separate fascinating claims from the methods that scientists use to establish the facts of nature. Journalists, and the public, thrive on controversial and stunning statements. But science is, basically, a way of knowing — in P. B. Medawar's apt words, "the art of the soluble." If the growing corps of popular science writers would focus on *how* scientists develop and defend those fascinating claims, they would make their greatest possible contribution to public understanding.

Consider three ideas, proposed in perfect seriousness to explain that greatest of all titillating puzzles — the extinction of dinosaurs. Since these three notions invoke the primally fascinating themes of our culture — sex, drugs, and violence — they surely reside in the category of fascinating claims. I want to show why two of them rank as silly speculation, while the other represents science at its grandest and most useful.

Science works with the testable proposals. If, after much compilation and scrutiny of data, new information continues to affirm a hypothesis, we may accept it provisionally and gain confidence as further evidence mounts. We can never be completely sure that a hypothesis is right, though we may be able to show with confidence that it is wrong. The best scientific hypotheses are also generous and expansive: They suggest extensions and implications that enlighten related, and even far distant, subjects. Simply

For biographical information on Stephen Jay Gould, see p. 650.

consider how the idea of evolution has influenced virtually every intellectual field.

Useless speculation, on the other hand, is restrictive. It generates no testable hypothesis, and offers no way to obtain potentially refuting evidence. Please note that I am not speaking of truth or falsity. The speculation may well be true; still, if it provides, in principle, no material for affirmation or rejection, we can make nothing of it. It must simply stand forever as an intriguing idea. Useless speculation turns in on itself and leads nowhere; good science, containing both seeds for its potential refutation and implications for more and different testable knowledge, reaches out. But, enough preaching. Let's move on to dinosaurs, and the three proposals for their extinction.

1. *Sex:* Testes function only in a narrow range of temperature (those of mammals hang externally in a scrotal sac because internal body temperatures are too high for their proper function). A worldwide rise in temperature at the close of the Cretaceous period caused the testes of dinosaurs to stop functioning and led to their extinction by sterilization of males.
2. *Drugs:* Angiosperms (flowering plants) first evolved toward the end of the dinosaurs' reign. Many of these plants contain psychoactive agents, avoided by mammals today as a result of their bitter taste. Dinosaurs had neither means to taste the bitterness nor livers effective enough to detoxify the substances. They died of massive overdoses.
3. *Disasters:* A large comet or asteroid struck the earth some 65 million years ago, lofting a cloud of dust into the sky and blocking sunlight, thereby suppressing photosynthesis and so drastically lowering world temperatures that dinosaurs and hosts of other creatures became extinct.

Before analyzing these three tantalizing statements, we must establish a basic ground rule often violated in proposals for the dinosaurs' demise. *There is no separate problem of the extinction of dinosaurs.* Too often we divorce specific events from their wider contexts and systems of cause and effect. The fundamental fact of dinosaur extinction is its synchrony with the demise of so many other groups across a wide range of habitats, from terrestrial to marine.

The history of life has been punctuated by brief episodes of mass extinction. A recent analysis by University of Chicago paleontologists Jack Sepkoski and Dave Raup, based on the best and most exhaustive tabulation of data ever assembled, shows clearly that five episodes of mass dying stand well above the "background" extinctions of normal times (when we consider all mass extinctions, large and small, they seem to fall in a regular 26-million-year cycle). The Cretaceous debacle, occurring 65 million years ago and separating the Mesozoic and Cenozoic eras of our geological time scale, ranks prominently among the five. Nearly all the marine plankton (single-celled floating creatures) died with geological suddenness; among marine invertebrates, nearly 15 percent of all families perished, including many previously dominant groups, especially the ammonites (relatives of squids in coiled shells). On land, the dinosaurs disappeared after more than 100 million years of unchallenged domination.

In this context, speculations limited to dinosaurs alone ignore the larger phenomenon. We need a coordinated explanation for a system of events that includes the extinction of dinosaurs as one component. Thus it makes little sense, though it may fuel our desire to view mammals as inevitable inheritors of the earth, to guess that dinosaurs died because small mammals ate their eggs (a perennial favorite among untestable speculations). It seems most unlikely that some disaster peculiar to dinosaurs befell these massive beasts — and that the debacle happened to strike just when one of history's five great dyings had enveloped the earth for completely different reasons.

The testicular theory, an old favorite from the 1940s, had its root in an interesting and thoroughly respectable study of temperature tolerances in the American alligator, published in the staid *Bulletin of the American Museum of Natural History* in 1946 by three experts on living and fossil reptiles — E. H. Colbert, my own first teacher in paleontology; R. B. Cowles; and C. M. Bogert.

The first sentence of their summary reveals a purpose beyond alligators: "This report describes an attempt to infer the reactions of extinct reptiles, especially the dinosaurs, to high temperatures as based upon reactions observed in the modern alligator." They studied, by rectal thermometry, the body temperatures of alligators under changing conditions of heating and cooling. (Well, let's face it, you wouldn't want to try sticking a thermometer under a 'gator's tongue.) The predictions under test go way back to an old theory first stated by Galileo in the 1630s — the unequal scaling of surfaces and volumes. As an animal, or any object, grows (provided its shape doesn't change), surface areas must increase more slowly than volumes — since surfaces get larger as length squared, while volumes increase much more rapidly, as length cubed. Therefore, small animals have high ratios of surface to volume, while large animals cover themselves with relatively little surface.

Among cold-blooded animals lacking any physiological mechanism for keeping their temperatures constant, small creatures have a hell of a time keeping warm — because they lose so much heat through their relatively large surfaces. On the other hand, large animals, with their relatively small surfaces, may lose heat so slowly that, once warm, they may maintain effectively constant temperatures against ordinary fluctuations of climate. (In fact, the resolution of the "hot-blooded dinosaur" controversy that burned so brightly a few years back may simply be that, while large dinosaurs possessed no physiological mechanism for con-

10

stant temperature, and were not therefore warm-blooded in the technical sense, their large size and relatively small surface area kept them warm.)

Colbert, Cowles, and Bogert compared the warming rates of small and large alligators. As predicted, the small fellows heated up (and cooled down) more quickly. When exposed to a warm sun, a tiny 50-gram (1.76-ounce) alligator heated up one degree Celsius every minute and a half, while a large alligator, 260 times bigger at 13,000 grams (28.7 pounds), took seven and a half minutes to gain a degree. Extrapolating up to an adult 10-ton dinosaur, they concluded that a one-degree rise in body temperature would take eighty-six hours. If large animals absorb heat so slowly (through their relatively small surfaces), they will also be unable to shed any excess heat gained when temperatures rise above a favorable level.

The authors then guessed that large dinosaurs lived at or near their optimum temperatures; Cowles suggested that a rise in global temperatures just before the Cretaceous extinction caused the dinosaurs to heat up beyond their optimal tolerance — and, being so large, they couldn't shed the unwanted heat. (In a most unusual statement within a scientific paper, Colbert and Bogert then explicitly disavowed this speculative extension of their empirical work on alligators.) Cowles conceded that this excess heat probably wasn't enough to kill or even to enervate the great beasts, but since testes often function only within a narrow range of temperature, he proposed that this global rise might have sterilized all the males, causing extinction by natural contraception.

The overdose theory has recently been supported by UCLA psychiatrist Ronald K. Siegel. Siegel has gathered, he claims, more than 2,000 records of animals who, when given access, administer various drugs to themselves — from a mere swig of alcohol to massive doses of the big H. Elephants will swill the equivalent of twenty beers at a time, but do not like alcohol in concentrations greater than 7 percent. In a silly bit of anthropocentric speculation, Siegel states that "elephants drink, perhaps, to forget . . . the anxiety produced by shrinking rangeland and the competition for food."

Since fertile imaginations can apply almost any hot idea to the ex- 15 tinction of dinosaurs, Siegel found a way. Flowering plants did not evolve until late in the dinosaurs' reign. These plants also produced an array of aromatic, amino-acid-based alkaloids — the major group of psychoactive agents. Most mammals are "smart" enough to avoid these potential poisons. The alkaloids simply don't taste good (they are bitter); in any case, we mammals have livers happily supplied with the capacity to detoxify them. But, Siegel speculates, perhaps dinosaurs could neither taste the bitterness nor detoxify the substances once ingested. He recently told members of the American Psychological Association: "I'm not suggesting that all dinosaurs OD'd on plant drugs, but it certainly was a factor." He also argued that death by overdose may help explain why so many dinosaur fossils are found in contorted positions. (Do not go gentle into that good night.)

Extraterrestrial catastrophes have long pedigrees in the popular literature of extinction, but the subject exploded again in 1979, after a long lull, when the father-son, physicist-geologist team of Luis and Walter Alvarez proposed that an asteroid, some 10 km in diameter, struck the earth 65 million years ago (comets, rather than asteroids, have since gained favor. Good science is self-corrective).

The force of such a collision would be immense, greater by far than the megatonnage of all the world's nuclear weapons. In trying to reconstruct a scenario that would explain the simultaneous dying of dinosaurs on land and so many creatures in the sea, the Alvarezes proposed that a gigantic dust cloud, generated by particles blown aloft in the impact, would so darken the earth that photosynthesis would cease and temperatures drop precipitously. (Rage, rage against the dying of the light.) The single-celled photosynthetic oceanic plankton, with life cycles measured in weeks, would perish outright, but land plants might survive through the dormancy of their seeds (land plants were not much affected by the Cretaceous extinction, and any adequate theory must account for the curious pattern of differential survival). Dinosaurs would die by starvation and freezing; small, warm-blooded mammals, with more modest requirements for food and better regulation of body temperature, would squeak through. "Let the bastards freeze in the dark," as bumper stickers of our chauvinistic neighbors in sunbelt states proclaimed several years ago during the Northeast's winter oil crisis.

All three theories, testicular malfunction, psychoactive overdosing, and asteroidal zapping, grab our attention mightily. As pure phenomenology, they rank about equally high on any hit parade of primal fascination. Yet one represents expansive science, the others restrictive and untestable speculation. The proper criterion lies in evidence and methodology; we must probe behind the superficial fascination of particular claims.

How could we possibly decide whether the hypothesis of testicular frying is right or wrong? We would have to know things that the fossil record cannot provide. What temperatures were optimal for dinosaurs? Could they avoid the absorption of excess heat by staying in the shade, or in caves? At what temperatures did their testicles cease to function? Were late Cretaceous climates ever warm enough to drive the internal temperatures of dinosaurs close to this ceiling? Testicles simply don't fossilize, and how could we infer their temperature tolerances even if they did? In short, Cowles's hypothesis is only an intriguing speculation leading nowhere. The most damning statement against it appeared right in the conclusion of Colbert, Cowles, and Bogert's paper, when they admitted: "It is difficult to advance any definite arguments against the hypothesis." My statement may seem paradoxical — isn't a hypothesis really good if you can't devise any arguments against it? Quite the contrary. It is simply untestable and unusable.

Siegel's overdosing has even less going for it. At least Cowles extrapo-   20
lated his conclusion from some good data on alligators. And he didn't completely violate the primary guideline of siting dinosaur extinction in the context of a general mass dying — for rise in temperature could be the root cause of a general catastrophe, zapping dinosaurs by testicular malfunction and different groups for other reasons. But Siegel's speculation cannot touch the extinction of ammonites or oceanic plankton (diatoms make their own food with good sweet sunlight; they don't OD on the chemicals of terrestrial plants). It is simply a gratuitous, attention-grabbing guess. It cannot be tested, for how can we know what dinosaurs tasted and what their livers could do? Livers don't fossilize any better than testicles.

The hypothesis doesn't even make any sense in its own context. Angiosperms were in full flower ten million years before dinosaurs went the way of all flesh. Why did it take so long? As for the pains of a chemical death recorded in contortions of fossils, I regret to say (or rather I'm pleased to note for the dinosaurs' sake) that Siegel's knowledge of geology must be a bit deficient: muscles contract after death and geological strata rise and fall with motions of the earth's crust after burial — more than enough reason to distort a fossil's pristine appearance.

The impact story, on the other hand, has a sound basis in evidence. It can be tested, extended, refined, and, if wrong, disproved. The Alvarezes did not just construct an arresting guess for public consumption. They proposed their hypothesis after laborious geochemical studies with Frank Asaro and Helen Michael had revealed a massive increase of iridium in rocks deposited right at the time of extinction. Iridium, a rare metal of the platinum group, is virtually absent from indigenous rocks of the earth's crust; most of our iridium arrives on extraterrestrial objects that strike the earth.

The Alverez hypothesis bore immediate fruit. Based originally on evidence from two European localities, it led geochemists throughout the world to examine other sediments of the same age. They found abnormally high amounts of iridium everywhere — from continental rocks of the western United States to deep sea cores from the South Atlantic.

Cowles proposed his testicular hypothesis in the mid-1940s. Where has it gone since then? Absolutely nowhere, because scientists can do nothing with it. The hypothesis must stand as a curious appendage to a solid study of alligators. Siegel's overdose scenario will also win a few press notices and fade into oblivion. The Alvarezes's asteroid falls into a different category altogether, and much of the popular commentary has missed this essential distinction by focusing on the impact and its attendant results, and forgetting what really matters to a scientist — the iridium. If you talk just about asteroids, dust, and darkness, you tell stories no better and no more entertaining than fried testicles or terminal trips. It is the iridium — the source of testable evidence — that counts and forges the crucial distinction between speculation and science.

The proof, to twist a phrase, lies in the doing. Cowles's hypothesis has generated nothing in thirty-five years. Since its proposal in 1979, the Alvarez hypothesis has spawned hundreds of studies, a major conference, and attendant publications. Geologists are fired up. They are looking for iridium at all other extinction boundaries. Every week exposes a new wrinkle in the scientific press. Further evidence that the Cretaceous iridium represents extraterrestrial impact and not indigenous volcanism continues to accumulate. As I revise this essay in November 1984 (this paragraph will be out of date when the book is published),[1] new data include chemical "signatures" of other isotopes indicating unearthly provenance, glass spherules of a size and sort produced by impact and not by volcanic eruptions, and high-pressure varieties of silica formed (so far as we know) only under the tremendous shock of impact.

My point is simply this: Whatever the eventual outcome (I suspect it will be positive), the Alvarez hypothesis is exciting, fruitful science because it generates tests, provides us with things to do, and expands outward. We are having fun, battling back and forth, moving toward a resolution, and extending the hypothesis beyond its original scope.

As just one example of the unexpected, distant cross-fertilization that good science engenders, the Alvarez hypothesis made a major contribution to a theme that has riveted public attention in the past few months — so-called nuclear winter. In a speech delivered in April 1982, Luis Alvarez calculated the energy that a ten-kilometer asteroid would release on impact. He compared such an explosion with a full nuclear exchange and implied that all-out atomic war might unleash similar consequences.

This theme of impact leading to massive dust clouds and falling temperatures formed an important input to the decision of Carl Sagan and a group of colleagues to model the climatic consequences of nuclear holocaust. Full nuclear exchange would probably generate the same kind of dust cloud and darkening that may have wiped out the dinosaurs. Temperatures would drop precipitously and agriculture might become impossible. Avoidance of nuclear war is fundamentally an ethical and political imperative, but we must know the factual consequences to make firm judgments. I am heartened by a final link across disciplines and deep concerns — another criterion, by the way, of science at its best.[2] A recognition of the very phenomenon that made our evolution possible by exterminating the previously dominant dinosaurs and clear-

---

[1] *The Flamingo's Smile* (1985), in which Gould collected this essay. — EDS.
[2] This quirky connection so tickles my fancy that I break my own strict rule about eliminating redundancies from [this essay]. . . . — GOULD'S NOTE.

ing a way for the evolution of large mammals, including us, might actually help to save us from joining those magnificent beasts in contorted poses among the strata of the earth.

1984

The Reader's Presence

1. Although the title of Stephen Jay Gould's essay focuses on the extinction of dinosaurs, his overriding interest is in demonstrating the way science works, and his purpose is to make that process fully accessible and understandable to the general public. Where does he lay out this central claim, and how does he demonstrate, clarify, and complicate it as his essay proceeds?

2. What distinctions does Gould draw among "testable proposals," "intriguing ideas," and "useless speculation"? What features of each does he identify? Reread his summary of the three proposals for the extinction of dinosaurs. Which of the three terms cited above would you use to characterize this summary? In what specific ways does Gould use them to demonstrate the limitations of popular presentations of scientific theory? What crucial piece of evidence does he omit from the summary? With what effect?

3. Reread Gould's essay, with special attention to his use of tone, diction, syntax, and metaphor. How does he use these compositional strategies to make information accessible to his readers? Point to passages where Gould uses the diction and syntax of a serious scientist. When — and with what effects — does his prose sound more colloquial? Does his tone remain consistent throughout the essay? If not, when and how does it change? With what effects?

34

Jeff Greenfield

The Black and White Truth about Basketball

The dominance of black athletes over professional basketball is beyond dispute. Two-thirds of the players are black, and the number would be greater were it not for the continuing practice of picking white bench warmers for the sake of balance. Over the last two decades, no more than three white players have been among the ten starting players on the National Basketball Association's All-Star team, and in the last quarter century, only two white players — Dave Cowens and Larry Bird of the Boston Celtics — have ever been chosen as the NBA's Most Valuable Player.

And at a time when a baseball executive can lose his job for asserting that blacks lack "the necessities" to become pro sports executives and when the National Football League only in 1989 had its first black head coach, the NBA stands as a pro sports league that hired its first black head coach in 1968 (Bill Russell) and its first black general manager in the early 1970s (Wayne Embry of the Milwaukee Bucks). What discrimination remains — lack of equal opportunity for speaking engagements and product endorsements — has more to do with society than with basketball.

This dominance reflects a natural inheritance: Basketball is a pastime of the urban poor. The current generation of black athletes are heirs to a tradition more than half a century old. In a neighborhood without the money for bats, gloves, hockey sticks and ice skates, or shoulder pads, basketball is an eminently accessible sport. "Once it was the game of the Irish and Italian Catholics in Rockaway and the Jews on Fordham Road in the Bronx," writes David Wolf in his brilliant book, *Foul!* "It was recreation, status, and a way out." But now the ethnic names have been changed: Instead of the Red Holzmans, Red Auerbachs, and the McGuire brothers, there are the Michael Jordans and Charles Barkleys, the Shaquille O'Neals

For biographical information on Jeff Greenfield, see p. 651.

and Patrick Ewings. And professional basketball is a sport with national television exposure and million-dollar salaries.

But the mark on basketball of today's players can be measured by more than money or visibility. It is a question of style. For there is a clear difference between "black" and "white" styles of play that is as clear as the difference between 155th Street at Eighth Avenue and Crystal City, Missouri. Most simply (remembering we are talking about culture, not chromosomes), "black" basketball is the use of superb athletic skill to adapt to the limits of space imposed by the game. "White" ball is the pulverization of that space by sheer intensity.[1]

It takes a conscious effort to realize how constricted the space is on a   5 basketball court. Place a regulation court (ninety-four by fifty feet) — on a football field, and it will reach from the back of the end zone to the twenty-one-yard line; its width will cover less than a third of the field. On a baseball diamond, a basketball court will reach from home plate to first base. Compared to its principal indoor rival, ice hockey, basketball covers about one-fourth the playing area. Moreover, during the normal flow of the game, most of the action takes place on the third of the court nearest the basket. It is in this dollhouse space that ten men, each of them half a foot taller than the average man, come together to battle each other.

There is, thus, no room; basketball is a struggle for the edge: the half step with which to cut around the defender for a lay-up, the half second of freedom with which to release a jump shot, the instant a head turns allowing a pass to a teammate breaking for the basket. It is an arena for the subtlest of skills: the head fake, the shoulder fake, the shift of body weight to the right and the sudden cut to the left. Deception is crucial to success; and to young men who have learned early and painfully that life is a battle for survival, basketball is one of the few pursuits in which the weapon of deception is a legitimate tactic rather than the source of trouble.

If there is, then, the need to compete in a crowd, to battle for the edge, then the surest strategy is to develop the *unexpected:* to develop a shot that is simply and fundamentally different from the usual methods of putting the ball in the basket. Drive to the hoop, but go under it and come up the other side; hold the ball at waist level and shoot from there instead of bringing the ball up to eye level; leap into the air, but fall away from the basket instead of toward it. All these tactics, which a fan can see embodied in the astonishing play of the Chicago Bulls' Michael Jordan, take maximum advantage of the crowding on the court. They also stamp uniqueness on young men who may feel it nowhere else.

[1]This distinction has nothing to do with the question of whether whites can play as "well" as blacks. In 1987, the Detroit Pistons' Isiah Thomas quipped that the Celtics' Larry Bird was "a pretty good player," but would be much less celebrated and wealthy if he were black. As Thomas later said, Bird was one of the greatest pro players in history. Nor is this distinction about "smart," although the ex-Los Angeles Laker great Magic Johnson was right when he said that too many journalists attribute brilliant strategic moves by black players to "innate" ability. — GREENFIELD'S NOTE.

"For many young men in the slums," David Wolf writes, "the school yard is the only place they can feel true pride in what they do, where they can move free of inhibitions and where they can, by being spectacular, rise for the moment against the drabness and anonymity of their lives. Thus, when a player develops extraordinary 'school yard' moves and shots . . . [they] become his measure as a man."

So the moves that begin as tactics for scoring soon become calling cards. You don't just lay the ball in for an uncontested basket; you take the ball in both hands, leap as high as you can, and slam the ball through the hoop. When you jump in the air, fake a shot, bring the ball back to your body, and throw up a shot, all without coming back down, you have proven your worth in uncontestable fashion.

This liquid grace is an integral part of "black" ball, almost exclusively   10
the province of the playground player. Some white stars like Bob Cousy, Billy Cunningham, Doug Collins, and Kevin McHale had it; John Stockton of the Utah Jazz has it now: the body control, the moves to the basket, the free-ranging mobility. Most of them also possessed the surface ease that is integral to the "black" style; an incorporation of the ethic of mean streets — to "make it" is not just to have wealth but to have it without strain. Whatever the muscles and organs are doing, the face of the "black" star almost never shows it. Magic Johnson of the Lakers could bring the ball downcourt with two men on him, whip a pass through an invisible opening, cut to the basket, take a return pass, and hit the shot all with no more emotion than a quick smile. So stoic was San Antonio Spurs' great George Gervin that he earned the nick-name "Ice Man." (Interestingly, a black coach like San Antonio's John Lucan exhibits far less emotion on the bench than a white counterpart like Portland's Rick Adelman.)

If there is a single trait that characterizes "black" ball it is leaping ability. Bob Cousy, ex-Celtic great and former pro coach, says that "when coaches get together, one is sure to say, 'I've got the one black kid in the country who can't jump.' When coaches see a white boy who can jump or who moves with extraordinary quickness, they say, 'He should have been born black, he's that good.'" This pervasive belief was immortalized by the title of the hit film: *White Men Can't Jump*.

Don Nelson, now a top executive with the Golden State Warriors, recalls that back in 1970, Dave Cowens, then a relatively unknown graduate of Florida State, prepared for his rookie pro season by playing in the Rucker League, an outdoor competition in Harlem playgrounds that pits pros against college kids and playground stars. So ferocious was Cowens's leaping ability, Nelson says, that "when the summer was over, everyone wanted to know who the white son of a bitch was who could jump so high." That's another way to overcome a crowd around the basket — just go over it.

Speed, mobility, quickness, acceleration, "the moves" — all of these are catch-phrases that surround the "black" playground athlete, the style of play. So does the most racially tinged of attributes, "rhythm." Yet rhythm is what the black stars themselves talk about: feeling the flow of the game, finding the tempo of the dribble, the step, the shot. It is an instinctive quality (although it stems from hundreds of hours of practice), and it is one that has led to difficulty between system-oriented coaches and free-form players. "Cats from the street have their own rhythm when they play," said college dropout Bill Spivey, onetime New York high school star. "It's not a matter of somebody setting you up and you shooting. You *feel* the shot. When a coach holds you back, you lose the feel and it isn't fun anymore."

When legendary Brooklyn playground star Connie Hawkins was winding up his NBA career under Laker coach Bill Sharman, he chafed under the methodical style of play. "He's systematic to the point where it begins to be a little too much. It's such an action-reaction type of game that when you have to do everything the same way, I think you lose some-thing."

There is another kind of basketball that has grown up in America. It is not played on asphalt playgrounds with a crowd of kids competing for the court; it is played on macadam driveways by one boy with a ball and a backboard nailed over the garage; it is played in gyms in the frigid winter of the rural Midwest and on Southern dirt courts. It is a mechanical, precise development of skills (when Don Nelson was an Iowa farm boy, his incentive to make his shots was that an errant rebound would land in the middle of chicken droppings). It is a game without frills, without flow, but with effectiveness. It is "white" basketball: jagged, sweaty, stumbling, intense. Where a "black" player overcomes an obstacle with finesse and body control, a "white" player reacts by outrunning or overpowering the obstacle.

By this definition, the Boston Celtics have been classically "white" regardless of the pigmentation of the players. They have rarely suited up a player with dazzling moves; indeed such a player would probably have made Red Auerbach swallow his cigar. Instead, the Celtic philosophy has been to wear you down with execution, with constant running, with the same play run again and again and again. The rebound by Bill Russell (or Dave Cowens or Robert Parrish) triggers the fast break, as everyone races downcourt; the ball goes to Bob Cousy (or John Havlicek, or Larry Bird), who pulls up and takes the shot, or who drives and then finds Sam Jones (or Kevin McHale or M. L. Carr) free for an easy basket.

Perhaps the most definitively "white" position is that of the quick forward, one without great moves to the basket, without highly developed shots, without the height and mobility for rebounding effectiveness. So what does he do?

He runs. He runs from the opening jump to the final buzzer. He runs up and down the court, from base line to base line, back and forth under the basket, looking for the opening, the pass, the chance to take a quick step, the high-percentage shot. To watch Detroit's Bill Laimbeer or the Suns' Dan Majerle, players without speed or obvious moves, is to wonder what they are doing in the NBA — until you see them swing free and throw up a shot that, without demanding any apparent skill, somehow goes in the basket more frequently than the shots of many of their more skilled team-mates. And to have watched the New York Knicks' (now U.S. Senator) Bill Bradley, or the Celtics' John Havlicek, is to have watched "white" ball at its best.

Havlicek or Laimbeer, or the Phoenix Suns' Danny Ainge, stand in dramatic contrast to Michael Jordan or to the Philadelphia 76ers' legend, Julius Erving. Erving had the capacity to make legends come true, leaping from the foul line and slam-dunking the ball on his way down; going up for a lay-up, pulling the ball to his body, and driving under and up the other side of the rim, defying gravity and probability with impossible moves and jumps. Michael Jordan of the Chicago Bulls has been seen by thousands spinning a full 360 degrees in midair before slamming the ball through the hoop.

When John Havlicek played, by contrast, he was the living embodi-   20
ment of his small-town Ohio background. He would bring the ball downcourt, weaving left, then right, looking for a path. He would swing the ball to a teammate, cut behind the pick, take the pass, and release the shot in a flicker of time. It looked plain, unvarnished. But it was a blend of skills that not more than half a dozen other players in the league possessed.

To former pro Jim McMillian, a black who played quick forward with "white" attributes, "it's a matter of environment. Julius Erving grew up in a different environment from Havlicek. John came from a very small town in Ohio. There everything was done the easy way, the shortest distance between two points. It's nothing fancy; very few times will he go one-on-one. He hits the lay-up, hits the jump shot, makes the free throw, and after the game you look up and say, 'How did he hurt us that much?' "

"White" ball, then, is the basketball of patience, method, and some-times brute strength. "Black" ball is the basketball of electric self-expression. One player has all the time in the world to perfect his skills, the other a need to prove himself. These are slippery categories, because a poor boy who is black can play "white" and a white boy of middle-class parents can play "black." Charles Oakley of the New York Knicks and John Paxson of the Chicago Bulls are athletes who seem to defy these categories.

And what makes basketball the most intriguing of sports is how these styles do not necessarily clash; how the punishing intensity of "white" players and the dazzling moves of the "blacks" can fit together, a fusion of cultures that seems more and more difficult in the world beyond the out-of-bounds line.

1993

The Reader's Presence

1. Summarize the principal differences Jeff Greenfield perceives be-tween black and white styles of playing professional basketball. To what origins, to what circumstances, to what specific reasons

does he attribute this "truth" about basketball? What specific language does Greenfield use to underscore the differences between the circumstances in which blacks and whites typically learn how to play basketball? What specific terms does he use to highlight the differences in the playing styles of blacks and whites? Which style does he seem to prefer? Why? To what extent is the evidence Greenfield provides to validate each of his claims dependent on stereotypes?

2. Reread Greenfield's essay, this time paying special attention to his metaphors and syntax. Consider, for example, the final sentence in paragraph 5: "It is in this dollhouse space that ten men, each of them half a foot taller than the average man, come together to battle each other." Evaluate the effectiveness of the two major metaphors in this sentence, and identify and assess the effectiveness of the later instances when Greenfield extends and amplifies these metaphors. In a similar manner, how does Greenfield use sentence length and verb choices to reflect the distinguishing features of this intense game played in a restricted space? How is his prose, like the game itself, a "struggle for the edge"?

3. Consider Greenfield's relationship with his readers. How knowledgeable do his readers need to be about the fundamentals and the subtleties of professional basketball in order to understand and appreciate the points he makes? In this respect, to what extent has Greenfield prepared his readers to accept the final, far larger claim of his essay: that the "punishing intensity of 'white' players and the dazzling moves of the 'blacks' can fit together, a fusion of cultures that seems more and more difficult in the world beyond the out-of-bounds line"?

35 ————————————

Pete Hamill

Crack and the Box

One sad rainy morning last winter, I talked to a woman who was addicted to crack cocaine. She was twenty-two, stiletto-thin, with eyes as old as tombs. She was living in two rooms in a welfare hotel with her children, who were two, three, and five years of age. Her story was the usual tangle of human woe: early pregnancy, dropping out of school, vanished men, smack and then crack, tricks with johns in parked cars to pay for the dope. I asked her why she did drugs. She shrugged in an empty way and couldn't really answer beyond "makes me feel good." While we talked and she told her tale of squalor, the children ignored us. They were watching television.

Walking back to my office in the rain, I brooded about the woman, her zombielike children, and my own callous indifference. I'd heard so many versions of the same story that I almost never wrote them anymore; the sons of similar women, glimpsed a dozen years ago, are now in Dannemora or Soledad or Joliet; in a hundred cities, their daughters are moving into the same loveless rooms. As I walked, a series of homeless men approached me for change, most of them junkies. Others sat in doorways, staring at nothing. They were additional casualties of our time of plague, demoralized reminders that although this country holds only 2 percent of the world's population, it consumes 65 percent of the world's supply of hard drugs.

Why, for God's sake? Why do so many millions of Americans of all ages, races, and classes choose to spend all or part of their lives stupefied? I've talked to hundreds of addicts over the years; some were my friends. But none could give sensible answers. They stutter about the pain of the world, about despair or boredom, the urgent need for magic or pleasure in a society empty of both. But then they just shrug. Americans have the money to buy drugs; the supply is plentiful. But almost nobody in power asks, *Why?* Least of all, George Bush and his drug warriors.

For biographical information on Pete Hamill, see p. 651.

William Bennett talks vaguely about the heritage of sixties permissiveness, the collapse of Traditional Values, and all that. But he and Bush offer the traditional American excuse: It Is Somebody Else's Fault. This posture set the stage for the self-righteous invasion of Panama, the bloodiest drug arrest in world history. Bush even accused Manuel Noriega of "poisoning our children." But he never asked *why* so many Americans demand the poison.

And then, on that rainy morning in New York, I saw another one of   5
those ragged men staring out at the rain from a doorway. I suddenly remembered the inert postures of the children in that welfare hotel, and I thought: *television.*

Ah, no, I muttered to myself: too simple. Something as complicated as drug addiction can't be blamed on television. Come on. . . . but I remembered all those desperate places I'd visited as a reporter, where there were no books and a TV set was always playing and the older kids had gone off somewhere to shoot smack, except for the kid who was at the mortuary in a coffin. I also remembered when I was a boy in the forties and early fifties, and drugs were a minor sideshow, a kind of dark little rumor. And there was one major difference between that time and this: television.

We had unemployment then; illiteracy, poor living conditions, racism, governmental stupidity, a gap between rich and poor. We didn't have the all-consuming presence of television in our lives. Now two generations of Americans have grown up with television from their earliest moments of consciousness. Those same American generations are afflicted by the pox of drug addiction.

Only thirty-five years ago, drug addiction was not a major problem in this country. There were drug addicts. We had some at the end of the nineteenth century, hooked on the cocaine in patent medicines. During the placid fifties, Commissioner Harry Anslinger pumped up the budget of the old Bureau of Narcotics with fantasies of reefer madness. Heroin was sold and used in most major American cities, while the bebop generation of jazz musicians got jammed up with horse.

But until the early sixties, narcotics were still marginal to American life; they weren't the $120-billion market they make up today. If anything, those years have an eerie innocence. In 1955 there were 31,700,000 TV sets in use in the country (the number is now past 184 million). But the majority of the audience had grown up without the dazzling new medium. They embraced it, were diverted by it, perhaps even loved it, but they weren't *formed* by it. That year, the New York police made a mere 1,234 felony drug arrests; in 1988 it was 43,901. They confiscated ninety-seven *ounces* of cocaine for the entire year; last year it was hundreds of pounds. During each year of the fifties in New York, there were only about a hundred narcotics-related deaths. But by the end of the sixties, when the first generation of children *formed* by television had come to maturity (and thus to the marketplace), the number of such deaths had risen to 1,200. The same phenomenon was true in every major American city.

In the last Nielsen survey of American viewers, the average family was   10
watching television seven hours a day. This has never happened before in
history. No people has ever been entertained for seven hours a *day*. The
Elizabethans didn't go to the theater seven hours a day. The pre-TV generation did not go to the movies seven hours a day. Common sense tells us
that this all-pervasive diet of instant imagery, sustained now for forty
years, must have changed us in profound ways.

Television, like drugs, dominates the lives of its addicts. And though
some lonely Americans leave their sets on without watching them, using
them as electronic companions, television usually absorbs its viewers the
way drugs absorb their users. Viewers can't work or play while watching
television; they can't read; they can't be out on the streets, falling in love
with the wrong people, learning how to quarrel and compromise with
other human beings. In short they are asocial. So are drug addicts.

One Michigan State University study in the early eighties offered a
group of four- and five-year-olds the choice of giving up television or giving up their fathers. Fully one third said they would give up Daddy. Given
a similar choice (between cocaine or heroin and father, mother, brother,
sister, wife, husband, children, job), almost every stoned junkie would do
the same.

There are other disturbing similarities. Television itself is a consciousness-
altering instrument. With the touch of a button, it takes you out of the
"real" world in which you reside and can place you at a basketball game,
the back alleys of Miami, the streets of Bucharest, or the cartoony living
rooms of Sitcom Land. Each move from channel to channel alters mood,
usually with music or a laugh track. On any given evening, you can laugh,
be frightened, feel tension, thump with excitement. You can even tune in
MacNeil/Lehrer and feel sober.

But none of these abrupt shifts in mood is *earned*. They are attained as
easily as popping a pill. Getting news from television, for example, is simply not the same experience as reading it in a newspaper. Reading is *active*.
The reader must decode little symbols called words, then create images or
ideas and make them connect; at its most basic level, reading is an act of
the imagination. But the television viewer doesn't go through that process.
The words are spoken to him by Dan Rather or Tom Brokaw or Peter
Jennings. There isn't much decoding to do when watching television, no
time to think or ponder before the next set of images and spoken words
appears to displace the present one. The reader, being active, works at
his or her own pace; the viewer, being passive, proceeds at a pace determined by the show. Except at the highest levels, television never demands that its audience take part in an act of imagination. Reading always does.

In short, television works on the same imaginative and intellectual   15
level as psychoactive drugs. If prolonged television viewing makes the
young passive (dozens of studies indicate that it does), then moving to
drugs has a certain coherence. Drugs provide an unearned high (in contrast

to the earned rush that comes from a feat accomplished, a human breakthrough earned by sweat or thought or love).

And because the television addict and the drug addict are alienated from the hard and scary world, they also feel they make no difference in its complicated events. For the junkie, the world is reduced to him and the needle, pipe, or vial; the self is absolutely isolated, with no desire for choice. The television addict lives the same way. Many Americans who fail to vote in presidential elections must believe they have no more control over such a choice than they do over the casting of *L.A. Law.*

The drug plague also coincides with the unspoken assumption of most television shows: Life should be *easy.* The most complicated events are summarized on TV news in a minute or less. Cops confront murder, chase the criminals, and bring them to justice (usually violently) within an hour. In commercials, you drink the right beer and you get the girl. *Easy!* So why should real life be a grind? Why should any American have to spend years mastering a skill or a craft, or work eight hours a day at an unpleasant job, or endure the compromises and crises of a marriage? Nobody *works* on television (except cops, doctors, and lawyers). Love stories on television are about falling in love or breaking up; the long, steady growth of a marriage — its essential *dailiness* — is seldom explored, except as comedy. Life on television is almost always simple: good guys and bad, nice girls and whores, smart guys and dumb. And if life in the real world isn't that simple, well, hey, man, have some dope, man, be happy, feel good.

The doper always whines about how he *feels;* drugs are used to enhance his feelings or obliterate them, and in this the doper is very American. No other people on earth spend so much time talking about their feelings; hundreds of thousands go to shrinks, they buy self-help books by the millions, they pour out intimate confessions to virtual strangers in bars or discos. Our political campaigns are about emotional issues now, stated in the simplicities of adolescence. Even alleged statesmen can start a sentence, "I feel that the Sandinistas should . . . " when they once might have said, "I *think* . . . " I'm convinced that this exaltation of cheap emotions over logic and reason is one by-product of hundreds of thousands of hours of television.

Most Americans under the age of fifty have now spent their lives absorbing television; that is, they've had the structures of drama pounded into them. Drama is always about conflict. So news shows, politics, and advertising are now all shaped by those structures. Nobody will pay attention to anything as complicated as the part played by Third World debt in the expanding production of cocaine; it's much easier to focus on Manuel Noriega, a character right out of *Miami Vice,* and believe that even in real life there's a Mister Big.

What is to be done? Television is certainly not going away, but its addictive qualities can be controlled. It's a lot easier to "just say no" to television than to heroin or crack. As a beginning, parents must take immediate control of the sets, teaching children to watch specific television *programs,* not "television," to get out of the house and play with other kids. Elementary and high schools must begin teaching television as a subject, the way literature is taught, showing children how shows are made, how to distinguish between the true and the false, how to recognize cheap emotional manipulation. All Americans should spend more time reading. And thinking.

For years, the defenders of television have argued that the networks are only giving the people what they want. That might be true. But so is the Medellín cartel.

1990

The Reader's Presence

1. Pete Hamill's attack on the addictive nature of television is grounded in his conviction that Americans — and particularly our government leaders — are asking the wrong questions about the national drug epidemic: Rather than asking why so many people are willing to sell drugs, he proposes that we ask why so many Americans are willing, even eager, to buy them. Outline each of the points Hamill makes as he unfolds this analogy, and analyze the series of connections Hamill makes between the life-style of escapism promoted on television and provided by drugs. How convincing do you find his explanations?

2. Hamill presents a great deal of statistical information to support his assertions about the causes and the effects of drug addiction in the United States. What sources does he invoke to validate his claims? What sense of authority does he create through citing this information? Explain how he reinforces this sense of authority by invoking his personal observations and experiences. See, for example, paragraphs 2 and 3. What general patterns do you notice in the ways he introduces his personal experience in these paragraphs? Show how these patterns are sustained — or altered — in the remainder of his article.

3. Consider Hamill's point of view and his tone in criticizing television's debilitating effects on American consciousness. Can you point to any evidence in his tone to suggest that Hamill, who makes his living writing newspaper columns and magazine articles, bears a prejudice toward television, especially toward its popularity? What assumptions about the relative cultural value of newspapers, magazines, and television does Hamill express in the article? What is their effect?

36 ———————————————

Daniel R. Harris

Effeminacy

In an age in which androgyny has become the essence of urban cool and radical chic, even the nattiest male trendsetter is still a good old boy in regard to the tribal imperative of masculinity. For all his *blasé,* he would undoubtedly bristle at the suggestion that his fashionable minimizing of gender is either coquettish or effeminate. Effeminacy, after all, has none of the cachet and all of the curse. Whereas androgyny creates its own mystique of sexual ambiguity and tasteful self-containment, effeminacy is animated, excessive, and engaged. Androgyny is tantalizingly withdrawn; effeminacy theatrical and extroverted, causing acute embarrassment and disgust not only among the intolerant but the socially progressive as well.

For this reason, some twenty years after gay liberation, neither a forum nor, for that matter, a *decorum* exists for the discussion of what amounts to an outlawed manner of walking and talking, a proscribed behavior that attracts few defenders at a time when activists of the boldest stripe have shown remarkable agility in flushing out new forms of prejudice and bigotry. Every gesture of the effeminate man, from his sinuous amble to the proverbial erect pinkie nervously sawing the air, is a direct affront to an unspoken ideology of the body. Written like a signature in the very register of the voice, in the gait, the demeanor, the sense of humor, and even the prose style, effeminacy is an unwilled form of radicalism, of unrepentant exaggeration, hands that rake the air rather than remaining clenched at the sides.

Is it possible to say that something as elusive and inconsequential as a walk that's too markedly feminine or laughter that tends to unravel into titters has a political dimension? In a society whose body language consists of firm grips and steely gazes, the gestural iconoclasm of effeminacy, its unconventional moves, sounds, and expressions, has more than just private

For biographical information on Daniel R. Harris, see p. 651.

and individual consequences. One has only to look at the media to appreciate the extent to which the quavering contralto of the effeminate voice and its accompanying mannerisms have been purged from public view on the grounds that they are untelegenic in comparison with the sanitized corporate physiques and monotonously melodic tenors and baritones of most newscasters. The media are allergic to effeminacy, as are the other most powerful professions in the country. Would a corporation, for instance, hire an effeminate C.E.O. whose grip melts into a glove of putty when he shakes the hand of an important client? Would a criminal hire an effeminate lawyer to defend him in court, or the electorate vote for an effeminate candidate in a major election? The absence of effeminacy and the predominance of such dour and conservative models of behavior in the masculine consortiums of power, our boardrooms, courts, media, and legislative chambers, raise a number of troubling political issues, and yet the practical effect of this most evasive of chauvinisms passes virtually unacknowledged.

Why does an age so conscious of its victims turn a blind eye to the politics of the flaccid handshake and the insufficiently rigid swagger? For a culture accustomed to measuring victimhood entirely in terms of the lack of money, charges of active discrimination go up in smoke when you consider that the majority of effeminate men — homosexuals — are gainfully employed, swimming in disposable income, and thus, according to the accepted mythology of oppression, too rich to be victims. With no underclass to shore up its credentials for persecution, effeminacy challenges and redefines our whole notion of what constitutes both a minority and an appropriate political response to an unorthodox form of oppression, with hilarious images of an "effeminacy rights" movement — marches on Washington, impassioned testimonials before glowering Congressional subcommittees — inevitably leaping to mind. In the eyes of society, the effeminate have no political identity, in part because what distinguishes them from others, something as insubstantial as a husky resonance in the voice or a languorous posture, is too impalpable to set them apart as a distinct group. Their movements are considered so irrepressibly demonstrative, clownish, and marginal that the effeminate are often unwilling to admit to themselves, much less to others, that they are effeminate and therefore take solace in a self-ignorance that undercuts the very foundation of organized political action.

For obvious social and professional reasons, the effeminate also submit   5
to a process of voluntary ghettoization that makes this most colorless of apartheids even more invisible, both to others and, more importantly, to themselves. When faced with the hostility they are likely to encounter in the staid sanctuaries of corporate America, they conveniently flee into an arty barrio of so-called "accepting" professions where their stylized mannerisms fade into a common idiom. Instead of being escorted out of the boardroom and into jobs less directly linked with the administration of power, they prefer to believe that they have skirted around these professions for personal reasons and misinterpret what is in fact a manly rebuff

on the part of the business world as a conscious decision on their part to enter a special subdivision of the work force, the beauty and entertainment industries — interior decoration, cosmetics, floristry, the theater, the fine arts. Unaware of the barriers that limit their choices, so many effeminate men become shopkeepers, hairdressers, and manicurists because they know their place, a place traditionally occupied by women, and have intuitively sought out those careers society has decided are unimportant enough to provide a refuge (or quarantine) for their unacceptable behavior. The purging of effeminacy from the media, courts, or boardrooms is not interpreted as exclusion or discrimination because it occurs with the full complicity of the discriminated party, who willingly shuffles to the back of the bus. With neither victim nor villain, this non-racial jim crow, this *self-imposed* ghettoization defuses and depoliticizes an issue that is in fact deeply political.

In another category altogether, the calculated understatements of androgyny, so successfully exploited by rock musicians like Prince, David Byrne, Mick Jagger, or David Bowie, constitute little more than a stylized and well-groomed imperviousness that preserves intact the conventionally masculine man's sullen independence and detachment. Far from being a liability, androgyny is just the banal and essentially retrograde poetic license that we give to urban youth and the commercialized hedonists of the music industry, whose behavior represents an insignificant departure from rigid gender paradigms. Moreover, the behavioral impact on established sex roles of a more genuine androgyny is severely restricted from the outset by the fact that it is a fashion to which men and women have unequal access: It is much easier for a woman to be androgynous than a man. The venerable tradition of the hard-boiled actress and the manly chanteuse, from Marlene Dietrich and Joan Crawford to Sigourney Weaver, Laurie Anderson, Patti Smith, and Annie Lennox, officially sanctions female experimentation with gender, whereas no comparable tradition exists in popular culture for men.

Unlike androgyny, effeminate behavior profoundly alters the hard and fast distinctions between the sexes, and, what's more, it does so in a way that is highly original and in no sense of the word imitative. Is effeminacy, as it is commonly understood, really an imitation of the opposite sex? Certainly, popular films and sitcoms construe it as such. In *The Odd Couple,* for instance, Tony Randall appears quite literally as a housewife in an apron furiously mowing the carpet with his Hoover or taking mad swipes with the feather duster in the wake of Jack Lemmon's exasperating masculinity. The effeminate man in both American public life and popular iconography is *always* a man impersonating a woman. He is allotted his marginal presence in TV and film only if he makes the terms of his impersonation abundantly clear, as Quentin Crisp does with his theatrical makeup and imperious capes or Boy George with his wide-brimmed bonnets and modish dresses. The only exception to this rule that comes immediately to mind is the conspicuously effeminate behavior of Michael Jackson, who is in no obvious way imitating the style and apparel of women but who is nonetheless poignantly, defenselessly effeminate. However much time, money, and effort his publicists have invested in burying the eccentric gestures and squeaking voice of the castrato under black shades and hoodish accoutrements, the embarrassing and unmarketable manner-isms of a real person, and not just a bland, pasteurized superstar, burn through the floodlights.

For the mass audience, effeminacy is comedy — the slapstick of *La Cage aux Folles* or the dizzy exaggerations of William Hurt in his mistak-enly rapturous performance in *Kiss of the Spider Woman*. Because it is almost impossible for people to view effeminacy as an entirely separate form of behavior with an integrity of its own, it is pigeonholed in popular culture as a ridiculous waste product of gender conflicts, the province of endearing grotesques and colorful transsexuals who strive unavailingly, with all of the attendant absurdities, to transform themselves into the op-posite sex. In reality, however, the effeminate man is not just a rowdy im-postor of women and a favorite cinematic gag. In fact, he is not so much imitative of women as he is *non-imitative* of men, for the state of effemi-nacy is characterized by complete inattention to gender, a kind of forgetful-ness of one's duty to uphold the rituals of the fellowship. It is so difficult to describe, not only because the embarrassment it causes interferes with our concentration on it and thus prevents us from fixing it in words, but also because it is defined by the *absence* rather than by the presence of specific qualities, by the lack of the preoccupying awareness most men have of their sex. The imitative view of effeminacy, the attempt to locate the analogue of every effeminate gesture in the body language of women, is fundamentally flawed because it presumes that these gestures are deliberate, however un-consciously, when in fact they are simply the outcome of total, anarchistic relaxation of one's vigilance in maintaining the masculine stance and de-meanor. In short, effeminacy is nonrepresentational, an imitation of noth-ing. It is not a routine, a futile act of sexual plagiarism, but an absence of the absorption and single-mindedness with which we conform to the strict code of conduct that our culture mandates for both men and women. In this sense, conventional masculinity and femininity are much more imita-tive, because masculine men and feminine women, far from being oblivious to their sex, are constantly attempting to achieve a successful approxima-tion of an abstract behavioral ideal considered appropriate to their gender, whereas the effeminate are heedless, if inadvertently so, of these often op-pressive expectations.

One would have anticipated that gay liberation and the commercial-ization of the lives of gay men in inner-city neighborhoods like the Castro and Christopher Street would have significantly changed the way that our culture views effeminacy, providing a new protective environment in which to experiment with unconventionally masculine forms of behavior. A cen-tral paradox of the birth of the subculture, however, is that in resisting the effeminate stereotypes and gestural paradigms that have tyrannized gay men in the past, we have created a new Frankenstein — the "good gay," masculine, assimilated, forceful, deliberate, his body no longer a boneless frenzy of threshing arms and legs but a militarized automaton patrolling his beat at a brisk goosestep. In liberating themselves from effeminacy, homosexuals have taken on yet another albatross, accepted more, not less rigid notions of how they should express their homosexuality, and essentially invented — to borrow a stereotype ridiculed in the black community — the gay oreo, effeminate on the inside, masculine without. In the final analysis, liberation has liberated homosexuals into a new totalitarian attitude toward their mannerisms, a new contempt for effeminacy, and above all a new body language, the masculine majority's depersonalizing Esperanto of frigid gestures and flinty smiles.

Nowhere is the resistance to effeminacy, the ultimatum to butch it up, 10 seen more clearly than in the de-sexing of many men's lives. Since the gay community has by and large ceased to be our culture's effeminate avant-garde, the effeminate man must now contend with both his ostracism and his lack of sex appeal. The language of self-censorship and self-fascism one finds in gay personal ads, the epithets of "straight-appearing" and "straight-acting," expresses a new anxiety on the part of gay men to strip themselves of the demasculinizing traces of the subculture, an anxiety they once clothed and shod and sexed up with the dated accoutrements of hard-line homosexual machismo: the boots and keys of the hard hat, the chaps and Stetson of the cowpoke, the olive drab and dog tags of the soldier, the leather jacket and motorcycle of the cop, or even the Lacoste shirts and penny loafers of the preppie. The subculture we thought would enable us to be more ourselves has in fact encouraged us to be less so, with the unfortunate result that the rise of the gay ghetto and our attempt to escape from the demeaning stereotypes of the swish have put us more at the mercy of heterosexual models for masculine behavior and sexual appeal than we have ever been before.

Which isn't to say that effeminate mannerisms — legs that involuntarily seek each other out and braid under the table or hands that oscillate like pendulums at the wrists — have been eradicated altogether, as anyone who has the most casual acquaintance with an inner-city ghetto can attest. Instead of disappearing entirely in the aftermath of the militarization of the gay libido, effeminacy is now governed by a new decorum: "camp," not "camp" in Susan Sontag's sense of the word but in the much more specific sense of "to camp," "camp it up," or "campy queen." These idioms are essential components of the vernacular of contemporary urban life, and they are part of a revolution in sensibility. The very fact that effeminate behavior has been given a name and, what's more, that one of the forms of the name is an intransitive verb, suggests that a major change has occurred in the way that gay men view themselves and their gestures. The verbal form "to camp" implies that effeminacy has become a specific kind of activity that one can choose to do, like "to sing" or "to dance" or "to laugh" — that it is not, in other words, an all-embracing style over which the effeminate have no control but rather that it is an *action* that one can will oneself to perform and likewise *not* to perform. To be effeminate is no longer something one *is* but something one *does*. What was once a largely unconscious attitude toward the self, an obliviousness or immunity to the erect carriage and poker face of The Real Man, has now become a willed form of behavior, a social mask or party drag of which the effeminate man is not the victim but the impresario, the emcee.

Camp, unlike effeminacy, is an alternative form of the self, a routine, a shtick, a persona, something that can be donned like formal wear for occasions of state and similarly doffed when the situation demands a low profile, like dining with your parents or careering at the office. Camp is effeminacy empowered by gay liberation, not the pre-Stonewall straight jacket of the flouncing pansy, the slave of his own gestures, but a heavily monitored and site-specific style which we can hide or flaunt as we choose. After twenty years of gay activism, our closets haven't really been ripped open, as those of us who have participated in gay liberation would like to believe, but simply equipped with swinging doors, slamming shut to enable the sober professional with his power suit and his attaché to embark for the office undetected, and then — after 6:00 — swinging wide open again to reveal the master of the revels no longer in his three-piece but in harlequin tights and a cap with jingling bells.

Gay liberation has inspired a new self-consciousness about the way that effeminacy isolates the individual and has encouraged men to reserve their effeminate behavior for colorful intermezzos of short duration policed by a harsh decorum. Camp is a new expression of their unsparingly objective view of their own mannerisms, a form of monologuing, grandstanding, and self-display in which effeminacy becomes a cunning and deliberate ceremony, a highly detached street mime or self-theater with its own repertoire of stock moves, parts, phrases, gags, bits — all of the elements of the outlandish cartoon, the "queen." Camp transforms the effeminate titter into a booming bray and the effeminate mince into a vampish slink with the man who is "on" batting away the imaginary tidal-wave curl. Camp, in short, is effeminacy in quotation marks. It is "about" itself, involving the burlesque of a style that once dictated the appearance of virtually every move the effeminate man made. In this sense, rather than endorsing effeminacy, gay liberation has led to the institutionalization of its ridicule.

The major difference between genuinely effeminate men like Little Richard, Michael Jackson, or even Paul Lynde from *Hollywood Squares* and camp goddesses like Divine (the star of John Waters's cult films), Holly Woodlawn (the transsexual heroine of Paul Morrissey's *Trash*), or the late Charles Ludlum (the brilliant drag-queen performer from The Ridiculous Theater Company) is that the former are unconscious of the restraints of gender and therefore nonimitative of women, whereas the latter are preoccupied with the ribald effects of the paradox of the boy-girl. Far from being spontaneous and individual personalities with a *sui generis* style, the camp stars of the American underground — San Francisco's Sisters of Perpetual

Indulgence (a group of gay men in full nuns' habits), the Trocadero (a dance company which performs full-length ballets in drag), or the late disco diva Sylvester — are imitative of at least three separate things: women, new media images of the female performer, and the effete mannerisms of the old-style homosexual. Unlike effeminacy, camp *is* representational. Whereas the effeminate man exists in solipsistic oblivion to masculinity, the campy queen is fully conscious, not only of his sex and the potential it offers for humorous paradoxes, but also of images of women disseminated by TV and film, the dense web of allusions to popular culture (to Judy Garland, Bette Davis, Marilyn Monroe, Barbara Stanwyck, Mae West, and any number of other celebrities) which constitutes the bedrock of camp, the sounding board off of which the queen is constantly bouncing his impersonations.

Why do men camp? While there is such a thing as good camp and bad 15 camp, camp that involves full-scale impersonations by men with an uncanny theatrical presence and camp that is as mundane and artless as a screeching falsetto, anyone who has ever seen quality camp knows how exhilarating it can be, both for the performer and for his audience. It is an indigenous style of stand-up comedy, and like many stand-up comedians, the most talented maintain a playfully mordant antagonism with members of their audiences, laughing at the way they're dressed or at their bashfulness in the face of his sour but ultimately good-natured intimidation. For the audience, the pleasure of such a performance is a good show and also the exciting sensation that you will be the next one singled out for inspection, the next sacrificial object of scorn. For the performer, the pleasure of camp is far more complex, involving feelings of power and superiority, of towering over your audience and being able to send them sprawling as you sweep past on a gust of outrageous barbs. Camp creates the illusion of incredible conversational omnipotence, of an urbanity and self-control that make your audience cower before you, full of admiration, fear, and obedience.

Because of this short-lived power-fix, camp has a particularly seductive appeal for gay men in that it sponsors the illusion of having a sort of power they often lack in their daily lives, a spurious mastery over others which they achieve by means of their skills as pantomimists and wordsmiths. It thus functions as a form of false politics: it allows effeminate men to live out fantasies of being conversational champions in a restrictive and permissive environment, whereas in the less restrictive environment of the workplace, they are so often cast in the role of the victim — not the loud and imperious *femme fatale* of camp's portable stage but a man hemmed in by the constraints of the still largely homophobic office world.

Does this mean that camp is a good thing or a bad thing, politics or playacting, a real source of power or a placebo? As someone who finds camp one of the inescapable elements of his life, something I take for granted like the air I breathe, it would be ridiculous for me to shower reproaches on a style of behavior that is a rich example of ethnic culture, an authentic form of urban folk art that enshrines the divided sensibility of the homosexual, of someone who has kept quiet and yet observed, and consequently recognizes on a visceral level the value of irony and parody. Yet camp, like all great things, most notably effeminacy itself, carries with it both a license and a responsibility: Those who acquire its addictive taste are in constant danger of falling prey to its seductive false politics which, rather than enabling effeminate men to resist ghettoization, will ultimately turn them into clowns and harlequins, dancing bears and bearded ladies.

1991

The Reader's Presence

1. Harris's essay is as much about the need for defining effeminacy as it is an extended definition of the term. Why does he believe it is necessary to devise a definition of effeminacy? What purpose does he hope to accomplish by defining it? What does he explain is at stake — personally, culturally, and politically — in defining the term? Where in the article does he make these points clear? What specific characteristics does he ascribe to effeminacy? What does he mean when he says (in paragraph 8) that "it is defined by the *absence* rather than by the presence of specific qualities"?

2. What does Harris assume about his audience's attitudes toward effeminacy? In what ways does he take into account his audience's divergent attitudes toward the word? toward homosexuality? Where in the essay does he address the issue of audience response to these subjects, and toward camp? What distinctions does Harris draw between the terms *effeminacy, androgyny,* and *camp?*

3. Reread the essay carefully, with special attention to the diction Harris uses when talking about effeminacy. What parts of speech dominate those sentences? What responses does Harris elicit from his audience by using such terms as "purging" and "*self-imposed* ghettoization"? What kinds of adjectives and verbs does Harris use to talk about androgyny? camp? How would you characterize Harris's tone toward androgyny, camp, and effeminacy? What specific techniques does he use to establish his attitude toward each? In this respect, pay particular attention to his use of irony. For example, what does he mean when he says: "In the final analysis, liberation has liberated homosexuals into a new totalitarian attitude toward their mannerisms, a new contempt for effeminacy, and above all a new body language, the masculine majority's depersonalizing Esperanto of frigid gestures and flinty smiles" (paragraph 9)?

37

Linda M. Hasselstrom

Why One Peaceful Woman Carries a Pistol

I'm a peace-loving woman. I also carry a pistol. For years, I've written about my decision in an effort to help other women make intelligent choices about gun ownership, but editors rejected the articles. Between 1983 and 1986, however, when gun sales to men held steady, gun ownership among women rose fifty-three percent, to more than twelve million. We learned that any female over the age of twelve can expect to be criminally assaulted some time in her life, that women aged thirty have a fifty-fifty chance of being raped, robbed, or attacked, and that many police officials say flatly that they cannot protect citizens from crime. During the same period, the number of women considering gun ownership quadrupled to nearly two million. Manufacturers began showing lightweight weapons with small grips, and purses with built-in holsters. A new magazine is called *Guns and Women,* and more than eight thousand copies of the video *A Woman's Guide to Firearms* were sold by 1988. Experts say female gun buyers are not limited to any particular age group, profession, social class, or area of the country, and most are buying guns to protect themselves. Shooting instructors say women view guns with more caution than do men, and may make better shots.

I decided to buy a handgun for several reasons. During one four-year period, I drove more than a hundred thousand miles alone, giving speeches, readings, and workshops. A woman is advised, usually by men, to protect herself by avoiding bars, by approaching her car like an Indian scout, by locking doors and windows. But these precautions aren't always enough. And the logic angers me: *Because* I am female, it is my responsibility to be extra careful.

For biographical information on Linda M. Hasselstrom, see p. 651.

As a responsible environmentalist, I choose to recycle, avoid chemicals on my land, minimize waste. As an informed woman alone, I choose to be as responsible for my own safety as possible: I keep my car running well, use caution in where I go and what I do. And I learned about self-protection — not an easy or quick decision. I developed a strategy of protection that includes handgun possession. The following incidents, chosen from a larger number because I think they could happen to anyone, helped make up my mind.

When I camped with another woman for several weeks, she didn't want to carry a pistol, and police told us Mace was illegal. We tucked spray deodorant into our sleeping bags, theorizing that any man crawling into our tent at night would be nervous anyway; anything sprayed in his face would slow him down until we could hit him with a frying pan, or escape. We never used our improvised weapon, because we were lucky enough to camp beside people who came to our aid when we needed them. I returned from that trip determined to reconsider.

At that time, I lived alone and taught night classes in town. Along a   5
city street I often traveled, a woman had a flat tire, called for help on her CB, and got a rapist; he didn't fix the tire either. She was afraid to call for help again and stayed in her car until morning. Also, CBs work best along line-of-sight; I ruled them out.

As I drove home one night, a car followed me, lights bright. It passed on a narrow bridge, while a passenger flashed a spotlight in my face, blinding me. I braked sharply. The car stopped, angled across the bridge, and four men jumped out. I realized the locked doors were useless if they broke my car windows. I started forward, hoping to knock their car aside so I could pass. Just then, another car appeared, and the men got back in their car, but continued to follow me, passing and repassing. I dared not go home. I passed no lighted houses. Finally, they pulled to the roadside, and I decided to use their tactic: fear. I roared past them inches away, horn blaring. It worked; they turned off the highway. But it was desperate and foolish, and I was frightened and angry. Even in my vehicle I was too vulnerable.

Other incidents followed. One day I saw a man in the field near my house, carrying a shotgun and heading for a pond full of ducks. I drove to meet him, and politely explained that the land was posted. He stared at me, and the muzzle of his shotgun rose. I realized that if he simply shot me and drove away, I would be a statistic. The moment passed; the man left.

One night, I returned home from class to find deep tire ruts on the lawn, a large gas tank empty, garbage in the driveway. A light shone in the house; I couldn't remember leaving it on. I was too embarrassed to wake the neighbors. An hour of cautious exploration convinced me the house was safe, but once inside, with the doors locked, I was still afraid. I put a .22 rifle by my bed, but I kept thinking of how naked I felt, prowling around my own house in the dark.

It was time to consider self-defense. I took a kung fu class and learned to define the distance to maintain between myself and a stranger. Once someone enters that space without permission, kung fu teaches appropriate evasive or protective action. I learned to move confidently, scanning for possible attack. I learned how to assess danger, and techniques for avoiding it without combat.

I also learned that one must practice several hours every day to be good at kung fu. By that time I had married George; when I practiced with him, I learned how *close* you must be to your attacker to use martial arts, and decided a 120-pound woman dare not let a six-foot, 220-pound attacker get that close unless she is very, very good at self-defense. Some women who are well trained in martial arts have been raped and beaten anyway.

Reluctantly I decided to carry a pistol. George helped me practice with his .357 and .22. I disliked the .357's recoil, though I later became comfortable with it. I bought a .22 at a pawn shop. A standard .22 bullet, fired at close range, can kill, but news reports tell of attackers advancing with five such bullets in them. I bought magnum shells, with more power, and practiced until I could hit someone close enough to endanger me. Then I bought a license making it legal for me to carry the gun concealed.

George taught me that the most important preparation was mental: convincing myself I could shoot someone. Few of us really wish to hurt or kill another human being. But there is no point in having a gun — in fact, gun possession might increase your danger — unless you know you can use it against another human being. A good training course includes mental preparation, as well as training in safety. As I drive or walk, I often rehearse the conditions which would cause me to shoot. Men grow up handling firearms, and learn controlled violence in contact sports, but women grow up learning to be subservient and vulnerable. To make ourselves comfortable with the idea that we are capable of protecting ourselves requires effort. But it need not turn us into macho, gun-fighting broads. We must simply learn to do as men do from an early age: believe in, and rely on, *ourselves* for protection. The pistol only adds an extra edge, an attention-getter; it is a weapon of last resort.

Because shooting at another person means shooting to kill. It's impossible even for seasoned police officers to be sure of only wounding an assailant. If I shot an attacking man, I would aim at the largest target, the chest. This is not an easy choice, but for me it would be better than rape.

In my car, my pistol is within instant reach. When I enter a deserted rest stop at night, it's in my purse, my hand on the grip. When I walk from a dark parking lot into a motel, it's in my hand, under a coat. When I walk my dog in the deserted lots around most motels, the pistol is in a shoulder holster, and I am always aware of my surroundings. In my motel room, it lies on the bedside table. At home, it's on the headboard.

Just carrying a pistol is not protection. Avoidance is still the best approach to trouble; watch for danger signs, and practice avoiding them. Develop your instinct for danger.

One day while driving to the highway mailbox, I saw a vehicle parked about halfway to the house. Several men were standing in the ditch, relieving themselves. I have no objection to emergency urination; we always need moisture. But they'd also dumped several dozen beer cans, which blow into pastures and can slash a cow's legs or stomach.

As I slowly drove closer, the men zipped their trousers ostentatiously while walking toward me. Four men gathered around my small foreign car, making remarks they wouldn't make to their mothers, and one of them demanded what the hell I wanted.

"This is private land; I'd like you to pick up the beer cans."

"What beer cans?" said the belligerent one, putting both hands on the car door, and leaning in my window. His face was inches from mine, the beer fumes were strong, and he looked angry. The others laughed. One tried the passenger door, locked; another put his foot on the hood and rocked the car. They circled, lightly thumping the roof, discussing my good fortune in meeting them, and the benefits they were likely to bestow upon me. I felt small and trapped; they knew it.

"The ones you just threw out," I said politely.   20

"I don't see no beer cans. Why don't you get out here and show them to me, honey?" said the belligerent one, reaching for the handle inside my door.

"Right over there," I said, still being polite, "there and over there." I pointed with the pistol, which had been under my thigh. Within one minute the cans and the men were back in the car, and headed down the road.

I believe this small incident illustrates several principles. The men were trespassing and knew it; their judgment may have been impaired by alcohol. Their response to the polite request of a woman alone was to use their size and numbers to inspire fear. The pistol was a response in the same language. Politeness didn't work; I couldn't intimidate them. Out of the car, I'd have been more vulnerable. The pistol just changed the balance of power.

My husband, George, asked one question when I told him. "What would you have done if he'd grabbed for the pistol?"

"I had the car in reverse; I'd have hit the accelerator, and backed up; if   25 he'd kept coming, I'd have fired straight at him." He nodded.

In fact, the sight of the pistol made the man straighten up; he cracked his head on the door frame. He and the two in front of the car stepped backward, catching the attention of the fourth, who joined them. They were all in front of me then, and as the car was still running and in reverse gear, my options had multiplied. If they'd advanced again, I'd have backed away, turning to keep the open window toward them. Given time, I'd have put the first shot into the ground in front of them, the second into the belligerent leader. It might have been better to wait until they were gone, pick up the beer cans, and avoid confrontation, but I believed it was reasonable and my right to make a polite request to strangers littering my property. Showing the pistol worked on another occasion when I was driving in a desolate part of Wyoming. A man played cat-and-mouse with me for thirty miles, ultimately trying to run my car off the road. When his car was only two inches from mine, I pointed my pistol at him, and he disappeared.

I believe that a handgun is like a car; both are tools for specific purposes; both can be lethal if used improperly. Both require a license, training, and alertness. Both require you to be aware of what is happening before and behind you. Driving becomes almost instinctive; so does handgun use. When I've drawn my gun for protection, I simply found it in my hand. Instinct told me a situation was dangerous before my conscious mind reacted; I've felt the same while driving. Most good drivers react to emergencies by instinct.

Knives are another useful tool often misunderstood and misused; some people acquire knives mostly for display, either on a wall or on a belt, and such knives are often so large as to serve no useful purpose. My pocket knives are always razor sharp, because a small, sharp knife will do most jobs. Skinning blades serve for cutting meat and splitting small kindling in camp. A *sgian dubh,* a four-inch flat blade in a wooden sheath, was easily concealed inside a Scotsman's high socks, and slips into my dress or work boots as well. Some buckskinners keep what they call a "grace knife" on a thong around their necks; the name may derive from *coup de grâce,* the welcome throat-slash a wounded knight asked from his closest friend, to keep him from falling alive into the hands of his enemies. I also have a push dagger, with a blade only three inches long, attached to a handle that fits into the fist so well that the knife would be hard to lose even in hand-to-hand combat. When I first showed it, without explanation, to an older woman who would never consider carrying a knife, she took one look and said, "Why, you could push that right into someone's stomach," and demonstrated with a flourish. That's what it's for. I wear it for decoration, because it was handmade by Jerry and fits my hand perfectly, but I am intently aware of its purpose. I like my knives, not because they are weapons, but because they are well designed, and beautiful, and because each is a tool with a specific purpose.

Women didn't always have jobs, or drive cars or heavy equipment, though western women did many of those things almost as soon as they arrived here. Men in authority argued that their attempt to do so would unravel the fabric of society. Women, they said, would become less feminine; they hadn't the intelligence to cope with the mechanics of a car, or the judgment to cope with emergencies. Since these ideas were so wrong, perhaps it is time women brought a new dimension to the wise use of handguns as well.

We can and should educate ourselves in how to travel safely, take self-defense courses, reason, plead, or avoid trouble in other ways. But some 30 men cannot be stopped by those methods; they understand only power. A man who is committing an attack already knows he's breaking laws; he has no concern for someone else's rights. A pistol is a woman's answer to his greater power. It makes her equally frightening. I have thought of revising the old Colt slogan: "God made man, but Sam Colt made them equal" to read "God made men *and women* but Sam Colt made them equal." Recently I have seen an ad for a popular gunmaker with a similar sentiment; perhaps this is an idea whose time has come, though the pacifist inside me will be saddened if the only way women can achieve equality is by carrying a weapon.

As a society, we were shocked in early 1989 when a female jogger in New York's Central Park was beaten and raped savagely and left in a coma. I was even more shocked when reporters interviewed children who lived near the victim and quoted a twelve-year-old as saying, "She had nothing to guard herself; she didn't have no man with her; she didn't have no Mace." And another sixth-grader said, "It is like she committed suicide." Surely this is not a majority opinion, but I think it is not so unusual, either, even in this liberated age. Yet there is no city or county in the nation where law officers can relax because all the criminals are in jail. Some authorities say citizens armed with handguns stop almost as many crimes annually as armed criminals succeed in committing, and that people defending themselves kill three times more attackers and robbers than police do. I don't suggest all criminals should be killed, but some can be stopped only by death or permanent incarceration. Law enforcement officials can't prevent crimes; later punishment may be of little comfort to the victim. A society so controlled that no crime existed would probably be too confined for most of us, and is not likely to exist any time soon. Therefore, many of us should be ready and able to protect ourselves, and the intelligent use of firearms is one way.

We must treat a firearm's power with caution. "Power tends to corrupt, and absolute power corrupts absolutely," as a man (Lord Acton) once said. A pistol is not the only way to avoid being raped or murdered in today's world, but a firearm, intelligently wielded, can shift the balance and provide a measure of safety.

1991

The Reader's Presence

1. The title of Linda M. Hasselstrom's essay announces her purpose. Outline each of the points she highlights in her defense of carrying a firearm. What alternatives to a handgun does she consider, and why does she reject each? How does she anticipate objections to her explanation? What kinds of preparation does she think necessary in order to "ready" herself to carry a pistol? What, finally, does she see as the most effective form of protection against trouble?

2. In what specific ways does Hasselstrom address the conventional perception that men are more likely to bear arms than women? When — and in what terms — does she make gender an issue in carrying a firearm? What specific words and phrases does she repeat to emphasize her own vulnerability and that of other women?

3. In the opening paragraphs of her detailed explanation of why she carries a gun, Hasselstrom announces to her readers the point of view from which she speaks: a "peace-loving woman," a freelance writer who lives on a ranch in western South Dakota. Recognizing that "handgun possession is a controversial subject," she immediately expresses her overall aim in writing: "perhaps my reasoning will interest others." Who might be included in the "others" she mentions here? Is there any evidence to suggest, for example, that she has women primarily in mind as her audience? If so, what evidence validates your reading? If, however, you believe that gender is not an important factor in determining who might be included in her audience for this article, what factors in her explanation might help you to identify her intended audience?

38

Satoshi Kamata

Six Months at Toyota

MONDAY, SEPTEMBER 18

My first workday. Up at 5:00 A.M. It's still dark when I go out. The eastern mountains are glowing faintly, but I can still see the stars shining brightly in the sky. The street is lit by a few scattered lamps. It's a forty-minute walk to the factory. Unfortunately, the plant I have to work in is at the farthest corner of the factory compound. I can't find the canteen and miss breakfast.

For biographical information on Satoshi Kamata, see p. 653.

I have really been fooled by the seeming slowness of the conveyor belt. No one can understand how it works without experiencing it. Almost as soon as I begin, I am dripping with sweat. Somehow, I learn the order of the work motions, but I'm totally unable to keep up with the speed of the line. My work gloves make it difficult to grab as many tiny bolts as I need, and how many precious seconds do I waste doing just that? I do my best, but I can barely finish one gear box out of three within the fixed length of time. If a different-model transmission comes along, it's simply beyond my capacity. Some skill is needed, and a new hand like me can't do it alone. I'm thirsty as hell, but workers can neither smoke nor drink water. Going to the toilet is out of the question. Who could have invented a system like this? It's designed to make workers do nothing *but* work and to prevent any kind of rest. Yet the man beside me the other day deftly handled his hammer, put the bolts into their grooves with both hands, and fastened them with a nut runner (a power screwdriver that can tighten six bolts simultaneously), seemingly with no difficulty.

The conveyor starts at 6:00 A.M. and doesn't stop until 11:00 A.M. One box of transmissions arrives on the conveyor belt every minute and twenty seconds with unerring precision. When the line stops at eleven o'clock, we tear off our gloves and leave our positions as quickly as we can. We wash our greasy hands and run to the toilet, then rush to the canteen about a hundred yards away where we wait in another line to get our food. After standing five hours, my legs are numb and stiff. My new safety shoes are so heavy that I feel I can barely move. I put my ticket into a box, take an aluminum tray, a pair of chopsticks, a plate of food, a tea cup, and a bowl of rice. I'm still unfamiliar with the routine and have a hard time finding a seat at one of the long tables. Finally, just as I'm settling down to eat, I have the sensation that the trays on the table are moving slowly sideways as if they're on a conveyor belt! At 11:45, the line starts again. There's not much time to rest since ten minutes before work starts we have to begin preparing a large enough supply of parts for the afternoon assemblage.

Above the line, a little to my right, there's a big electric display panel. Under the words "Transmission Assembly Conveyor," there are numbers from 1 to 15. When it is absolutely impossible to catch up with the conveyor, you have to push a button under the belt. This lights up your number in yellow on the board. To halt the line in an emergency, you have to push another button, which triggers a red light and stops the line. Although there are fifteen buttons on the line, there are now only eight workers. To increase production, Toyota decided to use two shifts starting this month. September is the beginning of the high-demand season, and I'm in the first group of seasonal workers hired under this new schedule.

The first shift ends at 2:15 P.M. Already, the man on the next shift is standing beside me, waiting for me to finish. As soon as I put my hammer down on the belt, he picks it up and begins precisely where I left off. A baton pass, and neatly done, too.

Still, it turns out I'm not finished! I have to spend thirty more minutes

5

replenishing the supply parts for the afternoon shift. I also have to pick up the parts I've scattered on the floor. Damn! My legs ache the entire forty-minute walk back to the dorm. I'm bone tired. Is this the life for a worker in a great enterprise, a famous auto company, proud of being tops in Japan and the third in the world? Somehow I'll have to get used to it.

Tonight Kudo, who had left at eight in the morning, comes back a little after seven. He also had to work two hours overtime. For some reason, the lights in the dorms have gone out. It's really depressing to return to a dark room after walking all the way from the plant.

Kudo is lying spread-eagled on the mat floor. "I didn't quite expect the work to be so hard," he says. Still, he tells me somewhat proudly that he's made 400 pieces today. I don't know how many I made myself, or for that matter, don't really know what I was making. Exactly what part of the gear box were they? I was much too busy to look at the other guys' operations. I didn't even have time to look at my watch. After a while, I felt like I was making some part of a child's plastic toy. What was I really doing? The sign in my shop has a word for it — "Assembly"!

Tonight, I'm too tired to sleep and awfully nervous about having to get up early tomorrow. I get up and go out to buy a can of beer. A picture of Ken Takakura, a famous actor, smiles down at me from the vending machine. Even beer is sold by machines. . . .

THURSDAY, SEPTEMBER 28

I went to take a bath downstairs this morning. When I came out, my   10
wooden clogs were gone. You're not often robbed these days, even in public baths. When I went to the dining room, there was nothing left to eat. Here every day is a small war.

There is a Safety First meeting ten minutes before the shift begins. It's not fair for management to force a meeting on the workers during their off time, but no one protests.

There are some complaints among the workers. When the company declared an increase in output, it promised that ten workers from another plant would be sent here as reinforcements. In the end, only eight came. The only way not to hold up the line was to offset the labor shortage by working overtime. Workers are angry.

"What we can't do, we can't do," one worker says. "The company should be satisfied."

"If we really care about Safety First," another says, "why don't they hire more workers? That's top priority."

But still, when the time comes, we all return to work without protest.   15
By 10:00 P.M. everyone is exhausted. It is all I can do to keep my hands in motion on the line. But strangely, time passes and the line moves on, and somehow each day's work ends.

I'm responsible for assembling two kinds of truck transmissions, and by now I can do about 90 percent of the required work. I'd give anything just to keep up with the murderous conveyor. I hate having to push the button to call the team chief and reveal my incompetence again and again.

Takeda, whose position is next to mine, helps me sometimes by rushing through his own work to give me a whole minute of his precious time. "Tell me how to do it and I'll help you. My job is simple. I can spare the minute."

I know he really can't spare the minute. Nobody on the line can afford the luxury of helping others. I am touched.

But there's another side to Takeda's generosity. He's dying from the monotony of his own work. I'm thankful for his help, of course, but Takeda also wants to try something new and strange, something that breaks the deadly boredom, the relentless repetition of the assembly line. There, where no amount of intelligence, creativity, or freedom is permitted, he can release some tension and refresh his energy by helping me, and that helps him get through the day.

Almost all the workers here are hardworking. In most factories, there are   20
those who work very hard and those who don't. But here, the conveyor-belt system makes everyone work at exactly the same pace. Even off the line, we all begin preparing parts even before our shift starts, time which is still our supper break, for without this preparation we'd never get the work done.

It is raining when work finishes. I am depressed, already worrying if I will make it through to next February, when my contract expires. Takeda asks Yoshizaki, who happens to live near my dorm, to give me a lift.

The joint at the base of my right third finger is numb. I can't bend it at all. . . .

THURSDAY, OCTOBER 5

A meeting after work. Mostly, we talk about our section manager's new order to check the tightness of all six bolts in the transmission. It's impossible for us to add one more operation. We're already too pressed for time. The team chief tries to force it on us, using the oldest excuse in the world:

"It's an order from the section manager."

One worker answers coldly, "Well, if it's an order, it's an order. But   25
the line's going to stop."

"I don't care. Let it stop."

"You say you don't care? But the people on the second shift will have to work overtime to make up for us."

Another worker exclaims, "They'll have to work until two or three o'clock in the morning! That's impossible. What sort of people do the management think we are?"

Everybody starts complaining all at once. Finally, the general foreman, a stout man with a white cap, proposes a compromise: "Well, we'll try measuring at only one point. I'll ask the management about it."

"One place is plenty!" someone shouts in disgust.   30

Suddenly the section manager, who issued the order, comes in. He's still young, about forty. The general foreman tells us rather ceremoniously, "Please pay special attention to safety." Then he stands and leaves in spite of our anger. The meeting has "ended." We also stand and leave the narrow locker room. As we're filing out, someone tells the section manager. "You've got to think more about us," but the words no longer have an icy edge. They're more like a joke. Even the experienced workers are getting upset. I'm relieved to know that others are as discontented as I am. . . .

THURSDAY, JANUARY 11

When I went to work last night, I knew immediately something was wrong. The team chief on the other shift stood there rather uneasily, and the workers who had just arrived surrounded him. I asked Miura, who works with me, if there had been an accident. He said that Kawamura, a seasonal worker, had been severely shocked. Kawamura is a young man from Hokkaido, where he worked as a carpenter. They carried him to the Toyota Hospital, and he'll probably be there for more than a week.

Before work started, the general foreman made one of his little speeches: "Kawamura's biorhythm chart shows that today is his worst day. Looks like the chart was right!"

The workers knew the real story. Going to get some parts he needed, Kawamura crossed over two small conveyor belts and touched a machine. But the machine (a parts feeder that fits washers in bolts) was so old that some of a 200-volt electric cord was frayed. And his gloves were wet. He received a severe shock and fell to the floor. He suffered a concussion and lost consciousness. Luckily the current passed through the base of his finger. If it had gone near his heart, he would have been killed instantly.

On the day of the accident, his team was short of workers, since two people hadn't showed up and one seasonal worker had quit. Superficially, the cause of the accident was that he took a shortcut to get the parts, but the real cause was the short circuit in the old machine, and also, the fact that there was no bridge over the line. But according to the general foreman (who's also a member of the union!), the problem was in the worker's biorhythm, and the key to safety is for all of us to be careful when our own biorhythms are bad.

This year's new slogan is written on the company's blackboard: "Whatever you do, be prepared to take responsibility for it." . . .

THURSDAY, JANUARY 18

They say we made 425 boxes today. Though we have no time to count, our production has increased by 25 boxes a day. Soon we'll be making 450 boxes a day. When I get back tonight, I find Kudo still there.

"Aren't you going to work?"

"No, not today. Not tomorrow, either."

"Are you feeling bad?"   40

"I'm leaving. Today I fell on the floor unconscious," he says, looking at me weakly.

Last night he worked the night shift, but as soon as he started, he felt sick. He tried to keep on working. When he checked the clock, it was 12:50 A.M. Ten minutes to go until the break for the midnight meal. When he looked at the clock again, three minutes had passed. Seven more minutes, he thought, and then he fell on the floor. When he came to he was lying on a bench, covered with the coat he had just bought. Someone must have opened his locker and put it over him. The foreman, who was standing beside him, told him that right after he fell, they had carried him to the Toyota Hospital, just outside the factory grounds. They had given him an injection, and then he had been transferred to the infirmary inside the factory. It was already morning when he came to. Why hadn't they left him to sleep in a soft hospital bed?

When he was carried to the hospital again, Kudo told them about the traffic accident he'd had before. The general foreman told Kudo, "Once you fall, you can't work any more. I'll see that your account is settled. Rest well at home, and then come and see us again." That was all; he was fired.

"At least I'm glad I'm alive," Kudo adds. "Well, I won't worry. Anyway, they need someone at home to shovel the snow off the roof. It's only forty-six days till the end of my contract, though. Then I could have gotten my bonus." His voice becomes choked with emotion and he can't talk any more.

I recall how he worked from eight to eight, but he reported to the shop   45
an hour early to prepare for work, wash parts, and melt wax. He wasn't paid for these jobs, but without doing them he wouldn't have been able to keep up with his work. He's a real craftsman. He wants to do his job well. Both of us just sit looking at each other for a while, and finally he speaks: "I'm feeling much better. I could go to work right now." . . .

SUNDAY, FEBRUARY 4

I rarely have time to sit and talk with the others in my team. But when we do talk over a glass of sake, they speak frankly of their discontent, even to a seasonal worker like me.

Worker A's story:

"Now the work is nearly three times tougher than when I came here six or seven years ago. Around 1965, they measured our work by stop-watch. Since then it's been getting tougher. But until a couple of years ago we still had enough workers, and the line used to stop ten minutes before finishing time. After the Tsutsumi plant was built in December 1970, everything really got worse. They changed from the daytime single shift to the two-consecutive-shift system, and now we've got day and night split shifts with time between shifts. And they keep speeding up the line. The faster the line gets, the harder we work to catch up, because we want to go home quickly. But when we finally get used to the speed, then they make it even faster. Right now it's a minute and fourteen seconds per unit, but I bet they'll speed it up. The new guys can't handle it any more. You read in the newspapers that Toyota workers are quick and active. We're not quick. We're forced to work quickly. It's the ones up there who benefit by exploiting us down here. I'm sure the section managers know very well how hard a time we're having. And the union, they're supported by our money, but they only work for the company. You can't expect anything from them because the leaders are all general foremen and foremen. They change every year, so nobody has enough time to get into the job seriously. If you complain to them, they just tell you to 'cooperate' and say. 'Unless you produce more your salary will not go up.'

"Two years ago we talked about ending overtime, but we realized that we couldn't make ends meet without it, so nothing changed. Personally, I enjoy physical labor. I like to work with my hands. But here, it's just too fast. I guess I can put up with the hard pace, but the trouble is I never know when I can go home. When I come home all I do is take a bath, have something to eat, and go to bed. I don't have more than an hour to talk with my wife. Nowadays I vomit whenever I'm not feeling well, and if I go see a doctor at Toyota Hospital, he just tells me to get back to work."

B's Story:

"You know Yamashita lost his finger, don't you? Or was that before you came? Anyway, during the break — we were on the second shift — the section manager came and made a speech on safety for about thirty minutes. So we were late for supper, and there were no noodles left at the canteen. We had some rice, but we all like to have a bowl of noodles at the end of the meal, you know. Afterwards we complained about this to the section manager. Then he took ten dollars out of his pocket and gave it to us. We handed it to our foreman, and he went out on his bicycle to buy some bread and ice cream. When he came back we stopped the line and sat around and ate. I was impressed. It was an amazing thing. I've decided to work for this section manager, and as long as he's here, I won't take any days off. I may be a fool, but I've never heard of anything like that happening at Toyota. Nobody would spend ten dollars out of his pocket for us. The section managers all think they have nothing to do with us.

"When I first came here the job was so tough I thought of quitting. I remember one morning I woke up and discovered I couldn't move my wrist. I wondered why I had to do work like this. And then I thought, once I've mastered the job it'll be a lot easier, and this idea kept me going. The people who stay here are the ones who have no other place to go and who like to endure pain. But in the end, we'll all be crushed by Toyota. There's hardly anyone at Toyota I can trust.

"The union? I hear they buy it off with women. I don't know if it's true or not, but I can't think of any other way. We all want to go home earlier. If you ask anybody, they'll say 'We don't want any more money, but let us go home without overtime.' When we come home late after overtime, we hardly have time to look at our wives, and they complain. That adds insult to injury. But they don't know what we go through. And I guess they'd better not find out. If they did, they'd tell us to quit. I don't want my wife to see what I'm doing here — it would make me feel even worse. I work for the sake of my children, and my only enjoyment here is having a good laugh over dumb jokes during the lunch break. Other than that, I don't have any hopes for this job.

"If you quit, Kamata, another guy'll take your place. With a new worker, the line'll stop again, and we won't be able to go home until we finish the day's quota. We'll be up shit creek."

Toyota's current slogan is "Toyota . . . Cars to Love, the World Over."   55
On television, a charming film star, Sayuri Yoshinaga, smiles and says, "It's the car with distinction, the car for someone special." The people who buy the cars never realize that they were made, quit literally, over the dead and mutilated bodies of workers who were given no "distinction" at all. . . .

THURSDAY, FEBRUARY 15

I wake up around five this morning and hear the clatter of empty cans echoing coldly on concrete as someone sorts them out of the trash cans. At 6:45 the sound of the morning chimes blares over the loudspeaker. Soon, I hear car engines warming up in the parking lot below my window. Then the clatter and hiss and banging of the heating system being turned on. Bright sunshine falls in through the cracks of my curtains. Fine weather. I couldn't sleep last night and stayed up until one. I was excited and nervous wondering if I could hold out one more day. . . .

At the end of the morning meeting, the foreman orders me to stand beside him in the center of a circle and says, "Thank you very much for working with us for such a long time." He seems sincere. During the lunch break, as I walk to the canteen, a regular worker joins me.

"Finally finishing, aren't you?"

"Yeah, I'm getting out of this prison."

"Us regulars are condemned to life imprisonment, I guess," he says,   60
looking at the ground.

During the break, a guy I've never had a chance to talk to comes up to me at the locker-room bench.

"You've only got three-and-a-half hours to go, haven't you? I wish I did, too. I've got to stay here for life. And no matter how hard I try, I doubt if I'll ever be able to wear a white general foreman's cap."

"Hey, you better not get too excited yet," someone else says."I know a guy, a seasonal, who drank the night he left and went walking with a girl and got run over by a car."

"Maybe that was the best thing that could've happened," another guy says. "Better to die happy than be killed little by little in this goddamn factory."

Finally, it's time to go. Shimoyama, who works two positions ahead of 65
me on the line, keeps coming over to tease me.

"You'll be hit by the impactor at the last second," he says.

"Only thirty minutes left!"

At 4:27 the foreman comes over to take my place. He smiles and says
simply, "OK. That's all. You need time to change. Somehow, it is all too
simple. I feel strange, as if resigning means simply changing places with
somebody. I go around the line and say good-bye to everyone. Shimoyama
holds out his hand. Takeda says with a big smile, "Thanks for everything."
One worker says, "If you come back, you'd better get a softer job in one of
the subcontracting companies." The line doesn't let us stop and talk. The
team chief and the deputy section manager in the office look at me as if I
don't exist. I go to the personnel office to get my pay and pick up some
papers for unemployment insurance. My wages for twelve days' work, including basic pay, overtime, night work, and other fringe allowances together with the final bonus of $43, come to $197.40. Net pay: $185.08. As
he hands me the money the clerk says, "Mr. Kamata, you earned it." He
knows how it is. "Isn't there anyone else finishing today?" I ask. "There
was one in December." Only two completed their contracts at the main
plant — only Yamamoto and I. Two! At first I can't believe it. After I get
my money, I take a last slow walk around the place. It all seems so simple
and matter-of-fact, putting an end to such hard work just like that. It isn't
so much a feeling of liberation as of weariness and emptiness. I have a dull
pain in my right wrist; my right fingers are stiff; my palms have shreds of
metal in them; my back is sore all over; I feel continually nauseated. These
are the only things I can take with me.

I return to my room and find Hamada still in bed. I show him my pay
slip and tell him how to read it. He looks at it closely and says, "I'll try hard
to complete my contract." I go to the dormitory office and return my key,
name tag, and bedding. The clerk glances at me, but doesn't say anything,
not even thank you. I'm still nothing more to them than a thing. My neighbor Miyamoto drives me to the nearest train station. As soon as I sit down
I'm overcome by fatigue, cold, and a deep desire to sleep. . . .

When I left Toyota in February 1973, assembly time at the Main Plant 70
for transmissions was one minute and fourteen seconds. This had been
shortened by six seconds in the six months since I had begun, while production had been increased by 100 to 415 units. Now, seven years later, the
assembly time is forty-five seconds and the production is 690 units. This
increase was achieved solely through accelerating the work pace. Knock-
down part packing at the Takaoka plant needed sixty minutes for a set
(which includes 20 cars) three years ago. Today it takes twelve minutes,
and still the manpower has been reduced from 50 to 40. Before, workers
stood in front of conveyors; now they rush around from one part to another, pushing mobile work desks with wheels.

At the assembly lines for passenger cars, parts have become larger and have increased in number, owing to exhaust-emission control. In addition, parts for various models come down the line all mixed together because of the simultaneous production of many models. Nevertheless, the speed of the conveyor belts only accelerates. The Tahara plant on the Chita Peninsula, which started its operation in January 1979, recently completed arrangements to produce 5000 small trucks and 5000 Corollas. To fill its manpower needs, many workers were taken from the other Toyota plants. Despite this loss, conveyor belts at each plant are running as if nothing had happened. Many workers have been moved onto the assembly line as "reinforcements." Workers are forced to work on Sundays and holidays. The reinforcement work and Sunday-holiday work are a lubricant without which the conveyors could not run.

At the management-union convention mentioned above, Executive Director Yoshiaki Yamamoto said: "In this day and age of uncertainty and severe competition, we must and shall concentrate our production on popular models and adjust the imbalance of work loads among shops. So please be cooperative in establishing flexible shop arrangements that will be able to respond quickly to requests for help."

Reinforcement work is feared by workers who have had no work experience on conveyor lines. Most workers begin losing weight within a few days. Even without the everyday work they're expected to do, inexperienced reinforcement workers would be exhausted by such difficult labor in a totally unfamiliar environment. A directive to management ("On Accepting Reinforcement Workers: Daily Guidance and Management") from the Takaoka plant personnel division shows that reinforcement workers have many complaints and dissatisfactions, more than half of which pertain to safety issues. But the guidance policy goes no farther than the following:

> Management personnel and the longtime workers in the shop should "say hello and a few words" to reinforcement workers at least once a day, and unit members should make an effort to create a congenial atmosphere so that the management and senior workers can easily "say hello and a few words." . . . It is not easy for reinforcement workers to speak out.

One evening, I met with workers from various plants. I wanted to know the facts behind Toyota's remarkable production records. What the workers counted on their fingers was the number of suicides — more than twenty in the past year. These were only cases that they remembered at that moment. They told me that in June there were three suicides within a couple of days. There was a twenty-seven-year-old worker at the Takaoka plant who reported to work and then disappeared; he had thrown himself into the sea. A team leader at the same plant drove his car into a reservoir. These were the only cases reported in the newspapers. The other cases were all related by those who had been close to the suicides. There are no statistics.

The number, they said, is particularly high at the Takaoka plant, whose products are popular and whose production cannot keep pace with demand. On June 28, a forty-five-year-old worker at the Tsutsumi plant hanged himself in his company-rented apartment. Around the same time, a Takaoka plant reinforcement worker from the Tsutsumi plant committed suicide in his dormitory by taking sleeping pills. He was depressed after having been blamed by the team leader for his tardiness and forced to "apologize to his fellow workers for the inconvenience he caused." Also around the same time, a team leader of the Maintenance Department in the Head Office hanged himself. A body found at the Takaoka plant dormitory was taken away by a member of the Security Division staff. Afterwards he complained that while playing pinball, he imagined he saw the suicide's face in the glass of the pinball machine. The workers who met with me that evening talked endlessly of similar cases. I had heard rumors of mentally disturbed workers and suicides many times while I worked at Toyota. But the rapid increase in their numbers is frightening.

1980

The Reader's Presence

1. Satoshi Kamata has written a powerful firsthand account of the working conditions at a Toyota assembly plant in Japan. Why do you think Kamata decided to present his report in the form of a diary? How much of his account is devoted to describing what he and others actually do on the assembly line? How does Kamata create a sense of immediacy in his account of working on the assembly line? At what point does he express his attitude toward this work? In this respect, pay particular attention to the way in which he works with verbs.

2. At the end of the entry dated "Thursday, January 11," Kamata quotes Toyota's new slogan: "Whatever you do, be prepared to take responsibility for it. . . . " What sense of responsibility emerges from Kamata's purpose in writing this firsthand account of life on the Toyota assembly line? How are these responsibilities expressed in relation to his co-workers? his readers? How is this sense of responsibility to both the workers and his readers expressed in his use of statistical information? Where in his account does Kamata most directly state his overriding point about life on the assembly line?

3. Kamata concludes the first paragraph in the section dated "Thursday, September 28," with the following notation: "Here every day is a small war." In what specific ways has he prepared his readers for this statement? Point to words and phrases that lead to this conclusion. When — and how — does he follow up on this metaphor? With what effect? Consider, more generally, Kamata's use of metaphor in his account of life on the assembly line. Which metaphors do you find most effective? Why? Comment in the same terms on his use of irony.

39

Maxine Hong Kingston

No Name Woman

"You must not tell anyone," my mother said, "what I am about to tell you. In China your father had a sister who killed herself. She jumped into the family well. We say that your father has all brothers because it is as if she had never been born.

"In 1924 just a few days after our village celebrated seventeen hurry-up weddings — to make sure that every young man who went 'out on the road' would responsibly come home — your father and his brothers and your grandfather and his brothers and your aunt's new husband sailed for America, the Gold Mountain. It was your grandfather's last trip. Those lucky enough to get contracts waved good-bye from the decks. They fed and guarded the stowaways and helped them off in Cuba, New York, Bali, Hawaii. 'We'll meet in California next year,' they said. All of them sent money home.

"I remember looking at your aunt one day when she and I were dressing; I had not noticed before that she had such a protruding melon of a stomach. But I did not think, 'She's pregnant,' until she began to look like other pregnant women, her shirt pulling and the white tops of her black pants showing. She could not have been pregnant, you see, because her husband had been gone for years. No one said anything. We did not discuss it. In early summer she was ready to have the child, long after the time when it could have been possible.

"The village had also been counting. On the night the baby was to be born the villagers raided our house. Some were crying. Like a great saw, teeth strung with lights, files of people walked zigzag across our land, tearing the rice. Their lanterns doubled in the disturbed black water, which drained away through the broken bunds. As the villagers closed in, we could see that some of them, probably men and women we knew well,

For biographical information on Maxine Hong Kingston, see p. 654.

290

wore white masks. The people with long hair hung it over their faces. Women with short hair made it stand up on end. Some had tied white bands around their foreheads, arms, and legs.

"At first they threw mud and rocks at the house. Then they threw eggs and began slaughtering our stock. We could hear the animals scream their deaths — the roosters, the pigs, a last great roar from the ox. Familiar wild heads flared in our night windows; the villagers encircled us. Some of the faces stopped to peer at us, their eyes rushing like searchlights. The hands flattened against the panes, framed heads, and left red prints.

"The villagers broke in the front and the back doors at the same time, even though we had not locked the doors against them. Their knives dripped with the blood of our animals. They smeared blood on the doors and walls. One woman swung a chicken, whose throat she had slit, splattering blood in red arcs about her. We stood together in the middle of our house, in the family hall with the pictures and tables of the ancestors around us, and looked straight ahead.

"At that time the house had only two wings. When the men came back we would build two more to enclose our courtyard and a third one to begin a second courtyard. The villagers pushed through both wings, even your grandparents' rooms, to find your aunt's, which was also mine until the men returned. From this room a new wing for one of the younger families would grow. They ripped up her clothes and shoes and broke her combs, grinding them underfoot. They tore her work from the loom. They scattered the cooking fire and rolled the new weaving in it. We could hear them in the kitchen breaking our bowls and banging the pots. They overturned the great waist-high earthenware jugs; duck eggs, pickled fruits, vegetables burst out and mixed in acrid torrents. The old woman from the next field swept a broom through the air and loosed the spirits-of-the-broom over our heads. 'Pig.' 'Ghost.' 'Pig,' they sobbed and scolded while they ruined our house.

"When they left, they took sugar and oranges to bless themselves. They cut pieces from the dead animals. Some of them took bowls that were not broken and clothes that were not torn. Afterward we swept up the rice and sewed it back up into sacks. But the smells from the spilled preserves lasted. Your aunt gave birth in the pigsty that night. The next morning when I went up for the water, I found her and the baby plugging up the family well.

"Don't let your father know that I told you. He denies her. Now that you have started to menstruate, what happened to her could happen to you. Don't humiliate us. You wouldn't like to be forgotten as if you had never been born. The villagers are watchful."

Whenever she had to warn us about life, my mother told stories that ran like this one, a story to grow up on. She tested our strength to establish realities. Those in the emigrant generations who could not reassert brute survival died young and far from home. Those of us in the first American generations have had to figure out how the invisible world the emigrants built around our childhoods fit in solid America.

   The emigrants confused the gods by diverting their curses, misleading
them with crooked streets and false names. They must try to confuse their
offspring as well, who, I suppose, threaten them in similar ways — always
trying to get things straight, always trying to name the unspeakable. The
Chinese I know hide their names; sojourners take new names when their
lives change and guard their real names with silence.

   Chinese-Americans, when you try to understand what things in you are
Chinese, how do you separate what is peculiar to childhood, to poverty, insan-
ities, one family, your mother who marked your growing with stories, from
what is Chinese? What is Chinese tradition and what is the movies?

   If I want to learn what clothes my aunt wore, whether flashy or ordinary,
I would have to begin, "Remember Father's drowned-in-the-well sister?" I
cannot ask that. My mother has told me once and for all the useful parts. She
will add nothing unless powered by Necessity, a riverbank that guides her life.
She plants vegetable gardens rather than lawns; she carries the odd-shaped
tomatoes home from the fields and eats food left for the gods.

   Whenever we did frivolous things, we used up energy; we flew high kites.
We children came up off the ground over the melting cones our parents
brought home from work and the American movie on New Years' Day —
Oh, You Beautiful Doll with Betty Grable one year, and *She Wore a Yellow
Ribbon* with John Wayne another year. After the one carnival ride each, we
paid in guilt; our tired father counted his change on the dark walk home.

   Adultery is extravagance. Could people who hatch their own chicks   15
and eat the embryos and the heads for delicacies and boil the feet in vinegar
for party food, leaving only the gravel, eating even the gizzard lining —
could such people engender a prodigal aunt? To be a woman, to have a
daughter in starvation time was a waste enough. My aunt could not have
been the lone romantic who gave up everything for sex. Women in the old
China did not choose. Some man had commanded her to lie with him and
be his secret evil. I wonder whether he masked himself when he joined the
raid on her family.

   Perhaps she encountered him in the fields or on the mountain where
the daughters-in-law collected fuel. Or perhaps he first noticed her in the
marketplace. He was not a stranger because the village housed no strangers. She had to have dealings with him other than sex. Perhaps he worked
an adjoining field, or he sold her the cloth for the dress she sewed and
wore. His demand must have surprised, then terrified her. She obeyed him;
she always did as she was told.

   When the family found a young man in the next village to be her husband, she stood tractably beside the best rooster, his proxy, and promised
before they met that she would be his forever. She was lucky that he was
her age and she would be the first wife, an advantage secure now. The
night she first saw him, he had sex with her. Then he left for America. She
had almost forgotten what he looked like. When she tried to envision him,
she only saw the black and white face in the group photograph the men
had had taken before leaving.

The other man was not, after all, much different from her husband. They both gave orders: she followed. "If you tell your family, I'll beat you. I'll kill you. Be here again next week." No one talked sex, ever. And she might have separated the rapes from the rest of living if only she did not have to buy her oil from him or gather wood in the same forest. I want her fear to have lasted just as long as rape lasted so that the fear could have been contained. No drawn-out fear. But women at sex hazarded birth and hence lifetimes. The fear did not stop but permeated everywhere. She told the man, "I think I'm pregnant." He organized the raid against her.

On nights when my mother and father talked about their life back home, sometimes they mentioned an "outcast table" whose business they still seemed to be settling, their voices tight. In a commensal tradition, where food is precious, the powerful older people made wrongdoers eat alone. Instead of letting them start separate new lives like the Japanese, who could become samurais and geishas, the Chinese family, faces averted but eyes glowering sideways, hung on to the offenders and fed them leftovers. My aunt must have lived in the same house as my parents and eaten at an outcast table. My mother spoke about the raid as if she had seen it, when she and my aunt, a daughter-in-law to a different household, should not have been living together at all. Daughters-in-law lived with their husbands' parents, not their own; a synonym for marriage in Chinese is "taking a daughter-in-law." Her husband's parents could have sold her, mortgaged her, stoned her. But they had sent her back to her own mother and father, a mysterious act hinting at disgraces not told me. Perhaps they had thrown her out to deflect the avengers.

She was the only daughter; her four brothers went with her father, husband, and uncles "out on the road" and for some years became western men. When the goods were divided among the family, three of the brothers took land, and the youngest, my father, chose an education. After my grandparents gave their daughter away to her husband's family, they had dispensed all the adventure and all the property. They expected her alone to keep the traditional ways, which her brothers, now among the barbarians, could fumble without detection. The heavy, deep-rooted women were to maintain the past against the flood, safe for returning. But the rare urge west had fixed upon our family, and so my aunt crossed boundaries not delineated in space.

The work of preservation demands that the feelings playing about in one's guts not be turned into action. Just watch their passing like cherry blossoms. But perhaps my aunt, my forerunner, caught in a slow life, let dreams grow and fade and after some months or years went toward what persisted. Fear at the enormities of the forbidden kept her desires delicate, wire and bone. She looked at a man because she liked the way the hair was tucked behind his ears, or she liked the question-mark line of a long torso curving at the shoulder and straight at the hip. For warm eyes or a soft voice or a slow walk — that's all — a few hairs, a line, a brightness, a sound, a pace, she gave up family. She offered us up for a charm that vanished with tiredness, a pigtail that didn't toss when the wind died. Why, the wrong lighting could erase the dearest thing about him.

It could very well have been, however, that my aunt did not take subtle enjoyment of her friend, but, a wild woman, kept rollicking company. Imagining her free with sex doesn't fit, though. I don't know any women like that, or men either. Unless I see her life branching into mine, she gives me no ancestral help.

To sustain her being in love, she often worked at herself in the mirror, guessing at the colors and shapes that would interest him, changing them frequently in order to hit on the right combination. She wanted to look back.

On a farm near the sea, a woman who tended her appearance reaped a reputation for eccentricity. All the married women blunt-cut their hair in flaps about their ears or pulled it back in tight buns. No nonsense. Neither style blew easily into heart-catching tangles. And at their weddings they displayed themselves in their long hair for the last time. "It brushed the backs of my knees," my mother tells me. "It was braided, and even so, it brushed the backs of my knees."

At the mirror my aunt combed individuality into her bob. A bun could 25 have been contrived to escape into black streamers blowing in the wind or in quiet wisps about her face, but only the older women in our picture album wear buns. She brushed her hair back from her forehead, tucking the flaps behind her ears. She looped a piece of thread, knotted into a circle between her index fingers and thumbs, and ran the double strand across her forehead. When she closed her fingers as if she were making a pair of shadow geese bite, the string twisted together catching the little hairs. Then she pulled the thread away from her skin, ripping the hairs out neatly, her eyes watering from the needles of pain. Opening her fingers, she cleaned the thread, then rolled it along her hairline and the tops of the eyebrows. My mother did the same to me and my sisters and herself. I used to believe that the expression "caught by the short hairs" meant a captive held with a depilatory string. It especially hurt at the temples, but my mother said we were lucky we didn't have to have our feet bound when we were seven. Sisters used to sit on their beds and cry together, she said, as their mothers or their slave removed the bandages for a few minutes each night and let the blood gush back into their veins. I hope that the man my aunt loved appreciated a smooth brow, that he wasn't just a tits-and-ass man.

Once my aunt found a freckle on her chin, at a spot that the almanac said predestined her for unhappiness. She dug it out with a hot needle and washed the wound with peroxide.

More attention to her looks than these pullings of hairs and pickings at spots would have caused gossip among the villagers. The owned work clothes and good clothes, and they wore good clothes for feasting the new seasons. But since a woman combing her hair hexes beginnings, my aunt rarely found an occasion to look her best. Women looked like great sea snails — the corded wood, babies, and laundry they carried were the whorls on their backs. The Chinese did not admire a bent back; goddesses and warriors stood straight. Still there must have been a marvelous freeing of beauty when a worker laid down her burden and stretched and arched.

Such commonplace loveliness, however, was not enough for my aunt. She dreamed of a lover for the fifteen days of New Year's, the time for families to exchange visits, money, and food. She plied her secret comb. And sure enough she cursed the year, the family, the village, and herself.

Even as her hair lured her imminent lover, many other men looked at her. Uncles, cousins, nephews, brothers would have looked, too, had they been home between journeys. Perhaps they had already been restraining their curiosity, and they left, fearful that their glances, like a field of nesting birds, might be startled and caught. Poverty hurt, and that was their first reason for leaving. But another, final reason for leaving the crowded house was the never-said.

She may have been unusually beloved, the precious only daughter, spoiled   30 and mirror-gazing because of the affection the family lavished on her. When her husband left, they welcomed the chance to take her back from the in-laws; she could live like the little daughter for just a while longer. There are stories that my grandfather was different from other people, "crazy ever since the little Jap bayoneted him in the head." He used to put his naked penis on the dinner table, laughing. And one day he brought home a baby girl, wrapped up inside his brown western-style greatcoat. He had traded one of his sons, probably my father, the youngest, for her. My grandmother made him trade back. When he finally got a daughter of his own, he doted on her. They must have all loved her, except perhaps my father, the only brother who never went back to China, having once been traded for a girl.

Brothers and sisters, newly men and women, had to efface their sexual color and present plain miens. Disturbing hair and eyes, a smile like no other, threatened the ideal of five generations living under one roof. To focus blurs, people shouted face to face and yelled from room to room. The immigrants I know have loud voices, unmodulated to American tones even after years away from the village where they called their friendships out across the fields. I have not been able to stop my mother's screams in public libraries or over telephones. Walking erect (knees straight, toes pointed forward, not pigeon-toed, which is Chinese-feminine) and speaking in an inaudible voice, I have tried to turn myself American-feminine. Chinese communication was loud, public. Only sick people had to whisper. But at the dinner table, where the family members came nearest one another, no one could talk, not the outcasts nor any eaters. Every word that falls from the mouth is a coin lost. Silently they gave and accepted food with both hands. A preoccupied child who took his bowl with one hand got a sideways glare. A complete moment of total attention is due everyone alike. Children and lovers have no singularity here, but my aunt used a secret voice, a separate attentiveness.

She kept the man's name to herself throughout her labor and dying; she did not accuse him that he be punished with her. To save her inseminator's name she gave silent birth.

He may have been somebody in her own household, but intercourse with a man outside the family would have been no less abhorrent. All the village were kinsmen, and the titles shouted in loud country voices never let kinship be forgotten. Any man within visiting distance would have been neutralized as a lover — "brother," "younger brother," "older brother" — 115 relationship titles. Parents researched birth charts probably not so much to assure good fortune as to circumvent incest in a population that has but one hundred surnames. Everybody has eight million relatives. How useless then sexual mannerisms, how dangerous.

As if it came from an atavism deeper than fear, I used to add "brother" silently to boys' names. It hexed the boys, who would or would not ask me to dance, and made them less scary and as familiar and deserving of benevolence as girls.

But, of course, I hexed myself also — no dates. I should have stood up,   35 both arms waving, and shouted out across libraries, "Hey, you! Love me back." I had no idea, though, how to make attraction selective, how to control its direction and magnitude. If I made myself American-pretty so that the five or six Chinese boys in the class fell in love with me, everyone else — the Caucasian, Negro, and Japanese boys — would too. Sisterliness, dignified and honorable, made much more sense.

Attraction eludes control so stubbornly that whole societies designed to organize relationships among people cannot keep order, not even when they bind people to one another from childhood and raise them together. Among the very poor and the wealthy, brothers married their adopted sisters, like doves. Our family allowed some romance, paying adult brides' prices and providing dowries so that their sons and daughters could marry strangers. Marriage promises to turn strangers into friendly relatives — a nation of siblings.

In the village structure, spirits shimmered among the live creatures, balanced and held in equilibrium by time and land. But one human being flaring up into violence could open up a black hole, a maelstrom that pulled in the sky. The frightened villagers, who depended on one another to maintain the real, went to my aunt to show her a personal, physical representation of the break she made in the "roundness." Misallying couples snapped off the future, which was to be embodied in true offspring. The villagers punished her for acting as if she could have a private life, secret and apart from them.

If my aunt had betrayed the family at a time of large grain yields and peace, when many boys were born, and wings were being built on many houses, perhaps she might have escaped such severe punishment. But the men — hungry, greedy, tired of planting in dry soil, cuckolded — had been forced to leave the village in order to send food-money home. There were ghost plagues, bandit plagues, wars with the Japanese, floods. My Chinese brother and sister had died of an unknown sickness. Adultery, perhaps only a mistake during good times, became a crime when the village needed food.

The round moon cakes and round doorways, the round tables of graduated size that fit one roundness inside another, round windows and rice bowls — these talismans had lost their power to warn this family of the law: A family must be whole, faithfully keeping the descent line by having sons to feed the old and the dead who in turn look after the family. The villagers came to show my aunt and lover-in-hiding a broken house. The villagers were speeding up the circling of events because she was too shortsighted to see that her infidelity had already harmed the village, that waves of consequences would return unpredictably, sometimes in disguise, as now, to hurt her. This roundness had to be made coin-sized so that she would see its circumference: Punish her at the birth of her baby. Awaken her to the inexorable. People who refused fatalism because they could invent small resources insisted on culpability. Deny accidents and wrest fault from the stars.

After the villagers left, their lanterns now scattering in various directions toward home, the family broke their silence and cursed her. "Aiaa, we're going to die. Death is coming. Death is coming. Look what you've done. You've killed us. Ghost! Dead Ghost! Ghost! You've never been born." She ran out into the fields, far enough from the house so that she could no longer hear their voices, and pressed herself against the earth, her own land no more. When she felt the birth coming, she thought that she had been hurt. Her body seized together. "They've hurt me too much," she thought. "This is gall, and it will kill me." With forehead and knees against the earth, her body convulsed and then relaxed. She turned on her back, lay on the ground. The black well of sky and stars went out and out forever; her body and her complexity seemed to disappear. She was one of the stars, a bright dot in blackness, without home, without a companion, in eternal cold and silence. An agoraphobia rose in her, speeding higher and higher, bigger and bigger; she would not be able to contain it; there would be no end to fear.

Flayed, unprotected against space, she felt pain return, focusing her body. This pain chilled her — a cold, steady kind of surface pain. Inside, spasmodically, the other pain, the pain of the child, heated her. For hours she lay on the ground, alternately body and space. Sometimes a vision of normal comfort obliterated reality: She saw the family in the evening gambling at the dinner table, the young people massaging their elders' backs. She saw them congratulating one another, high joy on the mornings the rice shoots came up. When these pictures burst, the stars drew yet further apart. Black space opened.

She got to her feet to fight better and remembered that old-fashioned women gave birth in their pigsties to fool the jealous, pain-dealing gods, who do not snatch piglets. Before the next spasms could stop her, she ran to the pigsty, each step a rushing out into emptiness. She climbed over the fence and knelt in the dirt. It was good to have a fence enclosing her, a tribal person alone.

Laboring, this woman who had carried her child as a foreign growth that sickened her every day, expelled it at last. She reached down to touch the hot, wet, moving mass, surely smaller than anything human, and could feel that it was human after all — fingers, toes, nails, nose. She pulled it up on to her belly, and it lay curled there, butt in the air, feet precisely tucked one under the other. She opened her loose shirt and buttoned the child inside. After resting, it squirmed and thrashed and she pushed it up to her breast. It turned its head this way and that until it found her nipple. There, it made little snuffling noises. She clenched her teeth at its preciousness, lovely as a young calf, a piglet, a little dog.

She may have gone to the pigsty as a last act of responsibility: She would protect this child as she had protected its father. It would look after her soul, leaving supplies on her grave. But how would this tiny child without family find her grave when there would be no marker for her anywhere, neither in the earth nor the family hall? No one would give her a family hall name. She had taken the child with her into the wastes. At its birth the two of them had felt the same raw pain of separation, a wound that only the family pressing tight could close. A child with no descent line would not soften her life but only trail after her, ghostlike, begging her to give it purpose. At dawn the villagers on their way to the fields would stand around the fence and look.

Full of milk, the little ghost slept. When it awoke, she hardened her 45 breasts against the milk that crying loosens. Toward morning she picked up the baby and walked to the well.

Carrying the baby to the well shows loving. Otherwise abandon it. Turn its face into the mud. Mothers who love their children take them along. It was probably a girl; there is some hope of forgiveness for boys.

"Don't tell anyone you had an aunt. Your father does not want to hear her name. She has never been born." I have believed that sex was unspeakable and words so strong and fathers so frail that "aunt" would do my father mysterious harm. I have thought that my family, having settled among immigrants who had also been their neighbors in the ancestral land, needed to clean their name, and a wrong word would incite the kinspeople even here. But there is more to this silence: They want me to participate in her punishment. And I have.

In the twenty years since I heard this story I have not asked for details nor said my aunt's name; I do not know it. People who comfort the dead can also chase after them to hurt them further — a reverse ancestor worship. The real punishment was not the raid swiftly inflicted by the villagers, but the family's deliberately forgetting her. Her betrayal so maddened them, they saw to it that she would suffer forever, even after death. Always hungry, always needing, she would have to beg food from other ghosts, snatch and steal it from those whose living descendants give them gifts. She would have to fight the ghosts massed at crossroads for the buns a few thoughtful citizens leave to decoy her away from village and home so that the ancestral spirits could feast unharassed. At peace, they could act like gods, not ghosts, their descent lines providing them with paper suits and dresses, spirit money, paper houses, paper automobiles, chicken, meat, and rice into eternity — essences delivered up in smoke and flames, steam and incense rising from each rice bowl. In an attempt to make the Chinese care for people outside the family, Chairman Mao encourages us now to give our paper replicas to the spirits of outstanding soldiers and workers, no matter whose ancestors they may be. My aunt remains forever hungry. Goods are not distributed evenly among the dead.

My aunt haunts me — her ghost drawn to me because now, after fifty years of neglect, I alone devote pages of paper to her, though not origamied into houses and clothes. I do not think she always means me well. I am telling on her, and she was a spite suicide, drowning herself in the drinking water. The Chinese are always very frightened of the drowned one, whose weeping ghost, wet hair hanging and skin bloated, waits silently by the water to pull down a substitute.

1975

The Reader's Presence

1. Maxine Hong Kingston's account of her aunt's life and death is a remarkable blend of fact and speculation. Consider the overall structure of "No Name Woman." How many versions of the aunt's story do we hear? Where, for example, does the mother's story end? Where does the narrator's begin? Which version do you find more compelling? Why? What does the narrator mean when she says that her mother's stories "tested our strength to establish realities" (paragraph 10)?

2. The narrator's version of her aunt's story is replete with such words and phrases as *perhaps* and *It could very well have been.* The narrator seems far more speculative about her aunt's life than her mother is. At what point does the narrator raise doubts about the veracity of her mother's version of the aunt's story? What purpose does the mother espouse in telling the aunt's story? Is it meant primarily to express family lore? to issue a warning? Point to specific passages to verify your response. What is the proposed moral of the story? Is that moral the same for the mother as for the narrator? Explain.

3. What does the narrator mean when she says "They must try to confuse their offspring as well, who, I suppose, threaten them in similar ways — always trying to get things straight, always trying to name the unspeakable" (paragraph 11)? What line does Kingston draw between the two cultures represented in the story: between the mother, a superstitious, cautious Chinese woman, and the narrator, an American-born child trying to "straighten out" her mother's confusing story? How does the narrator resolve the issue by thinking of herself as neither Chinese nor American, but as a Chinese American? How are these issues made matters of gender? Judging from the evidence in this story, how would you summarize — and characterize — Chinese expectations of men? of women? How much does the story depend on gender stereotypes, and how does the narrator explore the complexity of those roles in her version of her aunt's story?

40

Barry Lopez

The Stone Horse

1

The deserts of southern California, the high, relatively cooler and wetter Mojave and the hotter, dryer Sonoran to the south of it, carry the signatures of many cultures. Prehistoric rock drawings in the Mojave's Coso Range, probably the greatest concentration of petroglyphs in North America, are at least three thousand years old. Big-game-hunting cultures that flourished six or seven thousand years before that are known from broken spear tips, choppers, and burins left scattered along the shores of great Pleistocene lakes, long since evaporated. Weapons and tools discovered at China Lake may be thirty thousand years old; and worked stone from a quarry in the Calico Mountains is, some argue, evidence that human beings were here more than 200,000 years ago.

Because of the long-term stability of such arid environments, much of this prehistoric stone evidence still lies exposed on the ground, accessible to anyone who passes by — the studious, the acquisitive, the indifferent, the merely curious. Archaeologists do not agree on the sequence of cultural history beyond about twelve thousand years ago, but it is clear that these broken bits of chalcedony, chert, and obsidian, like the animal drawings and geometric designs etched on walls of basalt throughout the desert, anchor the earliest threads of human history, the first record of human endeavor here.

Western man did not enter the California desert until the end of the eighteenth century, 250 years after Coronado brought his soldiers into the Zuni pueblos in a bewildered search for the cities of Cibola. The earliest appraisals of the land were cursory, hurried. People traveled *through* it, en route to Santa Fe or the California coastal settlements. Only miners tarried.

For biographical information on Barry Lopez, see p. 655.

In 1823 what had been Spain's became Mexico's, and in 1848 what had been Mexico's became America's; but the bare, jagged mountains and dry lake beds, the vast and uniform plains of creosote bush and yucca plants, remained as obscure as the northern Sudan until the end of the nineteenth century.

Before 1940 the tangible evidence of twentieth-century man's passage here consisted of very little — the hard tracery of travel corridors; the widely scattered, relatively insignificant evidence of mining operations; and the fair expanse of irrigated fields at the desert's periphery. In the space of a hundred years or so the wagon roads were paved, railroads were laid down, and canals and high-tension lines were built to bring water and electricity across the desert to Los Angeles from the Colorado River. The dark mouths of gold, talc, and tin mines yawned from the bony flanks of desert ranges. Dust-encrusted chemical plants stood at work on the lonely edges of dry lake beds. And crops of grapes, lettuce, dates, alfalfa, and cotton covered the Coachella and Imperial valleys, north and south of the Salton Sea, and the Palo Verde Valley along the Colorado.

These developments proceeded with little or no awareness of earlier $\quad$ 5 human occupations by cultures that preceded those of the historic Indians — the Mohave, the Chemehuevi, the Quechan. (Extensive irrigation began actually to change the climate of the Sonoran Desert, and human settlements, the railroads, and farming introduced many new, successful plants into the region.)

During World War II, the American military moved into the desert in great force, to train troops and to test equipment. They found the clear weather conducive to year-round flying, the dry air and isolation very attractive. After the war, a complex of training grounds, storage facilities, and gunnery and test ranges was permanently settled on more than three million acres of military reservations. Few perceived the extent or significance of the destruction of the aboriginal sites that took place during tank maneuvers and bombing runs or in the laying out of highways, railroads, mining districts, and irrigated fields. The few who intuited that something like an American Dordogne Valley lay exposed here were (only) amateur archaeologists; even they reasoned that the desert was too vast for any of this to matter.

After World War II, people began moving out of the crowded Los Angeles basin into homes in Lucerne, Apple, and Antelope valleys in the western Mojave. They emigrated as well to a stretch of resort land at the foot of the San Jacinto Mountains that included Palm Springs, and farther out to old railroad and military towns like Twentynine Palms and Barstow. People also began exploring the desert, at first in military-surplus jeeps and then with a variety of all-terrain and off-road vehicles that became available in the 1960s. By the mid-1970s, the number of people using such vehicles for desert recreation had increased exponentially. Most came and went in innocent curiosity; the few who didn't wreaked a havoc all out of proportion to their numbers. The disturbance of previously isolated archaeological sites increased by an order of magnitude. Many sites were vandalized before archaeologists, themselves late to the desert, had any firm grasp of the bounds of human history in the desert. It was as though in the same moment an Aztec library had been discovered intact various lacunae had begun to appear.

The vandalism was of three sorts: the general disturbance usually caused by souvenir hunters and by the curious and the oblivious; the wholesale stripping of a place by professional thieves for black-market sale and trade; and outright destruction, in which vehicles were actually used to ram and trench an area. By 1980, the Bureau of Land Management estimated that probably 35 percent of the archaeological sites in the desert had been vandalized. The destruction at some places by rifles and shotguns, or by power winches mounted on vehicles, was, if one cared for history, demoralizing to behold.

In spite of public education, land closures, and stricter law enforcement in recent years, the BLM estimates that, annually, about 1 percent of the archaeological record in the desert continues to be destroyed or stolen.

2

A BLM archaeologist told me, with understandable reluctance, where   10
to find the intaglio. I spread my Automobile Club of Southern California map of Imperial County out on his desk, and he traced the route with a pink felt-tip pen. The line crossed Interstate 8 and then turned west along the Mexican border.

"You can't drive any farther than about here," he said, marking a small X. "There's boulders in the wash. You walk up past them."

On a separate piece of paper he drew a route in a smaller scale that would take me up the arroyo to a certain point where I was to cross back east, to another arroyo. At its head, on higher ground just to the north, I would find the horse.

"It's tough to spot unless you know it's there. Once you pick it up . . ." He shook his head slowly, in a gesture of wonder at its existence.

I waited until I held his eye. I assured him I would not tell anyone else how to get there. He looked at me with stoical despair, like a man who had been robbed twice, whose belief in human beings was offered without conviction.

I did not go until the following day because I wanted to see it at dawn.   15
I ate breakfast at four A.M. in El Centro and then drove south. The route was easy to follow, though the last section of road proved difficult, broken and drifted over with sand in some spots. I came to the barricade of boulders and parked. It was light enough by then to find my way over the ground with little trouble. The contours of the landscape were stark, without any masking vegetation. I worried only about rattlesnakes.

I traversed the stone plain as directed, but, in spite of the frankness of the land, I came on the horse unawares. In the first moment of recognition I was without feeling. I recalled later being startled, and that I held my breath. It was laid out on the ground with its head to the east, three times life size. As I took in its outline I felt a growing concentration of all my senses, as though my attentiveness to the pale rose color of the morning sky and other peripheral images had now ceased to be important. I was aware that I was straining for sound in the windless air, and I felt the uneven pressure of the earth hard against my feet. The horse, outlined in a standing profile on the dark ground, was as vivid before me as a bed of tulips.

I've come upon animals suddenly before, and felt a similar tension, a precipitate heightening of the senses. And I have felt the inexplicable but sharply boosted intensity of a wild moment in the bush, where it is not until some minutes later that you discover the source of electricity — the warm remains of a grizzly bear kill, or the still moist tracks of a wolverine.

But this was slightly different. I felt I had stepped into an unoccupied corridor. I had no familiar sense of history, the temporal structure in which to think: This horse was made by Quechan people three hundred years ago. I felt instead a headlong rush of images: people hunting wild horses with spears on the Pleistocene veld of southern California; Cortés riding across the causeway into Montezuma's Tenochtitlán; a short-legged Comanche, astride his horse like some sort of ferret, slashing through cavalry lines of young men who rode like farmers; a hood exploding past my face one morning in a corral in Wyoming. These images had the weight and silence of stone.

When I released my breath, the images softened. My initial feeling, of facing a wild animal in a remote region, was replaced with a calm sense of antiquity. It was then that I became conscious, like an ordinary tourist, of what was before me, and thought: this horse was probably laid out by Quechan people. But when? I wondered. The first horses they saw, I knew, might have been those that came north from Mexico in 1692 with Father Eusebio Kino. But Cocopa people, I recalled, also came this far north on occasion, to fight with their neighbors, the Quechan. And *they* could have seen horses with Melchior Díaz, at the mouth of the Colorado River in the fall of 1540. So, it could be four hundred years old. (No one in fact knows.)

I still had not moved. I took my eyes off the horse for a moment to look 20 south over the desert plain into Mexico, to look east past its head at the brightening sunrise, to situate myself. Then, finally, I brought my trailing foot slowly forward and stood erect. Sunlight was running like a thin sheet of water over the stony ground and it threw the horse into relief. It looked as though no hand had ever disturbed the stones that gave it its form.

The horse had been brought to life on ground called desert pavement, a tight, flat matrix of small cobbles blasted smooth by sand-laden winds. The uniform, monochromatic blackness of the stones, a patina of iron and magnesium oxides called desert varnish, is caused by long-term exposure to the sun. To make this type of low-relief ground glyph, or intaglio, the artist either selectively turns individual stones over to their lighter side or removes areas of stone to expose the lighter soil underneath, creating a negative image. This horse, about eighteen feet from brow to rump and eight feet from withers to hoof, had been made in the latter way, and its outline was bermed at certain points with low ridges of stone a few inches high to enhance its three-dimensional qualities. (The left side of the horse was in full profile; each leg was extended at 90 degrees to the body and fully visible, as though seen in three-quarter profile.)

I was not eager to move. The moment I did I would be back in the flow of time, the horse no longer quivering in the same way before me. I did not want to feel again the sequence of quotidian events — to be drawn off into deliberation and analysis. A human being, a four-footed animal, the open land. That was all that was present — and a "thoughtless" understanding of the very old desires bearing on this particular animal: to hunt it, to render it, to fathom it, to subjugate it, to honor it, to take it as a companion.

What finally made me move was the light. The sun now filled the shallow basin of the horse's body. The weighted line of the stone berm created the illusion of a mane and the distinctive roundness of an equine belly. The change in definition impelled me. I moved to the left, circling past its rump, to see how the light might flesh the horse out from various points of view. I circled it completely before squatting on my haunches. Ten or fifteen minutes later I chose another view. The third time I moved, to a point near the rear hooves, I spotted a stone tool at my feet. I stared at it a long while, more in awe than disbelief, before reaching out to pick it up. I turned it over in my left palm and took it between my fingers to feel its cutting edge. It is always difficult, especially with something so portable, to rechannel the desire to steal.

I spent several hours with the horse. As I changed positions and as the angle of the light continued to change I noticed a number of things. The angle at which the pastern carried the hoof away from the ankle was perfect. Also, stones had been placed within the image to suggest at precisely the right spot the left shoulder above the foreleg. The line that joined thigh and hock was similarly accurate. The muzzle alone seemed distorted — but perhaps these stones had been moved by a later hand. It was an admirably accurate representation, but not what a breeder would call perfect conformation. There was the suggestion of a bowed neck and an undershot jaw, and the tail, as full as a winter coyote's, did not appear to be precisely to scale.

The more I thought about it, the more I felt I was looking at an individual horse, a unique combination of generic and specific detail. It was easy to imagine one of Kino's horses as a model, or a horse that ran off from one of Coronado's columns. What kind of horses would these have been? I wondered. In the sixteenth century the most sought-after horses in Europe were Spanish, the offspring of Arabian stock and Barbary horses that the Moors brought to Iberia and bred to the older, eastern European strains brought in by the Romans. The model for this horse, I speculated, could easily have been a palomino, or a descendant of horses trained for lion hunting in North Africa. 25

A few generations ago, cowboys, cavalry quartermasters, and draymen would have taken this horse before me under consideration and not let up their scrutiny until they had its heritage fixed to their satisfaction. Today, the distinction between draft and harness horses is arcane knowledge, and no image may come to mind for a blue roan or a claybank horse. The loss of such refinement in everyday conversation leaves me unsettled. People praise the Eskimo's ability to distinguish among forty types of snow but forget the skill of others who routinely differentiate between overo and tobiano pintos. Such distinctions are made for the same reason. You have to do it to be able to talk clearly about the world.

For parts of two years I worked as a horse wrangler and packer in Wyoming. It is dim knowledge now; I would have to think to remember if a buckskin was a kind of dun horse. And I couldn't throw a double-diamond hitch over a set of panniers — the packer's basic tie-down — without guidance. As I squatted there in the desert, however, these more personal memories seemed tenuous in comparison with the sweep of this animal in human time. My memories had no depth. I thought of the Hittite cavalry riding against the Syrians 3,500 years ago. And the first of the Chinese emperors, Ch'in Shih Huang, buried in Shensi Province in 210 B.C. with thousands of life-size horses and solders, a terra-cotta guardian army. What could I know of what was in the mind of whoever made this horse? Was there some racial memory of it as an animal that had once fed the artist's ancestors and then disappeared from North America? And then returned in this strange alliance with another race of men?

Certainly, whoever it was, the artist had observed the animal very closely. Certainly the animal's speed had impressed him. Among the first things the Quechan would have learned from an encounter with Kino's horses was that their own long-distance runners — men who could run down mule deer — were no match for this animal.

From where I squatted I could look far out over the Mexican plain. Juan Bautista de Anza passed this way in 1774, extending El Camino Real into Alta California from Sinaloa. He was followed by others, all of them astride the magical horse; *gente de razón,* the people of reason, coming into the country of *los primitivos.* The horse, like the stone animals of Egypt, urged these memories upon me. And as I drew them up from some forgotten corner of my mind — huge horses carved in the white chalk downs of southern England by an Iron Age people; Spanish horses rearing and wheeling in fear before alligators in Florida — the images seemed tethered before me. With this sense of proportion, a memory of my own — the morning I almost lost my face to a horse's hoof — now had somewhere to fit.

I rose up and began to walk slowly around the horse again. I had taken the first long measure of it and was now looking for a way to depart, a new angle of light, a fading of the image itself before the rising sun, that would break its hold on me. As I circled, feeling both heady and serene at the encounter, I realized again how strangely vivid it was. It had been created on a barren bajada between two arroyos, as nondescript a place as one could imagine. The only plant life here was a few wands of ocotillo cactus. The ground beneath my shoes was so hard it wouldn't take the print of a heavy animal even after a rain. The only sounds I heard here were the voices of quail.

The archaeologist had been correct. For all its forcefulness, the horse is inconspicuous. If you don't care to see it you can walk right past it. That pleases him, I think. Unmarked on the bleak shoulder of the plain, the site signals to no one; so he wants no protective fences here, no informative plaque, to act as beacons. He would rather take a chance that no motorcyclist, no aimless wanderer with a flair for violence and a depth of ignorance, will ever find his way here.

The archaeologist had given me something before I left his office that now seemed peculiar — an aerial photograph of the horse. It is widely believed that an aerial view of an intaglio provides a fair and accurate depiction. It does not. In the photograph the horse looks somewhat crudely constructed; from the ground it appears far more deftly rendered. The photograph is of a single moment, and in that split second the horse seems vaguely impotent. I watched light pool in the intaglio at dawn; I imagine you could watch it withdraw at dusk and sense the same animation I did. In those prolonged moments its shape and so, too, its general character changed — noticeably. The living quality of the image, its immediacy to the eye, was brought out by the light-in-time, not, at least here, in the camera's frozen instant.

Intaglios, I thought, were never meant to be seen by gods in the sky above. They were meant to be seen by people on the ground, over a long period of shifting light. This could even be true of the huge figures on the Plain of Nazca in Peru, where people could walk for the length of a day beside them. It is our own impatience that leads us to think otherwise.

This process of abstraction, almost unintentional, drew me gradually away from the horse. I came to a position of attention at the edge of the sphere of its influence. With a slight bow I paid my respects to the horse, its maker, and the history of us all, and departed.

3

A short distance away I stopped the car in the middle of the road to   35 make a few notes. I could not write down what I was thinking when I was with the horse. It would have seemed disrespectful, and it would have required another kind of attention. So now I patiently drained my memory of the details it had fastened itself upon. The road I'd stopped on was adjacent to the All American Canal, the major source of water for the Imperial and Coachella valleys. The water flowed west placidly. A disjointed flock of coots, small, dark birds with white bills, was paddling against the current, foraging in the rushes.

I was peripherally aware of the birds as I wrote, the only movement in the desert, and of a series of sounds from a village a half-mile away. The first sounds from this collection of ramshackle houses in a grove of cottonwoods were the distracted dawn voices of dogs. I heard them intermingled with the cries of a rooster. Later, the high-pitches voices of children calling out to each other came disembodied through the dry desert air. Now, a little after seven, I could hear someone practicing on the trumpet, the same rough phrases played over and over. I suddenly remembered how as children we had tried to get the rhythm of a galloping horse with hands against our thighs, or by fluttering our tongues against the roofs of our mouths.

After the trumpet, the impatient calls of adults summoning children. Sunday morning. Wood smoke hung like a lens in the trees. The first car starts — a cold eight-cylinder engine, of Chrysler extraction perhaps, goosed to life, then throttled back to murmur through dual mufflers, the obbligato music of a shade-tree mechanic. The rote bark of mongrel dogs at dawn, the jagged outcries of men and women, an engine coming to life. Like a thousand villages from West Virginia to Guadalajara.

I finished my notes — where was I going to find a description of the horses that came north with the conquistadors? Did their manes come forward prominently over the brow, like this one's, like the forelocks of Blackfeet and Assiniboin men in nineteenth-century paintings? I set the notes on the seat beside me.

The road followed the canal for a while and then arced north, toward Interstate 8. It was slow driving and I fell to thinking how the desert had changed since Anza had come through. New plants and animals — the MacDougall cottonwood, the English house sparrow, the chukar from India — have about them now the air of the native born. Of the native species, some — no one knows how many — are extinct. The populations of many others, especially the animals, have been sharply reduced. The idea of a desert impoverished by agricultural poisons and varmint hunters, by off-road vehicles and military operations, did not seem as disturbing to me, however, as this other horror, now that I had been those hours with the horse. The vandals, the few who crowbar rock art off the desert's walls, who dig up graves, who punish the ground that holds intaglios, are people who devour history. Their self-centered scorn, their disrespect for ideas and images beyond their ken, create the awful atmosphere of loose ends in which totalitarianism thrives, in which the past is merely curious or wrong.

I thought about the horse sitting out there on the unprotected plain. I enumerated its qualities in my mind until a sense of its vulnerability receded and it became an anchor for something else. I remembered that history, a history like this one, which ran deeper than Mexico, deeper than the Spanish, was a kind of medicine. It permitted the great breadth of human expression to reverberate, and it did not urge you to locate its apotheosis in the present.

Each of us, individuals and civilizations, has been held upside down like Achilles in the River Styx. The artist mixing his colors in the dim light of Altamira; an Egyptian ruler lying still now, wrapped in his byssus,[1] stored against time in a pyramid; the faded Dorset culture of the Arctic; the

---

[1]*byssus:* Ancient cloth. — Eds.

Hmong and Samburu and Walbiri of historic time; the modern nations. This great, imperfect stretch of human expression is the clarification and encouragement, the urging and the reminder, we call history. And it is inscribed everywhere in the face of the land, from the mountain passes of the Himalayas to a nameless bajada in the California desert.

Small birds rose up in the road ahead, startled, and flew off. I prayed no infidel would ever find that horse.

1986

The Reader's Presence

1. Barry Lopez artfully blends historical information about archeological treasures with personal narrative and reflection in "The Stone Horse." Outline the overall structure of his essay, and indicate the sections in which history, aesthetics, narrative, and reflection dominate his thinking in writing. What, for example, does Lopez accomplish in the opening section of his essay, where he recounts the development of the California desert and the destruction of its archeological sites? Show how Lopez's reflections at the end pull the different strands of the essay together into a compelling conclusion.

2. "The Stone Horse" is also a masterful exercise in observation and inference. What specific sources does Lopez draw on for his vocabulary as he describes the stone horse? Based on the details Lopez provides in his description, do you have enough information to prepare a sketch of the stone horse? This essay originally appeared in *Anteaus,* a literary periodical, and was printed without an accompanying photograph of the stone horse. Given what you know of what Lopez says about such photographs, why do you think he decided to print his essay without one? Why does he remain unsatisfied when he is shown an aerial photograph of the horse? What kinds of information do his sentences provide that are lacking in the aerial photograph?

3. At the beginning of paragraph 25, Lopez announces: "The more I thought about it, the more I felt I was looking at an individual horse, a unique combination of generic and specific detail." As you reread Lopez's essay, show how his description of the stone horse does indeed reflect "a unique combination of generic and specific detail." A few paragraphs later, Lopez culminates his description by drawing several distinctions about the horse, noting such distinctions are necessary in order "to be able to talk clearly about the world." Show how the distinctions he makes about the stone horse are finally a matter of shifting his point of view in observing it.

41 ⸻

Paule Marshall

From the Poets in the Kitchen

Some years ago, when I was teaching a graduate seminar in fiction at Columbia University, a well-known male novelist visited my class to speak on his development as a writer. In discussing his formative years, he didn't realize it but he seriously endangered his life by remarking that women writers are luckier than those of his sex because they usually spend so much time as children around their mothers and their mothers' friends in the kitchen.

What did he say that for? The women students immediately forgot about being in awe of him and began readying their attack for the question and answer period later on. Even I bristled. There again was that awful image of women locked away from the world in the kitchen with only each other to talk to, and their daughters locked in with them.

But my guest wasn't really being sexist or trying to be provocative or even spoiling for a fight. What he meant — when he got around to examining himself more fully — was that, given the way children are (or were) raised in our society, with little girls kept closer to home and their mothers, the woman writer stands a better chance of being exposed, while growing up, to the kind of talk that goes on among women, more often than not in the kitchen; and that this experience gives her an edge over her male counterpart by instilling in her an appreciation for ordinary speech.

It was clear that my guest lecturer attached great importance to this, which is understandable. Common speech and the plain, workaday words that make it up are, after all, the stock in trade of some of the best fiction writers. They are the principal means by which a character in a novel or story reveals himself and gives voice sometimes to profound feelings and complex ideas about himself and the world. Perhaps the proper measure of

For biographical information on Paule Marshall, see p. 656.

a writer's talent is his skill in rendering everyday speech — when it is appropriate to his story — as well as his ability to tap, to exploit, the beauty, poetry, and wisdom it often contains.

"If you say what's on your mind in the language that comes to you   5
from your parents and your street and friends you'll probably say something beautiful." Grace Paley tells this, she says, to her students at the beginning of every writing course.

It's all a matter of exposure and a training of the ear for the would-be writer in those early years of his or her apprenticeship. And, according to my guest lecturer, this training, the best of it, often takes place in as unglamorous a setting as the kitchen.

He didn't know it, but he was essentially describing my experience as a little girl. I grew up among poets. Now they didn't look like poets — whatever that breed is supposed to look like. Nothing about them suggested that poetry was their calling. They were just a group of ordinary housewives and mothers, my mother included, who dressed in a way (shapeless housedresses, dowdy felt hats and long, dark, solemn coats) that made it impossible for me to imagine they had ever been young.

Nor did they do what poets were supposed to do — spend their days in an attic room writing verses. They never put pen to paper except to write occasionally to their relatives in Barbados. "I take my pen in hand hoping these few lines will find you in health as they leave me fair for the time being," was the way their letters invariably began. Rather, their day was spent "scrubbing floor," as they described the work they did.

Several mornings a week these unknown bards would put an apron and a pair of old house shoes in a shopping bag and take the train or streetcar from our section of Brooklyn out to Flatbush. There, those who didn't have steady jobs would wait on certain designated corners for the white housewives in the neighborhood to come along and bargain with them over pay for a day's work cleaning their houses. This was the ritual even in the winter.

Later, armed with the few dollars they had earned, which in their vo-   10
cabulary became "a few raw-mouth pennies," they made their way back to our neighborhood, where they would sometimes stop off to have a cup of tea or cocoa together before going home to cook dinner for their husbands and children.

The basement kitchen of the brownstone house where my family lived was the usual gathering place. Once inside the warm safety of its walls the women threw off the drab coats and hats, seated themselves at the large center table, drank their cups of tea or cocoa, and talked. While my sister and I sat at a smaller table over in a corner doing our homework, they talked — endlessly, passionately, poetically, and with impressive range. No subject was beyond them. True, they would indulge in the usual gossip: whose husband was running with whom, whose daughter looked slightly "in the way" (pregnant) under her bridal gown as she walked down the aisle. That sort of thing. But they also tackled the great issues of the time.

They were always, for example, discussing the state of the economy. It was the mid and late thirties then, and the aftershock of the Depression, with its soup lines and suicides on Wall Street, was still being felt.

Some people, they declared, didn't know how to deal with adversity. They didn't know that you had to "tie up your belly" (hold in the pain, that is) when things got rough and go on with life. They took their image from the bellyband that is tied around the stomach of a newborn baby to keep the navel pressed in.

They talked politics. Roosevelt was their hero. He had come along and rescued the country with relief and jobs, and in gratitude they christened their sons Franklin and Delano and hoped they would live up to the names.

If F.D.R. was their hero, Marcus Garvey was their God. The name of the fiery, Jamaican-born black nationalist of the twenties was constantly invoked around the table. For he had been their leader when they first came to the United States from the West Indies shortly after World War I. They had contributed to his organization, the United Negro Improvement Association (UNIA), out of their meager salaries, bought shares in his ill-fated Black Star Shipping Line, and at the height of the movement they had marched as members of his "nurses' brigade" in their white uniforms up Seventh Avenue in Harlem during the great Garvey Day parades. Garvey: He lived on through the power of their memories.

And their talk was of war and rumors of wars. They raged against   15 World War II when it broke out in Europe, blaming it on the politicians. "It's these politicians. They're the ones always starting up all this lot of war. But what they care? It's the poor people got to suffer and mothers with their sons." If it was *their* sons, they swore they would keep them out of the Army by giving them soap to eat each day to make their hearts sound defective. Hitler? He was for them "the devil incarnate."

Then there was home. They reminisced often and at length about home. The old country. Barbados — or Bimshire, as they affectionately called it. The little Caribbean island in the sun they loved but had to leave. "Poor — poor but sweet" was the way they remembered it.

And naturally they discussed their adopted home. America came in for both good and bad marks. They lashed out at it for the racism they encountered. They took to task some of the people they worked for, especially those who gave them only a hard-boiled egg and a few spoonfuls of cottage cheese for lunch. "As if anybody can scrub floor on an egg and some cheese that don't have no taste to it!"

Yet although they caught H in "this man country," as they called America, it was nonetheless a place where "you could at least see your way to make a dollar." That much they acknowledged. They might even one day accumulate enough dollars, with both them and their husbands working, to buy the brownstone houses which, like my family, they were only leasing at that period. This was their consuming ambition: to "buy house" and to see the children through.

There was no way for me to understand it at the time, but the talk that filled the kitchen those afternoons was highly functional. It served as therapy, the cheapest kind available to my mother and her friends. Not only did it help them recover from the long wait on the corner that morning and the bargaining over their labor, it restored them to a sense of themselves and reaffirmed their self- worth. Through language they were able to overcome the humiliations of the work-day.

But more than therapy, that freewheeling, wide-ranging, exuberant   20
talk functioned as an outlet for the tremendous creative energy they possessed. They were women in whom the need for self-expression was strong, and since language was the only vehicle readily available to them they made of it an art form that — in keeping with the African tradition in which art and life are one — was an integral part of their lives.

And their talk was a refuge. They never really ceased being baffled and overwhelmed by America — its vastness, complexity, and power. Its strange customs and laws. At a level beyond words they remained fearful and in awe. Their uneasiness and fear were even reflected in their attitude toward the children they had given birth to in this country. They referred to those like myself, the little Brooklyn-born Bajans (Barbadians), as "these New York children" and complained that they couldn't discipline us properly because of the laws here. "You can't beat these children as you would like, you know, because the authorities in this place will dash you in jail for them. After all, these is New York children." Not only were we different, American, we had, as they saw it, escaped their ultimate authority.

Confronted therefore by a world they could not encompass, which even limited their rights as parents, and at the same time finding themselves permanently separated from the world they had known, they took refuge in language. "Language is the only homeland," Czeslaw Milosz, the emigré Polish writer and Nobel Laureate, has said. This is what it became for the women at the kitchen table.

It served another purpose also, I suspect. My mother and her friends were after all the female counterpart of Ralph Ellison's invisible man. Indeed, you might say they suffered a triple invisibility, being black, female, and foreigners. They really didn't count in American society except as a source of cheap labor. But given the kind of women they were, they couldn't tolerate the fact of their invisibility, their powerlessness. And they fought back, using the only weapon at their command: the spoken word.

Those late afternoon conversations on a wide range of topics were a way for them to feel they exercised some measure of control over their lives and the events that shaped them. "Soully-gal, talk yuh talk!" they were always exhorting each other. "In this man world you got to take yuh mouth and make a gun!" They were in control, if only verbally and if only for the two hours or so that they remained in our house.

For me, sitting over in the corner, being seen but not heard, which was   25
the rule for children in those days, it wasn't only what the women talked about — the content — but the way they put things — their style. The insight, irony, wit, and humor they brought to their stories and discussions

and their poet's inventiveness and daring with language — which of course I could only sense but not define back then.

They had taken the standard English taught them in the primary schools of Barbados and transformed it into an idiom, an instrument that more adequately described them — changing around the syntax and imposing their own rhythm and accent so that the sentences were more pleasing to their ears. They added the few African sounds and words that had survived, such as the derisive suck-teeth sound and the word "yam," meaning to eat. And to make it more vivid, more in keeping with their expressive quality, they brought to bear a raft of metaphors, parables, biblical quotations, sayings, and the like:

"The sea ain' got no back door," they would say, meaning that it wasn't like a house where if there was a fire you could run out the back. Meaning that it was not to be trifled with. And meaning perhaps in a larger sense that man should treat all of nature with caution and respect.

"I has read hell by heart and called every generation blessed!" They sometimes went in for hyperbole.

A woman expecting a baby was never said to be pregnant. They never used that word. Rather, she was "in the way" or, better yet, "tumbling big." "Guess who I butt up on in the market the other day tumbling big again!"

And a woman with a reputation of being too free with her sexual favors was known in their book as a "thoroughfare" — the sense of men like a steady stream of cars moving up and down the road of her life. Or she might be dubbed "a free-bee," which was my favorite of the two. I liked the image it conjured up of a woman scandalous perhaps but independent, who flitted from one flower to another in a garden of male beauties, sampling their nectar, taking her pleasure at will, the roles reversed.   30

And nothing, no matter how beautiful, was ever described as simply beautiful. It was always "beautiful-ugly": the beautiful-ugly dress, the beautiful-ugly house, the beautiful-ugly car. Why the word "ugly," I used to wonder, when the thing they were referring to was beautiful, and they knew it. Why the antonym, the contradiction, the linking of opposites? It used to puzzle me greatly as a child.

There is the theory in linguistics which states that the idiom of a people, the way they use language, reflects not only the most fundamental views they hold of themselves and the world but their very conception of reality. Perhaps in using the term "beautiful-ugly" to describe nearly everything, my mother and her friends were expressing what they believed to be a fundamental dualism in life: the idea that a thing is at the same time its opposite, and that these opposites, these contradictions make up the whole. But theirs was not a Manichaean[1] brand of dualism that sees mat-

---

[1]*Manichaean:* Pertaining to the dualistic religion of the Persian prophet Manes (A.D. 216?–276?), whose basic doctrine consists of a universal conflict between light and dark, good and evil. — EDS.

ter, flesh, the body, as inherently evil, because they constantly addressed each other as "soully-gal" — soul: spirit; gal: the body, flesh, the visible self. And it was clear from their tone that they gave one as much weight and importance as the other. They had never heard of the mind/body split.

As for God, they summed up His essential attitude in a phrase. "God," they would say, "don' love ugly and He ain' stuck on pretty."

Using everyday speech, the simple commonplace words — but always with imagination and skill—they gave voice to the most complex ideas. Flannery O'Connor would have approved of how they made ordinary language work, as she put it, "double-time," stretching, shading, deepening its meaning. Like Joseph Conrad they were always trying to infuse new life in the "old old words worn thin . . . by . . . careless usage." And the goals of their oral art were the same as his: "to make you hear, to make you feel . . . to make you *see*." This was their guiding esthetic.

By the time I was eight or nine, I graduated from the corner of the kitchen to the neighborhood library, and thus from the spoken to the written word. The Macon Street Branch of the Brooklyn Public Library was an imposing half-block-long edifice of heavy gray masonry, with glass-paneled doors at the front and two tall metal torches symbolizing the light that comes of learning flanking the wide steps outside.

The inside was just as impressive. More steps — of pale marble with gleaming brass railings at the center and sides — led up to the circulation desk, and a great pendulum clock gazed down from the balcony stacks that faced the entrance. Usually stationed at the top of the steps like the guards outside Buckingham Palace was the custodian, a stern-faced West Indian type who for years, until I was old enough to obtain an adult card, would immediately shoo me with one hand into the Children's Room and with the other threaten me into silence, a finger to his lips. You would have thought he was the chief librarian and not just someone whose job it was to keep the brass polished and the clock wound. I put him in a story called "Barbados" years later and had terrible things happen to him at the end.

I was sheltered from the storm of adolescence in the Macon Street library, reading voraciously, indiscriminately, everything from Jane Austen to Zane Grey, but with a special passion for the long, full-blown, richly detailed eighteenth- and nineteenth-century picaresque tales: *Tom Jones. Great Expectations. Vanity Fair.*

But although I loved nearly everything I read and would enter fully into the lives of the characters — indeed, would cease being myself and become them — I sensed a lack after a time. Something I couldn't quite define was missing. And then one day, browsing in the poetry section, I came across a book by someone called Paul Laurence Dunbar, and opening it I found the photograph of a wistful, sad-eyed poet who to my surprise was black. I turned to a poem at random. "Little brown-baby wif spa'klin' / eyes / Come to yo' pappy an' set on his knee." Although I had a little difficulty at first with the words in dialect, the poem spoke to me as nothing I had read before of the closeness, the special relationship I had had

35

with my father, who by then had become an ardent believer in Father Divine and gone to live in Father's "kingdom" in Harlem. Reading it helped to ease somewhat the tight knot of sorrow and longing I carried around in my chest that refused to go away. I read another poem. "Lias! Lias! Bless de Lawd! Don' you know de day's / erbroad? / Ef you don' get up, you scamp / Dey'll be trouble in dis camp." I laughed. It reminded me of the way my mother sometimes yelled at my sister and me to get out of bed in the mornings.

And another: "Seen my lady home las' night / Jump back, honey, jump back. / Hel' huh han' an' sque'z it tight . . . " About love between a black man and a black woman. I had never seen that written about before and it roused in me all kinds of delicious feelings and hopes.

And I began to search then for books and stories and poems about 40 "The Race" (as it was put back then), about my people. While not abandoning Thackeray, Fielding, Dickens, and the others, I started asking the reference librarian, who was white, for books by Negro writers, although I must admit I did so at first with a feeling of shame — the shame I and many others used to experience in those days whenever the word "Negro" or "colored" came up.

No grade school literature teacher of mine had ever mentioned Dunbar or James Weldon Johnson or Langston Hughes. I didn't know that Zora Neale Hurston existed and was busy writing and being published during those years. Nor was I made aware of people like Frederick Douglass and Harriet Tubman — their spirit and example — or the great nineteenth-century abolitionist and feminist Sojourner Truth. There wasn't even Negro History Week when I attended P.S. 35 on Decatur Street!

What I needed, what all the kids — West Indian and native black American alike — with whom I grew up needed, was an equivalent of the Jewish shul, someplace where we could go after school — the schools that were shortchanging us — and read works by those like ourselves and learn about our history.

It was around that time also that I began harboring the dangerous thought of someday trying to write myself. Perhaps a poem about an apple tree, although I had never seen one. Or the story of a girl who could magically transplant herself to wherever she wanted to be in the world — such as Father Divine's kingdom in Harlem. Dunbar — his dark, eloquent face, his large volume of poems — permitted me to dream that I might someday write, and with something of the power with words my mother and her friends possessed.

When people at readings and writers' conferences ask me who my major influences were, they are sometimes a little disappointed when I don't immediately name the usual literary giants. True, I am indebted to those writers, white and black, whom I read during my formative years and still read for instruction and pleasure. But they were preceded in my life by another set of giants whom I always acknowledge before all others: the group of women around the table long ago. They taught me my first lesson in the narrative art. They trained my ear. They set a standard of excellence. This is why the best of my work must be attributed to them; it stands as testimony to the rich legacy of language and culture they so freely passed on to me in the wordshop of the kitchen.

1983

The Reader's Presence

1. Paule Marshall celebrates the evocative power and eloquence of "ordinary speech," "the kind of talk that goes on among women, more often than not in the kitchen." Marshall discusses this language in terms of its substance and style. What major characteristics does Marshall attribute to this kind of talk? From what — and where — does its power derive? She also discusses such language in terms of its functions. Identify as many of these functions as possible. Which do you find most important? Why? Which seem less important? Explain. What does this language enable these women to do each day?

2. Marshall's essay also includes an affectionate portrait of her mother and the neighborhood women who gathered around the kitchen table each day. What subjects do they discuss? In what ways do these conversations challenge the stereotypes of women on such occasions? Near the beginning of paragraph 23, Marshall observes that "My mother and her friends were after all the female counterpart of Ralph Ellison's invisible man. Indeed, you might say they suffered a triple invisibility. . . . " Discuss the nature of this "triple invisibility," and explain how language — how even the most ordinary language — enabled them to "fight back."

3. At the beginning of paragraph 32, Marshall notes: "There is the theory in linguistics which states that the idiom of a people, the way they use language, reflects not only the most fundamental views they hold of themselves and the world but their very conception of reality." She then explains that her mother and friends were "expressing what they believed to be a fundamental dualism in life: the idea that a thing is at the same time its opposite, and that these opposites, these contradictions make up the whole." What are the "opposites" she presents in this essay, and how do they "make up the whole"? How are these opposites matters of race? gender? economics? linguistics? style? culture? How does Marshall demonstrate her commitment to "rendering everyday speech" in her own prose style? Point to specific words and phrases to support and clarify your response.

42

Judith Martin

The Pursuit of Politeness

The problem that baffled Thomas Jefferson was an etiquette problem. It was, and remains, the great American etiquette problem: how to adapt European systems of etiquette, based on court life and hereditary social classes, to a democracy. A number of other American etiquetteers have struggled with this mighty problem as well — Benjamin Franklin, Ralph Waldo Emerson, Harriet Beecher Stowe, Eleanor Roosevelt. How is it possible to express equality, individual freedom, social mobility, and the dignity of labor in the hierarchical language of polite social behavior? What is democratic etiquette? How may it be invented?

In do-your-own-thing America, there is no longer much distinction between etiquette, the codified rules of behavior, and manners, the social premises from which they are derived. There is a distinction, however, which must be preserved. Manners, which pertain to the outer person, must not be confused with morals. Those who deal in both, such as Cotton Mather[1] and his friend God, do not always make that distinction clear. Religions tend to put regulations about eating, dress, and washing in the same category as areas for sinning that promise more fun. Acts forbidden by law in Puritan America included making nasty faces, jeering at people (or leering at them, depending on how attractive one found them), flirting, swearing, gossiping, and finger-sticking.

The failure to distinguish between manners and morals suggests, erroneously, that acceptable social behavior follows effortlessly from personal virtue. All you need is a good heart, and the rest will take care of itself. You don't have to write thank-you letters. I think, to the contrary, that it is safer to hope that practicing proper behavior eventually encourages virtuous feeling; that if you write enough thank-you letters, you may actually feel a flicker of gratitude. At the very least, good manners can put

---

For biographical information on Judith Martin, see p. 656.
[1]*Cotton Mather:* Influential Puritan theologian and writer (1663–1728). — EDS.

a decent cover over ugly feelings. Charming villains have always had a decided social advantage over crass people who mean well.

The belief that natural behavior is beautiful and that civilization and
its manners spoil the essential goodness inherent in all of us noble savages
is, of course, the Jean-Jacques Rousseau[2] school of etiquette. A major influence in Jefferson's time, Rousseau's philosophy survives in the pop-
psychology and "human potential" movements of today (the concept that
civilization is corrupt and nature is benign is particularly popular in earth-
quake- and flood-ridden California) and in the child-rearing philosophy
that has given us so many little — savages. The natural approach to human
relations presumes that to know any person well enough is to love him,
that the only human problem is a communication problem. This denies
that people might be separated by basic, deeply held, and genuinely irreconcilable differences — philosophical, political, or religious. One has to
believe that all such differences are no more than misunderstandings.

Many forms of etiquette are employed exactly to disguise the antipa-   5
thies that arise from irreconcilable differences, in order to prevent may-
hem. Thus, the charge is often made against etiquette that it is artificial.
Indeed, it is. Civilization is artificial. When people extol the virtues of nat-
uralness, honesty, informality, intimacy, and creativity — watch out. They
are about to insult you to your face.

The idea that people can behave "naturally," without resorting to an
artificial code tacitly agreed upon by their own society, is as silly as the idea
that they can communicate by a spoken language without commonly accepted semantic and grammatical rules. Like language, a code of manners
can be used with more or with less skill, for laudable or for evil purposes,
to express a great variety of ideas and emotions. Like language, manners
continually undergo slow changes and adaptations, but these changes have
to be global, not atomic. For if everyone improvises his own manners, no
one will understand the meaning of anyone else's behavior, and the result
will be social chaos, or about what we have now.

Ordinarily, etiquette, like language, is learned by children imitating
their elders, with the difference that parents occasionally have to assist the
imitative efforts by saying, "Stop that! That's disgusting!" The transmission from generation to generation occurs nonreflectively, so that the cor-
pus of traditional etiquette is tacitly conserved. But at certain times and
under certain conditions, people deliberately fool with the system — for
philosophical or aesthetic reasons (Classical Greece and the Renaissance
were times of great interest in etiquette, for instance) or to redefine, because of upheaval or uncertainty, who is in now and who is out. The best
way to play In and Out is to keep devising new rules of etiquette so that
only the nimble can keep up, as was done at the court of Louis XIV.

---

[2]*Jean-Jacques Rousseau:* French philosopher and educational reformer (1712–1778). —
EDS.

British Victorian manners were notoriously complicated for a similar reason: A threatened aristocracy was trying to fight off the inevitable rise of newly rich industrialists. (Money is never mentioned in a properly fought social war; the polite way of saying you cannot stand new people, still in use today among people who do not like those whom their children are marrying, is "Those people simply do not know how to behave.") Meanwhile, the nouveaux riches were putting their money into new types of forks with which to fend off their former neighbors and friends. But in the end — as we know from Victorian novels — aristocrats and parvenus, after much crossing of forks, got together and lived happily ever after on his title and her money.

(The fork, by the way, has a venerable history as a weapon in class warfare. The earliest example I have come across was St. Peter Damian moralizing, in 1005, on the death of the young dogaressa of Venice. She had had the plague, and a great percentage of the population also died of the plague, but he attributed this young woman's death to God's retribution against her uppitiness, as demonstrated by the fact that she ate with a fork. She also took an occasional bath in fresh water. No wonder God struck her down. The idea that good table manners indicate a lack of humility is still with us; to this day a great many people brag about not knowing which fork to use.)

Inventing a whole new system of etiquette, however, is bound to create   10 certain problems. Etiquette is folk custom, and people have emotional ties to the forms of their youth. That is one reason why there is such hostility between generations in times of rapid change; their manners being different, each feels affronted by the other. Another obstacle to implementing wholesale changes in manners is that the changes cannot be the least bit subtle or complicated, because everything has to be learned instantly, not gradually assimilated during childhood. That would seem to be fine with Americans, as — following Jefferson's example — we value simplicity of style as suitable to an unpretentious country. But this leads to an avoidance of the indirect, which removes the very ambiguity that often saves us from fully understanding one another, and thus from scorn and ridicule.

Finally, the trouble with inventing etiquette forms is that it is a game everybody can play. Each person not only claims the right to design his own etiquette, but also to be insulted if others do not observe it, even if he has not troubled to acquaint them with his preferences. Consider forms of address. In present-day America, there is no consensus on usage of titles and names. One man is insulted to be addressed by his first name, when it implies intimacy that he does not want; another is insulted to be addressed by title and surname, because he says it makes him seem too old for intimacy. One woman complains that calling her Mrs. with her husband's name insults her by implying she is his property; another is insulted to be addressed any other way because, she announces, she is proud of being his wife. And listening to the rationales for everyone's tiniest acts has certainly added to the boredom of modern life.

Similarly, it has never been easier to insult people inadvertently. A gentleman opens a door for a lady because his mother taught him that ladies appreciate such courtesies, but this one turns around and spits in his eye because he has insulted her womanhood. A young lady offers her seat in a crowded bus to an elderly, frail gentleman, and he gives her a filthy look, because she has insulted his manhood. Moreover, it has never been harder to insult people intentionally. If you say, "You are horrid and I hate you," people reply, "Oh, you're feeling hostile; I'll wait until you feel better." The idea that explaining motivation justifies any violation is perhaps essential in a world of flying insults, where the all-purpose psychiatric excuse, "I'm depressed," is considered to absolve one of any obligation or responsibility.

This lack of standardization in American manners results in an anger-ridden, chaotic society, where each trivial act is interpreted as a revelation of the moral philosophy of the individual actor, who is left standing there naked in his mores.

Thomas Jefferson certainly did not mean to make such a mess with his forays into etiquette. He was only trying to codify his social ideals. Given his belief that there was a need to invent democratic etiquette and protocol, what should it be like? There was little precedent to go on. The abolition of *ancien régime* etiquette by French revolutionaries was all very well, but nobody wants to have to watch a bunch of revolutionaries eating dinner.

Jefferson's solution was to abolish rank entirely. He called it Pell-Mell etiquette. When he was in the White House, even foreign diplomats representing undemocratic countries were stripped of their personal and professional ranks. "When brought together in society," Jefferson wrote in a directive to his cabinet, probably the least edifying document he left a grateful nation, "all are perfectly equal, whether foreign or domestic, titled or untitled, in or out of office." Nowadays, he might have worn a tag: "Hello! My name is Tom. What's yours?" A nobleman, representing his country in an exalted position — probably sent abroad because he was disgracing his family at home, a personnel policy that used to make diplomatic social life so interesting — would be treated exactly the same as the flunky sent to clean up after him. The one success of Jefferson's novel system of democratic etiquette was that it gave everyone equal offense. He was forced to modify it, and President Madison abolished it. But although he made such a mess, Jefferson (who, by the way, was as susceptible as the next Virginia gentleman to the charm of polished French manners) had addressed a very important question.

My misgivings about the invention of new manners notwithstanding, I certainly agree with the Jeffersonian premise of universal human dignity, and am frightfully upset when snobbery makes a democratic people ape aristocratic forms. I had to grab for my smelling salts when an American chief of protocol curtseyed to British royalty — we fought a war over that point, and we won. I have no patience with those who claim that they eat European style because "it's more efficient"; if there is one thing our doctors agree on, it is that we should eat less efficiently, not more. What is more, the American style of switching the fork from left hand to right was the older European style that came here and stayed, while the fast-food approach developed over there.

Still, despite the nobility of Jefferson's ideal, the notion that we are above petty symbols of rank is unfortunately not true. Our leaders may use limousine service, private office dining rooms, and the like, only to save valuable time, but that does not explain why President Reagan gives out gold and navy-blue enameled cuff links to his close associates — in two grades of enamel. (Everybody in the administration has learned to distinguish the two grades at a glance, and the flashing of cuffs at state functions is astounding.) Nevertheless, the Jeffersonian system of protocol after all these years is creeping back into international usage. Foreign countries where forms of royalty and nobility are no longer as appropriate as they used to be also need modern forms to demonstrate their ideologies. The ill-fitting double-breasted suit, for example, is thought to symbolize deep commitment to the egalitarian precepts of Marxism-Leninism. This symbolism does not always work. When world leaders call each other "Ronnie" and "Maggie" and kiss hello, they are, whether they realize it or not, using the traditional forms of reigning royalty, who, possibly because they were more times related than was good for their health, identified more with one another than with their subjects. (The correct written address among royalty, even if the correspondents are not of the same race, much less the same family, is *"Madame ma soeur,"* and *"Monsieur mon frère."*)[3]

The Jeffersonian system of nonhierarchical etiquette is now even more widely practiced in the society at large. The nearly universal use of first names and other features of the model of instant-intimacy have all but erased such de facto distinctions as age, degree of education, professional rank, and increasingly, gender. Everybody is treated alike. This is the system, remember, that never did work.

We must standardize American manners, then, not only to complete Jefferson's sidetracked project of developing a democratic etiquette, but to make order out of the current chaos and to relieve people of the burden of developing and defending their own choices in the most common, everyday matters. But what exactly do we want? The ideals we have in mind, Mr. Jefferson and I, are equality and individual freedom and dignity of labor. I

---

[3]*Madame . . . frère:* In French, literally "Madam, my sister" and "Mister, my brother." — EDS.

shall take the liberty of adding equality for women, whose interests, along with those of a few other people, he unaccountably overlooked.

I hope that we can take it for granted that individual freedom must be   20
tempered somewhat by the need for maintaining a harmonious society. I am not the only crank who is being driven mad by the abrasiveness of modern America. The modern etiquette problem is not that people don't know how to eat artichokes properly (the artichoke can defend itself — it has prickles) but that the citizens are screaming at one another in the streets. When I am told nowadays of a "return to manners," I am forced to reply that that is not quite accurate. People have indeed come to realize that they hate being treated rudely by others, but the solution they seek is the "put-down," a method of returning rudeness with even greater rudeness. It is surely a premise of democracy that the rules apply equally to everyone.

Equality, then, is something we all agree belongs in American behavior. But when we interpret it to mean a complete lack of recognizable distinctions among types of people on any basis whatsoever, and a thorough leveling of all hierarchies — a universal kindergarten, where everyone wears the same play clothes for all occasions and is addressed by nickname — then equality does not work.

The truth is that nobody believes in it. Nobody really likes it. The de facto equality we have, of everyone's being treated at the lowest humanly possible standard of behavior, has not prevented tremendous striving to establish a recognizable class system. It seems to be a human instinct, once one has had the least advantage in life, to point out to as many people as possible that they have not.

Unlike a hereditary class system, where titles fix the position of the upper classes, a fluid system requires blatant outward manifestations for constant confirmation of status. The argument is often made that an institutionalized class system is better, in a way, because people at least know where they belong and are relieved from constant competition. (I have noticed that this argument is always advanced by people who are satisfied that if a class system were newly declared, they would come out on top.) American class distinctions, however, are made with money. Indeed, class distinctions everywhere have always been made with money, or its equivalent in land, never mind what may have been said here or in any other society about blood or breeding or education or taste or nobility of character. Fine feelings, intellectual, aesthetic, philanthropic or spiritual, require at least temporary indifference to one's immediate financial gain. Generally, but not always, this means that one has already satisfied one's material wants.

Under a hereditary system, the hard-working dynastic founder who makes the money does not fully enjoy the spending of it. That is left for the next generation, the children who are brought up gently to acquire the fine taste and breeding that comes to be called nobility of character. In subsequent generations, the founder's money and their taste accumulate possessions, and the patina of age is more highly valued than the shine of the new. (In England, the traditional insult is, "They're the sort of people who buy their silver.") In Europe, there was always that clear-cut division between those who made the money and those who enjoyed it. One was either in trade, or one was in society, but it was impossible to be in both. The essence of being in trade is working to get ever ahead, while the essence of being in society is knowing how to enjoy the leisure afforded by having arrived.

Solving this problem diachronically, with earlier generations in trade and later ones in society, is obviously not suitable in the land of the self-made man, where everyone is created equal. In nineteenth-century America, a synchronic solution was found, a sexual division of the tasks of making and spending within one generation of the same family. Until fairly recently, the pattern was that the father and sons worked, and, to whatever extent their earnings allowed, the mother and daughters were supposed to display culture, religion, luxury, and other assorted fine feelings of society — in addition to seeing that the housework got done.

This system of working men and supposedly leisured women is not as old as those who are trying to root out the remains of it (or to revive it) seem to imagine. Before the rise of the middle class during the Industrial Revolution, gender had little to do with whether one worked. All the poor — men, women, and children — worked, and all the rich did not work. (The nonworking of the rich was known as "looking after the property," a unisex form of housewifery, except that the men looked after the estate manager who looked after the outdoor property, and women looked after the household staff who looked after the indoor property.)

But the American-style family division, by gender, of earning and spending, made trouble right away. When the women became socially mobile — Mama taking the daughters to Europe perhaps, and finding them noble husbands unsullied by work — the last thing they needed to have around was old, vulgar, money-grubbing Papa. And in recent years, we have finally noticed that dividing the tasks of work and leisure by gender leaves a lot of dissatisfied people — overburdened men and bored women.

This system has now come to an end. It took a remarkably long time for people to notice the simple fact that everyone needs some sort of challenging work in his or her life, and that everyone needs a personal life, complete with noncompetitive leisure. Now even aristocratic societies are abandoning the idea of full-time leisure. There is not a countess left in Europe who doesn't run a boutique, or aspire to; and every idiot son of an old family identifies himself as a photographer.

A new social problem is replacing the old one. Now that virtually everyone works, including middle-class women and upper-class men, the private realm has all but disappeared. There is no one left to run it. Everything is business. What is referred to as "society" in the newspapers consists of parties celebrating merchants or new merchandise, or of charity luncheons or balls to which tickets are sold. More exclusively, so-called private, social life is routinely used unabashedly for opportunities to further the guests' careers.

Just about every etiquette question I receive concerning weddings pro-   30
vides financial information as the presumptive basis for my ruling on social matters. "We're paying for it ourselves, so why do we have to invite my mother's cousins whom I can't stand?" "If my stepfather is paying for the liquor, shouldn't he give me away, rather than my father, who's only paying for the flowers?" "How can we tell people that we already have all the household things we want and prefer cash?" There seems to be a general belief that social, and even family, honors are for sale, and that there is an acknowledged admission charge to wedding guests.

Business techniques are applied to the most personal situations. If you are ready to fall in love, you run a classified advertisement announcing a vacancy and including a job description with the most detailed skill requirements. It is permissible to fire lovers, but only with cause. "I don't love you anymore" is not considered acceptable; "You don't meet my present needs" is more suitably businesslike. In what used to be known as free love, contractual obligation after obligation is being established until, ultimately, the free lovers will have reinvented marriage. Friends are only friends, moreover, if they fit exactly with one's stage of life and momentary interests. That person whose agenda is to find romance does not bother with married people, and married couples only bother with people who are childless, if they are, or else have children of the same age group they do. Acquiring or losing a spouse means, therefore, that one also loses one's friends.

I suppose one could not argue with using business techniques to run personal life if they worked. But it is, after all, the goal of business to get things done and to move ahead; while the whole idea of society, not to mention love, is to enjoy being where you are.

Meanwhile, the empty forms of social behavior survive inappropriately in business situations, where there is a pretense, by using the social model, that professional inequalities do not exist. "Hi, I'm Kimberly, and I'm going to be bringing you dinner. How ya doing?" "We're not just your bank, we're your friend." Never trust your luggage to an airline that has promised to be your friend, because that means that the business will not be held accountable any more than a friend would. If a friend does his best, or has an excuse, or just botches something, or does not feel like it, it is rude to berate him for not doing a favor.

This confusion of friendship and business not only blinds people to their own interests, but leads them to unrealistic expectations from others. I always have to start the New Year reading pitiful letters from those who, thinking the office Christmas party a social occasion where everyone is equal, used it to have a frank talk with the boss. I do not in the least mean

to suggest that I do not approve of an unashamed recognition of the importance of trade in American life, and of the dignity of all honest labor. But
how can the ideological equality of all citizens be represented symbolically
in the decidedly unequal world of business, where some people are bosses
and others are their employees? It cannot. Only in the private realm, where
each citizen can exercise autonomy and choice, is full equality possible.

When there is no private realm, rank derives only from jobs; and a   35
person without a job, no matter how rich, is a person without social identification or standing. This is why women who were once proud of single-
handedly maintaining private, domestic, community, social, and cultural
life for men (who could manage only one job) are now ashamed of or defensive about being housewives. Those clearly low on the job scale — or
even high but not satisfied with their positions — also harbor terrible resentment because they feel they do not have the equality they were promised as Americans. By equality, they mean not only equal opportunity, but
being considered "just as good as anyone else" at whatever level they
occupy.

Of course, according to the American tradition, anyone who is dissatisfied ought to be able to work his or her way up. But even if this tradition
accurately reflected the possibilities, the climb would rarely be quick or
high enough. Nor is there any one rung on the ladder that commands universal respect, unless it is that of celebrity, the new super-category based on
the lucky accident of having become conspicuous for whatever reason,
good or bad. Perhaps that is because it skips over the old work ethic, which
seems too slow and tedious now that everything depends on it. It is not the
climbing Horatio Alger[4] whom we admire now, but the sitting Lana
Turner,[5] who is discovered at Schwab's Pharmacy and rewarded for simply
being — whatever it is that she is. The only identity one can still have as a
person is as a personality, which seems to be something less than a person
blown up to look like more.

Consumer competition does remain another, related, form of ranking,
but blatant consumerism makes inequalities even more obvious. It is now
carried out by the very same people who make the money, which may seem
only fair, but which means that the relative worth of the goods must be
recognizable to people who have not had sufficient leisure to learn to make
subtle judgments. Clothes with labels — designers' names — on the outside, where everyone can read them, are designed to meet this need. In this
competition, success is judged not by how old possessions are, but how
newly acquired, demonstrating the ability to afford the latest designated
symbol, even if that means buying up someone else's heirlooms.

[4]***Horatio Alger:*** Popular American author (1834–1899) whose "rags-to-riches" novels
contributed to a national myth of personal success. — EDS.

[5]***Lana Turner:*** Film star (b. 1920) whose discovery at a popular soda fountain became a
legend of Hollywood success. — EDS.

Curiously, this has come to mean that the rich — who were traditionally courted and served by the commercial classes — have now put themselves at the service of those very persons who have a financial interest in the competition for social standing. A lady has arrived socially when her hairdresser and dressmaker consent to grace her dinner table. Some of the credit for this clever inversion must go to the middlemen of modern art — the critics, dealers, and curators who, early in this century, managed to convince their patrons that by using their own money in the exercise of their own taste, they would make hopeless fools of themselves. Now the principle of the incompetence of the rich regarding the spending of their own money has been extended from art to most other luxury purchases. A person who can afford it has an interior decorator to arrange his house, as he has a psychoanalyst to arrange his feelings. There is a professional expert for every aspect of life. No one who has enough money needs to worry about spending it in ways of which merchants might disapprove.

And so the role of social arbiter, of judging today's placements on the social scale, has been turned over to middlemen who make money at it. Popular articles about "making it" invariably state that the ultimate sign of success is recognition and approval from headwaiters. If the owner of the restaurant interrupts your dinner to greet you, life can hold no further glory. The expensive restaurant, with its mysterious allocations of good and bad tables, whatever that may mean, is apparently the temple of judgment, along with a new place on Fifth Avenue called Trumpery Tower. Or something.

We need, again, a coherent code of manners. And this should be based   40 not on commerce-dictated expenditure, but on gentility of behavior. I believe that the only hope for equality in this society is reestablishing the dualism of the commercial and the personal realms. Instead of assigning people to one or the other by gender, we need to change the society so that everyone can enjoy some of each.

I think we will probably eventually adopt a system of precedence based on age, rather than gender, and I rather think that is a good idea, as it gives everyone a shot at being last and then first. But there are some changes that more immediately need to be made. For example, the business realm must be structured to recognize that both men and women have personal lives. The pattern of the man being free to work all the time because he has a sham family and social life, which is actually entirely run by a woman, is disappearing; both men and women are less willing to settle for half a life. Moreover, the requirement of mobility for many careers is already becoming unfeasible. Couples who work require two satisfactory slots if they are to move. Constant moving also means that one's contacts are job-related, and effectively rules out community life. Employers will have to recognize that employees — and not only women employees — have families, and therefore require certain scheduling adjustments to accommodate child-rearing and other personal duties and pleasures.

Then there is that oxymoron, business entertaining. The chief purpose of business entertaining is to confuse people into applying social standards, such as loyalty regardless of merit, to business dealings. I do not think it works. It does not require much sophistication to figure out how to accept free drinks but still clear one's head for business. The foreign service and corporate America are also finding that women are refusing to devote themselves, for free, to making those burdensome social schedules function.

Tax advantages for business entertaining, and deductions for memberships in clubs and other nominally recreational organizations, invite abuses of all sorts. It is commonplace for people to claim that their clubs are private when fairness requirements are mentioned, and part of the business world when that is profitable. Why should the government, through the tax laws, so involve itself in the social realm?

Freedom ought to include the right to bestow friendship as one chooses. If we truly believe in the dignity of labor, any task can be performed with pride, because no honest work can demean the basic dignity of a human being.

Equality means that one does not take one's identity in society from 45 the job slot one happens to fill. I would hope that a revival of the private realm would preclude hierarchies in which absolute standards, such as job titles and money, rather than personal qualities, mark some individuals as obviously superior to others.

I think my colleague Thomas Jefferson would agree. I'm not so sure about my colleague Cotton Mather.

1984

The Reader's Presence

1. Martin uses many words with valuative connotations. How, for example, are you meant to read "do-your-own-thing America"? Does she intend that expression to be read positively or negatively? How do you know? Can you identify other similar terms and expressions?

2. We ordinarily use the words *etiquette* and *manners* as synonyms. What distinction does Martin make between these words? Why does she believe this distinction is important? Is it a distinction you would find in a dictionary? Do you think her distinction is valid?

3. "I am not the only crank," Martin says, "who is being driven mad by the abrasiveness of modern America." What does she find "abrasive" about today's society? Why does she refer to herself as a "crank"? How self-critical do you think she is being? In rereading her essay, what characteristics would you consider "cranky"?

43 _____

John McPhee

Pieces of the Frame

On the edge of Invermoriston Forest, I was trying to explain raised beaches, the fifty-foot beaches of Scotland, so called because they are about that far above the sea. Waves never touch them. Tides don't come near reaching them. Shell and shingle, whitened like bones, they are aftereffects of the ice, two miles thick, that once rested on Scotland and actually shoved Scotland down into the earth. When the ice melted, the sea slowly came up, but so did the land, sluggishly recovering its buoyancy over the molten center of things. After the sea had increased as much as it was going to, the land kept rising, and beaches were lifted into the air, some as much as fifty feet.

That was how I understood the story, and I was doing what I could to say it in a way that would make it intelligible to an audience of four children (mine — all girls, and all quite young), but the distractions were so numerous that I never really had a chance. My family and I were having a lakeside lunch — milk, potato sticks, lambs' tongues, shortbread, white chocolate, Mini-Dunlop cheese — beside a stream in a grove of birches that was backed by dense reforested pines. The pines covered steep slopes toward summits two thousand feet above us. It was late spring, but there were snowfields up there nonetheless, and the water we drank had been snow in the mountains that morning.

Near us, another family, also with small children, was having what was evidently a birthday picnic. They had arrived after we were already settled, and they had chosen — I don't know why, with acre upon acre of unpeopled and essentially similar terrain to move about in — to unpack all their special effects (a glistening white cake, noisemakers, conical cardboard orange hats) only forty or fifty yards away. I tried to ignore them

For biographical information on John McPhee, see p. 657.

and go on with my ruminations on the raised beaches. There were no raised beaches in that place, at least not in the usual form, but the children had seen them and had played on them elsewhere in the Highlands, and I thought that if they could understand how such phenomena had come to be, they might in turn be able to imagine the great, long lake now before them — Loch Ness — as the sea loch, the arm of the Atlantic, that it once was, and how marine creatures in exceptional variety had once freely moved in and out of it, some inevitably remaining.

Losing interest in the birthday party, my youngest daughter said, "I want to see the monster."

This had already become another distraction. In much the way that, in the United States, NO HUNTING signs are posted on every other tree along blacktop country roads, cardboard signs of about the same size had been tacked to trees and poles along the lake. There were several in the birch grove. Printed in royal blue on a white background, they said, "Any members of the general public who genuinely believe they have seen an unusual creature or object in or on the shores of Loch Ness are requested to report the occurrence to Expedition Headquarters at Achnahannet, two miles south of Urquhart Castle. If unable to report in person, they may telephone the Expedition (No. Drumnadrochit 358). Reports will only be of interest from people willing to give their full name and address and fill in a Sighting Report Form, which will be sent on request. Thank you for your cooperation. Published by the Loch Ness Phenomena Investigation Bureau, 23 Ashley Place, London, S.W. 1, and printed at the Courier Office, Inverness."

"What makes you think the monster wants to see *you?*" I said to my youngest one. "There won't be any sightings today, anyway. There's too much wind out there."

The wind on the lake was quite strong. It was blowing from the north. There were whitecaps, and the ranks of the waves were uniform in our perspective, which was high. Watching the waves, I remembered canoe trips when I was ten or eleven years old, trying to achieve some sort of momentum against white-capping headwinds between Rogers Rock and Sabbath Day Point on Lake George. Lake George was for beginners, who could learn in its unwild basin the essentials they would need to know on longer trips in later years in wildernesses they would seek out. But now, watching the north wind go down the lake in Scotland, I could not remember headwinds anywhere as powerful and savage as they had been in that so-styled lake for beginners, and I could feel again the skin rubbed off my hands. The likeness was in more than the wind, however. It was in the appearance, the shape, and the scale — about a mile from side to side — of Loch Ness, which, like the American lake, is at least twenty times longer than it is wide, a long deep cleft, positioned like some great geophysical ax-cut between its lateral hills. I remember being told, around the fire at night, stories of the first white man who saw Lake George. He was a travelling French priest, intent on converting the Mohawks and other nations

of the Iroquois. He had come from Orléans. He said that the lake was
the most beautiful he had ever seen, and he named it the Lake of the
Blessed Sacrament. The Indians, observing that the priest blessed them
with his right hand, held him down and chewed away his fingers until
the fingers were stumps and the hand was pulp. Later, when the priest
did not stop his work, the Indians axed the top of his skull, and then cut
off his head.

Lake George is so clear that objects far below its surface, such as white
stones or hovering bass, can be seen in total definition. The water of Loch
Ness is so dark with the tints of peat that on a flat-calm day it looks like
black glass. Three or four feet below the surface is an obscurity so complete
that experienced divers have retreated from it in frustration, and in some
cases in fear. A swimmer looking up toward a bright sky from a distance of
inches beneath the surface has the impression that he is afloat in very dark
tea. Lake George is nearly two hundred feet deep in places, has numerous
islands, and with its bays and points, is prototypal of beautiful mountain
lakes of grand dimension in every part of the world. Loch Ness is like almost no other lake anywhere. Its shores are formidably and somewhat un-
naturally parallel. It has no islands. Its riparian walls go straight down. Its
bottom is flat, and in most places is seven hundred feet deep, a mean depth
far greater than the mean depth of the North Sea. Loch Ness holds a fantastic volume of water, the entire runoff of any number of northern glens
— Glen Affric, Glen Cannich, Glen Moriston, Glen Farrar, Glen Urquhart.
All of these valleys, impressive in themselves, are petals to Glen More, the
Great Glen. Loch Ness is the principal basin of the Great Glen, and the
Great Glen is the epicenter of the Highlands. A few miles of silt, carried
into the lake by the rivers, long ago dammed the seaward end, changing the
original sea loch into a freshwater lake, but so slowly that marine creatures
trapped within it had a chance to adapt themselves. Meanwhile the land
kept rising, and with it the new lake. The surface of Loch Ness is fifty-two
feet above sea level.

My wife listened with some interest when, repeating all this, I made an
expanded attempt to enrich everyone's experience, but nothing was going
through to the children. "I want to see the monster," the youngest one said
again, speaking for all. They didn't want to know how or why the so-called
monster might have come into that particular lake. They just wanted to see
it. But the wind was not slowing up out there on the lake.

All of us looked now at the family that was having the birthday picnic, 10
for the father had stood up shouting and had flung a large piece of the
birthday cake at his wife. It missed her and spattered in bits in the branches
of a tree. She shouted back at him something to the effect that he was
depraved and cruel, and he in turn bellowed that she was a carbon of her
bloody mother and that he was fed up. She said she had had all she could
ever take, and was going home — to England, apparently. With that, she
ran up the hillside and soon was out of sight in the pines. At first, he did
not follow, but he suddenly was on his feet and shouting serial threats as

he too went out of range in the pines. Meanwhile, their children, all but one, were crying. The one that wasn't crying was the girl whose birthday it was, and she just sat without moving, under a conical orange hat, staring emptily in the direction of the lake.

We went to our car and sat in it for some time, trying not to be keeping too obvious an eye on the children in the birch grove, who eventually began to play at being the bailiffs of the birthday picnic and made such a mess that finally the girl whose birthday it was began to cry, and she was still crying when her father came out of the pines. I then drove north.

The road — the A-82 — stayed close to the lake, often on ledges that had been blasted into the mountainsides. The steep forests continued, broken now and again, on one shore or the other, by fields of fern, clumps of bright-yellow whin, and isolated stands of cedar. Along the far shore were widely separated houses and farms, which to the eyes of a traveller appeared almost unbelievably luxuriant after the spare desolation of some of the higher glens. We came to the top of the rise and suddenly saw, on the right-hand side of the road, on the edge of a high meadow that sloped sharply a considerable distance to the lake, a cluster of caravans and other vehicles, arranged in the shape of a C, with an opening toward the road — much like a circle of prairie schooners, formed for protection against savage attack. All but one or two of the vehicles were painted bright lily-pad green. The compound, in its compact half acre, was surrounded by a fence, to keep out, among other things, sheep, which were grazing all over the slope in deep-green turf among buttercups, daisies, and thistles. Gulls above beat hard into the wind, then turned and planed toward the south. Gulls are inland birds in Scotland, there being so little distance from anywhere to the sea. A big fireplace had been made from rocks of the sort that were scattered all over the meadow. And on the lakeward side a platform had been built, its level eminence emphasizing the declivity of the hill, which dropped away below it. Mounted on the platform was a thirty-five-millimeter motion-picture camera with an enormous telephoto lens. From its point of view, two hundred feet above the lake and protruding like a gargoyle, the camera could take in a bedazzling panorama that covered thousands of acres of water.

This was Expedition Headquarters, the principal field station of the Loch Ness Phenomena Investigation Bureau — dues five pounds per annum, life membership one hundred pounds, tax on donations recoverable under covenant. Those who join the bureau receive newsletters and annual reports, and are eligible to participate in the fieldwork if they so desire. I turned into the compound and parked between two bright-green reconditioned old London taxis. The central area had long since been worn grassless, and was covered at this moment with fine-grain dust. People were coming and going. The place seemed rather public, as if it were a depot. No one even halfway interested in the natural history of the Great

Glen would think of driving up the A-82 without stopping in there. Since the A-82 is the principal route between Glasgow and Inverness, it is not surprising that the apparently amphibious creature as yet unnamed, the so-called Loch Ness Monster, has been seen not only from the highway but on it.

The atmosphere around the headquarters suggested a scientific frontier and also a boom town, much as Cape Canaveral and Cocoa Beach do. There were, as well, cirrus wisps of show business and fine arts. Probably the one word that might have been applied to everyone present was adventurer. There was, at any rate, nothing emphatically laboratorial about the place, although the prevailing mood seemed to be one not of holiday but of matter-of-fact application and patient dedication. A telephone call came in that day, to the caravan that served as an office, from a woman who owned an inn south of Inverarigaig, on the other side of the lake. She said that she had seen the creature that morning just forty yards offshore — three humps, nothing else to report, and being very busy just now, thank you very much, good day. This was recorded, with no particular display of excitement, by an extremely attractive young woman who appeared to be in her late twenties, an artist from London who had missed but one summer at Loch Ness in seven years. She wore sandals, dungarees, a firmly stretched black pullover, and gold earrings. Her name was Mary Piercy, and her toes were painted pink. The bulletin board where she recorded the sighting resembled the kind used in railway stations for the listing of incoming trains.

The office walls were decorated with photographs of the monster in various postures — basking, cruising, diving, splashing, looking up inquisitively. A counter was covered with some of the essential bibliography: the bureau's annual report (twenty-nine sightings the previous year), J. A. Carruth's *Loch Ness and Its Monster* (The Abbey Press, Fort Augustus), Tim Dinsdale's *Loch Ness Monster* (Routledge and Kegan Paul, London), and a report by the Joint Air Reconnaissance Center of the Royal Air Force on a motion picture of the monster swimming about half a mile on the lake's surface. These books and documents could, in turn, lead the interested reader to less available but nonetheless highly relevant works such as R. T. Gould's *The Loch Ness Monster and Others* and Constance Whyte's *More Than a Legend*.

My children looked over the photographs with absorption but not a great deal of awe, and they bought about a dozen postcards with glossy prints of a picture of the monster — three humps showing, much the same sight that the innkeeper had described — that had been taken by a man named Stuart, directly across the lake from Urquhart Castle. The three younger girls then ran out into the meadow and began to pick daisies and buttercups. Their mother and sister sat down in the sun to read about the creature in the lake, and to write postcards. We were on our way to Inverness, but with no need to hurry. "Dear Grammy, we came to see the monster today."

From the office to the camera-observation platform to the caravan that served as a pocket mess hall, I wandered around among the crew, was offered and accepted tea, and squinted with imaginary experience up and down the lake, where the whitecaps had, if anything, increased. Among the crew at the time were two Canadians, a Swede, an Australian, three Americans, two Englishmen, a Welshman, and one Scot. Two were women. When I asked one of the crew members if he knew what some of the others did, vocationally, when they were not at Loch Ness, he said, "I'm not sure what they are. We don't go into that." This was obviously a place where now was all that mattered, and in such a milieu it is distinctly pleasant to accept that approach to things. Nonetheless, I found that I couldn't adhere completely to this principle, and I did find out that one man was a medical doctor, another a farmer, another a retired naval officer, and that several, inevitably, were students. The daily watch begins at four in the morning and goes on, as one fellow put it, "as long as we can stand up." It has been the pattern among the hundreds of sightings reported that the early-morning hours are the most promising ones. Camera stations are manned until ten at night, dawn and sunset being so close to midnight at that latitude in summer, but the sentries tend to thin out with the lengthening of the day. During the autumn, the size of the crew reduces precipitously toward one.

One man lives at the headquarters all year long. His name is Clem Lister Skelton. "I've been staring at that bloody piece of water since five o'clock," he said, while he drank tea in the mess caravan.

"Is there a technique?" I asked him.

"Just look," he said. "Look. Run your eye over the water in one quick   20 skim. What we're looking for is not hard to see. You just sit and sort of gaze at the loch, that's all. Mutter a few incantations. That's all there is to do. In wintertime, very often, it's just myself. And of course one keeps a very much more perfunctory watch in the winter. I saw it once in a snowstorm, though, and that was the only time I've had a clear view of the head and neck. The neck is obviously very mobile. The creature was quite big, but it wasn't as big as a seventy-foot MFV. Motor fishing vessel. I'd been closer to it, but I hadn't seen as much of it before, I've seen it eight times. The last time was in September. Only the back. Just the sort of upturned boat, which is the classic view of it."

Skelton drank some more tea, and refilled a cup he had given me. "I must know what it is," he went on. "I shall never rest peacefully until I know what it is. Some of the largest creatures in the world are out there, and we can't name them. It may take ten years, but we're going to identify the genus. Most people are not as fanatical as I, but I would like to see this through to the end, if I don't get too broke first."

Skelton is a tall, offhand man, English, with reddish hair that is disheveled in long strings from the thinning crown of his head. In outline, Skelton's life there in the caravan on the edge of the high meadow over the lake, in a place that must be uncorrectably gloomy during the wet rains of winter, seemed cagelike and hopeless to me — unacceptably lonely. The impression he gave was of a man who had drawn a circle around himself many hundreds of miles from the rest of his life. But how could I know? He was saying that he had flown Supermarine Spitfires for the R.A.F. during the Second World War. His father had been a solider, and when Skelton was a boy, he lived, as he put it, "all over the place." As an adult, he became first an actor, later a writer and director of films. He acted in London in plays like *March Hare* and *Saraband for Dead Lovers*. One film he directed was, in his words, "a dreadful thing called *Saul and David.*" These appearances on the surface apparently did not occur so frequently that he needed to do nothing else for a livelihood. He also directed, in the course of many years, several hundred educational films. The publisher who distributed some of these films was David James, a friend of Skelton's, and at that time a Member of Parliament. James happened to be, as well, the founder of the Loch Ness Phenomena Investigation Bureau — phenomena, because, for breeding purposes, there would have to be at least two monsters living in the lake at any one time, probably more, and in fact two had on occasion been sighted simultaneously. James asked Skelton if he would go up to the lake and give the bureau the benefit of his technical knowledge of movie cameras. "Anything for a laugh," Skelton had said to James. This was in the early nineteen-sixties. "I came for a fortnight," Skelton said now, in the caravan. "And I saw it. I wanted to know what it was, and I've wanted to know what it was ever since. I thought I'd have time to write up here, and I haven't. I don't do anything now except hunt this beast."

Skelton talked on about what the monster might be — a magnified newt, a long-necked variety of giant seal, an unextinct *Elasmosaurus*. Visitors wandered by in groups outside the caravan, and unexplained strangers kept coming in for tea. In the air was a feeling, utterly belied by the relative permanence of the place, of a country carnival on a two-night stand. The caravans themselves, in their alignment, suggested a section of a midway. I remembered a woman shouting to attract people to a big caravan on a carnival midway one night in May in New Jersey. That was some time ago. I must have been nineteen. The woman, who was standing on a small platform, was fifty or sixty, and she was trying to get people to go into the caravan to see big jungle cats, I suppose, and brown bears — "Ferocious Beasts," at any rate, according to block lettering on the side of the caravan. A steel cage containing a small black bear had been set up on two sawhorses outside the caravan — a fragment to imply what might be found on a larger scale inside.

So young that it was no more than two feet from nose to tail, the bear was engaged in desperate motion, racing alone one side of the cage from corner to corner, striking the steel bars bluntly with its nose. Whirling then, tossing its head over its shoulder like a racing swimmer, it turned and bolted crazily for the opposite end. Its eyes were deep red, and shining in a kind of full-sighted blindness. It had gone mad there in the cage, and its motion, rhythmic and tortured, never ceased, back and forth, back and forth, the head tossing with each jarring turn. The animal abraded its flanks on the steel bars as it ran. Hair and skin had scraped from its sides so that pink flesh showed in the downpour of the carnival arc lights. Blood drained freely through the thinned hair of its belly and dropped onto the floor of the cage. What had a paralyzing effect on me was the animal's almost perfect and now involuntary rhythm — the wild toss of the head after the crash into the corner, the turn, the scraping run, the crash again at the other end, never stopping, metronomic — the exposed interior of some brutal and organic timepiece.

Beside the cage, the plump, impervious woman, red-faced, red-nosed, 25 kept shouting to the crowds, but she said to me, leaning down, her own eyes bloodshot, "Why don't you move on, sonny, if you ain't going to buy a ticket? Beat it. Come on, now. Move on."

"We argue about what it is," Skelton said. "I'm inclined to think it's a giant slug, but there is an amazingly impressive theory for its being a worm. You can't rule out that it's one of the big dinosaurs, but I think this is more wishful thinking than anything else." In the late nineteen-thirties, a large and exotic footprint was found along the shore of Loch Ness. It was meticulously studied by various people and was assumed, for a time, to be an impression from a foot or flipper of the monster. Eventually, the print was identified. Someone who owned the preserved foot of a hippo-potamus had successfully brought off a hoax that put layers of mockery and incredibility over the creature in the lake for many years. The Second World War further diverted any serious interest that amateurs or naturalists might have taken. Sightings continued, however, in a consistent pattern, and finally, in the early nineteen-sixties, the Loch Ness Phenomena Investigation Bureau was established. "I have no plans whatever for leaving," Skelton said. "I am prepared to stay here ad infinitum. All my worldly goods are here."

A dark-haired young woman had stepped into the caravan and poured herself a cup of tea. Skelton, introducing her to me, said, "If the beast has done nothing else, it has brought me a wife. She was studying Gaelic and Scottish history at Edinburgh University, and she walked into the glen one day, and I said, 'That is the girl I am going to marry.'" He gestured toward a window of the caravan, which framed a view of the hills and the lake. "The Great Glen is one of the most beautiful places in the world," he continued. "It is peaceful here. I'd be happy here all my life, even if there were nothing in the loch. I've even committed the unforgivable sin of going to sleep in the sun during a flat calm. With enough time, we could shoot the beast with a crossbow and a line, and get a bit of skin. We could also shoot a small transmitter into its hide and learn more than we know now about its habits and characteristics."

The creature swims with remarkable speed, as much as ten or fifteen knots when it is really moving. It makes no noise other than seismic splashes, but it is apparently responsive in a highly sensitive way to sound. A shout, an approaching engine, any loud report, will send it into an immediate dive, and this shyness is in large part the cause of its inaccessibility, and therefore of its mystery. Curiously, though, reverberate sound was what apparently brought the creature widespread attention, for the first sequence of frequent sightings occurred in 1933, when the A-82 was blasted into the cliffsides of the western shore of the lake. Immense boulders kept falling into the depths, and shock waves from dynamite repeatedly ran through the water, causing the creature to lose confidence in its environment and to alter, at least temporarily, its shy and preferentially nocturnal life. In that year it was first observed on land, perhaps attempting to seek a way out forever from the detonations that had alarmed it. A couple named Spicer saw it, near Inverarigaig, and later described its long, serpentine neck, followed by an ungainly hulk of body, lurching toward the lake and disappearing into high undergrowth as they approached.

With the exception of one report recorded in the sixth century, which said that a monster (fitting the description of the contemporary creatures in the lake) had killed a man with a single bite, there have been no other examples of savagery on its part. To the contrary, its sensitivity to people seems to be acute, and it keeps a wide margin between itself and mankind. In all likelihood, it feeds on fish and particularly on eels, of which there are millions in the lake. Loch Ness is unparalleled in eel-fishing circles, and has drawn commercial eel fishermen from all over the United Kingdom. The monster has been observed with its neck bent down in the water, like a swan feeding. When the creatures die, they apparently settle into the seven-hundred-foot floor of the lake, where the temperature is always forty-two degrees Fahrenheit — so cold that the lake is known for never giving up its dead. Loch Ness never freezes, despite its high latitude, so if the creature breathes air, as has seemed apparent from the reports of observers who have watched its mouth rhythmically opening and closing, it does not lose access to the surface in winter. It clearly prefers the smooth, sunbaked waterscapes of summer, however, for it seems to love to bask in the sun, like an upturned boat, slowly rolling, plunging, squirming around with what can only be taken as pleasure. By observers' reports, the creature has two pairs of lateral flippers, and when it swims off, tail thrashing, it leaves behind it a wake as impressive as the wake of a small warship. When it dives from a still position, it inexplicably goes down without leaving a bubble. When it dives as it swims, it leaves on the surface a churning signature of foam.

Skelton leaned back against the wall of the caravan in a slouched and   30
nonchalant posture. He was wearing a dark blue tie that was monogrammed in small block letters sewn with white thread — L.N.I. (Loch Ness Investigation). Above the monogram and embroidered also in white thread was a small depiction of the monster — humps undulant, head

high, tail extending astern. Skelton gave the tie a flick with one hand. "You get this with a five-pound membership," he said.

The sea-serpent effect given by the white thread on the tie was less a stylization than an attempt toward a naturalistic sketch. As I studied it there, framed on Skelton's chest, the thought occurred to me that there was something inconvenient about the monster's actual appearance. In every sense except possibly the sense that involves cruelty, the creature in Loch Ness is indeed a monster. An average taken from many films and sightings gives its mature length at about forty feet. Its general appearance is repulsive, in the instant and radical sense in which reptiles are repulsive to many human beings, and any number of people might find difficulty in accepting a creature that looks like the one that was slain by St. George. Its neck, about six feet long, columnar, powerfully muscled, is the neck of a serpent. Its head, scarcely broader than the neck, is a serpent's head, with uncompromising, lenticular eyes. Sometimes as it swims it holds its head and neck erect. The creature's mouth is at least a foot wide. Its body undulates. Its skin glistens when wet and appears coarse, mottled, gray, and elephantine when exposed to the air long enough to become dry. The tail, long and columnar, stretches back to something of a point. It seemed to me, sitting there at Headquarters, that the classical, mythical, dragon likeness of this animate thing — the modified dinosaur, the fantastically exaggerated newt — was an impediment to the work of the investigation bureau, which has no pertinent interest in what the monster resembles or calls to mind but a great deal in what it actually is, the goal being a final and positive identification of the genus.

"What we need is a good, lengthy, basking sighting," Skelton said. "We've had one long surfacing — twenty-five minutes. I saw it. Opposite Urquhart Castle. We only had a twelve-inch lens then, at four and a half miles. We have thirty-six-inch lenses now. We need a long, clear, close-up — in color."

My children had watched, some months earlier, the killing of a small snake on a lawn in Maryland. About eighteen inches long, it came out from a basement-window well, through a covering lattice of redwood, and was noticed with shouts and shrieks by the children and a young retriever that barked at the snake and leaped about it in a circle. We were the weekend guests of another family, and eight children in all crowded around the snake, which had been gliding slowly across the lawn during the moments after it had been seen, but had now stopped and was turning its head from side to side in apparent indecision. Our host hurried into his garage and came running back to the lawn with a long shovel. Before he killed the snake, his wife urged him not to. She said the snake could not possibly be poisonous. He said, "How do you know?" The children, mine and theirs, looked back and forth from him to her. The dog began to bark more rapidly and at a higher pitch.

"It has none of the markings. There is nothing triangular about its head," she told him.

"That may very well be," he said. "But you can't be sure."   35
"It is *not* poisonous. Leave it alone. Look at all these children."
"I can't help that."
"It is *not* poisonous."
"How do you know?"
"I know."
He hit the snake with the flat of the shovel, and it writhed. He hit it   40
again. It kept moving. He hit it a third time, and it stopped. Its underside,
whitish green, segmental, turned up. The children moved in for a closer
look.

                                                                    1975

The Reader's Presence

1. McPhee "frames" his essay with two anecdotes: the opening
   story about the family on a picnic and the closing story about
   the snake. What is the effect of these incidents? What do they
   have in common? What relationship do they bear to the main
   topic?
2. Note how McPhee introduces what appears to be extraneous information. But how extraneous is it? Can you see any point to his
   account of the "first white man who saw Lake George" or the biography of Clem Lister Skelton? How do these stories fit into the
   scope of his exposition?
3. In rereading the essay, pay close attention to McPhee's attitude.
   Do you think he believes in the existence of the Loch Ness monster? What evidence persuades you one way or the other?

44 _____

N. Scott Momaday

A First American Views His Land

First Man
behold:
the earth
glitters
with leaves;
the sky
glistens
with rain.
Pollen
is borne
on winds
that low
and lean
upon
mountains.
Cedars
blacken
the slopes —
and pines.[1]

One hundred centuries ago. There is a wide, irregular landscape in what is now northern New Mexico. The sun is a dull white disk, low in the south; it is a perfect mystery, a deity whose coming and going are inexorable. The gray sky is curdled, and it bears very close upon the earth. A cold wind runs along the ground, dips and spins, flaking drift from a pond in the bottom of a ravine. Beyond the wind the silence is acute. A man crouches

---

For biographical information on N. Scott Momaday, see p. 657.
[1]The poem woven into this selection is drawn from Momaday's book, *The Gourd Dancer* (1976). — EDS.

in the ravine, in the darkness there, scarcely visible. He moves not a muscle; only the wind lifts a lock of his hair and lays it back along his neck. He wears skins and carries a spear. These things in particular mark his human intelligence and distinguish him as the lord of the universe. And for him the universe is especially *this* landscape; for him the landscape is an element like the air. The vast, virgin wilderness is by and large his whole context. For him there is no possibility of existence elsewhere.

Directly there is a blowing, a rumble of breath deeper than the wind, above him, where some of the hard clay of the bank is broken off and the clods roll down into the water. At the same time there appears on the skyline the massive head of a long-horned bison, then the hump, then the whole beast, huge and black on the sky, standing to a height of seven feet at the hump, with horns that extend six feet across the shaggy crown. For a moment it is poised there; then it lumbers obliquely down the bank to the pond. Still the man does not move, though the beast is now only a few steps upwind. There is no sign of what is about to happen; the beast meanders; the man is frozen in repose.

Then the scene explodes. In one and the same instant the man springs to his feet and bolts forward, his arm cocked and the spear held high, and the huge animal lunges in panic, bellowing, its whole weight thrown violently into the bank, its hooves churning and chipping earth into the air, its eyes gone wide and wild and white. There is a moment in which its awful, frenzied motion is wasted, and it is mired and helpless in its fear, and the man hurls the spear with his whole strength, and the point is driven into the deep, vital flesh, and the bison in its agony staggers and crashes down and dies.

This ancient drama of the hunt is enacted again and again in the landscape. The man is preeminently a predator, the most dangerous of all. He hunts in order to survive; his very existence is simply, squarely established upon that basis. But he hunts also because he can, because he has the means; he has the ultimate weapon of his age, and his prey is plentiful. His relationship to the land has not yet become a moral equation.

But in time he will come to understand that there is an intimate, vital   5
link between the earth and himself, a link that implies an intricate network of rights and responsibilities. In some unimagined future he will understand that he has the ability to devastate and perhaps destroy his environment. That moment will be one of extreme crisis in his evolution.

The weapon is deadly and efficient. The hunter has taken great care in its manufacture, especially in the shaping of the flint point, which is an extraordinary thing. A larger flake has been removed from each face, a groove that extends from the base nearly to the tip. Several hundred pounds of pressure, expertly applied, were required to make these grooves. The hunter then is an artisan, and he must know how to use rudimentary tools. His skill, manifest in the manufacture of this artifact, is unsurpassed for its time and purpose. By means of this weapon is the Paleo-Indian hunter eminently able to exploit his environment.

Thousands of years later, about the time that Columbus begins his first voyage to the New World, another man, in the region of the Great Lakes, stands in the forest shade on the edge of a sunlit brake. In a while a deer enters into the pool of light. Silently the man fits an arrow to a bow, draws aim, and shoots. The arrow zips across the distance and strikes home. The deer leaps and falls dead.

But this latter-day man, unlike his ancient predecessor, is only incidentally a hunter; he is also a fisherman, a husbandman, even a physician. He fells trees and builds canoes; he grows corn, squash, and beans, and he gathers fruits and nuts; he uses hundreds of species of wild plants for food, medicine, teas, and dyes. Instead of one animal, or two or three, he hunts many, none to extinction as the Paleo-Indian may have done. He has fitted himself far more precisely into the patterns of the wilderness than did his ancient predecessor. He lives on the land; he takes his living from it; but he does not destroy it. This distinction supports the fundamental ethic that we call conservation today. In principle, if not yet in name, this man is a conservationist.

These two hunting sketches are far less important in themselves than is that long distance between them, that whole possibility within the dimension of time. I believe that in that interim there grew up in the mind of man an idea of the land as sacred.

> *At dawn*
> *eagles*
> *lie and*
> *hover*
> *above*
> *the plain*
> *where light*
> *gathers*
> *in pools.*
> *Grasses*
> *shimmer*
> *and shine.*
> *Shadows*
> *withdraw*
> *and lie*
> *away*
> *like smoke.*

"The earth is our mother. The sky is our father." This concept of nature, which is at the center of the Native American world view, is familiar to us all. But it may well be that we do not understand entirely what the concept is in its ethical and philosophical implications.

I tell my students that the American Indian has a unique investment in   10 the American landscape. It is an investment that represents perhaps thirty thousand years of habitation. That tenure has to be worth something in itself — a great deal, in fact. The Indian has been here a long time; he is at home here. That simple and obvious truth is one of the most important realities of the Indian world, and it is integral in the Indian mind and spirit.

How does such a concept evolve? Where does it begin? Perhaps it begins with the recognition of beauty, the realization that the physical world *is* beautiful. We don't know much about the ancient hunter's sensibilities. It isn't likely that he had leisure in his life for the elaboration of an aesthetic ideal. And yet the weapon he made was beautiful as well as functional. It has been suggested that much of the minute chipping along the edges of his weapon served no purpose but that of aesthetic satisfaction.

A good deal more is known concerning that man of the central forests. He made beautiful boxes and dishes out of elm and birch bark, for example. His canoes were marvelous, delicate works of art. And this aesthetic perception was a principle of the whole Indian world of his time, as indeed it is of our time. The contemporary Native American is a man whose strong aesthetic perceptions are clearly evident in his arts and crafts, in his religious ceremonies, and in the stories and songs of his rich oral tradition. This, in view of the pressures that have been brought to bear upon the Indian world and the drastic changes that have been effected in its landscape, is a blessing and an irony.

Consider for example the Navajos of the Four Corners area. In recent years an extensive coal-mining operation has mutilated some of their most sacred land. A large power plant in that same region spews a contamination into the sky that is visible for many miles. And yet, as much as any people of whom I have heard, the Navajos perceive and celebrate the beauty of the physical world.

There is a Navajo ceremonial song that celebrates the sounds that are made in the natural world, the particular voices that beautify the earth:

Voice above,
Voice of thunder,
Speak from the
dark of clouds;
Voice below,
Grasshopper voice,
Speak from the
green of plants;
So may the earth
be beautiful.

There is in the motion and meaning of this song a comprehension of the world that is peculiarly native, I believe, that is integral in the Native American mentality. Consider: The singer stands at the center of the natural world, at the source of its sound, of its motion, of its life. Nothing of that world is inaccessible to him or lost upon him. His song is filled with reverence, with wonder and delight, and with confidence as well. He knows something about himself and about the things around him — and he knows that he knows. I am interested in what he sees and hears; I am interested in the range and force of his perception. Our immediate impression may be that his perception is narrow and deep — vertical. After all, "voice above . . . voice below," he sings. But is it vertical only? At each level of his expression there is an extension of his awareness across the whole landscape. The voice above is the voice of thunder, and thunder rolls. Moreover, it issues from the impalpable dark clouds and runs upon their horizontal range. It is a sound that integrates the whole of the atmosphere. And even so, the voice below, that of the grasshopper, issues from the broad plain and multiplicity of plants. And of course the singer is mindful of much more than thunder and insects; we are given in his song the wide angle of his vision and his hearing — and we are given the testimony of his dignity, his trust, and his deep belief.

This comprehension of the earth and air is surely a matter of morality, 15 for it brings into account not only man's instinctive reaction to his environment but the full realization of his humanity as well, the achievement of his intellectual and spiritual development as an individual and as a race.

In my own experience I have seen numerous examples of this regard for nature. My grandfather Mammedaty was a farmer in his mature years; his grandfather was a buffalo hunter. It was not easy for Mammedaty to be a farmer; he was a Kiowa, and the Kiowas never had an agrarian tradition. Yet he had to make his living, and the old, beloved life of roaming the plains and hunting the buffalo was gone forever. Even so, as much as any man before him, he fitted his mind and will and spirit to the land; there was nothing else. He could not have conceived of living apart from the land.

In *The Way to Rainy Mountain* I set down a small narrative that belongs in the oral tradition of my family. It indicates something essential about the Native American attitude toward the land:

"East of my grandmother's house, south of the pecan grove, there is buried a woman in a beautiful dress. Mammedaty used to know where she is buried, but now no one knows. If you stand on the front porch of the house and look eastward towards Carnegie, you know that the woman is buried somewhere within the range of your vision. But her grave is unmarked. She was buried in a cabinet, and she wore a beautiful dress. How beautiful it was! It was one of those fine buckskin dresses, and it was decorated with elk's teeth and beadwork. That dress is still there, under the ground."

It seems to me that this statement is primarily a declaration of love for the land, in which the several elements — the woman, the dress, and this plain — are at last become one reality, one expression of the beautiful in nature. Moreover, it seems to me a peculiarly Native American expression in this sense: that the concentration of things that are explicitly remembered — the general landscape, the simple, almost abstract nature of the burial, above all the beautiful dress, which is wholly singular in kind (as well as in its function within the narrative) — is especially Indian in character. The things that are *not* explicitly remembered — the woman's name, the exact location of her grave — are the things that matter least in the special view of the storyteller. What matters here is the translation of the woman into the landscape, a translation particularly signified by means of the beautiful and distinctive dress, an *Indian* dress.

When I was a boy, I lived for several years at Jemez Pueblo, New Mex-   20
ico. The Pueblo Indians are perhaps more obviously invested in the land than are other people. Their whole life is predicated upon a thorough perception of the physical world and its myriad aspects. When I first went there to live, the cacique, or chief, of the Pueblos was a venerable old man with long, gray hair and bright, deep-set eyes. He was entirely dignified and imposing — and rather formidable in the eyes of a boy. He excited my imagination a good deal. I was told that this old man kept the calendar of the tribe, that each morning he stood on a certain spot of ground near the center of the town and watched to see where the sun appeared on the skyline. By means of this solar calendar did he know and announce to his people when it was time to plant, to harvest, to perform this or that ceremony. This image of him in my mind's eye — the old man gazing each morning after the ranging sun — came to represent for me the epitome of that real harmony between man and the land that signifies the Indian world.

One day when I was riding my horse along the Jemez River, I looked up to see a long caravan of wagons and people on horseback and on foot. Men, women, and children were crossing the river ahead of me, moving out to the west, where most of the cultivated fields were, the farmland of the town. It was a wonderful sight to see, this long procession, and I was immediately deeply curious. I wanted to investigate, but it was not in me to do so at once, for that racial reserve, that sense of propriety that is deep-seated in Native American culture, stayed me, held me up. Then I saw someone coming toward me on horseback, galloping. It was a friend of mine, a boy of my own age. "Come on," he said. "Come with us," "Where are you going?" I asked casually. But he would not tell me. He simply laughed and urged me to come along, and of course I was very glad to do so. It was a bright spring morning, and I had a good horse under me, and the prospect of adventure was delicious. We moved far out across the eroded plain to the farthest fields at the foot of a great red mesa, and there we planted two large fields of corn. And afterward, on the edge of the fields, we sat on blankets and ate a feast in the shade of a cottonwood grove. Later I learned it was the cacique's fields we planted. And this is an ancient tradition at Jemez. The people of the town plant and tend and harvest the cacique's fields, and in the winter the hunters give to him a portion of the meat that they bring home from the mountains. It is as if the cacique is himself the translation of man, every man, into the landscape.

I have not forgotten that day, nor shall I forget it. I remember the warm earth of the fields, the smooth texture of seeds in my hands, and the brown water moving slowly and irresistibly among the rows. Above all I remember the spirit in which the procession was made, the work was done, and the feasting was enjoyed. It was a spirit of communion, of the life of each man in relation to the life of the planet and of the infinite distance and silence in which it moves. We made, in concert, an appropriate expression of that spirit.

One afternoon an old Kiowa woman talked to me, telling me of the place in Oklahoma in which she had lived for a hundred years. It was the place in which my grandparents, too, lived; and it is the place where I was born. And she told me of a time even further back, when the Kiowas came down from the north and centered their culture in the red earth of the southern plains. She told wonderful stories, and as I listened, I began to feel more and more sure that her voice proceeded from the land itself. I asked her many things concerning the Kiowas, for I wanted to understand all that I could of my heritage. I told the old woman that I had come there to learn from her and from people like her, those in whom the old ways were preserved. And she said simply: "It is good that you have come here." I believe that her word "good" meant many things; for one thing it meant *right*, or *appropriate*. And indeed it was appropriate that she should speak of the land. She was eminently qualified to do so. She had a great reverence for the land, and an ancient perception of it, a perception that it acquired only in the course of many generations.

It is this notion of the appropriate, along with that of the beautiful, that forms the Native American perspective on the land. In a sense these considerations are indivisible; Native American oral tradition is rich with songs and tales that celebrate natural beauty, the beauty of the natural world. What is more appropriate to our world than that which is beautiful:

> At *noon*
> turtles
> enter
> slowly
> into
> the warm
> dark loam.
> Bees hold
> the swarm.
> Meadows
> recede
> through planes
> of heat
> and pure
> distance.

Very old in the Native American world view is the conviction that the earth is vital, that there is a spiritual dimension to it, a dimension in which man rightly exists. It follows logically that there are ethical imperatives in this matter. I think: Inasmuch as I am in the land, it is appropriate that I should affirm myself in the spirit of the land. I shall celebrate my life in the world and the world in my life. In the natural order man invests himself in the landscape and at the same time incorporates the landscape into his own most fundamental experience. This trust is sacred.

The process of investment and appropriation is, I believe, preeminently   25
a function of the imagination. It is accomplished by means of an act of the imagination that is especially ethical in kind. We are what we imagine ourselves to be. The Native American is someone who thinks of himself, imagines himself in a particular way. By virtue of his experience his idea of himself comprehends his relationship to the land.

And the quality of this imagining is determined as well by racial and cultural experience. The Native American's attitudes toward this landscape have been formulated over a long period of time, a span that reaches back to the end of the Ice Age. The land, *this* land, is secure in his racial memory.

In our society as a whole we conceive of the land in terms of ownership and use. It is a lifeless medium of exchange; it has for most of us, I suspect, no more spirituality than has an automobile, say, or a refrigerator. And our laws confirm us in this view, for we can buy and sell the land, we can exclude each other from it, and in the context of ownership we can use it as we will. Ownership implies use, and use implies consumption.

But this way of thinking of the land is alien to the Indian. His cultural intelligence is opposed to these concepts; indeed, for him they are all but inconceivable quantities. This fundamental distinction is easier to understand with respect to ownership than to use, perhaps. For obviously the Indian does use, and has always used, the land and the available resources in it. The point is that *use* does not indicate in any real way his idea of the land. "Use" is neither his word nor his idea. As an Indian I think: "You say that I *use* the land, and I reply, yes, it is true; but it is not the first truth. The first truth is that I *love* the land; I see that it is beautiful; I delight in it; I am alive in it."

In the long course of his journey from Asia and in the realization of himself in the New World, the Indian has assumed a deep ethical regard for the earth and sky, a reverence for the natural world that is antipodal to that strange tenet of modern civilization that seemingly has it that man must destroy his environment. It is this ancient ethic of the Native American that must shape our efforts to preserve the earth and the life upon and within it.

> *At dusk*
> *the gray*
> *foxes*
> *stiffen*
> *in cold;*
> *blackbirds*
> *are fixed*
> *in white*
> *branches.*
> *Rivers*
> *follow*

the moon,
the long
white track
of the
full moon.

1976

The Reader's Presence

1. N. Scott Momaday has written a powerful account of the relationship between Native Americans and the land. What does he identify as the essential characteristics of the Native American's perspective on the land? What does he mean when, in paragraph 4, he speaks of a person's relationship to the land as "a moral equation"? What "ethical imperatives" — in relation to his own behavior as well as the behavior of others — does Momaday see as resulting from this "moral equation"? In paragraph 5, he announces that there is "a vital link" between the earth and the Native American, "a link that implies a network of rights and responsibilities." How does he develop this point throughout the essay?

2. Momaday tells us that the Native American belief that the land is sacred may well result from their recognition of the physical world's beauty. In what specific ways is that sense of beauty the same as, and different from, that of other Americans? How is this sense of beauty understood as "a matter of morality" by Native Americans? In what ways does it affect their behavior? How are these issues related to the Native Americans' realization of their own sense of humanity?

3. Reread the opening four paragraphs of Momaday's essay, in which he summarizes two different versions of the "ancient drama of the hunt." Compare and contrast the structure of his sentences, diction, and especially his verb choices in each version. Why is the first so detailed in its description and the second so brief? What functions do the interspersed poetry and song serve in the essay? Consider, too, Momaday's use of narrative throughout the essay. How, for example, is his narrative about the buried woman "a declaration of love for the land" (paragraph 19)? Why doesn't it matter that the woman has no name? Why is the attention to her dress so significant? Comment on the overall structure of the essay. What sources, in addition to narrative, does Momaday draw on to illustrate his points about the distinctiveness of Native American world views?

45

Gloria Naylor

A Question of Language

Language is the subject. It is the written form with which I've managed to keep the wolf away from the door and, in diaries, to keep my sanity. In spite of this, I consider the written word inferior to the spoken, and much of the frustration experienced by novelists is the awareness that whatever we manage to capture in even the most transcendent passages falls far short of the richness of life. Dialogue achieves its power in the dynamics of a fleeting moment of sight, sound, smell, and touch.

I'm not going to enter the debate here about whether it is language that shapes reality or vice versa. That battle is doomed to be waged whenever we seek intermittent reprieve from the chicken and egg dispute. I will simply take the position that the spoken word, like the written word, amounts to a nonsensical arrangement of sounds or letters without a consensus that assigns "meaning." And building from the meanings of what we hear, we order reality. Words themselves are innocuous; it is the consensus that gives them true power.

I remember the first time I heard the word *nigger*. In my third-grade class, our math tests were being passed down the rows, and as I handed the papers to a little boy in back of me, I remarked that once again he had received a much lower mark than I did. He snatched his test from me and spit out that word. Had he called me a nymphomaniac or a necrophiliac, I couldn't have been more puzzled. I didn't know what a nigger was, but I knew that whatever it meant, it was something he shouldn't have called me. This was verified when I raised my hand, and in a loud voice repeated what he had said and watched the teacher scold him for using a "bad"

For biographical information on Gloria Naylor, see p. 658.

word. I was later to go home and ask the inevitable question that every black parent must face — "Mommy, what does 'nigger' mean?"

And what exactly did it mean? Thinking back, I realize that this could not have been the first time the word was used in my presence. I was part of a large extended family that had migrated from the rural South after World War II and formed a close-knit network that gravitated around my maternal grandparents. Their ground-floor apartment in one of the buildings they owned in Harlem was a weekend mecca for my immediate family, along with countless aunts, uncles, and cousins who brought along assorted friends. It was a bustling and open house with assorted neighbors and tenants popping in and out to exchange bits of gossip, pick up an old quarrel, or referee the ongoing checkers game in which my grandmother cheated shamelessly. They were all there to let down their hair and put up their feet after a week of labor in the factories, laundries, and shipyards of New York.

Amid the clamor, which could reach deafening proportions — two   5
or three conversations going on simultaneously, punctuated by the sound of a baby's crying somewhere in the back rooms or out on the street — there was still a rigid set of rules about what was said and how. Older children were sent out of the living room when it was time to get into the juicy details about "you-know-who" up on the third floor who had gone and gotten herself "p-r-e-g-n-a-n-t!" But my parents, knowing that I could spell well beyond my years, always demanded that I follow the others out to play. Beyond sexual misconduct and death, everything else was considered harmless for our young ears. And so among the anecdotes of the triumphs and disappointments in the various workings of their lives, the word *nigger* was used in my presence, but it was set within contexts and inflections that caused it to register in my mind as something else.

In the singular, the word was always applied to a man who had distinguished himself in some situation that brought their approval for his strength, intelligence, or drive:

"Did Johnny really do that?"

"I'm telling you, that nigger pulled in $6,000 of overtime last year. Said he got enough for a down payment on a house."

When used with a possessive adjective by a woman — "my nigger" — it became a term of endearment for husband or boyfriend. But it could be more than just a term applied to a man. In their mouths it became the pure essence of manhood — a disembodied force that channeled their past history of struggle and present survival against the odds into a victorious statement of being: "Yeah, that old foreman found out quick enough — you don't mess with a nigger."

In the plural, it became a description of some group within the commu-   10
nity that had overstepped the bounds of decency as my family defined it: Parents who neglected their children, a drunken couple who fought in public, people who simply refused to look for work, those with excessively

dirty mouths or unkempt households were all "trifling niggers." This particular circle could forgive hard times, unemployment, the occasional bout of depression — they had gone through all of that themselves — but the unforgivable sin was lack of self-respect.

A woman could never be a *nigger* in the singular, with its connotation of confirming worth. The noun *girl* was its closest equivalent in that sense, but only when used in direct address and regardless of the gender doing the addressing. *Girl* was a token of respect for a woman. The one-syllable word was drawn out to sound like three in recognition of the extra ounce of wit, nerve, or daring that the woman had shown in the situation under discussion.

"G-i-r-l, stop. You mean you said that to his face?"

But if the word was used in a third-person reference or shortened so that it almost snapped out of the mouth, it always involved some element of communal disapproval. And age became an important factor in these exchanges. It was only between individuals of the same generation, or from an older person to a younger (but never the other way around), that "girl" would be considered a compliment.

I don't agree with the argument that use of the word *nigger* at this social stratum of the black community was an internalization of racism. The dynamics were the exact opposite: the people in my grandmother's living room took a word that whites used to signify worthlessness or degradation and rendered it impotent. Gathering there together, they transformed *nigger* to signify the varied and complex human beings they knew themselves to be. If the word was to disappear totally from the mouths of even the most liberal of white society, no one in that room was naïve enough to believe it would disappear from white minds. Meeting the word head-on, they proved it had absolutely nothing to do with the way they were determined to live their lives.

So there must have been dozens of times that the word *nigger* was spoken in front of me before I reached the third grade. But I didn't "hear" it until it was said by a small pair of lips that had already learned it could be a way to humiliate me. That was the word I went home and asked my mother about. And since she knew that I had to grow up in America, she took me in her lap and explained.   15

1986

The Reader's Presence

1. Gloria Naylor analyzes the various meanings of the word *nigger,* meanings that are agreed to by consensus and that vary according to the speaker, the audience, and the context within which the word is spoken. Outline the different meanings of *nigger,* and evaluate the effectiveness of the example she provides to illustrate each definition. Do the same for her definitions of *girl.* Can you think of any other examples to reinforce the points she makes in each definition, or any examples that challenge her definitions?

2. Where — and how — does Naylor make her own point of view clear in this essay? How does she reveal her personal stake in the issues addressed in the essay? Consider her use of personal narrative in the essay. Comment, for example, on the effectiveness of paragraphs 4 and 5. What do they contribute to the overall point of her essay? What does this description of the circumstances of her extended family in Harlem add to the essay?

3. Gloria Naylor creates a two-part structure for her essay: two generalized, abstract opening paragraphs, followed by a series of extended illustrations of her definitions of the words *nigger* and *girl*. In the first paragraph she talks about the nature of language and its inadequacy in conveying the fullness and complexity of an experience. In the second she asserts the need for consensus in order to establish meaning. Where does she announce the overriding point of her essay? Review the different definitions she provides. What inferences can you draw from these definitions about the values of the communities she describes? What do these definitions tell us about what is important to these communities? about what kinds of behavior are to be avoided and censured?

46

Itabari Njeri

Who Is Black?

My cousin Jeffrey looked like Ricky Nelson and always wanted to be the baddest nigger on the block.

"Little girl, come here. What you doin' with that white man?" the black supermarket clerk asked, eyeing me with concern.

"He's not white, that's my cousin," I told him, then ran to catch up with Jeff several aisles away in the Safeway.

"That man wanted to know if I was white, didn't he?" Jeff asked.

For biographical information on Itabari Njeri, see p. 658.

"No, he didn't," I said, my face as fixed as granite. Jeff looked me   5
straight in the eye, but I didn't blink. I knew nothing made him feel worse
than people calling him a white man.

I was in grade school then and Jeffrey was sixteen. I remember him as
tall but pudgy in his teens. The extra flesh contributed to the altar-boy
innocence of his face. He was a good Catholic kid who attended parochial
school for years. He could take apart and put together anything electrical.
He could have been an engineer. But he was the son of my moll aunt and a
gangster father. He was a black male surrounded by the hustling life without a counterweight, without a sense of options. He bought into the street
life, but because of his looks, the price of admission was made exceedingly
high. He looked too much like the enemy, and always had to prove he
wasn't.

When he was being sent to prison, the judge, examining his record,
called him a white man. My cousin pointed to our brown-skin grandmother in the courtroom and said, "If she's black, I'm black, too." Then he
demanded to be treated just like any other black. The judge obliged and
added a year to his sentence.

When Jeff was found dead on a Harlem rooftop, his bloated body
pierced by bullets, it was because he'd spent his short life trying to prove
how bad he was in the eyes of other black men.

Two decades after I walked out of that Safeway with Jeff, his sister —
fair-skinned, golden-haired, living in a tenement above crack-infested Harlem — hopes her second baby looks *black, black, black,* because that will
validate her in the eyes of other black people, she says. In the meantime,
she'd like to give her elder child to somebody else to raise because he's so
light, light, light.

I, too, know the pain at the other end of the color spectrum: the extent   10
of our psychic anguish over the hurt many suffered because of the parent
or grandparent who rejected the darkest among us, told us we had coffee-
cooler lips or "bad" hair because it was short and kinky.

When I'm not weeping over this color madness, I silently scream,
When will it end?

I realize Jeffrey didn't look like a redbone, a high yellow, or anything
else in the nomenclature of color members of the African diaspora use to
distinguish our varied complexions. Like me, he was a West Indian and
black American of African, French, East Indian, English, and Arawak descent who happened to come out looking like one of Ozzie and Harriet's
kids. But what's unusual about that? African Americans are the product of
a New World culture: It's been estimated that 80 percent of us have poly-
genetic backgrounds. And while U.S. custom and law have denied that
multiethnic reality to perpetuate its own system of apartheid, calling America on it wouldn't be the first time black people got hip to a trick bag —
and out of it.

It was in this state of mind that I began writing about ethnic identity
and conflict five years ago. It was then that I began to explore the concerns

of the nation's proliferating "multiracial" population — especially those of partial African descent. The trigger for this examination was both my family's history and the massive population shifts that will lead to a new majority in twenty-first-century America: people of color. Demographers predict that whites will be a minority by the middle of the next century. Latino and Asian immigration, the higher birthrate among Latinos and blacks, and intermarriage among all groups are key factors in the rise of the multiethnic population.

Tagged an "emerging" population by social scientists, multiethnic Americans may be the most significant group to spring from a newly pluralistic America. Their demand for recognition is stimulating what I think will be a decades-long debate — one that will force all Americans to confront the myths that surround "race" and ethnicity in the United States.

While the concerns of this emerging group need to be addressed be- 15 cause they illuminate important issues about the nature of race and culture in the United States, how the issues are framed also frequently contributes to confusion.

High on the political agenda of many now-vocal multiethnic Americans is the demand for a new multiracial census category that specifically identifies ethnically and racially mixed citizens. The size of the multiracial population may be about five million, according to Ramona Douglas, the vice president of the Biracial Family Network in Chicago. The exact numbers are unknown because the census requires people to either identify with one race or ethnic group or to check "other" when filling out data for the Census Bureau.

The ranks of multiethnic activists are being bolstered by their monoethnic kin — parents, grandparents, and spouses — who have helped form support groups in Atlanta, Buffalo, Chicago, Houston, Los Angeles, Omaha, San Diego, Seattle, San Francisco, Pittsburgh, and Washington, D.C. Similar support groups are popping up on college campuses, particularly in California, a center of multicultural activism. While these activists failed to get a new multiethnic designation on the 1990 census, they are pushing to see one established for the year 2000.

In general, supporters of the category want recognition and political representation for people of mixed heritage. Opponents say minority groups would shrink if such a designation is allowed. The issue is of particular importance to black people because of the way in which race has been traditionally defined in America: Socially, any known African ancestry makes you black.

"If you consider yourself black for political reasons, raise your hand," Charles Stewart said to a predominantly African-American audience at the National Association of Black Journalists convention in Los Angeles last year. "The overwhelming majority raised their hands. When I asked how many people here believe that they are of pure African descent, without any mixture, nobody raised their hands." The point, says Stewart, chief deputy to California State Senator Diane Watson (D-Los Angeles), is this: "If you advocate a category that includes people who are multiracial to the detriment of their black identification, you will replicate what you saw — an empty room. We cannot afford to have an empty room. We cannot afford to have a race empty of black people — not so long as we are struggling against discrimination based on our identification as black people."

But Velina Hasu Houston eschews the little-dab'll-do-you school of   20 genetics. An award-winning Los Angeles playwright and executive director of the Amerasian League, she has an identity that is a metaphor for the new type of diversity shaping America at the dawn of a millennium. Of Japanese, African-American, and Native-American ancestry, Houston represents the sushi-and-grits generation of multicultural diversity.

"African Americans want us to be their political slaves," Houston charges. "They are saying, 'Come join us.' But it's not because of some great brother or sister love — it's political. If their numbers decrease, their chances of getting public funds decrease — as well as political representation. To me, that's a totally unethical way of saying that you want people to be members of your community."

As she sits in a Santa Monica café, Houston's delicate body belies the dragon within. Without recognition as a unique group, multiethnic people are "just not heard," she says with the quiet intensity of water at a low boil. One of the "big pushes of the Amerasian League," an educational and support group for multiracial Asians, "is raising funds to start a Big Brother/Big Sister network for refugee Amerasians. Many of them have African-American fathers," Houston points out.

"I just saw a boy who is seventeen years old who is half African-American; his mother is Vietnamese. He can't speak English very well and he needs help," says Houston. "But the people who make the most fun of him, give him the hardest time, are African Americans," she adds. "So there's a lot of work to be done if African Americans are going to take on the multiracial community. It means ownership of everything; it doesn't just mean ownership of our head count."

Yet Houston thinks the idea of mutual identification or broad-based cooperation among blacks and multiethnics at this point is slim. She cites as proof of this the hostile reception she felt she received when she appeared on a panel with Charles Stewart at the National Association of Black Journalists convention last year. "Those people were vicious," she says of the audience. "It was frightening. These were journalists — educated African Americans — hissing at me. Hissing!"

Such has been the nature of her relationships with most African Ameri-   25 cans throughout her life, Houston laments. Her mother, a Japanese war bride married to an African American, "raised me the only way she knew how, as a Japanese daughter, and I don't apologize for that. At the same time, I have never been ashamed of any part of my heritage," says Houston, whose plays have been staged by the Negro Ensemble Company and the Old Globe Theatre in San Diego.

On the days Houston brought sushi to lunch as a youngster, African-American children teased her. But their mild teasing escalated to schoolyard terrorism: A group of African-American girls once pushed her down and cut off her long, dark hair. Even as an adult there have been indignities: A black cop in Los Angeles ignored her pleas for help after a car accident injured her light-skinned son and then called her a "half-breed bitch."

From her perspective, the dark-brown, long-haired, Polynesian-looking, and Japanese-speaking Houston has been hearing hisses all her life. "Communities of color are the most severe in doling out this kind of oppression," she says grimly. "The oppressed seem to oppress more."

The increasingly acrimonious nature of the debate among multiethnic Americans and the African-American community has become, in too many cases, a dialogue of the deaf: so-called multiracial Americans viewing the behavior of African Americans through a veil of pain, failing to grasp the deep well of daily fortified anguish fueling black rage toward them. It is well fed by a contemporary white racism that still gives economic and aesthetic preference to the least African-looking among us.

At the other end of the silence are African Americans in denial over the pain we inflict on mixed-looking members of our ethnic group — even when they want to be embraced by the black community, as my cousin did.

The real issue that must be addressed among people of color is inter-   30 nalized oppression. That is what has us in a ridiculous fight over who's black and who's not, and holding on to a slave master's definition of race. It's part of the politics of distraction that keeps an oppressive system in place.

"I define internalized oppression as that process whereby a set of beliefs, attitudes, and misinformation about members of a target or oppressed group are put out by the dominant group to justify their subordination," says Dr. Barbara J. Love, a professor of education at the University of Massachusetts at Amherst. "That misinformation becomes embedded in the psyche — the emotional domain of that target group.

"There is extensive internalized oppression within the black community," Love states unequivocally. "It was a deliberate part of the system of dehumanizing Africans who were brought to the United States and making them fit to be slaves. We were not fit to be slaves when we came here, so we had to be made to be fit — that is, to go along with and participate in an oppressive system. And that process continues to this day."

Among the consequences of that internalized oppression are "the ways in which we put each other down. The ways in which we play out the dehumanization that got inflicted on *us,* at *each other*," Love continues.

Love relates that her own sister — the opposite of Love in appearance — had long hair and light skin. "If she tossed her hair in a certain way, she was accused of trying to act like a white girl," Love explains. "And they [other kids] jumped her." Why? "Because we have internalized this set of notions about what it means to be beautiful," says Love. "And what it means to beautiful in this society is to be like whites.

"What the oppression says is that by definition black people cannot be   35
beautiful — and we internalized that notion about ourselves. But if someone — because of our genetically mixed heritage — comes along looking
like the dominant group, we say 'if you're black you are not beautiful —
that is, you can't have long hair and here you've got long hair. It's wrong.
We'll fix it. We'll cut it off and we'll put you back in your place. Because
your place is to be like us: nobody.'"

But just to blame white oppression is not enough. African Americans
have proven that we are not merely prisoners of history. We have engaged
our fate in the past and changed it. We can do so again. Love explains:
"The process I teach is called Reevaluation Counseling. One has to begin
with the places we got hurt, both as a result of the oppression and the ways
we vented our pain on others, usually within our own communities of
color."

When people are able to identify, talk about, and discharge their pain
with the help of an aware, supportive human being, "you can take the
information, minus the painful emotions" and reevaluate the behavior,
says Love. "It's when the information is covered over with all that painful
emotion that we get stuck and end up hurting one another rather than
responding to one another from a rational place of thinking."

Getting the personal pain healed is one piece, but the process has to be
placed in a larger social context. "The question of whether there should be
a new racial category has to be considered aside from personal pain and
personal history," Love says. Personal wishes have to be viewed in the context of what it means to live in an oppressive society where inequality is
based on social identity groups. And where *race* is the fundamental criterion on which those groupings and thus divisions are made.

Says Love: "From my point of view, if you go at it from a sociological
rather than a personal standpoint, it is disastrous to create a new category,
because the oppression itself is based on exactly that kind of division. We
should be putting our energies into using the historic juncture of the year
2000 as a time when we will abolish all racial categories."

Many multiethnic activists would argue that this is a progressive-   40
sounding argument to deny them recognition and representation. But if
their interest is the elimination of oppression — and not social vengeance
against blacks — then the elimination of classifications based on race is the
only solution that makes sense.

However, if African Americans continue to vent their internalized oppression through the physical and psychological abuse of multiethnic people who have black ancestry but do not identify solely with the African-
American community, what alternative is there for people like Velina Hasu
Houston than to reject us?

Right now, the last plantation is the mind. We need an ongoing dialogue in every black home to discuss the issue of colorism among us, conflict with other ethnic groups of color — remember, we are going to be the majority one day — and a definition of African American that discards overly romantic attachments to Africa and the equally ridiculous notion of ourselves as solely the products of U.S. slavery.

"There are so many pieces of us that we have simply not had the opportunity to embrace," says Love. "If we could just get freed up for two minutes of history not to have to protect, defend, and react, but think creatively about who we are — our bouquet ancestry — we might come up with something that may surprise us. After all, when I pour libations into the earth, which of my ancestors knows who it's for?"

                                                                        1991

The Reader's Presence

1. Why do you think Njeri began her essay with an anecdote about a family member? How does the anecdote dramatize the central issue of the selection? Do you think it represents most multiethnic experiences? Explain why or why not.

2. How would you describe Njeri's audience for the essay? When she says "We need . . . " in paragraph 42, which specific group is being addressed? Which group is she identified with? Which groups — if any — do you think she is excluding from "we"?

3. In rereading the essay, pay close attention to the way Njeri uses quotations. How many interview sources does she rely on? How reliable do these sources seem to you? Which sources do you think she is most comfortable with? Do you come across any instances in the essay when you aren't sure whether a position or statement is Njeri's or that of her sources?

47

Irene Oppenheim

On Waitressing

In September of 1985 I needed a job that would give me a regular income for a few months. I hadn't worked as a waitress for more than a decade, and at first didn't consider that a possibility. But as I searched for more demure employment, I found that one after another of my interviewers would glance at my resume, sadly mumble something about "all that writing," and proceed, making as much eye-contact as I'd permit, to ask "sincerely" about my intentions, naming anything less than full commitment a form of deceit. Unable to assuage their concern with a convincingly forthright response, I soon found myself applying for work at Canter's, a sprawling twenty-four-hour-a-day Jewish (though non-kosher) bakery, delicatessen, and restaurant which for the past forty-five years has been dishing up kishka and knishes in the Fairfax district of Los Angeles. I knew that neither of my most recent waitress references would check out — Herb of Herb's Hamburgers in San Francisco had thrown down his spatula some years ago and gone to work in a hardware store, while the Sand Dollar Cafe in Stinson Beach had changed owners, so no one there would remember just how deftly I could sling hash. I told all this to Jackie Canter who, in her early twenties, is among a number of Canter relations working in the family business. She hesitated, but I was hired anyway.

While I don't wish to discredit my powers of persuasion, getting hired at Canter's was hardly a difficult affair. The "Help Wanted" sign in Canter's front window was a faded, permanent fixture. And in the two months I ultimately worked at the restaurant, the volume of employee comings and goings was never less than impressive. There were, however, exceptions to this transitoriness, and some among the large Canter crew had been with the restaurant for ten, twenty, or even thirty years. These

For biographical information on Irene Oppenheim, see p. 659.

were mostly older women who remained through a combination of loyalty, age, narrow skills, and inertia. The younger people tended to find the work too demanding and the income increasingly unreliable. Canter's heyday had been in the pre-McDonalds, pre-cholesterol days of the 1950s and 60s. And while the erosion was gradual, it was clear that the combination of fast food and *nouvelle cuisine* was steadily reducing Canter's corned beef/pastrami/chopped liver clientele. Despite trendy additions to the menu, such as an avocado melt sandwich (not bad) and the steamed vegetable plate (not good), there were now many quiet afternoons when the older waitresses, wiping off ketchup bottles and filling napkin holders to pass the time, would tell you about the days when the lines for Canter's stretched right down from the door to the corner of Beverly Boulevard.

Canter's could still get enormously busy — on holidays, for instance, or weekend nights. Sometimes for no reason at all the place would suddenly be mobbed. But it all had become unpredictable. And while this unpredictability made the owners niggardly and anxious, its more immediate toll was on the waiters and waitresses, who were almost totally dependent on customer tips. Canter's is a "union house," which means that for sixteen dollars a month the workers are covered by a not-too-respected grievance procedure and a well-loved medical/dental plan. The pay for waiting on tables, however, remains $3.37 per hour (two cents above minimum wage), so at Canter's, as with most restaurants, any real money has to come from tips.

Until a few years ago these tips were untaxed, which made waitressing a tough but reasonably lucrative profession. Now tips have to be regularly declared, and through a complicated process that involves the IRS taking eight percent of a restaurant's gross meal receipts and dividing that amount up among the number of food servers, a per-employee tip figure is arrived at, and any waiter who declares less than that may very well be challenged. In some restaurants the management automatically deducts the estimated amount from the paychecks. At Canter's each individual makes a weekly declaration. But in either case there's great bitterness among the table waiters about the way the tax is estimated. In every restaurant, for instance, some shifts are far more profitable than others, a subtlety the IRS doesn't take into account. There's also a built-in bias toward "class" operations where the bills are high and the tips generally run fifteen to twenty percent, while at Canter's with its soup and sandwich fare, ten percent or less is the norm. Also, waitresses and waiters volubly and resentfully claim that others in service professions, such as porters, cab drivers, or hairdressers, are left to make simple declarations, without the income of the business being involved.

Where it is possible, most restaurant workers under-declare their tips and simply hope they can get away with it. But a few of them at Canter's had been called in each year, and the more canny of the waitresses told me I should keep a daily tally of all my checks in case the IRS claimed I'd made not just more than I'd declared, but more than I really took in. What all this meant in terms of an actual paycheck was that, after meal deductions, regular taxes, and taxes declared on my tips, my average check for a forty-hour week was $74.93 or, in the first week of the month, when union fees were due, $58.93. Whatever else I took home was in the form of tips, and if business wasn't good these could become a unnervingly scarce commodity.

Still, most waitresses at Canter's made more than they would as bank tellers, store clerks, or non-managerial office workers. And even for those whose options were somewhat less grim, waitressing was not without its alluring aspects. The range of tips — which, depending on how many customers of what kind you got on a shift, might be as low as twelve dollars or as high as eighty — gave the job a gambling flavor which appealed to some. (Gambling, in fact, was rather a big item at Canter's. More than a few of the waitresses played as much bingo as paying their rent allowed, while the kitchen help would, almost every day, pool their money and purchase long strings of lottery tickets, with any winnings divided among the buyers.) Others among the waitresses worked there because they preferred the restaurant's physical demands to the boredom of paper work, and several were performers or students who took advantage of the night hours and flexible scheduling. But no one was really happy to be at Canter's. It simply wasn't a very happy place.

I've never worked anywhere that had more rules than Canter's. The staff bulletin board was so crammed with admonitions that the overflow had to be taped to the adjacent wall. The topics of these missives varied. One sign, for example, warned that bags and purses might be checked on the way out for purloined food; another that those who didn't turn up for their shifts on holidays such as Christmas (Canter's is open every day of the year except Rosh Hashanah and Yom Kippur) would be automatically dismissed; a third firmly stated that no food substitutions were permitted, which meant that it was against regulations to give a customer who requested it a slice of tomato instead of a pickle. When working on the floor, one encountered even more elaborate rules. All ice cream, juice, or bakery items, for instance, had to be initialed on your check by that shift's hostess, lest you serve something without writing it down. To further complicate matters, orders for deli sandwiches had to be written on a slip of paper along with your waitress number (mine was #35), and these slips were then matched against your checks to make sure, for example, that if you ordered two pastrami sandwiches the customer had paid for two. I was castigated by Jackie one day for — along with the more major infraction of not charging fifty cents extra for a slice of cheese — charging ten cents too little for a cup of potato salad. It seems like a small thing, said Jackie (I concurred), but then she added grimly that little mistakes like mine with the potato salad cost the restaurant many thousands of dollars each year. I was tempted to point out that undoubtedly an equal number of errors were made in the restaurant's favor. But I held my tongue, knowing by then that, in the face of a documented Canter's money loss, anything that could be construed as less than acute remorse would only serve to bring my checks under even closer scrutiny.

The waitresses were generally good to each other, though such camaraderie didn't often run deep and rarely extended to any auxiliary personnel such as the bus boys. These were constantly (and mostly unjustly) suspected of stealing tips from the tables and thereby adding to their required tips from the waitresses (I'm not sure exactly what this came to per individual bus boy, but every waitress contributed about twenty dollars a week which was divided up among the bus boys). At one time Canter's bus boy positions had been filled by strapping immigrant Jewish boys from places such as Bulgaria and Lithuania. But now the bus boys were almost all Hispanic, as were the cooks, and a troublesome plate of blintzes or latkes would be garnished by a storm of Spanish curses. In the back kitchen, too, where they made the soups and mixed together enormous vats of tuna salad, the workers were mostly Spanish-speaking. Things in the back kitchen were usually less frantic than in the front, and the back kitchen guys would smile and try to make conversation as you negotiated your way over the wooden floor slats to the bathroom or the time clock. From the deli and kitchen men, however, surliness was a virtual constant, with their black moods frequently exacerbated into anger by such things as the restaurant's awkward design and organization. It was required, for example, that a waitress serving a cheddar cheese omelette first write a slip for the cheese, which had to be sliced and picked up at the front deli counter, and then, after writing another slip for the kitchen, hand-carry the cheese back to the grill. When the place got busy, tempers also ran short among the waitresses themselves, who would swear at the always recalcitrant toasters, at the bagels (or lack of them), or at each other, as fast movers stumbled into slower ones. But in the arena of churlishness the waitresses never came close to competing with the hardworking deli men. Brandishing knives and hunks of meat with a rhythmic skill and an admirable — even graceful — economy of movement, they set the tone at Canter's. And I remember a time when, having made a mistake, I said to one of the deli men, by way of apology, that I'd try to improve. "Don't try," he snarled back. "Do."

One of the more graphic symbols of Canter's changing times was the uniform closet. The male waiters — a relative novelty at Canter's — were allowed to work in a black-pants/white-shirt combo, with some of them opting to appear in the "I Love Canter's" T-shirt available for eight dollars (*their* eight dollars) at the front cash register.

The women could get "I Love Canter's" stenciled free on the off-work shirt of their choice, but their on-the-job dress code was more severe. No 10 one's memory reached back to a time when Canter's waitresses had worn anything other than cream-colored outfits with a single brown stripe running down from each shoulder. There were many of these lined up in the

uniform closet. In most cases the uniforms were well-worn, with under-
arms stained an irreparable gray and hems which had been let up or down
more than once. But their dominant characteristic was size. Most of the
available uniforms could have doubled as small tents. And no matter how
many pins or tucks you employed, material would billow out over your
tightly pulled apron strings, an irrepressible tribute to the amplitude of
your predecessors.

Although there was a locker room at Canter's it was deemed dangerous for reasons I never explored, and I always arrived with my uniform
already on. At first I'd worked various shifts — twelve P.M. to eight P.M.,
eight P.M. to four A.M. — but finally was assigned to days, primarily because I was considered easy-going and the day shift had a contentious reputation. My first task was to relieve Pauline at the counter. She went on
duty at six A.M., and technically I was to relieve her at nine A.M. when my
shift began. Though the management preferred you didn't clock it in, the
rules at Canter's required you to be on the floor fifteen minutes before your
shift time, and I'd generally show up around 8:40, which would give Pauline a chance to finish off her checks and put together her own breakfast —
usually a mixture of Frosted Flakes and Wheaties from the little boxes kept
on display right near the coffee machine.

There was nothing contentious about Pauline. She was a slow, heavy
woman in her early sixties. She was having tooth problems during the time
I knew her. But her feet were also troublesome, and she'd made long knife
cuts in the front of her white shoes so that, defying the beige of her nylons,
the flesh of each foot pushed out rosy-pink between the slits. Pauline had
been working at Canter's for twenty-five years, and was the only one of the
waitresses left who had her name machine-embroidered onto her uniform.
The rest of us were given pins with our first names punched out on a black
dymo label. But Pauline's was sewn right in, so you knew she represented
a different, less transient era at the restaurant. You could tell by watching
her, too, by the deliberate way she moved, that this was a place she was
intimately familiar with.

Only one part of the counter was open in the morning. It sat around
fourteen people and included, as part of the station, three adjacent two-
person booths as well as any take-out coffee orders. Almost everyone hated
working the counter because the turnover could be impossibly fast and the
tips were always small. On the other hand, the counter didn't involve as
much running around as the other stations, and Pauline preferred it. She'd
move as though she were doing a little dance, reaching toward the coffee
machine, and then the toaster, and then scooping up packets of strawberry
jam (strawberry was the only jam flavor Canter's served), with a steady
elegance that belied her girth — a factor substantial enough to make it virtually unfeasible for both of us to work behind the counter at once.

Pauline was always glad to see me, for the half-hour's rest I represented
would be the longest break she'd have until getting off work at two P.M. I
liked Pauline too, and we got along well, but the counter was another mat-

ter. Generally two kinds of people showed up at the counter: those who were alone and in a hurry to get somewhere else, and a group of "regulars" for whom time was not a consideration. This latter group was dominated by retired men who met at Canter's punctually each day to have windy discussions which would begin focused on a single topic — such as how people on welfare should be prevented from buying lottery tickets — that would gradually merge into a broader lament about the disintegration of the neighborhood, the city, the nation, and onward. From my standpoint, both these counter groups meant trouble: Those who were alone tended to be impatient, while those who came in every day expected special treatment which included remembering details about their preferences (water without ice, or a cherry danish heated with soft butter on the side), and they'd become belligerent if these idiosyncrasies were forgotten or if they felt some mere counter itinerant were getting better service. But there were other regulars too, lonely souls who were not part of the clique. As you stopped for a moment to write out their check, they'd start to tell you about painful cataracts or distant children. I remember one woman who liked her single piece of rye toast burnt almost black. She'd occasionally whisper, so that I had to bend down to hear her, that she was short of cash, and would ask to borrow a dollar from me to pay the bill. I'd always do it. And next day the loan would be stealthily but triumphantly repaid, the dollar slipped into my hand or pocket with a conspiratorial smile as though this act of trust and complicity had secretly bonded us together.

My Canter's career was to come to an unfortunately abrupt end. A 15 restaurant as large as Canter's was bound to have "walk-outs" who'd leave without paying their checks, and I'd had a few. There was one obese woman who asked me a couple of times if she could pay with a credit card (Canter's didn't accept them) and then left me a tip before managing to get away without paying for her hamburger and coke. Another man had me take his bacon and eggs back to the kitchen twice for repairs; he left me a tip too, but the eggs and bacon went unpaid for. Though there was an element of disgrace in having a walk-out, these small incidents were too common for much of a fuss to be made. But one busy Saturday I had a party of seven who each ordered around ten dollars worth of food and then made a calculated escape while I was in the back adding up their check. Jackie sat me down at the staff table and grimly said that while she didn't blame me for what happened, she did want me to know that it was the largest walk-out loss in the history of Canter's. Nothing was mentioned about my leaving, though Jackie did say that from this point on she wanted me immediately to report to her or the hostess any of my customers who seemed suspicious. I worked the rest of my shift, but everyone I served began to look vaguely suspicious. And with my reputation securely if infamously etched into Canter's history, it seemed time to move on.

1986

The Reader's Presence

1. What overall impression does Irene Oppenheim create in her account of working the day shift at Canter's restaurant in Los Angeles? How does she characterize the people with whom she works? The patrons of the restaurant? What compositional strategies does she use to make this place — and the people who frequent it — seem so vibrant and vivid?

2. What reasons does Oppenheim give for working at Canter's? What reasons convinced her to leave? What role does trust play in her decision to leave? When — and in what other forms — does the issue of trust surface in this essay? What is Oppenheim's attitude toward the issue of trust? What other points of view does Oppenheim introduce into her essay on this and other subjects? Does she seem to prefer one point of view more than others? Consider, for example, the moment when the manager scolds her for undercharging a customer. The manager notes that such errors, though seemingly small, cost the restaurant "many thousands of dollars each year." Explain how Oppenheim's response typifies her view of such matters, as well as, more generally, her view of work and of the people who patronize the restaurant. What is the point of her detailed explanation in paragraph 4 of the process of calculating the tax due on the tips she earns?

3. Characterize the tone of Irene Oppenheim's account of working the day shift at Canter's. When — and how — does she convey her attitude toward her experience as a waitress? Does she treat her experience there with bitterness? resentment? understanding? sympathy? humor? some combination of these? Something else? What does she gain (and lose) as a result of her decision to write in the first person? What "conclusions" does she draw from her experience as a waitress at Canter's? How explicit is she in articulating the significance of her experience there?

48

George Orwell

Politics and the English Language

Most people who bother with the matter at all would admit that the English language is in a bad way, but it is generally assumed that we cannot by conscious action do anything about it. Our civilization is decadent and our language — so the argument runs — must inevitably share in the general collapse. It follows that any struggle against the abuse of language is a sentimental archaism, like preferring candles to electric light or hansom cabs to airplanes. Underneath this lies the half-conscious belief that language is a natural growth and not an instrument which we shape for our own purposes.

Now, it is clear that the decline of a language must ultimately have political and economic causes: It is not due simply to the bad influence of this or that individual writer. But an effect can become a cause, reinforcing the original cause and producing the same effect in an intensified form, and so on indefinitely. A man may take to drink because he feels himself to be a failure, and then fail all the more completely because he drinks. It is rather the same thing that is happening to the English language. It becomes ugly and inaccurate because our thoughts are foolish, but the slovenliness of our language makes it easier for us to have foolish thoughts. The point is that the process is reversible. Modern English, especially written English, is full of bad habits which spread by imitation and which can be avoided if one is willing to take the necessary trouble. If one gets rid of these habits one can think more clearly, and to think clearly is a necessary first step towards political regeneration: so that the fight against bad English is not frivolous and is not the exclusive concern of professional writers. I will come back to this presently, and I hope that by that time the meaning of

For biographical information on George Orwell, see p. 659.

what I have said here will have become clearer. Meanwhile, here are five specimens of the English language as it is now habitually written.

These five passages have not been picked out because they are especially bad — I could have quoted far worse if I had chosen — but because they illustrate various of the mental vices from which we now suffer. They are a little below the average, but are fairly representative samples. I number them so that I can refer back to them when necessary:

(1) I am not, indeed, sure whether it is not true to say that the Milton who once seemed not unlike a seventeenth-century Shelley had not become, out of an experience ever more bitter in each year, more alien [*sic*] to the founder of that Jesuit sect which nothing could induce him to tolerate.

Professor Harold Laski (Essay in *Freedom of Expression*).

(2) Above all, we cannot play ducks and drakes with a native battery of idioms which prescribes such egregious collections of vocables as the Basic *put up with* for *tolerate* or *put at a loss* for *bewilder*.

Professor Lancelot Hogben (*Interglossa*).

(3) On the one side we have the free personality: By definition it is not neurotic, for it has neither conflict nor dream. Its desires, such as they are, are transparent, for they are just what institutional approval keeps in the forefront of consciousness; another institutional pattern would alter their number and intensity; there is little in them that is natural, irreducible, or culturally dangerous. But *on the other side,* the social bond itself is nothing but the mutual reflection of these self-secure integrities. Recall the definition of love. Is not this the very picture of a small academic? Where is there a place in this hall of mirrors for either personality or fraternity?

Essay on psychology in *Politics* (New York).

(4) All the "best people" from the gentlemen's clubs, and all the frantic fascist captains, united in common hatred of Socialism and bestial horror of the rising tide of the mass revolutionary movement, have turned to acts of provocation, to foul incendiarism, to medieval legends of poisoned wells, to legalize their own destruction of proletarian organizations, and rouse the agitated petty-bourgeoisie to chauvinistic fervor on behalf of the fight against the revolutionary way out of the crisis.

Communist pamphlet.

(5) If a new spirit *is* to be infused into this old country, there is one thorny and contentious reform which must be tackled, and that is the humanization and galvanization of the B.B.C. Timidity here will bespeak cancer and atrophy of the soul. The heart of Britain may be sound and of strong beat, for instance, but the British lion's roar at present is like that of Bottom in Shakespeare's *Midsummer Night's Dream* — as gentle as any sucking dove. A virile new Britain cannot continue indefinitely to be traduced in the eyes or rather ears, of the world by the effete languors of Langham Place, brazenly masquerading as "standard English." When the Voice of Britain is heard at nine o'clock, better far and infinitely less ludicrous to hear aitches honestly dropped than the present priggish, inflated, inhibited, school-ma'amish arch braying of blameless bashful mewing maidens!

Letter in *Tribune*.

Each of these passages has faults of its own, but, quite apart from avoidable ugliness, two qualities are common to all of them. The first is staleness of imagery: The other is lack of precision. The writer either has a meaning and cannot express it, or he inadvertently says something else, or he is almost indifferent as to whether his words mean anything or not. This mixture of vagueness and sheer incompetence is the most marked characteristic of modern English prose, and especially of any kind of political writing. As soon as certain topics are raised, the concrete melts into the abstract and no one seems able to think of turns of speech that are not hackneyed: Prose consists less and less of *words* chosen for the sake of their meaning, and more and more of *phrases* tacked together like the sections of a prefabricated hen-house. I list below, with notes and examples, various of the tricks by means of which the work of prose-construction is habitually dodged:

Dying Metaphors. A newly invented metaphor assists thought by evoking a visual image, while on the other hand a metaphor which is technically "dead" (e.g., *iron resolution*) has in effect reverted to being an ordinary word and can generally be used without loss of vividness. But in between these two classes there is a huge dump of worn-out metaphors which have lost all evocative power and are merely used because they save people the trouble of inventing phrases for themselves. Examples are: *Ring the changes on, take up the cudgels for, toe the line, ride roughshod over, stand shoulder to shoulder with, play into the hands of, no axe to grind, grist to the mill, fishing in troubled waters, rift within the lute, on the order of the day, Achilles' heel, swan song, hotbed.* Many of these are used without knowledge of their meaning (what is a "rift," for instance?), and incompatible metaphors are frequently mixed, a sure sign that the writer is not interested in what he is saying. Some metaphors now current have been twisted out of their original meaning without those who use them even being aware of the fact. For example, *toe the line* is sometimes written *tow the line.* Another example is *the hammer and the anvil,* now always used with the implication that the anvil gets the worst of it. In real life it is always the anvil that breaks the hammer, never the other way about: A writer who stopped to think what he was saying would be aware of this, and would avoid perverting the original phrase.

Operators or Verbal False Limbs. These save the trouble of picking out appropriate verbs and nouns, and at the same time pad each sentence with extra syllables which give it an appearance of symmetry. Characteristic phrases are *render inoperative, militate against, make contact with, be subjected to, give rise to, give grounds for, have the effect of, play a leading part (role) in, make itself felt, take effect, exhibit a tendency to, serve the purpose of, etc., etc.* The keynote is the elimination of simple verbs. Instead of being a single word, such as *break, stop, spoil, mend, kill,* a verb becomes a *phrase,* made up of a noun or adjective tacked on to some general-purpose verb such as *prove, serve, form, play, render.* In addition, the passive voice is wherever possible used in preference to the active, and noun constructions are used instead of gerunds (*by examination of* instead of *by examining*). The range of verbs is further cut down by means of the *-ize* and *de-* formation, and the banal statements are given an appearance of profundity by means of the *not un-* formation. Simple conjunctions and prepositions are replaced by such phrases as *with respect to, having regard to, the fact that, by dint of, in view of, in the interests of, on the hypothesis that;* and the ends of sentences are saved from anticlimax by such resounding commonplaces as *greatly to be desired, cannot be left out of account, a development to be expected in the near future, deserving of serious consideration, brought to a satisfactory conclusion,* and so on and so forth.

Pretentious Diction. Words like *phenomenon, element, individual* (as noun), *objective, categorical, effective, virtual, basic, primary, promote, constitute, exhibit, exploit, utilize, eliminate, liquidate,* are used to dress up simple statements and give an air of scientific impartiality to biased judgments. Adjectives like *epoch-making, epic, historic, unforgettable, triumphant, age-old, inevitable, inexorable, veritable,* are used to dignify the sordid processes of international politics, while writing that aims at glorifying war usually takes on an archaic color, its characteristic words being: *realm, throne, chariot, mailed fist, trident, sword, shield, buckler, banner, jackboot, clarion.* Foreign words and expressions such as *cul de sac, ancien régime, deus ex machina, mutatis mutandis, status quo, gleichschaltung, weltanschauung,* are used to give an air of culture and elegance. Except for the useful abbreviations *i.e., e.g.,* and *etc.,* there is no real need for any of the hundreds of foreign phrases now current in English. Bad writers, and especially scientific, political, and sociological writers, are nearly always haunted by the notion that Latin or Greek words are grander than Saxon ones, and unnecessary words like *expedite, ameliorate, predict, extraneous, deracinated, clandestine, subaqueous,* and hundreds of others constantly gain ground from their Anglo-Saxon opposite numbers.[1] The jargon peculiar to Marxist writing (*hyena, hangman, cannibal, petty bourgeois, these gentry, lackey, flunkey, mad dog, White Guard, etc.*) consists largely of words and phrases translated from Russian, German, or French; but the normal way of coining a new word is to use a Latin or Greek root with the appropriate affix and, where necessary, the *-ize* formation. It is often easier to make up words of this kind (*deregionalize, impermissible, extramarital, nonfragmentatory,* and so forth) than to think up the English words that will cover one's meaning. The result, in general, is an increase in slovenliness and vagueness.

---

[1] An interesting illustration of this is the way in which the English flower names which were in use till very recently are being ousted by Greek ones, *snapdragon* becoming *antirrhinum, forget-me-not* becoming *myosotis,* etc. It is hard to see any practical reason for this change of fashion: It is probably due to an instinctive turning away from the more homely word and a vague feeling that the Greek word is scientific. — ORWELL'S NOTE.

Meaningless Words. In certain kinds of writing, particularly in art criticism and literary criticism, it is normal to come across long passages which are almost completely lacking in meaning.[2] Words like *romantic, plastic, values, human, dead, sentimental, natural, vitality,* as used in art criticism, are strictly meaningless, in the sense that they not only do not point to any discoverable object, but are hardly ever expected to do so by the reader. When one critic writes, "The outstanding feature of Mr. X's work is its living quality," while another writes, "The immediately striking thing about Mr. X's work is its peculiar deadness," the reader accepts this as a simple difference of opinion. If words like *black* and *white* were involved, instead of the jargon words *dead* and *living,* he would see at once that language was being used in an improper way. Many political words are similarly abused. The word *Fascism* has now no meaning except in so far as it signifies "something not desirable." The words *democracy, socialism, freedom, patriotic, realistic, justice,* have each of them several different meanings which cannot be reconciled with one another. In the case of a word like *democracy,* not only is there no agreed definition, but the attempt to make one is resisted from all sides. It is almost universally felt that when we call a country democratic we are praising it: Consequently the defenders of every kind of regime claim that it is a democracy, and fear that they might have to stop using the word if it were tied down to any one meaning. Words of this kind are often used in a consciously dishonest way. That is, the person who uses them has his own private definition, but allows his hearer to think he means something quite different. Statements like *Marshal Pétain*[3] *was a true patriot, The Soviet Press is the freest in the world, The Catholic Church is opposed to persecution,* are almost always made with intent to deceive. Other words used in variable meanings, in most cases more or less dishonestly, are: *class, totalitarian, science, progressive, reactionary, bourgeois, equality.*

Now that I have made this catalogue of swindles and perversions, let me give another example of the kind of writing that they lead to. This time it must of its nature be an imaginary one. I am going to translate a passage of good English into modern English of the worst sort. Here is a well-known verse from *Ecclesiastes:*

---

[2]Example: Comfort's catholicity of perception and image, strangely Whitmanesque in range, almost the exact opposite in aesthetic compulsion, continues to evoke that trembling atmospheric accumulative hinting at a cruel, an inexorably serene timelessness. . . . Wrey Gardiner scores by aiming at simple bull's-eyes with precision. Only they are not so simple, and through this contented sadness runs more than the surface bitter-sweet of resignation." (*Poetry Quarterly.*) — ORWELL'S NOTE.

[3]*Pétain:* Henri Phillipe Pétain was a World War I French military hero who served as chief of state in France from 1940 to 1945, after France surrendered to Germany. A controversial figure, Pétain was regarded by some to be a patriot who had sacrificed himself for his country, while others considered him to be a traitor. He was sentenced to life imprisonment in 1945, the year before Orwell wrote this essay. — EDS.

> I returned and saw under the sun, that the race is not to the swift, nor the
> battle to the strong, neither yet bread to the wise, nor yet riches to men of
> understanding, nor yet favor to men of skill; but time and chance
> happeneth to them all.

Here it is in modern English:

> Objective consideration of contemporary phenomena compels the conclu-
> sion that success or failure in competitive activities exhibits no tendency to
> be commensurate with innate capacity, but that a considerable element of
> the unpredictable must invariably be taken into account.

This is a parody, but not a very gross one. Exhibit (3), above, for in-   10
stance, contains several patches of the same kind of English. It will be seen
that I have not made a full translation. The beginning and ending of the
sentence follow the original meaning fairly closely, but in the middle the
concrete illustrations — race, battle, bread — dissolve into the vague
phrase "success or failure in competitive activities." This had to be so, because no modern writer of the kind I am discussing — no one capable of
using phrases like "objective consideration of contemporary phenomena"
— would ever tabulate his thoughts in that precise and detailed way. The
whole tendency of modern prose is away from concreteness. Now analyze
these two sentences a little more closely. The first contains forty-nine
words but only sixty syllables, and all its words are those of everyday life.
The second contains thirty-eight words of ninety syllables: Eighteen of its
words are from Latin roots, and one from Greek. The first sentence contains six vivid images, and only one phrase ("time and chance") that could
be called vague. The second contains not a single fresh, arresting phrase,
and in spite of its ninety syllables it gives only a shortened version of the
meaning contained in the first. Yet without a doubt it is the second kind of
sentence that is gaining ground in modern English. I do not want to exaggerate. This kind of writing is not yet universal, and outcrops of simplicity
will occur here and there in the worst-written page. Still, if you or I were
told to write a few lines on the uncertainty of human fortunes, we should
probably come much nearer to my imaginary sentence than to the one from
Ecclesiastes.

As I have tried to show, modern writing at its worst does not consist in
picking out words for the sake of their meaning and inventing images in
order to make the meaning clearer. It consists in gumming together long
strips of words which have already been set in order by someone else, and
making the results presentable by sheer humbug. The attraction of this way
of writing is that it is easy. It is easier — even quicker once you have the
habit — to say *In my opinion it is a not unjustifiable assumption that* than
to say *I think*. If you use ready-made phrases, you not only don't have to
hunt about for words; you also don't have to bother with the rhythms of
your sentences, since these phrases are generally so arranged as to be more
or less euphonious. When you are composing in a hurry — when you are

dictating to a stenographer, for instance, or making a public speech — it is natural to fall into a pretentious, Latinized style. Tags like *a consideration which we should do well to bear in mind* or *a conclusion to which all of us would readily assent* will save many a sentence from coming down with a bump. By using stale metaphors, similes, and idioms, you save much mental effort, at the cost of leaving your meaning vague, not only for your reader but for yourself. This is the significance of mixed metaphors. The sole aim of a metaphor is to call up a visual image. When these images clash — as in *The Fascist octopus has sung its swan song, the jackboot is thrown into the melting pot* — it can be taken as certain that the writer is not seeing a mental image of the objects he is naming; in other words he is not really thinking. Look again at the examples I gave at the beginning of this essay. Professor Laski (1) uses five negatives in fifty-three words. One of these is superfluous, making nonsense of the whole passage, and in addition there is the slip — *alien* for akin — making further nonsense, and several avoidable pieces of clumsiness which increase the general vagueness. Professor Hogben (2) plays ducks and drakes with a battery which is able to write prescriptions, and, while disapproving of the everyday phrase *put up with,* is unwilling to look *egregious* up in the dictionary and see what it means; (3), if one takes an uncharitable attitude towards it, is simply meaningless: Probably one could work out its intended meaning by reading the whole of the article in which it occurs. In (4), the writer knows more or less what he wants to say, but an accumulation of stale phrases chokes him like tea leaves blocking a sink. In (5), words and meaning have almost parted company. People who write in this manner usually have a general emotional meaning — they dislike one thing and want to express solidarity with another — but they are not interested in the detail of what they are saying. A scrupulous writer, in every sentence that he writes, will ask himself at least four questions, thus: What am I trying to say? What words will express it? What image or idiom will make it clearer? Is this image fresh enough to have an effect? And he will probably ask himself two more: Could I put it more shortly? Have I said anything that is avoidably ugly? But you are not obliged to go to all this trouble. You can shirk it by simply throwing your mind open and letting the ready-made phrases come crowding in. They will construct your sentences for you — even think your thoughts for you, to a certain extent — and at need they will perform the important service of partially concealing your meaning even from yourself. It is at this point that the special connection between politics and the debasement of language becomes clear.

In our time it is broadly true that political writing is bad writing. Where it is not true, it will generally be found that the writer is some kind of rebel, expressing his private opinions and not a "party line." Orthodoxy, of whatever color, seems to demand a lifeless, imitative style. The political dialects to be found in pamphlets, leading articles, manifestos, White Papers, and the speeches of under-secretaries do, of course, vary from party to party, but they are all alike in that one almost never finds in them a fresh, vivid, home-made turn of speech. When one watches some tired hack on the platform mechanically repeating the familiar phrases — *bestial atrocities, iron heel, bloodstained tyranny, free peoples of the world, stand shoulder to shoulder* — one often has a curious feeling that one is not watching a live human being but some kind of dummy: a feeling which suddenly becomes stronger at moments when the light catches the speaker's spectacles and turns them into blank discs which seem to have no eyes behind them. And this is not altogether fanciful. A speaker who uses that kind of phraseology has gone some distance towards turning himself into a machine. The appropriate noises are coming out of his larynx, but his brain is not involved as it would be if he were choosing his words for himself. If the speech he is making is one that he is accustomed to make over and over again, he may be almost unconscious of what he is saying, as one is when one utters the responses in church. And this reduced state of consciousness, if not indispensable, is at any rate favorable to political conformity.

In our time, political speech and writing are largely the defense of the indefensible. Things like the continuance of British rule in India, the Russian purges and deportations, the dropping of the atom bombs on Japan, can indeed be defended, but only by arguments which are too brutal for most people to face, and which do not square with the professed aims of political parties. Thus political language has to consist largely of euphemism, question-begging, and sheer cloudy vagueness. Defenseless villages are bombarded from the air, the inhabitants driven out into the countryside, the cattle machine-gunned, the huts set on fire with incendiary bullets: This is called *pacification*. Millions of peasants are robbed of their farms and sent trudging along the roads with no more than they can carry: This is called *transfer of population* or *rectification of frontiers*. People are imprisoned for years without trial, or shot in the back of the neck or sent to die of scurvy in Arctic lumber camps[4]: This is called *elimination of unreliable elements*. Such phraseology is needed if one wants to name things without calling up mental pictures of them. Consider for instance some comfortable English professor defending Russian totalitarianism. He cannot say outright, "I believe in killing off your opponents when you get good results by doing so." Probably, therefore, he will say something like this:

"While freely conceding that the Soviet régime exhibits certain features which the humanitarian may be inclined to deplore, we must, I think, agree that a certain curtailment of the right to political opposition is an unavoidable concomitant of transitional periods, and that the rigors which the Russian people have been called upon to undergo have been amply justified in the sphere of concrete achievement."

---

[4]*People . . . camps:* Though Orwell is decrying all totalitarian abuse of language, his examples are mainly pointed at the Soviet purges under Stalin. — EDS.

The inflated style is itself a kind of euphemism. A mass of Latin words 15
falls upon the facts like soft snow, blurring the outlines and covering up all
the details. The great enemy of clear language is insincerity. When there is
a gap between one's real and one's declared aims, one turns as it were instinctively to long words and exhausted idioms, like a cuttlefish squirting
out ink. In our age there is no such thing as "keeping out of politics." All
issues are political issues, and politics itself is a mass of lies, evasions, folly,
hatred, and schizophrenia. When the general atmosphere is bad, language
must suffer. I should expect to find — this is a guess which I have not sufficient knowledge to verify — that the German, Russian, and Italian languages have all deteriorated in the last ten or fifteen years, as a result of
dictatorship.

But if thought corrupts language, language can also corrupt thought. A
bad usage can spread by tradition and imitation, even among people who
should and do know better. The debased language that I have been discussing is in some ways very convenient. Phrases like *a not unjustifiable assumption, leaves much to be desired, would serve no good purpose, a consideration which we should do well to bear in mind,* are a continuous
temptation, a packet of aspirins always at one's elbow. Look back through
this essay, and for certain you will find that I have again and again committed the very faults I am protesting against. By this morning's post I have
received a pamphlet dealing with conditions in Germany. The author tells
me that he "felt impelled" to write it. I open it at random, and here is
almost the first sentence that I see: "(The Allies) have an opportunity not
only of achieving a radical transformation of Germany's social and political structure in such a way as to avoid a nationalistic reaction in Germany
itself, but at the same time of laying the foundations of a co-operative and
unified Europe." You see, he "feels impelled" to write — feels, presumably, that he has something new to say — and yet his words, like cavalry
horses answering the bugle, group themselves automatically into the familiar dreary pattern. This invasion of one's mind by ready-made phrases (*lay
the foundations, achieve a radical transformation*) can only be prevented if
one is constantly on guard against them, and every such phrase anaesthe-
tizes a portion of one's brain.

I said earlier that the decadence of our language is probably curable.
Those who deny this would argue, if they produced an argument at all, that
language merely reflects existing social conditions, and that we cannot influence its development by any direct tinkering with words and constructions. So far as the general tone or spirit of a language goes, this may be
true, but it is not true in detail. Silly words and expressions have often
disappeared, not through any evolutionary process but owing to the conscious action of a minority. Two recent examples were *explore every avenue* and *leave no stone unturned,* which were killed by the jeers of a few
journalists. There is a long list of flyblown metaphors which could similarly be got rid of if enough people would interest themselves in the job;
and it should also be possible to laugh the *not un-* formation out of exis-

tence,[5] to reduce the amount of Latin and Greek in the average sentence, to drive out foreign phrases and strayed scientific words, and, in general, to make pretentiousness unfashionable. But all these are minor points. The defense of the English language implies more than this, and perhaps it is best to start by saying what it does *not* imply.

To begin with it has nothing to do with archaism, with the salvaging of obsolete words and turns of speech, or with the setting up of a "standard English" which must never be departed from. On the contrary, it is especially concerned with the scrapping of every word or idiom which has outworn its usefulness. It has no thing to do with correct grammar and syntax, which are of no importance so long as one makes one's meaning clear, or with the avoidance of Americanisms, or with having what is called a "good prose style." On the other hand it is not concerned with fake simplicity and the attempt to make written English colloquial. Nor does it even imply in every case preferring the Saxon word to the Latin one, though it does imply using the fewest and shortest words that will cover one's meaning. What is above all needed is to let the meaning choose the word, and not the other way about. In prose, the worst thing one can do with words is to surrender to them. When you think of a concrete object, you think wordlessly, and then, if you want to describe the thing you have been visualizing you probably hunt about till you find the exact words that seem to fit. When you think of something abstract you are more inclined to use words from the start, and unless you make a conscious effort to prevent it, the existing dialect will come rushing in and do the job for you, at the expense of blurring or even changing your meaning. Probably it is better to put off using words as long as possible and get one's meaning as clear as one can through pictures or sensations. Afterwards one can choose — not simply *accept* — the phrases that will best cover the meaning, and then switch round and decide what impression one's words are likely to make on another person. This last effort of the mind cuts out all stale or mixed images, all prefabricated phrases, needless repetitions, and humbug and vagueness generally. But one can often be in doubt about the effect of a word or a phrase, and one needs rules that one can rely on when instinct fails. I think the following rules will cover most cases:

(i) Never use a metaphor, simile, or other figure of speech which you are used to seeing in print.
(ii) Never use a long word where a short one will do.
(iii) If it is possible to cut a word out, always cut it out.
(iv) Never use the passive where you can use the active.
(v) Never use a foreign phrase, a scientific word, or a jargon word if you can think of an everyday English equivalent.
(vi) Break any of these rules sooner than say anything outright barbarous.

[5]One can cure oneself of the *not un-* formation by memorizing this sentence: *A not unblack dog was chasing a not unsmall rabbit across a not ungreen field.* — ORWELL'S NOTE.

These rules sound elementary, and so they are, but they demand a deep change in attitude in anyone who has grown used to writing in the style now fashionable. One could keep all of them and still write bad English, but one could not write the kind of stuff that I quoted in those five specimens at the beginning of this article.

I have not here been considering the literary use of language, but merely language as an instrument for expressing and not for concealing or preventing thought. Stuart Chase and others have come near to claiming that all abstract words are meaningless, and have used this as a pretext for advocating a kind of political quietism. Since you don't know what Fascism is, how can you struggle against Fascism? One need not swallow such absurdities as these, but one ought to recognize that the present political chaos is connected with the decay of language, and that one can probably bring about some improvement by starting at the verbal end. If you simplify your English, you are freed from the worst follies of orthodoxy. You cannot speak any of the necessary dialects, and when you make a stupid remark its stupidity will be obvious, even to yourself. Political language — and with variations this is true of all political parties, from Conservatives to Anarchists — is designed to make lies sound truthful and murder respectable, and to give an appearance of solidity to pure wind. One cannot change this all in a moment, but one can at least change one's own habits, and from time to time one can even, if one jeers loudly enough, send some worn-out and useless phrase — some *jackboot, Achilles' heel, hotbed, melting pot, acid test, veritable inferno,* or other lump of verbal refuse — into the dustbin where it belongs.

1946

The Reader's Presence

1. Look carefully at Orwell's five examples of bad prose. Would you have identified this writing as "bad" writing if you had come across it in the course of your college reading? What do the examples remind you of?
2. What characteristics of Orwell's own writing demonstrate his six rules for writing good prose? Can you identify five examples in which Orwell practices what he preaches? Can you identify any moments when he seems to slip?
3. Note that Orwell does not provide *positive* examples of political expression. Why do you think this is so? Is Orwell implying that all political language — regardless of party or position — is corrupt? From this essay can you infer his political philosophy? Explain your answer.

49

Walker Percy

The Loss of the Creature

I

Every explorer names his island Formosa, beautiful. To him it is beautiful because, being first, he has access to it and can see it for what it is. But to no one else is it ever as beautiful — except the rare man who manages to recover it, who knows that it has to be recovered.

Garcia López de Cárdenas discovered the Grand Canyon and was amazed at the sight. It can be imagined: One crosses miles of desert, breaks through the mesquite, and there it is at one's feet. Later the government set the place aside as a national park, hoping to pass along to millions the experience of Cárdenas. Does not one see the same sight from the Bright Angel Lodge that Cárdenas saw?

The assumption is that the Grand Canyon is a remarkably interesting and beautiful place and that if it had a certain value P for Cárdenas, the same value P may be transmitted to any number of sightseers — just as Banting's discovery of insulin can be transmitted to any number of diabetics. A counterinfluence is at work, however, and it would be nearer the truth to say that if the place is seen by a million sightseers, a single sightseer does not receive value P but a millionth part of value P.

It is assumed that since the Grand Canyon has the fixed interest value P, tours can be organized for any number of people. A man in Boston decides to spend his vacation at the Grand Canyon. He visits his travel bureau, looks at the folder, signs up for a two-week tour. He and his family take the tour, see the Grand Canyon, and return to Boston. May we say

For biographical information on Walker Percy, see p. 659.

that this man has seen the Grand Canyon? Possibly he has. But it is more likely that what he has done is the one sure way not to see the canyon.

Why is it almost impossible to gaze directly at the Grand Canyon   5
under these circumstances and see it for what it is — as one picks up a strange object from one's back yard and gazes directly at it? It is almost impossible because the Grand Canyon, the thing as it is, has been appropriated by the symbolic complex which has already been formed in the sightseer's mind. Seeing the canyon under approved circumstances is seeing the symbolic complex head on. The thing is no longer the thing as it confronted the Spaniard; it is rather that which has already been formulated — by picture postcard, geography book, tourist folders, and the words *Grand Canyon*. As a result of this preformulation, the source of the sightseer's pleasure undergoes a shift. Where the wonder and delight of the Spaniard arose from his penetration of the thing itself, from a progressive discovery of depths, patterns, colors, shadows, etc., now the sightseer measures his satisfaction *by the degree to which the canyon conforms to the preformed complex*. If is does so, if it looks just like the postcard, he is pleased; he might even say, "Why it is every bit as beautiful as a picture postcard!" He feels he has not been cheated. But if it does not conform, if the colors are somber, he will not be able to see it directly; he will only be conscious of the disparity between what it is and what it is supposed to be. He will say later that he was unlucky in not being there at the right time. The highest point, the term of the sightseer's satisfaction, is not the sovereign discovery of the thing before him; it is rather the measuring up of the thing to the criterion of the preformed symbolic complex.

Seeing the canyon is made even more difficult by what the sightseer does when the moment arrives, when sovereign knower confronts the thing to be known. Instead of looking at it, he photographs it. There is no confrontation at all. At the end of forty years of preformulation and with the Grand Canyon yawning at his feet, what does he do? He waives his right of seeing and knowing and records symbols for the next forty years. For him there is no present; there is only the past of what has been formulated and seen and the future of what has been formulated and not seen. The present is surrendered to the past and the future.

The sightseer may be aware that something is wrong. He may simply be bored; or he may be conscious of the difficulty: that the great thing yawning at his feet somehow eludes him. The harder he looks at it, the less he can see. It eludes everybody. The tourist cannot see it; the bellboy at the Angel Lodge cannot see it: For him it is only one side of the space he lives in, like one wall of a room; to the ranger it is a tissue of everyday signs relevant to his own prospects — the blue haze down there means that he will probably get rained on during the donkey ride.

How can the sightseer recover the Grand Canyon? He can recover it in any number of ways, all sharing in common the stratagem of avoiding the approved confrontation of the tour and the Park Service.

It may be recovered by leaving the beaten track. The tourist leaves the tour, camps in the back country. He arises before dawn and approaches the South Rim through a wild terrain where there are no trails and no railed-in lookout points. In other words, he sees the canyon by avoiding all the facilities for seeing the canyon. If the benevolent Park Service hears about this fellow and thinks he has a good idea and places the following notice in the Bright Angel Lodge: *Consult ranger for information on getting off the beaten track* — the end result will only be the closing of another access to the canyon.

It may be recovered by a dialectical movement which brings one back   10
to the beaten track but at a level above it. For example, after a lifetime of avoiding the beaten track and guided tours, a man may deliberately seek out the most beaten track of all, the most commonplace tour imaginable: He may visit the canyon by a Greyhound tour in the company of a party from Terre Haute — just as a man who has lived in New York all his life may visit the Statue of Liberty. (Such dialectical savorings of the *familiar* as the familiar are, of course, a favorite stratagem of *The New Yorker* magazine.) The thing is recovered from familiarity by means of an exercise in familiarity. Our complex friend stands behind the fellow tourists at the Bright Angel Lodge and sees the canyon through them and their predicament, their picture taking and busy disregard. In a sense, he exploits his fellow tourists; he stands on their shoulders to see the canyon.

Such a man is far more advanced in the dialectic than the sightseer who is trying to get off the beaten track — getting up at dawn and approaching the canyon through the mesquite. This stratagem is, in fact, for our complex man the weariest, most beaten track of all.

It may be recovered as a consequence of a breakdown of the symbolic machinery by which the experts present the experience to the consumer. A family visits the canyon in the usual way. But shortly after their arrival, the park is closed by an outbreak of typhus in the south. They have the canyon to themselves. What do they mean when they tell the home folks of their good luck: "We had the whole place to ourselves"? How does one see the thing better when the others are absent? Is looking like sucking: the more lookers, the less there is to see? They could hardly answer, but by saying this they testify to a state of affairs which is considerably more complex than the simple statement of the schoolbook about the Spaniard and the millions who followed him. It is a state in which there is a complex distribution of sovereignty, of zoning.

It may be recovered in a time of national disaster. The Bright Angel Lodge is converted into a rest home, a function that has nothing to do with the canyon a few yards away. A wounded man is brought in. He regains consciousness; there outside his window is the canyon.

The most extreme case of access by privilege conferred by disaster is the Huxleyan[1] novel of the adventures of the surviving remnant after the

---

[1]*Huxleyan:* A reference to the English novelist Aldous Huxley (1894–1963), best known for his anti-utopian novel, *Brave New World* (1932). — EDS.

great wars of the twentieth century. An expedition from Australia lands in Southern California and heads east. They stumble across the Bright Angel Lodge, now fallen into ruins. The trails are grown over, the guard rails fallen away, the dime telescope at Battleship Point rusted. But there is the canyon, exposed at last. Exposed by what? By the decay of those facilities which were designed to help the sightseer.

This dialectic of sightseeing cannot be taken into account by planners,   15
for the object of the dialectic is nothing other than the subversion of the efforts of the planners.

The dialectic is not known to objective theorists, psychologists, and the like. Yet it is quite well known in the fantasy-consciousness of the popular arts. The devices by which the museum exhibit, the Grand Canyon, the ordinary thing, is recovered have long since been stumbled upon. A movie shows a man visiting the Grand Canyon. But the moviemaker knows something the planner does not know. He knows that one cannot take the sight frontally. The canyon must be approached by the stratagems we have mentioned: the Inside Track, the Familiar Revisited, the Accidental Encounter. Who is the stranger at the Bright Angel Lodge? Is he the ordinary tourist from Terre Haute that he makes himself out to be? He is not. He has another objective in mind, to revenge his wronged brother, counterespionage, etc. By virtue of the fact that he has other fish to fry, he may take a stroll along the rim after supper and then we can see the canyon through him. The movie accomplishes its purpose by concealing it. Overtly the characters (the American family marooned by typhus) and we the onlookers experience pity for the sufferers, and the family experience anxiety for themselves; covertly and in truth they are the happiest of people and we are happy through them, for we have the canyon to ourselves. The movie cashes in on the recovery of sovereignty through disaster. Not only is the canyon now accessible to the remnant: The members of the remnant are now accessible to each other; a whole new ensemble of relations becomes possible — friendship, love, hatred, clandestine sexual adventures. In a movie when a man sits next to a woman on a bus, it is necessary either that the bus break down or that the woman lose her memory. (The question occurs to one: Do you imagine there are sightseers who see sights just as they are supposed to? a family who live in Terre Haute, who decide to take the canyon tour, who go there, see it, enjoy it immensely, and go home content? a family who are entirely innocent of all the barriers, zones, losses of sovereignty I have been talking about? Wouldn't most people be sorry if Battleship Point fell into the canyon, carrying all one's fellow passengers to their death, leaving one alone on the South Rim? I cannot answer this. Perhaps there are such people. Certainly a great many American families would swear they had no such problems, that they came, saw, and went away happy. Yet it is just these families who would be happiest if they had gotten the Inside Track and been among the surviving remnant.)

It is now apparent that as between the many measures which may be taken to overcome the opacity, the boredom, of the direct confrontation of the thing or creature in its citadel of symbolic investiture, some are less authentic than others. That is to say, some stratagems obviously serve other purposes than that of providing access to being — for example, various unconscious motivations which it is not necessary to go into here.

Let us take an example in which the recovery of being is ambiguous, where it may under the same circumstances contain both authentic and unauthentic components. An American couple, we will say, drives down into Mexico. They see the usual sights and have a fair time of it. Yet they are never without the sense of missing something. Although Taxco and Cuernavaca are interesting and picturesque as advertised, they fall short of "it." What do the couple have in mind by "it"? What do they really hope for? What sort of experience could they have in Mexico so that upon their return, they would feel that "it" had happened? We have a clue: Their hope has something to do with their own role as tourists in a foreign country and the way in which they conceive this role. It has something to do with other American tourists. Certainly they feel that they are very far from "it" when, after traveling five thousand miles, they arrive at the plaza in Guanajuato only to find themselves surrounded by a dozen other couples from the Midwest.

Already we may distinguish authentic and unauthentic elements. First, we see the problem the couple faces and we understand their efforts to surmount it. The problem is to find an "unspoiled" place. "Unspoiled" does not mean only that a place is left physically intact; it means also that it is not encrusted by renown and by the familiar (as in Taxco), that it has not been discovered by others. We understand that the couple really want to get at the place and enjoy it. Yet at the same time we wonder if there is not something wrong in their dislike of their compatriots. Does access to the place require the exclusion of others?

Let us see what happens.   20

The couple decide to drive from Guanajuato to Mexico City. On the way they get lost. After hours on a rocky mountain road, they find themselves in a tiny valley not even marked on the map. There they discover an Indian village. Some sort of religious festival is going on. It is apparently a corn dance in supplication of the rain god.

The couple know at once that this is "it." They are entranced. They spend several days in the village, observing the Indians and being themselves observed with friendly curiosity.

Now may we not say that the sightseers have at last come face to face with an authentic sight, a sight which is charming, quaint, picturesque, unspoiled, and that they see the sight and come away rewarded? Possibly this may occur. Yet it is more likely that what happens is a far cry indeed from an immediate encounter with being, that the experience, while masquerading as such, is in truth a rather desperate impersonation. I use the word *desperate* advisedly to signify an actual loss of hope.

The clue to the spuriousness of their enjoyment of the village and the festival is a certain restiveness in the sightseers themselves. It is given expression by their repeated exclamations that "this is too good to be true," and by their anxiety that it may not prove to be so perfect, and finally by their downright relief at leaving the valley and having the experience in the bag, so to speak — that is, safely embalmed in memory and movie film.

What is the source of their anxiety during the visit? Does it not mean   25 that the couple are looking at the place with a certain standard of performance in mind? Are they like Fabre,[2] who gazed at the world about him with wonder, letting it be what it is; or are they not like the overanxious mother who sees her child as one performing, now doing badly, now doing well? The village is their child and their love for it is an anxious love because they are afraid that at any moment it might fail them.

We have another clue in their subsequent remark to an ethnologist friend. "How we wished you had been there with us! What a perfect goldmine of folkways! Every minute we would say to each other, if only you were here! You must return with us." This surely testifies to a generosity of spirit, a willingness to share their experience with others, not at all like their feelings toward their fellow Iowans on the plaza at Guanajuato!

I am afraid this is not the case at all. It is true that they longed for their ethnologist friend, but it was for an entirely different reason. They wanted him, not to share their experience, but to certify their experience as genuine.

"This is it" and "Now we are really living" do not necessarily refer to the sovereign encounter of the person with the sight that enlivens the mind and gladdens the heart. It means that now at last we are having the acceptable experience. The present experience is always measured by a prototype, the "it" of their dreams. "Now I am really living" means that now I am filling the role of sightseer and the sight is living up to the prototype of sights. This quaint and picturesque village is measured by a Platonic ideal of the Quaint and the Picturesque.

Hence their anxiety during the encounter. For at any minute something could go wrong. A fellow Iowan might emerge from a 'dobe hut; the chief might show them his Sears catalogue. (If the failures are "wrong" enough, as these are, they might still be turned to account as rueful conversation pieces: "There we were expecting the chief to bring us a churinga and he shows up with a Sears catalogue!") They have snatched victory from disaster, but their experience always runs the danger of failure.

They need the ethnologist to certify their experience as genuine. This is   30 borne out by their behavior when the three of them return for the next corn dance. During the dance, the couple do not watch the goings-on; instead they watch the ethnologist! Their highest hope is that their friend should find the dance interesting. And if he should show signs of true absorption, an interest in the goings-on so powerful that he becomes oblivious of his friends — then their cup is full. "Didn't we tell you?" they say at last. What

---

[2]*Fabre:* Jean-Henri Fabre (1823–1913), French scientist who wrote numerous books on insects (*The Life of the Fly, The Life of the Spider,* etc.) based on careful observation. — Eds.

they want from him is not ethnological explanations; all they want is his approval.

What has taken place is a radical loss of sovereignty over that which is as much theirs as it is the ethnologist's. The fault does not lie with the ethnologist. He has no wish to stake a claim to the village; in fact, he desires the opposite: He will bore his friends to death by telling them about the village and the meaning of the folkways. A degree of sovereignty has been surrendered by the couple. It is the nature of the loss, moreover, that they are not aware of the loss, beyond a certain uneasiness. (Even if they read this and admitted it, it would be very difficult for them to bridge the gap in their confrontation of the world. Their consciousness of the corn dance cannot escape their consciousness of their consciousness, so that with the onset of the first direct enjoyment, their higher consciousness pounces and certifies: "Now you are doing it! Now you are really living!" and, in certifying the experience, sets it at nought.)

Their basic placement in the world is such that they recognize a priority of title of the expert over his particular department of being. The whole horizon of being is staked out by "them," the experts. The highest satisfaction of the sightseer (not merely the tourist but any layman seer of sights) is that his sight should be certified as genuine. The worst of this impoverishment is that there is no sense of impoverishment. The surrender of title is so complete that it never even occurs to one to reassert title. A poor man may envy the rich man, but the sightseer does not envy the expert. When a caste system becomes absolute, envy disappears. Yet the caste of layman-expert is not the fault of the expert. It is due altogether to the eager surrender of sovereignty by the layman so that he may take up the role not of the person but of the consumer.

I do not refer only to the special relation of layman to theorist. I refer to the general situation in which sovereignty is surrendered to a class of privileged knowers, whether these be theorists or artists. A reader may surrender sovereignty over that which has been written about, just as a consumer may surrender sovereignty over a thing which has been theorized about. The consumer is content to receive an experience just as it has been presented to him by theorists and planners. The reader may also be content to judge life by whether it has or has not been formulated by those who know and write about life. A young man goes to France. He too has a fair time of it, sees the sights, enjoys the food. On his last day, in fact as he sits in a restaurant in Le Havre waiting for his boat, something happens. A group of French students in the restaurant get into an impassioned argument over a recent play. A riot takes place. Madame la concierge joins in, swinging her mop at the rioters. Our young American is transported. This is "it." And he had almost left France without seeing "it"!

But the young man's delight is ambiguous. On the one hand, it is a pleasure for him to encounter the same Gallic temperament he had heard about from Puccini and Rolland.[3] But on the other hand, the source of his pleasure testifies to a certain alienation. For the young man is actually barred from a direct encounter with anything French excepting only that which has been set forth, authenticated by Puccini and Rolland — those who know. If he had encountered the restaurant scene without reading Hemingway, without knowing that the performance was so typically, charmingly French, he would not have been delighted. He would only have been anxious at seeing things get out of hand. The source of his delight is the sanction of those who know.

This loss of sovereignty is not a marginal process, as might appear   35 from my example of estranged sightseers. It is a generalized surrender of the horizon to those experts within whose competence a particular segment of the horizon is thought to lie. Kwakiutls are surrendered to Franz Boas;[4] decaying Southern mansions are surrendered to Faulkner and Tennessee Williams. So that, although it is by no means the intention of the expert to expropriate sovereignty — in fact he would not even know what sovereignty meant in this context — the danger of theory and consumption is a seduction and deprivation of the consumer.

In the New Mexican desert, natives occasionally come across strange-looking artifacts which have fallen from the skies and which are stenciled: *Return to U.S. Experimental Project, Alamogordo. Reward.* The finder returns the object and is rewarded. He knows nothing of the nature of the object he has found and does not care to know. The sole role of the native, the highest role he can play, is that of finder and returner of the mysterious equipment.

The same is true of the layman's relation to *natural* objects in a modern technical society. No matter what the object or event is, whether it is a star, a swallow, a Kwakiutl, a "psychological phenomenon," the layman who confronts it does not confront it as a sovereign person, as Crusoe confronts a seashell he finds on the beach. The highest role he can conceive himself as playing is to be able to recognize the title of the object, to return it to the appropriate expert, and have it certified as a genuine find. He does not even permit himself to see the thing — as Gerard Hopkins[5] could see a rock or a cloud or a field. If anyone asks him why he doesn't look, he may reply that he didn't take that subject in college (or he hasn't read Faulkner).

This loss of sovereignty extends even to oneself. There is the neurotic who asks nothing more of his doctor than that his symptoms should prove interesting. When all else fails, the poor fellow has nothing to offer but his own neurosis. But even this is sufficient if only the doctor will show interest

[3]***Puccini:*** Giacomo Puccini (1853–1924), the Italian composer of such well-known operas as *La Bohème* (1896) and *Madame Butterfly* (1904); ***Rolland:*** Romain Rolland (1866–1944), Nobel-prize-winning French novelist and dramatist. — Eds.

[4]***Boas:*** Franz Boas (1858–1942), influential German-born American anthropologist who specialized in the languages of and cultures of Native Americans; in 1886 he began studying the Kwakiutl tribe of British Columbia. — Eds.

[5]***Hopkins:*** Gerard Manley Hopkins (1844–1889), English poet admired for his observations of nature and his innovative use of rhythm and metrics. — Eds.

when he says, "Last night I had a curious sort of dream; perhaps it will be significant to one who knows about such things. It seems I was standing in a sort of alley — " (I have nothing else to offer you but my own unhappiness. Please say that it, at least, measures up, that it is a *proper* sort of unhappiness.)

II

A young Falkland Islander walking along a beach and spying a dead dogfish and going to work on it with his jackknife has, in a fashion wholly unprovided in modern educational theory, a great advantage over the Scarsdale high-school pupil who finds the dogfish on his laboratory desk. Similarly the citizen of Huxley's *Brave New World* who stumbles across a volume of Shakespeare in some vine-grown ruins and squats on a potsherd to read it is in a fairer way of getting at a sonnet than the Harvard sophomore taking English Poetry II.

The educator whose business it is to teach students biology or poetry is   40 unaware of a whole ensemble of relations which exist between the student and the dogfish and between the student and the Shakespeare sonnet. To put it bluntly: A student who has the desire to get at a dogfish or a Shakespeare sonnet may have the greatest difficulty in salvaging the creature itself from the educational package in which it is presented. The great difficulty is that he is not aware that there is a difficulty; surely, he thinks, in such a fine classroom, with such a fine textbook, the sonnet must come across! What's wrong with me?

The sonnet and the dogfish are obscured by two different processes. The sonnet is obscured by the symbolic package which is formulated not by the sonnet itself but by the *media* through which the sonnet is transmitted, the media which the educators believe for some reason to be transparent. The new textbook, the type, the smell of the page, the classroom, the aluminum windows and the winter sky, the personality of Miss Hawkins — these media which are supposed to transmit the sonnet may only succeed in transmitting themselves. It is only the hardiest and cleverest of students who can salvage the sonnet from this many-tissued package. It is only the rarest student who knows that the sonnet must be salvaged from the package. (The educator is well aware that something is wrong, that there is a fatal gap between the student's learning and the student's life: The student reads the poem, appears to understand it, and gives all the answers. But what does he recall if he should happen to read a Shakespeare sonnet twenty years later? Does he recall the poem or does he recall the smell of the page and the smell of Miss Hawkins?)

One might object, point out that Huxley's citizen reading his sonnet in the ruins and the Falkland Islander looking at his dogfish on the beach also receive them in a certain package. Yes, but the difference lies in the fundamental placement of the student in the world, a placement which makes it possible to extract the thing from the package. The pupil at Scarsdale High sees himself placed as a consumer receiving an experience-package; but the Falkland Islander exploring his dogfish is a person exercising the sovereign right of a person in his lordship and mastery of creation. He too could use an instructor and a book and a technique, but he would use them as his subordinates, just as he uses his jackknife. The biology student does not use his scalpel as an instrument; he uses it as a magic wand! Since it is a "scientific instrument," it should do "scientific things."

The dogfish is concealed in the same symbolic package as the sonnet. But the dogfish suffers an additional loss. As a consequence of this double deprivation, the Sarah Lawrence student who scores A in zoology is apt to know very little about a dogfish. She is twice removed from the dogfish, once by the symbolic complex by which the dogfish is concealed, once again by the spoliation of the dogfish by theory which renders it invisible. Through no fault of zoology instructors, it is nevertheless a fact that the zoology laboratory at Sarah Lawrence College is one of the few places in the world where it is all but impossible to see a dogfish.

The dogfish, the tree, the seashell, the American Negro, the dream, are rendered invisible by a shift of reality from concrete thing to theory which Whitehead[6] has called the fallacy of misplaced concreteness. It is the mistaking of an idea, a principle, an abstraction, for the real. As a consequence of the shift, the "specimen" is seen as less real than the theory of the specimen. As Kierkegaard[7] said, once a person is seen as a specimen of a race or a species, at that very moment he ceases to be an individual. Then there are no more individuals but only specimens.

To illustrate: A student enters a laboratory which, in the pragmatic view, offers the student the optimum conditions under which an educational experience may be had. In the existential view, however — that view of the student in which he is regarded not as a receptacle of experience but as a knowing being whose peculiar property it is to see himself as being in a certain situation — the modern laboratory could not have been more effectively designed to conceal the dogfish forever. 45

The student comes to his desk. On it, neatly arranged by his instructor, he finds his laboratory manual, a dissecting board, instruments, and a mimeographed list:

Exercise 22: Materials
1 dissecting board
1 scalpel
1 forceps
1 probe
1 bottle india ink and syringe
1 specimen of *Squalus acanthias*

---

[6]*Whitehead:* Alfred North Whitehead (1861–1947), prominent British philosopher and mathematician. — EDS.
[7]*Kierkegaard:* Sören Aabye Kierkegaard (1813–1855), Danish philosopher and theologian. — EDS.

The clue to the situation in which the student finds himself is to be found in the last item: 1 specimen of *Squalus acanthias*.

The phrase *specimen of* expresses in the most succinct way imaginable the radical character of the loss of being which has occurred under his very nose. To refer to the dogfish, the unique concrete existent before him, as a "specimen of *Squalus acanthias*" reveals by its grammar the spoliation of the dogfish by the theoretical method. This phrase, *specimen of,* example of, instance of, indicates the ontological status of the individual creature in the eyes of the theorist. The dogfish itself is seen as a rather shabby expression of an ideal reality, the species *Squalus acanthias*. The result is the radical devaluation of the individual dogfish. (The *reductio ad absurdum*[8] of Whitehead's shift is Toynbee's[9] employment of it in his historical method. If a gram of NaCl is referred to by the chemist as a "sample of" NaCl, one may think of it as such and not much is missed by the oversight of the act of being of this particular pinch of salt, but when the Jews, and the Jewish religion are understood as — in Toynbee's favorite phrase — a "classical example of" such and such a kind of *Voelkerwanderung*,[10] we begin to suspect that something is being left out.)

If we look into the ways in which the student can recover the dogfish (or the sonnet), we will see that they have in common the stratagem of avoiding the educator's direct presentation of the object as a lesson to be learned and restoring access to sonnet and dogfish as beings to be known, reasserting the sovereignty of knower over known.

In truth, the biography of scientists and poets is usually the story of the discovery of the indirect approach, the circumvention of the educator's presentation — the young man who was sent to the *Technikum*[11] and on his way fell into the habit of loitering in book stores and reading poetry; or the young man dutifully attending law school who on the way became curious about the comings and goings of ants. One remembers the scene in *The Heart Is a Lonely Hunter*[12] where the girl hides in the bushes to hear the Capehart in the big house play Beethoven. Perhaps she was the lucky one after all. Think of the unhappy souls inside, who see the record, worry about scratches, and most of all worry about whether they are *getting it*, whether they are bona fide music lovers. What is the best way to hear Beethoven: sitting in a proper silence around the Capehart or eavesdropping from an azalea bush?

However it may come about, we notice two traits of the second situa-

---

[8]*reductio ad absurdum:* "A reduction to absurdity" (Latin); the argumentative method by which one shows that a statement carried to its logical conclusion leads to an absurdity. — EDS.

[9]*Toynbee:* Arnold Toynbee (1889–1975), British historian who believed that civilizations were formed out of responses to adversity. — EDS.

[10]*Voelkerwanderung:* Barbarian invasion (German). — EDS.

[11]*Technikum:* Technical school (German). — EDS.

[12]*The Heart Is a Lonely Hunter:* A 1940 novel by Carson McCullers (1917–1967). — EDS.

tion: (1) an openness of the thing before one — instead of being an exercise to be learned according to an approved mode, it is a garden of delights which beckons to one; (2) a sovereignty of the knower — instead of being a consumer of a prepared experience, I am a sovereign wayfarer, a wanderer in the neighborhood of being who stumbles into the garden.

One can think of two sorts of circumstances through which the thing may be restored to the person. (There is always, of course, the direct recovery: A student may simply be strong enough, brave enough, clever enough to take the dogfish and the sonnet by storm, to wrest control of it from the educators and the educational package.) First by ordeal: The Bomb falls; when the young man recovers consciousness in the shambles of the biology laboratory, there not ten inches from his nose lies the dogfish. Now all at once he can see it, directly and without let,[13] just as the exile or the prisoner or the sick man sees the sparrow at his window in all its inexhaustibility; just as the commuter who has had a heart attack sees his own hand for the first time. In these cases, the simulacrum of everydayness and of consumption has been destroyed by disaster; in the case of the bomb, literally destroyed. Secondly, by apprenticeship to a great man: One day a great biologist walks into the laboratory; he stops in front of our student's desk; he leans over, picks up the dogfish, and ignoring instruments and procedure, probes with a broken fingernail into the little carcass. "Now here is a curious business," he says, ignoring also the proper jargon of the specialty. "Look here how this little duct reverses its direction and drops into the pelvis. Now if you would look into a coelacanth, you would see that it — " And all at once the student can see. The technician and the sophomore who loves his textbooks are always offended by the genuine research man because the latter is usually a little vague and always humble before the thing; he doesn't have much use for the equipment or the jargon. Whereas the technician is never vague and never humble before the thing; he holds the thing disposed of by the principle, the formula, the textbook outline; and he thinks a great deal of equipment and jargon.

But since neither of these methods of recovering the dogfish is pedagogically feasible — perhaps the great man even less so than the Bomb — I wish to propose the following educational technique which should prove equally effective for Harvard and Shreveport High School. I propose that English poetry and biology should be taught as usual, but that at irregular intervals, poetry students should find dogfishes on their desks and biology students should find Shakespeare sonnets on their dissection boards. I am serious in declaring that a Sarah Lawrence English major who began poking about in a dogfish with a bobby pin would learn more in thirty minutes than a biology major in a whole semester; and that the latter upon reading on her dissecting board

---

[13]*let:* Hindrance. Used here in its older sense: The dogfish is seen "without hindrance." Related to the tennis call "let ball," meaning the net interfered with (hindered) the ball. — EDS.

That time of year Thou may'st in me behold
When yellow leaves, or none, or few, do hang
Upon those boughs which shake against the cold —
Bare ruin'd choirs where late the sweet birds sang.[14]

might catch fire at the beauty of it.

The situation of the tourist at the Grand Canyon and the biology student are special cases of a predicament in which everyone finds himself in a modern technical society — a society, that is, in which there is a division between expert and layman, planner and consumer, in which experts and planners take special measures to teach and edify the consumer. The measures taken are measures appropriate to the consumer: The expert and the planner *know* and *plan,* but the consumer *needs* and *experiences.*

There is a double deprivation. First, the thing is lost through its packaging. The very means by which the thing is presented for consumption, the very techniques by which the thing is made available as an item of need-satisfaction, these very means operate to remove the thing from the sovereignty of the knower. A loss of title occurs. The measures which the museum curator takes to present the thing to the public are self-liquidating. The upshot of the curator's efforts are not that everyone can see the exhibit but that no one can see it. The curator protests: Why are they so indifferent? Why do they even deface the exhibit? Don't they know it is theirs? But it is not theirs. It is his, the curator's. By the most exclusive sort of zoning, the museum exhibit, the park oak tree, is part of an ensemble, a package, which is almost impenetrable to them. The archaeologist who puts his find in a museum so that everyone can see it accomplishes the reverse of his expectations. The result of his action is that no one can see it now but the archaeologist. He would have done better to keep it in his pocket and show it now and then to strangers.

The tourist who carves his initials in a public place, which is theoretically "his" in the first place, has good reasons for doing so, reasons which the exhibitor and planner know nothing about. He does so because in his role of consumer of an experience (a "recreational experience" to satisfy a "recreational need") he knows that he is disinherited. He is deprived of his title over being. He knows very well that he is in a very special sort of zone in which his only rights are the rights of a consumer. He moves like a ghost through schoolroom, city streets, trains, parks, movies. He carves his initials as a last desperate measure to escape his ghostly role of consumer. He is saying in effect: I am not a ghost after all; I am a sovereign person. And he establishes title the only way remaining to him, by staking his claim over one square inch of wood or stone.

Does this mean that we should get rid of museums? No, but it means

55

that the sightseer should be prepared to enter into a struggle to recover a sight from a museum.

The second loss is the spoliation of the thing, the tree, the rock, the swallow, by the layman's misunderstanding of scientific theory. He believes that the thing is *disposed of* by theory, that it stands in the Platonic relation of being a *specimen of* such and such an underlying principle. In the transmission of scientific theory from theorist to layman, the expectation of the theorist is reversed. Instead of the marvels of the universe being made available to the public, the universe is disposed of by theory. The loss of sovereignty takes this form: As a result of the science of botany, trees are not made available to every man. On the contrary. The tree loses its proper density and mystery as a concrete existent and, as merely another *specimen of* a species, becomes itself nugatory.

Does this mean that there is no use taking biology at Harvard and Shreveport High? No, but it means that the student should know what a fight he has on his hands to rescue the specimen from the educational package. The educator is only partly to blame. For there is nothing the educator can do to provide for this need of the student. Everything the educator does only succeeds in becoming, for the student, part of the educational package. The highest role of the educator is the maieutic role of Socrates: to help the student come to himself not as a consumer of experience but as a sovereign individual.

The thing is twice lost to the consumer. First, sovereignty is lost: It is theirs, not his. Second, it is radically devalued by theory. This is a loss which has been brought about by science but through no fault of the scientist and through no fault of scientific theory. The loss has come about as a consequence of the seduction of the layman by science. The layman will be seduced as long as he regards beings as consumer items to be experienced rather than prizes to be won, and as long as he waives his sovereign rights as a person and accepts his role of consumer as the highest estate to which the layman can aspire.

As Mounier said, the person is not something one can study and provide for; he is something one struggles for. But unless he also struggles for himself, unless he knows that there is a struggle, he is going to be just what the planners think he is.

1975

The Reader's Presence

1. Walker Percy's essay is about the difficulties of seeing the world around us. At the beginning of paragraph 5, Percy asks: "Why is it almost impossible to gaze directly at the Grand Canyon under these circumstances and see it for what it is . . . because the Grand Canyon . . . has been appropriated by the symbolic complex

which has already been formed in the sightseer's mind." What does he mean when he talks about "these circumstances" and "the symbolic complex"? In the next sentence Percy mentions seeing the Grand Canyon "under approved circumstances." What does he mean here, and how does he extend this point beyond seeing to learning as well?

2. What would you identify as Percy's overall purpose in writing this essay? Where does he announce this purpose? With what terms? Consider Percy's diction. From what sources does he derive his vocabulary? What, for example, do such terms as *authenticity, appropriation, expropriate,* and *sovereignty* have in common? What point of view does he express about each of these terms and, more generally, about seeing the world directly? How would you characterize Percy's tone of voice in this essay? Is it, for example, pessimistic or optimistic? What attitude does he finally express about the individual's ability to discover and/or recover the world? Where is this theme of discovery and recovery first introduced in the essay? How is it developed?

3. Outline the structure of Percy's essay. In what specific ways does the structure of the first part of his essay reappear in the second part? What is the general subject of the second part, and how does Percy connect it to the subject of the first part? Percy builds his case for experiencing the world first-hand by exploring a series of examples. Work through several of these examples, and show how they not only support the points he makes but eventually take on a life of their own. Consider, for example, the moment in paragraph 53 when he announces: "I propose that English poetry and biology should be taught as usual, but that at irregular intervals, poetry students should find dogfishes on their desks and biology students should find Shakespeare sonnets on their dissection boards." What sense do you make of this statement? How does it represent Percy's attitude about education? about seeing the world?

50

Ishmael Reed

America: The Multinational Society

> At the annual Lower East Side Jewish Festival yesterday, a Chinese
> woman ate a pizza slice in front of Ty Thuan Duc's Vietnamese gro-
> cery store. Beside her a Spanish-speaking family patronized a cart
> with two signs: "Italian Ices" and "Kosher by Rabbi Alper." And
> after the pastrami ran out, everybody ate knishes.
> — *NEW YORK TIMES,* 23 June 1983

On the day before Memorial Day, 1983, a poet called me to describe a
city he had just visited. He said that one section included mosques, built by
the Islamic people who dwelled there. Attending his reading, he said, were
large numbers of Hispanic people, forty thousand of whom lived in the
same city. He was not talking about a fabled city located in some mysterious region of the world. The city he'd visited was Detroit.

A few months before, as I was leaving Houston, Texas, I heard it announced on the radio that Texas's largest minority was Mexican-American,
and though a foundation recently issued a report critical of bilingual education, the taped voice used to guide the passengers on the air trams con-
necting terminals in Dallas Airport is in both Spanish and English. If the
trend continues, a day will come when it will be difficult to travel through
some sections of the country without hearing commands in both English
and Spanish; after all, for some western states, Spanish was the first written
language and the Spanish style lives on in the western way of life.

Shortly after my Texas trip, I sat in an auditorium located on the campus of the University of Wisconsin at Milwaukee as a Yale professor —
whose original work on the influence of African cultures upon those of the
Americas has led to his ostracism from some monocultural intellectual circles — walked up and down the aisle, like an old-time southern evangelist,

For biographical information on Ishmael Reed, see p. 660.

dancing and drumming the top of the lectern, illustrating his points before some serious Afro-American intellectuals and artists who cheered and applauded his performance and his mastery of information. The professor was "white." After his lecture, he joined a group of Milwaukeeans in a conversation. All of the participants spoke Yoruban, though only the professor had ever traveled to Africa.

One of the artists told me that his paintings, which included African and Afro-American mythological symbols and imagery, were hanging in the local McDonald's restaurant. The next day I went to McDonald's and snapped pictures of smiling youngsters eating hamburgers below paintings that could grace the walls of any of the country's leading museums. The manager of the local McDonald's said, "I don't know what you boys are doing, but I like it," as he commissioned the local painters to exhibit in his restaurant.

Such blurring of cultural styles occurs in everyday life in the United   5
States to a greater extent than anyone can imagine and is probably more prevalent than the sensational conflict between people of different backgrounds that is played up and often encouraged by the media. The result is what the Yale professor Robert Thompson referred to as a cultural bouillabaisse, yet members of the nation's present educational and cultural Elect still cling to the notion that the United States belongs to some vaguely defined entity they refer to as "Western civilization," by which they mean, presumably, a civilization created by the people of Europe, as if Europe can be viewed in monolithic terms. Is Beethoven's Ninth Symphony, which includes Turkish marches, a part of Western civilization, or the late nineteenth- and twentieth-century French paintings, whose creators were influenced by Japanese art? And what of the cubists, through whom the influence of African art changed modern painting, or the surrealists, who were so impressed with the art of the Pacific Northwest Indians that, in their map of North America, Alaska dwarfs the lower forty-eight in size?

Are the Russians, who are often criticized for their adoption of "Western" ways by Tsarist dissidents in exile, members of Western civilization? And what of the millions of Europeans who have black African and Asian ancestry, black Africans having occupied several countries for hundreds of years? Are these "Europeans" members of Western civilization, or the Hungarians, who originated across the Urals in a place called Greater Hungary, or the Irish, who came from the Iberian Peninsula?

Even the notion that North America is part of Western civilization because our "system of government" is derived from Europe is being challenged by Native American historians who say that the founding fathers, Benjamin Franklin especially, were actually influenced by the system of government that had been adopted by the Iroquois hundreds of years prior to the arrival of large numbers of Europeans.

Western civilization, then, becomes another confusing category like Third World, or Judeo-Christian culture, as man attempts to impose his small-screen view of political and cultural reality upon a complex world.

Our most publicized novelist recently said that Western civilization was the greatest achievement of mankind, an attitude that flourishes on the street level as scribbles in public restrooms: "White Power," "Niggers and Spics Suck," or "Hitler was a prophet," the latter being the most telling, for wasn't Adolph Hitler the archetypal monoculturalist who, in his pigheaded arrogance, believed that one way and one blood was so pure that it had to be protected from alien strains at all costs? Where did such an attitude, which has caused so much misery and depression in our national life, which has tainted even our noblest achievements, begin? An attitude that caused the incarceration of Japanese-American citizens during World War II, the persecution of Chicanos and Chinese-Americans, the near-extermination of the Indians, and murder and lynchings of thousands of Afro-Americans.

Virtuous, hard-working, pious, even though they occasionally would wander off after some fancy clothes, or rendezvous in the woods with the town prostitute, the Puritans are idealized in our schoolbooks as "a hardy band" of no-nonsense patriarchs whose discipline razed the forest and brought order to the New World (a term that annoys Native American historians). Industrious, responsible, it was their "Yankee ingenuity" and practicality that created the work ethic. They were simple folk who produced a number of good poets, and they set the tone for the American writing style, of lean and spare lines, long before Hemingway. They worshiped in churches whose colors blended in with the New England snow, churches with simple structures and ornate lecterns.

The Puritans were a daring lot, but they had a mean streak. They hated 10
the theater and banned Christmas. They punished people in a cruel and inhuman manner. They killed children who disobeyed their parents. When they came in contact with those whom they considered heathens or aliens, they behaved in such a bizarre and irrational manner that this chapter in the American history comes down to us as a late-movie horror film. They exterminated the Indians, who taught them how to survive in a world unknown to them, and their encounter with the calypso culture of Barbados resulted in what the tourist guide in Salem's Witches' House refers to as the Witchcraft Hysteria.

The Puritan legacy of hard work and meticulous accounting led to the establishment of a great industrial society; it is no wonder that the American industrial revolution began in Lowell, Massachusetts, but there was the other side, the strange and paranoid attitudes toward those different from the Elect.

The cultural attitudes of that early Elect continue to be voiced in every-day life in the United States: the president of a distinguished university, writing a letter to the *Times,* belittling the study of African civilizations; the television network that promoted its show on the Vatican art with the boast that this art represented "the finest achievement of the human spirit." A modern up-tempo state of complex rhythms that depends upon contacts with an international community can no longer behave as if it dwelled in a "Zion Wilderness" surrounded by beasts and pagans.

When I heard a schoolteacher warn the other night about the invasion of the American educational system by foreign curriculums, I wanted to yell at the television set, "Lady, they're already here." It has already begun because the world is here. The world has been arriving at these shores for at least ten thousand years from Europe, Africa, and Asia. In the late nineteenth and early twentieth centuries, large numbers of Europeans arrived, adding their cultures to those of the European, African, and Asian settlers who were already here, and recently millions have been entering the country from South America and the Caribbean, making Yale Professor Bob Thompson's bouillabaisse richer and thicker.

One of our most visionary politicians said that he envisioned a time when the United States could become the brain of the world, by which he meant the repository of all of the latest advanced information systems. I thought of that remark when an enterprising poet friend of mine called to say that he had just sold a poem to a computer magazine and that the editors were delighted to get it because they didn't carry fiction or poetry. Is that the kind of world we desire? A humdrum homogeneous world of all brains and no heart, no fiction, no poetry; a world of robots with human attendants bereft of imagination, of culture? Or does North America deserve a more exciting destiny? To become a place where the cultures of the world crisscross. This is possible because the United States is unique in the world: The world is here.

1988

The Reader's Presence

1. Examine Reed's opening paragraph. How does he set it up to be a surprise? What is the surprise? How does it reinforce the main theme of his essay? Were you surprised?

2. As an exercise in reading, try this experiment. Choose a significant paragraph of the essay and place a plus sign (+) above every word or phrase you think Reed is using positively. Then put a minus sign (–) above every word he uses negatively. Do this for several paragraphs and see how certain positive and negative terms cluster. To what extent do these words have positive or negative meanings in general speech? To what extent does Reed give them their positive or negative connotations? Why does a word we often use negatively, such as *blurring* (paragraph 5), have positive connotations in this context? (Note: This simple exercise can be applied to any piece of reading you do, and it often produces interesting results.)

3. Reed ends his essay by saying that "The world is here." What does he mean by this assertion? To what extent do you think he has proved it? If what he says is true, then how would you define the specific problem his essay appears to be addressing?

51

Phyllis Rose

Shopping and Other Spiritual Adventures in America Today

Last year a new Waldbaum's Food Mart opened in the shopping mall on Route 66. It belongs to the new generation of superduper-markets open twenty-four hours that have computerized checkout. I went to see the place as soon as it opened and I was impressed. There was trail mix in Lucite bins. There was freshly made pasta. There were coffee beans, four kinds of tahini, ten kinds of herb teas, raw shrimp in shells and cooked shelled shrimp, fresh-squeezed orange juice. Every sophistication known to the big city, even goat's cheese covered with ash, was now available in Middletown, Conn. People raced from the warehouse aisle to the bagel bin to the coffee beans to the fresh fish market, exclaiming at all the new things. Many of us felt elevated, graced, complimented by the presence of this food palace in our town.

This is the wonderful egalitarianism of American business. Was it Andy Warhol who said that the nice thing about Coke is, no can is any better or worse than any other? Some people may find it dull to cross the country and find the same chain stores with the same merchandise from coast to coast, but it means that my town is as good as yours, my shopping mall as important as yours, equally filled with wonders.

Imagine what people ate during the winter as little as seventy-five years ago. They ate food that was local, long-lasting, and dull, like acorn squash, turnips, and cabbage. Walk into an American supermarket in February and the world lies before you: grapes, melons, artichokes, fennel, lettuce, peppers, pistachios, dates, even strawberries, to say nothing of ice cream. Have you ever considered what a triumph of civilization it is to be able to buy a

For biographical information on Phyllis Rose, see p. 661.

pound of chicken livers? If you lived on a farm and had to kill a chicken when you wanted to eat one, you wouldn't ever accumulate a pound of chicken livers.

Another wonder of Middletown is Caldor, the discount department store. Here is man's plenty: tennis racquets, panty hose, luggage, glassware, records, toothpaste. Timex watches, Cadbury's chocolate, corn poppers, hair dryers, warm-up suits, car wax, light bulbs, television sets. All good quality at low prices with exchanges cheerfully made on defective goods. There are worse rules to live by. I feel good about America whenever I walk into this store, which is almost every midwinter Sunday afternoon, when life elsewhere has closed down. I go to Caldor the way English people go to pubs: out of sociability. To get away from my house. To widen my horizons. For culture's sake. Caldor provides me too with a welcome sense of seasonal change. When the first outdoor grills and lawn furniture appear there, it's as exciting a sign of spring as the first crocus or robin.

Someone told me about a Soviet emigré who practices English by   5
declaiming, at random, sentences that catch his fancy. One of his favorites is, "Fifty percent off all items today only." Refugees from Communist countries appreciate our supermarkets and discount department stores for the wonders they are. An Eastern European scientist visiting Middletown wept when she first saw the meat counter at Waldbaum's. On the other hand, before her year in America was up, her pleasure turned sour. She wanted everything she saw. Her approach to consumer goods was insufficiently abstract, too materialistic. We Americans are beyond a simple, possessive materialism. We're used to abundance and the possibility of possessing things. The things, and the possibility of possessing them, will still be there next week, next year. So today we can walk the aisles calmly.

It is a misunderstanding of the American retail store to think we go there necessarily to buy. Some of us shop. There's a difference. Shopping has many purposes, the least interesting of which is to acquire new articles. We shop to cheer ourselves up. We shop to practice decision-making. We shop to be useful and productive members of our class and society. We shop to remind ourselves how much is available to us. We shop to remind ourselves how much is to be striven for. We shop to assert our superiority to the material objects that spread themselves before us.

Shopping's function as a form of therapy is widely appreciated. You don't really need, let's say, another sweater. You need the feeling of power that comes with buying or not buying it. You need the feeling that someone wants something you have — even if it's just your money. To get the benefit of shopping, you needn't actually purchase the sweater, any more than you have to marry every man you flirt with. In fact, window-shopping, like flirting, can be more rewarding, the same high without the distressing commitment, the material encumbrance. The purest form of shopping is provided by garage sales. A connoisseur goes out with no goal in mind, open to whatever may come his or her way, secure that it will cost very little. Minimum expense, maximum experience. Perfect shopping.

I try to think of the opposite, a kind of shopping in which the object is all-important, the pleasure of shopping at a minimum. For example, the purchase of blue jeans. I buy new blue jeans as seldom as possible because the experience is so humiliating. For every pair that looks good on me, fifteen look grotesque. But even shopping for blue jeans at Bob's Surplus on Main Street — no frills, bare-bones shopping — is an event in the life of the spirit. Once again I have to come to terms with the fact that I will never look good in Levi's. Much as I want to be mainstream, I never will be.

In fact, I'm doubly an oddball, neither Misses nor Junior, but Misses Petite. I look in the mirror, I acknowledge the disparity between myself and the ideal, I resign myself to making the best of it: I will buy the Lee's Misses Petite. Shopping is a time of reflection, assessment, spiritual self-discipline.

It is appropriate, I think, that Bob's Surplus has a communal dressing   10
room. I used to shop only in places where I could count on a private dressing room with a mirror inside. My impulse then was to hide my weaknesses. Now I believe in sharing them. There are other women in the dressing room at Bob's Surplus trying on blue jeans who look as bad as I do. We take comfort from one another. Sometimes a woman will ask me which of two items looks better. I always give a definite answer. It's the least I can do. I figure we are all in this together, and I emerge from the dressing room not only with a new pair of jeans but with a renewed sense of belonging to a human community.

When a Solzhenitsyn rants about American materialism, I have to look at my digital Timex and check what year this is. Materialism? Like conformism, a hot moral issue of the fifties, but not now. How to spread the goods, maybe. Whether the goods are the Good, no. Solzhenitsyn, like the visiting scientist who wept at the beauty of Waldbaum's meat counter but came to covet everything she saw, takes American materialism too materialistically. He doesn't see its spiritual side. Caldor, Waldbaum's, Bob's Surplus — these, perhaps, are our cathedrals.

1987

The Reader's Presence

1. Consider the title of Phyllis Rose's essay. How seriously do you
   think her readers should take the title before they read her essay?
   after they have finished it? In what specific ways is shopping "a
   spiritual adventure"? What other examples of spiritual language
   can you locate in the essay? What effects does such language elicit
   from Rose's readers? How would you characterize the other

sources of diction Rose draws on to create these lasting impressions of the pleasures — and the frustrations — of shopping? Comment on the role irony plays in her essay. How, finally, would you characterize Rose's own attitude, the nature of her presence, in this essay?

2. From what point of view is this essay presented? When — and how — is this made a matter of gender? In what ways does Rose account for a masculine view of shopping? At the beginning of paragraph 2, Rose praises "the wonderful egalitarianism of American business." What examples does she use to validate and develop this point? What does she tell us are the various functions of shopping? What purposes does it serve in contemporary American culture? What does she mean when she reports that the response of Eastern Europeans to shopping "was insufficiently abstract"?

3. Consider the purposes and effects of Rose's litany of the names of American department stores, the lists of goods available there, and their trademarks. How would you characterize the sound of her voice in these moments? Consider, for example, the opening paragraph. Reread it, this time aloud. Where have you heard this kind of language, this tone of voice before? How does the sound of the speaker's voice in the opening paragraph anticipate the last line of the essay? What evidence can you point to in order to support your reading of how seriously Rose's readers ought to take the closing line? In what specific ways, then, is Rose's essay a critique and/or a celebration of America's consumer culture?

52

Lynne Sharon Schwartz

Beggaring Our Better Selves

> Hark, hark, the dogs do bark! The beggars are coming to town . . .
> – MOTHER GOOSE

A family legend: New York, the Bowery, early 1950s, a man comes up to my father and asks for money for something to eat. What most Bowery beggars really want is a drink, my father knows. But food is healthier. "You're hungry? Okay, come on, I'll buy you lunch." And he does.

The story was meant to be touching — how generous my father was with time, money, wisdom — and for a long time I found it so. I could hear my father's voice, like the snapping of a finger — "Come on, I'll buy you lunch" — and picture the swift, peremptory jerk of his head in the direction of the nearest restaurant, a simple but decent place. How gallantly he led the beggar to a table, appropriating two illustrated menus coated in plastic and handing him one. "Anything you like," he would say rather grandly. Did the beggar order a substantial meal, steaming pot roast nestled in simmered carrots and onions, or something more austere, like an egg salad sandwich?

Knowing my father, I assumed they did not eat in silence. Did he use the opportunity to expound on his political views, making provocative statements, raising his voice and blood pressure? And was the beggar gregarious, eager to tell his tale of adversity, or taciturn, paying for the meal with his only abundant possession, his endurance?

Did my father finally dab sauvely at his mustache, toss down his napkin, and extend his hand for a gentlemanly parting? And how did the beggar respond to that? Alas, the story was never told as I would have liked to

For biographical information on Lynne Sharon Schwartz, see p. 662.

hear it, with each nuance of gesture and dialogue, setting and timing, the shifting underpinnings of emotion and small stirrings of heart and mind as revealed in the face and voice, all of which, to me, *were* the story, as opposed to the bare events. Still, it was a good story, despite its ambiguities.

Until many years later, that is, when I told it to my friend A. She was   5 aghast. My father's act showed the worst kind of condescension, she informed me heatedly. Giving was his free choice, but how to spend the gift was the beggar's choice. Otherwise giving is an abuse of power. An ego trip.

A. had a good case, and I was downcast, my moment of nostalgia ruined. Yet wasn't my father's behavior valid in his life and times? His own scramble for success proved that he knew how to go about things; doing good, by his lights, was scattering abroad his earned knowledge. How could I scorn him when I myself would not have given my time to an unappealing stranger? True, A. might have done it. She would have taken him to a bar, I thought bitterly.

Long after my father's episode, I happened to see, from a third-floor window, another lunch given away on the Bowery. A raggedy grizzled man shuffled northward across Delancey Street. A young black woman wearing shorts and a halter and biting into a frankfurter crossed in the opposite direction. When they met, he held out his hand, palm up. Barely breaking stride — for the light was changing and four lanes of impatient traffic would instantly engulf them — she handed him the half-eaten frankfurter. Between the north and south corners of Delancey Street the frankfurter passed from one pair of lips to another, as the milk from Rose of Sharon's breast passed to the lips of the dying man in *The Grapes of Wrath*.

Now, of course, our streets are so thick with beggars that people of my father's virtuous persuasion could take a beggar to lunch every day, ten times a day, incensing the politically correct. Or, in keeping with "lite" aesthetics, they might follow B.'s strategy: Overcome by the clamor of the hungry, she has begun fixing daily packets of sandwiches — whatever she herself is having for lunch — and hands out the neat tinfoil squares to whoever asks. "What's in it today?" one of her regulars inquired. "Peanut butter and jelly." He scowled, hesitated, but in the end accepted it indulgently, as if *she* were the beggar, asking to be relieved of the burden of good fortune.

Indeed, social roles have become so fluid that askers and givers change places with the agility of partners at a square dance. As the numbers of beggars increased, C., like B., came to loathe the impotence of his assigned role. No more awkward doling out of futile coins, he decided. He would give a significant sum every couple of weeks, like paying a bill, a sum that might make a real, if temporary, difference in a beggar's life. No class-bound judgments either: He wouldn't choose the apparently deserving or speculate on how the money might be spent. A gratuitous act, a declaration of freedom from the conventional etiquette of beggardom. The first time he tried it, the beggar looked at the bill handed to him, then up at C. "But this is twenty dollars." "Yes, I know," said C. "Hey, this is terrific! Come on, I'll take you to lunch."

Some hold that begging is a job, not one which anyone would aspire to but which a share of the population regularly does, through family tradition, lack of drive or opportunity, possibly even natural talent. George Orwell puts it best in *Down and Out in Paris and London:*

> There is no *essential* difference between a beggar's livelihood and that of numberless respectable people. Beggars do not work, it is said; but then, what is *work?* A navvy works by swinging a pick. An accountant works by adding up figures. A beggar works by standing out of doors in all weathers and getting varicose veins, chronic bronchitis, etc. It is a trade like any other; quite useless, of course — but, then, many reputable trades are quite useless . . . A beggar . . . has not, more than most modern people, sold his honour; he has merely made the mistake of choosing a trade at which it is impossible to grow rich.

But in the United States begging evokes too much shock and horror ever to be accepted as a career. The pursuit of happiness works as a command as well as a right, and part of the pursuit is ambition, labor, sweat. Then there is the famous liberal guilt at being privileged in a supposedly classless society. Above all, our horror is attached to a certain pride: We are enlightened enough to be horrified at beggary, if not enough to do anything significant about it.

Before the First World War, according to my mother's sentimental stories, hoboes turning up on her parents' doorstep were given lunch in exchange for sweeping the yard or hauling the garbage — a fairly clear and guilt-free transaction compared with begging and giving. These days few city people are at home to offer lunch — they're out doing what Orwell so disparagingly calls "work" — while those who are would hardly open their doors to a stranger.

Today's beggars baffle us. Unlike the working poor, they haven't always been with us, not lining the streets, at any rate, in such a vast and variegated array: from bedraggled to shabbily decent to casually hip; sick or drugged-out to robust; pathetic to friendly to arrogant.

To confuse matters further, not all beggars see their situation in an Orwellian light, as my friend D.'s experience illustrates. The opposite of shy, D. can say with impunity virtually anything to anybody. She marches up to the regular on her street corner and asks, "Look here, why can't a healthy, strapping young man like you get a job?" He talks about the sad state of the job market, how demoralizing it is to be turned away. "Look here," says D., undaunted, very much like my father in her certainty of what is right, "we've all had some bad luck with jobs. You've got to get back in there and keep trying." So the conversation goes. And, as in my father's time, enduring it is how the beggar earns his keep. When he feels he's put in enough time for the money, he says, "Look here, I'll decide when the vacation is over."

The beggars become an index of our state of affairs: Who we are is   15 revealed in our response. We range from openhanded A., who sets forth staunchly with a pocketful of change and gives democratically to all — "If they're desperate enough to ask . . . " — to otherwise kindly Z., who never gives because she suspects every beggar is making a fool of her. To give, she feels, is to be taken.

In themselves, A. and Z. do not represent extremes of generosity and meanness, wealth and poverty, or political left and right. A. may have more money, but Z. is far from penury. Nor is she stingy and insensitive; a therapist working in a social agency, she gives at the office, as it were. What can be read from their actions is their degree of suspicion of the world and safety in it, their reflexive response to the unexpected and unwelcome. Maybe their whole psychic structure could be discovered, had we enough data.

On my way to the supermarket recently I saw a familiar beggar approach — a tall, slender, woebegone man with watery eyes, graying hair, and neat gray clothes, whose beat was slightly to the south. Immediately came the usual and wearisome chain of thoughts. Do I have any change on me? Do I feel like it today? How am I today anyway, that is, how firm is my place in the world? — a question usually reserved for the murky insomniac hours. The unsettling thing about beggars is that, unless one has a very thick skin or, like A. and Z., a strict policy, their presence compels such questions many times a day. Like public clocks that drive compulsives to check their watches, beggars make us check our inner dials of plenitude or neediness, well-being or instability. The readings determine whether and what we give.

In the midst of my reckonings, the man passed me by without even an acknowledgment. Imagine! I was just another face in the crowd. He wasn't soliciting because he wasn't yet at work. Why assume begging is a twenty-four-hour-a-day job any more than plumbing or typing? Any more an identity than grocer or engineer? Maybe I assume it because quite a few beggars in mufti — spiffy, sprightly — stroll past with such a gracious good morning that I'm moved to answer in kind. Then, with my attention snagged, comes the touch, a mutual joke at my expense: Ha, ha, and you thought I was only being friendly.

Some in rags, and some in tags. And one in a velvet gown.

It didn't begin, this age of beggary, on an appointed day, the way Errol   20 Flynn in an old movie announced with a flourish of his sword the opening thrust of the Thirty Years' War, but sneaked up some seven or eight years ago, just as the cult of money was enjoying a passionate revival. At first people were appalled. Not here; this wasn't Calcutta, after all. There was sympathy, naturally. We stared uneasily, clucked somberly, catalogued:

young, old, black, white, male, female. Sickly and strong. Addicts? Hard to tell. In rags and tags and velvet gowns.

There was curiosity, too. The beggars offered a new genre of performance art amid other lively street phenomena, and we the audience compared offerings, whipped up impromptu reviews around our dinner tables. As with any art form, early samples ranged from the banal — I'm not really a beggar but an unemployed carpenter with five hungry children — to the memorable — pardon my odor but I have no place to take a shower like you folks. Successful beggars, like successful stand-up comics, must display uniqueness of personality in a few swift, arresting strokes. Their stories require a certain narrative flair. Verisimilitude aside, we treasure sheer inventiveness.

A justly renowned beggar works the rowdy nocturnal subway cars returning from New York's Shea Stadium during the baseball season. He enters ominously, carrying a tarnished trumpet blotched with holes. He brings it to his lips; the sound that emerges is a Dantean assault. The passengers blink and shudder, like romping children startled by an ogre. At last he mercifully lowers the trumpet and announces genially, "I'm not going to stop till you folks give me some money." A tense moment? Not at all. The crowd laughs, and gives. A good-humored crowd, they've paid for their tickets and beer and hot dogs and subway ride; they'll shell out for peace too, and for a laugh. It's part of the price of the sportive outing, a surtax. By some mad urban alchemy it is acceptable to be assailed by this grotesque noise and have to pay to make it stop. He plays a few more measures, goading the recalcitrant, then moves on to the next car to repeat the performance, becoming part of the legend of the city, O splendiferous city full of assaults and of relief, where you pay for both.

Our reactions followed a predictable trajectory. As the initial surprise wore off along with the entertainment value, as we got used to seeing beggars everywhere (but not for long, surely — whatever political glitch brought them out would soon be repaired), our interest became more defined. Refined. We found we have *tastes* in beggars as in everything else. E. will not give to those who look young and healthy, for why are they not out hustling for a living as he is? F. always gives to women because they seem more vulnerable, their lot harder to bear than men's. G. gives only outside his immediate neighborhood so as not to encourage beggars to congregate there, while H., careful of her spiritual integrity, will give only out of genuine sympathy, not to get rid of a nuisance. J. will not give to anyone who comes too close: She has strong feelings about her personal "space" being invaded. K. is too afraid to take out her purse on the street: She views beggars and, in fact, all passersby as potential thieves.

L. gives exclusively to those who ask humbly and politely. If he must be solicited and possibly "taken" (shades of Z.), he feels the beggars should at the very least make a pretense of a civil transaction, to save face all around. Anyone claiming his contribution as if by right is out of luck. If L. is not thanked, he will not give again. Sensitive M. prefers not to be thanked. "There but for the grace of God . . . ," she murmurs. She will gladly engage in non-grateful repartee, though, while N., who also shuns gratitude, wants the briefest verbal exchange: He gives willingly but cannot stomach long-winded explanations or autobiography.

Quite unlike O., who must say a few words with his donation and wants a few in return; he needs to act out an ordinary exchange between ordinary people, one of whom happens to be in straitened circumstances. P. went still further: He made friends with a local beggar, learned his story, occasionally met him for coffee, and introduced him around. Now living elsewhere, P. inquires after him and sends news through friends.

Q. resists giving when pressured or manipulated — for instance, when beggars act as obsequious doormen at the threshold of banks, an explicit reminder: You have reason to enter a bank while I do not, and what is a bank but the stony emblem of what distinguishes us? R., too, resists urgent pleas but yields to the beggar who with grinning aplomb requests ten dollars for a steak dinner or five hundred for a trip to Hawaii. An epicure, he waits for a beggar worthy of his attentions, a beggar of kindred, subtle sensibility, an accomplice. Then he can forget the mutual mortification.

With the passage of time, sympathy and selective appreciation slid into frustration. We had given, we were giving, yet the beggars remained rooted to their posts, holding out the everlasting Styrofoam cups. (S., in an expansive mood, dropped a quarter into a Styrofoam cup and coffee splashed forth.) Our tone, when we spoke of them, was somewhat distraught.

So we cast around for reasons to harden our hearts. In all probability, our handouts encouraged the drug trade, crime, and personal degeneration. Shouldn't legitimate beggars avail themselves of social services through official channels? (A Brechtian notion, given the nature of the services.) One way or another, we tempered generosity with righteousness.

Meanwhile the beggars grew intemperate. No more meek charm and witty eccentricities. Their banter took on a hard edge. A nagging beggar trailed T. until she announced firmly, "Look, I'm having a really bad day. I feel lousy, would you please leave me alone?" "Oh, I'm sorry," he replied. "Anything I can do?" "No thanks, I'll be okay. Just let me alone." "Well, in that case how about a dollar sixty-five for a hamburger?" Caving in, T. fished around and came up with sixty cents. "Here." "But it's not enough," the man said evenly.

Irritation took root. We had given and given, surely enough to expiate our blessings. Now could we have our streets back? As if we needed to give only to a certain point, as we need to give taxes or suffer unto the death. In response the beggars became aggressive — after all, they had been asking for as long as we had been giving. They implored, nagged, demanded. They hounded, pursued, and menaced, accepting small change grudgingly, muttering, even shouting their contempt, a form of blackmail, embarrassing us publicly as if we — we! — were the outcasts. Once I had no bills less than five dollars and gave my only coin, a dime, to a sickly young beggar wrapped in a blanket. "You can keep your ten cents, lady," he shouted through the crowd. Maybe he threw it back at me — I didn't turn to look. It would have cost me less to give him a five.

As I lugged my crammed shopping cart home, I was stopped by the woebegone man who had earlier failed to recognize me. This time my first thought was atavistic — those stories about hoboes sweeping the porch for a hot lunch. If only he would offer to pull my cart home. Yes, by rights he should earn the money with dignity for a change. But this is not 1910: The social contract has altered, along with the connotations of "rights" and "earn" and "dignity." Whatever tasks I might need done were not his concern. If he noticed at all, chances are he resented my cornucopia on wheels. Or perhaps he prized his freedom from the banality of shopping carts, like the hoboes of legend. I gave him some coins and he drifted past and away — to the bar, to McDonald's, the crack dealer, or his hungry family? We were farther apart than my grandmother and her pre-war vagrants, the distance greater with each step: no common life, no basis for business, between us.

Nowadays we want to pick and choose our stimuli. Sealed cars and windows, shopping malls, suburbs, and retirement communities shut out the natural inevitabilities of weather, noise, dirt, and chaos, while the technology of exclusion is hard at work on pain and death. But the beggars simply will not vanish. And when they are truculent and defy our wishes, we sullenly withhold our aid. In turn, when we deny the full measure of their requests, they withhold their gratitude.

In the end the beggars became tiresome, like TV sitcoms. Their plots were always the same, leaning heavily on flashback and ending with the extended cup. We got bored. Soon came boredom's handmaiden: We are indifferent. Yes, a few, like A., still give with a kind of moral fervor. Some try to renovate housing, others work in soup kitchens or hand out used clothing. But no matter what small efforts we make, still the beggars remain. They line the crazed streets, a serpentine fun-house mirror, confounding us, giving us our images *in extremis,* distorting our best instincts, exaggerating our worst.

At jarring moments they reflect us all too well. My friend U.'s street is a gathering place for beggars, among them a relentless badgerer. In a vindictive mood, she gave a pittance every few feet but bypassed this least favorite. He chased after her, yelling, "Hey, what about me? I'm a person too!" A cry from the soul. A universal truth that brought U. to a repentant halt. She turned, her hand already burrowing in the grit of her pocket, but the imploring face, the timbre of his plea resounding in her ears, sent a streak of revulsion through her. That endless self-assertion, that merciless need: Why, he was a replica of the inexhaustibly demanding husband she was on the point of leaving. She wheeled around and walked on.

I think all the forms of giving, with their elaborate rationales, come 35 down to two modes, the way art can be crudely divided into classic and romantic. We give from a feeling that the beggars are different from us or that they are the same. Social philosopher Philip Slater has written that love of others is what we have left over when self-love has been satisfied. To give from a feeling of plenitude and aloofness adds to our self-satisfaction. To give out of kinship is the more accurate impulse, though, as well as the more raw and painful.

I tend to give when feeling least in need, when the world has provided me with my share and maybe more. When I feel neglected, abused, invisible, unloved, and surly — a bit like a beggar myself — I resist. What makes you think I'm any different from you? I want to say. That I have anything to spare, that I don't need help too? Of course my feelings are irrelevant to beggars (though theirs are not irrelevant to me, making for a deeper inequity and unease). They are not asking for my existential well-being but for my spare change, and while my well-being may vary from day to day, I always have spare change. I can afford subtle distinctions. To the beggars, though, money is not metaphor.

Just as slavery imprisons masters as well as slaves, beggary beggars us. We are solicited and must solicit in turn, asking that the performances represent the world as we wish it to be, so that our place in it holds steady. We beg the beggars not to jostle too noticeably the abstractions we have constituted in our heads and imprinted on the physical matter around us.

Small wonder that beggars are resented. Unlike slaves, they appear to have opted out, gotten away with something, while we earn our bread by the sweat of our brow. And yet they certainly sweat, and also shiver. A paradox. Often we would like not to work either — more than a dash of envy sours our tangled response — but we surely don't want to sweat quite so much. There they outdo us. We imagine what kinds of beggars we would make, as we have idly imagined what kinds of politicians or pitchers or violinists we would make, and shrink from the image. What a relief, then, how glad we are of our lives. The next instant brings a faint needling: But are we living right? Do our lives make sense? Any more than theirs? What do their lives say about our own? The worst suspicion, the one we must not look at too closely, is that our lives and theirs amount to more or less the same thing — sweating, shivering, waiting to die, only some far more comfortably than others. For then we would have to wonder, in more than a glancing way, why as a people we feel no need to remedy this.

Our finely wrought distinctions, from A. to Z., shape a peculiar aesthetics of giving, fittingly traced on the urban fresco of blank or battered faces. The pattern reveals how much we can give without feeling destitute, how far we can unclench our fists without feeling powerless. It becomes a moral fever chart, as morality always underlies aesthetics, showing what we feel ourselves entitled to and how much we feel the entitlement of others falls on us to fulfill. In the end its import is quite simple: Either we are our brothers' keepers or we are not. The government's answer has the virtue of being cruelly clear: It is no one's keeper but its own. Our individual answers are not cruel, only ambiguous. Like aesthetics.

1991

The Reader's Presence

1. What criteria does Schwartz establish as the basis for classifying various kinds of beggars? various kinds of responses to begging? How does she use the same criteria to express her own reactions to beggars and begging? Point to specific words and phrases to support your response. How does she characterize her father's story about his response to begging? Her mother's? Which does she prefer? Why? What, more generally, does she believe can be inferred from people's reactions to begging?

2. This essay attempts far more than to classify beggars. For example, what assumptions about begging does the essay challenge? Schwartz also encourages her readers to think about what has become a commonplace experience in contemporary American life from strikingly fresh perspectives. Choose two examples of her discussion of beggars — as well as of her consideration of those who respond to them — and demonstrate the nature of Schwartz's incisiveness. What does she find most unsettling about the increase in the number of beggars? In what specific ways does she demonstrate that begging is a "new genre of performance art" (paragraph 21)? What does she mean when she speaks of "the technology of exclusion" (paragraph 32)?

3. Identify Schwartz's own point of view in this essay and characterize her tone of voice. Does it remain consistent? If not, when and how does it change? With what effects? What does she mean when she says: "We beg the beggars not to jostle too noticeably the abstractions we have constituted in our heads and imprinted on the physical matter around us" (paragraph 37)? At the end of paragraph 21, Schwartz reminds her readers that "Verisimilitude aside, we treasure sheer inventiveness." Examine Schwartz's inventiveness, as reflected in her sentence structure, diction, and metaphors. What are the principal features of the style she uses, and how do these features enable her to discuss beggars and begging without becoming either caustic or maudlin?

53

Lewis Thomas

The World's Biggest Membrane

Viewed from the distance of the moon, the astonishing thing about the earth, catching the breath, is that it is alive. The photographs show the dry, pounded surface of the moon in the foreground, dead as an old bone. Aloft, floating free beneath the moist, gleaming membrane of bright blue sky, is the rising earth, the only exuberant thing in this part of the cosmos. If you could look long enough, you would see the swirling of the great drifts of white cloud, covering and uncovering the half-hidden masses of land. If you had been looking for a very long, geologic time, you could have seen the continents themselves in motion, drifting apart on their crustal plates held afloat by the fire beneath. It has the organized, self-contained look of a live creature, full of information, marvelously skilled in handling the sun.

It takes a membrane to make sense out of disorder in biology. You have to be able to catch energy and hold it, storing precisely the needed amount and releasing it in measured shares. A cell does this, and so do the organelles inside. Each assemblage is poised in the flow of solar energy, tapping off energy from metabolic surrogates of the sun. To stay alive, you have to be able to hold out against equilibrium, maintain imbalance, bank against entropy, and you can only transact this business with membranes in our kind of world.

When the earth came alive it began constructing its own membrane for the general purpose of editing the sun. Originally, in the time of prebiotic elaboration of peptides and nucleotides from inorganic ingredients in the water on the earth, there was nothing to shield out ultraviolet radiation except the water itself. The first thin atmosphere came entirely from the degassing of the earth as it cooled, and there was only a vanishingly small

For biographical information on Lewis Thomas, see p. 665.

trace of oxygen in it. Theoretically, there could have been some production of oxygen by photodissociation of water vapor in ultraviolet light, but not much. This process would have been self-limiting, as Urey showed, since the wave lengths needed for photolysis are the very ones screened out selectively by oxygen; the production of oxygen would have been cut off almost as soon as it occurred.

The formation of oxygen had to await the emergence of photosynthetic cells, and these were required to live in an environment with sufficient visible light for photosynthesis but shielded at the same time against lethal ultraviolet. Berkner and Marshall calculate that the green cells must therefore have been about ten meters below the surface of water, probably in pools and ponds shallow enough to lack strong convection currents (the ocean could not have been the starting place).

You could say that the breathing of oxygen into the atmosphere was   5
the result of evolution, or you could turn it around and say that evolution was the result of oxygen. You can have it either way. Once the photosynthetic cells had appeared, very probably counterparts of today's blue-green algae, the future respiratory mechanism of the earth was set in place. Early on, when the level of oxygen had built up to around 1 per cent of today's atmospheric concentration, the anaerobic life of the earth was placed in jeopardy, and the inevitable next stage was the emergence of mutants with oxidative systems and ATP.[1] With this, we were off to an explosive developmental stage in which great varieties of respiring life, including the multicellular forms, became feasible.

Berkner has suggested that there were two such explosions of new life, like vast embryological transformations, both dependent on threshold levels of oxygen. The first, at 1 per cent of the present level, shielded out enough ultraviolet radiation to permit cells to move into the surface layers of lakes, rivers, and oceans. This happened around 600 million years ago, at the beginning of the Paleozoic era, and accounts for the sudden abundance of marine fossils of all kinds in the record of this period. The second burst occurred when oxygen rose to 10 per cent of the present level. At this time, around 400 million years ago, there was a sufficient canopy to allow life out of the water and onto the land. From here on it was clear going, with nothing to restrain the variety of life except the limits of biologic inventiveness.

It is another illustration of our fantastic luck that oxygen filters out the very bands of ultraviolet light that are most devastating for nucleic acids and proteins, while allowing full penetration of the visible light needed for photosynthesis. If it had not been for this semipermeability, we could never have come along.

---

[1]*ATP:* Adenosine triphosphate, a chemical in cells that produces energy for physiological responses. — EDS.

The earth breathes, in a certain sense. Berkner suggests that there may have been cycles of oxygen production and carbon dioxide consumption, depending on relative abundances of plant and animal life, with the ice ages representing periods of apnea. An overwhelming richness of vegetation may have caused the level of oxygen to rise above today's concentration, with a corresponding depletion of carbon dioxide. Such a drop in carbon dioxide may have impaired the "greenhouse" property of the atmosphere, which holds in the solar heat otherwise lost by radiation from the earth's surface. The fall in temperature would in turn have shut off much of living, and, in a long sigh, the level of oxygen may have dropped by 90 per cent. Berkner speculates that this is what happened to the great reptiles; their size may have been all right for a richly oxygenated atmosphere, but they had the bad luck to run out of air.

Now we are protected against lethal ultraviolet rays by a narrow rim of ozone, thirty miles out. We are safe, well ventilated, and incubated, provided we can avoid technologies that might fiddle with that ozone, or shift the levels of carbon dioxide. Oxygen is not a major worry for us, unless we let fly with enough nuclear explosives to kill off the green cells in the sea; if we do that, of course, we are in for strangling.

It is hard to feel affection for something as totally impersonal as the   10
atmosphere, and yet there it is, as much a part and product of life as wine or bread. Taken all in all, the sky is a miraculous achievement. It works, and for what it is designed to accomplish it is as infallible as anything in nature. I doubt whether any of us could think of a way to improve on it, beyond maybe shifting a local cloud from here to there on occasion. The word "chance" does not serve to account well for structures of such magnificence. There may have been elements of luck in the emergence of chloroplasts, but once these things were on the scene, the evolution of the sky became absolutely ordained. Chance suggests alternatives, other possibilities, different solutions. This may be true for gills and swim-bladders and forebrains, matters of detail, but not for the sky. There was simply no other way to go.

We should credit it for what it is: For sheer size and perfection of function, it is far and away the grandest product of collaboration in all of nature.

It breathes for us, and it does another thing for our pleasure. Each day, millions of meteorites fall against the outer limits of the membrane and are burned to nothing by the friction. Without this shelter, our surface would long since have become the pounded powder of the moon. Even though our receptors are not sensitive enough to hear it, there is comfort in knowing that the sound is there overhead, like the random noise of rain on the roof at night.

1973

The Reader's Presence

1. Lewis Thomas presents the controlling metaphor of the atmosphere as a membrane so engagingly and incisively that we not only think differently about the atmosphere but experience it differently. Thomas announces in the first sentence that the earth "is alive." Trace the specific ways in which he develops and extends this metaphor throughout the essay. Where — and with what consequences — does he pull back from this metaphor, from his earlier insistence that the earth is actually a living, breathing creature? In paragraph 2, Thomas seems to be using the word *membrane* literally; he describes how membranes function in cells. How does Thomas's summary of the properties of a membrane in paragraph 2 serve to organize the remainder of his essay?

2. Thomas's essay counters the stereotype, one that still lingers in the academy, that scientific writing can be readily identified by its reliance on the passive voice, dense syntax, and the elimination of any traces of a writer's presence. Where — and in what specific ways — does Thomas's essay demonstrate that clear scientific thinking and an emotional response to a subject are not fundamentally incompatible? Consider, for example, the diction in paragraph 1. What attitude does Thomas reveal in such word choices as *gleaming, exuberant, astonishing,* and *marvelously*? In paragraph 10, Thomas suggests that his readers should feel "affection" for the atmosphere. How do his choices of metaphors elicit a personal response to so impersonal a subject?

3. Thomas's essay is also an insightful exercise in point of view. What point of view is established in the opening sentences of the selection? When does Thomas shift this point of view as the essay develops? How do these shifts enrich and complicate his readers' view of the atmosphere? How does Thomas encourage his readers to view the earth differently in the concluding paragraphs?

54

Sallie Tisdale

A Weight that Women Carry

I don't know how much I weigh these days, though I can make a good guess. For years I'd known that number, sometimes within a quarter pound, known how it changed from day to day and hour to hour. I want to weigh myself now; I lean toward the scale in the next room, imagine standing there, lining up the balance. But I don't do it. Going this long, starting to break the scale's spell — it's like waking up suddenly sober.

By the time I was sixteen years old I had reached my adult height of five feet six inches and weighed 164 pounds. I weighed 164 pounds before and after a healthy pregnancy. I assume I weigh about the same now; nothing significant seems to have happened to my body, this same old body I've had all these years. I usually wear a size 14, a common clothing size for American women. On bad days I think my body looks lumpy and misshapen. On my good days, which are more frequent lately, I think I look plush and strong; I think I look like a lot of women whose bodies and lives I admire.

I'm not sure when the word "fat" first sounded pejorative to me, or when I first applied it to myself. My grandmother was a petite woman, the only one in my family. She stole food from other people's plates, and hid the debris of her own meals so that no one would know how much she ate. My mother was a size 14, like me, all her adult life; we shared clothes. She fretted endlessly over food scales, calorie counters, and diet books. She didn't want to quit smoking because she was afraid she would gain weight, and she worried about her weight until she died of cancer five years ago. Dieting was always in my mother's way, always there in the conversations above my head, the dialogue of stocky women. But I was strong and healthy and didn't pay too much attention to my weight until I was grown.

For biographical information on Sallie Tisdale, see p. 666.

It probably wouldn't have been possible for me to escape forever. It doesn't matter that whole human epochs have celebrated big men and women, because the brief period in which I live does not; since I was born, even the voluptuous calendar girl has gone. Today's models, the women whose pictures I see constantly, unavoidably, grow more minimal by the day. When I berate myself for not looking like — whomever I think I should look like that day, I don't really care that no one looks like that. I don't care that Michelle Pfeiffer doesn't look like the photographs I see of Michelle Pfeiffer, I want to look — think I should look — like the photographs. I want her little miracles; the makeup artists, photographers, and computer imagers who can add a mole, remove a scar, lift the breasts, widen the eyes, narrow the hips, flatten the curves. The final product is what I see, have seen my whole adult life. And I've seen this: Even when big people become celebrities, their weight is constantly remarked upon and scrutinized; their successes seem always to be *in spite of* their weight. I thought my successes must be, too.

I feel myself expand and diminish from day to day, sometimes from hour to hour. If I tell someone my weight, I change in their eyes: I become bigger or smaller, better or worse, depending on what that number, my weight, means to them. I know many men and women, young and old, gay and straight, who look fine, whom I love to see and whose faces and forms I cherish, who despise themselves for their weight. For their ordinary, human bodies. They and I are simply bigger than we think we should be. We always talk about weight in terms of gains and losses, and don't wonder at the strangeness of the words. In trying always to lose weight, we've lost hope of simply being seen for ourselves.

My weight has never actually affected anything — it's never seemed to mean anything one way or the other to how I lived. Yet for the last ten years I've felt quite bad about it. After a time, the number on the scale became my totem, more important than my experience — it was layered, metaphorical, *metaphysical,* and it had bewitching power. I thought if I could change that number I could change my life.

In my mid-twenties I started secretly taking diet pills. They made me feel strange, half-crazed, vaguely nauseated. I lost about twenty-five pounds, dropped two sizes, and bought new clothes. I developed rituals and taboos around food, ate very little, and continued to lose weight. For a long time afterward I thought it only coincidental that with every passing week I also grew more depressed and irritable.

I could recite the details, but they're remarkable only for being so common. I lost more weight until I was rather thin, and then I gained it all back. It came back slowly, pound by pound, in spite of erratic and melancholy and sometimes frantic dieting, dieting I clung to even though being thin had changed nothing, had meant nothing to my life except that I was thin. Looking back, I remember blinding moments of shame and lightning-bright moments of clearheadedness, which inevitably gave way to rage at the time I'd wasted — rage that eventually would become, once again, self-disgust and the urge to lose weight. So it went, until I weighed exactly what I'd weighed when I began.

I used to be attracted to the sharp angles of the chronic dieter — the caffeine-wild, chain-smoking, skinny women I see sometimes. I considered them a pinnacle not of beauty but of will. Even after I gained back my weight, I wanted to be like that, controlled and persevering, live that underfed life so unlike my own rather sensual and disorderly existence. I felt I should always be dieting, for the dieting of it; dieting had become a rule, a given, a constant. Every ordinary value is distorted in this lens. I felt guilty for not being completely absorbed in my diet, for getting distracted, for not caring enough all the time. The fat person's character flaw is a lack of narcissism. She's let herself go.

So I would begin again — and at first it would all seem so . . . easy.   10
Simple arithmetic. After all, 3,500 calories equal one pound of fat — so the books and articles by the thousands say. I would calculate how long it would take to achieve the magic number on the scale, to succeed, to win. All past failures were suppressed. If 3,500 calories equal one pound, all I needed to do was cut 3,500 calories out of my intake every week. The first few days of a new diet would be colored with a sense of control — organization and planning, power over the self. Then the basic futile misery took over.

I would weigh myself with foreboding, and my weight would determine how went the rest of my day, my week, my life. When 3,500 calories didn't equal one pound lost after all, I figured it was my body that was flawed, not the theory. One friend, who had tried for years to lose weight following prescribed diets, made what she called "an amazing discovery." The real secret to a diet, she said, was that you had to be willing to be hungry *all the time.* You had to eat even less than the diet allowed.

I believed that being thin would make me happy. Such a pernicious, enduring belief. I lost weight and wasn't happy and saw that elusive happiness disappear in a vanishing point, requiring more — more self-disgust, more of the misery of dieting. Knowing all that I know now about the biology and anthropology of weight, knowing that people naturally come in many shapes and sizes, knowing that diets are bad for me and won't make me thin — sometimes none of this matters. I look in the mirror and think: Who am I kidding? *I've got to do something about myself.* Only then will this vague discontent disappear. Then I'll be loved.

For ages humans believed that the body helped create the personality, from the humors of Galen to W. H. Sheldon's somatotypes. Sheldon distinguished between three templates — endomorph, mesomorph, and ectomorph — and combined them into hundreds of variations with physical, emotional, and psychological characteristics. When I read about weight now, I see the potent shift in the last few decades: The modern culture of dieting is based on the idea that the personality creates the body. Our size must be in some way voluntary, or else it wouldn't be subject to change. A lot of my misery over my weight wasn't about how I looked at all. I was miserable because I believed *I* was bad, not my body. I felt truly reduced then, reduced to being just a body and nothing more.

Fat is perceived as an *act* rather than a thing. It is antisocial, and curable through the application of social controls. Even the feminist revisions of dieting, so powerful in themselves, pick up the theme: the hungry, empty heart; the woman seeking release from sexual assault, or the man from the loss of the mother, through food and fat. Fat is now a symbol not of the personality but of the soul — the cluttered, neurotic, and immature soul.

Fat people eat for "mere gratification," I read, as though no one else   15 does. Their weight is *intentioned,* they simply eat "too much," their flesh is lazy flesh. Whenever I went on a diet, eating became cheating. One pretzel was cheating. Two apples instead of one was cheating — a large potato instead of a small, carrots instead of broccoli. It didn't matter which diet I was on; diets have failure built in, failure is in the definition. Every substitution — even carrots for broccoli — was a triumph of desire over will. When I dieted, I didn't feel pious just for sticking to the rules. I felt condemned for the act of eating itself, as though my hunger were never normal. My penance was to not eat at all.

My attitude toward food became quite corrupt. I came, in fact, to subconsciously believe food itself was corrupt. Diet books often distinguish between "real" and "unreal" hunger, so that *correct* eating is hollowed out, unemotional. A friend of mine who thinks of herself as a compulsive eater says she feels bad only when she eats for pleasure. "Why?" I ask, and she says, "Because I'm eating food I don't need." A few years ago I might have admired that. Now I try to imagine a world where we eat only food we need, and it seems inhuman. I imagine a world devoid of holidays and wedding feasts, wakes and reunions, a unique shared joy. "What's wrong with eating a cookie because you like cookies?" I ask her, and she hasn't got an answer. These aren't rational beliefs, any more than the unnecessary pleasure of ice cream is rational. Dieting presumes pleasure to be an insignificant, or at least malleable, human motive.

I felt no joy in being thin — it was just work, something I had to do. But when I began to gain back the weight, I felt despair. I started reading about the "recidivism" of dieting. I wondered if I had myself to blame not only for needing to diet in the first place but for dieting itself, the weight inevitably regained. I joined organized weight-loss programs, spent a lot of money, listened to lectures I didn't believe on quack nutrition, ate awful, processed diet foods. I sat in groups and applauded people who'd lost a half pound, feeling smug because I'd lost a pound and a half. I felt ill much of the time, found exercise increasingly difficult, cried often. And I thought that if I could only lose a little weight, everything would be all right.

When I say to someone, "I'm fat," I hear, "Oh, no! You're not *fat*! You're just — " What? Plump? Big-boned? Rubenesque? I'm just *not thin*. That's crime enough. I began this story by stating my weight. I said it all at once, trying to forget it and take away its power; I said it to be done being scared. Doing so, saying it out loud like that, felt like confessing a mortal sin. I have to bite my tongue not to seek reassurance, not to defend myself, not to plead. I see an old friend for the first time in years, and she comments on how much my fourteen-year-old son looks like me — "except, of course, he's not chubby." "Look who's talking," I reply, through clenched teeth. This pettiness is never far away; concern with my weight evokes the smallest, meanest parts of me. I look at another woman passing on the street and think, "At least I'm not *that* fat."

Recently I was talking with a friend who is naturally slender about a mutual acquaintance who is quite large. To my surprise my friend reproached this woman because she had seen her eating a cookie at lunchtime. "How is she going to lose weight that way?" my friend wondered. When you are as fat as our acquaintance is, you are primarily, fundamentally, seen as fat. It is your essential characteristic. There are so many presumptions in my friend's casual, cruel remark. She assumes that this woman should diet all the time — and that she *can*. She pronounces whole categories of food to be denied her. She sees her unwillingness to behave in this externally prescribed way, even for a moment, as an act of rebellion. In his story "A Hunger Artist," Kafka writes that the guards of the fasting man were "usually butchers, strangely enough." Not so strange, I think.

I know that the world, even if it views me as overweight (and I'm not   20 sure it really does), clearly makes a distinction between me and this very big woman. I would rather stand with her and not against her, see her for all she is besides fat. But I know our experiences aren't the same. My thin friend assumes my fat friend is unhappy because she is fat: Therefore, if she loses weight she will be happy. My fat friend has a happy marriage and family and a good career, but insofar as her weight is a source of misery, I think she would be much happier if she could eat her cookie in peace, if people would shut up and leave her weight alone. But the world never lets up when you are her size; she cannot walk to the bank without risking insult. Her fat is seen as perverse bad manners. I have no doubt she would be rid of the fat if she could be. If my left-handedness invited the criticism her weight does, I would want to cut that hand off.

In these last several years I seem to have had an infinite numbers of conversations about dieting. They are really all the same conversation — weight is lost, then weight is gained back. This repetition finally began to sink in. Why did everyone sooner or later have the same experience? (My friend who had learned to be hungry all the time gained back all the weight she had lost and more, just like the rest of us.) Was it really our bodies that were flawed? I began reading the biology of weight more carefully, reading the fine print in the endless studies. There is, in fact, a preponderance of evidence disputing our commonly held assumptions about weight.

The predominant biological myth of weight is that thin people live longer than fat people. The truth is far more complicated. (Some deaths of fat people attributed to heart disease seem actually to have been the result of radical dieting.) If health were our real concern, it would be dieting we questioned, not weight. The current ideal of thinness has never been held before, except as a religious ideal; the underfed body is the martyr's body. Even if people can lose weight, maintaining an artificially low weight for any period of time requires a kind of starvation. Lots of people are naturally thin, but for those who are not, dieting is an unnatural act; biology rebels. The metabolism of the hungry body can change inalterably, making it ever harder and harder to stay thin. I think chronic dieting made me gain weight — not only pounds, but fat. This equation seemed so strange at first that I couldn't believe it. But the weight I put back on after losing was much more stubborn than the original weight. I had lost it by taking diet pills and not eating much of anything at all for quite a long time. I haven't touched the pills again, but not eating much of anything no longer works.

When Oprah Winfrey first revealed her lost weight, I didn't envy her. I thought, She's in trouble now. I knew, I was certain, she would gain it back; I believed she was biologically destined to do so. The tabloid headlines blamed it on a cheeseburger or mashed potatoes, they screamed OPRAH PASSES 200 POUNDS, and I cringed at her misery and how the world wouldn't let up, wouldn't leave her alone, wouldn't let her be anything else. How dare the world do this to anyone? I thought, and then realized I did it to myself.

The "Ideal Weight" charts my mother used were at their lowest acceptable-weight ranges in the 1950s, when I was a child. They were based on sketchy and often inaccurate actuarial evidence, using, for the most part, data on northern Europeans and allowing for the most minimal differences in size for a population of less than half a billion people. I never fit those weight charts, I was always just outside the pale. As an adult, when I would join an organized diet program, I accepted their version of my Weight Goal as gospel, knowing it would be virtually impossible to reach. But reach I tried; that's what one does with gospel. Only in the last few years have the weight tables begun to climb back into the world of the average human. The newest ones distinguish by gender, frame, and age. And suddenly I'm not off the charts anymore. I have a place.

A man who is attracted to fat women says, "I actually have less specific 25 physical criteria than most men. I'm attracted to women who weigh 170 or 270 or 370. Most men are only attracted to women who weigh between 100 and 135. So who's got more of a fetish?" We look at fat as a problem of the fat person. Rarely do the tables get turned, rarely do we imagine that it might be the viewer, not the viewed, who is limited. What the hell is wrong with *them*, anyway? Do they believe everything they see on television?

My friend Phil, who is chronically and almost painfully thin, admitted that in his search for a partner he finds himself prejudiced against fat women. He seemed genuinely bewildered by this. I didn't jump to reassure him that such prejudice is hard to resist. What I did was bite my tongue at my urge to be reassured by him, to be told that I, at least, wasn't fat. That over the centuries humans have been inclined to prefer extra flesh rather than the other way around seems unimportant. All we see now tells us otherwise. Why does my kindhearted friend criticize another woman for eating a cookie when she would never dream of commenting in such a way on another person's race or sexual orientation or disability? Deprivation is the dystopian idea.

My mother called her endless diets "reducing plans." Reduction, the diminution of women, is the opposite of feminism, as Kim Chernin points out in *The Obsession.* Smallness is what feminism strives against, the smallness that women confront everywhere. All of women's spaces are smaller than those of men, often inadequate, without privacy. Furniture designers distinguish between a man's and a woman's chair, because women don't spread out like men. (A sprawling woman means only one thing.) Even our voices are kept down. By embracing dieting I was rejecting a lot I held dear, and the emotional dissonance that created just seemed like one more necessary evil.

A fashion magazine recently celebrated the return of the "well-fed" body; a particular model was said to be "the archetype of the new womanly woman . . . stately, powerful." She is a size 8. The images of women presented to us, images claiming so maliciously to be the images of women's whole lives, are not merely social fictions. They are *absolute* fictions; they can't exist. How would it feel, I began to wonder, to cultivate my own real womanliness rather than despise it? Because it was my fleshy curves I wanted to be rid of, after all. I dreamed of having a boy's body, smooth, hipless, lean. A body rapt with possibility, a receptive body suspended before the storms of maturity. A dear friend of mine, nursing her second child, weeps at her newly voluptuous body. She loves her children and hates her own motherliness, wanting to be unripened again, to be a bud and not a flower.

Recently I've started shopping occasionally at stores for "large women," where the smallest size is a 14. In department stores the size 12 and 14 and 16 clothes are kept in a ghetto called the Women's Department. (And who would want that, to be the size of a woman? We all dream of being "juniors" instead.) In the specialty stores the clerks are usually big women and the customers are big, too, big like a lot of women in my life — friends, my sister, my mother and aunts. Not long ago I bought a pair of jeans at Lane Bryant and then walked through the mall to the Gap, with its shelves of generic clothing. I flicked through the clearance rack and suddenly remembered the Lane Bryant shopping bag in my hand and its enormous weight, the sheer heaviness of that brand name shouting to the world. The shout is that I've let myself go. I still feel like crying out sometimes: Can't I feel *satisfied?* But I am not supposed to be satisfied, not allowed to be satisfied. My discontent fuels the market; I need to be afraid in order to fully participate.

American culture, which has produced our dieting mania, does more   30
than reward privation and acquisition at the same time: it actually associates them with each other. Read the ads: the virtuous runner's reward is a
new pair of $180 running shoes. The fat person is thought to be impulsive,
indulgent, but insufficiently or incorrectly greedy, greedy for the wrong
thing. The fat person lacks ambition. The young executive is complimented
for being "hungry"; he is "starved for success." We are teased with what
we will *have* if we are willing to *have not* for a time. A dieting friend,
avoiding the food on my table, says, "I'm just dying for a bite of that."

Dieters are the perfect consumers: They never get enough. The dieter
wistfully imagines food without substance, food that is not food, that begs
the definition of food, because food is the problem. Even the ways we *don't
eat* are based in class. The middle class don't eat in support groups. The
poor can't afford not to eat at all. The rich hire someone to not eat with
them in private. Dieting is an emblem of capitalism. It has a venal heart.

The possibility of living another way, living without dieting, began to
take root in my mind a few years ago, and finally my second trip through
Weight Watchers ended dieting for me. This last time I just couldn't stand
the details, the same kind of details I'd seen and despised in other programs, on other diets: the scent of resignation, the weighing-in by the quarter pound, the before and after photographs of group leaders prominently
displayed. Jean Nidetch, the founder of Weight Watchers, says, "Most fat
people need to be hurt badly before they do something about themselves."
She mocks every aspect of our need for food, of a person's sense of entitlement to food, of daring to *eat what we want.* Weight Watchers refuses to
release its own weight charts except to say they make no distinction for
frame size; neither has the organization ever released statistics on how
many people who lose weight on the program eventually gain it back. I
hated the endlessness of it, the turning of food into portions and exchanges,
everything measured out, permitted, denied. I hated the very idea of "maintenance." Finally I realized I didn't just hate the diet. I was sick of the way
I acted on a diet, the way I whined, my niggardly, penny-pinching behavior. What I liked in myself seemed to shrivel and disappear when I dieted.
Slowly, slowly I saw these things. I saw that my pain was cut from whole
cloth, imaginary, my own invention. I saw how much time I'd spent on
something ephemeral, something that simply wasn't important, didn't matter. I saw that the real point of dieting is dieting — to not be done with it,
ever.

I looked in the mirror and saw a woman, with flesh, curves, muscles, a
few stretch marks, the beginnings of wrinkles, with strength and softness in
equal measure. My body is the one part of me that is always, undeniably,
here. To like myself means to be, literally, shameless, to be wanton in the
pleasures of being inside a body. I feel *loose* this way, a little abandoned, a
little dangerous. That first feeling of liking my body — not being resigned
to it or despairing of change, but actually *liking* it — was tentative and

guilty and frightening. It was alarming, because it was the way I'd felt as a child, before the world had interfered. Because surely I was wrong; I knew, I'd known for so long, that my body wasn't all right this way. I was afraid even to act as though I were all right: I was afraid that by doing so I'd be acting a fool.

For a time I was thin, I remember — and what I remember is nothing special — strain, a kind of hollowness, the same troubles and fears, and no magic. So I imagine losing weight again. If the world applauded, would this comfort me? Or would it only compromise whatever approval the world gives me now? What else will be required of me besides thinness? What will happen to me if I get sick, or lose the use of a limb, or, God forbid, grow old?

By fussing endlessly over my body, I've ceased to inhabit it. I'm trying 35 to reverse this equation now, to trust my body and enter it again with a whole heart. I know more now than I used to about what constitutes "happy" and "unhappy," what the depths and textures of contentment are like. By letting go of dieting, I free up mental and emotional room. I have more space, I can move. The pursuit of another, elusive body, the body someone else says I should have, is a terrible distraction, a sidetracking that might have lasted my whole life long. By letting myself go, I go places.

Each of us in this culture, this twisted, inchoate culture, has to choose between battles: one battle is against the cultural ideal, and the other is against ourselves. I've chosen to stop fighting myself. Maybe I'm tilting at windmills; the cultural ideal is ever-changing, out of my control. It's not a cerebral journey, except insofar as I have to remind myself to stop counting, to stop thinking in terms of numbers. I know, even now that I've quit dieting and eat what I want, how many calories I take in every day. If I eat as I please, I eat a lot one day and very little the next; I skip meals and snack at odd times. My nourishment is good—as far as nutrition is concerned. I'm in much better shape than when I was dieting. I know that the small losses and gains in my weight over a period of time aren't simply related to the number of calories I eat. Someone asked me not long ago how I could possibly know my calorie intake if I'm not dieting (the implication being, perhaps, that I'm dieting secretly). I know because calorie counts and grams of fat and fiber are embedded in me. I have to work to *not* think of them, and I have to learn to not think of them in order to really live without fear.

When I look, *really* look, at the people I see every day on the street, I see a jungle of bodies, a community of women and men growing every which way like lush plants, growing tall and short and slender and round, hairy and hairless, dark and pale and soft and hard and glorious. Do I look around at the multitudes and think all these people — all these people who are like me and not like me, who are various and different — are not loved or lovable? Lately, everyone's body interests me, every body is desirable in some way. I see how muscles and skin shift with movement; I sense a cornucopia of flesh in the world. In the midst of it I am a little capacious and unruly.

I repeat with Walt Whitman, "I dote on myself . . . there is that lot of me, and all so luscious." I'm eating better, exercising more, feeling fine — and then I catch myself thinking, *Maybe I'll lose some weight.* But my mood changes or my attention is caught by something else, something deeper, more lingering. Then I can catch a glimpse of myself by accident and think only: That's me. My face, my hips, my hands. Myself.

1993

The Reader's Presence

1. Sallie Tisdale's essay on the compulsion to diet in American society offers a revealing look at the prejudices, standards, and values associated with being "fat" and "thin" in contemporary life. Summarize the stereotypes Tisdale presents about "fat" people. How are they characterized by others, and especially by thin people? What assumptions about their personalities are embedded in these stereotypes? For example, what does Tisdale mean when she says: "Fat is perceived as an *act* rather than a thing" (paragraph 14)? What, more generally, does she offer as the "preponderance of evidence disputing our commonly held assumptions about weight" (paragraph 21)?

2. What does Tisdale mean when, at the end of paragraph 5, she reminds her readers that "We always talk about weight in terms of gains and losses, and don't wonder at the strangeness of the words"? What is so "strange" about the language of dieting? What metaphors are most often used to talk about dieting? To what extent do irony and paradox play important roles in the ways in which Americans are encouraged to think and talk about dieting? Point to specific examples to support your response. At what point does Tisdale suggest that one's perspective on being fat is finally quite relative, a matter of point of view? How convincing do you find her analysis at this point and at related moments?

3. Tisdale shapes her information into a series of illustrative anecdotes about fat people and the American mania about dieting. What patterns do you notice in the sequence of examples she presents? Does the fact that Tisdale announces that she is five foot six inches and weighs 164 pounds make it easier — or more difficult — for you as a reader to be drawn to and convinced by her analysis of dieting, its mythology, and its social and individual consequences? What does she "gain" and "lose" by providing us with this information in the first paragraph? How persuasive do you find the alternatives to dieting that she presents in the conclusion of her essay? What, finally, is the overriding purpose of her essay?

55

Mark Twain

The Damned Human Race

I have been studying the traits and dispositions of the "lower animals" (so-called), and contrasting them with the traits and dispositions of man. I find the result humiliating to me. For it obliges me to renounce my allegiance to the Darwinian[1] theory of the Ascent of Man from the Lower Animals; since it now seems plain to me that that theory ought to be vacated in favor of a new and truer one, this new and truer one to be named the *Des*cent of Man from the Higher Animals.

In proceeding toward this unpleasant conclusion I have not guessed or speculated or conjectured, but have used what is commonly called the scientific method. That is to say, I have subjected every postulate that presented itself to the crucial test of actual experiment, and have adopted it or rejected it according to the result. Thus I verified and established each step of my course in its turn before advancing to the next. These experiments were made in the London Zoological Gardens, and covered many months of painstaking and fatiguing work.

Before particularizing any of the experiments, I wish to state one or two things which seem to more properly belong in this place than further along. This in the interest of clearness. The massed experiments established to my satisfaction certain generalizations, to wit:

1. That the human race is of one distinct species. It exhibits slight variations — in color, stature, mental caliber, and so on — due to climate, environment, and so forth; but it is a species by itself, and not to be confounded with any other.

2. That the quadrupeds are a distinct family, also. This family exhibits   5

For biographical information on Mark Twain, see p. 666.

[1]Charles Darwin (1809–1882) published *The Descent of Man* in 1871, a highly controversial book in which he argued that humankind had descended from "lower" forms of life. — EDS.

variations — in color, size, food preferences and so on; but it is a family by itself.

3. That the other families — the birds, the fishes, the insects, the reptiles, etc. — are more or less distinct, also. They are in the procession. They are links in the chain which stretches down from the higher animals to man at the bottom.

Some of my experiments were quite curious. In the course of my reading I had come across a case where, many years ago, some hunters on our Great Plains organized a buffalo hunt for the entertainment of an English earl — that, and to provide some fresh meat for his larder. They had charming sport. They killed seventy-two of those great animals; and ate part of one of them and left the seventy-one to rot. In order to determine the difference between an anaconda and an earl — if any — I caused seven young calves to be turned into the anaconda's cage. The grateful reptile immediately crushed one of them and swallowed it, then lay back satisfied. It showed no further interest in the calves, and no disposition to harm them. I tried this experiment with other anacondas; always with the same result. The fact stood proven that the difference between an earl and an anaconda is that the earl is cruel and the anaconda isn't; and that the earl wantonly destroys what he has no use for, but the anaconda doesn't. This seemed to suggest that the anaconda was not descended from the earl. It also seemed to suggest that the earl was descended from the anaconda, and had lost a good deal in the transition.

I was aware that many men who have accumulated more millions of money than they can ever use have shown a rabid hunger for more, and have not scrupled to cheat the ignorant and the helpless out of their poor servings in order to partially appease that appetite. I furnished a hundred different kinds of wild and tame animals the opportunity to accumulate vast stores of food, but none of them would do it. The squirrels and bees and certain birds made accumulations, but stopped when they had gathered a winter's supply, and could not be persuaded to add to it either honestly or by chicane. In order to bolster up a tottering reputation the ant pretended to store up supplies, but I was not deceived. I know the ant. These experiments convinced me that there is this difference between man and the higher animals: He is avaricious and miserly, they are not.

In the course of my experiments I convinced myself that among the animals man is the only one that harbors insults and injuries, broods over them, waits till a chance offers, then takes revenge. The passion of revenge is unknown to the higher animals.

Roosters keep harems, but it is by consent of their concubines; therefore no wrong is done. Men keep harems, but it is by brute force, privileged by atrocious laws which the other sex were allowed no hand in making. In this matter man occupies a far lower place than the rooster.

Cats are loose in their morals, but not consciously so. Man, in his descent from the cat, has brought the cat's looseness with him but has left the unconsciousness behind — the saving grace which excuses the cat. The cat is innocent, man is not.

Indecency, vulgarity, obscenity — these are strictly confined to man; he invented them. Among the higher animals there is no trace of them. They hide nothing; they are not ashamed. Man, with his soiled mind, covers himself. He will not even enter a drawing room with his breast and back naked, so alive are he and his mates to indecent suggestion. Man is "The Animal that Laughs." But so does the monkey, as Mr. Darwin pointed out; and so does the Australian bird that is called the laughing jackass. No — Man is the Animal that Blushes. He is the only one that does it — or has occasion to.

At the head of this article[2] we see how "three monks were burnt to death" a few days ago, and a prior "put to death with atrocious cruelty." Do we inquire into the details? No; or we should find out that the prior was subjected to unprintable mutilations. Man — when he is a North American Indian — gouges out his prisoner's eyes; when he is King John, with a nephew to render untroublesome, he uses a red-hot iron; when he is a religious zealot dealing with heretics in the Middle Ages, he skins his captive alive and scatters salt on his back; in the first Richard's time he shuts up a multitude of Jew families in a tower and sets fire to it; in Columbus's time he captures a family of Spanish Jews and — but *that* is not printable; in our day in England a man is fined ten shillings for beating his mother nearly to death with a chair, and another man is fined forty shillings for having four pheasant eggs in his possession without being able to satisfactorily explain how he got them. Of all the animals, man is the only one that is cruel. He is the only one that inflicts pain for the pleasure of doing it. It is a trait that is not known to the higher animals. The cat plays with the frightened mouse; but she has this excuse, that she does not know that the mouse is suffering. The cat is moderate — unhumanly moderate: She only scares the mouse, she does not hurt it; she doesn't dig out its eyes, or tear off its skin, or drive splinters under its nails — man-fashion; when she is done playing with it she makes a sudden meal of it and puts it out of its trouble. Man is the Cruel Animal. He is alone in that distinction.

The higher animals engage in individual fights, but never in organized masses. Man is the only animal that deals in that atrocity of atrocities, War. He is the only one that gathers his brethren about him and goes forth in cold blood and with calm pulse to exterminate his kind. He is the only animal that for sordid wages will march out, as the Hessians did in our

[2]In his nonfiction Twain often introduced newsclippings as evidence of human atrocity. In this instance the article has been lost, but Twain is most likely referring to the religious persecutions that followed the 1897 Cretan revolt. — EDS.

Revolution,[3] and as the boyish Prince Napoleon did in the Zulu war,[4] and help to slaughter strangers of his own species who have done him no harm and with whom he has no quarrel.

Man is the only animal that robs his helpless fellow of his country — takes possession of it and drives him out of it or destroys him. Man has done this in all the ages. There is not an acre of ground on the globe that is in possession of its rightful owner, or that has not been taken away from owner after owner, cycle after cycle, by force and bloodshed.

Man is the only Slave. And he is the only animal who enslaves. He has always been a slave in one form or another, and has always held other slaves in bondage under him in one way or another. In our day he is always some man's slave for wages, and does that man's work; and this slave has other slaves under him for minor wages, and they do *his* work. The higher animals are the only ones who exclusively do their own work and provide their own living.

Man is the only Patriot. He sets himself apart in his own country, under his own flag, and sneers at the other nations, and keeps multitudinous uniformed assassins on hand at heavy expense to grab slices of other people's countries, and keep *them* from grabbing slices of *his*. And in the intervals between campaigns he washes the blood off his hands and works for "the universal brotherhood of man" — with his mouth.

Man is the Religious Animal. He is the only Religious Animal. He is the only animal that has the True Religion — several of them. He is the only animal that loves his neighbor as himself, and cuts his throat if his theology isn't straight. He has made a graveyard of the globe in trying his honest best to smooth his brother's path to happiness and heaven. He was at it in the time of the Caesars, he was at it in Mahomet's time, he was at it in the time of the Inquisition, he was at it in France a couple of centuries, he was at it in England in Mary's day,[5] he has been at it ever since he first saw the light, he is at it today in Crete — as per the telegrams quoted above — he will be at it somewhere else tomorrow. The higher animals have no religion. And we are told that they are going to be left out, in the Hereafter. I wonder why? It seems questionable taste.

Man is the Reasoning Animal. Such is the claim. I think it is open to dispute. Indeed, my experiments have proven to me that he is the Unreasoning Animal. Note his history, as sketched above. It seems plain to me

15

---

[3]***Revolution:*** Approximately 17,000 mercenaries from Hesse, a part of Germany, fought for the British during the American Revolution. — EDS.

[4]***Zulu war:*** Napolean III's son died while fighting for the British during the 1879 Zulu rebellion in what is now the Republic of South Africa. Great Britain annexed the Zulu territory shortly after, and that is the context for Twain's remarks in the next paragraph. — EDS.

[5]***Mary's day:*** In the time of Mary I, who reigned as Queen of England between 1553 and 1558; her vigorous persecution of Protestants earned her the nickname "Bloody Mary." — EDS.

that whatever he is he is *not* a reasoning animal. His record is the fantastic record of a maniac. I consider that the strongest count against his intelligence is the fact that with that record back of him he blandly sets himself up as the head animal of the lot: Whereas by his own standards he is the bottom one.

In truth, man is incurably foolish. Simple things which the other 20 animals easily learn, he is incapable of learning. Among my experiments was this. In an hour I taught a cat and a dog to be friends. I put them in a cage. In another hour I taught them to be friends with a rabbit. In the course of two days I was able to add a fox, a goose, a squirrel and some doves. Finally a monkey. They lived together in peace; even affectionately.

Next, in another cage I confined an Irish Catholic from Tipperary, and as soon as he seemed tame I added a Scotch Presbyterian from Aberdeen. Next a Turk from Constantinople; a Greek Christian from Crete; an Armenian; a Methodist from the wilds of Arkansas; a Buddhist from China; a Brahman from Benares. Finally, a Salvation Army Colonel from Wapping. Then I stayed away two whole days. When I came back to note results, the cage of Higher Animals was all right, but in the other there was but a chaos of gory odds and ends of turbans and fezzes and plaids and bones and flesh — not a specimen left alive. These Reasoning Animals had disagreed on a theological detail and carried the matter to a Higher Court.

One is obliged to concede that in true loftiness of character, Man cannot claim to approach even the meanest of the Higher Animals. It is plain that he is constitutionally incapable of approaching that altitude; that he is constitutionally afflicted with a Defect which must make such approach forever impossible, for it is manifest that this defect is permanent in him, indestructible, ineradicable.

I find this Defect to be *the Moral Sense*. He is the only animal that has it. It is the secret of his degradation. It is the quality *which enables him to do wrong*. It has no other office. It is incapable of performing any other function. It could never have been intended to perform any other. Without it, man could do no wrong. He would rise at once to the level of the Higher Animals.

Since the Moral Sense has but the one office, the one capacity — to enable man to do wrong — it is plainly without value to him. It is as valueless to him as is disease. In fact, it manifestly *is* a disease. *Rabies* is bad, but it is not so bad as this disease. Rabies enables a man to do a thing which he could not do when in a healthy state: kill his neighbor with a poisonous bite. No one is the better man for having rabies. The Moral Sense enables a man to do wrong. It enables him to do wrong in a thousand ways. Rabies is an innocent disease, compared to the Moral Sense. No one, then, can be the better man for having the Moral Sense. What, now, do we find the Primal Curse to have been? Plainly what it was in the beginning: the infliction upon man of the Moral Sense; the ability to distinguish good from evil; and with it, necessarily, the ability to *do* evil; for there can be no evil act without the presence of consciousness of it in the doer of it.

And so I find that we have descended and degenerated, from some far ancestor — some microscopic atom wandering at its pleasure between the mighty horizons of a drop of water perchance — insect by insect, animal by animal, reptile by reptile, down the long highway of smirchless innocence, till we have reached the bottom stage of development — namable as the Human Being. Below us — nothing. Nothing but the Frenchman.

There is only one possible stage below the Moral Sense; that is the Immoral Sense. The Frenchman has it. Man is but little lower than the angels. This definitely locates him. He is between the angels and the French.

Man seems to be a rickety poor sort of a thing, any way you take him; a kind of British Museum of infirmities and inferiorities. He is always undergoing repairs. A machine that was as unreliable as he is would have no market. On top of his specialty — the Moral Sense — are piled a multitude of minor infirmities; such a multitude, indeed, that one may broadly call them countless. The higher animals get their teeth without pain or inconvenience. Man gets his through months and months of cruel torture; and at a time of life when he is but ill able to bear it. As soon as he has got them they must all be pulled out again, for they were of no value in the first place, not worth the loss of a night's rest. The second set will answer for a while, by being reinforced occasionally with rubber or plugged up with gold; but he will never get a set which can really be depended on till a dentist makes him one. This set will be called "false" teeth — as if he had ever worn any other kind.

In a wild state — a natural state — the Higher Animals have a few diseases; diseases of little consequence; the main one is old age. But man starts in as a child and lives on diseases till the end, as a regular diet. He has mumps, measles, whooping cough, croup, tonsillitis, diphtheria, scarlet fever, almost as a matter of course. Afterward, as he goes along, his life continues to be threatened at every turn: by colds, coughs, asthma, bronchitis, itch, cholera, cancer, consumption, yellow fever, bilious fever, typhus fevers, hay fever; ague, chilblains, piles, inflammation of the entrails, indigestion, toothache, earache, deafness, dumbness, blindness, influenza, chicken pox, cowpox, smallpox, liver complaint, constipation, bloody flux, warts, pimples, boils, carbuncles, abscesses, bunions, corns, tumors, fistulas, pneumonia, softening of the brain, melancholia and fifteen other kinds of insanity; dysentery, jaundice, diseases of the heart, the bones, the skin, the scalp, the spleen, the kidneys, the nerves, the brain, the blood; scrofula, paralysis, leprosy, neuralgia, palsy, fits, headache, thirteen kinds of rheumatism, forty-six of gout, and a formidable supply of gross and unprintable disorders of one sort and another. Also — but why continue the list? The mere names of the agents appointed to keep this shackly machine out of repair would hide him from sight if printed on his body in the smallest type known to the founder's art. He is but a basket of pestilent corruption provided for the support and entertainment of swarming armies of bacilli — armies commissioned to rot him and destroy him, and each army equipped with a special detail of the work. The process of waylaying him, persecuting him, rotting him, killing him, begins with his first breath, and there is no mercy, no pity, no truce till he draws his last one.

Look at the workmanship of him, in certain of its particulars. What are his tonsils for? They perform no useful function; they have no value. They have no business there. They are but a trap. They have but the one office, the one industry: to provide tonsillitis and quinsy and such things for the possessor of them. And what is the vermiform appendix for? It has no value; it cannot perform any useful service. It is but an ambuscaded enemy whose sole interest in life is to lie in wait for stray grapeseeds and employ them to breed strangulated hernia. And what are the male's mammals for? For business, they are out of the question; as an ornament, they are a mistake. What is his beard for? It performs no useful function; it is a nuisance and a discomfort; all nations hate it; all nations persecute it with a razor. And because it is a nuisance and a discomfort, Nature never allows the supply of it to fall short, in any man's case, between puberty and the grave. You never see a man bald-headed on his chin. but his hair! It is a graceful ornament, it is a comfort, it is the best of all protections against certain perilous ailments, man prizes it above emeralds and rubies. And because of these things Nature puts it on, half the time, so that it won't stay. Man's sight, smell, hearing, sense of locality — how inferior they are. The condor sees a corpse at five miles; man has no telescope that can do it. The bloodhound follows a scent that is two days old. The robin hears the earthworm burrowing his course under the ground. The cat, deported in a closed basket, finds its way home again through twenty miles of country which it has never seen.

Certain functions lodged in the other sex perform in a lamentably infe- 30
rior way as compared with the performance of the same functions in the Higher Animals. In the human being, menstruation, gestation and parturition are terms which stand for horrors. In the Higher Animals these things are hardly even inconveniences.

For style, look at the Bengal tiger — that ideal of grace, beauty, physical perfection, majesty. And then look at Man — that poor thing. He is the Animal of the Wig, the Trepanned Skull, the Ear Trumpet, the Glass Eye, the Pasteboard Nose, the Porcelain Teeth, the Silver Windpipe, the Wooden Leg — a creature that is mended and patched all over, from top to bottom. If he can't get renewals of his bric-a-brac in the next world, what will he look like?

He has just one stupendous superiority. In his intellect he is supreme. The Higher Animals cannot touch him there. It is curious, it is noteworthy, that no heaven has ever been offered him wherein his one sole superiority was provided with a chance to enjoy itself. Even when he himself has imagined a heaven, he has never made provision in it for intellectual joys. It is a striking omission. It seems a tacit confession that heavens are provided for the Higher Animals alone. This is matter for thought; and for serious thought. And it is full of a grim suggestion: that we are not as important, perhaps, as we had all along supposed we were.

1938

The Reader's Presence

1. What conventional attitudes does Twain satirize in this essay? How does he reverse our sense of higher and lower? In what ways is the essay a response to Darwin's theory of evolution? What does Twain expect his readers to know of that theory?
2. How would you specifically identify the target of Twain's satire? What idea or ideas is he making fun of? What groups of people is he making fun of? Who might be shocked by his reasoning? Do you find any parts of the essay intellectually or religiously shocking? Explain why or why not.
3. Why do you think Twain puts his essay into the form of a scientific report of experiments? What effect does that have upon the reader? How "scientific" do you think his experiments are? Do you think Twain is also making fun of scientific reasoning? What evidence would you bring in from the essay to say he is or isn't?

56

Alice Walker

In Search of Our Mothers' Gardens

I described her own nature and temperament. Told how they needed
a larger life for their expression. . . . I pointed out that in lieu of
proper channels, her emotions had overflowed into paths that dissi-
pated them. I talked, beautifully I thought, about an art that would
be born, an art that would open the way for women the likes of her.
I asked her to hope, and build up an inner life against the coming of
that day. . . . I sang, with a strange quiver in my voice, a promise
song.

> – "Avey," JEAN TOOMER, CANE
> The poet speaking to a prostitute who
> falls asleep while he's talking.

When the poet Jean Toomer[1] walked through the South in the early
twenties, he discovered a curious thing: black women whose spirituality
were so intense, so deep, so *unconscious,* they were themselves unaware of
the richness they held. They stumbled blindly through their lives: creatures
so abused and mutilated in body, so dimmed and confused by pain, that
they considered themselves unworthy even of hope. In the selfless abstractions their bodies became to the men who used them, they became more
than "sexual objects," more even than mere women: They became
"Saints." Instead of being perceived as whole persons, their bodies became
shrines: What was thought to be their minds became temples suitable for
worship. These crazy Saints stared out at the world, wildly, like lunatics —
or quietly, like suicides; and the "God" that was in their gaze was as mute
as a great stone.

For biographical information on Alice Walker, see p. 666.
[1]*Jean Toomer* (1894–1967): A black poet, novelist, and leading figure of the Harlem
Renaissance who wrote *Cane* in 1923. — EDS.

Who were these Saints? These crazy, loony, pitiful women?

Some of them, without a doubt, were our mothers and grandmothers.

In the still heat of the post-Reconstruction South, this is how they seemed to Jean Toomer: exquisite butterflies trapped in an evil honey, toiling away their lives in an era, a century, that did not acknowledge them, except as "the *mule* of the world." They dreamed dreams that no one knew — not even themselves, in any coherent fashion — and saw visions no one could understand. They wandered or sat about the countryside crooning lullabies to ghosts, and drawing the mother of Christ in charcoal on courthouse walls.

They forced their minds to desert their bodies and their striving spirits   5
sought to rise, like frail whirlwinds from the hard red clay. And when those frail whirlwinds fell, in scattered particles, upon the ground, no one mourned. Instead, men lit candles to celebrate the emptiness that remained, as people do who enter a beautiful but vacant space to resurrect a God.

Our mothers and grandmothers, some of them: moving to music not yet written. And they waited.

They waited for a day when the unknown thing that was in them would be made known; but guessed, somehow in their darkness, that on the day of their revelation they would be long dead. Therefore to Toomer they walked, and even ran, in slow motion. For they were going nowhere immediate, and the future was not yet within their grasp. And men took our mothers and grandmothers, "but got no pleasure from it." So complex was their passion and their calm.

To Toomer, they lay vacant and fallow as autumn fields, with harvest time never in sight: and he saw them enter loveless marriages, without joy; and become prostitutes, without resistance; and become mothers of children, without fulfillment.

For these grandmothers and mothers of ours were not Saints, but Artists; driven to a numb and bleeding madness by the springs of creativity in them for which there was no release. They were Creators, who lived lives of spiritual waste, because they were so rich in spirituality — which is the basis of Art — that the strain of enduring their unused and unwanted talent drove them insane. Throwing away this spirituality was their pathetic attempt to lighten the soul to a weight their work-worn, sexually abused bodies could bear.

What did it mean for a black woman to be an artist in our grand-   10
mothers' time? In our great-grandmothers' day? It is a question with an answer cruel enough to stop the blood.

Did you have a genius of a great-great-grandmother who died under some ignorant and depraved white overseer's lash? Or was she required to bake biscuits for a lazy backwater tramp, when she cried out in her soul to paint watercolors of sunsets, or the rain falling on the green and peaceful pasturelands? Or was her body broken and forced to bear children (who were more often than not sold away from her) — eight, ten, fifteen, twenty children — when her one joy was the thought of modeling heroic figures of rebellion, in stone or clay?

How was the creativity of the black woman kept alive, year after year and century after century, when for most of the years black people have been in America, it was a punishable crime for a black person to read or write? And the freedom to paint, to sculpt, to expand the mind with action did not exist. Consider, if you can bear to imagine it, what might have been the result if singing, too, had been forbidden by law. Listen to the voices of Bessie Smith, Billie Holiday, Nina Simone, Roberta Flack, and Aretha Franklin, among others and imagine those voices muzzled for life. Then you may begin to comprehend the lives of our "crazy," "Sainted" mothers and grandmothers. The agony of the lives of women who might have been Poets, Novelists, Essayists, and Short-Story Writers (over a period of centuries), who died with their real gifts stifled within them.

And, if this were the end of the story, we would have cause to cry out in my paraphrase of Okot p'Bitek's great poem:

O, my clanswomen
Let us all cry together!
Come,
Let us mourn the death of our mother,
The death of a Queen
The ash that was produced
By a great fire!
O, this homestead is utterly dead
Close the gates
With lacari *thorns,*
For our mother
The creator of the Stool is lost!
And all the young men
Have perished in the wilderness!

But this is not the end of the story, for all the young women — our mothers and grandmothers, *ourselves* — have not perished in the wilderness. And if we ask ourselves why, and search for and find the answer, we will know beyond all efforts to erase it from our minds, just exactly who, and of what, we black American women are.

One example, perhaps the most pathetic, most misunderstood one, can   15
provide a backdrop for our mothers' work: Phillis Wheatley,[2] a slave in the 1700s.

Virginia Woolf, in her book *A Room of One's Own*, wrote that in order for a woman to write fiction she must have two things, certainly:

---

[2]*Phillis Wheatley* (ca. 1754–1784): A slave in a prosperous Boston family; published her first poetry at the age of thirteen and enjoyed an international reputation, acclaimed by such figures as Voltaire, George Washington, and Benjamin Franklin. She died, however, in poverty and obscurity. — EDS.

a room of her own (with key and lock) and enough money to support herself.

What then are we to make of Phillis Wheatley, a slave, who owned not even herself? This sickly, frail black girl who required a servant of her own at times — her health was so precarious — and who, had she been white, would have been easily considered the intellectual superior of all the women and most of the men in the society of her day.

Virginia Woolf wrote further, speaking of course not of our Phillis, that "any woman born with a great gift in the sixteenth century [insert "eighteenth century," insert "black woman," insert "born or made a slave"] would certainly have gone crazed, shot herself, or ended her days in some lonely cottage outside the village, half witch, half wizard [insert "Saint"], feared and mocked at. For it needs little skill and psychology to be sure that a highly gifted girl who had tried to use her gift of poetry would have been so thwarted and hindered by contrary instincts [add "chains, guns, the lash, the ownership of one's body by someone else, submission to an alien religion"], that she must have lost her health and sanity to a certainty."

The key words, as they relate to Phillis, are "contrary instincts." For when we read the poetry of Phillis Wheatley — as when we read the novels of Nella Larsen or the oddly false-sounding autobiography of that freest of all black women writers, Zora Hurston — evidence of "contrary instincts" is everywhere. Her loyalties were completely divided, as was, without question, her mind.

But how could this be otherwise? Captured at seven, a slave of   20 wealthy, doting whites who instilled in her the "savagery" of the Africa they "rescued" her from . . . one wonders if she was even able to remember her homeland as she had known it, or as it really was.

Yet, because she did try to use her gift for poetry in a world that made her a slave, she was "so thwarted and hindered by . . . contrary instincts, that she . . . lost her health . . . " In the last years of her brief life, burdened not only with the need to express her gift but also with a penniless, friendless "freedom" and several small children for whom she was forced to do strenuous work to feed, she lost her health, certainly. Suffering from malnutrition and neglect and who knows what mental agonies, Phillis Wheatley died.

So torn by "contrary instincts" was black, kidnapped, enslaved Phillis that her description of "the Goddess" — as she poetically called the Liberty she did not have — is ironically, cruelly humorous. And, in fact, has held Phillis up to ridicule for more than a century. It is usually read prior to hanging Phillis's memory as that of a fool. She wrote:

The Goddess comes, she moves divinely fair,
Olive and laurel binds her golden hair.
Wherever shines this native of the skies,
Unnumber'd charms and recent graces rise. [My emphasis]

It is obvious that Phillis, the slave, combed the "Goddess's" hair every morning; prior, perhaps, to bringing in the milk, or fixing her mistress's lunch. She took her imagery from the one thing she saw elevated above all others.

With the benefit of hindsight we ask, "How could she?"

But at last, Phillis, we understand. No more snickering when your stiff, struggling, ambivalent lines are forced on us. We know now that you were not an idiot or a traitor; only a sickly little black girl, snatched from your home and country and made a slave; a woman who still struggled to sing the song that was your gift, although in a land of barbarians who praised you for your bewildered tongue. It is not so much what you sang, as that you kept alive, in so many of our ancestors, *the notion of song.*

Black women are called, in the folklore that so aptly identifies one's status in society, "the *mule* of the world," because we have been handed the burdens that everyone else — *everyone* else — refused to carry. We have also been called "Matriarchs," "Superwomen," and "Mean and Evil Bitches." Not to mention "Castraters" and "Sapphire's Mama." When we have pleaded for understanding, our character has been distorted; when we have asked for simple caring, we have been handed empty inspirational appellations, then stuck in the farthest corner. When we have asked for love, we have been given children. In short, even our plainer gifts, our labors of fidelity and love, have been knocked down our throats. To be an artist and a black woman, even today, lowers our status in many respects, rather than raises it: And yet, artists we will be.

Therefore we must fearlessly pull out of ourselves and look at and identify with our lives the living creativity some of our great-grandmothers were not allowed to know. I stress *some* of them because it is well known that the majority of our great-grandmothers knew, even without "knowing" it, the reality of their spirituality, even if they didn't recognize it beyond what happened in the singing at church — and they never had any intention of giving it up.

How they did it — those millions of black women who were not Phillis Wheatley, or Lucy Terry or Frances Harper or Zora Hurston or Nella Larsen or Bessie Smith; or Elizabeth Catlett, or Katherine Dunham, either — brings me to the title of this essay, "In Search of Our Mothers' Gardens," which is a personal account that is yet shared, in its theme and its meaning, by all of us. I found, while thinking about the far-reaching world of the creative black woman, that often the truest answer to a question that really matters can be found very close.

In the late 1920s my mother ran away from home to marry my father. Marriage, if not running away, was expected of seventeen-year-old girls. By the time she was twenty, she had two children and was pregnant with a third. Five children later, I was born. And this is how I came to know my mother: She seemed a large, soft, loving-eyed woman who was rarely impatient in our home. Her quick, violent temper was on view only a few times a year, when she battled with the white landlord who had the misfortune to suggest to her that her children did not need to go to school.

She made all the clothes we wore, even my brothers' overalls. She made all the towels and sheets we used. She spent the summers canning vegetables and fruits. She spent the winter evenings making quilts enough to cover our beds.

During the "working" day, she labored beside — not behind — my father in the fields. Her day began before sunup, and did not end until late at night. There was never a moment for her to sit down, undisturbed, to unravel her own private thoughts; never a time free from interruption — by work or the noisy inquiries of her many children. And yet, it is to my mother — and all our mothers who were not famous — that I went in search of the secret of what has fed that muzzled and often mutilated, but vibrant, creative spirit that the black woman has inherited, and that pops out in wild and unlikely places to this day.

But when, you will ask, did my overworked mother have time to know or care about feeding the creative spirit?

The answer is so simple that many of us have spent years discovering it. We have constantly looked high, when we should have looked high — and low.

For example: In the Smithsonian Institution in Washington, D.C., there hangs a quilt unlike any other in the world. In fanciful, inspired, and yet simple and identifiable figures, it portrays the story of the Crucifixion. It is considered rare, beyond price. Though it follows no known pattern of quilt-making, and though it is made of bits and pieces of worthless rags, it is obviously the work of a person of powerful imagination and deep spiritual feeling. Below this quilt I saw a note that says it was made by "an anonymous Black woman in Alabama, a hundred years ago."

If we could locate this "anonymous" black woman from Alabama, she would turn out to be one of our grandmothers — an artist who left her mark in the only materials she could afford, and in the only medium her position in society allowed her to use.

As Virginia Woolf wrote further, in *A Room of One's Own:*

> Yet genius of a sort must have existed among women as it must have existed among the working class. [Change this to "slaves" and "the wives and daughters of sharecroppers."] Now and again an Emily Brontë or a Robert Burns [change this to "a Zora Hurston or a Richard Wright"] blazes out and proves its presence. But certainly it never got itself on to paper. When, however, one reads of a witch being ducked, of a woman possessed by devils [or "Sainthood"], of a wise woman selling herbs [our root workers], or even a very remarkable man who had a mother, then I think we are on the track of a lost novelist, a suppressed poet, or some mute and inglorious Jane Austen.... Indeed, I would venture to guess

that Anon, who wrote so many poems without signing them, was often a woman. . . .

And so our mothers and grandmothers have, more often than not anonymously, handed on the creative spark, the seed of the flower they themselves never hoped to see: or like a sealed letter they could not plainly read.

And so it is, certainly, with my own mother. Unlike "Ma" Rainey's songs, which retained their creator's name even while blasting forth from Bessie Smith's mouth, no song or poem will bear my mother's name. Yet so many of the stories that I write, that we all write, are my mother's stories. Only recently did I fully realize this: That through years of listening to my mother's stories of her life, I have absorbed not only the stories themselves, but something of the manner in which she spoke, something of the urgency that involves the knowledge that her stories — like her life — must be recorded. It is probably for this reason that so much of what I have written is about characters whose counterparts in real life are so much older than I am.

But the telling of these stories, which came from my mother's lips as naturally as breathing, was not the only way my mother showed herself as an artist. For stories, too, were subject to being distracted, to dying without conclusion. Dinners must be started, and cotton must be gathered before the big rains. The artist that was and is my mother showed itself to me only after many years. This is what I finally noticed:

Like Mem, a character in *The Third Life of Grange Copeland*,[3] my mother adorned with flowers whatever shabby house we were forced to live in. And not just your typical straggly country stand of zinnias, either. She planted ambitious gardens — and still does — with over fifty different varieties of plants that bloom profusely from early March until late November. Before she left home for the fields, she watered her flowers, chopped up the grass, and laid out new beds. When she returned from the fields, she might divide clumps of bulbs, dig a cold pit, uproot and replant roses, or prune branches from her taller bushes or trees — until night came and it was too dark to see.

Whatever she planted grew as if by magic, and her fame as a grower of flowers spread over three counties. Because of her creativity with her flowers, even my memories of poverty are seen through a screen of blooms — sunflowers, petunias, roses, dahlias, forsythia, spirea, delphiniums, verbena . . . and on and on.

And I remember people coming to my mother's yard to be given cuttings from her flowers; I hear again the praise showered on her because whatever rocky soil she landed on, she turned into a garden. A garden so brilliant with colors, so original in its design, so magnificent with life and

40

---

[3]*The Third Life of Grange Copeland:* Walker's first novel, published in 1970. — Eds.

creativity, that to this day people drive by our house in Georgia — perfect strangers and imperfect strangers — and ask to stand or walk among my mother's art.

I notice that it is only when my mother is working in her flowers that she is radiant, almost to the point of being invisible — except as Creator: hand and eye. She is involved in work her soul must have. Ordering the universe in the image of her personal conception of Beauty.

Her face, as she prepares the Art that is her gift, is a legacy of respect she leaves to me, for all that illuminates and cherishes life. She has handed down respect for the possibilities — and the will to grasp them.

For her, so hindered and intruded upon in so many ways, being an 45 artist has still been a daily part of her life. This ability to hold on, even in very simple ways, is work black women have done for a very long time.

This poem is not enough, but it is something, for the woman who literally covered the holes in our walls with sunflowers:

> *They were women then*
> *My mamma's generation*
> *Husky of voice — Stout of*
> *Step*
> *With fists as well as*
> *Hands*
> *How they battered down*
> *Doors*
> *And ironed*
> *Starched white*
> *Shirts*
> *How they led*
> *Armies*
> *Headragged Generals*
> *Across mined*
> *Fields*
> *Booby-trapped*
> *Kitchens*
> *To discover books*
> *Desks*
> *A place for us*
> *How they knew what we*
> *Must know*
> *Without knowing a page*
> *Of it*
> *Themselves*

Guided by my heritage of a love of beauty and a respect for strength — in search of my mother's garden, I found my own.

And perhaps in Africa over two hundred years ago, there was just such a mother; perhaps she painted vivid and daring decorations in oranges and yellows and greens on the walls of her hut; perhaps she sang — in a voice

like Roberta Flack's — *sweetly* over the compounds of her village; perhaps
she wove the most stunning mats or told the most ingenious stories of all
the village storytellers. Perhaps she was herself a poet — though only her
daughter's name is signed to the poems that we know.

Perhaps Phillis Wheatley's mother was also an artist.

Perhaps in more than Phillis Wheatley's biological life is her mother's   50
signature made clear.

1974

The Reader's Presence

1. The *our* of the essay's title signals an identification of the author
   with an audience. Why didn't Walker title her essay "In Search of
   My Mother's Garden"? Does Walker's *our* include everyone who
   reads the essay — or is her audience more restricted? Explain
   your answer.
2. Consider carefully Walker's image of the garden. What does it
   mean both to her and to other women? What is the connection
   between gardens and a woman's "living creativity"? What
   other objects or activities in the essay are related to the idea of
   gardens?
3. In rereading the essay, note the many quotations throughout.
   Consider the way Walker uses quotation in general. Can you detect any patterns? What sort of "presence" do they convey? Why
   do you think she brought in so many quotations in an essay
   about silence? How does her use of quotations contribute to her
   overall theme?

57 _____

Virginia Woolf

The Death of the Moth

Moths that fly by day are not properly to be called moths; they do not excite that pleasant sense of dark autumn nights and ivy-blossom which the commonest yellow-underwing asleep in the shadow of the curtain never fails to rouse in us. They are hybrid creatures, neither gay like butterflies nor somber like their own species. Nevertheless the present specimen, with his narrow hay-colored wings, fringed with a tassel of the same color, seemed to be content with life. It was a pleasant morning, mid-September, mild, benignant, yet with a keener breath than that of the summer months. The plough was already scoring the field opposite the window, and where the share had been, the earth was pressed flat and gleamed with moisture. Such vigor came rolling in from the fields and the down beyond that it was difficult to keep the eyes strictly turned upon the book. The rooks too were keeping one of their annual festivities; soaring round the tree tops until it looked as if a vast net with thousands of black knots in it had been cast up into the air; which, after a few moments sank slowly down upon the trees until every twig seemed to have a knot at the end of it. Then, suddenly, the net would be thrown into the air again in a wider circle this time, with the utmost clamor and vociferation, as though to be thrown into the air and settle slowly down upon the tree tops were a tremendously exciting experience.

The same energy which inspired the rooks, the ploughmen, the horses, and even, it seemed, the lean bare-backed downs, sent the moth fluttering from side to side of his square of the windowpane. One could not help watching him. One, was, indeed, conscious of a queer feeling of pity for him. The possibilities of pleasure seemed that morning so enormous and so various that to have only a moth's part in life, and a day moth's at that,

---

For biographical information on Virginia Woolf, see p. 668.

appeared a hard fate, and his zest in enjoying his meager opportunities to the full, pathetic. He flew vigorously to one corner of his compartment, and after waiting there a second, flew across to the other. What remained for him but to fly to a third corner and then to a fourth? That was all he could do, in spite of the size of the downs, the width of the sky, the far-off smoke of houses, and the romantic voice, now and then, of a steamer out at sea. What he could do he did. Watching him, it seemed as if a fiber, very thin but pure, of the enormous energy of the world had been thrust into his frail and diminutive body. As often as he crossed the pane, I could fancy that a thread of vital light became visible. He was little or nothing but life.

Yet, because he was so small, and so simple a form of the energy that was rolling in at the open window and driving its way through so many narrow and intricate corridors in my own brain and in those of other human beings, there was something marvelous as well as pathetic about him. It was as if someone had taken a tiny bead of pure life and decking it as lightly as possible with down and feathers, had set it dancing and zigzagging to show us the true nature of life. Thus displayed one could not get over the strangeness of it. One is apt to forget all about life, seeing it humped and bossed and garnished and cumbered so that it has to move with the greatest circumspection and dignity. Again, the thought of all that life might have been had he been born in any other shape caused one to view his simple activities with a kind of pity.

After a time, tired by his dancing apparently, he settled on the window ledge in the sun, and, the queer spectacle being at an end, I forgot about him. Then, looking up, my eye was caught by him. He was trying to resume his dancing, but seemed either so stiff or so awkward that he could only flutter to the bottom of the windowpane; and when he tried to fly across it he failed. Being intent on other matters I watched these futile attempts for a time without thinking, unconsciously waiting for him to resume his flight, as one waits for a machine, that has stopped momentarily, to start again without considering the reason of its failure. After perhaps a seventh attempt he slipped from the wooden ledge and fell, fluttering his wings, on to his back on the windowsill. The helplessness of his attitude roused me. It flashed upon me that he was in difficulties; he could no longer raise himself; his legs struggled vainly. But, as I stretched out a pencil, meaning to help him to right himself, it came over me that the failure and awkwardness were the approach of death. I laid the pencil down again.

The legs agitated themselves once more. I looked as if for the enemy   5 against which he struggled. I looked out of doors. What had happened there? Presumably it was midday, and work in the fields had stopped. Stillness and quiet had replaced the previous animation. The birds had taken themselves off to feed in the brooks. The horses stood still. Yet the power was there all the same, massed outside, indifferent, impersonal, not attending to anything in particular. Somehow it was opposed to the little hay-colored moth. It was useless to try to do anything. One could only watch the extraordinary efforts made by those tiny legs against an oncoming doom which could, had it chosen, have submerged an entire city, not merely a city, but masses of human beings; nothing, I knew had any chance against death. Nevertheless after a pause of exhaustion the legs fluttered again. It was superb this last protest, and so frantic that he succeeded at last in righting himself. One's sympathies, of course, were all on the side of life. Also, when there was nobody to care or to know, this gigantic effort on the part of an insignificant little moth, against a power of such magnitude, to retain what no one else valued or desired to keep, moved one strangely. Again, somehow, one saw life, a pure bead. I lifted the pencil again, useless though I knew it to be. But even as I did so, the unmistakable tokens of death showed themselves. The body relaxed, and instantly grew stiff. The struggle was over. The insignificant little creature now knew death. As I looked at the dead moth, this minute wayside triumph of so great a force over so mean an antagonist filled me with wonder. Just as life had been strange a few minutes before, so death was now as strange. The moth having righted himself now lay most decently and uncomplainingly composed. O yes, he seemed to say, death is stronger than I am.

1942

The Reader's Presence

1. Woolf calls her essay "The Death of *the* Moth" rather than "The Death of *a* Moth." Describe what difference this makes. What quality does the definite article add to the essay?
2. Can you find any connections between what happens to the moth and what happens outside the window? Why do you think Woolf brings in the outside world? Of what importance is it to the essay?
3. Reread the essay paying special attention not to the moth but to the writer. What presence does Woolf establish for herself in the essay? How does the act of writing itself get introduced? Of what significance is the pencil? Can you discover any connection between the essay's subject and its composition?

Part III

Contending with Issues

58

James Baldwin

Stranger in the Village

From all available evidence no black man had ever set foot in this tiny Swiss village before I came. I was told before arriving that I would probably be a "sight" for the village; I took this to mean that people of my complexion were rarely seen in Switzerland, and also that city people are always something of a "sight" outside of the city. It did not occur to me — possibly because I am an American — that there could be people anywhere who had never seen a Negro.

It is a fact that cannot be explained on the basis of the inaccessibility of the village. The village is very high, but it is only four hours from Milan and three hours from Lausanne. It is true that it is virtually unknown. Few people making plans for a holiday would elect to come here. On the other hand, the villagers are able, presumably, to come and go as they please — which they do: to another town at the foot of the mountain, with a population of approximately five thousand, the nearest place to see a movie or go to the bank. In the village there is no movie house, no bank, no library, no theater; very few radios, one jeep, one station wagon; and, at the moment, one typewriter, mine, an invention which the woman next door to me here had never seen. There are about six hundred people living here, all Catholic — I conclude this from the fact that the Catholic church is open all year round, whereas the Protestant chapel, set off on a hill a little removed from the village, is open only in the summertime when the tourists arrive. There are four or five hotels, all closed now, and four or five bistros, of which, however, only two do any business during the winter. These two do not do a great deal, for life in the village seems to end around nine or ten o'clock. There are a few stores, butcher, baker, *épicerie*,[1] a hardware store, and a money-changer — who cannot change travelers' checks, but

For biographical information on James Baldwin, see p. 642.
[1] *épicerie:* A grocery store (French). — EDS.

must send them down to the bank, an operation which takes two or three days. There is something called the *Ballet Haus,* closed in the winter and used for God knows what, certainly not ballet, during the summer. There seems to be only one schoolhouse in the village, and this for the quite young children; I suppose this to mean that their older brothers and sisters at some point descend from these mountains in order to complete their education — possibly, again, to the town just below. The landscape is absolutely forbidding, mountains towering on all four sides, ice and snow as far as the eye can reach. In this white wilderness, men and women and children move all day, carrying washing, wood, buckets of milk or water, sometimes skiing on Sunday afternoons. All week long boys and young men are to be seen shoveling snow off the rooftops, or dragging wood down from the forest in sleds.

The village's only real attraction, which explains the tourist season, is the hot spring water. A disquietingly high proportion of these tourists are cripples, or semi-cripples, who come year after year — from other parts of Switzerland, usually — to take the waters. This lends the village, at the height of the season, a rather terrifying air of sanctity, as though it were a lesser Lourdes. There is often something beautiful, there is always something awful, in the spectacle of a person who has lost one of his faculties, a faculty he never questioned until it was gone, and who struggles to recover it. Yet people remain people, on crutches or indeed on deathbeds; and wherever I passed, the first summer I was here, among the native villagers or among the lame, a wind passed with me — of astonishment, curiosity, amusement, and outrage. That first summer I stayed two weeks and never intended to return. But I did return in the winter, to work; the village offers, obviously, no distractions whatever and has the further advantage of being extremely cheap. Now it is winter again, a year later, and I am here again. Everyone in the village knows my name, though they scarcely ever use it, knows that I come from America — though, this, apparently, they will never really believe: black men come from Africa — and everyone knows that I am the friend of the son of a woman who was born here, and that I am staying in their chalet. But I remain as much a stranger today as I was the first day I arrived, and the children shout *Neger! Neger!* as I walk along the streets.

It must be admitted that in the beginning I was far too shocked to have any real reaction. In so far as I reacted at all, I reacted by trying to be pleasant — it being a great part of the American Negro's education (long before he goes to school) that he must make people "like" him. This smile-and-the-world-smiles-with-you routine worked about as well in this situation as it had in the situation for which it was designed, which is to say that it did not work at all. No one, after all, can be liked whose human weight and complexity cannot be, or has not been, admitted. My smile was simply another unheard-of phenomenon which allowed them to see my teeth — they did not, really, see my smile and I began to think that, should I take to snarling, no one would notice any difference. All of the physical characteristics of the Negro which had caused me, in America, a very different and almost forgotten pain were nothing less than miraculous — or infernal — in the eyes of the village people. Some thought my hair was the color of tar, that it had the texture of wire, or the texture of cotton. It was jocularly suggested that I might let it all grow long and make myself a winter coat. If I sat in the sun for more than five minutes some daring creature was certain to come along and gingerly put his fingers on my hair, as though he were afraid of an electric shock, or put his hand on my hand, astonished that the color did not rub off. In all of this, in which it must be conceded there was the charm of genuine wonder and in which there was certainly no element of intentional unkindness, there was yet no suggestion that I was human: I was simply a living wonder.

I knew that they did not mean to be unkind, and I know it now; it is necessary, nevertheless, for me to repeat this to myself each time I walk out of the chalet. The children who shout *Neger!* have no way of knowing the echoes this sound raises in me. They are brimming with good humor and the more daring swell with pride when I stop to speak with them. Just the same, there are days when I cannot pause and smile, when I have no heart to play with them; when, indeed, I mutter sourly to myself, exactly as I muttered on the streets of a city these children have never seen, when I was no bigger than these children are now: *Your* mother *was a nigger.* Joyce is right about history being a nightmare — but it may be the nightmare from which no one *can* awaken. People are trapped in history and history is trapped in them.

There is a custom in the village — I am told it is repeated in many villages — of "buying" African natives for the purpose of converting them to Christianity. There stands in the church all year round a small box with a slot for money, decorated with a black figurine, and into this box the villagers drop their francs. During the *carnaval* which precedes Lent, two village children have their faces blackened — out of which bloodless darkness their blue eyes shine like ice — and fantastic horsehair wigs are placed on their blond heads; thus disguised, they solicit among the villagers for money for the missionaries in Africa. Between the box in the church and the blackened children, the village "bought" last year six or eight African natives. This was reported to me with pride by the wife of one of the bistro owners and I was careful to express astonishment and pleasure at the solicitude shown by the village for the souls of black folk. The bistro owner's wife beamed with a pleasure far more genuine than my own and seemed to feel that I might now breathe more easily concerning the souls of at least six of my kinsmen.

I tried not to think of these so lately baptized kinsmen, of the price paid for them, or the peculiar price they themselves would pay, and said nothing about my father, who having taken his own conversion too literally never, at bottom, forgave the white world (which he described as heathen) for having saddled him with a Christ in whom, to judge at least from their treatment of him, they themselves no longer believed. I thought of white men

5

arriving for the first time in an African village, strangers there, as I am a stranger here, and tried to imagine the astounded populace touching their hair and marveling at the color of their skin. But there is a great difference between being the first white man to be seen by Africans and being the first black man to be seen by whites. The white man takes the astonishment as tribute, for he arrives to conquer and to convert the natives, whose inferiority in relation to himself is not even to be questioned; whereas I, without a thought of conquest, find myself among a people whose culture controls me, has even, in a sense, created me, people who have cost me more in anguish and rage than they will ever know, who yet do not even know of my existence. The astonishment with which I might have greeted them, should they have stumbled into my African village a few hundred years ago, might have rejoiced their hearts. But the astonishment with which they greet me today can only poison mine.

And this is so despite everything I may do to feel differently, despite my friendly conversations with the bistro owner's wife, despite their three-year-old son who has at last become my friend, despite the *saluts* and *bonsoirs* which I exchange with people as I walk, despite the fact that I know that no individual can be taken to task for what history is doing, or has done. I say that the culture of these people controls me — but they can scarcely be held responsible for European culture. America comes out of Europe, but these people have never seen America, nor have most of them seen more of Europe than the hamlet at the foot of their mountain. Yet they move with an authority which I shall never have; and they regard me, quite rightly, not only as a stranger in their village but as a suspect latecomer, bearing no credentials, to everything they have — however unconsciously — inherited.

For this village, even were it incomparably more remote and incredibly more primitive, is the West, the West onto which I have been so strangely grafted. These people cannot be, from the point of view of power, strangers anywhere in the world; they have made the modern world, in effect, even if they do not know it. The most illiterate among them is related, in a way that I am not, to Dante, Shakespeare, Michelangelo, Aeschylus, Da Vinci, Rembrandt, and Racine; the cathedral at Chartres says something to them which it cannot say to me, as indeed would New York's Empire State Building, should anyone here ever see it. Out of their hymns and dances come Beethoven and Bach. Go back a few centuries and they are in their full glory — but I am in Africa, watching the conquerors arrive.

The rage of the disesteemed is personally fruitless, but it is also abso-   10
lutely inevitable; this rage, so generally discounted, so little understood even among the people whose daily bread it is, is one of the things that makes history. Rage can only with difficulty, and never entirely, be brought under the domination of the intelligence and is therefore not susceptible to any arguments whatever. This is a fact which ordinary representatives of the *Herrenvolk*, having never felt this rage and being unable to imagine it, quite fail to understand. Also, rage cannot be hidden, it can only

be dissembled. This dissembling deludes the thoughtless, and strengthens rage, and adds, to rage, contempt. There are, no doubt, as many ways of coping with the resulting complex of tensions as there are black men in the world, but no black man can hope ever to be entirely liberated from this internal warfare — rage, dissembling, and contempt having inevitably accompanied his first realization of the power of white men. What is crucial here is that, since white men represent in the black man's world so heavy a weight, white men have for black men a reality which is far from being reciprocal; and hence all black men have toward all white men an attitude which is designed, really, either to rob the white man of the jewel of his naïveté, or else to make it cost him dear.

The black man insists, by whatever means he finds at his disposal, that the white man cease to regard him as an exotic rarity and recognize him as a human being. This is a very charged and difficult moment, for there is a great deal of will power involved in the white man's naïveté. Most people are not naturally reflective any more than they are naturally malicious, and the white man prefers to keep the black man at a certain human remove because it is easier for him thus to preserve his simplicity and avoid being called to account for crimes committed by his forefathers, or his neighbors. He is inescapably aware, nevertheless, that he is in a better position in the world than black men are, nor can he quite put to death the suspicion that he is hated by black men therefor. He does not wish to be hated, neither does he wish to change places, and at this point in his uneasiness he can scarcely avoid having recourse to those legends which white men have created about black men, the most usual effect of which is that the white man finds himself enmeshed, so to speak, in his own language which describes hell, as well as the attributes which lead one to hell, as being as black as night.

Every legend, moreover, contains its residuum of truth, and the root function of language is to control the universe by describing it. It is of quite considerable significance that black men remain, in the imagination, and in overwhelming numbers in fact, beyond the disciplines of salvation; and this despite the fact that the West has been "buying" African natives for centuries. There is, I should hazard, an instantaneous necessity to be divorced from this so visibly unsaved stranger, in whose heart, moreover, one cannot guess what dreams of vengeance are being nourished; and, at the same time, there are few things on earth more attractive than the idea of the unspeakable liberty which is allowed the unredeemed. When, beneath the black mask, a human being begins to make himself felt one cannot escape a certain awful wonder as to what kind of human being it is. What one's imagination makes of other people is dictated, of course, by the laws of one's own personality and it is one of the ironies of black-white relations that, by means of what the white man imagines the black man to be, the black man is enabled to know who the white man is.

I have said, for example, that I am as much a stranger in this village today as I was the first summer I arrived, but this is not quite true. The villagers wonder less about the texture of my hair than they did then, and wonder rather more about me. And the fact that their wonder now exists on another level is reflected in their attitudes and in their eyes. There are the children who make those delightful, hilarious, sometimes astonishing grave overtures of friendship in the unpredictable fashion of children; other children, having been taught that the devil is a black man, scream in genuine anguish as I approach. Some of the older women never pass without a friendly greeting, never pass, indeed, if it seems that they will be able to engage me in conversation; other women look down or look away or rather contemptuously smirk. Some of the men drink with me and suggest that I learn how to ski — partly, I gather, because they cannot imagine what I would look like on skis — and want to know if I am married, and ask questions about my métier. But some of the men have accused *le sale négre* — behind my back — of stealing wood and there is already in the eyes of some of them that peculiar intent, paranoiac malevolence which one sometimes surprises in the eyes of American white men when, out walking with their Sunday girl, they see a Negro male approach.

There is a dreadful abyss between the streets of this village and the streets of the city in which I was born, between the children who shout *Neger!* today and those who shouted *Nigger!* yesterday — the abyss is experience, the American experience. The syllable hurled behind me today expresses, above all, wonder: I am a stranger here. But I am not a stranger in America and the same syllable riding on the American air expresses the war my presence has occasioned in the American soul.

For this village brings home to me this fact: that there was a day, and   15
not really a very distant day, when Americans were scarcely Americans at all but discontented Europeans, facing a great unconquered continent and strolling, say, into a marketplace and seeing black men for the first time. The shock this spectacle afforded is suggested, surely, by the promptness with which they decided that these black men were not really men but cattle. It is true that the necessity on the part of the settlers of the New World of reconciling their moral assumptions with the fact — and the necessity — of slavery enhanced immensely the charm of this idea, and it is also true that this idea expresses, with a truly American bluntness, the attitude which to varying extents all masters have had toward all slaves.

But between all former slaves and slave-owners and the drama which begins for Americans over three hundred years ago at Jamestown, there are at least two differences to be observed. The American Negro slave could not suppose, for one thing, as slaves in past epochs had supposed and often done, that he would ever be able to wrest the power from his master's hands. This was a supposition which the modern era, which was to bring about such vast changes in the aims and dimensions of power, put to death; it only begins, in unprecedented fashion, and with dreadful implications, to be resurrected today. But even had this supposition persisted with undiminished force, the American Negro slave could not have used it to lend his condition dignity, for the reason that this supposition rests on another: that the slave in exile yet remains related to his past, has some means — if only in memory — of revering and sustaining the forms of his former life, is able, in short, to maintain his identity.

This was not the case with the American Negro slave. His is unique among the black men of the world in that his past was taken from him, almost literally, at one blow. One wonders what on earth the first slave found to say to the first dark child he bore. I am told that there are Haitians able to trace their ancestry back to African kings, but any American Negro wishing to go back so far will find his journey through time abruptly arrested by the signature on the bill of sale which served as the entrance paper for his ancestor. At the time — to say nothing of the circumstances — of the enslavement of the captive black man who was to become the American Negro, there was not the remotest possibility that he would ever take power from his master's hands. There was no reason to suppose that his situation would ever change, nor was there, shortly, anything to indicate that his situation had ever been different. It was his necessity, in the words of E. Franklin Frazier, to find a "motive for living under American culture or die." The identity of the American Negro comes out of this extreme situation, and the evolution of this identity was a source of the most intolerable anxiety in the minds and the lives of his masters.

For the history of the American Negro is unique also in this: that the question of his humanity, and of his rights therefore as a human being, became a burning one for several generations of Americans, so burning a question that it ultimately became one of those used to divide the nation. It is out of this argument that the venom of the epithet *Nigger!* is derived. It is an argument which Europe has never had, and hence Europe quite sincerely fails to understand how or why the argument arose in the first place, why its effects are so frequently disastrous and always so unpredictable, why it refuses until today to be entirely settled. Europe's black possessions remained — and do remain — in Europe's colonies, at which remove they represented no threat to European identity. If they posed any problem at all for the European conscience, it was a problem which remained comfortingly abstract: in effect, the black man, *as a man,* did not exist for Europe. But in America, even as a slave, he was an inescapable part of the general social fabric and no American could escape having an attitude toward him. Americans attempt until today to make an abstraction of the Negro, but the very nature of these abstractions reveals the tremendous effects the presence of the Negro has had on the American character.

When one considers the history of the Negro in America it is of the greatest importance to recognize that the moral beliefs of a person, or a people, are never really as tenuous as life — which is not moral — very often causes them to appear; these create for them a frame of reference and a necessary hope, the hope being that when life has done its worst they will be enabled to rise above themselves and to triumph over life. Life would scarcely be bearable if this hope did not exist. Again, even when the worst has been said, to betray a belief is not by any means to have put oneself beyond its power; the betrayal of a belief is not the same thing as ceasing to believe. If this were not so there would be no moral standards in the world at all. Yet one must also recognize that morality is based on ideas and that all ideas are dangerous — dangerous because ideas can only lead to action and where the action leads no man can say. And dangerous in this respect: that confronted with the impossibility of remaining faithful to one's beliefs, and the equal impossibility of becoming free of them, one can be driven to the most inhuman excesses. The ideas on which American beliefs are based are not, though Americans often seem to think so, ideas which originated in America. They came out of Europe. And the establishment of democracy on the American continent was scarcely as radical a break with the past as was the necessity, which Americans faced, of broadening this concept to include black men.

This was, literally, a hard necessity. It was impossible, for one thing, for Americans to abandon their beliefs, not only because these beliefs alone seemed able to justify the sacrifices they had endured and the blood that they had spilled, but also because these beliefs afforded them their only bulwark against a moral chaos as absolute as the physical chaos of the continent it was their destiny to conquer. But in the situation in which Americans found themselves, these beliefs threatened an idea which, whether or not one likes to think so, is the very warp and woof of the heritage of the West, the idea of white supremacy.

Americans have made themselves notorious by the shrillness and the brutality with which they have insisted on this idea, but they did not invent it; and it has escaped the world's notice that those very excesses of which Americans have been guilty imply a certain, unprecedented uneasiness over the idea's life and power, if not, indeed, the idea's validity. The idea of white supremacy rests simply on the fact that white men are the creators of civilization (the present civilization, which is the only one that matters; all previous civilizations are simply "contributions" to our own) and are therefore civilization's guardians and defenders. Thus it was impossible for Americans to accept the black man as one of themselves, for to do so was to jeopardize their status as white men. But not so to accept him was to deny his human reality, his human weight and complexity, and the strain of denying the overwhelmingly undeniable forced Americans into rationalizations so fantastic that they approached the pathological.

At the root of the American Negro problem is the necessity of the American white man to find a way of living with the Negro in order to be able to live with himself. And the history of this problem can be reduced to the means used by Americans — lynch law and law, segregation and legal acceptance, terrorization and concession — either to come to terms with this necessity, or to find a way around it, or (most usually) to find a way of doing both these things at once. The resulting spectacle, at once foolish and dreadful, led someone to make the quite accurate observation that "the Negro-in-America is a form of insanity which overtakes white men."

In this long battle, a battle by no means finished, the unforeseeable effects of which will be felt by many future generations, the white man's motive was the protection of his identity; the black man was motivated by the need to establish an identity. And despite the terrorization which the Negro in America endured and endures sporadically until today, despite the cruel and totally inescapable ambivalence of his status in his country, the battle for his identity has long ago been won. He is not a visitor to the West, but a citizen there, an American, as American as the Americans who despise him, the Americans who fear him, the Americans who love him — the Americans who became less than themselves, or rose to be greater than themselves by virtue of the fact that the challenge he represented was inescapable. He is perhaps the only black man in the world whose relationship to white men is more terrible, more subtle, and more meaningful than the relationship of bitter possessed to uncertain possessor. His survival depended, and his development depends, on his ability to turn his peculiar status in the Western world to his own advantage and, it may be, so the very great advantage of that world. It remains for him to fashion out of his experience that which will give him sustenance, and a voice.

The cathedral of Chartres, I have said, says something to the people of this village which it cannot say to me; but it is important to understand that this cathedral says something to me which it cannot say to them. Perhaps they are struck by the power of the spires, the glory of the windows; but they have known God, after all, longer than I have known him, and in a different way, and I am terrified by the slippery bottomless well to be found in the crypt, down which heretics were hurled to death, and by the obscene, inescapable gargoyles jutting out of the stone and seeming to say that God and the devil can never be divorced. I doubt that the villagers think of the devil when they face a cathedral because they have never been identified with the devil. But I must accept the status which myth, if nothing else, gives me in the West before I can hope to change the myth.

Yet, if the American Negro has arrived at his identity by virtue of the 25 absoluteness of his estrangement from his past, American white men still nourish the illusion that there is some means of recovering the European innocence, of returning to a state in which black men do not exist. This is one of the greatest errors Americans can make. The identity they fought so hard to protect has, by virtue of that battle, undergone a change: Americans are as unlike any other white people in the world as it is possible to be. I do not think, for example, that it is too much to suggest that the American vision of the world — which allows so little reality, generally speaking, for any of the darker forces in human life, which tends until today to paint moral issues in glaring black and white — owes a great deal to the battle waged by Americans to maintain between themselves and black men a human separation which could not be bridged. It is only now beginning to be borne in on us — very faintly, it must be admitted, very slowly, and very much against our will — that this vision of the world is dangerously inaccurate, and perfectly useless. For it protects our moral high-mindedness at the terrible expense of weakening our grasp of reality. People who shut their eyes to reality simply invite their own destruction, and anyone who insists on remaining in a state of innocence long after that innocence is dead turns himself into a monster.

The time has come to realize that the interracial drama acted out on the American continent has not only created a new black man, it has created a new white man, too. No road whatever will lead Americans back to the simplicity of this European village where white men still have the luxury of looking on me as a stranger. I am not, really, a stranger any longer for any American alive. One of the things that distinguishes Americans from other people is that no other people has ever been so deeply involved in the lives of black men, and vice versa. This fact faced, with all its implications, it can be seen that the history of the American Negro problem is not merely shameful, it is also something of an achievement. For even when the worst has been said, it must also be added that the perpetual challenge posed by this problem was always, somehow, perpetually met. It is precisely this black-white experience which may prove of indispensable value to us in the world we face today. This world is white no longer, and it will never be white again.

1953

The Reader's Presence

1. Baldwin opens the essay with an account of himself as a stranger in an actual Swiss village. But how do we begin to see him as a stranger in more general ways? What does the village come to represent? What is the relation of the Swiss village to Baldwin's America?

2. This is an essay that moves from autobiography to argument. In rereading it, can you find the place where Baldwin's autobiography begins to disappear and where his argument begins to take over? Try stating Baldwin's central argument in your own terms. To what extent is his argument historical?

3. In paragraph 21, Baldwin writes about the denial of "human weight and complexity." What role does such complexity play in this essay? In rereading the essay, locate several sentences in which you think Baldwin's ideas resist simplification. Study these sentences carefully. What do they have in common? How do they illustrate the kind of complexity that Baldwin sees as essentially human?

59

Susan Brownmiller

Let's Put Pornography Back in the Closet

Free speech is one of the great foundations on which our democracy rests. I am old enough to remember the Hollywood Ten, the screenwriters who went to jail in the late 1940s because they refused to testify before a congressional committee about their political affiliations. They tried to use the First Amendment as a defense, but they went to jail because in those days there were few civil liberties lawyers around who cared to champion the First Amendment right to free speech, when the speech concerned the Communist party.

The Hollywood Ten were correct in claiming the First Amendment. Its high purpose is the protection of unpopular ideas and political dissent. In the dark, cold days of the 1950s, few civil libertarians were willing to declare themselves First Amendment absolutists. But in the brighter, though frantic, days of the 1960s, the principle of protecting unpopular political speech was gradually strengthened.

It is fair to say now that the battle has largely been won. Even the American Nazi party has found itself the beneficiary of the dedicated, tireless work of the American Civil Liberties Union. But — and please notice the quotation marks coming up — "To equate the free and robust exchange of ideas and political debate with commercial exploitation of obscene material demeans the grand conception of the First Amendment and its high purposes in the historic struggle for freedom. It is a misuse of the great guarantees of free speech and free press."

I didn't say that, although I wish I had, for I think the words are thrilling. Chief Justice Warren Burger said it in 1973, in the United States Supreme Court's majority opinion in *Miller v. California*. During the same decades that the right to political free speech was being

For biographical information on Susan Brownmiller, see p. 644.

strengthened in the courts, the nation's obscenity laws also were undergoing extensive revision.

It's amazing to recall that in 1934 the question of whether James   5
Joyce's *Ulysses* should be banned as pornographic actually went before the Court. The battle to protect *Ulysses* as a work of literature with redeeming social value was won. In later decades, Henry Miller's *Tropic* books, *Lady Chatterley's Lover,* and the *Memoirs of Fanny Hill* also were adjudged not obscene. These decisions have been important to me. As the author of *Against Our Will,* a study of the history of rape that does contain explicit sexual material, I shudder to think how my book would have fared if James Joyce, D. H. Lawrence, and Henry Miller hadn't gone before me.

I am not a fan of *Chatterley* or the *Tropic* books, I should quickly mention. They are not to my literary taste, nor do I think they represent female sexuality with any degree of accuracy. But I would hardly suggest that we ban them. Such a suggestion wouldn't get very far anyway. The battle to protect these books is ancient history. Time does march on, quite methodically. What, then, is unlawfully obscene, and what does the First Amendment have to do with it?

In the Miller case of 1973 (not Henry Miller, by the way, but a porn distributor who sent unsolicited stuff through the mails), the Court came up with new guidelines that it hoped would strengthen obscenity laws by giving more power to the states. What it did in actuality was throw everything into confusion. It set up a three-part test by which materials can be adjudged obscene. The materials are obscene if they depict patently offensive, hard-core sexual conduct; lack serious scientific, literary, artistic, or political value; and appeal to the prurient interest of an average person — as measured by contemporary community standards.

"Patently offensive," prurient interest," and "hard-core" are indeed words to conjure with. "Contemporary community standards" are what we're trying to redefine. The feminist objection to pornography is not based on prurience, which the dictionary defines as lustful, itching desire. We are not opposed to sex and desire, with or without the itch, and we certainly believe that explicit sexual material has its place in literature, art, science, and education. Here we part company rather swiftly with old-line conservatives who don't want sex education in the high schools, for example.

No, the feminist objection to pornography is based on our belief that pornography represents hatred of women, that pornography's intent is to humiliate, degrade, and dehumanize the female body for the purpose of erotic stimulation and pleasure. We are unalterably opposed to the presentation of the female body being stripped, bound, raped, tortured, mutilated, and murdered in the name of commercial entertainment and free speech.

These images, which are standard pornographic fare, have nothing   10
to do with the hallowed right of political dissent. They have everything

to do with the creation of a cultural climate in which a rapist feels he is merely giving in to a normal urge and a woman is encouraged to believe that sexual masochism is healthy, liberated fun. Justice Potter Stewart once said about hard-core pornography, "You know it when you see it," and that certainly used to be true. In the good old days, pornography looked awful. It was cheap and sleazy, and there was no mistaking it for art.

Nowadays, since the porn industry has become a multimillion dollar business, visual technology has been employed in its service. Pornographic movies are skillfully filmed and edited, pornographic still shots using the newest tenets of good design artfully grace the covers of *Hustler, Penthouse,* and *Playboy,* and the public — and the courts — are sadly confused.

The Supreme Court neglected to define "hard-core" in the Miller decision. This was a mistake. If "hard-core" refers only to explicit sexual intercourse, then that isn't good enough. When women or children or men — no matter how artfully — are shown tortured or terrorized in the service of sex, that's obscene. And "patently offensive," I would hope, to our "contemporary community standards."

Justice William O. Douglas wrote in his dissent to the Miller case that no one is "compelled to look." This is hardly true. To buy a paper at a corner newsstand is to subject oneself to a forcible immersion in pornography, to be demeaned by an array of dehumanized, chopped-up parts of the female anatomy, packaged like cuts of meat at the supermarket. I happen to like my body and I work hard at the gym to keep it in good shape, but I am embarrassed for my body and for the bodies of all women when I see the fragmented parts of us so frivolously, and so flagrantly, displayed.

Some constitutional theorists (Justice Douglas was one) have maintained that any obscenity law is a serious abridgment of free speech. Others (and Justice Earl Warren was one) have maintained that the First Amendment was never intended to protect obscenity. We live quite compatibly with a host of free-speech abridgments. There are restraints against false and misleading advertising or statements — shouting "fire" without cause in a crowded movie theater, etc. — that do not threaten, but strengthen, our societal values. Restrictions on the public display of pornography belong in this category.

The distinction between permission to publish and permission to display publicly is an essential one and one which I think consonant with First Amendment principles. Justice Burger's words which I quoted above support this without question. We are not saying "Smash the presses" or "Ban the bad ones," but simply "Get the stuff out of our sight." Let the legislatures decide — using realistic and humane contemporary community standards — what can be displayed and what cannot. The courts, after all, will be the final arbiters.

1979

The Reader's Presence

1. Susan Brownmiller presents a strong argument in support of what she calls "the feminist objection to pornography." Her essay contains a clear explanation of the nature of obscenity, especially as it was defined by the Supreme Court in the early 1970s. How does she define *pornography?* What are the major criteria in her definition? In what specific ways is her definition similar to — or different from — your own? your community's? Where might you find definitions of pornography in your local community? How, for example, is that term understood by the owners of your local newsstand, movie theater, and video store — given what is available at each place? How is the term defined in local state ordinances? How does each draw the line between what is pornographic and what is sexually explicit?

2. In the middle of paragraph 8, Brownmiller shifts her pronouns from *I* and *my* to *we* and *our.* On what basis does Brownmiller claim to speak for feminists? for women in general? What is the essential nature of the feminist objection to pornography? Explain the distinction she draws between "permission to publish and permission to display?" What objections does she raise to earlier legal rulings on obscenity? How are those issues related to the question of pornography?

3. What does Brownmiller argue would be the most sensible solution to the issue of pornography in relation to First Amendment rights? In what specific ways do you find her argument compelling? convincing? flawed? How would you characterize the nature of Brownmiller's presence in this essay? Comment, for example, on her tone of voice. Would you describe it as outraged? urgent?

60

Leslie Epstein

Civility and Its Discontents

I have set myself a moral puzzle. What would I do if I were a college president and had to decide the fate of a student who had been caught writing racial and ethnic epithets — *niggers back to Africa, Hitler didn't finish the job* — on the doors of, respectively, a black and Jewish classmate, and was suspected of writing *gays suck!* in the entryway of an openly bisexual dorm? Hangdog or defiant, the miscreant is brought before me. In real life I expect my reactions would run something like this: righteousness, rage even, before the door opened, along with a fixed determination to expel the criminal from our midst; and a sudden surge of curiosity, zeal for reformation, and a form of fellow feeling, once the flesh-and-blood chap appeared on the other side of my desk. That's one good reason why the destiny of others should not be placed in my hands.

To expel or not expel? Even in the abstract, on paper, the question leaves me divided. My emotions boil at the prospect of having to share a campus with such bad apples in it. By my mind, which has its instincts too, raises the flag of caution. I've lived in this democracy long enough to know that the First Amendment ought not to be monkeyed with and that the more absolute its protections the better off all of us are (well not *all*: not those libeled, or, more to the point, not those threatened on campus). I am a member of the ACLU. I am also a writer, with a writer's concern for minimizing the role of the censor in American life.

Wait a minute: the truth is, my view of censorship is more complicated than that. The worst thing that can happen to any artist is to be shot dead by Stalin. The second worst is to be told that anything goes. I suppose the third worst is to be dragooned, by an NEA grant, into respecting the diversity of one's fellow citizens' beliefs. The point is, if there are no taboos in society, there will be few in the psyche. So much, then, for the disguises, the

For biographical information on Leslie Epstein, see p. 648.

tricks and sleight of hand, that the public, which shares the magician's re-
pressions, calls art.

How could I favor expulsion, moreover, when I had suffered that fate
myself, and more than once, in the fifties? The first occasion was at the
Webb School, in California, when one of the preppies asked, "What's
this?" as the turnips and gruel were plopped on his plate.

"The week's profit," quipped I. Papa Webb wasn't one to tolerate   5
teenage quipsters. Gone. Rusticated. Dismissed. Expelled.

A few years later the same wise guy was standing on York Street, in
New Haven, when the mayor came out of Phil's Barber Shop and stepped
into Fenn-Feinstein next door. "What's the mayor doing?" asked my current straight man, as His Honor emerged from the doorway and ducked
into the entrance of Barrie Shoes. "Wednesday. Two-thirty," I replied, just
loud enough. "Time to collect." This was, remember, the fifties. The next
thing I knew I had been thrust up against the side of a car, had handed over
my wallet, and been ordered to be at the dean's office the next morning at
ten. By eleven, I was no longer a Son of Eli.

Hard to believe? Even those who lived through those days might find
it difficult to recall the atmosphere that lingered on campus well after Senator McCarthy's demise. The master of my residential college was a particularly despotic fellow. During my junior year a number of my pals secretly
published a mimeographed newspaper, *The Trumbullian,* and at three in
the morning shoved them under everyone's door. "Ape Rape in Trumbull
Lounge" was the leading headline. Doc Nick, as he was known to his subjects, responded by calling in the FBI. For a week afterward we watched as
a crack team of pale young men in dark suits went about dusting for finger-
prints, and testing our typewriters, as they had recently done for the Hiss
trial, for telltale keys.

To return to the tale, both my expulsions had been effected in order to
remove from two bastions of Civilization, and Christendom, a threat to
what is generally called, especially by those who do the expelling these
days, civility. How can one learn, so goes the argument, in a boorish atmosphere, especially when one might be subjected to crude, offensive, even
inflammatory remarks? The premise deserves explanation. My own feeling
is that Miss Manners, and anyone else who thinks the university must be
governed by a special code of decorum, have, slightly, but crucially, missed
the point. Webb might be a finishing school, but Yale is not. At least not
any longer. "When Jews and other scum beyond human ken make Yale
fraternities. . ." The line is from the famed Yale *Record,* 1917 (and not, as
you thought, from the *Dartmouth Review,* 1990), and there was enough of
that attitude left forty years later to make our class of '60, if not quite
Judenrein, then at least controlled by a quota so strict we could count the
total number of blacks and Asians on the fingers of one hand, and which,
of course, allowed for no women at all.

Many are the sins hidden behind the cloak of gentility; enough of them were revealed in the decade following my graduation to make me forever suspicious of those who invest much of their energy in attempting to make the tattered garment whole. Oddly enough, the worst of those sins was intellectual sloth. I saw this most clearly at Oxford, not long after my adventures in New Haven. Talk about finishing schools! I know of one student, an Englishman, whose tutor advised him to stay on an extra year, "because you haven't quite got the accent yet." My own tutor, a world-renowned figure, used to wave away my fears of Armageddon with the repeated mantra: "Epstein! You Americans and your atom bomb! Have another ale!" So frantic were the dons and dullards about their civilization being violated by a good hard thought that they had institutionalized the sconce as a means of ensuring that no one did much more than dally at tea or punt along the Isis. This is how the OED defines the term:

> At Oxford, a fine of a tankard of ale or the like, imposed by undergraduates on one of their number for some breach of customary rule when dining in hall.

At Merton, the customary rule forbade any conversation about one's 10 studies, about politics, or anything roughly resembling an idea. This left, as topics, the girls at St. Hilda's and cricket.

I can't resist relating how, one night, an uncouth American, Michael Fried, now a distinguished critic of art, thoughtlessly let slip a remark about Marx or Freud. An awful hush fell upon the hall. At high table, the dons froze, their asparagus savories hanging above their mouths. Down at the benches, the undergraduates let the peas roll off their knives. Behind the malefactor a waiter appeared, with the customary bloodshot cheeks and bushy mustache, holding a foaming chalice of ale. Fried, deep in discussion, paid no mind. The ruddy servant — in his white apron he looked the kosher butcher — tapped him on the shoulder and held up the tankard with a grin and a wink. Fried whirled around. "What am I supposed to do with this?" he asked, as if unaware that custom dictated he drink down the contents and order an equal portion for all those at table. "Shove it up your ass?" Thus, on the shores of England, did the sixties arrive.

Universities exist not to inculcate manners or teach propriety but to foster inquiry, pass on the story of what has been best thought and done in the past, and to search for the truth. There is no proof that this teaching and this search can be done only when people are being polite to each other. Indeed, there is much evidence, beginning with Socrates, to suggest that it can be done best when people rub hard, and the wrong way, against each other, ruffling feathers, making sparks.

Does this mean, then, that one student may call another *fag* or *nigger* or *kike*? As a college president I would have no trouble allowing anyone on campus who wished to argue that homosexuality was contrary to nature, that blacks were intellectually inferior to whites, or that the Holocaust never happened. Such visitations are far different than hurled epithets. To the awful arguments one may at least offer arguments of one's own, display one's charts and graphs and statistics, confident that the truth will out. But what argument can one make against a slur — even one that is not anonymous? If anything, an epithet is designed to short-circuit rationality, to inflame feelings, to draw a curtain, the color of boiling blood, across the life of the mind. Further, it is not just the life of the mind that is threatened: behind the word "nigger" hangs the noose, just as the ovens burn and smoke hovers behind the word "kike."

This distinction — between, if you will, inquiry and invective — carries almost enough weight with me to force a decision: if anyone seeks to destroy another's ability to join the intellectual life of the university, that is, to reason freely, to search dispassionately, to think, he ought not to have any role in that community himself. Almost. The strongest voice against passing sentence comes not from civil libertarians (to whose arguments I hope to turn soon) but from a Yale Law School student, himself the recipient of an anonymous letter ("Now you know why we call you niggers"), who recently told the Yale *Herald*, "It infantilizes people of color to say we can't handle people saying mean things about us. . . . It's much better for people of color to know what people think of us. I'd feel much, much better if people said exactly what they think." Back, for the moment, on the fence.

I began the discussion of this moral puzzle by listing a number of reasons why I am, through intellectual makeup and personal experience, drawn toward a merciful resolution of the dilemma. Not the least of these reasons has to do with the allies I would rather not have should I choose to expel. I am thinking, of course, of the movement whose members — though "movement" and "members" are clearly misnomers — have become the most censorious figures on college campuses. It is the politically correct who call for strict codes to define what is and is not permissable speech and who have exercised the will to enforce them.

Now I want to make it clear at once that if I have problems with the PC crowd, I am no happier with what seems to be the orchestrated campaign of attack against them, a campaign whose sole purpose is to transform the last institution in American life not already controlled by the right. I'm caught, for friends, between people who call for the hide of others; or others, who have suddenly seen the virtue of the Bill of Rights, like Representative Henry Hyde. (The congressman's bill states that "federally assisted institutions cannot discipline students if their spoken or printed views are found to be repugnant, offensive, or emotionally distressing to others on the campus." This from a man who voted to force recipients of grants from the National Endowment for the Arts to consider their fellow citizens' beliefs!)

Everyone has a favorite example — at Michigan, for instance, a male student is officially proscribed from saying "women just aren't as good in this field as men" — of PC excess. Because I'm trying to keep these remarks as personal as possible, I'll turn to my own town, Brookline, which

15

once had a first-rate school system. Nowadays it has embarked on a "hundred-year plan" to do away with what an assistant superintendent of curriculum calls the "traditional" white male perspective. Among the things this plan would eliminate is the "vertical" white male notion of excellence, along with disciplined thinking, logic, and what this same superintendent calls the "incredible abomination" of Black History Month, whose sin is to reinforce privileged ideas of excellence by pointing out "pinnacle people" who are "outstanding exceptions to their group."

A few weeks ago, a good thirty-two years after my undergraduate days, I took part in a panel on censorship at what is probably Yale's most prestigious, and certainly its most open-minded, senior society. The current delegation was there, class of '91, together with representatives of delegations going back almost to the days when the *Record* could speak of subhuman scum. The discussion, as you might imagine, was lively. At one point a contemporary of mine, an artist, told the story of how the curators of a Gauguin exhibition had been lobbied to take down half the paintings because they demonstrated "an exploitative colonialist perspective." An appreciative chuckle went round the room. We codgers elbowed each other. Such an absurdity! Suddenly a member of the current delegation rose from his bench. "I'd like to point out," he said, in a voice that was only slightly shaking, "that no people of color are laughing." True enough. Nor was anyone much below the age of thirty-five.

I hope it isn't necessary for me to say how much I like these students. They are bright, sensitive, idealistic, and — at Yale, anyway — they work every bit as hard as I did in the fifties. They may be bamboozled, but these bits of zaniness are no more indicative of a totalitarian spirit than the knee-jerk liberalism I still feel a twitch of on rainy days. At the same time, there are elements of a kind of conformity that cannot be laughed away. To stick to my current campus, I've been present when a harassment officer browbeat my colleagues — who merely grinned and bore it — about how to notice sexist attitudes among its members and how to turn the offenders in to her office. And I know of a department that voted to offer a talented young assistant professor ("enchanting" was the word his students used to describe his teaching) the normal extension of his contract, then reversed itself twenty-four hours later, largely because of his supposed sexism (he had, as an example, observed a lousy performance by a graduate student and suggested that perhaps her advanced pregnancy had created a strain). Kaput career. There's more than a whiff of Peking in the air when professors are forced, as they have been, to recant, or apologize for their opinions, or sent to special classes for reeducation.

Yet even the thought police are not what worries me most about political correctness, or what tie these worries to the subject at hand. Perhaps I can best get at what I mean by reiterating what I told my daughter, who is struggling with these issues herself as a college junior, when she asked me for a one-sentence definition of PC. "Well," I said, perhaps less clumsily 20 than this, "I guess this is a way of seeing society as a system of oppression, and that the interests of its victims ought to dictate our thinking and behavior, to the exclusion of pretty much any other consideration." What I didn't add was that the "other consideration" I had in mind was the very idea of objective reality, stubborn and recalcitrant as the law of gravity; and that it was this reality, with its laws, its truth, and — tricky, this — its values that the university was founded to discover, nurture, and pass on.

Which leads me to note that during that debate at Yale, the most engaged and vociferous students invariably turned out to be English majors. No surprise there. They were well versed in deconstruction and other reader-response theories, which together have provided the ideological underpinnings of political correctness. Here, from Jane Tompkins, a leading feminist scholar, is a nutshell version of how these students have been taught to approach a test:

> Critics deny that criticism has . . . an objective basis because they deny the existence of objective texts and indeed the possibility of objectivity altogether. . . . The net result of this epistemological revolution is to politicize literature and literary criticism. When discourse is responsible for reality and not merely a reflection of it, then whose discourse prevails makes all the difference.

Literary texts, then, have no inherent meaning or even a claim to existence, apart from the baggage of the culture in which they were written and now are read. Free speech? Value? Objective standards? Timeless verities? Reality itself? Truth becomes simply an opinion, whatever has been ferreted out as the reigning myth; and knowledge is the triumph of one ideology over another. It is this academic version of might makes right, with its inherent nihilism, that has helped me to solve the puzzle I set myself these many paragraphs back.

That is to say, there are *two* slopes that lead from the heights of academe, one as slippery as the other. The first has, with good reason, preoccupied those concerned with civil liberties: Once we begin proscribing some speech, what other restrictions will follow? To what end will we come? We already have the answer: to the harassment code at the University of Connecticut, which forbids "inconsiderate jokes," misdirected laughter," and "conspicuous exclusion from conversation." Yet even these grotesqueries do not resolve our dilemma. If the City College of New York were to prohibit Leonard Jeffries of its Black Studies Department from saying that blacks are superior to whites because of the melanin in their skins, or silence Michael Levin, a professor of philosophy at the same institution, who believes that blacks are inherently inferior, it would surely be exercising a form of thought control. The trouble is, *not* censoring the kind of racial epithet whose effect is to undermine the very processes of logic is a form of thought control as well.

Perhaps the solution, or at least a legal rationale for a solution, to this dilemma lies as near to hand as my daily newspaper. On page 41 of today's *Boston Globe,* under the headline *Black workers at Maine plant win in bias suit,* is the story of how three black men from the South were recruited to work at the International Paper Co. in Auburn, Maine. Once there they were harassed by "ugly oral racial epithets and graffiti," and by co-workers "in Ku Klux Klan–like garb 'prancing' around their work stations."

The United States District Court ruled that in creating "a hostile and   25 offensive workplace" and by substantially altering the plaintiffs' working conditions, International Paper had violated Maine's human rights act. The three workers were awarded $55,000 each. Now there is similar harassment legislation in every state of the union. Is there any reason why, of all the institutions in America, only those of higher education should be exempt from these statutes? The only response is a truism: that a university, with its special mission and need for forceful debate, and comprehensive points of view, is not a paper mill. It is precisely the role of the university, its vulnerability, and its fate in modern history, that leads me to look at the second, and steeper, of the slippery slopes.

The grease for this chute is applied by that same belief in the relativity of all values that now prevails on so many campuses. Here are the words of one university president:

> Every people in every period must form its life according to its own law and fate, and to this law of its own, scholarship, with all other spheres of life, is also subject. . . . The idea of humanism, with the teaching of pure human reason and absolute spirit founded upon it, is a philosophical principle of the eighteenth century caused by the conditions of that time. It is in no sense binding upon us as we live under different conditions and under a different fate.

The speaker is Ernst Krick, rector of Frankfort University, and the occasion was the 550th anniversary of the University of Heidelberg in 1936.

At the bottom of this slope lies totalitarianism of one kind or another. The movement of nihilism is both centrifugal and centripetal, moving outward from literary texts — which, since they have no enduring value, are all too easily burned — through discipline after discipline, in ever widening circles until even the obdurate laws of nature herself are subject to challenge. Hence, in the universities of the Third Reich, biology became "National Socialist biology," psychoanalysis became "mongrel psychology," and the theory of relativity was "Jewish physics."

If there are no lasting truths, nothing to be handed down from one generation to another, then the only source of authority shrinks centripetally in narrower and narrower circles until one arrives at the fountainhead of truth, which in the German formula was the Fuehrer. What Hitler set out to destroy was Western culture and intelligence itself — and not in the name of diversity! On the contrary it was the Fuehrer, who became the only thinker, the sole author, the one biologist, legal expert, psychologist, and knower of nature's secrets.

The Weimar Republic had as many laws against harassment as has,   30
these days, the state of Maine. Dueling societies were banned (and with
them the practice of refusing to duel with Jews), as were all remarks tending to incite racial hatred or campus strife. The trouble was, the rules were
not enforced — or worse, enforced selectively. The book has yet to be written as to why the right has always felt free ruthlessly to suppress the liberal
left, and why the liberal left, and liberalism in general, has stood by,
Hamlet-like, unable to repress the forces of the right. (The image of Hamlet
is appropriate, since, according to the "mongrel science," the reason he
cannot strike Claudius is that his uncle has enacted the very crimes — murdering his father and sleeping with his mother — that he wished, in the
depths of his unconscious, to commit himself. The liberal may see, in the
nationalist, the racist, and the fanatic, the embodiment of the passions he
has smothered in his own breast.)

Hence Hitler, after the beer-hall putsch, was put in a cell with a view
and handed a paper and pencil. In the name of academic freedom, Weimar
permitted every atrocity, even the assassinations it half-heartedly prosecuted and feebly punished. The result was that, well before Hitler took
power, the universities had become such hotbeds of anti-Semitism and ul-
tranationalism that the professorate, of all the classes in Germany, became
the most devoted followers of his cause.

The fundamental mistake of Weimar Germany, and of liberalism in
general, is the belief that, confronted by nihilistic fervor, one may yet count
on a triumph of reason. Theodor Mommsen, the great German historian,
wore himself out (and lost his job) in the attempt to defend what he called
the "legacy of Lessing" against "racial hatred and the fanaticism of the
Middle Ages." In the end he came to realize:

> You are mistaken if you believe that anything at all could be achieved
> by reason. In years past I thought so myself and kept protesting against
> the monstrous infamy that is anti-Semitism. But it is useless, completely
> useless. Whatever I or anybody else could tell you are in the last analysis
> reasons, logical and ethical arguments which no anti-Semite will listen to.
> They listen only to their own envy and hatred, to the meanest instincts.
> Nothing else counts for them. They are deaf to reason, right morals. One
> cannot influence them.

Let us return to that Yale Law School student (his name is Anthony K.
Jones) who faced with equanimity and no small amount of courage the
prospect of a fellow student calling him nigger. What would he feel, I wonder, when faced by *two* screaming students? Or four? Eventually he would
have to run, as others have before him, a gauntlet. Is there any prospect
that, hounded by what Mommsen called "the mob of the streets or the
parlors," anything resembling the free exchange of ideas could take place?

I cannot remain, even in my imagination, a university president if I do
not believe in certain things — chief among them the belief that reality can
be known and its truths both taught and learned. Free speech, far from

being an end in itself, is an instrument in a process of discovery. When it impedes or perverts that process — for instance by denying a student the exercise of his intellect or putting him in fear for his body — something must be done.

But what? About that I have come, through however tortuous a route, 35 to a decision. It is perhaps natural that, since my ideas have been divided against themselves, this conclusion should take the form of a paradox. Because the tactics of the civil libertarians, and liberalism in general, are unavailing against men and women seized by nihilistic fervor, I shall have to adopt those that belong to the fervent themselves. I do so not so much to circumscribe those who are politically correct, but to guard against those, like the young man about to be brought before me, who have been provoked to react — in what is always a deadly dance — against them.

Here he comes now. Of course he shall have due process. And we shall have to go into every detail, each aspect of his case. But at bottom it is his unwillingness to engage others as free spirits, his attempt to extinguish reason within them, that dooms him. I shall not attempt to put ideas he does not feel into his head or words he does not feel into his mouth: no people's court here! Instead, I shall steel myself against my own nature and ask him to leave the university. Perhaps he might reapply and, if his self-knowledge has grown, be readmitted (as it happens, I got back into Webb and Yale, although the fifties might have been more forgiving than present times). And in passing this harsh sentence I shall turn, as college presidents like to do, to authority — this time, appropriately enough, to the man who above all others believed in the imperishability of ideas. Punishment, Plato said, is the most salutary thing one can do for a man who has done wrong.

1991

The Reader's Presence

1. Reread Epstein's third paragraph carefully. How does his list of the three "worst" things that could happen reflect the complexity of his position? Why would he want to let the reader know this about himself at the outset?
2. What kind of presence does Epstein create for himself in the essay? How does he use his personal experience to advance his argument? Do you think that the same experiences could be used to advance the other side of the argument? Explain.
3. Were you surprised by Epstein's final decision? Reread his opening paragraphs. Were there any clues that he would decide this way right from the start? Or do you think the essay honestly shows the *process* of his reaching a decision? Explain your response.

61

Susan Faludi

Blame It on Feminism

To be a woman in America at the close of the twentieth century —
what good fortune. That's what we keep hearing anyway. The barricades
have fallen, politicians assure us. Women have "made it," Madison Avenue cheers. Women's fight for equality has "largely been won," *Time* magazine announces. Enroll at any university, join any law firm, apply for
credit at any bank. Women have so many opportunities now, corporate
leaders say, that they don't really need opportunity policies. Women are so
equal now, lawmakers say, that they no longer need an Equal Rights
Amendment. Women have "so much," former president Ronald Reagan
says, that the White House no longer needs to appoint them to high office.
Even American Express ads are saluting a woman's right to charge it. At
last, women have received their full citizenship papers.

And yet . . .

Behind this celebration of the American woman's victory, behind the
news, cheerfully and endlessly repeated, that the struggle for women's
rights is won, another message flashes: You may be free and equal now,
but you have never been more miserable.

This bulletin of despair is posted everywhere — at the newsstand, on
the TV set, at the movies, in advertisements and doctors' offices and academic journals. Professional women are suffering "burnout" and succumb-
ing to an "infertility epidemic." Single women are grieving from a "man
shortage." The *New York Times* reports: Childless women are "depressed
and confused" and their ranks are swelling. *Newsweek* says: Unwed
women are "hysterical" and crumbling under a "profound crisis of confidence." The health-advice manuals inform: High-powered career women
are stricken with unprecedented outbreaks of "stress-induced disorders,"
hair loss, bad nerves, alcoholism, and even heart attacks. The psychology

---

For biographical information on Susan Faludi, see p. 648.

books advise: Independent women's loneliness represents "a major mental-health problem today." Even founding feminist Betty Friedan has been spreading the word: She warns that women now suffer from "new problems that have no name."

How can American women be in so much trouble at the same time that 5
they are supposed to be so blessed? If women got what they asked for, what could possibly be the matter now?

The prevailing wisdom of the past decade has supported one, and only one, answer to this riddle: It must be all that equality that's causing all that pain. Women are unhappy precisely because they are free. Women are enslaved by their own liberation. They have grabbed at the gold ring of independence, only to miss the one ring that really matters. They have gained control of their fertility, only to destroy it. They have pursued their own professional dreams — and lost out on romance, the greatest female adventure. "Our generation was the human sacrifice" to the women's movement, writer Elizabeth Mehren contends in a *Time* cover story. Baby-boom women, like her, she says, have been duped by feminism: "We believed the rhetoric." In *Newsweek,* writer Kay Ebeling dubs feminism the "Great Experiment That Failed" and asserts, "Women in my generation, its perpetrators, are the casualties."

In the eighties, publications from the *New York Times* to *Vanity Fair* to *The Nation* have issued a steady stream of indictments against the women's movement, with such headlines as "When Feminism Failed" or "The Awful Truth About Women's Lib." They hold the campaign for women's equality responsible for nearly every woe besetting women, from depression to meager savings accounts, from teenage suicides to eating disorders to bad complexions. The *Today* show says women's liberation is to blame for bag ladies. A guest columnist in the *Baltimore Sun* even proposes that feminists produced the rise in slasher movies. By making the "violence" of abortion more acceptable, the author reasons, women's rights activists made it all right to show graphic murders on screen.

At the same time, other outlets of popular culture have been forging the same connection: in Hollywood films, of which *Fatal Attraction* is only the most famous, emancipated women with condominiums of their own slink wild-eyed between bare walls, paying for their liberty with an empty bed, a barren womb. "My biological clock is ticking so loud it keeps me awake at night," Sally Field cries in the film *Surrender,* as, in an all-too-common transformation in the cinema of the eighties, an actress who once played scrappy working heroines is now showcased groveling for a groom. In prime-time television shows, from *thirtysomething* to *Family Man,* single, professional, and feminist women are humiliated, turned into harpies, or hit by nervous breakdowns; the wise ones recant their independent ways by the closing sequence. In popular novels, from Gail Parent's *A Sign of the Eighties* to Stephen King's *Misery,* unwed women shrink to sniveling spinsters or inflate to fire-breathing she-devils; renouncing all aspirations but marriage, they beg for wedding bands from strangers or swing axes at reluctant bachelors. Even Erica Jong's high-flying independent heroine literally crashes by the end of the decade, as the author supplants *Fear of Flying's* saucy Isadora Wing, an exuberant symbol of female sexual emancipation in the seventies, with an embittered careerist-turned-recovering-"codependent" in *Any Woman's Blues* — a book that is intended, as the narrator bluntly states, "to demonstrate what a dead end the so-called sexual revolution had become and how desperate so-called free women were in the last few years of our decadent epoch."

Popular psychology manuals peddle the same diagnosis for contemporary female distress. "Feminism, having promised her a stronger sense of her own identity, has given her little more than an identity *crisis*," the bestselling advice manual *Being a Woman* asserts. The authors of the era's self-help classic, *Smart Women/Foolish Choices,* proclaim that women's distress was "an unfortunate consequence of feminism" because "it created a myth among women that the apex of self-realization could be achieved only through autonomy, independence, and career."

In the Reagan and Bush years, government officials have needed no   10
prompting to endorse this thesis. Reagan spokeswoman Faith Ryan Whittlesey declared feminism a "straitjacket" for women, in one of the White House's only policy speeches on the status of the American female population — entitled "Radical Feminism in Retreat." The U.S. attorney general's Commission on Pornography even proposed that women's professional advancement might be responsible for rising rape rates: With more women in college and at work now, the commission members reasoned in their report, women just have more opportunities to be raped.

Legal scholars have railed against the "equality trap." Sociologists have claimed that "feminist-inspired" legislative reforms have stripped women of special "protections." Economists have argued that well-paid working women have created a "less stable American family." And demographers, with greatest fanfare, have legitimated the prevailing wisdom with so-called neutral data on sex ratios and fertility trends; they say they actually have the numbers to prove that equality doesn't mix with marriage and motherhood.

Finally, some "liberated" women themselves have joined the lamentations. In *The Cost of Loving: Women and the New Fear of Intimacy,* Megan Marshall, a Harvard-pedigreed writer, asserts that the feminist "Myth of Independence" has turned her generation into unloved and unhappy fast-trackers, "dehumanized" by careers and "uncertain of their gender identity." Other diaries of mad Superwomen charge that "the hardcore feminist viewpoint," as one of them puts it, has relegated educated executive achievers to solitary nights of frozen dinners and closet drinking. The triumph of equality, they report, has merely given women hives, stomach cramps, eye "twitching" disorders, even comas.

But what "equality" are all these authorities talking about?

If American women are so equal, why do they represent two-thirds of all poor adults? Why are more than 70 percent of full-time working women making less than twenty-five thousand dollars a year, nearly double the number of men at that level? Why are they still far more likely than men to live in poor housing, and twice as likely to draw no pension? If women "have it all," then why don't they have the most basic requirements to achieve equality in the work force: Unlike that of virtually all other industrialized nations, the U.S. government still has no family-leave and childcare programs.

If women are so "free," why are their reproductive freedoms in   15 greater jeopardy today than a decade earlier? Why, in their own homes, do they still shoulder 70 percent of the household duties — while the only major change in the last fifteen years is that now men *think* they do more around the house? In thirty states, it is still generally legal for husbands to rape their wives; and only ten states have laws mandating arrest for domestic violence — even though battering is the leading cause of injury to women (greater than rapes, muggings, and auto accidents combined).

The word may be that women have been "liberated," but women themselves seem to feel otherwise. Repeatedly in national surveys, majorities of women say they are still far from equality. In poll after poll in the decade, overwhelming majorities of women said they need equal pay and equal job opportunities, they need an Equal Rights Amendment, they need the right to an abortion without government interference, they need a federal law guaranteeing maternity leave, they need decent child-care services. They have none of these. So how exactly have women "won" the war for women's rights?

Seen against this background, the much ballyhooed claim that feminism is responsible for making women miserable becomes absurd — and irrelevant. The afflictions ascribed to feminism, from "the man shortage" to "the infertility epidemic" to "female burnout" to "toxic day care," have had their origins not in the actual conditions of women's lives but rather in a closed system that starts and ends in the media, popular culture, and advertising — an endless feedback loop that perpetuates and exaggerates its own false images of womanhood. And women don't see feminism as their enemy, either. In fact, in national surveys, 75 to 95 percent of women credit the feminist campaign with *improving* their lives, and a similar proportion say that the women's movement should keep pushing for change.

If the many ponderers of the Woman Question really wanted to know what is troubling the American female population, they might have asked their subjects. In public-opinion surveys, women consistently rank their own *inequality,* at work and at home, among their most urgent concerns. Over and over, women complain to pollsters of a lack of economics, not marital, opportunities; they protest that working men, not working women, fail to spend time in the nursery and the kitchen. It is justice for their gender, not wedding rings and bassinets, that women believe to be in desperately short supply.

As the last decade ran its course, the monitors that serve to track slippage in women's status have been working overtime. Government and private surveys are showing that women's already vast representation in the lowliest occupations is rising, their tiny presence in higher-paying trade and craft jobs stalled or backsliding, their minuscule representation in upper management posts stagnant or falling, and their pay dropping in the very occupations where they have made the most "progress."

In national politics, the already small numbers of women in both elective posts and political appointments fell during the eighties. In private life, the average amount that a divorced man paid in child support fell by about 25 percent from the late seventies to the mid-eighties (to a mere $140 a month). And government records chronicled a spectacular rise in sexual violence against women. Reported rapes more than doubled from the early seventies — at nearly twice the rate of all other violent crimes and four times the overall crime rate in the United States.

The truth is that the last decade has seen a powerful counterassault on women's rights, a backlash, an attempt to retract the handful of small and hard-won victories that the feminist movement did manage to win for women. This counterassault is largely insidious: In a kind of pop-culture version of the big lie, it stands the truth boldly on its head and proclaims that the very steps that have elevated women's position have actually led to their downfall.

The backlash is at once sophisticated and banal, deceptively "progressive" and proudly backward. It deploys both the "new" findings of "scientific research" and the dime-store moralism of yesteryear; it turns into media sound bites both the glib pronouncements of pop-psych trendwatchers and the frenzied rhetoric of New Right preachers. The backlash has succeeded in framing virtually the whole issue of women's rights in its own language. Just as Reaganism shifted political discourse far to the right and demonized liberalism, so the backlash convinced the public that women's "liberation" was the true contemporary American scourge — the source of an endless laundry list of personal, social, and economic problems.

But what has made women unhappy in the last decade is not their "equality" — which they don't yet have — but the rising pressure to halt, and even reverse, women's quest for that equality. The "man shortage" and the "infertility epidemic" are not the price of liberation; in fact, they do not even exist. But these chimeras are part of a relentless whittling-down process — much of it amounting to outright propaganda — that has served to stir women's private anxieties and break their political wills. Identifying feminism as women's enemy only furthers the ends of a backlash against women's equality by simultaneously deflecting attention from the backlash's central role and recruiting women to attack their own cause.

Some social observers may well ask whether the current pressures on women actually constitute a backlash — or just a continuation of American society's long-standing resistance to women's equal rights. Certainly hostility to female independence has always been with us. But if fear and loathing of feminism is a sort of perpetual viral condition in our culture, it is not always in an acute stage; its symptoms subside and resurface periodically. And it is these episodes of resurgence, such as the one we face now, that can accurately be termed "backlashes" to women's advancement. If we trace these occurrences in American history, we find such flare-ups are hardly random; they have always been triggered by the perception — accurate or not — that women are making great strides. These outbreaks are backlashes because they have always arisen in reaction to women's "progress," caused not simply by a bedrock of misogyny but by the specific efforts of contemporary women to improve their status, efforts that have been interpreted time and again by men — especially men grappling with real threats to their economic and social well-being on other fronts — as spelling their own masculine doom.

The most recent round of backlash first surfaced in the late seventies 25 on the fringes, among the evangelical Right. By the early eighties, the fundamentalist ideology had shouldered its way into the White House. By the mideighties, as resistance to women's rights acquired political and social acceptability, it passed into the popular culture. And in every case, the timing coincided with signs that women were believed to be on the verge of a breakthrough.

Just when the women's quest for equal rights seemed closest to achieving its objectives, the backlash struck it down. Just when a "gender gap" at the voting booth surfaced in 1980, and women in politics began to talk of capitalizing on it, the Republican party elevated Ronald Reagan and both political parties began to shunt women's rights off their platforms. Just when support for feminism and the Equal Rights Amendment reached a record high in 1981, the amendment was defeated the following year. Just when women were starting to mobilize against battering and sexual assaults, the federal government cut funding for battered-women's programs, defeated bills to fund shelters, and shut down its Office of Domestic Violence — only two years after opening it in 1979. Just when record numbers of younger women were supporting feminist goals in the mid-eighties (more of them, in fact, than older women) and a majority of all women were calling themselves feminists, the media declared the advent of a younger "postfeminist generation" that supposedly reviled the women's movement. Just when women racked up their largest percentage ever supporting the right to abortion, the U.S. Supreme Court moved toward reconsidering it.

In other words, the antifeminist backlash has been set off not by women's achievement of full equality but by the increased possibility that they might win it. It is a preemptive strike that stops women long before they reach the finish line. "A backlash may be an indication that women really have had an effect," feminist psychiatrist Dr. Jean Baker Miller has written, "but backlashes occur when advances have been small, before changes are sufficient to help many people. . . . It is almost as if the leaders of backlashes use the fear of change as a threat before major change has occurred." In the last decade, some women did make substantial advances before the backlash hit, but millions of others were left behind, stranded. Some women now enjoy the right to legal abortion — but not the forty-four million women, from the indigent to the military worker, who depend on the federal government for their medical care. Some women can now walk into high-paying professional careers — but not the millions still in the typing pools or behind the department-store sales counters. (Contrary to popular myth about the "have-it-all" baby-boom women, the largest percentage of women in this generation remain in office support roles.)

As the backlash has gathered force, it has cut off the few from the many — and the few women who have advanced seek to prove, as a social survival tactic, that they aren't so interested in advancement after all. Some of them parade their defection from the women's movement, while their working-class peers founder and cling to the splintered remains of the feminist cause. While a very few affluent and celebrity women who are showcased in news stories boast about going home to "bake bread," the many working-class women appeal for their economic rights — flocking to unions in record numbers, striking on their own for pay equity, and establishing their own fledgling groups for working-women's rights. In 1986, while 41 percent of upper-income women were claiming in the Gallup poll that they were not feminists, only 26 percent of low-income women were making the same claim.

Women's advances and retreats are generally described in military terms: battles won, battles lost, points and territory gained and surrendered. The metaphor of combat is not without its merits in this context, and, clearly, the same sort of martial accounting and vocabulary is already surfacing here. But by imagining the conflict as two battalions neatly arrayed on either side of the line, we miss the entangled nature, the locked embrace, of a "war" between women and the male culture they inhabit. We miss the reactive nature of a backlash, which, by definition, can exist only in response to another force.

In times when feminism is at a low ebb, women assume the reactive role — privately and, most often, covertly struggling to assert themselves against the dominant cultural tide. But when feminism itself become the tide, the opposition doesn't simply go along with the reversal: It digs in its heels, brandishes its fists, builds walls and dams. And its resistance creates countercurrents and treacherous undertows.

The force and furor of the backlash churn beneath the surface, largely invisible to the public eye. On occasion in the last decade, they have burst into view. We have seen New Right politicians condemn women's independence, antiabortion protesters firebomb women's clinics, fundamentalist preachers damn feminists as "whores." Other signs of the backlash's wrath, by their sheer brutality, can push their way into public consciousness for a time — the sharp increase in rape, for example, or the rise in pornography that depicts extreme violence against women.

More subtle indicators in popular culture may receive momentary, and often bemused, media notice, then quickly slip from social awareness: a report, for instance, that the image of women on prime-time TV shows has suddenly degenerated. A survey of mystery fiction finding the number of tortured and mutilated female characters mysteriously multiplying. The puzzling news that, as one commentator put it, "so many hit songs have the B word [bitch] to refer to women that some rap music seems to be veering toward rape music." The ascendancy of violently misogynist comics like Andrew Dice Clay, who calls women "pigs" and "sluts," or radio hosts like Rush Limbaugh, whose broadsides against "femi-Nazi" feminists helped make his syndicated program the most popular radio talk show in the nation. Or word that, in 1987, the American Women in Radio and Television couldn't award its annual prize to ads that feature women positively: It could find no ad that qualified.

These phenomena are all related, but that doesn't mean they are somehow coordinated. The backlash is not a conspiracy, with a council dispatching agents from some central control room, nor are the people who serve its ends often aware of their role; some even consider themselves feminists. For the most part, its workings are encoded and internalized, diffuse and chameleonic. Not all of the manifestations of the backlash are of equal weight or significance, either; some are mere ephemera thrown up by a culture machine that is always scrounging for a "fresh" angle. Taken as a whole, however, these codes and cajolings, these whispers and threats and myths, move overwhelmingly in one direction: They try to push women back into their "acceptable" roles — whether as Daddy's girl or fluttery romantic, active nester or passive love object.

Although the backlash is not an organized movement, that doesn't make it any less destructive. In fact, the lack of orchestration, the absence of a single string-puller, only makes it harder to see — and perhaps more effective. A backlash against women's rights succeeds to a degree that it appears *not* to be political, that it appears not to be a struggle at all. It is most powerful when it goes private, when it lodges inside a woman's mind and turns her vision inward, until she imagines the pressure is all in her head, until she begins to enforce the backlash, too — on herself.

In the last decade, the backlash has moved through the culture's secret 35 chambers, traveling through passageways of flattery and fear. Along the way, it has adopted disguises: a mask of mild derision or the painted face of deep "concern." Its lips profess pity for any women who won't fit the mold, while it tries to clamp the mold around her ears. It pursues a divide-and-conquer strategy: single versus married women, working women versus homemakers, middle versus working class. It manipulates a system of rewards and punishments, elevating women who follow its rules, isolating those who don't. The backlash remarkets old myths about women as new facts and ignores all appeals to reason. Cornered, it denies its own existence, points an accusatory finger at feminism, and burrows deeper underground.

Backlash happens to be the title of a 1947 Hollywood movie in which a man frames his wife for a murder he's committed. The backlash against women's rights works in much the same way: Its rhetoric charges feminists with all the crimes it perpetrates. The backlash line blames the women's movement for the "feminization of poverty" — while the backlash's own instigators in Washington have pushed through the budget cuts that have helped impoverish millions of women, have fought pay-equity proposals, and undermined equal-opportunity laws. The backlash line claims the women's movement cares nothing for children's rights — while its own representatives in the capital and state legislatures have blocked one bill after another to improve child care, slashed billions of dollars in aid for children, and relaxed state licensing standards for day-care centers. The backlash line accuses the women's movement of creating a generation of unhappy single and childless women — but its purveyors in the media are the ones guilty of making single and childless women feel like circus freaks.

To blame feminism for women's "lesser life" is to miss its point entirely, which is to win women a wider range of experience. Feminism remains a pretty simple concept, despite repeated — and enormously effective — efforts to dress it up in greasepaint and turn its proponents into gargoyles. As Rebecca West wrote sardonically in 1913, "I myself have never been able to find out precisely what feminism is: I only know that people call me a feminist whenever I express sentiments that differentiate me from a doormat."

The meaning of the word "feminism" has not really changed since it first appeared in a book review in *The Athenaeum* on April 27, 1895, describing a woman who "has in her the capacity of fighting her way back to independence." It is the basic proposition that, as Nora put it in Ibsen's *A Doll's House* a century ago, "Before everything else I'm a human being." It is the simply worded sign hoisted by a little girl in the 1970 Women's Strike for Equality: "I AM NOT A BARBIE DOLL." Feminism asks the world to recognize at long last that women aren't decorative ornaments, worthy vessels, members of a "special-interest group." They are half (in fact, now more than half) of the national population, and just as deserving of rights and opportunities, just as capable of participating in the world's events, as the other half. Feminism's agenda is basic: It asks that women not be forced to "choose" between public justice and private happiness. It asks that women be free to define themselves — instead of having their identity defined for them, time and again, by their culture and their men.

The fact that these are still such incendiary notions should tell us that American women have a way to go before they enter the promised land of equality.

1991

The Reader's Presence

1. How would you describe the tone of voice Faludi adopts in her opening paragraph? What is her attitude toward the opinions she cites? Do you think she wants her readers to recognize her attitude immediately? Is it possible to read the paragraph and think she agrees with all of the opinions she cites? What sort of reader is she counting on?

2. What is a backlash? How does Faludi use the term? What proof does she offer that a backlash against feminism is occurring? To what extent does she hold women themselves as responsible? Which groups does she view as most responsible for the backlash? Why?

3. In rereading the essay, take careful note of the way Faludi supports her contention that a backlash is occurring. List all of the evidence she offers. Can you find any similarities among her sources? To what extent does she depend upon personal experience? upon interviews? upon experts? upon research? upon inference? Which evidence strikes you as the strongest? as the weakest?

62

Paul Fussell

A Well-regulated Militia

In the spring Washington swarms with high school graduating classes. They come to the great pulsating heart of the Republic — which no one has yet told them is Wall Street — to be impressed by the White House and the Capitol and the monuments and the Smithsonian and the space capsules. Given the state of public secondary education, I doubt if many of these young people are at all interested in language and rhetoric, and I imagine few are fascinated by such attendants of power and pressure as verbal misrepresentation and disingenuous quotation. But any who are can profit from a stroll past the headquarters of the National Rifle Association of America, its slick marble façade conspicuous at 1600 Rhode Island Avenue, NW.

There they would see an entrance flanked by two marble panels offering language, and language more dignified and traditional than that customarily associated with the Association's gun-freak constituency, with its T-shirts reading GUNS, GUTS, AND GLORY ARE WHAT MADE AMERICA GREAT and its belt buckles proclaiming I'LL GIVE UP MY GUN WHEN THEY PRY MY COLD DEAD FINGERS FROM AROUND IT. The marble panel on the right reads, "The right of the people to keep and bear arms shall not be infringed," which sounds familiar. So familiar that the student naturally expects the left-hand panel to honor the principle of symmetry by presenting the first half of the quotation, namely: "A well-regulated Militia, being necessary to the security of a free state, . . ." But looking to the left, the inquirer discovers not that clause at all but rather this lame list of NRA functions and specializations: "Firearms Safety Education. Marksmanship Training. Shooting for Recreation." It's as if in presenting its well-washed, shiny public face the NRA doesn't want to remind anyone of the crucial dependent clause of the Second Amendment, whose latter half alone it is so

For biographical information on Paul Fussell, see p. 649.

fond of invoking to urge its prerogatives. (Some legible belt buckles of members retreat further into a seductive vagueness, reading only, "Our American Heritage: the Second Amendment.") We infer that for the Association, the less emphasis on the clause about the militia, the better. Hence its pretence on the front of its premises that the quoted main clause is not crucially dependent on the now unadvertised subordinate clause — indeed, it's meaningless without it.

Because flying .38- and .45-caliber bullets rank close to cancer, heart disease, and AIDS as menaces to public health in this country, the firearm lobby, led by the NRA, comes under liberal attack regularly, and with special vigor immediately after an assault on some conspicuous person like Ronald Reagan or John Lennon. Thus *The New Republic,* in April 1981, deplored the state of things but offered as a solution only the suggestion that the whole Second Amendment be perceived as obsolete and amended out of the Constitution. This would leave the NRA with not a leg to stand on.

But here as elsewhere a better solution would be not to fiddle with the Constitution but to take it seriously, the way we've done with the First Amendment, say, or with the Thirteenth, the one forbidding open and avowed slavery. And by taking the Second Amendment seriously I mean taking it literally. We should "close read" it and thus focus lots of attention on the grammatical reasoning of its two clauses. This might shame the NRA into pulling the dependent clause out of the closet, displaying it on its façade, and accepting its not entirely pleasant implications. These could be particularized in an Act of Congress providing:

(1) that the Militia shall now, after these many years, be "well-regulated," as the Constitution requires.

(2) that any person who has chosen to possess at home a gun of any kind, and who is not a member of the police or the military or an appropriate government agency, shall be deemed to have enrolled automatically in the Militia of the United States. Members of the Militia, who will be issued identifying badges, will be organized in units of battalion, company, or platoon size representing counties, towns, or boroughs. If they bear arms while not proceeding to or from scheduled exercises of the Militia, they will be punished "as a court martial may direct."

(3) that any gun owner who declines to join the regulated Militia may opt out by selling his firearms to the federal government for $1,000 each. He will sign an undertaking that if he ever again owns firearms he will be considered to have enlisted in the Militia.

(4) that because the Constitution specifically requires that the Militia shall be "well regulated," a regular training program, of the sort familiar to all who have belonged to military units charged with the orderly management of small arms, shall be instituted. This will require at least eight hours of drill each Saturday at some con-

venient field or park, rain or shine or snow or ice. There will be
weekly supervised target practice (separation from the service,
publicly announced, for those who can't hit a barn door). And
there will be ample practice in digging simple defense works, like
foxholes and trenches, as well as necessary sanitary installations
like field latrines and straddle trenches. Each summer there will
be a six-week bivouac (without spouses), and this, like all the
other exercises, will be under the close supervision of long-service
noncommissioned officers of the United States Army and the Marine Corps. On bivouac, liquor will be forbidden under extreme
penalty, but there will be an issue every Friday night of two cans
of 3.2 beer, and feeding will follow traditional military lines, the
cuisine consisting largely of shit-on-a-shingle, sandwiches made of
bull dick (baloney) and choke-ass (cheese), beans, and fatty pork.
On Sundays and holidays, powdered eggs for breakfast. Chlorinated water will often be available, in Lister Bags. Further obligatory exercises designed to toughen up the Militia will include
twenty-five-mile hikes and the negotiation of obstacle courses. In
addition, there will be instruction of the sort appropriate to other
lightly armed, well-regulated military units: in map-reading, the
erection of double-apron barbed-wire fences, and the rudiments
of military courtesy and the traditions of the Militia, beginning
with the Minute Men. Per diem payments will be made to those
participating in these exercises.

(5) that since the purpose of the Militia is, as the Constitution says,
to safeguard "the security of a free state," at times when invasion
threatens (perhaps now the threat will come from Nicaragua, national security no longer being menaced by North Vietnam) all
units of the Militia will be trucked to the borders for the duration
of the emergency, there to remain in field conditions (here's
where the practice in latrine-digging pays off) until Congress declares that the emergency has passed. Congress may also order
the Militia to perform other duties consistent with its constitutional identity as a regulated volunteer force: for example, flood
and emergency and disaster service (digging, sandbag filling, res-
cuing old people); patrolling angry or incinerated cities; or controlling crowds at large public events like patriotic parades,
motor races, and professional football games.

(6) that failure to appear for these scheduled drills, practices, biv-
ouacs, and mobilizations shall result in the Militiaperson's dis-
missal from the service and forfeiture of badge, pay, and firearm.

Why did the Framers of the Constitution add the word *bear* to the   5
phrase "keep and bear arms?" Because they conceived that keeping arms at
home implied the public obligation to bear them in a regulated way for
"the security of" not a private household but "a free state." If interstate

bus fares can be regulated, it is hard to see why the Militia can't be, especially since the Constitution says it must be. *The New Republic* has recognized that "the Second Amendment to the Constitution clearly connects the right to bear arms to the 18th-century national need to raise a militia." But it goes on: "That need is now obsolete, and so is the amendment." And it concludes: "If the only way this country can get control of firearms is to amend the Constitution, then it's time for Congress to get the process under way."

I think not. Rather, it's time not to amend Article II of the Bill of Rights (and Obligations) but to read it, publicize it, embrace it, and enforce it. That the Second Amendment stems from concerns that can be stigmatized as "18th-century" cuts little ice. The First Amendment stems precisely from such concerns, and no one but Yahoos wants to amend it. Also "18th-century" is that lovely bit in Section 9 of Article I forbidding any "Title of Nobility" to be granted by the United States. That's why we've been spared Lord Annenberg and Sir Leonard Bernstein, Knight. Thank God for the eighteenth century, I say. It understood not just what a firearm is and what a Militia is. It also understood what "well regulated" means. It knew how to compose a constitutional article and it knew how to read it. And it assumed that everyone, gun lobbyists and touring students alike, would understand and correctly quote it. Both halves of it.

1988

The Reader's Presence

1. Here is the Second Amendment of the Bill of Rights: "A well-regulated Militia being necessary to the security of a free state, the right of the people to keep and bear arms shall not be infringed." Why does Fussell point out that the first part of the amendment does not appear on the marble facade of the National Rifle Association headquarters in Washington, D.C.? Why does he believe that the first half of the amendment is crucial to a correct understanding of the second half? Do you agree? Can you think of an alternative interpretation?

2. Though he is a proponent of gun control, why doesn't Fussell believe the Second Amendment should be repealed or revised? In what ways does his interpretation preserve the Second Amendment? Do you think the National Rifle Association would endorse Fussell's proposal? Do you think it would support any aspects of it? Explain.

3. Suppose Congress took Fussell's proposal seriously. Could it enact the kind of regulations Fussell recommends? What practical problems might arise? For example, how would the Militia be maintained? How expensive would it be? What parts of Fussell's plan do you think are meant to be taken seriously? What parts are intended as humorous? How can you tell the difference?

63

bell hooks

Feminism: A Transformational Politic

We live in a world in crisis — a world governed by politics of domination, one in which the belief in a notion of superior and inferior, and its concomitant ideology — that the superior should rule over the inferior — affects the lives of all people everywhere, whether poor or privileged, literate or illiterate. Systematic dehumanization, worldwide famine, ecological devastation, industrial contamination, and the possibility of nuclear destruction are realities which remind us daily that we are in crisis. Contemporary feminist thinkers often cite sexual politics as the origin of this crisis. They point to the insistence on difference as that factor which becomes the occasion for separation and domination and suggest that differentiation of status between females and males globally is an indication that patriarchal domination of the planet is the root of the problem. Such an assumption has fostered the notion that elimination of sexist oppression would necessarily lead to the eradication of all forms of domination. It is an argument that has led influential Western white women to feel that feminist movement should be *the* central political agenda for females globally. Ideologically, thinking in this direction enables Western women, especially privileged white women, to suggest that racism and class exploitation are merely the offspring of the parent system: patriarchy. Within feminist movement in the West, this had led to the assumption that resisting patriarchal domination is a more legitimate feminist action than resisting racism and other forms of domination. Such thinking prevails despite radical critiques made by black women and other women of color who question this proposition. To speculate that an oppositional division between men and women existed in early human communities is to impose on the past, on these non-

For biographical information on bell hooks, see p. 652.

white groups, a world view that fits all too neatly within contemporary feminist paradigms that name man as the enemy and woman as the victim.

Clearly, differentiation between strong and weak, powerful and powerless, has been a central defining aspect of gender globally, carrying with it the assumption that men should have greater authority than women, and should rule over them. As significant and important as this fact is, it should not obscure the reality that women can and do participate in politics of domination, as perpetrators as well as victims — that we dominate, that we are dominated. If focus on patriarchal domination masks this reality or becomes the means by which women deflect attention from the real conditions and circumstances of our lives, then women cooperate in suppressing and promoting false consciousness, inhibiting our capacity to assume responsibility for transforming ourselves and society.

Thinking speculatively about early human social arrangement, about women and men struggling to survive in small communities, it is likely that the parent-child relationship with its very real imposed survival structure of dependency, of strong and weak, of powerful and powerless, was a site for the construction of a paradigm of domination. While this circumstance of dependency is not necessarily one that leads to domination, it lends itself to the enactment of a social drama wherein domination could easily occur as a means of exercising and maintaining control. This speculation does not place women outside the practice of domination, in the exclusive role of victim. It centrally names women as agents of domination, as potential theoreticians, and creators of a paradigm for social relationships wherein those groups of individuals designated as "strong" exercise power both benevolently and coercively over those designated as "weak."

Emphasizing paradigms of domination that call attention to woman's capacity to dominate is one way to deconstruct and challenge the simplistic notion that man is the enemy, woman the victim; the notion that men have always been the oppressors. Such thinking enables us to examine our role as women in the perpetuation and maintenance of systems of domination. To understand domination, we must understand that our capacity as women and men to be either dominated or dominating is a point of connection, of commonality. Even though I speak from the particular experience of living as a black woman in the United States, a white-supremacist, capitalist, patriarchal society, where small numbers of white men (and honorary "white men") constitute ruling groups, I understand that in many places in the world oppressed and oppressor share the same color. I understand that right here in this room, oppressed and oppressor share the same gender. Right now as I speak, a man who is himself victimized, wounded, hurt by racism and class exploitation, is actively dominating a woman in his life — that even as I speak, women who are ourselves exploited, victimized, are dominating children. It is necessary for us to remember, as we think critically about domination, that we all have the capacity to act in ways that oppress, dominate, wound (whether or not that power is institutionalized). It is necessary to remember that it is first the potential oppressor within that we must resist — the potential victim within that we must rescue — otherwise we cannot hope for an end to domination, for liberation.

This knowledge seems especially important at this historical moment   5
when black women and other women of color have worked to create awareness of the ways in which racism empowers white women to act as exploiters and oppressors. Increasingly this fact is considered a reason we should not support feminist struggle even though sexism and sexist oppression is a real issue in our lives as black women (see, for example, Vivian Gordon's *Black Women, Feminism, Black Liberation: Which Way?*). It becomes necessary for us to speak continually about the convictions that inform our continued advocacy of feminist struggle. By calling attention to interlocking systems of domination — sex, race, and class — black women and many other groups of women acknowledge the diversity and complexity of female experience, of our relationship to power and domination. The intent is not to dissuade people of color from becoming engaged in feminist movement. Feminist struggle to end patriarchal domination should be of primary importance to women and men globally not because it is the foundation of all other oppressive structures but because it is that form of domination we are most likely to encounter in an ongoing way in everyday life.

Unlike other forms of domination, sexism directly shapes and determines relations of power in our private lives, in familiar social spaces, in that most intimate context — home — and in that most intimate sphere of relations — family. Usually, it is within the family that we witness coercive domination and learn to accept it, whether it be domination of parent over child, or male over female. Even though family relations may be, and most often are, informed by acceptance of a politic of domination, they are simultaneously relations of care and connection. It is this convergence of two contradictory impulses — the urge to promote growth and the urge to inhibit growth — that provides a practical setting for feminist critique, resistance, and transformation.

Growing up in a black, working-class, father-dominated household, I experienced coercive adult male authority as more immediately threatening, as more likely to cause immediate pain than racist oppression or class exploitation. It was equally clear that experiencing exploitation and oppression in the home made one feel all the more powerless when encountering dominating forces outside the home. This is true for many people. If we are unable to resist and end domination in relations where there is care, it seems totally unimaginable that we can resist and end it in other institutionalized relations of power. If we cannot convince the mothers and/or fathers who care not to humiliate and degrade us, how can we imagine convincing or resisting an employer, a lover, a stranger who systematically humiliates and degrades?

Feminist effort to end patriarchal domination should be of primary concern precisely because it insists on the eradication of exploitation and oppression in the family context and in all other intimate relationships. It is that political movement which most radically addresses the person — the personal — citing the need for transformation of self, of relationships, so that we might be better able to act in a revolutionary manner, challenging and resisting domination, transforming the world outside the self. Strategically, feminist movement should be a central component of all other liberation struggles because it challenges each of us to alter our person, our personal engagement (either as victims or perpetrators or both) in a system of domination.

Feminism, as liberation struggle, must exist apart from and as a part of the larger struggle to eradicate domination in all its forms. We must understand that patriarchal domination shares an ideological foundation with racism and other forms of group oppression, that there is no hope that it can be eradicated while these systems remain intact. This knowledge should consistently inform the direction of feminist theory and practice. Unfortunately, racism and class elitism among women have frequently led to the suppression and distortion of this connection so that it is now necessary for feminist thinkers to critique and revise much feminist theory and the direction of feminist movement. This effort at revision is perhaps most evident in the current widespread acknowledgment that sexism, racism, and class exploitation constitute interlocking systems of domination — that sex, race, and class, and not sex alone, determine the nature of any female's identity, status, and circumstance, the degree to which she will or will not be dominated, the extent to which she will have the power to dominate.

While acknowledgement of the complex nature of woman's status   10 (which has been most impressed upon everyone's consciousness by radical women of color) is a significant corrective, it is only a starting point. It provides a frame of reference which must serve as the basis for thoroughly altering and revising feminist theory and practice. It challenges and calls us to rethink popular assumptions about the nature of feminism that have had the deepest impact on a large majority of women, on mass consciousness. It radically calls into question the notion of a fundamentally common female experience which has been seen as the prerequisite for our coming together, for political unity. Recognition of the interconnectedness of sex, race, and class highlights the diversity of experience, compelling redefinition of the terms for unity. If women do not share "common oppression," what then can serve as a basis for our coming together?

Unlike many feminist comrades, I believe women and men must share a common understanding — a basic knowledge of what feminism is — if it is ever to be a powerful mass-based political movement. In *Feminist Theory: from margin to center,* I suggest that defining feminism broadly as a "movement to end sexism and sexist oppression" would enable us to have a common political goal. We would then have a basis on which to build solidarity. Multiple and contradictory definitions of feminism create confusion and undermine the effort to construct feminist movement so that it addresses everyone. Sharing a common goal does not imply that women and men will not have radically divergent perspectives on how that goal might be reached. Because each individual starts the process of engagement in feminist struggle at a unique level of awareness, very real differences in experience, perspective, and knowledge make developing varied strategies for participation and transformation a necessary agenda.

Feminist thinkers engaged in radically revisioning central tenets of feminist thought must continually emphasize the importance of sex, race, and class as factors which *together* determine the social construction of femaleness, as it has been so deeply ingrained in the consciousness of many women active in feminist movement that gender is the sole factor determining destiny. However, the work of education for critical consciousness (usually called consciousness-raising) cannot end there. Much feminist consciousness-raising has in the past focused on identifying the particular ways men oppress and exploit women. Using the paradigm of sex, race, and class means that the focus does not begin with men and what they do to women, but rather with women working to identify both individually and collectively the specific character of our social identity.

Imagine a group of women from diverse backgrounds coming together to talk about feminism. First they concentrate on working out their status in terms of sex, race, and class using this as the standpoint from which they begin discussing patriarchy or their particular relations with individual men. Within the old frame of reference, a discussion might consist solely of talk about their experiences as victims in relationship to male oppressors. Two women — one poor, the other quite wealthy — might describe the process by which they have suffered physical abuse by male partners and find certain commonalities which might serve as a basis for bonding. Yet if these same two women engaged in a discussion of class, not only would the social construction and expression of femaleness differ, so too would their ideas about how to confront and change their circumstances. Broadening the discussion to include an analysis of race and class would expose many additional differences even as commonalities emerged.

Clearly the process of bonding would be more complex, yet this broader discussion might enable the sharing of perspectives and strategies for change that would enrich rather than diminish our understanding of gender. While feminists have increasingly given "lip service" to the idea of diversity, we have not developed strategies of communication and inclusion that allow for the successful enactment of this feminist vision.

Small groups are no longer the central place for feminist consciousness- 15 raising. Much feminist education for critical consciousness takes place in women's studies classes or at conferences which focus on gender. Books are a primary source of education, which means that already masses of people who do not read have no access. The separation of grass-roots ways of sharing feminist thinking across kitchen tables from the spheres where much of that thinking is generated, the academy, undermines feminist movement. It would further feminist movement if new feminist thinking could be once again shared in small group contexts, integrating critical analysis with discussion of personal experience. It would be useful to promote anew the small group setting as an arena for education for critical consciousness, so that women and men might come together in neighborhoods and communities to discuss feminist concerns.

Small groups remain an important place for education for critical consciousness for several reasons. An especially important aspect of the small group setting is the emphasis on communicating feminist thinking, feminist theory, in a manner that can be easily understood. In small groups, individuals do not need to be equally literate or literate at all because the information is primarily shared through conversation, in dialogue which is necessarily a liberatory expression. (Literacy should be a goal for feminists even as we ensure that it not become a requirement for participation in feminist education.) Reforming small groups would subvert the appropriation of feminist thinking by a select group of academic women and men, usually white, usually from privileged class backgrounds.

Small groups of people coming together to engage in feminist discussion, in dialectical struggle make a space where the "personal is political" as a starting point for education for critical consciousness can be extended to include politicization of the self that focuses on creating understanding of the ways sex, race, and class together determine our individual lot and our collective experience. It would further feminist movement if many well-known feminist thinkers would participate in small groups, critically reexamining ways their works might be changed by incorporating broader perspectives. All efforts at self-transformation challenge us to engage in ongoing, critical self-examination and reflection about feminist practice, about how we live in the world. This individual commitment, when coupled with engagement in collective discussion, provides a space for critical feedback which strengthens our efforts to change and make ourselves new. It is in this commitment to feminist principles in our words and deeds that the hope of feminist revolution lies.

Working collectively to confront difference, to expand our awareness of sex, race, and class as interlocking systems of domination, of the ways we reinforce and perpetuate these structures, is the context in which we learn the true meaning of solidarity. It is this work that must be the foundation of feminist movement. Without it, we cannot effectively resist patriarchal domination; without it, we remain estranged and alienated from one another. Fear of painful confrontation often leads women and men active in feminist movement to avoid rigorous critical encounter, yet if we cannot engage dialectically in a committed, rigorous, humanizing manner, we cannot hope to change the world. True politicization — coming to critical consciousness — is a difficult, "trying" process, one that demands that we give up set ways of thinking and being, that we shift our paradigms, that we open ourselves to the unknown, the unfamiliar. Undergoing this process, we learn what it means to struggle and in this effort we experience the dignity and integrity of being that comes with revolutionary change. If we do not change our consciousness, we cannot change our actions or demand change from others.

Our renewed commitment to a rigorous process of education for critical consciousness will determine the shape and direction of future feminist movement. Until new perspectives are created, we cannot be living symbols of the power of feminist thinking. Given the privileged lot of many leading feminist thinkers, both in terms of status, class, and race, it is harder these days to convince women of the primacy of this process of politicization. More and more, we seem to form select interest groups composed of individuals who share similar perspectives. This limits our capacity to engage in critical discussion. It is difficult to involve women in new processes of feminist politicization because so many of us think that identifying men as the enemy, resisting male domination, gaining equal access to power and privilege is the end of feminist movement. Not only is it not the end, it is not even the place we want revitalized feminist movement to begin. We want to begin as women seriously addressing ourselves, not solely in relation to men, but in relation to an entire structure of domination of which patriarchy is one part. While the struggle to eradicate sexism and sexist oppression is and should be the primary thrust of feminist movement, to prepare ourselves politically for this effort we must first learn how to be in solidarity, how to struggle with one another.

Only when we confront the realities of sex, race, and class, the ways 20 they divide us, make us different, stand us in opposition, and work to reconcile and resolve these issues will we be able to participate in the making of feminist revolution, in the transformation of the world. Feminism, as Charlotte Bunch emphasizes again and again in *Passionate Politics,* is a transformational politics, a struggle against domination wherein the effort is to change ourselves as well as structures. Speaking about the struggle to confront difference, Bunch asserts:

> A crucial point of the process is understanding that reality does not look the same from different people's perspective. It is not surprising that one way feminists have come to understand about differences has been through the love of a person from another culture or race. It takes persistence and motivation — which love often engenders — to get beyond one's ethnocentric assumptions and really learn about other perspectives. In this process and while seeking to eliminate oppression, we also discover new possibilities and insights that come from the experience and survival of other peoples.

Embedded in the commitment to feminist revolution is the challenge to love. Love can be and is an important source of empowerment when we struggle to confront issues of sex, race, and class. Working together to identify and face our differences — to face the ways we dominate and are dominated — to change our actions, we need a mediating force that can sustain us so that we are not broken in this process, so that we do not despair.

Not enough feminist work has focused on documenting and sharing ways individuals confront differences constructively and successfully. Women and men need to know what is on the other side of the pain experienced in politicization. We need detailed accounts of the ways our lives are fuller and richer as we change and grow politically, as we learn to live each moment as committed feminists, as comrades working to end domination. In reconceptualizing and reformulating strategies for future feminist movement, we need to concentrate on the politicization of love, not just in the context of talking about victimization in intimate relationships, but in a critical discussion where love can be understood as a powerful force that challenges and resists domination. As we work to be loving, to create a culture that celebrates life, that makes love possible, we move against dehumanization, against domination. In *Pedagogy of the Oppressed,* Paulo Freire evokes this power of love, declaring:

> I am more and more convinced that true revolutionaries must perceive the revolution, because of its creative and liberating nature, as an act of love. For me, the revolution, which is not possible without a theory of revolution — and therefore science — is not irreconcilable with love . . . The distortion imposed on the word "love" by the capitalist world cannot prevent the revolution from being essentially loving in character, nor can it prevent the revolutionaries from affirming their love of life.

That aspect of feminist revolution that calls women to love womanness, that calls men to resist dehumanizing concepts of masculinity, is an essential part of our struggle. It is the process by which we move from seeing ourselves as objects to acting as subjects. When women and men understand that working to eradicate patriarchal domination is a struggle rooted in the longing to make a world where everyone can live fully and freely, then we know our work to be a gesture of love. Let us draw upon that love to heighten our awareness, deepen our compassion, intensify our courage, and strengthen our commitment.

1989

The Reader's Presence

1. bell hooks opens her argument on behalf of "a transformational politic" with a summary of patriarchal domination. What does she see as the ideological consequences of this widespread belief?

How does hooks reshape this argument to include issues of race and class? In what specific ways does she challenge the belief that women are not perpetrators — but solely victims — of what she calls "the politics of domination"? What purpose does she articulate in doing so?

2. Do you agree with hooks's assertion that sexism is the "form of domination we are most likely to encounter in an ongoing way in everyday life"? What aspects of feminism does hooks seem intent on keeping in her vision of the future? What aspects of feminist theory and practice does she want to change? Does hooks seem more intent, for example, on preserving the content or the method of feminism? Point to specific passages to support your response. What rationale does she present for proposing that the home and the family be the site for beginning the work of articulating a "transformational politic"?

3. What can you infer about hooks's conception of education from her discussion of "critical consciousness" (usually called consciousness-raising)? Outline the areas in education that still need attention in hooks's view. In what specific ways does her purpose extend beyond any interest in dissuading "people of color from being engaged in the feminist movement"? What, in effect, is the nature of the "transformational politic" she is advocating? How convincing do you find her argument? What are its strengths? its weaknesses?

64

June Jordan

Nobody Mean More to Me than You[1] and the Future Life of Willie Jordan

Black English is not exactly a linguistic buffalo; as children, most of the thirty-five million Afro-Americans living here depend on this language for our discovery of the world. But then we approach our maturity inside a larger social body that will not support our efforts to become anything other than the clones of those who are neither our mothers nor our fathers. We begin to grow up in a house where every true mirror shows us the face of somebody who does not belong there, whose walk and whose talk will never look or sound "right," because that house was meant to shelter a family that is alien and hostile to us. As we learn our way around this environment, either we hide our original word habits, or we completely surrender our own voice, hoping to please those who will never respect anyone different from themselves: Black English is not exactly a linguistic buffalo, but we should understand its status as an endangered species, as a perishing, irreplaceable system of community intelligence, or we should expect its extinction, and, along with that, the extinguishing of much that constitutes our own proud, and singular identity.

What we casually call "English," less and less defers to England and its "gentlemen." "English" is no longer a specific matter of geography or an element of class privilege; more than thirty-three countries use this tool as a means of "intranational communication."[2] Countries as disparate as Zimbabwe and Malaysia, or Israel and Uganda, use it as their non-native

---

For biographical information on June Jordan, see p. 653.

[1]Black English aphorism crafted by Monica Morris, a Junior at S.U.N.Y. at Stony Brook, October, 1984. — JORDAN'S NOTE.

[2]*English Is Spreading, But What Is English?* A presentation by Professor S. N. Sridahr, Dept. of Linguistics, S.U.N.Y. at Stonybrook, April 9, 1985: Dean's Conversation Among the Disciplines. — JORDAN'S NOTE.

currency of convenience. Obviously, this tool, this "English," cannot function inside thirty-three discrete societies on the basis of rules and values absolutely determined somewhere else, in a thirty-fourth other country, for example.

In addition to that staggering congeries of non-native users of English, there are five countries, or 333,746,000 people, for whom this thing called "English" serves as a native tongue.[3] Approximately ten percent of these native speakers of "English" are Afro-American citizens of the U.S.A. I cite these numbers and varieties of human beings dependent on "English" in order, quickly, to suggest how strange and how tenuous is any concept of "Standard English." Obviously, numerous forms of English now operate inside a natural, an uncontrollable, continuum of development. I would suppose "the standard" for English in Malaysia is not the same as "the standard" in Zimbabwe. I know that standard forms of English for Black people in this country do not copy that of whites. And, in fact, the structural differences between these two kinds of English have intensified, becoming more Black, or less white, despite the expected homogenizing effects of television[4] and other mass media.

Nonetheless, white standards of English persist, supreme and unquestioned, in these United States. Despite our multilingual population, and despite the deepening Black and white cleavage within that conglomerate, white standards control our official and popular judgments of verbal proficiency and correct, or incorrect, language skills, including speech. In contrast to India, where at least fourteen languages co-exist as legitimate Indian languages, in contrast to Nicaragua, where all citizens are legally entitled to formal school instruction in their regional or tribal languages, compulsory education in America compels accommodation to exclusively white forms of "English." White English, in America, is "Standard English."

This story begins two years ago. I was teaching a new course, "In   5
Search of the Invisible Black Woman," and my rather large class seemed evenly divided between young Black women and men. Five or six white students also sat in attendance. With unexpected speed and enthusiasm we had moved through historical narratives of the 19th century to literature by and about Black women, in the 20th. I had assigned the first forty pages of Alice Walker's *The Color Purple,* and I came, eagerly, to class that morning:

"So!" I exclaimed, aloud. "What did you think? How did you like it?"

The students studied their hands, or the floor. There was no response. The tense, resistant feeling in the room fairly astounded me.

---

[3]Ibid. — JORDAN'S NOTE.
[4]*New York Times,* March 15, 1985, Section One, p. 14: Report on study by Linguistics at the University of Pennsylvania. — JORDAN'S NOTE.

At last, one student, a young woman still not meeting my eyes, muttered something in my direction:

"What did you say?" I prompted her.

"Why she have them talk so funny. It don't sound right." 10

"You mean the language?"

Another student lifted his head: "It don't look right, neither. I couldn't hardly read it."

At this, several students dumped on the book. Just about unanimously, their criticisms targeted the language. I listened to what they wanted to say and silently marveled at the similarities between their casual speech patterns and Alice Walker's written version of Black English.

But I decided against pointing to these identical traits of syntax; I wanted not to make them self-conscious about their own spoken language — not while they clearly felt it was "wrong." Instead I decided to swallow my astonishment. Here was a negative Black reaction to a prize winning accomplishment of Black literature that white readers across the country had selected as a best seller. Black rejection was aimed at the one irreducibly Black element of Walker's work: the language — Celie's Black English. I wrote the opening lines of *The Color Purple* on the blackboard and asked the students to help me translate these sentences into Standard English:

> *You better not never tell nobody but God. It'd kill your mammy.*
> Dear God,
>   I am fourteen years old. I have always been a good girl. Maybe you can give me a sign letting me know what is happening to me.
>   Last spring after Little Lucious come I heard them fussing. He was pulling on her arm. She say it too soon, Fonso. I aint well. Finally he leave her alone. A week go by, he pulling on her arm again. She say, Naw, I ain't gonna. Can't you see I'm already half dead, an all of the children.[5]

Our process of translation exploded with hilarity and even hysterical, shocked laughter: The Black writer, Alice Walker, knew what she was doing! If rudimentary criteria for good fiction includes the manipulation of language so that the syntax and diction of sentences will tell you the identity of speakers, the probable age and sex and class of speakers, and even the locale — urban/rural/southern/western — then Walker had written, perfectly. This is the translation into Standard English that our class produced:

> *Absolutely, one should never confide in anybody besides God. Your secrets could prove devastating to your mother.*
> Dear God,
>   I am fourteen years old, I have always been good. But now, could you help me to understand what is happening to me?
>   Last spring, after my little brother, Lucious, was born, I heard my parents fighting. My father kept pulling at my mother's arm. But she told him, "It's too soon for sex, Alfonso. I am still not feeling well." Finally,

---

[5]Alice Walker, *The Color Purple,* p. 11, Harcourt Brace, N.Y. — JORDAN'S NOTE.

my father left her alone. A week went by, and then he began bothering my mother, again: Pulling her arm. She told him, "No, I won't! Can't you see I'm already exhausted from all of these children?"

(Our favorite line was "It's too soon for sex, Alphonso.")   15

Once we could stop laughing, once we could stop our exponentially wild improvisations on the theme of Translated Black English, the students pushed me to explain their own negative first reactions to their spoken language on the printed page. I thought it was probably akin to the shock of seeing yourself in a photograph for the first time. Most of the students had never before seen a written facsimile of the way they talk. None of the students had ever learned how to read and write their own verbal system of communication: Black English. Alternatively, this fact began to baffle or else bemuse and then infuriate my students. Why not? Was it too late? Could they learn how to do it, now? And, ultimately, the final test question, the one testing my sincerity: Could I teach them? Because I had never taught anyone Black English and, as far as I knew, no one, anywhere in the United States, had ever offered such a course, the best I could say was "I'll try."

He looked like a wrestler.

He sat dead center in the packed room and, every time our eyes met, he quickly nodded his head as though anxious to reassure, and encourage, me.

Short, with strikingly broad shoulders and long arms, he spoke with a surprisingly high, soft voice that matched the soft bright movement of his eyes. His name was Willie Jordan. He would have seemed even more unlikely in the context of Contemporary Women's Poetry, except that ten or twelve other Black men were taking the course, as well. Still, Willie was conspicuous. His extreme fitness, the muscular density of his presence underscored the riveted, gentle attention that he gave to anything anyone said. Generally, he did not join the loud and rowdy dialogue flying back and forth, but there could be no doubt about his interest in our discussions. And, when he stood to present an argument he'd prepared, overnight, that nervous smile of his vanished and an irregular stammering replaced it, as he spoke with visceral sincerity, word by word.

That was how I met Willie Jordan. It was in between "In Search of the   20
Invisible Black Woman" and "The Art of Black English." I was waiting for Departmental approval and I supposed that Willie might be, so to speak, killing time until he, too, could study Black English. But Willie really did want to explore Contemporary Women's poetry and, to that end, volunteered for extra research and never missed a class.

Towards the end of that semester, Willie approached me for an independent study project on South Africa. It would commence the next semester. I thought Willie's writing needed the kind of improvement only intense practice will yield. I knew his intelligence was outstanding. But he'd wholeheartedly opted for "Standard English" at a rather late age, and the results were stilted and frequently polysyllabic, simply for the sake of having more syllables. Willie's unnatural formality of language seemed to me consistent with the formality of his research into South African apartheid. As he projected his studies, he would have little time, indeed, for newspapers. Instead, more than 90 percent of his research would mean saturation in strictly historical, if not archival, material. I was certainly interested. It would be tricky to guide him into a more confident and spontaneous relationship both with language and apartheid. It was going to be wonderful to see what happened when he could catch up with himself, entirely, and talk back to the world.

September, 1984: Breezy fall weather and much excitement! My class, "The Art of Black English," was full to the limit of the fire laws. And, in Independent Study, Willie Jordan showed up, weekly, fifteen minutes early for each of our sessions. I was pretty happy to be teaching, altogether!

I remember an early class when a young brother, replete with his ever present pork-pie hat, raised his hand and then told us that most of what he'd heard was "all right" except it was "too clean." "The brothers on the street," he continued, "they mix it up more. Like 'fuck' and "motherfuck.' Or like 'shit.'" He waited, I waited. Then all of us laughed a good while, and we got into a brawl about "correct" and "realistic" Black English that led to Rule 1.

Rule 1: *Black English is about a whole lot more than mothafuckin.*

As a criterion, we decided, "realistic" could take you anywhere you   25
want to go. Artful places. Angry places. Eloquent and sweetalkin places. Polemical places. Church. And the local Bar & Grill. We were checking out a language, not a mood or a scene or one guy's forgettable mouthing off.

It was hard. For most of the students, learning Black English required a fallback to patterns and rhythms of speech that many of their parents had beaten out of them. I mean *beaten*. And, in a majority of cases, correct Black English could be achieved only by striving for *incorrect* Standard English, something they were still pushing at, quite uncertainly. This state of affairs led to Rule 2.

Rule 2: *If it's wrong in Standard English it's probably right in Black English, or, at least, you're hot.*

It was hard. Roommates and family members ridiculed their studies, or remained incredulous, "You *studying* that shit? At school?" But we were beginning to feel the companionship of pioneers. And we decided that we needed another rule that would establish each one of us as equally important to our success. This was Rule 3.

Rule 3: *If it don't sound like something that come out somebody mouth then it don't sound right. If it don't sound right then it ain't hardly right. Period.*

This rule produced two weeks of compositions in which the students   30
agonizingly tried to spell the sound of the Black English sentence they wanted to convey. But Black English is, preeminently, an oral/spoken means of communication. *And spelling don't talk.* So we needed Rule 4.

Rule 4: *Forget about the spelling. Let the syntax carry you.*

Once we arrived at Rule 4 we started to fly because syntax, the structure of an idea, leads you to the world view of the speaker and reveals her values. The syntax of a sentence equals the structure of your consciousness. If we insisted that the language of Black English adheres to a distinctive Black syntax, then we were postulating a profound difference between white and Black people, *per se*. Was it a difference to prize or to obliterate?

There are three qualities of Black English — the presence of life, voice, and clarity — that testify to a distinctive Black value system that we became excited about and self-consciously tried to maintain.

1. Black English has been produced by a pre-technocratic, if not anti-technological, culture. More, our culture has been constantly threatened by annihilation or, at least, the swallowed blurring of assimilation. Therefore, our language is a system constructed by people constantly needing to insist that we exist, that we are present. Our language devolves from a culture that abhors all abstraction, or anything tending to obscure or delete the fact of the human being who is here and now/the truth of the person who is speaking or listening. Consequently, *there is no passive voice construction possible in Black English*. For example, you cannot say, "Black English is being eliminated." You must say, instead, "White people eliminating Black English." The assumption of the presence of life governs all of Black English. Therefore, overwhelmingly, *all action takes place in the language of the present indicative*. And every sentence assumes the living and active participation of at least two human beings, the speaker and the listener.

2. A primary consequence of the person-centered values of Black English is the delivery of voice. If you speak or write Black English, your ideas will necessarily possess that otherwise elusive attribute, *voice*.

3. One main benefit following from the person-centered values of Black English is that of *clarity*. If your idea, your sentence, assumes the presence of at least two living and active people, you will make it understandable because the motivation behind every sentence is the wish to say something real to somebody real.

As the weeks piled up, translation from Standard English into Black English or vice versa occupied a hefty part of our course work.

> Standard English (hereafter S.E.): "In considering the idea of studying Black English those questioned suggested — "
> (What's the subject? Where's the person? Is anybody alive in there, in that idea?)
> Black English (hereafter B.E.): "I been asking people what you think about somebody studying Black English and they answer me like this."

But there were interesting limits. You cannot "translate" instances of Standard English preoccupied with abstraction or with nothing/nobody evidently alive, into Black English. That would warp the language into uses antithetical to the guiding perspective of its community of users. Rather you must first change those Standard English sentences, themselves, into ideas consistent with the person-centered assumptions of Black English.

GUIDELINES FOR BLACK ENGLISH

1. Minimal number of words for every idea: This is the source for the aphoristic and/or poetic force of the language; eliminate every possible word.

2. Clarity: If the sentence is not clear it's not Black English.

3. Eliminate use of the verb *to be* whenever possible. This leads to the　40 deployment of more descriptive and, therefore, more precise verbs.

4. Use *be* or *been* only when you want to describe a chronic, ongoing state of things.

He *be* at the office, by 9. (He is always at the office by 9.)
He *been* with her since forever.

5. Zero copula: Always eliminate the verb *to be* whenever it would combine with another verb in Standard English.

S.E.: She is going out with him.
B.E.: She going out with him.

6. Eliminate *do* as in:

S.E.: What do you think? What do you want?
B.E.: What you think? What you want?

Rules number 3, 4, 5, and 6 provide for the use of the minimal number of verbs per idea and, therefore, greater accuracy in the choice of verb.

7. In general, if you wish to say something really positive, try to for-　45 mulate the idea using emphatic negative structure.

S.E.: He's fabulous.
B.E.: He bad.

8. Use double or triple negatives for dramatic emphasis.

S.E.: Tina Turner sings out of this world.
B.E.: Ain nobody sing like Tina.

9. Never use the *-ed* suffix to indicate the past tense of a verb.

S.E.: She closed the door.
B.E.: She close the door. Or, she have close the door.

10. Regardless of intentional verb time, only use the third person singular, present indicative, for use of the verb *to have,* as an auxiliary.

S.E.: He had his wallet then he lost it.
B.E.: He have him wallet then he lose it.
S.E.: He had seen that movie.
B.E.: We seen that movie. Or, we have see that movie.

11. Observe a minimal inflection of verbs. Particularly, never change from the first person singular forms to the third person singular.

S.E.: Present Tense Forms: He goes to the store.
B.E.: He go to the store.
S.E.: Past Tense Forms: He went to the store.
B.E.: He go to the store. Or, he gone to the store. Or, he been to the store.

12. The possessive case scarcely ever appears in Black English. Never 50
use an apostrophe ('s) construction. If you wander into a possessive case
component of an idea, then keep logically consistent: *ours, his, theirs,
mines*. But, most likely, if you bump into such a component, you have wandered outside the underlying world-view of Black English.

S.E.: He will take their car tomorrow.
B.E.: He taking they car tomorrow.

13. Plurality: Logical consistency, continued: If the modifier indicates
plurality then the noun remains in the singular case.

S.E.: He ate twelve doughnuts.
B.E.: He eat twelve doughnut.
S.E.: She has many books.
B.E.: She have many book.

14. Listen for, or invent, special Black English forms of the past tense,
such as: "He losted it. That what she felted." If they are clear and readily
understood, then use them.

15. Do not hesitate to play with words, sometimes inventing them:
e.g. "astropotomous" means huge like a hippo plus astronomical and,
therefore, signifies real big.

16. In Black English, unless you keenly want to underscore the past
tense nature of an action, stay in the present tense and rely on the overall
context of your ideas for the conveyance of time and sequence.

17. Never use the suffix *-ly* form of an adverb in Black English. 55

S.E.: The rain came down rather quickly.
B.E.: The rain come down pretty quick.

18. Never use the indefinite article *an* in Black English.

S.E.: He wanted to ride an elephant.
B.E.: He want to ride him a elephant.

19. Invarient syntax: in correct Black English it is possible to formulate an imperative, an interrogative, and a simple declarative idea with the
same syntax:

B.E.: You going to the store?
    You going to the store.
    You going to the store!

Where was Willie Jordan? We'd reached the mid-term of the semester.
Students had formulated Black English guidelines, by consensus, and they
were now writing with remarkable beauty, purpose, and enjoyment:

I ain hardly speakin for everybody but myself so understan that. — Kim Parks

Samples from student writings:

Janie have a great big ole hole inside her. Tea Cake the only thing that fit that hole . . .

   That pear tree beautiful to Janie, especial when bees fiddlin with the blossomin pear there growing large and lovely. But personal speakin, the love she get from staring at that tree ain the love what starin back at her in them relationship. (Monica Morris)

Love is a big theme in, *They Eye Was Watching God*. Love show people new corners inside theyself. It pull out good stuff and stuff back bad stuff . . . Joe worship the doing uh his own hand and need other people to worship him too. But he ain't think about Janie that she a person and ought to live like anybody common do. Queen life not for Janie. (Monica Morris)

In both life and writin, Black womens have varietous experience of love that be cold like a iceberg or fiery like a inferno. Passion got for the other partner involve, man or woman, seem as shallow, ankle-deep water or the most profoundest abyss. (Constance Evans)

Family love another bond that ain't never break under no pressure. (Constance Evans)

You know it really cold / When the friend you / Always get out the fire / Act like they don't know you / When you in the heat. (Constance Evans)

Big classroom discussion bout love at this time. I never take no class where us have any long arguin for and against for two or three day. New to me and great. I find the class time talkin a million time more interestin than detail bout the book. (Kathy Esseks)

As these examples suggest, Black English no longer limited the students, in any way. In fact, one of them, Philip Garfield, would shortly "translate" a pivotal scene from Ibsen's *Doll House,* as his final term paper.

NORA: I didn't gived no shit. I thinked you a asshole back then, too, you make it so hard for me save mines husband life.
KROGSTAD: Girl, it clear you ain't any idea what you done. You done exact what once done, and I losed my reputation over it.
NORA: You asks me believe you once act brave save you wife life?
KROGSTAD: Law care less why you done it.
NORA: Law must suck.
KROGSTAD: Suck or no, if I wants, judge screw you wid dis paper.
NORA: No way, man. (Philip Garfield)

But where was Willie? Compulsively punctual, and always thoroughly 60 prepared with neatly typed compositions, he had disappeared. He failed to show up for our regularly scheduled conference, and I received neither a note nor a phone call of explanation. A whole week went by. I wondered if

Willie had finally been captured by the extremely current happenings in South Africa: passage of a new constitution that did not enfranchise the Black majority, and militant Black South African reaction to that affront. I wondered if he'd been hurt, somewhere. I wondered if the serious work-load of weekly readings and writings had overwhelmed him and changed his mind about independent study. Where was Willie Jordan?

One week after the first conference that Willie missed, he called: "Hello, Professor Jordan? This is Willie. I'm sorry I wasn't there last week. But something has come up and I'm pretty upset. I'm sorry but I really can't deal right now."

I asked Willie to drop by my office and just let me see that he was okay. He agreed to do that. When I saw him I knew something hideous had happened. Something had hurt him and scared him to the marrow. He was all agitated and stammering and terse and incoherent. At last, his sadly jumbled account let me surmise, as follows: Brooklyn police had murdered his unarmed, twenty-five-year-old brother, Reggie Jordan. Neither Willie nor his elderly parents knew what to do about it. Nobody from the press was interested. His folks had no money. Police ran his family around and around, to no point. And Reggie was really dead. And Willie wanted to fight, but he felt helpless.

With Willie's permission I began to try to secure legal counsel for the Jordan family. Unfortunately Black victims of police violence are truly nu-merous while the resources available to prosecute their killers are truly scarce. A friend of mine at the Center for Constitutional Rights estimated that just the preparatory costs for bringing the cops into court normally approaches $180,000. Unless the execution of Reggie Jordan became a major community cause for organizing, and protest, his murder would sim-ply become a statistical item.

Again, with Willie's permission, I contacted every newspaper and media person I could think of. But the William Bastone feature article in *The Village Voice* was the only result from that canvassing.

Again, with Willie's permission, I presented the case to my class in   65
Black English. We had talked about the politics of language. We had talked about love and sex and child abuse and men and women. But the murder of Reggie Jordan broke like a hurricane across the room.

There are few "issues" as endemic to Black life as police violence. Most of the students knew and respected and liked Jordan. Many of them came from the very neighborhood where the murder had occurred. All of the students had known somebody close to them who had been killed by police, or had known frightening moments of gratuitous confrontation with the cops. They wanted to do everything at once to avenge death. Number One: They decided to compose personal statements of condolence to Willie Jordan and his family written in Black English. Number Two: They decided to compose individual messages to the police, in Black En-glish. These should be prefaced by an explanatory paragraph composed by the entire group. Number Three: These individual messages, with their lead paragraph, should be sent to *Newsday*.

The morning after we agreed on these objectives, one of the young women students appeared with an unidentified visitor, who sat through the class, smiling in a peculiar, comfortable way.

Now we had to make more tactical decisions. Because we wanted the messages published, and because we thought it imperative that our outrage be known by the police, the tactical question was this: Should the opening, group paragraph be written in Black English or Standard English?

I have seldom been privy to a discussion with so much heart at the dead heat of it. I will never forget the eloquence, the sudden haltings of speech, the fierce struggle against tears, the furious throwaway, and useless explosions that this question elicited.

That one question contained several others, each of them extraordinar-   70
ily painful to even contemplate. How best to serve the memory of Reggie Jordan? Should we use the language of the killers — Standard English — in order to make our ideas acceptable to those controlling the killers? But wouldn't what we had to say be rejected, summarily, if we said it in our own language, the language of the victim, Reggie Jordan? But if we sought to express ourselves by abandoning our language wouldn't that mean our suicide on top of Reggie's murder? But if we expressed ourselves in our own language wouldn't that be suicidal to the wish to communicate with those who, evidently, did not give a damn about us/Reggie/police violence in the Black community?

At the end of one of the longest, most difficult hours of my own life, the students voted, unanimously, to preface their individual messages with a paragraph composed in the language of Reggie Jordan. "*At least we don't give up nothing else. At least we stick to the truth: Be who we been. And stay all the way with Reggie.*"

It was heartbreaking to proceed, from that point. Everyone in the room realized that our decision in favor of Black English had doomed our writings, even as the distinctive reality of our Black lives always has doomed our efforts to "be who we been" in this country.

I went to the blackboard and took down this paragraph, dictated by the class:

> ... YOU COPS!
> WE THE BROTHER AND SISTER OF WILLIE JORDAN, A FELLOW STONY BROOK STUDENT WHO THE BROTHER OF THE DEAD REGGIE JORDAN. REGGIE, LIKE MANY BROTHER AND SISTER, HE A VICTIM OF BRUTAL RACIST POLICE, OCTOBER 25, 1984. US APPALL, FED UP, BECAUSE THAT ANOTHER SENSELESS DEATH WHAT OCCUR IN OUR COMMUNITY. THIS WHAT WE FEEL, THIS, FROM OUR HEART, FOR WE AIN'T STAYIN' SILENT NO MORE.

With the completion of this introduction, nobody said anything. I asked for comments. At this invitation, the unidentified visitor, a young

Black man, ceaselessly smiling, raised his hand. He was, it so happens, a rookie cop. He had just joined the force in September and, he said he thought he should clarify a few things. So he came forward and sprawled easily into a posture of barroom, or fireside, nostalgia:

"See," Officer Charles enlightened us, "most times when you out on   75
the street and something come down you do one of two things. Over-react or under-react. Now, if you under-react then you can get yourself kilt. And if you over-react then maybe you kill somebody. Fortunately it's about nine times out of ten and you will over-react. So the brother got kilt. And I'm sorry about that, believe me. But what you have to understand is what kilt him: Over-reaction. That's all. Now you talk about Black people and white police but see, now, I'm a cop myself. And (big smile) I'm Black. And just a couple months ago I was on the other side. But see it's the same for me. You a cop, you the ultimate authority: the Ultimate Authority. And you on the street, most of the time you can only do one of two things: over-react or under-react. That's all it is with the brother. Over-reaction. Didn't have nothing to do with race."

That morning Officer Charles had the good fortune to escape without being boiled alive. But barely. And I remember the pride of his smile when I read about the fate of Black policemen and other collaborators, in South Africa. I remember him, and I remember the shock and palpable feeling of shame that filled the room. It was as though that foolish, and deadly, young man had just relieved himself of his foolish, and deadly, explanation, face to face with the grief of Reggie Jordan's father and Reggie Jordan's mother. Class ended quietly. I copied the paragraph from the blackboard, collected the individual messages and left to type them up.

Newsday rejected the piece.

The Village Voice could not find room in their "Letters" section to print the individual messages from the students to the police.

None of the TV news reporters picked up the story.

Nobody raised $180,000 to prosecute the murder of Reggie Jordan.   80
Reggie Jordan is really dead.

I asked Willie Jordan to write an essay pulling together everything important to him from that semester. He was still deeply beside himself with frustration and amazement and loss. This is what he wrote, unedited, and in its entirety:

> Throughout the course of this semester I have been researching the effects of oppression and exploitation along racial lines in South Africa and its neighboring countries. I have become aware of South African police brutalization of native Africans beyond the extent of the law, even though the laws themselves are catalyst affliction upon Black men, women, and children. Many Africans die each year as a result of the deliberate use of police force to protect the white power structure.
>
> Social control agents in South Africa, such as policemen, are also used to force compliance among citizens through both overt and covert tactics. It is not uncommon to find bold-faced coercion and cold-blooded

killings of Blacks by South African police for undetermined and/or inadequate reasons. Perhaps the truth is that the only reasons for this heinous
treatment of Blacks rests in racial differences. We should also understand
that what is conveyed through the media is not always accurate and may
sometimes be construed as the tip of the iceberg at best.

I recently received a painful reminder that racism, poverty, and the
abuse of power are global problems which are by no means unique to
South Africa. On October 25, 1984, at approximately 3:00 P.M. my
brother, Mr. Reginald Jordan, was shot and killed by two New York City
policemen from the 75th precinct in the East New York section of Brooklyn. His life ended at the age of twenty-five. Even up to this current point
in time the Police Department has failed to provide my family, which consists of five brothers, eight sisters, and two parents, with a plausible reason for Reggie's death. Out of the many stories that were given to my
family by the Police Department, not one of them seems to hold water. In
fact, I honestly believe that the Police Department's assessment of my
brother's murder is nothing short of ABSOLUTE BULLSHIT, and thus far
no evidence had been produced to alter perception of the situation.

Furthermore, I believe that one of three cases may have occurred in
this incident. First, Reggie's death may have been the desired outcome of
the police officer's action, in which case the killing was premeditated. Or,
it was a case of mistaken identity, which clarifies the fact that the two
officers who killed my brother and their commanding parties are all
grossly incompetent. Or, both of the above cases are correct, i.e., Reggie's
murderers intended to kill him and the Police Department behaved insub-
ordinately.

Part of the argument of the officers who shot Reggie was that he had
attacked one of them and took his gun. This was their major claim. They
also said that only one of them had actually shot Reggie. The facts, however, speak for themselves. According to the Death Certificate and autopsy report, Reggie was shot eight times from point-blank range. The
Doctor who performed the autopsy told me himself that two bullets entered the side of my brother's head, four bullets were sprayed into his
back, and two bullets struck him in the back of his legs. It is obvious that
unnecessary force was used by the police and that it is extremely difficult
to shoot someone in his back when he is attacking or approaching you.

After experiencing a situation like this and researching South Africa I
believe that to a large degree, justice may only exist as rhetoric. I find it
difficult to talk of true justice when the oppression of my people both at
home and abroad attests to the fact that inequality and injustice are serious problems whereby Blacks and Third World people are perpetually
short-changed by society. Something has to be done about the way in
which this world is set up. Although it is a difficult task, we do have the
power to make a change.

— Willie J. Jordan, Jr.
EGL 487, Section 58, November 14, 1984

It is my privilege to dedicate this book to the future life of Willie J.
Jordan, Jr.

August 8, 1985

The Reader's Presence

1. How would you characterize June Jordan's tone at the outset of this essay? When and how does her tone of voice change as the essay proceeds? How, for example, would you describe her voice when she takes up the subject of Black English, and more particularly its history and grammar? In what specific ways does her tone change when she discusses her class and her experiences with them? when she discusses Willie Jordan and her course in contemporary women's poetry? In what specific ways does her diction change in each of these parts of her essay? What, more specifically, do you make of the section where Jordan experiments with "translating" Alice Walker? What point does she make here about the adequacy of Standard English to represent the nuances of an important dimension of American culture?

2. Consider the "Rules and Guidelines" Jordan and her students formulate about Black English. Summarize the rationale for each, and comment on the extent to which you are convinced by the logic of each proposition. Assess the specific strengths and weaknesses of the examples Jordan presents from her students' own writing. Explain why the question of whether the students should write their group preface to their message of protest is so sensitive. What sorts of issues are at stake in such a decision? What does Jordan mean when she says "our decision in favor of Black English had doomed our writings" (paragraph 72)? In what sense was the decision to write the protest in Black English courageous?

3. Reread the scene in which Officer Charles explains Reggie Jordan's death. What responses does this account elicit from the author? from her students? What diction and tone of voice does Jordan use to convey her attitude toward Officer Charles's apology for the system? What conclusions does Jordan draw from her experiences with this class? What connections does she make between the students' work with Black English and their response to Reggie Jordan's death?

65 _____

Jamaica Kincaid

On Seeing England for the First Time

When I saw England for the first time, I was a child in school sitting at a desk. The England I was looking at was laid out on a map gently, beautifully, delicately, a very special jewel; it lay on a bed of sky blue — the background of the map — its yellow form mysterious, because though it looked like a leg of mutton, it could not really look like anything so familiar as a leg of mutton because it was England — with shadings of pink and green, unlike any shadings of pink and green I had seen before, squiggly veins of red running in every direction. England was a special jewel all right, and only special people got to wear it. The people who got to wear England were English people. They wore it well and they wore it everywhere: in jungles, in deserts, on plains, on top of the highest mountains, on all the oceans, on all the seas, in places where they were not welcome, in places they should not have been. When my teacher had pinned this map up on the blackboard, she said, "This is England" — and she said it with authority, seriousness, and adoration, and we all sat up. It was as if she had said, "This is Jerusalem, the place you will go to when you die but only if you have been good." We understood then — we were meant to understand then — that England was to be our source of myth and the source from which we got our sense of reality, our sense of what was meaningful, our sense of what was meaningless — and much about our own lives and much about the very idea of us headed that last list.

At the time I was a child sitting at my desk seeing England for the first time, I was already very familiar with the greatness of it. Each morning before I left for school, I ate a breakfast of half a grapefruit, an egg, bread and butter and a slice of cheese, and a cup of cocoa; or half of grapefruit, a bowl of oat porridge, bread and butter and a slice of cheese, and a cup of

For biographical information on Jamaica Kincaid, see p. 654.

cocoa. The can of coca was often left on the table in front of me. It had written on it the name of the company, the year the company was established, and the words "Made in England." Those words, "Made in England," were written on the box the oats came in too. They would also have been written on the box the shoes I was wearing came in; a bolt of gray linen cloth lying on the shelf of a store from which my mother had bought three yards to make the uniform that I was wearing had written along its edge those three words. The shoes I wore were made in England; so were my socks and cotton undergarments and the satin ribbons I wore tied at the end of two plaits of my hair. My father, who might have sat next to me at breakfast, was a carpenter and cabinet maker. The shoes he wore to work would have been made in England, as were his khaki shirt and trousers, his underpants and undershirt, his socks and brown felt hat. Felt was not the proper material from which a hat that was expected to provide shade from the hot sun should be made, but my father must have seen and admired a picture of an Englishman wearing such a hat in England, and this picture that he saw must have been so compelling that it caused him to wear the wrong hat for a hot climate most of his long life. And this hat — a brown felt hat — became so central to his character that it was the first thing he put on in the morning as he stepped out of bed and the last thing he took off before he stepped back into bed at night. As we sat at breakfast a car might go by. The car, a Hillman or a Zephyr, was made in England. The very idea of the meal itself, breakfast, and its substantial quality and quantity was an idea from England; we somehow knew that in England they began the day with this meal called breakfast and a proper breakfast was a big breakfast. No one I knew liked eating so much food so early in the day; it made us feel sleepy, tired. But this breakfast business was Made in England like almost everything else that surrounded us, the exceptions being the sea, the sky, and the air we breathed.

At the time I saw this map — seeing England for the first time — I did not say to myself, "Ah, so that's what it looks like," because there was no longing in me to put a shape to those three words that ran through every part of my life, no matter how small; for me to have had such a longing would have meant that I lived in a certain atmosphere, an atmosphere in which those three words were felt as a burden. But I did not live in such an atmosphere. My father's brown felt hat would develop a hole in its crown, the lining would separate from the hat itself, and six weeks before he thought that he could not be seen wearing it — he was a very vain man — he would order another hat from England. And my mother taught me to eat my food in the English way: the knife in the right hand, the fork in the left, my elbows held still close to my side, the food carefully balanced on my fork and then brought up to my mouth. When I had finally mastered it, I overheard her saying to a friend, "Did you see how nicely she can eat?" But I knew then that I enjoyed my food more when I ate it with my bare hands, and I continued to do so when she wasn't looking. And when my teacher showed us the map, she asked us to study it carefully, because no test we would ever take would be complete without this statement: "Draw a map of England."

I did not know then that the statement "Draw a map of England" was something far worse than a declaration of war, for in fact a flat-out declaration of war would have put me on alert, and again in fact, there was no need for war — I had long ago been conquered. I did not know then that this statement was part of a process that would result in my erasure, not my physical erasure, but my erasure all the same. I did not know then that this statement was meant to make me feel in awe and small whenever I heard the word "England": awe at its existence, small because I was not from it. I did not know very much of anything then — certainly not what a blessing it was that I was unable to draw a map of England correctly.

After that there were many times of seeing England for the first time. I 5 saw England in history. I knew the names of all the kings of England. I knew the names of their children, their wives, their disappointments, their triumphs, the names of people who betrayed them, I knew the dates on which they were born and the dates they died. I knew their conquests and was made to feel glad if I figured in them; I knew their defeats. I knew the details of the year 1066 (the Battle of Hastings, the end of the reign of the Anglo-Saxon kings) before I knew the details of the year 1832 (the year slavery was abolished). It wasn't as bad as I make it sound now; it was worse. I did like so much hearing again and again how Alfred the Great, traveling in disguise, had been left to watch cakes, and because he wasn't used to this the cakes got burned, and Alfred burned his hands pulling them out of the fire, and the woman who had left him to watch the cakes screamed at him. I loved King Alfred. My grandfather was named after him; his son, my uncle, was named after King Alfred; my brother is named after King Alfred. And so there are three people in my family named after a man they have never met, a man who died over ten centuries ago. The first view I got of England then was not unlike the first view received by the person who named my grandfather.

This view, though — the naming of the kings, their deeds, their disappointments — was the vivid view, the forceful view. There were other views, subtler ones, softer, almost not there — but these were the ones that made the most lasting impression on me, these were the ones that made me really feel like nothing. "When morning touched the sky" was one phrase, for no morning touched the sky where I lived. The mornings where I lived came on abruptly, with a shock of heat and loud noises. "Evening approaches" was another, but the evenings where I lived did not approach; in fact, I had no evening — I had night and I had day and they came and went in a mechanical way: on, off; on, off. And then there were gentle mountains and low blue skies and moors over which people took walks for nothing but pleasure, when where I lived a walk was an act of labor, a burden, something only death or the automobile could relieve. And there were things that a small turn of a head could convey — entire worlds, whole lives would depend on this thing, a certain turn of a head. Everyday life could be quite tiring, more tiring than anything I was told not to do. I was told not to gossip, but they did that all the time. And they ate so much food, violating another of those rules they taught me: Do no indulge in gluttony. And the foods they ate actually: If only sometime I could eat cold cuts after theater, cold cuts of lamb and mint sauce, and Yorkshire pudding and scones, and clotted cream, and sausages that came from up-country (imagine, "up-country"). And having troubling thoughts at twilight, a good time to have troubling thoughts, apparently; and servants who stole and left in the middle of a crisis, who were born with a limp or some other kind of deformity, not nourished properly in their mother's womb (that last part I figured out for myself; the point was, oh to have an un-trustworthy servant); and wonderful cobbled streets onto which solid front doors opened; and people whose eyes were blue and who had fair skins and who smelled only of lavender, or sometimes sweet pea or primrose. And those flowers with those names: delphiniums, foxgloves, tulips, daffodils, floribunda, peonies: in bloom, a striking display, being cut and placed in large glass bowls, crystal, decorating rooms so large twenty families the size of mine could fit in comfortably but used only for passing through. And the weather was so remarkable because the rain fell gently always, only occasionally in deep gusts, and it colored the air various shades of gray, each an appealing shade for a dress to be worn when a portrait was being painted; and when it rained at twilight, wonderful things happened: People bumped into each other unexpectedly and that would lead to all sorts of turns of events — a plot, the mere weather caused plots. I saw that people rushed: They rushed to catch trains, they rushed toward each other and away from each other; they rushed and rushed and rushed. That word: rushed! I did not know what it was to do that. It was too hot to do that, and so I came to envy people who would rush, even though it had no mean-ing to me to do such a thing. But there they are again. They loved their children; their children were sent to their own rooms as a punishment, rooms larger than my entire house. They were special, everything about them said so, even their clothes; their clothes rustled, swished, soothed. The world was theirs, not mine; everything told me so.

If now as I speak of all this I give the impression of someone on the outside looking in, nose pressed up against a glass window, that is wrong. My nose was pressed up against a glass window all right, but there was an iron vise at the back of my neck forcing my head to stay in place. To avert my gaze was to fall back into something from which I had been rescued, a hole filled with nothing, and that was the word for everything about me, nothing. The reality of my life was conquests, subjugation, humiliation, enforced amnesia. I was forced to forget. Just for instance, this: I lived in a part of St. John's, Antigua, called Ovals. Ovals was made up of five streets, each of them named after a famous English seaman — to be quite frank, an officially sanctioned criminal: Rodney Street (after George Rodney), Nel-son Street (after Horatio Nelson), Drake Street (after Francis Drake), Hood Street, and Hawkins Street (after John Hawkins). But John Hawkins was knighted after a trip he made to Africa, opening up a new trade, the slave trade. He was then entitled to wear as his crest a Negro bound with a cord. Every single person living on Hawkins Street was descended from a slave. John Hawkins's ship, the one in which he transported the people he had bought and kidnapped, was called *The Jesus*. He later became the treasurer of the Royal Navy and rear admiral.

Again, the reality of my life, the life I led at the time I was being shown these views of England for the first time, for the second time, for the one-hundred-millionth time, was this: The sun shone with what sometimes seemed to be a deliberate cruelty; we must have done something to deserve that. My dresses did not rustle in the evening air as I strolled to the theater (I had no evening, I had no theater; my dresses were made of a cheap cotton, the weave of which would give way after not too many washings). I got up in the morning, I did my chores (fetched water from the public pipe for my mother, swept the yard), I washed myself, I went to a woman to have my hair combed freshly every day (because before we were allowed into our classroom our teachers would inspect us, and children who had not bathed that day, or had dirt under their fingernails, or whose hair had not been combed anew that day, might not be allowed to attend class). I ate that breakfast. I walked to school. At school we gathered in an auditorium and sang a hymn, "All Things Bright and Beautiful," and looking down on us as we sang were portraits of the Queen of England and her husband; they wore jewels and medals and they smiled. I was a Brownie. At each meeting we would form a little group around a flagpole, and after raising the Union Jack, we would say, "I promise to do my best, to do my duty to God and the Queen, to help other people every day and obey the scouts' law."

Who were these people and why had I never seen them, I mean really seen them, in the place where they lived? I had never been to England. No one I knew had ever been to England, or I should say, no one I knew had ever been and returned to tell me about it. All the people I knew who had gone to England had stayed there. Sometimes they left behind them their small children, never to see them again. England! I had seen England's representatives. I had seen the governor general at the public grounds at a ceremony celebrating the Queen's birthday. I had seen an old princess and I had seen a young princess. They had both been extremely not beautiful, but who of us would have told them that? I had never seen England, really seen it, I had only met a representative, seen a picture, read books, memorized its history. I had never set foot, my own foot, in it.

The space between the idea of something and its reality is always wide 10 and deep and dark. The longer they are kept apart — idea of thing, reality of thing — the wider the width, the deeper the depth, the thicker and darker the darkness. This space starts out empty, there is nothing in it, but it rapidly becomes filled up with obsession or desire or hatred or love — sometimes all of these things, sometimes some of these things, sometimes only one of these things. The existence of the world as I came to know it was a result of this: idea of thing over here, reality of thing way, way over there. There was Christopher Columbus, an unlikable man, an unpleasant man, a liar (and so, of course, a thief) surrounded by maps and schemes and plans, and there was the reality on the other side of that width, that depth, that darkness. He became obsessed, he became filled with desire, the hatred came later, love was never a part of it. Eventually, his idea met the longed-for reality. That the idea of something and its reality are often two completely different things is something no one ever remembers; and so when they meet and find that they are not compatible, the weaker of the two, idea or reality, dies. That idea Christopher Columbus had was more powerful than the reality he met, and so the reality he met died.

And so finally, when I was a grown-up woman, the mother of two children, the wife of someone, a person who resides in a powerful country that takes up more than its fair share of a continent, the owner of a house with many rooms in it and of two automobiles, with the desire and will (which I very much act upon) to take from the world more than I give back to it, more than I deserve, more than I need, finally then, I saw England, the real England, not a picture, not a painting, not through a story in a book, but England, for the first time. In me, the space between the idea of it and its reality had become filled with hatred, and so when at last I saw it I wanted to take it into my hands and tear it into little pieces and then crumble it up as if it were clay, child's clay. That was impossible, and so I could only indulge in not-favorable opinions.

There were monuments everywhere; they commemorated victories, battles fought between them and the people who lived across the sea from them, all vile people, fought over which of them would have dominion over the people who looked like me. The monuments were useless to them now, people sat on them and ate their lunch. They were like markers on an old useless trail, like a piece of old string tied to a finger to jog the memory, like old decoration in an old house, dirty, useless, in the way. Their skins were so pale, it made them look so fragile, so weak, so ugly. What if I had the power to simply banish them from their land, send boat after boatload of them on a voyage that in fact had no destination, force them to live in a place where the sun's presence was a constant? This would rid them of their pale complexion and make them look more like me, make them look more like the people I love and treasure and hold dear, and more like the people who occupy the near and far reaches of my imagination, my history, my geography, and reduce them and everything they have ever known to figurines as evidence that I was in divine favor, what if all this was in my power? Could I resist it? No one ever has.

And they were rude, they were rude to each other. They didn't like each other very much. They didn't like each other in the way they didn't like me, and it occurred to me that their dislike for me was one of the few things they agreed on.

I was on a train in England with a friend, an English woman. Before we were in England she liked me very much. In England she didn't like me at all. She didn't like the claim I said I had on England, she didn't like the views I had of England. I didn't like England, she didn't like England, but she didn't like me not liking it too. She said, "I want to show you my England, I want to show you the England that I know and love." I had told her many times before that I knew England and I didn't want to love it anyway. She no longer lived in England; it was her own country, but it had not been kind to her, so she left. On the train, the conductor was rude to her; she asked something, and he responded in a rude way. She became ashamed. She was ashamed at the way he treated her; she was ashamed at the way he behaved. "This is the new England," she said. But I liked the conductor being rude; his behavior seemed quite appropriate. Earlier this had happened: We had gone to a store to buy a shirt for my husband; it was meant to be a special present, a special shirt to wear on special occasions. This was a store where the Prince of Wales has his shirts made, but the shirts sold in this store are beautiful all the same. I found a shirt I thought my husband would like and I wanted to buy him a tie to go with it. When I couldn't decide which one to choose, the salesman showed me a new set. He was very pleased with these, he said, because they bore the crest of the Prince of Wales, and the Prince of Wales had never allowed his crest to decorate an article of clothing before. There was something in the way he said it; his tone was slavish, reverential, awed. It made me feel angry; I wanted to hit him. I didn't do that. I said, my husband and I hate princes, my husband would never wear anything that had a prince's anything on it. My friend stiffened. The salesman stiffened. They both drew themselves in, away from me. My friend told me that the prince was a symbol of her Englishness, and I could see that I had caused offense. I looked at her. She was an English person, the sort of English person I used to know at home, the sort who was nobody in England but somebody when they came to live among the people like me. There were many people I could have seen England with; that I was seeing it with this particular person, a person who reminded me of the people who showed me England long ago as I sat in church or at my desk, made me feel silent and afraid, for I wondered if, all these years of our friendship, I had had a friend or had been in the thrall of a racial memory.

I went to Bath — we, my friend and I, did this, but though we were together, I was no longer with her. The landscape was almost as familiar as my own hand, but I had never been in this place before, so how could that be again? And the streets of Bath were familiar, too, but I had never walked on them before. It was all those years of reading, starting with Roman Britain. Why did I have to know about Roman Britain? It was of no real use to me, a person living on a hot, drought-ridden island, and it is of no use to me now, and yet my head is filled with this nonsense, Roman Britain. In Bath, I drank tea in a room I had read about in a novel written in the eighteenth century. In this very same room, young women wearing those dresses that rustled and so on danced and flirted and sometimes disgraced

15

themselves with young men, soldiers, sailors, who were on their way to Bristol or someplace like that, so many places like that where so many adventures, the outcome of which was not good for me, began. Bristol, England. A sentence that began "That night the ship sailed from Bristol, England" would end not so good for me. And then I was driving through the countryside in an English motorcar, on narrow winding roads, and they were so familiar, though I had never been on them before; and through little villages the names of which I somehow knew so well though I had never been there before. And the countryside did have all those hedges and hedges, fields hedged in. I was marveling at all the toil of it, the planting of the hedges to begin with and then the care of it, all that clipping, year after year of clipping, and I wondered at the lives of the people who would have to do this, because wherever I see and feel the hands that hold up the world, I see and feel myself and all the people who look like me. And I said, "Those hedges" and my friend said that someone, a woman named Mrs. Rothchild, worried that the hedges weren't being taken care of properly; the farmers couldn't afford or find the help to keep up the hedges, and often they replaced them with wire fencing. I might have said to that, well if Mrs. Rothchild doesn't like the wire fencing, why doesn't she take care of the hedges herself, but I didn't. And then in those fields that were now hemmed in by wire fencing that a privileged woman didn't like was planted a vile yellow flowering bush that produced an oil, and my friend said that Mrs. Rothchild didn't like this either; it ruined the English countryside, it ruined the traditional look of the English countryside.

It was not at that moment that I wished every sentence, everything I knew, that began with England would end with "and then it all died; we don't know how, it just all died." At that moment, I was thinking, who are these people who forced me to think of them all the time, who forced me to think that the world I knew was incomplete, or without substance, or did not measure up because it was not England; that I was incomplete, or without substance, and did not measure up because I was not English. Who were these people? The person sitting next to me couldn't give me a clue; no one person could. In any case, if I had said to her, I find England ugly, I hate England; the weather is like a jail sentence, the English are a very ugly people, the food in England is like a jail sentence, the hair of English people is so straight, so dead looking, the English have an unbearable smell so different from the smell of people I know, real people of course, she would have said that I was a person full of prejudice. Apart from the fact that it is I — that is, the people who look like me — who made her aware of the unpleasantness of such a thing, the idea of such a thing, prejudice, she would have been only partly right, sort of right: I may be capable of prejudice, but my prejudices have no weight to them, my prejudices have no force behind them, my prejudices remain opinions, my prejudices remain my personal opinion. And a great feeling of rage and disappointment came over me as I looked at England, my head full of personal opinions that could not have public, my public, approval. The people I come from are powerless to do evil on grand scale.

The moment I wished every sentence, everything I knew, that began with England would end with "and then it all died, we don't know how, it just all died" was when I saw the white cliffs of Dover. I had sung hymns and recited poems that were about a longing to see the white cliffs of Dover again. At the time I sang the hymns and recited the poems, I could really long to see them again because I had never seen them at all, nor had anyone around me at the time. But there we were, groups of people longing for something we had never seen. And so there they were, the white cliffs, but they were not that pearly majestic thing I used to sing about, that thing that created such a feeling in these people that when they died in the place where I lived they had themselves buried facing a direction that would allow them to see the white cliffs of Dover when they were resurrected, as surely they would be. The white cliffs of Dover, when finally I saw them, were cliffs, but they were not white; you would only call them that if the word "white" meant something special to you; they were dirty and they were steep; they were so steep, the correct height from which all my views of England, starting with the map before me in my classroom and ending with the trip I had just taken, should jump and die and disappear forever.

1991

The Reader's Presence

1. What twist does Kincaid give the word *seeing* throughout the first half of her essay? What England does she see? For example, why doesn't she see the slums of London or the industrial squalor of Manchester? How might these sights have affected her point of view? Where does her information come from?

2. Note the details Kincaid provides in paragraph 6. Where do these details come from? Where do the quotations come from? How do you think she wants her readers to see and hear these details? What have they to do with the "idea of England" as opposed to the reality?

3. Note that Kincaid does not include the English language among the many things she hates about England and the English. Do you think she regards the language as one of the few satisfactory parts of England? Or do you think she resents the language as well? In rereading the essay, consider her use of English. Given her overall hostility to England, what can you infer about her attitude toward the language itself?

66 ———————————————————————

Martin Luther King, Jr.
Letter from Birmingham Jail

MARTIN LUTHER KING, JR.
Birmingham City Jail
April 16, 1963

Bishop C. C. J. CARPENTER
Bishop JOSEPH A. DURICK
Rabbi MILTON L. GRAFMAN
Bishop PAUL HARDIN
Bishop NOLAN B. HARMON
The Rev. GEORGE M. MURRAY
The Rev. EDWARD V. RAMAGE
The Rev. EARL STALLINGS

My dear Fellow Clergymen,

While confined here in the Birmingham City Jail, I came across your recent statement calling our present activities "unwise and untimely." Seldom, if ever, do I pause to answer criticism of my work and ideas. If I sought to answer all of the criticisms that cross my desk, my secretaries would be engaged in little else in the course of the day and I would have no time for constructive work. But since I feel that you are men of genuine good will and your criticisms are sincerely set forth, I would like to answer your statement in what I hope will be patient and reasonable terms.

I think I should give the reason for my being in Birmingham, since you have been influenced by the argument of "outsiders coming in." I have the honor of serving as president of the Southern Christian Leadership Conference, an organization operating in every Southern state with headquarters in Atlanta, Georgia. We have some eighty-five affiliate organizations all

For biographical information on Martin Luther King, Jr., see p. 654.

514

across the South — one being the Alabama Christian Movement for Human Rights. Whenever necessary and possible we share staff, educational, and financial resources with our affiliates. Several months ago our local affiliate here in Birmingham invited us to be on call to engage in a nonviolent direct action program if such were deemed necessary. We readily consented and when the hour came we lived up to our promises. So I am here, along with several members of my staff, because we were invited here. I am here because I have basic organizational ties here. Beyond this, I am in Birmingham because injustice is here. Just as the eighth century prophets left their little villages and carried their "thus saith the Lord" far beyond the boundaries of their home town, and just as the Apostle Paul left his little village of Tarsus and carried the gospel of Jesus Christ to practically every hamlet and city of the Graeco-Roman world, I too am compelled to carry the gospel of freedom beyond my particular home town. Like Paul, I must constantly respond to the Macedonian call for aid.

Moreover, I am cognizant of the interrelatedness of all communities and states. I cannot sit idly by in Atlanta and not be concerned about what happens in Birmingham. Injustice anywhere is a threat to justice everywhere. We are caught in an inescapable network of mutuality tied in a single garment of destiny. Whatever affects one directly affects all indirectly. Never again can we afford to live with the narrow, provincial "outside agitator" idea. Anyone who lives inside the United States can never be considered an outsider anywhere in this country.

You deplore the demonstrations that are presently taking place in Birmingham. But I am sorry that your statement did not express a similar concern for the conditions that brought the demonstrations into being. I am sure that each of you would want to go beyond the superficial social analyst who looks merely at effects, and does not grapple with underlying causes. I would not hesitate to say that it is unfortunate that so-called demonstrations are taking place in Birmingham at this time, but I would say in more emphatic terms that it is even more unfortunate that the white power structure of this city left the Negro community with no other alternative.

In any nonviolent campaign there are four basic steps: (1) collection of the facts to determine whether injustices are alive; (2) negotiation; (3) self-purification; and (4) direct action. We have gone through all of these steps in Birmingham. There can be no gainsaying of the fact that racial injustice engulfs this community. Birmingham is probably the most thoroughly segregated city in the United States. Its ugly record of police brutality is known in every section of this country. Its unjust treatment of Negroes in the courts is a notorious reality. There have been more unsolved bombings of Negro homes and churches in Birmingham than any city in this nation. These are the hard, brutal, and unbelievable facts. On the basis of these conditions Negro leaders sought to negotiate with the city fathers. But the political leaders consistently refused to engage in good faith negotiation.

Then came the opportunity last September to talk with some of the leaders of the economic community. In these negotiating sessions certain promises were made by the merchants — such as the promise to remove the humiliating racial signs from the stores. On the basis of these promises Rev. Shuttlesworth and the leaders of the Alabama Christian Movement for Human Rights agreed to call a moratorium on any type of demonstrations. As the weeks and months unfolded we realized that we were the victims of a broken promise. The signs remained. As in so many experiences of the past we were confronted with blasted hopes, and the dark shadow of a deep disappointment settled upon us. So we had no alternative except that of preparing for direct action, whereby we would present our very bodies as a means of laying our case before the conscience of the local and national community. We were not unmindful of the difficulties involved. So we decided to go through a process of self-purification. We started having workshops on nonviolence and repeatedly asked ourselves the questions, "Are you able to accept blows without retaliating?" "Are you able to endure the ordeals of jail?"

We decided to set our direct action program around the Easter season, realizing that with the exception of Christmas, this was the largest shopping period of the year. Knowing that a strong economic withdrawal program would be the by-product of direct action, we felt that this was the best time to bring pressure on the merchants for the needed changes. Then it occurred to us that the March election was ahead, and so we speedily decided to postpone action until after election day. When we discovered that Mr. Connor[1] was in the run-off, we decided again to postpone so that the demonstrations could not be used to cloud the issues. At this time we agreed to begin our nonviolent witness the day after the run-off.

This reveals that we did not move irresponsibly into direct action. We too wanted to see Mr. Connor defeated; so we went through postponement after postponement to aid in this community need. After this we felt that direct action could be delayed no longer.

You may well ask, "Why direct action? Why sit-ins, marches, etc.? Isn't negotiation a better path?" You are exactly right in your call for negotiation. Indeed, this is the purpose of direct action. Nonviolent direct action seeks to create such a crisis and establish such creative tension that a community that has constantly refused to negotiate is forced to confront the issue. It seeks so to dramatize the issue that it can no longer be ignored. I just referred to the creation of tension as a part of the work of the nonvio-

---

[1]**Mr. Connor:** Eugene "Bull" Connor and Albert Boutwell ran for mayor of Birmingham, Alabama, in 1963. Although Boutwell, the more moderate candidate, was declared the winner, Connor, the city commissioner of public safety, refused to leave office claiming that he had been elected to serve until 1965. While the issue was debated in the courts, Connor was on the street ordering the police to use force to suppress demonstrations against segregation. — EDS.

lent resister. This may sound rather shocking. But I must confess that I am not afraid of the word tension. I have earnestly worked and preached against violent tension, but there is a type of constructive nonviolent tension that is necessary for growth. Just as Socrates felt that it was necessary to create a tension in the mind so that individuals could rise from the bondage of myths and half-truths to the unfettered realm of creative analysis and objective appraisal, we must see the need of having nonviolent gadflies to create the kind of tension in society that will help men rise from the dark depths of prejudice and racism to the majestic heights of understanding and brotherhood. So the purpose of the direct action is to create a situation so crisis-packed that it will inevitably open the door to negotiation. We, therefore, concur with you in your call for negotiation. Too long has our beloved Southland been bogged down in the tragic attempt to live in monologue rather than dialogue.

One of the basic points in your statement is that our acts are untimely.   10
Some have asked, "Why didn't you give the new administration time to act?" The only answer that I can give to this inquiry is that the new administration must be prodded about as much as the outgoing one before it acts. We will be sadly mistaken if we feel that the election of Mr. Boutwell will bring the millennium to Birmingham. While Mr. Boutwell is much more articulate and gentle than Mr. Connor, they are both segregationists dedicated to the task of maintaining the status quo. The hope I see in Mr. Boutwell is that he will be reasonable enough to see the futility of massive resistance to desegregation. But he will not see this without pressure from the devotees of civil rights. My friends, I must say to you that we have not made a single gain in civil rights without determined legal and nonviolent pressure. History is the long and tragic story of the fact that privileged groups seldom give up their privileges voluntarily. Individuals may see the moral light and voluntarily give up their unjust posture; but as Reinhold Niebuhr has reminded us, groups are more immoral than individuals.

We know through painful experience that freedom is never voluntarily given by the oppressor; it must be demanded by the oppressed. Frankly I have never yet engaged in a direct action movement that was "well timed," according to the timetable of those who have not suffered unduly from the disease of segregation. For years now I have heard the word "Wait!" It rings in the ear of every Negro with a piercing familiarity. This "wait" has almost always meant "never." It has been a tranquilizing thalidomide, relieving the emotional stress for a moment, only to give birth to an ill-formed infant of frustration. We must come to see with the distinguished jurist of yesterday that "justice too long delayed is justice denied." We have waited for more than three hundred and forty years for our constitutional and God-given rights. The nations of Asia and Africa are moving with jet-like speed toward the goal of political independence, and we still creep at horse and buggy pace toward the gaining of a cup of coffee at a lunch counter.

I guess it is easy for those who have never felt the stinging darts of segregation to say wait. But when you have seen vicious mobs lynch your mothers and fathers at will and drown your sisters and brothers at whim; when you have seen hate-filled policemen curse, kick, brutalize, and even kill your black brothers and sisters with impunity; when you see the vast majority of your twenty million Negro brothers smothering in an air-tight cage of poverty in the midst of an affluent society; when you suddenly find your tongue twisted and your speech stammering as you seek to explain to your six-year-old daughter why she can't go to the public amusement park that has just been advertised on television, and see tears welling up in her little eyes when she is told that Funtown is closed to colored children, and see the depressing clouds of inferiority begin to form in her little mental sky, and see her begin to distort her little personality by unconsciously developing a bitterness toward white people; when you have to concoct an answer for a five-year-old son asking in agonizing pathos: "Daddy, why do white people treat colored people so mean?"; when you take a cross country drive and find it necessary to sleep night after night in the uncomfortable corners of your automobile because no motel will accept you; when you are humiliated day in and day out by nagging signs reading "white" men and "colored"; when your first name becomes "nigger" and your middle name becomes "boy" (however old you are) and your last name becomes "John," and when your wife and mother are never given the respected title "Mrs."; when you are harried by day and haunted by night by the fact that you are a Negro, living constantly at tip-toe stance never quite knowing what to expect next, and plagued with inner fears and outer resentments; when you are forever fighting a degenerating sense of "nobodiness"; — then you will understand why we find it difficult to wait. There comes a time when the cup of endurance runs over, and men are no longer willing to be plunged into an abyss of injustice where they experience the bleakness of corroding despair. I hope, sirs, you can understand our legitimate and unavoidable impatience.

You express a great deal of anxiety over our willingness to break laws. This is certainly a legitimate concern. Since we so diligently urge people to obey the Supreme Court's decision of 1954 outlawing segregation in the public schools, it is rather strange and paradoxical to find us consciously breaking laws. One may well ask, "How can you advocate breaking some laws and obeying others?" The answer is found in the fact that there are two types of laws. There are *just* laws and there are *unjust* laws. I would be the first to advocate obeying just laws. One has not only a legal but moral responsibility to obey just laws. Conversely, one has a moral responsibility to disobey unjust laws. I would agree with Saint Augustine that "An unjust law is no law at all."

Now what is the difference between the two? How does one determine when a law is just or unjust? A just law is a man-made code that squares with the moral law or the law of God. An unjust law is a code that is out of harmony with the moral law. To put it in the terms of Saint Thomas

Aquinas, an unjust law is a human law that is not rooted in eternal and natural law. Any law that uplifts human personality is just. Any law that degrades human personality is unjust. All segregation statutes are unjust because segregation distorts the soul and damages the personality. It gives the segregator a false sense of superiority and the segregated a false sense of inferiority. To use the words of Martin Buber, the great Jewish philosopher, segregation substitutes an "I-it" relationship for the "I-thou" relationship, and ends up relegating persons to the status of things. So segregation is not only politically, economically, and sociologically unsound, but it is morally wrong and sinful. Paul Tillich[2] has said that sin is separation. Isn't segregation an existential expression of man's tragic separation, an expression of his awful estrangement, his terrible sinfulness? So I can urge men to obey the 1954 decision of the Supreme Court[3] because it is morally right, and I can urge them to disobey segregation ordinances because they are morally wrong.

Let us turn to a more concrete example of just and unjust laws. An   15
unjust law is a code that a majority inflicts on a minority that is not binding on itself. This is *difference* made legal. On the other hand a just law is a code that a majority compels a minority to follow that it is willing to follow itself. This is *sameness* made legal.

Let me give another explanation. An unjust law is a code inflicted upon a minority which that minority had no part in enacting or creating because they did not have the unhampered right to vote. Who can say the legislature of Alabama which set up the segregation laws was democratically elected? Throughout the state of Alabama all types of conniving methods are used to prevent Negroes from becoming registered voters and there are some counties without a single Negro registered to vote despite the fact that the Negro constitutes a majority of the population. Can any law set up in such a state be considered democratically structured?

These are just a few examples of unjust and just laws. There are some instances when a law is just on its face but unjust in its application. For instance, I was arrested Friday on a charge of parading without a permit. Now there is nothing wrong with an ordinance which requires a permit for a parade, but when the ordinance is used to preserve segregation and to deny citizens the First Amendment privilege of peaceful assembly and peaceful protest, then it becomes unjust.

I hope you can see the distinction I am trying to point out. In no sense do I advocate evading or defying the law as the rabid segregationist would do. This would lead to anarchy. One who breaks an unjust law must do it *openly, lovingly* (not hatefully as the white mothers did in New Orleans

---

[2]*Paul Tillich* (1886–1965): Theologian and philosopher. — EDS.
[3]*1954 decision of the Supreme Court: Brown* vs. *Board of Education,* the case in which the Supreme Court ruled racial segregation in the nation's public schools unconstitutional. — EDS.

when they were seen on television screaming "nigger, nigger, nigger") and with a willingness to accept the penalty. I submit that an individual who breaks a law that conscience tells him is unjust, and willingly accepts the penalty by staying in jail to arouse the conscience of the community over its injustice, is in reality expressing the very highest respect for law.

Of course there is nothing new about this kind of civil disobedience. It was seen sublimely in the refusal of Shadrach, Meshach, and Abednego to obey the laws of Nebuchadnezzar because a higher moral law was involved. It was practiced superbly by the early Christians who were willing to face hungry lions and the excruciating pain of chopping blocks, before submitting to certain unjust laws of the Roman Empire. To a degree academic freedom is a reality today because Socrates practiced civil disobedience.

We can never forget that everything Hitler did in Germany was "legal"   20
and everything the Hungarian freedom fighters[4] did in Hungary was "illegal." It was "illegal" to aid and comfort a Jew in Hitler's Germany. But I am sure that, if I had lived in Germany during that time, I would have aided and comforted my Jewish brothers even though it was illegal. If I lived in a communist country today where certain principles dear to the Christian faith are suppressed, I believe I would openly advocate disobeying those antireligious laws.

I must make two honest confessions to you, my Christian and Jewish brothers. First I must confess that over the last few years I have been gravely disappointed with the white moderate. I have almost reached the regrettable conclusion that the Negroes' great stumbling block in the stride toward freedom is not the White Citizens' "Counciler" or the Ku Klux Klanner, but the white moderate who is more devoted to "order" than to justice; who prefers a negative peace which is the absence of tension to a positive peace which is the presence of justice; who constantly says "I agree with you in the goal you seek, but I can't agree with your methods of direct action"; who paternalistically feels that he can set the timetable for another man's freedom; who lives by the myth of time and who constantly advises the Negro to wait until a "more convenient season." Shallow understanding from people of good will is more frustrating than absolute misunderstanding from people of ill will. Lukewarm acceptance is much more bewildering than outright rejection.

I had hoped that the white moderate would understand that law and order exist for the purpose of establishing justice, and that when they fail to do this they become the dangerously structured dams that block the flow of social progress. I had hoped that the white moderate would understand that the present tension in the South is merely a necessary phase of the transition from an obnoxious negative peace, where the Negro passively

---

[4]***Hungarian freedom fighters:*** Those who fought in the unsuccessful 1956 revolt against Soviet oppression. — EDS.

accepted his unjust plight, to a substance-filled positive peace, where all men will respect the dignity and worth of human personality. Actually, we who engage in nonviolent direct action are not the creators of tension. We merely bring to the surface the hidden tension that is already alive. We bring it out in the open where it can be seen and dealt with. Like a boil that can never be cured as long as it is covered up but must be opened with all its pus-flowing ugliness to the natural medicines of air and light, injustice must likewise be exposed, with all of the tension its exposing creates, to the light of human conscience and the air of national opinion before it can be cured.

In your statement you asserted that our actions, even though peaceful, must be condemned because they precipitate violence. But can this assertion be logically made? Isn't this like condemning the robbed man because his possession of money precipitated the evil act of robbery? Isn't this like condemning Socrates because his unswerving commitment to truth and his philosophical delvings precipitated the misguided popular mind to make him drink the hemlock? Isn't this like condemning Jesus because His unique God consciousness and never-ceasing devotion to His will precipitated the evil act of crucifixion? We must come to see, as federal courts have consistently affirmed, that it is immoral to urge an individual to withdraw his efforts to gain his basic constitutional rights because the quest precipitates violence. Society must protect the robbed and punish the robber.

I had also hoped that the white moderate would reject the myth of time. I received a letter this morning from a white brother in Texas which said: "All Christians know that the colored people will receive equal rights eventually, but is it possible that you are in too great of a religious hurry? It has taken Christianity almost 2000 years to accomplish what it has. The teachings of Christ take time to come to earth." All that is said here grows out of a tragic misconception of time. It is the strangely irrational notion that there is something in the very flow of time that will inevitably cure all ills. Actually time is neutral. It can be used either destructively or constructively. I am coming to feel that the people of ill will have used time much more effectively than the people of good will. We will have to repent in this generation not merely for the vitriolic words and actions of the bad people, but for the appalling silence of the good people. We must come to see that human progress never rolls in on wheels of inevitability. It comes through the tireless efforts and persistent work of men willing to be co-workers with God, and without this hard work time itself becomes an ally of the forces of social stagnation.

We must use time creatively, and forever realize that the time is always 25 ripe to do right. Now is the time to make real the promise of democracy, and transform our pending national elegy into a creative psalm of brotherhood. Now is the time to lift our national policy from the quicksand of racial injustice to the solid rock of human dignity.

You spoke of our activity in Birmingham as extreme. At first I was rather disappointed that fellow clergymen would see my nonviolent efforts as those of the extremist. I started thinking about the fact that I stand in the middle of two opposing forces in the Negro community. One is a force of complacency made up of Negroes who, as a result of long years of oppression, have been so completely drained of self-respect and a sense of "somebodiness" that they have adjusted to segregation, and of a few Negroes in the middle class who, because of a degree of academic and economic security, and because at points they profit by segregation, have unconsciously become insensitive to the problems of the masses. The other force is one of bitterness and hatred and comes perilously close to advocating violence. It is expressed in the various black nationalist groups that are springing up over the nation, the largest and best known being Elijah Muhammad's Muslim movement.[5] This movement is nourished by the contemporary frustration over the continued existence of racial discrimination. It is made up of people who have lost faith in America, who have absolutely repudiated Christianity, and who have concluded that the white man is an incurable "devil." I have tried to stand between these two forces saying that we need not follow the "do-nothing-ism" of the complacent or the hatred and despair of the black nationalist. There is the more excellent way of love and nonviolent protest. I'm grateful to God that, through the Negro church, the dimension of nonviolence entered our struggle. If this philosophy had not emerged I am convinced that by now many streets of the South would be flowing with floods of blood. And I am further convinced that if our white brothers dismiss us as "rabble rousers" and "outside agitators" — those of us who are working through the channels of nonviolent direct action — and refuse to support our nonviolent efforts, millions of Negroes, out of frustration and despair, will seek solace and security in black nationalist ideologies, a development that will lead inevitably to a frightening racial nightmare.

Oppressed people cannot remain oppressed forever. The urge for freedom will eventually come. This is what has happened to the American Negro. Something within has reminded him of his birthright of freedom; something without has reminded him that he can gain it. Consciously and unconsciously, he has been swept in by what the Germans call the *Zeitgeist*,[6] and with his black brothers of Africa, and his brown and yellow brothers of Asia, South America, and the Caribbean, he is moving with a sense of cosmic urgency toward the promised land of racial justice. Recognizing this vital urge that has engulfed the Negro community, one should readily understand public demonstrations. The Negro has many pent-up resentments and latent frustrations. He has to get them out. So let him march sometime; let him have his prayer pilgrimages to the city hall; under-

---

[5]*Elijah Muhammad's Muslim movement:* Led by Elijah Muhammad, the Black Muslims opposed integration and promoted the creation of a black nation within the United States. — EDS.

[6]*Zeitgeist:* A German word meaning spirit of the time. — EDS.

stand why he must have sit-ins and freedom rides. If his repressed emotions do not come out in these nonviolent ways, they will come out in ominous expressions of violence. This is not a threat; it is a fact of history. So I have not said to my people, "Get rid of your discontent." But I have tried to say that this normal and healthy discontent can be channeled through the creative outlet of nonviolent direct action. Now this approach is being dismissed as extremist. I must admit that I was initially disappointed in being so categorized.

But as I continued to think about the matter I gradually gained a bit of satisfaction from being considered an extremist. Was not Jesus an extremist in love? "Love your enemies, bless them that curse you, pray for them that despitefully use you." Was not Amos an extremist for justice — "Let justice roll down like waters and righteousness like a mighty stream." Was not Paul an extremist for the gospel of Jesus Christ — "I bear in my body the marks of the Lord Jesus." Was not Martin Luther an extremist — "Here I stand; I can do none other so help me God." Was not John Bunyan an extremist — "I will stay in jail to the end of my days before I make a butchery of my conscience." Was not Abraham Lincoln an extremist — "This nation cannot survive half slave and half free." Was not Thomas Jefferson an extremist — "We hold these truths to be self evident that all men are created equal." So the question is not whether we will be extremist but what kind of extremist will we be. Will we be extremists for hate or will we be extremists for love? Will we be extremists for the preservation of injustice — or will we be extremists for the cause of justice? In that dramatic scene on Calvary's hill three men were crucified. We must never forget that all three were crucified for the same crime — the crime of extremism. Two were extremists for immorality, and thus fell below their environment. The other, Jesus Christ, was an extremist for love, truth, and goodness, and thereby rose above His environment. So, after all, maybe the South, the nation, and the world are in dire need of creative extremists.

I had hoped that the white moderate would see this. Maybe I was too optimistic. Maybe I expected too much. I guess I should have realized that few members of a race that has oppressed another race can understand or appreciate the deep groans and passionate yearnings of those that have been oppressed, and still fewer have the vision to see that injustice must be rooted out by strong, persistent, and determined action. I am thankful, however, that some of our white brothers have grasped the meaning of this social revolution and committed themselves to it. They are still all too small in quantity, but they are big in quality. Some like Ralph McGill, Lillian Smith, Harry Golden, and James Dabbs have written about our struggle in eloquent, prophetic, and understanding terms. Others have marched with us down nameless streets of the South. They have languished in filthy, roach-infested jails, suffering the abuse and brutality of angry policemen who see them as "dirty nigger lovers." They, unlike so many of their moderate brothers and sisters, have recognized the urgency of the moment and sensed the need for powerful "action" antidotes to combat the disease of segregation.

Let me rush on to mention my other disappointment. I have been so 30 greatly disappointed with the white Church and its leadership. Of course there are some notable exceptions. I am not unmindful of the fact that each of you has taken some significant stands on this issue. I commend you, Rev. Stallings, for your Christian stand on this past Sunday, in welcoming Negroes to your worship service on a nonsegregated basis. I commend the Catholic leaders of this state for integrating Springhill College several years ago.

But despite these notable exceptions I must honestly reiterate that I have been disappointed with the Church. I do not say that as one of those negative critics who can always find something wrong with the Church. I say it as a minister of the gospel, who loves the Church; who was nurtured in its bosom; who has been sustained by its spiritual blessings and who will remain true to it as long as the cord of life shall lengthen.

I had the strange feeling when I was suddenly catapulted into the leadership of the bus protest in Montgomery[7] several years ago that we would have the support of the white Church. I felt that the white ministers, priests, and rabbis of the South would be some of our strongest allies. Instead, some have been outright opponents, refusing to understand the freedom movement and misrepresenting its leaders; all too many others have been more cautious than courageous and have remained silent behind the anesthetizing security of stained glass windows.

In spite of my shattered dreams of the past, I came to Birmingham with the hope that the white religious leadership of the community would see the justice of our cause and, with deep moral concern, serve as the channel through which our just grievances could get to the power structure. I had hoped that each of you would understand. But again I have been disappointed.

I have heard numerous religious leaders of the South call upon their worshippers to comply with a desegregation decision because it is the law, but I have longed to hear white ministers say follow this decree because integration is morally right and the Negro is your brother. In the midst of blatant injustices inflicted upon the Negro, I have watched white churches stand on the sideline and merely mouth pious irrelevancies and sanctimonious trivialities. In the midst of a mighty struggle to rid our nation of racial and economic injustice, I have heard so many ministers say, "Those are social issues with which the Gospel has no real concern," and I have watched so many churches commit themselves to a completely other-

---

[7]***bus protest in Montgomery:*** After Rosa Parks was arrested on December 1, 1955, in Montgomery, Alabama, for refusing to give her seat on a bus to a white male passenger, a bus boycott began, which lasted nearly one year and was supported by almost all of the city's black residents. — EDS.

wordly religion which made a strange distinction between body and soul, the sacred and the secular.

So here we are moving toward the exit of the twentieth century with a 35 religious community largely adjusted to the status quo, standing as a tail-light behind other community agencies rather than a headlight leading men to higher levels of justice.

I have travelled the length and breadth of Alabama, Mississippi, and all the other Southern states. On sweltering summer days and crisp autumn mornings I have looked at her beautiful churches with their spires pointing heavenward. I have beheld the impressive outlay of her massive religious education buildings. Over and over again I have found myself asking: "Who worships here? Who is their God? Where were their voices when the lips of Governor Barnett[8] dripped with words of interposition and nullification? Where were they when Governor Wallace[9] gave the clarion call for defiance and hatred? Where were their voices of support when tired, bruised, and weary Negro men and women decided to rise from the dark dungeons of complacency to the bright hills of creative protest?"

Yes, these questions are still in my mind. In deep disappointment, I have wept over the laxity of the Church. But be assured that my tears have been tears of love. There can be no deep disappointment where there is not deep love. Yes, I love the Church; I love her sacred walls. How could I do otherwise? I am in the rather unique position of being the son, the grandson, and the great grandson of preachers. Yes, I see the Church as the body of Christ. But, oh! How we have blemished and scarred that body through social neglect and fear of being nonconformists.

There was a time when the Church was very powerful. It was during that period when the early Christians rejoiced when they were deemed worthy to suffer for what they believed. In those days the Church was not merely a thermometer that recorded the ideas and principles of popular opinion; it was a thermostat that transformed the mores of society. Wherever the early Christians entered a town the power structure got disturbed and immediately sought to convict them for being "disturbers of the peace" and "outside agitators." But they went on with the conviction that they were a "colony of heaven" and had to obey God rather than man. They were small in number but big in commitment. They were too God-intoxicated to be "astronomically intimidated." They brought an end to such ancient evils as infanticide and gladiatorial contest.

Things are different now. The contemporary Church is so often a weak, ineffectual voice with an uncertain sound. It is so often the

---

[8]*Governor Barnett:* Ross R. Barnett, governor of Mississippi from 1960 to 1964. — EDS.
[9]*Governor Wallace:* George C. Wallace served as governor of Alabama from 1963 to 1966, 1971 to 1979, and 1983 to 1987. — EDS.

archsupporter of the status quo. Far from being disturbed by the presence of the Church, the power structure of the average community is consoled by the Church's silent and often vocal sanction of things as they are.

But the judgment of God is upon the Church as never before. If the   40
Church of today does not recapture the sacrificial spirit of the early Church, it will lose its authentic ring, forfeit the loyalty of millions, and be dismissed as an irrelevant social club with no meaning for the twentieth century. I am meeting young people every day whose disappointment with the Church has risen to outright disgust.

Maybe again I have been too optimistic. Is organized religion too inextricably bound to the status quo to save our nation and the world? Maybe I must turn my faith to the inner spiritual Church, the church within the Church, as the true *ecclesia*[10] and the hope of the world. But again I am thankful to God that some noble souls from the ranks of organized religion have broken loose from the paralyzing chains of conformity and joined us as active partners in the struggle for freedom. They have left their secure congregations and walked the streets of Albany, Georgia, with us. They have gone through the highways of the South on torturous rides for freedom. Yes, they have gone to jail with us. Some have been kicked out of their churches and lost the support of their bishops and fellow ministers. But they have gone with the faith that right defeated is stronger than evil triumphant. These men have been the leaven in the lump of the race. Their witness has been the spiritual salt that has preserved the true meaning of the Gospel in these troubled times. They have carved a tunnel of hope through the dark mountain of disappointment.

I hope the Church as a whole will meet the challenge of this decisive hour. But even if the Church does not come to the aid of justice, I have no despair about the future. I have no fear about the outcome of our struggle in Birmingham, even if our motives are presently misunderstood. We will reach the goal of freedom in Birmingham and all over the nation, because the goal of America is freedom. Abused and scorned though we may be, our destiny is tied up with the destiny of America. Before the pilgrims landed at Plymouth, we were here. Before the pen of Jefferson etched across the pages of history the majestic words of the Declaration of Independence, we were here. For more than two centuries our foreparents labored in this country without wages; they made cotton "king"; and they built the homes of their masters in the midst of brutal injustice and shameful humiliation — and yet out of a bottomless vitality they continued to thrive and develop. If the inexpressible cruelties of slavery could not stop us, the opposition we now face will surely fail. We will win our freedom because the sacred heritage of our nation and the eternal will of God are embodied in our echoing demands.

---

[10]*ecclesia:* The Latin word for church. — EDS.

I must close now. But before closing I am impelled to mention one other point in your statement that troubled me profoundly. You warmly commended the Birmingham police force for keeping "order" and "preventing violence." I don't believe you would have so warmly commended the police force if you had seen its angry violent dogs literally biting six unarmed, nonviolent Negroes. I don't believe you would so quickly commend the policemen if you would observe their ugly and inhuman treatment of Negroes here in the city jail; if you would watch them push and curse old Negro women and young Negro girls; if you would see them slap and kick old Negro men and young Negro boys; if you will observe them, as they did on two occasions, refuse to give us food because we wanted to sing our grace together. I'm sorry that I can't join you in your praise for the police department.

It is true that they have been rather disciplined in their public handling of the demonstrators. In this sense they have been rather publicly "nonviolent." But for what purpose? To preserve the evil system of segregation. Over the last few years I have consistently preached that nonviolence demands that the means we use must be as pure as the ends we seek. So I have tried to make it clear that it is wrong to use immoral means to attain moral ends. But now I must affirm that it is just as wrong, or even more so, to use moral means to preserve immoral ends. Maybe Mr. Connor and his policemen have been rather publicly nonviolent, as Chief Pritchett[11] was in Albany, Georgia, but they have used the moral means of nonviolence to maintain the immoral end of flagrant racial injustice. T. S. Eliot has said that there is no greater treason than to do the right deed for the wrong reason.

I wish you had commended the Negro sit-inners and demonstrators of   45
Birmingham for their sublime courage, their willingness to suffer, and their amazing discipline in the midst of the most inhuman provocation. One day the South will recognize its real heroes. They will be the James Merediths,[12] courageously and with a majestic sense of purpose, facing jeering and hostile mobs and the agonizing loneliness that characterizes the life of the pioneer. They will be old, oppressed, battered Negro women, symbolized in a seventy-two year old woman of Montgomery, Alabama, who rose up with a sense of dignity and with her people decided not to ride the segregated buses, and responded to one who inquired about her tiredness with ungrammatical profundity: "My feets is tired, but my soul is rested." They will be young high school and college students, young ministers of the gospel and a host of the elders, courageously and nonviolently sitting in at

[11]*Chief Pritchett:* Laurie Prichett served as police chief in Albany, Georgia during nonviolent demonstrations in 1961 and 1962. Chief Pritchett responded to the nonviolent demonstrations with nonviolence, refusing to allow his officers to physically or verbally abuse the demonstrators. — EDS.

[12]*James Merediths:* Under the protection of federal marshals and the National Guard in 1962, James Meredith was the first black to enroll at the University of Mississippi. — EDS.

lunch counters and willingly going to jail for conscience sake. One day the South will know that when these disinherited children of God sat down at lunch counters they were in reality standing up for the best in the American dream and the most sacred values in our Judeo-Christian heritage, and thus carrying our whole nation back to great wells of democracy which were dug deep by the founding fathers in the formulation of the Constitution and the Declaration of Independence.

Never before have I written a letter this long (or should I say a book?). I'm afraid that it is much too long to take your precious time. I can assure you that it would have been much shorter if I had been writing from a comfortable desk, but what else is there to do when you are alone for days in the dull monotony of a narrow jail cell other than write long letters, think strange thoughts, and pray long prayers?

If I have said anything in this letter that is an overstatement of the truth and is indicative of an unreasonable impatience, I beg you to forgive me. If I have said anything in this letter that is an understatement of the truth and is indicative of my having a patience that makes me patient with anything less than brotherhood, I beg God to forgive me.

I hope this letter finds you strong in the faith. I also hope that circumstances will soon make it possible for me to meet each of you, not as an integrationist or a civil rights leader, but as a fellow clergyman and a Christian brother. Let us all hope that the dark clouds of racial prejudice will soon pass away and the deep fog of misunderstanding will be lifted from our fear-drenched communities and in some not too distant tomorrow the radiant stars of love and brotherhood will shine over our great nation with all of their scintillating beauty.

Yours for the cause of
Peace and Brotherhood
MARTIN LUTHER KING, JR.
1963

The Reader's Presence

1. Martin Luther King, Jr. wrote this letter in response to the eight clergymen identified at the beginning of the letter, who had declared that the civil rights activities of King and his associates were "unwise and untimely." What does King gain by characterizing his "Fellow Clergymen" as "men of genuine good will," whose criticisms are "sincerely set forth"? What evidence can you point to in King's letter to verify the claim that his audience extends far beyond the eight clergymen he explicitly addresses? Comment on the overall structure of King's letter. What principle of composition underpins the structure of his response?

2. King establishes the tone of his response to the criticisms of the

clergymen at the end of the opening paragraph: "I would like to answer your statement in what I hope will be patient and reasonable terms." As you reread his letter, identify specific words and phrases — as well as argumentative strategies — that satisfy these self-imposed criteria. In what specific sense does King use the word *hope* here? As you reread his letter, point to each subsequent reference to hope. How does King emphasize the different meanings and connotations of the word as he unfolds his argument? Do the same for his use of the word *disappointment*. What distinctions does he draw about the word *tension?* How are these distinctions related to his argument?

3. On what historical sources does King rely to create a precedent for his actions in Birmingham? With what religious figure does King most closely identify? With what effects? What more general analogy does he draw between the circumstances in Birmingham and elsewhere? What argument does he offer in support of this specific claim? Comment on the nature — and the extent — of his use of metaphors. Does he use metaphor primarily to clarify and reinforce a point? to introduce an element of emotion? Some combination of these? Something else? In what ways does King base his argument on an appeal to his readers' emotions? Point to particular examples to clarify and support your response. What purposes does he identify in his definition of — and justification of — "nonviolent direct action"?

67 _____

Jonathan Kozol

Distancing the Homeless

It is commonly believed by many journalists and politicians that the homeless of America are, in large part, former patients of large mental hospitals who were deinstitutionalized in the 1970s — the consequence, it is sometimes said, of misguided liberal opinion, which favored the treatment of such persons in community-based centers. It is argued that this policy, and the subsequent failure of society to build such centers or to provide them in sufficient number, is the primary cause of homelessness in the United States.

Those who work among the homeless do not find that explanation satisfactory. While conceding that a certain number of the homeless are, or have been, mentally unwell, they believe that, in the case of most unshelterd people, the primary reason is economic rather than clinical. The cause of homelessness, they say with disarming logic, is the lack of homes and of income with which to rent or acquire them.

They point to the loss of traditional jobs in industry (two million every year since 1980) and to the fact that half of those who are laid off end up in work that pays a poverty-level wage. They point to the parallel growth of poverty in families with children, noting that children, who represent one quarter of our population, make up forty percent of the poor: since 1968, the number of children in poverty has grown by three million, while welfare benefits to families with children have declined by 35 percent.

And they note, too, that these developments have coincided with a time in which the shortage of low-income housing has intensified as the gentrification of our major cities has accelerated. Half a million units of low-income housing have been lost each year to condominium conversion as well as to arson, demolition, or abandonment. Between 1978 and 1980,

For biographical information on Jonathan Kozol, see p. 655.

median rents climbed 30 percent for people in the lowest income sector, driving many of these families into the streets. After 1980, rents rose at even faster rates. In Boston, between 1982 and 1984, over 80 percent of the housing units renting below three hundred dollars disappeared, while the number of units renting above six hundred dollars nearly tripled.

Hard numbers, in this instance, would appear to be of greater help 5 then psychiatric labels in telling us why so many people become homeless. Eight million American families now pay half or more of their income for rent or a mortgage. Six million more, unable to pay rent at all, live doubled up with others. At the same time, federal support for low-income housing dropped from $30 billion (1980) to $9 billion (1986). Under Presidents Ford and Carter, five hundred thousand subsidized private housing units were constructed. By President Reagan's second term, the number had dropped to twenty-five thousand. "We're getting out of the housing business, period," said a deputy assistant secretary of the Department of Housing and Urban Development in 1985.

One year later, the *Washington Post* reported that the number of homeless families in Washington, D.C., had grown by 500 percent over the previous twelve months. In New York City, the waiting list for public housing now contains two hundred thousand names. The waiting is eighteen years.

Why, in the face of these statistics, are we impelled to find a psychiatric explanation for the growth of homelessness in the United States?

A misconception, once it is implanted in the popular imagination, is not easy to uproot, particularly when it serves a useful social role. The notion that the homeless are largely psychotics who belong in institutions, rather than victims of displacement at the hands of enterprising realtors, spares us from the need to offer realistic solutions to the fact of deep and widening extremes of wealth and poverty in the United States. It also enables us to tell ourselves that the despair of homeless people bears no intimate connection to the privileged existence we enjoy — when, for example, we rent or purchase one of those restored townhouses that once provided shelter for people now huddled in the street.

But there may be another reason to assign labels to the destitute. Terming economic victims "psychotic" or "disordered" helps to place them at a distance. It says that they aren't quite like us — and, more important, that we could not be like them. The plight of homeless families is a nightmare. It may not seem natural to try to banish human beings from our midst, but it *is* natural to try to banish nightmares from our minds.

So the rituals of clinical contamination proceed uninterrupted by the 10 economic facts described above. Research that addresses homelessness as an *injustice* rather than as a medical *misfortune* does not win the funding of foundations. And the research which *is* funded, defining the narrowed borders of permissible debate, diverts our attention from the antecedent to the secondary cause of homelessness. Thus it is that perfectly ordinary women whom I know in New York City — people whose depression or anxiety is a realistic consequence of months and even years in crowded shelters or the streets — are interrogated by invasive research scholars in an effort to decode their poverty, to find clinical categories for their despair and terror, to identify the secret failing that lies hidden in their psyche.

Many pregnant women without homes are denied prenatal care because they constantly travel from one shelter to another. Many are anemic. Many are denied essential dietary supplements by recent federal cuts. As a consequence, some of their children do not live to see their second year of life. Do these mothers sometimes show signs of stress? Do they appear disorganized, depressed, disordered? Frequently. They are immobilized by pain, traumatized by fear. So it is no surprise that when researchers enter the scene to ask them how they "feel," the resulting reports tell us that the homeless are emotionally unwell. The reports do not tell us we have *made* these people ill. They do not tell us that illness is a natural response to intolerable conditions. Nor do they tell us of the strength and the resilience that so many of these people still retain despite the miseries they must endure. They set these men and women apart in capsules labeled "personality disorder" or "psychotic," where they no longer threaten our complacence.

I visited Haiti not many years ago, when the Duvalier family was still in power. If an American scholar were to have made a psychological study of the homeless families living in the streets of Port-au-Prince — sleeping amidst rotten garbage, bathing in open sewers — and if he were to return to the United States to tell us that the reasons for their destitution were "behavioral problems" or "a lack of mental health," we would be properly suspicious. Knowledgeable Haitians would not merely be suspicious. They would be enraged. Even to initiate such research when economic and political explanations present themselves so starkly would appear grotesque. It is no less so in the United States.

One of the more influential studies of this nature was carried out in 1985 by Ellen Bassuk, a psychiatrist at Harvard University. Drawing upon interviews with eight homeless parents. Dr. Bassuk contends, according to the *Boston Globe,* that "90 percent [of these people] have problems other than housing and poverty that are so acute they would be unable to live successfully on their own." She also precludes the possibility that illness, where it does exist, may be provoked by destitution. "Our data," she writes, "suggest that mental illness tends to precede homelessness." She concedes that living in the streets can make a homeless person's mental illness worse; but she insists upon the fact of prior illness.

The executive director of the Massachusetts Commission on Children and Youth believes that Dr. Bassuk's estimate is far too high. The staff of Massachusetts Human Services Secretary Phillip Johnston believes the appropriate number is closer to 10 percent.

In defending her research, Bassuk challenges such critics by claiming 15 that they do not have data to refute her. This may be true. Advocates for the homeless do not receive funds to defend the sanity of the people they represent. In placing the burden of proof upon them, Dr. Bassuk has created an extraordinary dialectic: How does one prove that people aren't unwell? What homeless mother would consent to enter a procedure that might "prove" her mental health? What overburdened shelter operator would divert scarce funds to such an exercise? Is it an unnatural, offensive, and dehumanizing challenge.

Dr. Bassuk's work, however, isn't the issue I want to raise here; the issue is the use or misuse of that work by critics of the poor. For example, in a widely syndicated essay published in 1986, the newspaper columnist Charles Krauthammer argued that the homeless are essentially a deranged segment of the population and that we must find the "political will" to isolate them from society. We must do this, he said, "whether they like it or not." Arguing even against the marginal benefits of homeless shelters, Krauthammer wrote: "There is a better alternative, however, though no one dares speak its name." Krauthammer dares: that better alternative, he said, is "asylum."

One of Mr. Krauthammer's colleagues at the *Washington Post*, the columnist George Will, perceives the homeless as a threat to public cleanliness and argues that they ought to be consigned to places where we need not see them. "It is," he says, "simply a matter of public hygiene" to put them out of sight. Another journalist, Charles Murray, writing from the vantage point of a social Darwinist, recommends the restoration of the almshouses of the 1800s. "Granted Dickensian horror stories about almshouses," he begins, there were nonetheless "good almshouses"; he proposes "a good correctional 'halfway house'" as a proper shelter for a mother and child with no means of self-support.

In the face of such declarations, the voices of those who work with and know the poor are harder to hear.

Manhattan Borough President David Dinkins made the following observation on the basis of a study commissioned in 1986: "No facts support the belief that addiction or behavioral problems occur with more frequency in the homeless family population than in a similar socioeconomic population. Homeless families are not demographically different from other public assistance families when they enter the shelter system. . . . Family homelessness is typically a housing and income problem: the unavailability of affordable housing and the inadequacy of public assistance income."

In a "hypothetical world," write James Wright and Julie Lam of the   20
University of Massachusetts, "where there were no alcoholics, no drug addicts, no mentally ill, no deinstitutionalization . . . indeed, no personal social pathologies at all, there would still be a formidable homelessness problem, simply because at this stage in American history, there is not enough low-income housing" to accommodate the poor.

New York State's respected commissioner of social services, Cesar Perales, makes the point in fewer words: "Homelessness is less and less a result of personal failure, and more and more is caused by larger forces. There is no longer affordable housing in New York City for people of poor and modest means."

Even the words of medical practitioners who care for homeless people have been curiously ignored. A study published by the Massachusetts Medical Society, for instance, has noted that the most frequent illnesses among a sample of the homeless population, after alcohol and drug use, are trauma (31 percent), upper respiratory disorders (28 percent), limb disorders (19 percent), mental illness (16 percent), skin diseases (15 percent), hypertension (14 percent), and neurological illnesses (12 percent). (Excluded from this tabulation are lead poisoning, malnutrition, acute diarrhea, and other illnesses especially common among homeless infants and small children.) Why, we may ask, of all these calamities, does mental illness command so much political and press attention? The answer may be that the label of mental illness places the destitute outside the sphere of ordinary life. It personalizes an anguish that is public in its genesis; it individualizes a misery that is both general in cause and general in application.

The rate of tuberculosis among the homeless is believed to be ten times that of the general population. Asthma, I have learned in countless interviews, is one of the most common causes of discomfort in the shelters. Compulsive smoking, exacerbated by the crowding and the tension, is more common in the shelters than in any place that I have visited except prison. Infected and untreated sores, scabies, diarrhea, poorly set limbs, protruding elbows, awkwardly distorted wrists, bleeding gums, impacted teeth, and other untreated dental problems are so common among children in the shelters that one rapidly forgets their presence. Hunger and emaciation are everywhere. Children as well as adults can bring to mind the photographs of people found in camps for refugees of war in 1945. But these miseries bear no stigma, and mental illness does. It conveys a stigma in the Soviet Union. It conveys a stigma in the United States. In both nations the label is used, whether as a matter of deliberate policy or not, to isolate and treat as special cases those who, by deed or word or by sheer presence, represent a threat to national complacence. The two situations are obviously not identical, but they are enough alike to give Americans reason for concern.

Last summer, some twenty-eight thousand homeless people were afforded shelter by the city of New York. Of this number, twelve thousand were children and six thousand were parents living together in families. The average child was six years old, the average parent twenty-seven. A typical homeless family included a mother with two or three children, but in about one-fifth of these families two parents were present. Roughly ten thousand single persons, then, made up the remainder of the population of the city's shelters.

These proportions vary somewhat from one area of the nation to another. In all areas, however, families are the fastest-growing sector of the homeless population, and in the Northeast they are by far the largest sector   25 already. In Massachusetts, three-fourths of the homeless now are families with children; in certain parts of Massachusetts — Attleboro and Northhampton, for example — the proportion reaches ninety percent. Two-thirds of the homeless children studied recently in Boston were less than five years old.

Of an estimated two to three million homeless people nationwide, about 500,000 are dependent children, according to Robert Hayes, counsel to the National Coalition for the Homeless. Including their parents, at least 750,000 homeless people in America are family members.

What is to be made, then, of the supposition that the homeless are primarily the former residents of mental hospitals, persons who were carelessly released during the 1970s? Many of them are, to be sure. Among the older men and women in the streets and shelters, as many as one-third (some believe as many as one-half) may be chronically disturbed, and a number of these people were deinstitutionalized during the 1970s. But in a city like New York, where nearly half the homeless are small children with an average age of six, to operate on the basis of such a supposition makes no sense. Their parents, with an average age of twenty-seven, are not likely to have been hospitalized in the 1970s, either.

Nor is it easy to assume, as was once the case, that single men — those who come closer to fitting the stereotype of the homeless vagrant, the drifting alcoholic of an earlier age — are the former residents of mental hospitals. The age of homeless men has dropped in recent years; many of them are only twenty-one to twenty-eight years old. Fifty percent of homeless men in New York City shelters in 1984 were there for the first time. Most had previously had homes and jobs. Many had never before needed public aid.

A frequently cited set of figures tells us that in 1955, the average daily census of nonfederal psychiatric institutions was 677,000, and that by 1984, the number had dropped to 151,000. Subtract the second number from the first, conventional logic tells us, and we have an explanation for the homelessness of half a million people. A closer look at the same number offers us a different lesson.

The sharpest decline in the average daily census of these institutions 30 occurred prior to 1978, and the largest part of that decline, in fact, appeared at least a decade earlier. From 677,000 in 1955, the census dropped to 378,000 in 1972. The 1974 census was 307,000. In 1976 it was 230,000; in 1977 it was 211,000; and in 1978 it was 190,000. In no year since 1978 has the average daily census dropped by more than 9,000 persons, and in the six-year period from 1978 to 1984, the total decline was 39,000 persons. Compared with a decline of 300,000 from 1955 to 1972, and of nearly 200,000 more from 1972 to 1978, the number is small. But the years since 1980 are the period in which the present homeless crisis surfaced. Only since 1983 have homeless individuals overflowed the shelters.

If the large numbers of the homeless lived in hospitals before they reappeared in subway stations and in public shelters, we need to ask where they were and what they had been doing from 1972 to 1980. Were they living under bridges? Were they waiting out the decade in the basements of deserted buildings?

No. The bulk of those who had been psychiatric patients and were released from hospitals during the 1960s and early 1970s had been living in the meantime in low-income housing, many in skid-row hotels or boarding houses. Such housing — commonly known as SRO (single-room occupancy) units — was drastically diminished by the gentrification of our cities that began in 1970. Almost 50 percent of SRO housing was replaced by luxury apartments or by office buildings between 1970 and 1980, and the remaining units have been disappearing at even faster rates. As recently as 1986, after New York City had issued a prohibition against conversion of such housing, a well-known developer hired a demolition team to destroy a building in Times Square that had previously been home to indigent people. The demolition took place in the middle of the night. In order to avoid imprisonment, the developer was allowed to make a philanthropic gift to homeless people as a token of atonement. This incident, bizarre as it appears, reminds us that the profit motive for displacement of the poor is very great in every major city. It also indicates a more realistic explanation for the growth of homelessness during the 1980s.

Even for those persons who are ill and were deinstitutionalized during the decades before 1980, the precipitating cause of homelessness in 1987 is not illness but loss of housing. SRO housing, unattractive as it may have been, offered low-cost sanctuaries for the homeless, providing a degree of safety and mutual support for those who lived within them. They were a demeaning version of the community health centers that society had promised; they were the de facto "halfway houses" of the 1970s. For these people too, then — at most half of the homeless single persons in America — the cause of homelessness is lack of housing.

A writer in the *New York Times* describes a homeless woman standing on a traffic island in Manhattan. "She was evicted from her small room in the hotel just across the street," and she is determined to get revenge. Until she does, "nothing will move her from that spot. . . . Her argumentativeness and her angry fixation on revenge, along with the apparent absence of hallucinations, mark her as a paranoid." Most physicians, I imagine, would be more reserved in passing judgment with so little evidence, but this author makes his diagnosis without hesitation. "The paranoids of the street," he says, "are among the most difficult to help."

Perhaps so. But does it depend on who is offering the help? Is anyone 35
offering to help this woman get back her home? Is it crazy to seek vengeance for being thrown into the street? The absence of anger, some psychiatrists believe, might indicate much greater illness.

The same observer sees additional symptoms of pathology ("negative symptoms," he calls them) in the fact that many homeless persons demon-

strate a "gross deterioration in their personal hygiene" and grooming, leading to "indifference" and "apathy." Having just identified one woman as
unhealthy because she is so far from being "indifferent" as to seek revenge,
he now sees apathy as evidence of illness; so consistency is not what we are
looking for in this account. But how much less indifferent might the homeless be if those who decide their fate were less indifferent themselves? How
might their grooming and hygiene be improved if they were permitted access to a public toilet?

In New York City, as in many cities, homeless people are denied the
right to wash in public bathrooms, to store their few belongings in a public
locker, or, in certain cases, to make use of public toilets altogether. Shav-
ing, cleaning of clothes, and other forms of hygiene are prohibited in the
men's rooms of Grand Central Station. The terminal's three hundred lock-
ers, used in former times by homeless people to secure their goods, were
removed in 1986 as "a threat to public safety," according to a study made
by the New York City Council.

At one-thirty every morning, homeless people are ejected from the station. Many once attempted to take refuge on the ramp that leads to Forty-
second Street because it was protected from the street by wooden doors
and thus provided some degree of warmth. But the station management
responded to this challenge in two ways. The ramp was mopped with a
strong mixture of ammonia to produce a noxious smell, and when the people sleeping there brought cardboard boxes and newspapers to protect
them from the fumes, the entrance doors were chained wide open. Temperatures dropped some nights to ten degrees. Having driven these people to
the streets, city officials subsequently determined that their willingness to
risk exposure to cold weather could be taken as further evidence of mental
illness.

At Pennsylvania Station in New York, homeless women are denied the
use of toilets. Amtrak police come by and herd them off each hour on the
hour. In June 1985, Amtrak officials issued this directive to police: "It is
the policy of Amtrak to not allow the homeless and undesirables to remain. . . . Officers are encouraged to eject all undesirables. . . . Now is the
time to train and educate them that their presence will not be tolerated as
cold weather sets in." In an internal memo, according to CBS, an Amtrak
official asked flatly: "Can't we get rid of this trash?"

I have spent many nights in conversation with the women who are   40
huddled in the corridors and near the doorway of the public toilets in Penn
Station. Many are young. Most are cogent. Few are dressed in the familiar
rags suggested by the term *bag ladies*. Unable to bathe or use the toilets in
the station, almost all are in conditions of intolerable physical distress. The
sight of clusters of police officers, mostly male, guarding a toilet from use
by homeless women speaks volumes about the public conscience of New
York.

Where do these women defecate? How do they bathe? What will we
do when, in her physical distress, a woman finally disrobes in public and

begins to urinate right on the floor? "Gross deterioration," someone will call it, evidence of mental illness. In the course of an impromptu survey in the streets last September, Mayor Koch observed a homeless woman who had soiled her own clothes. Not only was the woman crazy, said the mayor, but those who differed with him on his diagnosis must be crazy, too. "I am the number one social worker in this town — with sanity," said he.

It may be that this woman was psychotic, but the mayor's comment says a great deal more about his sense of revulsion and the moral climate of a decade in which words like these may be applauded than about her mental state.

A young man who had lost his job, then his family, then his home, all in the summer of 1986, spoke with me for several hours in Grand Central Station on the weekend following Thanksgiving. "A year ago," he said, "I never thought that somebody like me would end up in a shelter. Nothing you've ever undergone prepares you. You walk into the place [a shelter on the Bowery] — the smell of sweat and urine hits you like a wall. Unwashed bodies and the look of absolute despair on many, many faces there would make you think you were in Dante's Hell. . . . What you fear is that you will be here forever. You do not know if it is ever going to end. You think to yourself: it is a dream and I will awake. Sometimes I think: It's an experiment. They are watching you to find out how much you can take. . . . I was a pretty stable man. Now I tremble when I meet somebody in the ordinary world. I'm trembling right now. . . . For me, the loss of work and loss of wife had left me rocking. Then the welfare regulations hit me. I began to feel that I would be reduced to trash. . . . Half the people that I know are suffering from chest infections and sleep deprivation. The lack of sleep leaves you debilitated, shaky. You exaggerate your fears. If a psychiatrist came along he'd say that I was crazy. But I was an ordinary man. There was nothing wrong with me. I lost my kids. I lost my home. Now would you say that I was crazy if I told you I was feeling sad?"

"If the plight of homeless adults is the shame of America," writes Fred Hechinger in the *New York Times,* "the lives of homeless children are the nation's crime."

In November 1984, a fact already known to advocates for the home-   45
less was given brief attention by the press. Homeless families, the *New York Times* reported, "mostly mothers and young children, have been sleeping on chairs, counters, and floors of the city's emergency welfare offices." Reacting to such reports, the mayor declared: "The woman is sitting on a chair or on a floor. It is not because we didn't offer her a bed. We provide a shelter for every single person who knocks on our door." On the same day, however, the city reported that in the previous eleven weeks it had been unable to give shelter to 153 families, and in the subsequent year, 1985, the city later reported that about two thousand children slept in welfare offices because of lack of shelter space.

Some eight hundred homeless infants in New York City, reported the

National Coalition for the Homeless, "routinely go without sufficient food, cribs, health care, and diapers." The lives of these children "are put at risk," while "high-risk pregnant women" are repeatedly forced to sleep in unsafe "barracks shelters" or welfare offices called Emergency Assistance Units (EAUs). "Coalition monitors, making sporadic random checks, found eight women in their *ninth* month of pregnancy sleeping in EAUs. . . . Two women denied shelter began having labor contractions at the EAU." In one instance, the Legal Aid Society was forced to go to court after a woman lost her child by miscarriage while lying on the floor of a communal bathroom in a shelter which the courts had already declared unfit to house pregnant women.

The coalition also reported numerous cases in which homeless mothers were obliged to choose between purchasing food or diapers for their infants. Federal guidelines issued in 1986 deepened the nutrition crisis faced by mothers in the welfare shelters by counting the high rent paid to the owners of the buildings as a part of family income, rendering their residents ineligible for food stamps. Families I interviewed who had received as much as $150 in food stamps monthly in June 1986 were cut back to $33 before Christmas.

"Now you're hearing all kinds of horror stories," said President Reagan, "about the people that are going to be thrown out in the snow to hunger and [to] die of cold and so forth. . . . We haven't cut a single budget." But in the four years leading up to 1985, according to the *New Republic,* Aid to Families with Dependent Children had been cut by $4.8 billion, child nutrition programs by $5.2 billion, food stamps by $6.8 billion. The federal government's authority to help low-income families with housing assistance was cut from $30 billion to $11 billion in Reagan's first term. In his fiscal 1986 budget, the president proposed to cut that by an additional 95 percent.

"If even one American child is forced to go to bed hungry at night," the president said on another occasion, "that is a national tragedy. We are too generous a people to allow this." But in the years since the president spoke these words, thousands of poor children in New York alone have gone to bed too sick to sleep and far too weak to rise the next morning to attend a public school. Thousands more have been unable to attend school at all because their homeless status compels them to move repeatedly from one temporary shelter to another. Even in the affluent suburbs outside New York City, hundreds of homeless children are obliged to ride as far as sixty miles twice a day in order to obtain an education in the public schools to which they were originally assigned before their families were displaced. Many of these children get to school too late to eat their breakfast; others are denied lunch at school because of federal cuts in feeding programs.

Many homeless children die — and others suffer brain damage — as a   *50* direct consequence of federal cutbacks in prenatal programs, maternal nutrition, and other feeding programs. The parents of one such child shared with me the story of the year in which their child was delivered, lived, and died. The child, weighing just over four pounds at birth, grew deaf and blind soon after, and for these reasons had to stay in the hospital for several months. When he was released on Christmas Eve of 1984, his mother and father had no home. He lived with his parents in the shelters, subways, streets, and welfare offices of New York City for four winter months, and was readmitted to the hospital in time to die in May 1985.

When we met and spoke the following year, the father told me that his wife had contemplated and even attempted suicide after the child's death, while he had entertained the thought of blowing up the welfare offices of New York City. I would tell him that to do so would be illegal and unwise. I would never tell him it was crazy.

"No one will be turned away," says the mayor of New York City, as hundreds of young mothers with their infants are turned from the doors of shelters season after season. That may sound to some like denial of reality. "Now you're hearing all these stories," says the president of the United States as he denies that anyone is cold or hungry or unhoused. On another occasion he says that the unsheltered "are homeless, you might say, by choice." That sounds every bit as self-deceiving.

The woman standing on the traffic island screaming for revenge until her room has been restored to her sounds relatively healthy by comparison. If three million homeless people did the same, and all at the same time, we might finally be forced to listen.

                                                                      1988

The Reader's Presence

1. Reread Kozol's first two paragraphs. How does he set out the terms of the argument? Why does he identify the two sides of the argument with particular groups? With which group does he identify himself? Can you tell from the first two paragraphs alone?

2. Reread paragraph 34. What does Kozol find offensive about the *New York Times* account of the homeless woman? Why does he believe the reporter's interpretation is wrong? Why does he believe it is inconsistent? How does this paragraph reveal the center of Kozol's position?

3. Reread Kozol's conversation with the homeless young man at Grand Central Station (paragraph 43). What do the man's comments suggest about homeless people? Do you think the manner and substance of his remarks weaken or reinforce Kozol's position? Put yourself in Kozol's place. What questions would *you* ask the man? What details of his life would you like to know? How would your questions reveal your point of view? How do Kozol's reveal his?

68

Audre Lorde

The Master's Tools Will Never Dismantle the Master's House[1]

I agreed to take part in a New York University Institute for the Humanities conference a year ago, with the understanding that I would be commenting upon papers dealing with the role of difference within the lives of american women: difference of race, sexuality, class, and age. The absence of these considerations weakens any feminist discussion of the personal and the political.

It is a particular academic arrogance to assume any discussion of feminist theory without examining our many differences, and without a significant input from poor women, Black and Third World women, and lesbians. And yet, I stand here as a Black lesbian feminist, having been invited to comment within the only panel at this conference where the input of Black feminists and lesbians is represented. What this says about the vision of this conference is sad, in a country where racism, sexism, and homophobia are inseparable. To read this program is to assume that lesbian and Black women have nothing to say about existentialism, the erotic, women's culture and silence, developing feminist theory, or heterosexuality and power. And what does it mean in personal and political terms when even the two Black women who did present here were literally found at the last hour? What does it mean when the tools of a racist patriarchy are used to examine the fruits of that same patriarchy? It means that only the most narrow perimeters of change are possible and allowable.

The absence of any consideration of lesbian consciousness or the con-

For biographical information on Audre Lorde, see p. 655.
[1]Comments at "The Personal and the Political Panel," Second Sex Conference, New York, September 29, 1979. — LORDE'S NOTE.

sciousness of Third World women leaves a serious gap within this conference and within the papers presented here. For example, in a paper on
material relationships between women, I was conscious of an either/or
model of nurturing which totally dismissed my knowledge as a Black lesbian. In this paper there was no examination of mutuality between women,
no systems of shared support, no interdependence as exists between lesbians and women-identified women. Yet it is only in the patriarchal model of
nurturance that women "who attempt to emancipate themselves pay perhaps too high a price for the results," as this paper states.

For women, the need and desire to nurture each other is not pathological but redemptive, and it is within that knowledge that our real power is
rediscovered. It is this real connection which is so feared by a patriarchal
world. Only within a patriarchal structure is maternity the only social
power open to women.

Interdependency between women is the way to a freedom which al-   5
lows the *I* to *be*, not in order to be used, but in order to be creative. This is
a difference between the passive *be* and the active *being*.

Advocating the mere tolerance of difference between women is the
grossest reformism. It is a total denial of the creative function of difference
in our lives. Difference must be not merely tolerated, but seen as a fund of
necessary polarities between which our creativity can spark like a dialectic.
Only then does the necessity for interdependency become unthreatening.
Only within that interdependency of different strengths, acknowledged
and equal, can the power to seek new ways of being in the world generate, as well as the courage and sustenance to act where there are no
charters.

Within the interdependence of mutual (nondominant) differences lies
that security which enables us to descend into the chaos of knowledge and
return with true visions of our future, along with the concomitant power to
effect those changes which can bring that future into being. Difference is
that raw and powerful connection from which our personal power is
forged.

As women, we have been taught either to ignore our differences, or to
view them as causes for separation and suspicion rather than as forces for
change. Without community there is no liberation, only the most vulnerable and temporary armistice between an individual and her oppression. But
community must not mean a shedding of our differences, nor the pathetic
pretense that these differences do not exist.

Those of us who stand outside the circle of this society's definition of
acceptable women; those of us who have been forged in the crucibles of
difference — those of us who are poor, who are lesbians, who are Black,
who are older — know that *survival is not an academic skill*. It is learning
how to stand alone, unpopular and sometimes reviled, and how to make
common cause with those others identified as outside the structures in
order to define and seek a world in which we can all flourish. It is learning
how to take our differences and make them strengths. *For the master's*

tools will never dismantle the master's house. They may allow us temporarily to beat him at his own game, but they will never enable us to bring about genuine change. And this fact is only threatening to those women who still define the master's house as their only source of support.

Poor women and women of Color know there is a difference between   10
the daily manifestations of marital slavery and prostitution because it is our daughters who line 42nd Street. If white american feminist theory need not deal with the differences between us, and the resulting difference in our oppressions, then how do you deal with the fact that the women who clean your houses and tend your children while you attend conferences on feminist theory are, for the most part, poor women and women of Color? What is the theory behind racist feminism?

In a world of possibility for us all, our personal visions help lay the groundwork for political action. The failure of academic feminists to recognize difference as a crucial strength is a failure to reach beyond the first patriarchal lesson. In our world, divide and conquer must become define and empower.

Why weren't other women of Color found to participate in this conference? Why were two phone calls to me considered a consultation? Am I the only possible source of names of Black feminists? And although the Black panelist's paper ends on an important and powerful connection of love between women, what about interracial cooperation between feminists who don't love each other?

In academic feminist circles, the answer to these questions is often, "We did not know who to ask." But that is the same evasion of responsibility, the same cop-out, that keeps Black women's art out of women's exhibitions, Black women's work out of most feminist publications except for the occasional "Special Third World Women's Issue," and Black women's texts off your reading lists. But as Adrienne Rich pointed out in a recent talk, white feminists have educated themselves about such an enormous amount over the past ten years, how come you haven't also educated yourselves about Black women and the differences between us — white and Black — when it is key to our survival as a movement?

Women of today are still being called upon to stretch across the gap of male ignorance and to educate men as to our existence and our needs. This is an old and primary tool of all oppressors to keep the oppressed occupied with the master's concerns. Now we hear that it is the task of women of Color to educate white women — in the face of tremendous resistance — as to our existence, our differences, our relative roles in our joint survival. This is a diversion of energies and a tragic repetition of racist patriarchal thought.

Simone de Beauvoir once said: "It is in the knowledge of the genuine   15
conditions of our lives that we must draw our strength to live and our reasons for acting."

Racism and homophobia are real conditions of all our lives in this place and time. *I urge each one of us here to reach down into that deep place of knowledge inside herself and touch that terror and loathing of any difference that lives there. See whose face it wears.* Then the personal as the political can begin to illuminate all our choices.

The Reader's Presence

1. From what point of view does Lorde address the issues she raises in this essay? How does she define *difference*? What does she see as its creative — and sustaining — functions? What does she mean when she says: "Within the interdependence of mutual (nondominant) differences lies that security which enables us to descend into the chaos of knowledge and return with true visions of our future, along with the concomitant power to effect those changes which can bring that future into being" (paragraph 7)?

2. What would you identify as Lorde's thesis in this essay? Where does she make this assertion? What is her attitude toward academic discussions of feminist theory? What examples does she offer to clarify and support her point that *"survival is not an academic skill"*? What, specifically, does she identify as the failures of academic feminists? Given your initial reading of this essay, what rationale might you offer for why she chooses not to capitalize the word *american*?

3. In paragraph 2, Lorde asserts that "racism, sexism, and homophobia are inseparable" in this country. What evidence does she provide to validate this assertion? What prospects does Lorde see for change? How does she define and illustrate what she calls "the patriarchal model of nurturance" (paragraph 3)? What specific strategies does she identify to create freedom for the female "I"?

69 _____

Nancy Mairs

A Letter to Matthew

July 1983

My Dear Child —

Last night Daddy and I watched, on William F. Buckley, Jr.'s *Firing Line,* a debate whether women "have it as good as men," and I have been talking to you in my head ever since. Odd not to be able to talk with you in person — I'm not yet used to your absence — but I thought I would put onto paper some of the things I would say if you were here. They are not the sort of things I would say to Mr. Buckley if ever I met him. Mr. Buckley is an elderly man, fixed by his circumstances within a range of experiences so narrow that new ideas and new behaviors cannot squeeze through the boundaries. He is complete as he is. But you are just emerging into young manhood, still fluid, still making the choices that will determine the shape that manhood will take. I, as your mother and as a feminist, hope that the choices you make—you individually and your generation as a whole — will be transformative, that the manhood you develop will be so radically new that the question in Mr. Buckley's debate, smacking as it does of competition for goods and goodness, will no longer have any more meaning than questions like "Do pigs have it as good as fiddlehead ferns?" or, more aptly, "Do pigs have it as good as pigs?"

In many ways, of course, you've dashed my hopes already. You have, after all, lived for fourteen years in a dangerously patriarchal society, and you have put on much of the purple that Mr. Buckley wears with such aplomb. When I find myself disliking you — and I find myself disliking you with about the same regularity, I imagine, as you find yourself disliking me — I can usually tell that I'm responding to some behavior that I identify as peculiarly "masculine." I dislike your cockiness, for instance.

For biographical information on Nancy Mairs, see p. 656.

When you first began to work with computers, I remember, you immediately assumed the attitude that you knew all that was worth knowing about computers; when you took up racquetball, right away you set yourself up as a champion. This kind of swaggering strikes me as a very old pattern of masculine behavior (I think of Beowulf and Unferth at Heorot), the boast designed to establish superiority and domination, which trigger challenge and thus conflict. Related to your cockiness is your quickness to generalize and, from your generalizations, to pronounce judgments: Calculus is a waste of time; Christians are stupidly superstitious; classical music is boring; Jerry Falwell and the Moral Majority are idiots. This is just the kind of uninformed thinking that empowers Jerry Falwell and the Moral Majority in the first place, of course, this refusal to experience and explore the ambiguities of whatever one is quick to condemn. More seriously, such a pattern of response enables men to create the distinctions between Us and Them — the good guys and the bad guys, the left wing and the right, the Americans and the Russians — that lead to suspicion, fear, hatred, and finally the casting of stones.

Well then, have you shattered *all* my hopes? By no means. For you are not merely arrogant and opinionated. These qualities are overshadowed by another, one I have seldom seen in men: your extraordinary empathic capacity, your willingness to listen for and try to fulfill the needs of others. When Sean was threatening suicide, you were genuinely engaged in his pain. When Katherine needed a male model to encourage her creepy little fifth-grade boys to dance, you leaped in with psychological (if not physical!) grace. When Anne left us for good, I felt your presence supporting and soothing me despite your relief at being an only child at last. Women have long been schooled in this sensitivity to others; but men have been trained to hold themselves aloof, to leave the emotional business of life to their mothers and sisters and wives. I think you are learning to conduct some of that business on your own.

Clearly I believe that the ability to do so is a benefit and not the curse our patriarchal culture has made it out to be. In fact, in an ironic way the answer to Mr. Buckley's question might be that women have it better than men, and it is the fear of such an answer that keeps men nervously posing the question in the first place. You'll remember that Freud ascribed to women a problem he called "penis envy"; a later psychoanalyst, Lacan, called it a "lack." If I've learned anything during the years I've spent in psychotherapy, I've learned that the feelings and motives I ascribe to others tell me little about them but much about myself, for I am projecting my own feelings and motives onto them. Freud ascribed to women penis envy; ascription = projection; therefore Freud was really suffering from womb envy. QED. A man, lacking the womb and yearning to return to his early identity with the mother, tries to hide his pain by denigrating everything associated with the womb: the blood, the babies, the intuitive and nurturing behaviors of child-rearing. The very condition of having a womb in the first place he labels a pathology: hysteria. If I haven't got it, he tells himself, it can't be worth having. (But maybe, he whispers so softly that even he can't hear, maybe it *is*.)

I'm more than half serious, you know, amid this high-flown silliness.   5
But I don't seriously believe, despite some psychological advantages, that in
the "real world" women have it as good as men. In some highly visible
ways they have it very bad indeed: They are raped, battered, prostituted,
abandoned to raise their children in poverty. Less visibly but no less ruin-
ously, they are brainwashed (often by their mothers and sisters as well as
their fathers, brothers, lovers, and husbands) into believing that whatever
they get is what they deserve, being only women. Imagine this, Matthew, if
you can — and maybe you can, since you are just emerging from childhood, and children are often treated like women in our society. Imagine
thinking yourself lucky to get *any* job, no matter how servile or poorly
paid, *any* partner, no matter how brutal or dull, *any* roof over your head,
no matter how costly the psychic mortgage payment. Imagine believing
that's what you deserve. Imagine feeling guilty if you fail to feel grateful.

If you have trouble imagining such conditions, I'm not surprised. I
have trouble too; and for many years I held back from calling myself a
feminist because I couldn't conceive problems I hadn't experienced. The
men in our family do not smack their women and children around. They
seldom raise their voices, let alone their palms. They are gentle, courteous,
witty, companionable, solicitous. And yet, of late, I've begun to recognize in
them certain behaviors and attitudes which suggest that they, too, share a set
of cultural assumptions about male power and rights which devalue women's
lives. But our men worship their women, you may say; they put them right up
on what one of my students once called a "pedastool." True enough, but tell
me, how much actual living could you get done confined to a tiny platform
several feet above the ground, especially if you had acrophobia?

Look, now that you're staying with them, at Aunt Helen and Uncle
Ted, for instance. For forty-eight years they have sustained a relationship
founded on domination and submission if ever there was one. Daddy has
often insisted that their relationship is fine as long as it works for them. For
a long time I tried to accept it too, because I believed that he must be right.
I tend, as you know, to believe that Daddy is always right: I'm the product
of a patriarchal society too, after all. But now I believe that he's wrong.
Although I admire much about their marriage, especially its durability and
friendliness, I balk at its basis in a kind of human sacrifice. Trying, I suppose, to compensate for not having graduated from high school, Uncle Ted
kept Aunt Helen, a college graduate, confined in a life containing only himself, their one son, and the housework to maintain them. She could have
worked, of course — she had the education, and they always needed the
money — but Uncle Ted's manly pride insisted on his being the breadwin-
ner, and her job became to stretch the crusts and crumbs from one meager
meal to the next. So little had she to occupy her that she grieved for years
after her child left for college, and clung to her housework to give her days
meaning. Once, in the late sixties, I asked her why she didn't replace her
old-fashioned washing machine with an automatic (my mother had had
one since 1952), and she replied, "But then what would I do on Mon-
days?" Worse than the deprivation of stimulating activity has been the

undermining of her self-confidence. Even her statements sound like questions, and she repeatedly turns to her husband: "Isn't that right, Ted?" She tiptoes through space as through conversation like our Lionel Tigress, cautious, timorous, whiskers twitching, ready to dash under the bed at a strange voice or a heavy footfall. I like to watch her bake a cake. There in her kitchen she plants her feet firmly and even, sometimes, rattles the pans.

Is Uncle Ted then a monster, some Bluebeard glowering and dangling the incriminating key that represents some independent act that will cost Aunt Helen her head? Hardly. He is a man of sincerity and rectitude, who has lived scrupulously, at considerable cost to himself, according to the code by which he was raised, a code that Rudyard Kipling, whom he admires, described as the "white man's burden." In it, women (among others, such as our "darker brethren") require the kind of protection and control they are unable, being more "natural" creatures, to provide themselves. He adores Aunt Helen, I do believe, and wants to do only what's best for her. But he assumes that he knows what's best for her, and so does she. In the name of manhood, he has taken from her the only authentic power a human being can hold: that of knowing and choosing the good. Such theft of power results in mastery. There is no mistressy.

I've been uneasy, as you know, about your spending this summer with them, largely, I suppose, because I don't want Uncle Ted to make a "man" of you. And I've encouraged you to subvert their patterns of interaction in a small way, by helping Aunt Helen with her chores just as you help Uncle Ted with his, even when he tries to divert you and she tells you to run along with him, not so that you can change those patterns (you can't) but so that you'll remain aware of them. You may well be tempted to fall into them because what Uncle Ted construes as "men's work" is infinitely more interesting than "women's work." You already know what a drag it is to set the table knowing that within an hour the dishes will be streaked and gummy, to wash those dishes knowing that they'll go right back on the table for breakfast, to fold a whole line of clothes that will crawl straight back into the hamper, muddy and limp, to be washed and hung out again. How much more pleasant and heartening to tramp through the woods checking the line from the brook, to ride the lawn mower round and round on the sweet falling grass, to plot traps for porcupines and saw down trees and paddle the canoe across the pond spreading algicide and possibly falling in. If everyone washed the dishes together, of course, everyone could go for a walk in the woods. How one would tell the men from the women, though, I'm not sure.

But then, so what if you do fall into the patterns? Surely the world 10 won't end if you and Uncle Ted take the fishing rods down to the Battenkill to catch a few trout for breakfast, leaving Aunt Helen to make the beds? Well yes, I think in a way it will, and that's why I'm writing you this letter. For Aunt Helen and Uncle Ted's marriage is not in the least extraordinary. On the contrary, the interactions between them, despite some idiosyncracies, are being played out in millions of relationships throughout the world, including, in its own way, Daddy's and mine, within which you have lived your whole life. One partner is telling the other (though seldom in words) that she is weaker physically and intellectually, that her concerns are less meaningful to the world at large, that she is better suited (or even formed by God) to serve his needs in the privacy of his home than to confront the tangled problems of the public sphere. And instead of ignoring his transparent tactics for enhancing his uncertain self-image and increasing his own comfort, she is subordinating her needs to his, accepting the limits he decrees, and thereby bolstering the artificial pride that enables him to believe himself a "superior" creature. As soon as he feels superiority, he is capable of dividing his fellow creatures into Us and Them and of trying to dominate Them. That is, he is ready to make war.

This connection — between the private male who rules his roost and keeps his woman, however lovingly, in her place and the public male who imposes his will by keeping blacks poor and pacifying Vietnamese villages and shipping arms and men to Central America — is far from new. Virginia Woolf made it in *Three Guineas* nearly fifty years ago. "The public and the private worlds are inseparably connected," she wrote; "the tyrannies and servilities of the one are the tyrannies and servilities of the other." But *Three Guineas* has been largely ignored or denigrated: One male critic called it "neurotic," "morbid"; another, "cantankerous." (You know, I am sure, that when a man speaks out, he is assertive, forthright; when a woman speaks her "mind," she is sick or bitchy.) Moreover, its feminism has been labeled "old-fashioned," as though already in 1938 the problems Woolf named had been solved. If so, why do we stand today in the same spot she stood then, looking at the same photographs of dead bodies and burned villages? No, her feminism isn't out of date, though such a label shows a desperate attempt to set it aside. Rather, it says something, valid today, that men still do not want to hear: that if humanity — men and women — is to have it any good at all, men must give up their pleasure in domination, their belief in their superiority, the adulation of their fellow creatures, at the personal and private level of their lives. Now. They must stop believing that whoever they love will perish without their "protection," for the act of protecting leads to a sense of possession, and it necessitates enemies to protect from. They must completely and radically revise their relationships with themselves, their wives and children, their business associates, the men and women in the next block, the next city, the next country. They must learn to say to every other who enters their lives not, "You're over there, and you're bad," but, "You're over there, and you're me."

Can they do it? Some feminists think not. They say that we should simply kill men off (except perhaps for the babies) and start fresh. I understand the anger that fuels such a proposal and the desire to sweep the rubbishy world clean. But I reject it because it perpetuates the violence that distinguishes masculine solutions to conflict. Our cultural heritage would still be based on killing, our mythology rooted in massacre.

No, I think that I will let you live. Will you let me live? If so, the terms of your existence must be transformed. What's been good enough for Aunt Helen and Uncle Ted, for Mr. Buckley, for Ronald Reagan and the other men who govern us and every other nation, for the Catholic Church, for the medical and legal professions, for the universities, for all the patriarchy, cannot be good enough for you. (And I address you personally, though obviously I mean all young men everywhere, because moral choice is always a lonely matter. You may all encourage one another — in fact, if the transformation is working, you will — but each will have to choose his way of being for himself.) You must learn to develop your identity through exploring the ways you are like, not different from or better than, others. You must learn to experience power through your connections with people, your ability to support their growth, not through weakening them by ridicule or patronage or deprivation. If this means dancing with the little boys, then dance your heart out; they'll dance on into the future with more assurance because of you. And who can shoot straight while he's dancing?

I am demanding something of you that takes more courage than entering a battle: not to enter the battle. I am asking you to say *no* to the values that have defined manhood through the ages — prowess, competition, victory — and to grow into a manhood that has not existed before. If you do, some men and women will ridicule and even despise you. They may call you spineless, possibly even (harshest of curses) womanish. But your life depends on it. My life depends on it. I wish you well.

Now go help Aunt Helen with the dishes.   15

I love you —
Mother
1986

The Reader's Presence

1. Essays in the form of letters are usually addressed to one person; thus we can specifically identify Nancy Mairs's intended reader. But are there indications in the essay to show that Mairs wants a wider readership than one other person? In other words, do you think this was a "real" letter that she sent her son — or one she intended to be a published essay? What aspects of the selection make you feel one way or the other about this question?

2. The recipient of this letter is fourteen years old. In what ways do you think Mairs takes the age of her son into account? Are there times when you think she doesn't make adjustments because of age? How do her adjustments or lack of adjustments reflect her overall purpose in writing the letter?

3. What is Mairs attempting to persuade her son to do? How would you describe her persuasive efforts? What does she appeal to? How does she use both criticism and praise? How does her son's immediate situation — that he is staying with relatives — affect the terms of her appeal? Put yourself in Matthew's place as the reader. Explain whether this letter would transform your behavior or not.

70 _____

Little Rock Reed

Broken Treaties, Broken Promises

For Native Americans, the 500th anniversary of Christopher Columbus's arrival in the Americas is a painful reminder of the first in a long series of events which have stripped us of our land, our culture, and our religion. These five hundred years have seen the betrayal, mistreatment, and systematic destruction of Native Americans at the hands of European settlers. We have been denied our way of life, our expression of faith, and the lands on which we have lived for thousands of years.

The work of many Native American organizations this year has brought a heightened awareness of what colonization has meant for us. It is encouraging that some Europeans, for the first time, are beginning to come to terms with the sins of their forebears.

Yet we will gain little from this heightened awareness if all attention is focused on the past. Thankfully, the U.S. government, for the most part, has discontinued the horrifying military subjugation and outright extermination of Native Americans which dominated its relations with our community for hundreds of years. But newer, "enlightened" policies designed to assimilate Native Americans into the dominant European culture have been no less destructive to the religions and culture of more recent generations of Native Americans.

The political, cultural, and religious forms of tribal life are inseparable. U.S. church and political leaders have always known that to "Americanize" the Indian population, they must suppress tribal religious activity. By the mid-1800s, the United States had banned most forms of Indian religion on the reservations. Indians who maintained tribal customs were subject to imprisonment, forced labor, and even punishment by starvation. Indian dress, ceremony, dances, and singing were forbidden. Sacred instruments, medicine, and pipes were confiscated and destroyed. Even Indian names and hairstyles were forbidden by law.

In *On the Road to Wounded Knee,* Robert Burnette and John Koster   5

For biographical information on Little Rock Reed, see p. 660.

note that there were "on file orders from the Department of the Army and the Department of the Interior authorizing soldiers and Bureau of Indian Affairs agents to destroy every vestige of Indian religion, that is, to destroy the Indian's whole view of the world and his place in the universe." As late as the 1930s, the BIA openly promulgated the Indian Offenses Act which forbade all practice of Indian religion, including the rites of the Native American Church, which was a fusion of Christian and Indian beliefs.

When it comes to Native Americans, the United States can't claim to have shown much inclination toward the separation of church and state. In a previous article . . . , I discussed some of the measures the U.S. government has taken to control the education of Native American children, measures which separated generations of children from their heritage, culture, and religion.

In the early and mid-nineteenth century, the government negotiated with various Christian sects, dividing the Indians among them. Missionaries worked diligently to stomp out Native American religion and to separate Native American children from their "heathen" parents and relatives in hopes of raising them from their savage state to a "civilized" Christianity. With continuing European immigration and an increased need for more settleable lands, the government involved itself in Native American education in a more direct way. The establishment of the first boarding school — at Carlisle Barracks in Pennsylvania in 1878 — marked the beginning of a systematic attack on our religions and culture through the de-Indianization of our children.

In 1973, U.S. Supreme Court Justice William O. Douglas correctly stated the purpose of these rigid boarding schools: "The express policy was stripping the Indian child of cultural heritage and identity. They were designed to separate children from their reservation and family, strip them of tribal lore and mores, force complete abandonment of their native language, and prepare them for never again returning to their people." Many children were kidnapped or captured by the military at gunpoint and taken to distant schools, often at very early ages.

Everything in the boarding schools was designed to make the Native American ashamed of Indian values, dress, customs, and speech. Expression of tribal religions was prohibited, while Christianity was often forced upon the children. One graduate of these schools recalled "they cut our hair, shaved our heads, and forced us to go to Sunday school, where they showed us pictures of this man with long hair and a beard and told us he loved us."

Students who disobeyed or refused to give up Indian practices and heritage received torturous psychological and physical punishment which left some children permanently scarred. Although some students knew only their native tongue, the speaking of tribal languages was a physically punishable offense, as it continues to be in some boarding schools. "Unmanageable" students were regularly handcuffed or beaten in some schools. Girls were humiliated with lifted-dress spankings; boys were sometimes   10 forced to wear dresses. Some schools were forced to bar their windows because so many students died from exposure in attempting to run away and return to their families.

White-run boarding schools for Native Americans are a continuing part of the government's assimilation campaign. While military kidnapping is no longer practiced, many boarding-school students are welfare referrals. Schools are used to avoid providing increased family assistance. Parents are penalized for being poor by having their children shipped off to distant boarding institutions.

The practice of educating Indian children in non-Indian schools is a direct attack on Native American religion. Our religions and culture are one and the same. It is impossible to take away one without taking away the other. If an Indian is forcibly removed from Indian culture, he or she is also deprived of his or her religion. Denial of a people's culture and religion is no less than genocide.

The U.S. Constitution guarantees the free exercise of religion to all people, at least in theory. But, in practice, courts routinely use standards and tests rooted in Judeo-Christian concepts to determine what constitutes a religious belief worthy of protection. Since the regularly scheduled meetings, books of sacred writings, clergy, churches, and temples which characterize most world religions are absent from most traditional Indian religions, court decisions have routinely violated sacred traditions and beliefs of Native Americans.

A prime example of how the United States has destroyed Indian culture and religions can be found in its adamant refusal to recognize and respect the sacredness of land to Indian nations. Native Americans see the land as an integral and sacred aspect of the creation, something no one can own, sell, or buy any more than one can own, sell, or buy the air we breathe. The land is God's, and we are merely its stewards, vested with the responsibility to care for our Mother Earth that she might care for her children of future generations (which include not only humans, but all living creatures, both plant and animal).

The General Allotment Act of 1887 violated every treaty between the   15 United States and Indian tribes and nations. The act authorized the U.S. president to break up tribes by "allotting" communal lands to individual Indians. After allotments were made, "surplus" land was reopened to White settlement, resulting in the transfer of over ninety million acres of Native American land to non-Indians during the next half-century.

According to the framers of the act, its purpose was to teach the Indians to become good, "civilized" farmers. Unfortunately, most reservation land was originally allotted to the tribes precisely because it was not suitable for farming. Additionally, Indians had neither the capital nor the desire to become farmers. The very thought of tilling (or cutting into the face of) the Earth Mother was terrifying to most Indians due to their deep and abiding reverence for the earth.

Even today, the United States refuses to respect the sacredness of various geographical locations to Indian nations. Congress attempted to appease the Indian people and correct this bias by passing the American Indian Religious Freedom Act of 1978. However, American Indians have lost every court case involving this act. For Native Americans, the act clearly isn't worth the paper it was written on.

The San Francisco peaks in Arizona have been the home and sacred land of the Hopi, Navajo, and other groups since long before Whites realized they could sail over the ocean without falling off the edge. The values and beliefs of these people are expressed through cycles of ceremonies which pervade every aspect of their daily lives according to the will of the Creator. Theirs is a deeply religious way of life, tied intimately to the land.

In Hopi religious tradition, it is believed that the Creator destroyed the world for its evil. Only a few who remained faithful were chosen to survive, protected within the Mother Earth, from which the faithful were then born. They were sent out on four migrations. Finally they came to Oraibi (Arizona) where they settled. There, at the crossroads of the four migrations, their villages are guarded by the kachinas, spirits of the four major clans of the Hopi, who reside in the high points which surround the area.

Hopi, Navajo, and other native people go to this natural cathedral to   20
fast and pray. The protection of the peaks is integral to the religious ceremonial cycle of the Navajo and Hopi, and thus the survival of their people.

The Navajo and Hopi for many years have had problems with corporate developers wanting to build in these sacred areas. About thirty years ago, Indian people reached an agreement with corporate developers who wanted to build ski resorts in the peaks. Most Hopis and Navajos agreed to allow people to ski and commune with nature in this sacred area, while developers agreed to respect the sacred peaks, and not expand further.

In the early eighties, a wealthy Mormon developer came up with a new plan for expansion of the resort, with a hundred-acre parking lot and a four-lane access road. During debate on the issue, Hopi villages were flooded with Mormon missionaries, and many Hopis, including the tribal chairperson, became Mormon.

Not coincidentally, Hopis who became Mormon no longer saw the shrine as sacred. The controversy became so political and heated that the spiritual heart of the issue became overshadowed. In the end, the decision was handed off to the Secretary of the Interior in Washington, D.C., who is vested with nearly absolute power over all decisions affecting Indian people. In a short time, James Watt approved the development and expansion of the ski area, betraying the original agreements with the Native Americans and blatantly ignoring the religious claims of the Hopi and Navajo people.

The tribes appealed to U.S. courts, who held that Hopis and Navajos can practice their religion elsewhere.

Today not far from the San Francisco Peaks, the University of Arizona   25
has proposed the development of an astrophysical observatory atop Mount Graham. If completed, the telescope complex will be located on the summit of Big Seated Mountain, a site sacred to the Apaches. Although the re-

search could be done from several other sites, the university and its collaborators (which include the Smithsonian, the Vatican, the Max Planck Institute, Ohio State University, Arcetri Observatory, and several congressional representatives) have chosen to ignore the religious traditions of the Apache people.

Unfortunately, such cases are the rule of Anglo-Indian relations, not the exception. U.S. history is a trail of broken promises, ignored treaties, and unconstitutional violation of Indian religions.

The Black Hills of South Dakota are on land reserved for the Lakota (Sioux) Nation in the Fort Laramie Treaty of 1868. This land was "for the absolute and undisturbed use and occupation of the Indians" and the treaty provided that no unauthorized persons "shall ever be permitted to pass over, settle upon, or reside" in the territory without express consent of the Sioux people. Sioux believe the Black Hills to be the source and heart of their religion and culture.

In direct violation of this treaty, the U.S. Forest Service claimed this land. On April 4, 1981, Lakota traditional elders and their supporters returned to occupy Yellow Thunder Camp, at the heart of the seized sacred land in the Black Hills.

The religious importance of Yellow Thunder Camp was originally upheld by the courts. Yet in 1988, that decision was overturned by the Eighth Circuit Court of Appeals. On June 26, 1989, the U.S. Supreme Court refused to hear an appeal on behalf of the Lakota people. The caretakers of Yellow Thunder Camp were given one month to dismantle the camp and remove all ceremonial structures.

The Lakota people have been struggling throughout this century for   30
the recovery of their land. The United States takes the position that the Sioux peoples' rights to the Black Hills have been legally extinguished because the government has offered monetary compensation. They believe the Lakota have no right to refuse to accept money for their sacred land.

In another Black Hills case, Lakota and Tsistsistas (Cheyenne) nations sought to have the courts end the ongoing development of tourist facilities in Bear Butte, a most sacred place to the tribes, now a state park. Parking lots, visitors platforms, and recreational facilities all but ensure the disruption of sacred ceremonies, many of which require isolation. But the U.S. District Court held that a "compelling state interest" in promoting tourism is more important than the right of Indians to exercise their beliefs at Bear Butte — on Sioux land.

The Navajo people at Big Mountain in Arizona have been ordered by Congress to vacate their sacred ancestral lands so mineral companies can reap the rich deposits of coal, oil, and uranium found there. To "encourage" the thousands of Navajo people to relocate, for the last eighteen years the United States has made it a criminal offense for Navajos there to rejuvenate their homes or construct new ones. Residents believe federal agents may even have been sent to reduce the area's livestock (the Navajo's main source of subsistence) in hopes of starving them into submission.

Navajo elders and youth alike have been arrested for their peaceful resistance to a forced relocation which would spell an end to their
traditional religion and culture. In its campaign of pressuring and har-
assing the Navajo people, the government enlists the assistance of the
military, the Bureau of Indian Affairs, and even Hopi and Navajo "tribal councils." The majority of these councils were created through governmental coercion and do not represent the true concerns of the Indian
people.

In decision after decision, U.S. courts have failed to uphold the rights
of Native Americans to lands originally designated to them. The Rainbow
Bridge National Monument is a sacred shrine of the Navajo, separated
from the Navajo Reservation without tribal consent by a 1910 executive
order — a blatant violation of international law. Yet a 1980 court ruled
that the public's interest in low-cost electricity and tourism (the area was
flooded to create Lake Powell) was sufficient grounds to allow this land to
be taken from the Navajo people. In 1981, the U.S. Supreme Court refused
to review the decision.

In another case, Northern California District Court Judge Stanley A.   35
Weigel issued an order that would have prevented the construction of a
logging road through the Six Rivers National Forest. Weigel had ruled that
the road would desecrate sacred sites central to the religion of several peoples, including the Karuk, Yurok, Tolowa, and Hupa Indians.

But an April 1988 Supreme Court ruling reversed this decision. While
admitting that the road would have "devastating effects on traditional Indian religious practices," it nevertheless ruled that the economic "needs
and desires" of commercial interests must take precedence over the religious rights of Native Americans. The court ruled that actions which in-
fringe upon or destroy American Indian religions are not in violation of the
U.S. Constitution as long as 1) the government's purpose is secular and not
specifically aimed at infringing upon or destroying the religion, and 2) the
government's action does not coerce individuals to act contrary to their
religious beliefs.

We may suppose the U.S. Department of Energy is within the realm of
this decision as it continues to detonate nuclear bombs at the Nevada Test
Site, which is on land retained by the Shoshone Indians according to the
1863 Treaty of Ruby Valley. In fact, the government might be in compliance with the Constitution even if they blew up the Shoshone people during religious ceremonies on their land, provided the "specific aim" of the
detonation was to "test" the weapons and the radiation and explosions did
not "coerce" the victims into acting contrary to their beliefs.

In 1893, the native Hawaiian government was overthrown by U.S.
businessmen in an action which President Grover Cleveland called an illegal "act of war" in which "without the authority of Congress, the government of a feeble but friendly people was overthrown." Yet the U.S. businessmen labeled their organization the "Republic of Hawaii" and
celebrated its new constitution on July 4, 1894. To this day, the United

States has no true legal jurisdiction in Hawaii. Hawaii is a stolen land, with an illegal government.

Of course, when confronted with the land claims of Native Americans (and Native Hawaiians and Alaskans), nearly all North Americans say the same thing — it would be ludicrous to expect the United States to "give back" the land to the natives. But what of the lands that have not yet been squatted on by greedy businessmen? Must the theft taking place today be irresponsibly attributed to the bad deeds of someone's great-grandparents?

The United States and Hawaiian governments currently support the 40 destruction of Wao Kele O Puna, Hawaii's only tropical rain forest, near the Kilauea Volcano. Wao Kele O Puna Natural Forest Reserve is part of a 1.5 million-acre area of land held in trust by the State of Hawaii for two beneficiaries: the Native Hawaiians and the general public. However, the state breached this trust in 1985 by giving twenty-seven thousand acres of the forest to the Campbell Estate in exchange for twenty-five thousand acres at Kahauale'a, about half of which is covered with freshly erupted lava.

Campbell Estate needed the land exchange after the volcano erupted right on land where they originally planned to have the True/Midpacific Geothermal Company of Wyoming dig geothermal wells. The corporate goal is to turn the east rift of the Kilauea Volcano into one of the world's largest geothermal power plants. The company wants to dig two hundred wells and build as many as five power plants.

The problems with the project are numerous. No technology exists for the undersea cable which the company hopes will transport electricity to Oahu. The forest will have to be cleared to allow for miles of roads, pipelines, and transmission lines, not to mention cooling towers and dropout ponds which could leak and pollute the local water table. Like the existing plant at Pohoiki, the new plants will emit foul odors and poisonous gases that cause respiratory sickness and kill native forest life. Dangers of leakage, faulting, and even collapse are extreme in a power plant built on an active volcano.

Yet on May 4, 1990, the 9th Circuit Court of Appeals, in keeping with the tradition of U.S. granddaddies, affirmed a lower court's decision to dismiss Native Hawaiians' claims that the land swap was illegal. But of even greater concern to the native population is the danger that geothermal development will destroy the rain forest completely. Geothermal hazardous waste is totally unregulated in Hawaii. Developers have shown little regard for the health concerns of residents and have disposed of hazardous waste within one half mile of a town water well and children's playgrounds.

The struggle for the preservation of the only rain forest native to the United States has important health and environmental motivations. Yet the situation at Wao Kele O Puna also illustrates that theft of Native American lands continues today with the full endorsement of the U.S. government. Wao Kele O Puna is sacred land to Native Hawaiians, just as the San Francisco Peaks are to the Hopi and Navajo. Hawaiians believe it is a sacrilege to drill holes into their Mother's body, to capture her steam, to destroy her forests — and yet U.S. courts refuse to take such beliefs seriously or consider native religions worthy of constitutional protection. The impending devastation of the Puna rain forest threatens not only the beautiful land of Hawaii, but the religion and culture of its people.

In April of 1990, the U.S. Supreme Court ruled that states may criminally charge and imprison American Indians for possession and use of peyote regardless of the role that such possession plays in the religious system of the community. The government attributes such a decision to its interest in controlling substance abuse. Yet this attack of the "War on Drugs" has more to do with racial discrimination, ethnocentrism, and lack of respect for Native American religion and customs than any imaginary goal of controlling substance abuse.   45

U.S. law prohibits serving alcohol to minors. Yet one wonders if the court would rule similarly if the case involved Christian religious ceremonies where children are served wine. The U.S. statistics on alcohol as a drug are frightening. Twenty percent of drinking males and 10 percent of drinking females report signs of dependence on alcohol. The majority of homicides and aggravated assaults, and a significant proportion of rapes, are alcohol-related. Twenty-five thousand people are killed each year in car accidents involving alcohol. More death, disease, and financial and emotional loss result from alcohol than from all other psychoactive drugs combined. The annual economic cost of drinking exceeds $60 billion. It's tough to argue with C. H. McCaphy's assertion that "alcohol clearly constitutes America's greatest drug problem."

The statistics on alcohol abuse among Native Americans are even higher — so much so that alcoholism is considered not only the greatest drug problem in our communities but also the greatest social and health problem. Yet, it has been documented that the Native American Church, whose members use peyote in their purification and healing rituals, has been more successful in combating alcoholism among Indians than any other therapeutic program in existence. It seems that those states which refuse to grant exemptions to Native Americans from the laws on peyote use are defeating the goal of their own "war on drugs."

The Supreme Court may feel it has the power and authority to rewrite the U.S. Constitution so that religious freedom is no more than a myth for American Indians. Yet the Court remains subordinate to the International Bill of Human Rights, which states that religious freedoms should be limited only "to protect public safety, order, health, morals, or the fundamental rights of others." None of these are jeopardized by the use of peyote for religious purposes. It seems ironic that a government intent on "taking a bite out of crime" would focus such attention on the peaceful and harmless practice of one religion. And a nation which complains about the high cost of imprisoning criminal offenders has no business imprisoning Native Americans who use peyote as a central element in their religious beliefs.

The historical treatment of Native Americans by the United States has instilled a sickening fear in every native of this land. Our land has been stolen. Our children have been kidnapped, mistreated, and indoctrinated. Our tribal religions and sacred customs have been dragged through the courts and halls of Washington, D.C.

But recent court decisions should not be of concern only to Native 50 Americans. They should alarm every person in this land who values freedom. For our mistreatments point to a day, not far away, when all religions will inevitably fear to tread through the halls of Washington.

Rhythm of the Heart: Spiritual reflections from a Native American's prison cell . . .

Like all of you, brothers and sisters inside and outside these iron houses, I've faced many injustices. Sometimes injustice comes down on us with such crushing force that we want to lie down and cry ourselves to sleep and never wake up again. Other times we react with thoughts of how we'd like to pay back those who do us wrong, and rage, bitterness, hatred, and violence threaten to engulf our minds and hearts.

When we were made from the vessel of our Creator's heart, we were given our original instructions: to live in harmony with all our relations and to walk lightly upon the earth, our Mother, with love and respect. As I look around, it's pretty easy to see that things are out of balance and many of us seem to have forgotten these instructions.

The way I see it, that's because we've been given the ability to use our minds and hearts, to choose our own paths. And it seems that within each of us is a pair of twins: one which wants to hear and follow the heartbeat of the Creator, and another which will not hear and wants to go its own way. And these twins constantly struggle with each other.

The elders say that long ago so many humans had turned away from 55 the original instructions that the earth had to be cleansed by a great flood. Later, the earth was repopulated; but again, the people fell away, and the Creator began to consider destroying the human race.

At first, no one came forward to plead for the humans. No one dared ask for mercy. But finally the eagle came forward. The eagle knew about the wickedness on earth, and he knew there were only a few who remained faithful to the Creator's way. But on behalf of those few, the eagle begged for mercy, pleading with the Grandfather all night long.

At last, the Creator, though saddened by the evil on the earth, decided to give the human race another chance. And the Creator appointed the eagle to fly above the earth, searching for those remaining faithful to the Creator's way and encouraging them.

Our ancestors rejoiced in the love the Creator had shown. They rejoiced that they had been given a helper toward faithfulness. They rejoiced that the Creator had forgiven them and offered them another chance.

The elders say we are all called to show the same kind of forgiveness to the undeserving. We are called to never give up on each other.

I began a fast recently and asked my Grandfather to help me find some 60 good thoughts. I was looking for a way to understand how people can be so cruel to each other, how there can be so much injustice in the world, how a handful of people can be so greedy that they accumulate enormous material wealth while so many women, children, and elders go without food, shelter, and other necessities. Sometimes these thoughts overwhelm me, as they did when I was fasting.

But then another thought came to me. It's kind of strange, since I'm not a Christian, but in my mind I saw Jesus on the cross — nailed there, breathing his final breaths on earth. At that moment of his life, he was suffering his ultimate persecution and pain at the hands of the same kind of people who make us suffer. And yet, in that moment of his greatest suffering, he looked up in the sky and asked the Creator to have pity on them because they didn't realize what they were doing. And I thought to myself, "That's how it is."

At that moment, I realized I can no longer hate my enemies and those who cause pain and suffering in the world. I gotta have pity on them instead. I gotta pray for them.

We all have one Creator. We're all part of the same Creator. Even our enemies are our brothers and sisters. If I ignore that, I ignore the rhythm of the Creator's heart. With this thought I pray:

Tunkasila, Wakan Tanka, lean down to hear my pitiful voice. I ask for a blessing for me and all my relatives who struggle today. We need your guidance, your blessing, so we will be strong and our footsteps sure.

We can't do it without you, Grandfather. We are pitiful. Please have   65 pity on us. Give us the wisdom to see the things you place before us, the strength to pick these things up, and the courage to walk with them in a good way. Help us to set a good example so that our brothers and sisters whose good twins are asleep might see themselves reflected there and wake up and remember your original instructions.

And, Grandfather, bless us with our strength and courage to use the most powerful medicine you've given us, LOVE, which we seem to have forgotten how to use. Help us, with that medicine, to heal each other's hurts and dry each other's tears. Help and guide us, Tunkasila, to use the gifts you have given us — our skills, talents, minds, hearts — to the best of our ability to carry out your instructions and live in harmony with all creation.

Kunsik'un, Grandmother, thank you for the many things we take for granted in our daily living. Thank you for the warmth of shelter that we too often take without thought for the many people on this sacred earth whose bodies ache with cold because they have no place to sleep in warmth and peace. Thank you for the food we eat, and help us remember the many millions of children whose stomachs burn with hunger because they don't even have a crust of bread. Thank you for the water we sometimes take for granted without thinking of those who die each day for want of it.

Grandfather, mitunkasila, Wakan Tanka, I give thanks for this day, and for all my blessings. Please help me to use them wisely and humbly, so that when it is time for me to join my grandfathers, I will do so without shame.

Thank you for this prayer. Mitakuye Oyasin. — Inyan Cikala (Little Rock Reed)

1991

The Reader's Presence

1. Consider the organization of Reed's essay. What sequence does he create to demonstrate his overriding assertion — that "These five hundred years have seen the betrayal, mistreatment, and systematic destruction of Native Americans at the hands of European settlers"? What sort of evidence does Reed rely on in formulating his argument? To what extent does he anticipate opposing points of view in building his case? How successfully does he counter each of those arguments?

2. At the outset of paragraph 4, Reed asserts: "The political, cultural, and religious forms of tribal life are inseparable." As you reread the essay, assess the proportion of time Reed devotes to each of these three forms of tribal life. In which does he seem most interested? What evidence does he provide to support his claim that the establishment of the Carlisle Barracks in Pennsylvania in 1878 "marked the beginning of a systematic attack on our religions and culture through the de-Indianization of our children" (paragraph 7)?

3. Reed underscores his belief that the United States government has engaged in "a systematic attack" on Native Americans by repeating the word *systematic* and several variations of it. In what specific ways is Reed's use of this word related to his interest in documenting the government's suppression of Native American rights and culture through legal decisions? What does Reed gain (and lose) by emphasizing legal issues in his account of U.S. history as "a trail of broken promises, ignored treaties, and unconstitutional violation" of Native American rights and culture? In this respect, comment on Reed's use of metaphor, analogy, and especially irony to emphasize his points. Consider, for example, his report on the government's decision to detonate nuclear bombs in Nevada, on the land retained by the Shoshone Indians in the 1863 Treaty of Ruby Valley, as well as on the Supreme Court's ruling about the possession and use of peyote in Native American religion.

71 _____

Richard Rodriguez

Toward an American Language

For a hundred years Americans have resorted to Huckleberry Finn's American summer for refreshment. As much as Huck, Americans resist the coming of fall, the chill in the woods, the starched shirt, the inimical expectation of the schoolmarm. All city ways. Individualism is the source of America, the source of our greatness. But America is a city now and individualism has become our national dilemma.

America's individualism derives from low-church Protestantism. They taught us well, those old Puritans. Distrust the tyranny of the plural. Seek God with a singular pronoun. They didn't stop there. Puritans advised fences. Build a fence around what you hold dear and respect other fences.

TO SUIT ANY TASTE

The antisocial inclination of eighteenth-century Puritans paradoxically allowed for the immigrant America of the nineteenth century. Lacking a communal sense of itself — there was no "we" here — how could America resist the coming of strangers? America became a multiracial, multireligious society because a small band of Puritans didn't want the world.

The outsider is not the exception to America, rather the outsider is the archetypal citizen. In him, and only in him, in her — suitcase in hand, foreign-speaking, bewildered by the crowd — can Americans recognize ourselves. We recognize the stranger in us. For we are a nation of immigrants, we are accustomed to remind ourselves. We see ourselves as strangers to one another, all of us bewildered by the city.

For biographical information on Richard Rodriguez, see p. 661.

Immigrants may be appalled by the individualism they find when they   5
get here — skateboards; slang; disrespect; Daisy Miller; Deadheads — it's
all the same. But this same individualism allows the immigrant to purchase
a new life. Each new immigrant has a stake in the perpetuation of American individualism. Here the immigrant is freed from the collective fate of
his village. Once here, the immigrant has already eluded the destiny of his
father.

The limits of American generosity are the limits of Puritan individualism. We accept the stranger, sure we do, but we are suspicious of any assimilationist insinuation such as that the stranger might eventually change
us: Two in their meeting are changed.

With the exception of the army, the classroom is the most subversive
institution of America. The classroom works against our historical inclination by chipping away at any tangible distance between us. In the classroom, children are taught that they belong to a group. Children are taught
that there is a national culture, a public language, a plural pronoun implied
by the singular assertion of the Pledge of Allegiance.

About fifteen years ago, I got involved in the national debate over bilingual education. Proponents of bilingual classrooms argued that non-
English-speaking children would have an easier time of it in school if they
could keep a hold on heritage as a kind of trainer-wheel; if they would be
allowed to use their "family language" in classrooms.

What I knew from my own education was that such a scheme would
betray public education. There is no way for a child to use her family language in a classroom unless we diminish the notion of public school, unless
we confuse the child utterly about what is expected of her. Bilingual classrooms imply we are going to expect less.

BECAUSE IT'S GOOD FOR YOU

Family language distinguishes one child from all others. Classroom   10
language, on the other hand, is unyielding, impersonal, blind, public —
there are rules, there are limits, there are inevitable embarrassments, but
there are no exceptions. The child is expected to speak up, to make himself understood to an audience of boys and girls. It is an unsentimental
business.

At the time — in the mid-1970s — I took bilingual enthusiasts to be a
romantic lot, a fringe of the Ethnic Left. Fifteen years have passed and bilingual education has become a bureaucracy. I still believe that bilingualism is a confused ideology. But I now believe the confusion is willful and
characteristically American. Americans have always been at war with the
idea of school. We shrink from the idea of uniformity — as our Puritan
fathers would shrink — as from the image of the melting pot. We say we
want the advantages of public life, but we do not want to relinquish our
separateness for it. We want to coexist, not change.

In my mind, bilingual education belongs to those sentimental and violent American years, the sixties, when my generation imagined we had discovered individualism. There was a conveniently dishonorable war to protest. But Americans went to war against the idea of America. We went to war against anyone over thirty, against our parents, against memory. We marched in the name of "the people," exclusive of at least half the population.

The radical sixties were not such an isolated time. In the nineteenth century there were nativist riots against an expanding notion of America, against any idea of a plural pronoun. Should we now, in retrospect, be surprised that the black civil rights movement (the heroic march toward integration) was undermined, finally, by subsequent cries for black separatism? Another example of American ambivalence.

We think we are united only by a clean consent, and yet the rest of the world can spot us a mile off. America exists. Americans end up behaving more like each other alive, even in disagreement, than we resemble dead ancestors. There is a discernible culture about us, tangible in the spaces between us, that connects Thomas Jefferson with Martin Luther King, Jr. Trouble is, the lesson of that culture, the indoctrination of that culture in schools, implies that we form a "we." Our professors have lost the conviction of it. A unifying canon — an intellectual line which might implicate us all by virtue of our arrival here — seems an impossibility. Our professors have begun to fish in other streams, seeking alternatives to Western Civ.

In 1989 the majority of immigrants do not come from Europe. Now   15
Americans describe the distance we maintain from one another as "diversity." The problem of our national diversity becomes, with a little choke on logic, the solution to itself. "We should celebrate diversity," teachers, bureaucrats, join to tell us — that is what America means, they say. And they are right.

FAVORITE FLAVORS

Traditionally it has been pragmatism that forced Americans to yield to the fiction of a nation indivisible. War, for example. The U.S. Army took your darling boy, with his allergies and his moles and his favorite flavor and reduced him to a uniform. The workplace is very nearly as unsentimental.

In the nineteenth century, America compromised Puritanism with pragmatism. In order to work, to continue existing as a country, America required some uniform sense of itself.

In the nineteenth century, even as the American city was building, Samuel Clemens romanced the nation with a celebration of the wildness of the American river. But in the redbrick cities, and on streets without trees, the river became an idea, a learned idea, a civilizing idea, taking all to itself.

Women, usually women, tireless, overworked women, stood in front of rooms filled with the children of immigrants, teaching those children a common language. For language is not just another classroom skill, as today's bilingualists would have it. Language is the lesson of *grammar* school. And from the schoolmarm's achievement came the possibility of a shared history and a shared future. To my mind, this achievement of the nineteenth century classroom was an honorable one, comparable to the opening of the plains, the building of bridges. Grammar school teachers forged a nation.

My own first attempts to read *Huckleberry Finn* ended in defeat. I entered the classroom as a Spanish-speaking boy. I learned English with difficulty, but rightly enough. Huck spoke a dialect English, not the English I learned. ("You don't know about me without you have read. . . . ") Eventually, but this was long after, I was able to discern in Huck's dilemma — how he chafed so at school! — a version of my own. And, later still, to discern in him a version of the life of our nation: Huck as the archetypal bilingual child!

My fear is that today Huck Finn would emerge as the simple winner. The schoolmarm would be shown up as a tyrannical supremacist. I tell you the schoolmarm is the hero of America. My suspicion is that many of our children — dropouts and graduates alike — are learning the lesson of communality remedially, from the workplace. At the bank or behind the counter at McDonald's, or in the switch room of the telephone company, people from different parts of town and different parts of the country, and different countries of the world learn that they have one thing or another in common. Initially, a punch clock. A supervisor. A paycheck. A shared irony. A takeout lunch. Some nachos, some bagels, a pizza. And here's a fortune cookie for you: Two in their meeting are changed.

All the while the professors speak limply of diversity, which is truly our strength. But diversity which is not shared is no virtue. Diversity which is not shared is a parody nation.

The river owes its flux and its swell and its entire strength to its tributaries. But America was created in autumn by the schoolmarm, mistress of all she surveyed.

1989

The Reader's Presence

1. The leverage point in Rodriguez's case against bilingualism is his claim: "With the exception of the army, the classroom is the most subversive institution of America" (paragraph 7). What does he see as the principal contributions of the classroom — and of what he calls "the schoolmarm" — to the development of a shared American language? In what respect is the notion of a *public* school central to his argument? Draw on your own experience as

a basis for agreeing (or disagreeing) with his assertion that "public school" minimizes diversity and that the nineteenth-century "schoolmarm is the hero of America."

2. Identify the point of view from which Rodriguez speaks. What do you make of his repetition of *our* in the opening paragraph? Explain why you do (or do not) feel comfortable identifying with this use of *our* — and his subsequent use of *us*. What are the principal sources of his diction, metaphors, and allusions? How do you respond to the image of those who view bilingual education as "a kind of trainer-wheel" (paragraph 8)? Consider also what Rodriguez gains (and loses) by opening his argument by alluding to Mark Twain's *Huckleberry Finn.* In what ways is this moment similar to — and different from — his assertion near the beginning of paragraph 2: "They taught us well, those old Puritans"?

3. Discuss the extent to which you agree with Rodriguez's claim that Puritan values and ethics lie at the center of American society. How does Rodriguez reconcile this notion with his subsequent statement: "The outsider is not the exception to America, rather the outsider is the archetypal citizen" (paragraph 4)? Is Rodriguez's own view of this issue articulated from the vantage point of an outsider? Point to specific words and phrases — as well as to compositional strategies — to validate your response.

72 _____

Richard Selzer

What I Saw at the Abortion

I am a surgeon. Particularities of sick flesh is everyday news. Escaping blood, all the outpourings of disease — phlegm, pus, vomitus, even those occult meaty tumors that terrify — I see as blood, disease, phlegm, and so on. I touch them to destroy them. But I do not make symbols of them.

For biographical information on Richard Selzer, see p. 662.

What I am saying is that I have seen and I am used to seeing. We are talking about a man who has a trade, who has practiced it long enough to see no news in any of it. Picture this man, then. A professional. In his forties. Three children. Lives in a university town — so, necessarily, well — enlightened? Enough, anyhow. Successful in his work, yes. No overriding religious posture. Nothing special, then, your routine fellow, trying to do his work and doing it well enough. Picture him, this professional, a sort of scientist, if you please, in possession of the standard admirable opinions, positions, convictions, and so on — on this and that matter — on *abortion,* for example.

All right.

Now listen.

It is the western wing of the fourth floor of a great university hospital. 5 I am present because I asked to be present. I wanted to see what I had never seen. An abortion.

The patient is Jamaican. She lies on the table in that state of notable submissiveness I have always seen in patients. Now and then she smiles at one of the nurses as though acknowledging a secret.

A nurse draws down the sheet, lays bare the abdomen. The belly mounds gently in the twenty-fourth week of pregnancy. The chief surgeon paints it with a sponge soaked in red antiseptic. He does this three times, each time a fresh sponge. He covers the area with a sterile sheet, an aperture in its center. He is a kindly man who teaches as he works, who pauses to reassure the woman.

He begins.

A little pinprick, he says to the woman.

He inserts the point of a tiny needle at the midline of the lower portion 10 of her abdomen, on the downslope. He infiltrates local anesthetic into the skin, where it forms a small white bubble.

The woman grimaces.

That is all you will feel, the doctor says. Except for a little pressure. But no more pain.

She smiles again. She seems to relax. She settles comfortably on the table. The worst is over.

The doctor selects a three-and-one-half-inch needle bearing a central stylet. He places the point at the site of the previous injection. He aims it straight up and down, perpendicular. Next he takes hold of her abdomen with his left hand, palming the womb, steadying it. He thrusts with his right hand. The needle sinks into the abdominal wall.

Oh, says the woman quietly. 15

But I guess it is not pain that she feels. It is more a recognition that the deed is being done.

Another thrust and he has speared the uterus.

We are in, he says.

He has felt the muscular wall of the organ gripping the shaft of his needle. A further slight pressure on the needle advances it a bit more. He takes his left hand from the woman's abdomen. He retracts the filament of the stylet from the barrel of the needle. A small geyser of pale yellow fluid erupts.

We are in the right place, says the doctor. Are you feeling any pain? he   20 says.

She smiles, shakes her head. She gazes at the ceiling.

In the room we are six: two physicians, two nurses, the patient, and me.

The participants are busy, very attentive. I am not at all busy — but I am no less attentive. I want to see.

I see something!

It is unexpected, utterly unexpected, like a disturbance in the earth, a   25 tumultuous jarring. I see something other than what I expected here. I see a movement — a small one. But I have seen it.

And then I see it again. And now I see that it is the hub of the needle in the woman's belly that has jerked. First to one side. Then to the other side. Once more it wobbles, is *tugged,* like a fishing line nibbled by a sunfish.

Again! And I *know!*

It is the *fetus* that worries thus. It is the fetus struggling against the needle. Struggling? How can that be? I think: *That cannot be.* I think: The fetus feels no pain, cannot feel fear, has no *motivation.* It is merely reflex.

I point to the needle.

It is a reflex, says the doctor.   30

By the end of the fifth month, the fetus weighs about one pound, is about twelve inches long. Hair is on the head. There are eyebrows, eyelashes. Pale pink nipples show on the chest. Nails are present, at the fingertips, at the toes.

At the beginning of the sixth month, the fetus can cry, can suck, can make a fist. He kicks, he punches. The mother can feel this, can *see* this. His eyelids, until now closed, can open. He may look up, down, sideways. His grip is very strong. He could support his weight by holding with one hand.

A reflex, the doctor says.

I hear him. But I saw something. I saw *something* in that mass of cells *understand* that it must bob and butt. And I see it again! I have an impulse to shove to the table — it is just a step — seize that needle, pull it out.

We are not six, I think. I think we are *seven.*   35

Something strangles *there.* An effort, its effort, binds me to it.

I do not shove to the table. I take no little step. It would be . . . well, madness. Everyone here wants the needle where it is. Six do. No, *five* do.

I close my eyes. I see the inside of the uterus. It is bathed in ruby gloom.

I see the creature curled upon itself. Its knees are flexed. Its head is bent upon its chest. It is in fluid and gently rocks to the rhythm of the distant heartbeat.

It resembles . . . a sleeping infant.

Its place is entered by something. It is sudden. A point coming. A nee-   40
dle!

A spike of *daylight* pierces the chamber. Now the light is extinguished. The needle comes closer in the pool. The point grazes the thigh, and I stir. Perhaps I wake from dozing. The light is there again. I twist and straighten. My arms and legs *push*. My hand finds the shaft — grabs! I *grab*. I bend the needle this way and that. The point probes, touches on my belly. My mouth opens. Could I cry out? All is a commotion and a churning. There is a presence in the pool. An activity! The pool colors, reddens, darkens.

I open my eyes to see the doctor feeling a small plastic tube through the barrel of the needle into the uterus. Drops of pink fluid overrun the rim and spill onto the sheet. He withdraws the needle from around the plastic tubing. Now only the little tube protrudes from the woman's body. A nurse hands the physician a syringe loaded with a colorless liquid. He attaches it to the end of the tubing and injects it.

Prostaglandin, he says.

Ah, well, prostaglandin — a substance found normally in the body. When given in concentrated dosage, it throws the uterus into vigorous contraction. In eight to twelve hours, the woman will expel the fetus.

The doctor detaches the syringe but does not remove the tubing.   45

In case we must do it over, he says.

He takes away the sheet. He places gauze pads over the tubing. Over all this he applies adhesive tape.

I know. We cannot feed the great numbers. There is no more room. I know, I know. It is woman's right to refuse the risk, to decline the pain of childbirth. And an unwanted child is a very great burden. An unwanted child is a burden to himself. I know.

And yet . . . there is the flick of that needle. I *saw* it. I saw . . . I *felt* — in that room, a pace away, life prodded, life fending off. I saw life avulsed — swept by flood, blackening — then *out*.

There, says the doctor. It's all over. It wasn't too bad, was it? he says   50
to the woman.

She smiles. It is all over. Oh, yes.

And who would care to imagine that from a moist and dark commencement six months before there would ripen the cluster and globule, the sprout and pouch of man?

And who would care to imagine that trapped within the laked pearl and a dowry of yolk would lie the earliest stuff of dream and memory?

It is a persona carried here as well as person, I think. I think it is a signed piece, engraved with a hieroglyph of human genes.

I did not think this until I saw. The flick. The fending off.   55
We leave the room, the three of us, the doctors.

"Routine procedure," the chief surgeon says.

"All right," I say.

"Scrub nurse says first time you've seen one, Dick. First look at a purge," the surgeon says.

"That's right," I say. "First look."   60

"Oh, well," he says, "I guess you've seen everything else."

"Pretty much," I say.

"I'm not prying, Doctor," he says, "but was there something on your mind? I'd be delighted to field any questions. . . . "

"No," I say. "No, thanks. Just simple curiosity."

"Okay," he says, and we all shake hands, scrub, change, and go to our 65
calls.

I know, I know. The thing is normally done at sixteen weeks. Well, I've since seen it performed at that stage, too. And seen . . . the flick. But I also know that in the sovereign state of my residence it is hospital policy to warrant the procedure at twenty-four weeks. And that in the great state that is adjacent, policy is enlarged to twenty-eight weeks.

Does this sound like argument? I hope not. I am not trying to argue. I am only saying I've *seen*. The flick. Whatever else may be said in abortion's defense, the vision of that other defense will not vanish from my eyes.

What I saw I saw as that: a *defense*, a motion *from*, and effort *away*. And it has happened that you cannot reason with me now. For what can language do against the truth of what I saw?

1976

The Reader's Presence

1. What is Selzer's purpose in describing himself at the start of the essay? What does he want his reader to think of him? What authority does he claim?

2. The simplest words can at times be the most complex. Reread the essay, and consider Selzer's use of the word *saw*. Note the many occurrences of the act of seeing throughout the essay. How many senses of the word can you discover in the essay? Why is the word crucial to his position?

3. Does Selzer take various arguments about abortion into account? Is he stating and refuting different points of view? How does argument enter into his essay? Look carefully at the last two paragraphs. What have they to do with argument? Note the use of the word *defense*. What different meanings does Selzer give it? How do they relate to the essay's "argument"?

73

Randy Shilts

Talking AIDS to Death

*I'm talking to my friend Kit Herman when I notice a barely percep-
tible spot on the left side of his face. Slowly, it grows up his cheekbone,
down to his chin, and forward to his mouth. He talks on cheerfully, as
if nothing is wrong, and I'm amazed that I'm able to smile and chat on,
too, as if nothing were there. His eyes become sunken; his hair turns
gray; his ear is turning purple now, swelling into a carcinomatous cauliflower, and still we talk on. He's dying in front of me. He'll be dead
soon, if nothing is done.*

Dead soon, if nothing is done.

"Excuse me, Mr. Shilts, I asked if you are absolutely sure, if you can
categorically state that you definitely can*not* get AIDS from a mosquito."

I forget the early-morning nightmare and shift into my canned response. All my responses are canned now. I'm an AIDS talk-show jukebox.
Press the button, any button on the AIDS question list, and I have my
canned answer ready. Is this Chicago or Detroit?

"Of course you can get AIDS from a mosquito," I begin.   5

Here, I pause for dramatic effect. In that brief moment, I can almost
hear the caller murmur, "I *knew* it."

"If you have unprotected anal intercourse with an infected mosquito,
you'll get AIDS," I continue. "Anything short of that and you won't."

The talk-show host likes the answer. All the talk-show hosts like my
answers because they're short, punchy, and to the point. Not like those
boring doctors with long recitations of scientific studies so overwritten
with maybes and qualifiers that they frighten more than they reassure
an AIDS-hysteric public. I give good interview, talk-show producers

For biographical information on Randy Shilts, see p. 663.

agree. It's amazing, they say, how I always stay so cool and never lose my temper.

"Mr. Shilts, has there ever been a case of anyone getting AIDS from a gay waiter?"

"In San Francisco, I don't think they allow heterosexuals to be waiters.   10 This fact proves absolutely that if you could get AIDS from a gay waiter, all northern California would be dead by now."

I gave that same answer once on a Bay Area talk show, and my caller, by the sound of her a little old lady, quickly rejoined: "What if that gay waiter took my salad back into the kitchen and ejaculated into my salad dressing? Couldn't I get AIDS then?"

I didn't have a pat answer for that one, and I still wonder at what this elderly caller thought went on in the kitchens of San Francisco restaurants. Fortunately, this morning's phone-in — in Chicago, it turned out — is not as imaginative.

"You know, your question reminds me of a joke we had in California a couple of years back," I told the caller. "How many heterosexual waiters in San Francisco does it take to screw in a light bulb? The answer is both of them."

The host laughs, the caller is silent. Next comes the obligatory question about whether AIDS can be spread through coughing.

I had written a book to change the world, and here I was on talk shows   15 throughout America, answering questions about mosquitoes and gay waiters.

This wasn't exactly what I had envisioned when I began writing *And the Band Played On.* I had hoped to effect some fundamental changes. I really believed I could alter the performance of the institutions that had allowed AIDS to sweep through America unchecked.

AIDS had spread, my book attested, because politicians, particularly those in charge of federal-level response, had viewed the disease as a political issue, not an issue of public health — they deprived researchers of anything near the resources that were needed to fight it. AIDS had spread because government health officials consistently lied to the American people about the need for more funds, being more concerned with satisfying their political bosses and protecting their own jobs than with telling the truth and protecting the public health. And AIDS had spread because indolent news organizations shunned their responsibility to provide tough, adversarial reportage, instead basing stories largely on the Official Truth of government press releases. The response to AIDS was never even remotely commensurate with the scope of the problem.

I figured the federal government, finally exposed, would stumble over itself to accelerate the pace of AIDS research and put AIDS-prevention programs on an emergency footing. Once publicly embarrassed by the revelations of its years of shameful neglect, the media would launch serious investigative reporting on the epidemic. Health officials would step forward and finally lay bare the truth about how official disregard had cost this country hundreds of thousands of lives. And it would never happen again.

I was stunned by the "success" of my book. I quickly acquired all the trappings of bestsellerdom: *60 Minutes* coverage of my "startling" revelations, a Book-of-the-Month Club contract, a miniseries deal with NBC, translation into six languages, book tours on three continents, featured roles in movie-star-studded AIDS fund-raisers, regular appearances on network news shows, and hefty fees on the college lecture circuit. A central figure in my book became one of *People* magazine's "25 Most Intriguing People of 1987," even though he had been dead for nearly four years, and the *Los Angeles Herald Examiner* pronounced me one of the "in" authors of 1988. The mayor of San Francisco even proclaimed my birthday last year "Randy Shilts Day."

And one warm summer day as I was sunning at a gay resort in the   20
redwoods north of San Francisco, a well-toned, perfectly tanned young man slid into a chaise next to me and offered the ultimate testimony to my fifteen minutes of fame. His dark eyelashes rising and falling shyly, he whispered, "When I saw you on *Good Morning America* a couple weeks ago, I wondered what it would be like to go to bed with you."

"You're the world's first AIDS celebrity," enthused a friend at the World Health Organization, after hearing one of WHO's most eminent AIDS authorities say he would grant me an interview on one condition — that I autograph his copy of my book. "It must be great," he said.

It's not so great.

The bitter irony is, my role as an AIDS celebrity just gives me a more elevated promontory from which to watch the world make the same mistakes in the handling of the AIDS epidemic that I had hoped my work would help to change. When I return from network tapings and celebrity glad-handing, I come back to my home in San Francisco's gay community and see friends dying. The lesions spread from their cheeks to cover their faces, their hair falls out, they die slowly, horribly, and sometimes, suddenly, before anybody has a chance to know they're sick. They die in my arms and in my dreams, and nothing at all has changed.

Never before have I succeeded so well; never before have I failed so miserably.

I gave my first speech on the college lecture circuit at the University of   25
California [at] Los Angeles in January 1988. I told the audience that there were fifty thousand diagnosed AIDS cases in the United States as of that week and that within a few months there would be more people suffering from this deadly disease in the United States than there were Americans killed during the Vietnam War. There were audible gasps. During the question-and-answer session, several students explained that they had heard that the number of AIDS cases in America was leveling off.

In the next speech, at the University of Tennessee, I decided to correct such misapprehension by adding the federal government's projections —

the 270,000 expected to be dead or dying from AIDS in 1991, when the disease would kill more people than any single form of cancer, more than car accidents. When I spoke at St. Cloud State University in Minnesota three months later, I noted that the number of American AIDS cases had that week surpassed the Vietnam benchmark. The reaction was more a troubled murmur than a gasp.

By the time I spoke at New York City's New School for Social Research in June and there were sixty-five thousand AIDS cases nationally, the numbers were changing so fast that the constant editing made my notes difficult to read. By then as many as one thousand Americans a week were learning that they, too, had AIDS, or on the average, about one every fourteen minutes. There were new government projections to report, too: by 1993, some 450,000 Americans would be diagnosed with AIDS. In that year, one American will be diagnosed with the disease every thirty-six seconds. Again, I heard the gasps.

For my talk at a hospital administrators' conference in Washington in August, I started using little yellow stick-ons to update the numbers on my outline. That made it easier to read; there were now seventy-two thousand AIDS cases. Probably this month, or next, I'll tell another college audience that the nation's AIDS case load has topped one hundred thousand and there will be gasps again.

The gasps always amaze me. Why are they surprised? In epidemics, people get sick and die. That's what epidemics do to people and that's why epidemics are bad.

When Kit Herman was diagnosed with AIDS on May 13, 1986, his 30
doctor leaned over his hospital bed, took his hand, and assured him, "Don't worry, you're in time for AZT." The drug worked so well that all Kit's friends let themselves think he might make it. And we were bolstered by the National Institutes of Health's assurance that AZT was only the first generation of AIDS drugs, and that the hundreds of millions of federal dollars going into AIDS treatment research meant there would soon be a second and third generation of treatments to sustain life beyond AZT's effectiveness. Surely nothing was more important, considering the federal government's own estimates that between 1 and 1.5 million Americans were infected with the Human Immunodeficiency Virus (HIV), and virtually all would die within the next decade if nothing was done. The new drugs, the NIH assured everyone, were "in the pipeline," and government scientists were working as fast as they possibly could.

Despite my nagging, not one of dozens of public-affairs-show producers chose to look seriously into the development of those long-sought second and third generations of AIDS drugs. In fact, clinical trials of AIDS drugs were hopelessly stalled in the morass of bureaucracy at the NIH, but this story tip never seemed to cut it with producers. Clinical trials were not sexy. Clinical trials were boring.

I made my third *Nightline* appearance in January 1988 because new estimates had been released revealing that one in sixty-one babies born in New York City carried antibodies to the AIDS virus. And the link between those babies and the disease was intravenous drug use by one or both parents. Suddenly, junkies had become the group most likely to catch and spread AIDS through the heterosexual community. Free needles to junkies — now there was a sizzling television topic. I told the show's producers I'd talk about that, but that I was much more interested in the issue of AIDS treatments — which seemed most relevant to the night's program, since Ted Koppel's other guest was Dr. Anthony Fauci, associate NIH director for AIDS, and the Reagan administration's most visible AIDS official.

After fifteen minutes of talk on the ins and outs and pros and cons of free needles for intravenous drug users, I raised the subject of the pressing need for AIDS treatments. Koppel asked Fauci what was happening. The doctor launched into a discussion of treatments "in the pipeline" and how government scientists were working as fast as they possibly could.

I'd heard the same words from NIH officials for three years: Drugs were in the pipeline. Maybe it was true, but when were they going to come out of their goddamn pipeline? Before I could formulate a polite retort to Fauci's stall, however, the segment was over, Ted was thanking us, and the red light on the camera had blipped off. Everyone seemed satisfied that the government was doing everything it possibly could to develop AIDS treatments.

Three months later, I was reading a week-old *New York Times* in 35 Kit's room in the AIDS ward at San Francisco General Hospital. It was April, nearly two years after my friend's AIDS diagnosis. AZT had given him two years of nearly perfect health, but now its effect was wearing off, and Kit had suffered his first major AIDS-related infection since his original bout with pneumonia — cryptococcal meningitis. The meningitis could be treated, we all knew, but the discovery of this insidious brain infection meant more diseases were likely to follow. And the long-promised second and third generations of AIDS drugs were still nowhere on the horizon.

While perusing the worn copy of the *Times,* I saw a story about Dr. Fauci's testimony at a congressional hearing. After making Fauci swear an oath to tell the truth, a subcommittee headed by Representative Ted Weiss of New York City asked why it was taking so long to get new AIDS treatments into testing at a time when Congress was putting hundreds of millions of dollars into NIH budgets for just such purposes. At first Fauci talked about unavoidable delays. He claimed government scientists were working as fast as they could. Pressed harder, he finally admitted that the problem stemmed "almost exclusively" from the lack of staffing in his agency. Congress had allocated funds, it was true, but the Reagan administration had gotten around spending the money by stingily refusing to let Fauci hire anybody. Fauci had requested 127 positions to speed the development of AIDS treatments; the administration had granted him 11. And for a year, he had not told anyone. For a year, this spokesman for the public health answered reporters that AIDS drugs were in the pipeline and that government scientists had all the money they needed. It seemed that only when faced with the penalty of perjury would one of the administration's top AIDS officials tell the truth. That was the real story, I thought, but for some reason nobody else had picked up on it.

At the international AIDS conference in Stockholm two months later, the other reporters in "the AIDS pack" congratulated me on my success and asked what I was working on now. I admitted that I was too busy promoting the British and German release of my book to do much writing myself, and next month I had the Australian tour. But if I *were* reporting, I added with a vaguely conspiratorial tone, *I'd* look at the *scandal* in the NIH. Nobody had picked up that *New York Times* story from a few months ago about staffing shortages on AIDS clinical trials. The lives of 1.5 million HIV-infected Americans hung in the balance, and the only way you could get a straight answer out of an administration AIDS official was to put him under oath and make him face the charge of perjury. Where I went to journalism school, *that* was a news story.

One reporter responded to my tip with the question: "But who's going to play *you* in the miniseries?"

A few minutes later, when Dr. Fauci came into the press room, the world's leading AIDS journalists got back to the serious business of transcribing his remarks. Nobody asked him if he was actually telling the truth, or whether they should put him under oath to ensure a candid response to questions about when we'd get AIDS treatments. Most of the subsequent news accounts of Dr. Fauci's comments faithfully reported that many AIDS treatments were in the pipeline. Government scientists, he said once more, were doing all they possibly could.

The producer assured my publisher that Morton Downey, Jr., would   40
be "serious" about AIDS. "He's not going to play games on this issue," the producer said, adding solemnly: "His brother has AIDS. He understands the need for compassion." The abundance of Mr. Downey's compassion was implicit in the night's call-in poll question: "Should all people with AIDS be quarantined?"

Downey's first question to me was, "You *are* a homosexual, aren't you?"

He wasn't ready for my canned answer: "Why do you ask? Do you want a date or something?"

The show shifted into an earnest discussion of quarantine. In his television studio, Clearasil-addled high school students from suburban New Jersey held up MORTON DOWNEY FAN CLUB signs and cheered aggressively when the truculent, chain-smoking host appeared to favor a kind of homespun AIDS Auschwitz. The youths shouted down any audience member who stepped forward to defend the rights of AIDS sufferers, their howls growing particularly vitriolic if the speakers were gay. These kids were the ilk from which Hitler drew his Nazi youth. In the first commercial break, the other guest, an AIDS activist, and I told Downey we would walk off the show if he didn't tone down his gay-baiting rhetoric. Smiling amiably, Downey took a long drag on his cigarette and assured us, "Don't worry, I have a fallback position."

That comment provided one of the most lucid moments in my year as an AIDS celebrity. Downey's "fallback position," it was clear, was the opposite of what he was promoting on the air. Of course, he didn't *really* believe that people with AIDS, people like his brother, should all be locked up. This was merely a deliciously provocative posture to exploit the working-class resentments of people who needed someone to hate. AIDS sufferers and gays would do for this week. Next week, if viewership dropped and Downey needed a new whipping boy, maybe he'd move on to Arabs, maybe Jews. It didn't seem to matter much to him, since he didn't believe what he was saying anyway. For Morton Downey, Jr., talking about AIDS was not an act of conscience; it was a ratings ploy. He knew it, he let his guests know it, his producers certainly knew it, and his television station knew it. The only people left out of the joke were his audience.

The organizers of the Desert AIDS Project had enlisted actor Kirk 45 Douglas and CBS morning anchor Kathleen Sullivan to be honorary cochairs of the Palm Springs fundraiser. The main events would include a celebrity tennis match pitting Douglas against Mayor Sonny Bono, and a fifteen-hundred-dollar-a-head dinner at which I would receive a Lucite plaque for my contributions to the fight against AIDS. The next morning I would fly to L.A. to speak at still another event, this one with Shirley Mac-Laine, Valerie Harper, and Susan Dey of *L.A. Law.*

The desert night was exquisite. There were 130 dinner guests, the personification of elegance and confidence, who gathered on a magnificent patio of chocolate-brown Arizona flagstone at the home of one of Palm Springs's most celebrated interior designers. A lot of people had come simply to see what was regarded as one of the most sumptuous dwellings in this sumptuous town.

When I was called to accept my reward, I began with the same lineup of jokes I use on talk shows and on the college lecture circuit. They work every time.

I told the crowd about how you get AIDS from a mosquito.

Kirk Douglas laughed; everybody laughed.

Next, I did the how-many-gay-waiters joke. 50

Kirk Douglas laughed; everybody laughed.

Then I mentioned the woman who asked whether she could get AIDS from a waiter ejaculating in her salad dressing.

That one always has my college audiences rolling in the aisles, so I paused for the expected hilarity.

But in the utter stillness of the desert night air, all that could be heard was the sound of Kirk Douglas's steel jaw dropping to the magnificent patio of chocolate-brown Arizona flagstone. The rest was silence.

"You've got to remember that most of these people came because   55
they're my clients," the host confided later. "You said that, and all I could
think was how I'd have to go back to stitching slipcovers when this was
done."

It turned out that there was more to my lead-balloon remark than a
misjudged audience. Local AIDS organizers told me that a year earlier,
a rumor that one of Palm Spring's most popular restaurants was owned
by a homosexual, and that most of its waiters were gay, had terrified the
elite community. Patronage at the eatery quickly plummeted, and it had
nearly gone out of business. Fears that I dismissed as laughable were the
genuine concerns of my audience, I realized. My San Francisco joke was a
Palm Springs fable.

As I watched the busboys clear the tables later that night, I made a
mental note not to tell that joke before dinner again. Never had I seen so
many uneaten salads, so much wasted iceberg lettuce.

A friend had just tested antibody positive, and I was doing my best to
cheer him up as we ambled down the sidewalk toward a Castro Street restaurant a few blocks from where I live in San Francisco. It seems most of
my conversations now have to do with who has tested positive or lucked
out and turned up negative, or who is too afraid to be tested. We had
parked our car near Coming Home, the local hospice for AIDS patients
and others suffering from terminal illnesses, and as we stepped around a
nondescript, powder-blue van that blocked our path, two men in white
uniforms emerged from the hospice's side door. They carried a stretcher,
and on the stretcher was a corpse, neatly wrapped in a royal-blue blanket
and secured with navy-blue straps. My friend and I stopped walking. The
men quickly guided the stretcher into the back of the van, climbed in the
front doors, and drove away. We continued our walk but didn't say anything.

I wondered if the corpse was someone I had known. I'd find out Thursday when the weekly gay paper came out. Every week there are at least two
pages filled with obituaries of the previous week's departed. Each week,
when I turn to those pages, I hold my breath, wondering whose picture I'll
see. It's the only way to keep track, what with so many people dying.

Sometimes I wonder if an aberrant mother or two going to mass at the   60
Most Holy Redeemer Church across the street from Coming Home Hospice has ever warned a child, "That's where you'll end up if you don't obey
God's law." Or whether some youngster, feeling that first awareness of a
different sexuality, has looked at the doorway of this modern charnel
house with an awesome, gnawing dread of annihilation.

"Is the limousine here? Where are the dancers?"

The room fell silent. Blake Rothaus had sounded coherent until that
moment, but he was near death now and his brain was going. We were
gathered around his bed in a small frame house on a dusty street in Okla-

homa City. The twenty-four-year-old was frail and connected to life through a web of clear plastic tubing. He stared up at us and seemed to recognize from our looks that he had lapsed into dementia. A friend broke the uncomfortable silence.

"Of course, we all brought our dancing shoes," he said. "Nice fashionable pumps at that. I wouldn't go out without them."

Everyone laughed and Blake Rothaus was lucid again.

Blake had gone to high school in a San Francisco suburb. When he was 65 a sophomore, he told us, he and his best friend sometimes skipped school, sneaking to the city to spend their afternoons in the gay neighborhood around Castro Street.

It's a common sight, suburban teenagers playing hooky on Castro Street. I could easily imagine him standing on a corner not far from my house. But back in 1982, when he was eighteen, I was already writing about a mysterious, unnamed disease that had claimed 330 victims in the United States.

Blake moved back to Oklahoma City with his family after he graduated from high school. When he fell ill with AIDS, he didn't mope. Instead, he started pestering Oklahoma health officials with demands to educate people about this disease and to provide services for the sick. The state health department didn't recoil. At the age of twenty-two, Blake Rothaus had become the one-man nucleus for Oklahoma's first AIDS-patient services. He was the hero of the Sooner State's AIDS movement and something of a local legend.

Though the state had reported only 250 AIDS cases, Oklahoma City had a well-coordinated network of religious leaders, social workers, healthcare providers, gay-rights advocates, state legislators, and businessmen, all committed to providing a sane and humane response to this frightening new disease.

"I think it's the old Dust Bowl mentality," suggested one AIDS organizer. "When the hard times come, people pull together."

My past year's travels to twenty-nine states and talks with literally 70 thousands of people have convinced me of one thing about this country and AIDS: Most Americans want to do the right thing about this epidemic. Some might worry about mosquitoes and a few may be suspicious of their salad dressing. But beyond these fears is a reservoir of compassion and concern that goes vastly underreported by a media that needs conflict and heartlessness to fashion a good news hook.

In Kalamazoo, Michigan, when I visited my stepmother, I was buttonholed by a dozen middle-aged women who wondered anxiously whether we were any closer to a vaccine or a long-term treatment. One mentioned a hemophiliac nephew. Another had a gay brother in Chicago. A third went to a gay hairdresser who, she quickly added, was one of the finest people you'd ever meet. When I returned to my conservative hometown of Aurora, Illinois, nestled among endless fields of corn and soy, the local health department told me they receive more calls than they know what to do with from women's groups, parishes, and community organizations that want to do something to help. In New Orleans, the archconservative, pronuke, antigay bishop had taken up the founding of an AIDS hospice as a personal mission because, he said, when people are sick, you've got to help them out.

Scientists, reporters, and politicians privately tell me that of course *they* want to do more about AIDS, but they have to think about the Morton Downeys of the world, who argue that too much research or too much news space or too much official sympathy is being meted out to a bunch of miscreants. They do as much as they can, they insist; more would rile the resentments of the masses. So the institutions fumble along, convinced they must pander to the lowest common denominator, while the women and men of America's heartland pull me aside to fret about a dying cousin or co-worker and to plead, "When will there be a cure? When will this be over?"

"I think I'll make it through this time," Kit said to me, "but I don't have it in me to go through it again."

We were in room 3 in San Francisco General Hospital's ward 5A, the AIDS ward. The poplar trees outside Kit's window were losing their leaves, and the first winter's chill was settling over the city. I was preparing to leave for my fourth and, I hoped, final media tour, this time for release of the book in paperback and on audiocassette; Kit was preparing to die.

The seizures had started a week earlier, indicating he was suffering   75 either from toxoplasmosis, caused by a gluttonous protozoa that sets up housekeeping in the brain; or perhaps it was a relapse of cryptococcal meningitis; or, another specialist guessed, it could be one of those other nasty brain infections that nobody had seen much of until the past year. Now that AIDS patients were living longer, they fell victim to even more exotic infections than in the early days. But the seizures were only part of it. Kit had slowly been losing the sight in his left eye to a herpes infection. And the Kaposi's sarcoma lesions that had scarred his face were beginning to coat the inside of his lungs. When Kit mentioned he'd like to live until Christmas, the doctors said he might want to consider having an early celebration this year, because he wasn't going to be alive in December.

"I can't take another infection," Kit said.

"What does that mean?"

"Morphine," Kit answered, adding mischievously, "lots of it."

We talked briefly about the mechanics of suicide. We both knew people who'd made a mess of it, and people who had done it right. It was hardly the first time the subject had come up in conversation for either of us. Gay men facing AIDS now exchange formulas for suicide as casually as housewives swap recipes for chocolate-chip cookies.

Kit was released from the hospital a few days later. He had decided to   80 take his life on a Tuesday morning. I had to give my first round of interviews in Los Angeles that day, so I stopped on the way to the airport to say good-bye on Monday. All day Tuesday, while I gave my perfectly formed sound bites in a round of network radio appearances, I wondered: Is this the moment he's slipping out of consciousness and into that perfect darkness? When I called that night, it turned out he'd delayed his suicide until Thursday to talk to a few more relatives. I had to give a speech in Portland that day, so on the way to the airport I stopped again. He showed me the amber-brown bottle with the bubble-gum-pink morphine syrup, and we said another good-bye.

The next morning, Kit drank his morphine and fell into a deep sleep. That afternoon, he awoke and drowsily asked what time it was. When told it was five hours later, he murmured, "That's amazing. I should have been dead hours ago."

And then he went back to sleep.

That night, Kit woke up again.

"You know what they say about near-death experiences?" he asked. "Going toward the light?"

Shaking his head, he sighed, "No light. Nothing." 85

His suicide attempt a failure, Kit decided the timing of his death would now be up to God. I kept up on the bizarre sequence of events by phone and called as soon as I got back to San Francisco. I was going to tell Kit that his theme song should be "Never Can Say Good-by," but then the person on the other end of the phone told me that Kit had lapsed into a coma.

The next morning, he died.

Kit's death was like everything about AIDS — anticlimactic. By the time he actually did die, I was almost beyond feeling.

The next day, I flew to Boston for the start of the paperback tour, my heart torn between rage and sorrow. All week, as I was chauffeured to my appearances on *Good Morning America, Larry King Live,* and various CNN shows, I kept thinking, it's all going to break. I'm going to be on a TV show with some officious government health spokesman lying to protect his job, and I'm going to start shouting, "You lying son of a bitch. Don't you know there are people, real people, people I love out there dying?" Or I'll be on a call-in show and another mother will phone about her thirty-seven-year-old son who just died and it will hit me all at once, and I'll start weeping.

But day after day as the tour went on, no matter how many official lies 90 I heard and how many grieving mothers I talked to, the crackup never occurred. All my answers came out rationally in tight little sound bites about institutional barriers to AIDS treatments and projections about 1993 case loads.

By the last day of the tour, when a limousine picked me up at my Beverly Hills hotel for my last round of satellite TV interviews, I knew I had to stop. In a few weeks I'd return to being national correspondent for the *Chronicle,* and it was time to get off the AIDS celebrity circuit, end the interviews and decline the invitations to the star-studded fund-raisers, and get back to work as a newspaper reporter. That afternoon, there was just one last radio interview to a call-in show in the San Fernando Valley, and then it would be over.

The first caller asked why his tax money should go toward funding an AIDS cure when people got the disease through their own misdeeds.

I used my standard jukebox answer about how most cancer cases are linked to people's behavior but that nobody ever suggested we stop trying to find a cure for cancer.

A second caller phoned to ask why her tax money should go to funding an AIDS cure when these people clearly deserved what they got.

I calmly put a new spin on the same answer, saying in America you   95 usually don't sentence people to die for having a different lifestyle from yours.

Then a third caller phoned in to say that he didn't care if all those queers and junkies died, as did a fourth and fifth and sixth caller. By then I was shouting, "You stupid bigot. You just want to kill off everybody you don't like. You goddamn Nazi."

The talk-show host sat in stunned silence. She'd heard I was so *reasonable*. My anger baited the audience further, and the seventh and eighth callers began talking about "you guys," as if only a faggot like myself could give a shit about whether AIDS patients all dropped dead tomorrow.

In their voices, I heard the reporters asking polite questions of NIH officials. Of course, they had to be polite to the government doctors; dying queers weren't anything to lose your temper over. I heard the dissembling NIH researchers go home to their wives at night, complain about the lack of personnel, and shrug; this was just how it was going to have to be for a while. They'd excuse their inaction by telling themselves that if they went public and lost their jobs, worse people would replace them. It was best to go along. But how would they feel if *their* friends, *their* daughters were dying of this disease? Would they be silent — or would they shout? Maybe they'll forgive me for suspecting they believed that ultimately a bunch of fags weren't worth losing a job over. And when I got home, I was going to have to watch my friends get shoved into powder-blue vans, and it wasn't going to change.

The history of the AIDS epidemic, of yesterday and of today, was echoing in the voices of those callers. And I was screaming at them, and the show host just sat there stunned, and I realized I had rendered myself utterly and completely inarticulate.

I stopped, took a deep breath, and returned to compound-complex 100 sentences about the American tradition of compassion and the overriding need to overcome institutional barriers to AIDS treatments.

When I got home to San Francisco that night, I looked over some notes I had taken from a conversation I'd had with Kit during his last stay in the hospital. I was carping about how frustrated I was at the prospect of returning to my reporting job. If an internationally acclaimed best seller hadn't done shit to change the world, what good would mere newspaper stories do?

"The limits of information," Kit said. "There's been a lot written on it."

"Oh," I said.

Kit closed his eyes briefly and faded into sleep while plastic tubes fed him a cornucopia of antibiotics. After five minutes, he stirred, looked up, and added, as if we had never stopped talking, "But you don't really have a choice. You've got to keep on doing it. What else are you going to do?"

1989

The Reader's Presence

1. Consider the presence Shilts establishes for himself in the essay. How does he blend both professional expertise and private experience? How are these reflected in the structure of the essay itself?

2. Of what importance are television and radio talk shows to the essay? Why do you think Shilts included as much information as he did about them? What role do the callers play in the essay? What does the reader learn through them? How do the callers help Shilts structure his argument?

3. In what sense is this an essay about arguments? What happens to Shilts during the course of his arguments? Why is talking such a key part of the essay? Reread the section on the Palm Springs fund-raiser carefully (paragraphs 45–57). Why was Shilts surprised by the audience's reaction? How does his anecdote of that audience's response affect *your* response as an audience of the essay?

74

Gloria Steinem

Erotica vs. Pornography

Look at or imagine images of people making love; really making love. Those images may be very diverse, but there is likely to be a mutual pleasure and touch and warmth, an empathy for each other's bodies and nerve endings, a shared sensuality, and a spontaneous sense of two people who are there because they *want* to be.

Now look at or imagine images of sex in which there is force, violence, or symbols of unequal power. They may be very blatant: whips and chains of bondage, even torture and murder presented as sexually titillating, the clear evidence of wounds and bruises, or an adult's power being used sexually over a child. They may be more subtle: the use of class, race, authority, or just body poses to convey conqueror and victim; unequal nudity, with one person's body exposed and vulnerable while the other is armored with clothes; or even a woman by herself, exposed for an unseen but powerful viewer whom she clearly is trying to please. (It's interesting that, even when only the woman is seen, we often know whether she is there for her own pleasure or being displayed for someone else's.) But blatant or subtle, there is no equal power or mutuality. In fact, much of the tension and drama comes from the clear idea that one person is dominating another.

These two sorts of images are as different as love is from rape, as dignity is from humiliation, as partnership is from slavery, as pleasure is from pain. Yet they are confused and lumped together as "pornography" or "obscenity," "erotica" or "explicit sex," because sex and violence are so dangerously intertwined and confused. After all, it takes violence or the threat of it to maintain the unearned dominance of any group of human beings over another. Moreover, the threat must be the most persuasive

For biographical information on Gloria Steinem, see p. 664.

wherever men and women come together intimately and are most in danger of recognizing each other's humanity.

The confusion of sex with violence is most obvious in any form of sadomasochism. The gender-based barrier to empathy has become so great that a torturer or even murderer may actually believe pain or loss of life to be the natural fate of the victim; and the victim may have been so deprived of self-respect or of empathetic human contact that she expects pain or loss of freedom as the price of any intimacy or attention at all. It's unlikely that even a masochist expects death. Nonetheless, "snuff" movies and much current pornographic literature insist that a slow death from sexual torture is the final orgasm and ultimate pleasure. It's a form of "suicide" reserved for women. Though men in fact are far more likely to kill themselves, male suicide is almost never presented as sexually pleasurable. But sex is also confused with violence and aggression in all forms of popular culture, and in respectable theories of psychology and sexual behavior as well. The idea that aggression is a "normal" part of male sexuality, and that passivity or even the need for male aggression is a "normal" part of female sexuality, are part of the male-dominant culture we live in, the books we learn from, and the air we breathe.

Even the words we are given to express our feelings are suffused with the same assumptions. Sexual phrases are the most common synonyms for conquering and humiliation (*being had, being screwed, getting fucked*); the sexually aggressive woman is a *slut* or a *nymphomaniac,* but the sexually aggressive man is just *normal;* and real or scientific descriptions of sex may perpetuate the same roles; for instance, a woman is always *penetrated* by a man though she might also be said to have *enveloped* him.

5

Obviously, untangling sex from aggression and violence or the threat of it is going to take a very long time. And the process is going to be greatly resisted as a challenge to the very heart of male dominance and male centrality.

But we do have the common sense of our bodies to guide us. Pain is a warning of damage and danger. If that sensation is not mixed with all the intimacy we know as children, we are unlikely to confuse pain with pleasure and love. As we discover our free will and strength, we are also more likely to discover our own initiative and pleasure in sex. As men no longer can dominate and have to find an identity that doesn't depend on superiority, they also discover that cooperation is more interesting than submission, that empathy with their sex partner increases their own pleasure, and that anxieties about their own ability to "perform" tend to disappear along with stereotyped ideas about masculinity.

But women will be the main fighters of this new sexual revolution. It is our freedom, our safety, our lives, and our pleasure that are mostly at stake.

We began by trying to separate sex and violence in those areas where the physical danger was and is the most immediate: challenging rape as the one crime that was considered biologically irresistible for the criminal and perhaps invited by the victim; refusing to allow male-female beatings to be classified as "domestic violence" and ignored by the law; exposing forced prostitution and sexual slavery as national and international crimes. With the exception of wife beating, those challenges were made somewhat easier by men who wanted to punish other men for taking their female property. Women still rarely have the power to protect each other.

Such instances of real antiwoman warfare led us directly to the propa-   10
ganda that teaches and legitimizes them — pornography. Just as we had begun to separate rape from sex, we realized that we must find some way of separating pornographic depictions of sex as an antiwoman weapon from those images of freely chosen, mutual sexuality.

Fortunately, there is truth in the origin of words. *Pornography* comes from the Greek root *porné* (harlot, prostitute, or female captive) and *graphos* (writing about or description of). Thus, it means a description of either the purchase of sex, which implies an imbalance of power in itself, or sexual slavery.

This definition includes, and should include, all such degradation, regardless of whether it is females who are the slaves and males who are the captors or vice versa. There is certainly homosexual pornography, for instance, with a man in the "feminine" role of victim. There is also role-reversal pornography, with a woman whipping or punishing a man, though it's significant that this genre is created by men for their own pleasure, not by or for women, and allows men to *pretend* to be victims — but without real danger. There could also be lesbian pornography, with a woman assuming the "masculine" role of victimizing another woman. That women rarely choose this role of victimizer is due to no biological superiority, but a culture that doesn't addict women to violence. But whatever the gender of the participants, all pornography is an imitation of the male-female, conqueror-victim paradigm, and almost all of it actually portrays or implies enslaved woman and master.

Even the 1970 Presidential Commission on Obscenity and Pornography, whose report is often accused of suppressing or ignoring evidence of the causal link between pornography and violence against women, defined the subject of their study as pictorial or verbal descriptions of sexual behavior characterized by "the degrading and demeaning portrayal of the role and status of the human female.

In short, pornography is not about sex. It's about an imbalance of male-female power that allows and even requires sex to be used as a form of aggression.

Erotica may be the word that can differentiate sex from violence and   15
rescue sexual pleasure. It comes from the Greek root *eros* (sexual desire or passionate love, named for Eros, the son of Aphrodite), and so contains the idea of love, positive choice, and the yearning for a particular person. Unlike pornography's reference to a harlot or prostitute, *erotica* leaves en-

tirely open the question of gender. (In fact, we may owe its sense of shared power to the Greek idea that a man's love for another man was more worthy than love for a woman, but at least that bias isn't present in the word.) Though both erotica and pornography refer to verbal or pictorial representations of sexual behavior, they are as different as a room with doors open and one with doors locked. The first might be a home, but the second could only be a prison.

The problem is that there is so little erotica. Women have rarely been free enough to pursue erotic pleasure in our own lives, much less to create it in the worlds of film, magazines, art, books, television, and popular culture — all the areas of communication we rarely control. Very few male authors and filmmakers have been able to escape society's message of what a man should do, much less to imagine their way into the identity of a woman. Some women and men are trying to portray equal and erotic sex, but it is still not a part of popular culture.

And the problem is there is so much pornography. This underground stream of antiwoman propaganda that exists in all male-dominant societies has now become a flood in our streets and theaters and even our homes. Perhaps that's better in the long run. Women can no longer pretend pornography does not exist. We must either face our own humiliation and torture every day on magazine covers and television screens or fight back. There is hardly a newsstand without women's bodies in chains and bondage, in full labial display for the conquering male viewer, bruised or on our knees, screaming in real or pretended pain, pretending to enjoy what we don't enjoy. The same images are in mainstream movie theaters and respectable hotel rooms via closed-circuit TV for the traveling businessman. They are brought into our own homes not only in magazines, but in the new form of video cassettes. Even video games offer such features as a smiling, rope-bound woman and a male figure with an erection, the game's object being to rape the woman as many times as possible. (Like much of pornography, that game is fascist on racial grounds as well as sexual ones. The smiling woman is an Indian maiden, the rapist is General Custer, and the game is called "Custer's Revenge.") Though "snuff" movies in which real women were eviscerated and finally killed have been driven underground (in part because the graves of many murdered women were discovered around the shack of just one filmmaker in California), movies that simulate the torture murders of women are still going strong. (*Snuff* is the porn term for killing a woman for sexual pleasure. There is not even the seriousness of a word like *murder*.) So are the "kiddie porn" or "chicken porn" movies and magazines that show adult men undressing, fondling, and sexually using children; often with the titillating theme that "fathers" are raping "daughters." Some "chicken porn" magazines offer explicit tips on how to use a child sexually without leaving physical evidence of rape, the premise being that children's testimony is even less likely to be believed than that of adult women.

Add this pornography industry up, from magazines like *Playboy* and

Hustler, to movies like *Love Gestapo Style, Deep Throat,* or *Angels in Pain,* and the total sales come to a staggering eight billion dollars a year — more than all the sales of the conventional film and record industry combined. And that doesn't count the fact that many "conventional" film and music images are also pornographic, from gynocidal record jackets like the famous *I'm "Black and Blue" from the Rolling Stones — and I Love It!* (which showed a seminude black woman bound to a chair) to the hundreds of teenage sex-and-horror movies in which young women die sadistic deaths and rape is presented not as a crime but as sexual excitement. Nor do those industries include the sales of the supposedly "literary" forms of pornography, from *The Story of O* to the works of the Marquis de Sade.

If Nazi propaganda that justified the torture and killing of Jews were the theme of half of our most popular movies and magazines, would we not be outraged? If Ku Klux Klan propaganda that preached and even glamorized the enslavement of blacks were the subject of much-praised "classic" novels, would we not protest? We know that such racist propaganda precedes and justifies the racist acts of pogroms and lynchings. We know that watching a violent film causes test subjects to both condone more violence afterward and to be willing to perpetuate it themselves. Why is the propaganda of sexual aggression against women of all races the one form in which the "conventional wisdom" sees no danger? Why is pornography the only media violence that is supposed to be a "safety valve" to satisfy men's "natural" aggressiveness somewhere short of acting it out?

The first reason is the confusion of *all* nonprocreative sex with pornography. Any description of sexual behavior, or even nudity, may be called pornographic or obscene (a word whose Latin derivative means *dirty* or *containing filth*) by those who insist that the only moral purpose of sex is procreative, or even that any portrayal of sexuality or nudity is against the will of God.   20

In fact, human beings seem to be the only animals that experience the same sex drive and pleasure at times when we can and cannot conceive. Other animals experience periods of heat or estrus. Humans do not.

Just as we developed uniquely human capacities for language, planning, memory, and invention along our evolutionary path, we also developed sexuality as a form of expression, a way of communicating that is separable from our reproductive need. For human beings, sexuality can be and often is a way of bonding, of giving and receiving pleasure, bridging differentness, discovering sameness, and communicating emotion.

We developed this and other human gifts through our ability to change our environment, adapt to it physically, and so in the very long run to affect our own evolution. But as an emotional result of this spiraling path away from other animals, we seem to alternate between periods of exploring our unique abilities and feelings of loneliness in the unknown that we ourselves have created, a fear that sometimes sends us back to the comfort of the animal world by encouraging us to look for a sameness that is not there.

For instance, the separation of "play" from "work" is a feature of the human world. So is the difference between art and nature, or an intellectual accomplishment and a physical one. As a result, we celebrate play, art, and invention as pleasurable and important leaps into the unknown; yet any temporary trouble can send us back to a nostalgia for our primate past and a conviction that the basics of survival, nature, and physical labor are somehow more worthwhile or even more moral.

In the same way, we have explored our sexuality as separable from   25 conception: a pleasurable, empathetic, important bridge to others of our species. We have even invented contraception, a skill that has probably existed in some form since our ancestors figured out the process of conception and birth, in order to extend and protect this uniquely human gift. Yet we also have times of atavistic suspicion that sex is not complete, or even legal or intended by God, if it does not or could not end in conception.

No wonder the very different concepts of "erotica" and "pornography" can be so confused. Both assume that sex can be separated from conception; that human sexuality has additional uses and goals. This is the major reason why, even in our current culture, both may still be condemned as equally obscene and immoral. Such gross condemnation of all sexuality that isn't harnessed to childbirth (and to patriarchal marriage so that children are properly "owned" by men) has been increased by the current backlash against women's independence. Out of fear that the whole patriarchal structure will be eventually upset if we as women really have the autonomous power to decide our sexual and reproductive futures (that is, if we can control our own bodies, and thus the means of reproduction), anti-equality groups are not only denouncing sex education and family planning as "pornographic," but are trying to use obscenity laws to stop the sending of all contraceptive information through the mails. Any sex or nudity outside the context of patriarchal marriage and forced childbirth is their target. In fact, Phyllis Schlafly[1] has denounced the entire women's movement as "obscene."

Not surprisingly, this religious, visceral backlash has a secular, intellectual counterpart that relies heavily on applying the "natural" behavior of some selected part of the animal world to humans. This is questionable in itself, but such Lionel Tiger-ish[2] studies make their political purpose even more clear by the animals they choose and the habits they emphasize. For example, some male primates carry and generally

---

[1]*Phyllis Schlafly:* Conservative opponent of the women's movement. — EDS.
[2]*Lionel Tiger-ish:* The allusion is to anthropologist Lionel Tiger, author of *Men in Groups.* — EDS.

"mother" their infants, male lions care for their young, female elephants often lead the clan, and male penguins literally do everything except give birth, from hatching the eggs to sacrificing their own membranes to feed the new arrivals. Perhaps that's why many male supremacists prefer to discuss chimps and baboons (many of whom are studied in atypical conditions of captivity) whose behavior is suitably male-dominant. The message is that human females should accept their animal "destiny" of being sexually dependent and devote themselves to bearing and rearing their young.

Defending against such repression and reaction leads to the temptation to merely reverse the terms and declare that *all* nonprocreative sex is good. In fact, however, this human activity can be as constructive or destructive, moral or immoral, as any other. Sex as communication can send messages as different as mutual pleasure and dominance, life and death, "erotica" and "pornography."

The second kind of problem comes not from those who oppose women's equality in nonsexual areas, whether on grounds of God or nature, but from men (and some women, too) who present themselves as friends of civil liberties and progress. Their opposition may take the form of a concern about privacy, on the grounds that a challenge to pornography invades private sexual behavior and the philosophy of "whatever turns you on." It may be a concern about class bias, on the premise that pornography is just "workingmen's erotica." Sometimes, it's the simple argument that they themselves like pornography and therefore it must be okay. Most often, however, this resistance attaches itself to or hides behind an expressed concern about censorship, freedom of the press, and the First Amendment.

In each case, such liberal objections are more easily countered than the   30
anti-equality ones because they are less based on fact. It's true, for instance, that women's independence and autonomy would upset the whole patriarchal apple cart: The conservatives are right to be worried. It's not true, however, that pornography is a private concern. If it were just a matter of men making male-supremacist literature in their own basements to assuage their own sexual hang-ups, there would be sorrow and avoidance among women, but not the anger, outrage, and fear produced by being confronted with the preaching of sexual fascism on our newsstands, movie screens, television sets, and public streets. It is a multi-billion-dollar industry, which involves the making of public policy, if only to decide whether, as is now the case, crimes committed in the manufacture and sale of pornography will continue to go largely unprosecuted. Zoning regulations on the public display of pornography are not enforced, the sexual slavery and exploitation of children goes unpunished, the forcible use of teenage runaways is ignored by police, and even the torture and murder of prostitutes for men's sexual titillation is obscured by some mitigating notion that the women asked for it.

In all other areas of privacy, the limitation is infringement on the rights and lives and safety of others. That must become true for pornography. Right now, it is exempt: almost "below the law."

As for class bias, it's simply not accurate to say that pornography is erotica with less education. From the origins of the words, as well as the careful way that feminists working against pornography are trying to use them, it's clear there is a substantive difference, not an artistic or economic one. Pornography is about dominance. Erotica is about mutuality. (Any man able to empathize with women can easily tell the difference by looking at a photograph or film and putting himself in the woman's skin. There is some evidence that poor or discriminated-against men are better able to do this than rich ones.) Perhaps the most revealing thing is that this argument is generally made *on behalf* of the working class by propornography liberals, but not *by* working-class spokespeople themselves.

Of course, the idea that enjoying pornography makes it okay is an overwhelmingly male one. From Kinsey forward, research has confirmed that men are the purchasers of pornography, and that the majority of men are turned on by it, while the majority of women find it angering, humiliating, and not a turn-on at all. This was true even though women were shown sexually explicit material that may have included erotica, since Kinsey and others did not make that distinction. If such rare examples of equal sex were entirely deleted, pornography itself could probably serve as sex aversion-therapy for most women; yet many men and some psychologists continue to call women prudish, frigid, or generally unhealthy if they are not turned on by their own domination. The same men might be less likely to argue that anti-Semitic and racist literature was equally okay because it gave them pleasure, or that they wanted their children to grow up with the same feelings about people of other races, other classes, that had been inflicted on them. The problem is that the degradation of women of all races is still thought to be normal.

Nonetheless, there are a few well-meaning women who are both turned on by pornography and angered that other women are not. Some of their anger is misunderstanding: Objections to pornography are not condemnations of women who have been raised to believe sex and domination are synonymous, but objections to the idea that such domination is the only form that normal sexuality can take. Sometimes, this anger results from an underestimation of themselves: Being turned on by a rape fantasy is not the same thing as wanting to be raped. As Robin Morgan[3] has pointed out, the distinguishing feature of a fantasy is that the fantasizer herself is in control. Both men and women have "ravishment" fantasies in which we are passive while others act out our unspoken wishes — but they are still *our* wishes. And some anger, especially when it comes from women who consider themselves feminists, is a refusal to differentiate between

[3]***Robin Morgan:*** A feminist writer. — EDS.

what may be true for them now and what might be improved for all women in the future. To use a small but related example, a woman may now be attracted only to men who are taller, heavier, and older than she, but still understand that such superficial restrictions on the men she loves and enjoys going to bed with won't exist in a more free and less-stereotyped future. Similarly, some lesbians may find themselves following the masculine-feminine patterns that were our only model for intimate relationships, heterosexual or not, but still see these old patterns clearly and try to equalize them. It isn't that women attracted to pornography cannot also be feminists, but that pornography itself must be recognized as an adversary of women's safety and equality, and therefore, in the long run, of feminism.

Finally, there is the First Amendment argument against feminist anti-   35
pornography campaigns: the most respectable and public opposition, but also the one with the least basis in fact.

Feminist groups are not arguing for censorship of pornography, or for censorship of Nazi literature or racist propaganda of the Ku Klux Klan. For one thing, any societal definition of pornography in a male-dominant society (or of racist literature in a racist society) probably would punish the wrong people. Freely chosen homosexual expression might be considered more "pornographic" than snuff movies, or contraceptive courses for teenagers more "obscene" than bondage. Furthermore, censorship in itself, even with the proper definitions, would only drive pornography into more underground activity and, were it to follow the pattern of drug traffic,, into even more profitability. Most important, the First Amendment is part of a statement of individual rights against government intervention that feminism seeks to expand, not contract: for instance, a woman's right to decide whether and when to have children. When we protest against pornography and educate others about it, as I am doing now, we are strengthening the First Amendment by exercising it.

The only legal steps suggested by feminists thus far have been the prosecution of those pornography makers who are accused of murder or assault and battery, prosecution of those who use children under the age of consent, enforcement of existing zoning and other codes that are breached because of payoffs to law-enforcement officials and enormous rents paid to pornography's landlords, and use of public-nuisance statutes to require that pornography not be displayed in public places where its sight cannot reasonably be avoided. All of those measures involve enforcement of existing law, and none has been interpreted as a danger to the First Amendment.

Perhaps the reason for this controversy is less substance than smokescreen. Just as earlier feminist campaigns to combat rape were condemned by some civil libertarians as efforts that would end by putting only men of color or poor men in jail, or in perpetuating the death penalty, anti-pornography campaigns are now similarly opposed. In fact, the greater publicity given to rape exposed the fact that white psychiatrists, educators, and other professionals were just as likely to be rapists, and changes in the law reduced penalties to ones that were more appropriate and thus more likely to be administered. Feminist efforts also changed the definition to sexual assault so that men were protected, too.

Though there are no statistics on the purchasers of pornography, clerks, movie-house owners, video-cassette dealers, mail-order houses, and others who serve this clientele usually remark on their respectability, their professional standing, suits, briefcases, white skins, and middle-class zip codes. For instance, the last screening of a snuff movie showing a real murder was traced to the monthly pornographic film showings of a senior partner in a respected law firm; an event regularly held by him for a group of friends including other lawyers and judges. One who was present reported that many were "embarrassed" and "didn't know what to say." But not one man was willing to object, much less offer this evidence of murder to the police. Though some concern about censorship is sincere — the result of false reports that feminist anti-pornography campaigns were really calling for censorship, or of confusion with right-wing groups who both misdefine pornography and want to censor it — much of it seems to be a cover for the preservation of the pornographic status quo.

In fact, the obstacles to taking on pornography seem suspiciously 40 like the virgin-whore divisions that have been women's only choices in the past. The right wing says all that is not virginal or motherly is pornographic, and thus they campaign against sexuality and nudity in general. The left wing says all sex is good as long as it's male-defined, and thus pornography must be protected. Women who feel endangered by being the victim, and men who feel demeaned by being the victimizer, have a long struggle ahead. In fact, pornography will continue as long as boys are raised to believe they must control or conquer women as a measure of manhood, as long as society rewards men who believe that success or even functioning — in sex as in other areas of life — depends on women's subservience.

But we now have words to describe our outrage and separate sex from violence. We now have the courage to demonstrate publicly against pornography, to keep its magazines and films out of our houses, to boycott its purveyors, to treat even friends and family members who support it as seriously as we would treat someone who supported and enjoyed Nazi literature or the teachings of the Klan.

But until we finally untangle sexuality and aggression, there will be more pornography and less erotica. There will be little murders in our beds — and very little love.

1983

The Reader's Presence

1. Steinem's position depends on the extended distinction she draws between erotica and pornography. Summarize her distinction. Logicians sometimes use the phrase "a distinction without a difference" to refer to a contrast that is merely verbal. Do you think Steinem's distinction is without a difference, or is it an important distinction to make? Explain your answer.

2. Take a sheet of paper and draw a line down the middle. On top of one side of the line write the word *erotica*. On the other side, write *pornography*. Reread Steinem's essay and list the key words Steinem directly or indirectly associates with each term on the appropriate side of the line. For example, under which word would you put *play* or *violence* or *subservience*? Under which word would you put *sexuality*? Remember, you're working with her associations, not your own. Go over your work when completed, and see what the words in each list have in common. Describe how the relationship of terms in each list supports her basic distinction.

3. Who is Steinem's intended audience? What are its values? Does she feel part of this audience or at odds with it? How does her relation to her audience affect her purpose in the essay? How does it relate to the expository and informational aspects of her essay as opposed to the argumentative or persuasive?

75 _____

Jonathan Swift

A Modest Proposal

For Preventing the Children of Poor People in Ireland
from Being a Burden to Their Parents or Country,
and for Making Them Beneficial to the Public

It is a melancholy object to those who walk through this great town[1]
or travel in the country, when they see the streets, the roads, and cabin
doors, crowded with beggars of the female sex, followed by three, four, or
six children, all in rags and importuning every passenger for an alms. These
mothers, instead of being able to work for their honest livelihood, are
forced to employ all their time in strolling to beg sustenance for their helpless infants: who as they grow up either turn thieves for want of work, or
leave their dear native country to fight for the pretender in Spain,[2] or sell
themselves to the Barbadoes.[3]

I think it is agreed by all parties that this prodigious number of children in the arms, or on the backs, or at the heels of their mothers, and
frequently of their fathers, is in the present deplorable state of the kingdom
a very great additional grievance; and, therefore, whoever could find out a
fair, cheap, and easy method of making these children sound, useful members of the commonwealth, would deserve so well of the public as to have
his statute set up for a preserver of the nation.

But my intention is very far from being confined to provide only for the
children of professed beggars; it is of a much greater extent, and shall take

For biographical information on Jonathan Swift, see p. 664.

[1]*this great town:* Dublin. — EDS.

[2]*pretender in Spain:* James Stuart (1688–1766); exiled in Spain, he laid claim to the
English crown and had the support of many Irishmen who had joined an army hoping to
restore him to the throne. — EDS.

[3]*the Barbadoes:* Inhabitants of the British colony in the Caribbean where Irishmen emigrated to work as indentured servants in exchange for their passage. — EDS.

in the whole number of infants at a certain age who are born of parents in effect as little able to support them as those who demand our charity in the streets.

As to my own part, having turned my thoughts for many years upon this important subject, and maturely weighed the several schemes of our projectors,[4] I have always found them grossly mistaken in their computation. It is true, a child just dropped from its dam may be supported by her milk for a solar year, with little other nourishment; at most not above the value of 2s.,[5] which the mother may certainly get, or the value in scraps, by her lawful occupation of begging; and it is exactly at one year old that I propose to provide for them in such a manner as instead of being a charge upon their parents or the parish, or wanting food and raiment for the rest of their lives, they shall on the contrary contribute to the feeding, and partly to the clothing, of many thousands.

There is likewise another great advantage in my scheme, that it will   5 prevent those voluntary abortions, and that horrid practice of women murdering their bastard children, alas! too frequent among us! sacrificing the poor innocent babes I doubt more to avoid the expense than the shame, which would move tears and pity in the most savage and inhuman breast.

The number of souls in this kingdom being usually reckoned one million and a half, of these I calculate there may be about 200,000 couple whose wives are breeders; from which number I subtract 30,000 couple who are able to maintain their own children (although I apprehend there cannot be so many, under the present distress of the kingdom); but this being granted, there will remain 170,000 breeders. I again subtract 50,000 for those women who miscarry, or whose children die by accident or disease within the year. There only remain 120,000 children of poor parents annually born. The question therefore is, how this number shall be reared and provided for? which, as I have already said, under the present situation of affairs, is utterly impossible by all the methods hitherto proposed. For we can neither employ them in handicraft of agriculture; we neither build houses (I mean in the country) nor cultivate land; they can very seldom pick up a livelihood by stealing, till they arrive at six years old, except where they are of towardly parts;[6] although I confess they learn the rudiments much earlier; during which time they can, however, be properly looked upon only as probationers; as I have been informed by a principal gentleman in the county of Cavan, who protested to me that he never knew above one or two instances under the age of six, even in a part of the kingdom so renowned for the quickest proficiency in that art.

---

[4]*projectors:* Planners. — EDS.
[5]*2s.:* Two shillings; in Swift's time one shilling was worth less than twenty-five cents. Other monetary references in the essay are to pounds sterling ("£."), pence ("d."), a crown, and a groat. A pound consisted of twenty shillings; a shilling of twelve pence; a crown was five shillings; a groat was worth a few cents. — EDS.
[6]*towardly parts:* Natural abilities. — EDS.

I am assured by our merchants, that a boy or a girl before twelve years old is no salable commodity; and even when they come to this age they will not yield above 3£. or 3£. 2s. 6d. at most on the exchange; which cannot turn to account either to the parents or kingdom, the charge of nutriment and rags having been at least four times that value.

I shall now therefore humbly propose my own thoughts, which I hope will not be liable to the least objection.

I have been assured by a very knowing American of my acquaintance in London, that a young healthy child well nursed is at a year old a most delicious, nourishing, and wholesome food, whether stewed, roasted, baked, or broiled; and I make no doubt that it will equally serve in a fricassee or a ragout.[7]

I do therefore humbly offer it to public consideration that of the 120,000 children already computed, 20,000 may be reserved for breed, whereof only one-fourth part to be males; which is more than we allow to sheep, black cattle, or swine; and my reason is, that these children are seldom the fruits of marriage, a circumstance not much regarded by our savages; therefore one male will be sufficient to serve four females. That the remaining 100,000 may, at a year old, be offered in sale to the persons of quality and fortune through the kingdom; always advising the mother to let them suck plentifully in the last month, so as to render them plump and fat for a good table. A child will make two dishes at an entertainment for friends; and when the family dines alone, the fore and hind quarter will make a reasonable dish, and seasoned with a little pepper or salt will be very good boiled on the fourth day, especially in winter.

I have reckoned upon a medium that a child just born will weigh 12 pounds, and in a solar year, if tolerably nursed, will increase to 28 pounds.

I grant this food will be somewhat dear, and therefore very proper for landlords, who, as they have already devoured most of the parents, seem to have the best title to the children.

Infants' flesh will be in season throughout the year, but more plentiful in March, and a little before and after: for we are told by a grave author, an eminent French physician,[8] that fish being a prolific diet, there are more children born in Roman Catholic countries about nine months after Lent than at any other season; therefore, reckoning a year after Lent, the markets will be more glutted than usual, because the number of popish infants is at least three to one in this kingdom: and therefore it will have one other collateral advantage, by lessening the number of papists among us.

I have already computed the charge of nursing a beggar's child (in which list I reckon all cottagers, laborers, and four-fifths of the farmers) to be about 2s. per annum, rags included; and I believe no gentleman would

[10]

---

[7]*ragout:* A stew. — Eds.

[8]*French physician:* François Rabelais (c. 1494–1553), the great Renaissance humanist and author of the comic masterpiece *Gargantua and Pantagruel.* Swift is being ironic in calling Rabelais "grave." — Eds.

repine to give 10s. for the carcass of a good fat child, which, as I have said, will make four dishes of excellent nutritive meat, when he has only some particular friend or his own family to dine with him. Thus the squire will learn to be a good landlord, and grow popular among the tenants; the mother will have 8s. net profit, and be fit for work till she produces another child.

Those who are more thrifty (as I must confess the times require) may   15
flay the carcass; the skin of which artificially[9] dressed will make admirable gloves for ladies, and summer boots for fine gentlemen.

As to our city of Dublin, shambles[10] may be appointed for this purpose in the most convenient parts of it, and butchers we may be assured will not be wanting: although I rather recommend buying the children alive, and dressing them hot from the knife as we do roasting pigs.

A very worthy person, a true lover of his country, and whose virtues I highly esteem, was lately pleased in discoursing on this matter to offer a refinement upon my scheme. He said that many gentlemen of this kingdom, having of late destroyed their deer, he conceived that the want of venison might be well supplied by the bodies of young lads and maidens, not exceeding fourteen years of age nor under twelve; so great a number of both sexes in every country being now ready to starve for want of work and service; and these to be disposed of by their parents, if alive, or otherwise by their nearest relations. But with due deference to so excellent a friend and so deserving a patriot, I cannot be altogether in his sentiments; for as to the males, my American acquaintance assured me from frequent experience that their flesh was generally tough and lean, like that of our schoolboys by continual exercise, and their taste disagreeable; and to fatten them would not answer the charge. Then as to the females, it would, I think, with humble submission be a loss to the public, because they soon would become breeders themselves: and besides, it is not improbable that some scrupulous people might be apt to censure such a practice (although indeed very unjustly), as a little bordering upon cruelty; which, I confess, has always been with me the strongest objection against any project, how well soever intended.

But in order to justify my friend, he confessed that this expedient was put into his head by the famous Psalmanazar[11] a native of the island Formosa, who came from thence to London about twenty years ago: and in conversation told my friend, that in his country when any young person happened to be put to death, the executioner sold the carcass to persons of quality as a prime dainty; and that in his time the body of a plump girl of fifteen, who was crucified for an attempt to poison the emperor, was sold to his imperial majesty's prime minister of state, and other great mandarins

[9]*artificially:* Artfully. — EDS.

[10]*shambles:* Slaughterhouses. — EDS.

[11]*Psalmanazar:* George Psalmanazar (c. 1679–1763) was a Frenchman who tricked London society into believing he was a native of Formosa (now Taiwan). — EDS.

of the court, in joints from the gibbet, at 400 crowns. Neither indeed can I deny, that if the same use were made of several plump young girls in this town, who without one single groat to their fortunes cannot stir abroad without a chair,[12] and appear at the playhouse and assemblies in foreign fineries which they never will pay for, the kingdom would not be the worse.

Some persons of a desponding spirit are in great concern about the vast number of poor people, who are aged, diseased, or maimed, and I have been desired to employ my thoughts what course may be taken to ease the nation of so grievous an encumbrance. But I am not in the least pain upon that matter, because it is very well known that they are every day dying and rotting by cold and famine, and filth and vermin, as fast as can be reasonably expected. And as to the young laborers, they are now in as hopeful a condition: They cannot get work, and consequently pine away for want of nourishment, to a degree that if at any time they are accidentally hired to common labor, they have not strength to perform it; and thus the country and themselves are happily delivered from the evils to come.

I have too long digressed, and therefore shall return to my subject. I   20
think the advantages by the proposal which I have made are obvious and many, as well as of the highest importance.

For first, as I have already observed, it would greatly lessen the number of papists, with whom we are yearly overrun, being the principal breeders of the nation as well as our most dangerous enemies; and who stay at home on purpose to deliver the kingdom to the Pretender, hoping to take their advantage by the absence of so many good Protestants, who have chosen rather to leave their country than stay at home and pay tithes against their conscience to an Episcopal curate.

Secondly, The poor tenants will have something valuable of their own, which by law may be made liable to distress[13] and help to pay their landlord's rent, their corn and cattle being already seized, and money a thing unknown.

Thirdly, Whereas the maintenance of 100,000 children from two years old and upward, cannot be computed at less than 10s. a-piece per annum, the nation's stock will be thereby increased £50,000 per annum, beside the profit of a new dish introduced to the tables of all gentlemen of fortune in the kingdom who have any refinement in taste. And the money will circulate among ourselves, the goods being entirely of our own growth and manufacture.

Fourthly, The constant breeders beside the gain of 8s. sterling per annum by the sale of their children, will be rid of the charge of maintaining them after the first year.

Fifthly, This food would likewise bring great custom to taverns, where   25

---

[12]*a chair:* A sedan chair in which one is carried about. — EDS.
[13]*distress:* Seizure for payment of debt. — EDS.

the vintners will certainly be so prudent as to procure the best receipts[14] for dressing it to perfection, and consequently have their houses frequented by all the fine gentlemen, who justly value themselves upon their knowledge in good eating; and a skilful cook who understands how to oblige his guests, will contrive to make it as expensive as they please.

Sixthly, This would be a great inducement to marriage, which all wise nations have either encouraged by rewards or enforced by laws and penalties. It would increase the care and tenderness of mothers toward their children, when they were sure of a settlement for life to the poor babes, provided in some sort by the public, to their annual profit instead of expense. We should see an honest emulation among the married women, which of them would bring the fattest child to the market. Men would become as fond of their wives during the time of their pregnancy as they are now of their mares in foal, their cows in calf, their sows when they are ready to farrow; nor offer to beat or kick them (as is too frequent a practice) for fear of a miscarriage.

Many other advantages might be enumerated. For instance, the addition of some thousand carcasses in our exportation of barreled beef, the propagation of swine's flesh, and improvement in the art of making good bacon, so much wanted among us by the great destruction of pigs, too frequent at our table; which are no way comparable in taste or magnificence to a well-grown, fat, yearling child, which roasted whole will make a considerable figure at a lord mayor's feast or any other public entertainment. But this and many others I omit, being studious of brevity.

Supposing that 1,000 families in this city would be constant customers for infants' flesh, besides others who might have it at merry-meetings, particularly at weddings and christenings, I compute that Dublin would take off annually about 20,000 carcasses; and the rest of the kingdom (where probably they will be sold somewhat cheaper) the remaining 80,000.

I can think of no one objection that will possibly be raised against this proposal unless it should be urged that the number of people will be thereby much lessened in the kingdom. This I freely own, and it was indeed one principal design in offering it to the world. I desire the reader will observe, that I calculate my remedy for this one individual kingdom of Ireland and for no other that ever was, is, or I think ever can be upon earth. Therefore let no man talk to me of other expedients: of taxing our absentees at 5s. a pound: of using neither clothes nor household furniture except what is of our own growth and manufacture: of utterly rejecting the materials and instruments that promote foreign luxury: of curing the expensiveness of pride, vanity, idleness, and gaming in our women: of introducing a vein of parsimony, prudence, and temperance: of learning to love our country, in the want of which we differ even from Laplanders and the inhabitants of

---

[14]*receipts:* Recipes. — Eds.

Topinamboo:[15] of quitting our animosities and factions, nor acting any longer like the Jews, who were murdering one another at the very moment their city was taken:[16] of being a little cautious not to sell our country and conscience for nothing: of teaching landlords to have at least one degree of mercy toward their tenants: lastly, of putting a spirit of honesty, industry, and skill into our shopkeepers; who, if a resolution could now be taken to buy only our native goods, would immediately unite to cheat and exact upon us in the price the measure, and the goodness, nor could ever yet be brought to make one fair proposal of just dealing, though often and earnestly invited to it.

Therefore I repeat, let no man talk to me of these and the like expedients, till he has at least some glimpse of hope that there will be ever some hearty and sincere attempt to put them in practice.   30

But as to myself, having been wearied out for many years with offering vain, idle, visionary thoughts, and at length utterly despairing of success, I fortunately fell upon this proposal; which, as it is wholly new, so it has something solid and real, of no expense and little trouble, full in our own power, and whereby we can incur no danger in disobliging England. For this kind of commodity will not bear exportation, the flesh being of too tender a consistence to admit a long continuance in salt, although perhaps I could name a country which would be glad to eat up our whole nation without it.

After all, I am not so violently bent upon my own opinion as to reject any offer proposed by wise men, which shall be found equally innocent, cheap, easy, and effectual. But before something of that kind shall be advanced in contradiction to my scheme, and offering a better, I desire the author or authors will be pleased maturely to consider two points. First, as things now stand, how they will be able to find food and raiment for 100,000 useless mouths and backs. And secondly, there being a round million of creatures in human figure throughout this kingdom, whose subsistence put into a common stock would leave them in debt 2,000,000£. sterling, adding those who are beggars by profession to the bulk of farmers, cottagers, and laborers, with the wives and children who are beggars in effect; I desire those politicians who dislike my overture, and may perhaps be so bold as to attempt an answer, that they will first ask the parents of these mortals, whether they would not at this day think it a great happiness to have been sold for food at a year old in the manner I prescribe, and thereby have avoided such a perpetual scene of misfortunes as they have since gone through by the oppression of landlords, the impossibility of paying rent without money or trade, the want of common sustenance, with

---

[15]*Laplanders and the inhabitants of Topinamboo:* Lapland is the area of Scandinavia above the Arctic Circle; Topinamboo, in Brazil, was known in Swift's time for the savagery of its tribes. — EDS.

[16]*was taken:* A reference to the Roman seizure of Jerusalem (A.D. 70). — EDS.

neither house nor clothes to cover them from the inclemencies of the weather, and the most inevitable prospect of entailing the like or greater miseries upon their breed for ever.

I profess, in the sincerity of my heart, that I have not the least personal interest in endeavoring to promote this necessary work, having no other motive than the public good of my country, by advancing our trade, providing for infants, relieving the poor, and giving some pleasure to the rich. I have no children by which I can propose to get a single penny; the youngest being nine years old, and my wife past childbearing.

                                                                    1729

The Reader's Presence

1. Consider Swift's title. In what sense is the proposal "modest"? What is modest about it? What synonyms would you use for *modest* that appear in the essay? In what sense is the essay a "proposal"? Does it follow any format that resembles a proposal? What aspects of its language seem to resemble proposal writing?

2. For this essay Swift invents a speaker, an unnamed, fictional individual who "humbly" proposes a plan to relieve poverty in Ireland. What attitudes and beliefs in the essay do you attribute to the speaker? Which do you attribute to Swift, the author?

3. Having considered two authors (the speaker of the proposal and Swift), now consider two readers — the reader the speaker imagines and the reader Swift imagines. How do these two readers differ? Reread the final paragraph of the essay from the perspective of each of these readers. How do you think each reader is expected to respond?

76 _____

Henry David Thoreau
Civil Disobedience

I heartily accept the motto, — "That government is best which governs least"; and I should like to see it acted up to more rapidly and systematically. Carried out, it finally amounts to this, which also I believe, — "That government is best which governs not at all"; and when men are prepared for it, that will be the kind of government which they will have. Government is at best but an expedient; but most governments are usually, and all governments are sometimes, inexpedient. The objections which have been brought against a standing army, and they are many and weighty, and deserve to prevail, may also at last be brought against a standing government. The standing army is only an arm of the standing government. The government itself, which is only the mode which the people have chosen to execute their will, is equally liable to be abused and perverted before the people can act through it. Witness the present Mexican war, the work of comparatively a few individuals using the standing government as their tool; for, in the outset, the people would not have consented to this measure.

This American Government, — what is it but a tradition, though a recent one, endeavoring to transmit itself unimpaired to posterity, but each instant losing some of its integrity? It has not the vitality and force of a single living man; for a single man can bend it to his will. It is a sort of wooden gun to the people themselves. But it is not the less necessary for this; for the people must have some complicated machinery or other, and hear its din, to satisfy that idea of government which they have. Governments show thus how successfully men can be imposed on, even impose on themselves, for their own advantage. It is excellent, we must all allow. Yet this government never of itself furthered any enterprise, but by the alacrity with which it got out of its way. *It* does not keep the country free. *It* does

For biographical information on Henry David Thoreau, see p. 665.

not settle the West. *It* does not educate. The character inherent in the American people has done all that has been accomplished; and it would have done somewhat more, if the government had not sometimes got in its way. For government is an expedient by which men would fain succeed in letting one another alone; and, as has been said, when it is most expedient, the governed are most let alone by it. Trade and commerce, if they were not made of India-rubber, would never manage to bounce over the obstacles which legislators are continually putting in their way; and, if one were to judge these men wholly by the effects of their actions and not partly by their intentions, they would deserve to be classed and punished with those mischievous persons who put obstructions on the railroads.

But, to speak practically and as a citizen, unlike those who call themselves no-government men, I ask for, not at once no government, but *at once* a better government. Let every man make known what kind of government would command his respect, and that will be one step toward obtaining it.

After all, the practical reason why, when the power is once in the hands of the people, a majority are permitted, and for a long period continue, to rule is not because they are most likely to be in the right, nor because this seems fairest to the minority, but because they are physically the strongest. But a government in which the majority rule in all cases cannot be based on justice, even as far as men understand it. Can there not be a government in which majorities do not virtually decide right and wrong, but conscience? — in which majorities decide only those questions to which the rule of expediency is applicable? Must the citizen ever for a moment, or in the least degree, resign his conscience to the legislator? Why has every man a conscience, then? I think that we should be men first, and subjects afterward. It is not desirable to cultivate a respect for the law, so much as for the right. The only obligation which I have a right to assume is to do at any time what I think right. It is truly enough said, that a corporation has no conscience; but a corporation of conscientious men is a corporation *with* a conscience. Law never made men a whit more just; and, by means of their respect for it, even the well-disposed are daily made the agents of injustice. A common and natural result of any undue respect for law is, that you may see a file of soldiers, colonel, captain, corporal, privates, powder-monkeys, and all, marching in admirable order over hill and dale to the wars, against their wills, ay, against their common sense and consciences, which makes it very steep marching indeed, and produces a palpitation of the heart. They have no doubt that it is a damnable business in which they are concerned; they are all peaceably inclined. Now, what are they? Men at all? or small movable forts and magazines, at the service of some unscrupulous man in power? Visit the Navy-Yard, and behold a marine, such a man as an American government can make, or such as it can make a man with its black arts, — a mere shadow and reminiscence of humanity, a man laid out alive and standing, and already, as one may say, buried under arms with funeral accompaniments, it may be, —

> "Not a drum was heard, not a funeral note,
>   As his corse to the rampart we hurried;
> Not a solider discharged his farewell shot
>   O'er the grave where our hero we buried."[1]

The mass of men serve the state thus, not as men mainly, but as ma-   5
chines, with their bodies. They are the standing army, and the militia, jail-
ers, constables, posse comitatus, etc. In most cases there is no free exercise
whatever of the judgment or of the moral sense; but they put themselves on
a level with wood and earth and stones; and wooden men can perhaps be
manufactured that will serve the purpose as well. Such command no more
respect than men of straw or a lump of dirt. They have the same sort of
worth only as horses and dogs. Yet such as these even are commonly esteemed good citizens. Others — as most legislators, politicians, lawyers,
ministers, and office-holders — serve the state chiefly with their heads;
and, as they rarely make any moral distinctions, they are as likely to serve
the Devil, without *intending* it, as God. A very few, as heroes, patriots,
martyrs, reformers in the great sense, and *men*, serve the state with their
consciences also, and so necessarily resist it for the most part; and they are
commonly treated as enemies by it. A wise man will only be useful as a
man, and will not submit to be "clay," and "stop a hole to keep the wind
away,"[2] but leave that office to his dust at least: —

> "I am too high-born to be propertied,
> To be a secondary at control,
> Or useful serving-man and instrument
> To any sovereign state throughout the world."[3]

He who gives himself entirely to his fellow-men appears to them useless and selfish; but he who gives himself partially to them is pronounced a
benefactor and philanthropist.

How does it become a man to behave toward this American government to-day? I answer, that he cannot without disgrace be associated with
it. I cannot for an instant recognize that political organization as *my* government which is the *slave's* government also.

All men recognize the right of revolution; that is, the right to refuse
allegiance to, and to resist, the government, when its tyranny or its ineffi-
ciency are great and unendurable. But almost all say that such is not the
case now. But such was the case, they think, in the Revolution of '75. If one

---

[1]**"Not a drum was heard. . . .":** Lines from the Irish poet Charles Wolfe's "The Burial of
Sir John Moore of Corunna." — Eds.
[2]**"clay"** and **"stop a hole . . .":** From William Shakespeare's *Hamlet* (Act V, scene i). — Eds.
[3]**"I am too high-born. . . .":** From William Shakespeare's *Hamlet* (Act V, scene ii). — Eds.

were to tell me that this was a bad government because it taxed certain foreign commodities brought to its ports, it is most probable that I should not make an ado about it, for I can do without them. All machines have their friction; and possibly this does enough good to counterbalance the evil. At any rate, it is a great evil to make a stir about it. But when the friction comes to have its machine, and oppression and robbery are organized, I say, let us not have such a machine any longer. In other words, when a sixth of the population of a nation which has undertaken to be the refuge of liberty are slaves, and a whole country is unjustly overrun and conquered by a foreign army, and subjected to military law, I think that it is not too soon for honest men to rebel and revolutionize. What makes this duty the more urgent is the fact that the country so overrun is not our own, but ours is the invading army.

Paley,[4] a common authority with many on moral questions, in his chapter on the "Duty of Submission to Civil Government," resolves all civil obligation into expediency; and he proceeds to say, "that so long as the interest of the whole society requires it, that is, so long as the established government cannot be resisted or changed without public inconveniency, it is the will of God that the established government be obeyed, and no longer. . . . This principle being admitted, the justice of every particular case of resistance is reduced to a computation of the quantity of the danger and grievance on the one side, and of the probability and expense of redressing it on the other." Of this, he says, every man shall judge for himself. But Paley appears never to have contemplated those cases to which the rule of expediency does not apply, in which a people, as well as an individual, must do justice, cost what it may. If I have unjustly wrested a plank from a drowning man, I must restore it to him though I drown myself. This, according to Paley, would be inconvenient. But he that would save his life, in such a case, shall lose it. This people must cease to hold slaves, and to make war on Mexico, though it cost them their existence as a people.

In their practice, nations agree with Paley; but does any one think that Massachusetts does exactly what is right at the present crisis?   10

> "A drab of state, a cloth-o'-silver slut,
> To have her train borne up, and her soul trail in the dirt."[5]

Practically speaking, the opponents to a reform in Massachusetts are not a hundred thousand politicians at the South, but a hundred thousand merchants and farmers here, who are more interested in commerce and agriculture than they are in humanity, and are not prepared to do justice to the slave and to Mexico, *cost what it may.* I quarrel not with far-off foes, but

---

[4]*Paley:* William Paley (1743–1805), English philosopher and clergyman and the author of *Principles of Moral and Political Philosophy* (1785). — Eds.

[5]*"A drab of state. . . .":* See Cyril Tourneur's *The Revenger's Tragedy* (1607), (Act IV, scene iv). — Eds.

with those who, near at home, coöperate with, and do the bidding of, those far away, and without whom the latter would be harmless. We are accustomed to say, that the mass of men are unprepared; but improvement is slow, because the few are not materially wiser or better than the many. It is not so important that many should be as good as you, as that there be some absolute goodness somewhere; for that will leaven the whole lump. There are thousands who are *in opinion* opposed to slavery and to the war, who yet in effect do nothing to put an end to them; who, esteeming themselves children of Washington and Franklin, sit down with their hands in their pockets, and say that they know not what to do, and do nothing; who even postpone the question of freedom to the question of free-trade, and quietly read the prices-current along with the latest advices from Mexico, after dinner, and, it may be, fall asleep over them both. What is the price-current of an honest man and patriot to-day? They hesitate, and they regret, and sometimes they petition; but they do nothing in earnest and with effect. They will wait, well disposed, for others to remedy the evil, that they may no longer have it to regret. At most, they give only a cheap vote, and a feeble countenance and Godspeed, to the right, as it goes by them. There are nine hundred and ninety-nine patrons of virtue to one virtuous man. But it is easier to deal with the real possessor of a thing than with the temporary guardian of it.

All voting is a sort of gaming, like checkers or backgammon, with a slight moral tinge to it, a playing with right and wrong, with moral questions; and betting naturally accompanies it. The character of the voters is not staked. I cast my vote, perchance, as I think right; but I am not vitally concerned that that right should prevail. I am willing to leave it to the majority. Its obligation, therefore, never exceeds that of expediency. Even voting *for the right* is *doing* nothing for it. It is only expressing to men feebly your desire that it should prevail. A wise man will not leave the right to the mercy of chance, nor wish it to prevail through the power of the majority. There is but little virtue in the action of masses of men. When the majority shall at length vote for the abolition of slavery, it will be because they are indifferent to slavery, or because there is but little slavery left to be abolished by their vote. *They* will then be the only slaves. Only *his* vote can hasten the abolition of slavery who asserts his own freedom by his vote.

I hear of a convention to be held at Baltimore, or elsewhere, for the selection of a candidate for the Presidency, made up chiefly of editors, and men who are politicians by profession; but I think, what is it to any independent, intelligent, and respectable man what decision they may come to? Shall we not have the advantage of his wisdom and honesty, nevertheless? Can we not count upon some independent votes? Are there not many individuals in the country who do not attend conventions? But no: I find that the respectable man, so called, has immediately drifted from his position, and despairs of his country, when his country has more reason to despair of him. He forthwith adopts one of the candidates thus selected as the only *available* one, thus proving that he is himself *available* for any purposes of the demagogue. His vote is of no more worth than that of any unprincipled foreigner or hireling native, who may have been bought. O for a man who is a *man,* and, as my neighbor says, has a bone in his back which you cannot pass your hand through! Our statistics are at fault: The population has been returned too large. How many *men* are there to a square thousand miles in this country? Hardly one. Does not America offer any inducement for men to settle here? The American has dwindled into an Odd Fellow, — one who may be known by the development of his organ of gregariousness, and a manifest lack of intellect and cheerful self-reliance; whose first and chief concern, on coming into the world, is to see that the Almshouses are in good repair; and, before yet he has lawfully donned the virile garb, to collect a fund for the support of the widows and orphans that may be; who, in short, ventures to live only by the aid of the Mutual Insurance company, which has promised to bury him decently.

It is not a man's duty, as a matter of course, to devote himself to the eradication of any, even the most enormous wrong; he may still properly have other concerns to engage him; but it is his duty, at least, to wash his hands of it, and, if he gives it no thought longer, not to give it practically his support. If I devote myself to other pursuits and contemplations, I must first see, at least, that I do not pursue them sitting upon another man's shoulders. I must get off him first, that he may pursue his contemplations too. See what gross inconsistency is tolerated. I have heard some of my townsmen say, "I should like to have them order me out to help put down an insurrection of the slaves, or to march to Mexico; — see if I would go"; and yet these very men have each, directly by their allegiance, and so indirectly, at least, by their money, furnished a substitute. The soldier is applauded who refuses to serve in an unjust war by those who do not refuse to sustain the unjust government which makes the war; is applauded by those whose own act and authority he disregards and sets at naught; as if the state were penitent to that degree that it hired one to scourge it while it sinned, but not to that degree that it left off sinning for a moment. Thus, under the name of Order and Civil Government, we are all made at last to pay homage to and support our own meanness. After the first blush of sin comes its indifference; and from immoral it becomes, as it were, *un*moral, and not quite unnecessary to that life which we have made.

The broadest and most prevalent error requires the most disinterested virtue to sustain it. The slight reproach to which the virtue of patriotism is commonly liable, the noble are most likely to incur. Those who, while they disapprove of the character and measures of a government, yield to it their allegiance and support are undoubtedly its most conscientious supporters, and so frequently the most serious obstacles to reform. Some are petitioning the state to dissolve the Union, to disregard the requisitions of the President. Why do they not dissolve it themselves, — the union between themselves and the state, — and refuse to pay their quota into its treasury? Do not they stand in the same relation to the state that the state does to the Union? And have not the same reasons prevented the state from resisting the Union which have prevented them from resisting the state?

How can a man be satisfied to entertain an opinion merely, and enjoy   15
it? Is there any enjoyment in it, if his opinion is that he is aggrieved? If you are cheated out of a single dollar by your neighbor, you do not rest satisfied with knowing that you are cheated, or with saying that you are cheated, or even with petitioning him to pay you your due; but you take effectual steps at once to obtain the full amount, and see that you are never cheated again. Action from principle, the perception and the performance of right, changes things and relations; it is essentially revolutionary, and does not consist wholly with anything which was. It not only divides states and churches, it divides families; ay, it divides the *individual,* separating the diabolical in him from the divine.

Unjust laws exist: Shall we be content to obey them, or shall we endeavor to amend them, and obey them until we have succeeded, or shall we transgress them at once? Men generally, under such a government as this, think that they ought to wait until they have persuaded the majority to alter them. They think that, if they should resist, the remedy would be worse than the evil. But it is the fault of the government itself that the remedy *is* worse than the evil. *It* makes it worse. Why is it not more apt to anticipate and provide for reform? Why does it not cherish its wise minority? Why does it cry and resist before it is hurt? Why does it not encourage its citizens to be on the alert to point out its fault, and *do* better than it would have them? Why does it always crucify Christ, and excommunicate Copernicus and Luther, and pronounce Washington and Franklin rebels?

One would think, that a deliberate and practical denial of its authority was the only offense never contemplated by government; else, why has it not assigned its definite, its suitable and proportionate penalty? If a man who has no property refuses but once to earn nine shillings for the state, he is put in prison for a period unlimited by any law that I know, and determined only by the discretion of those who placed him there; but if he should steal ninety times nine shillings from the state, he is soon permitted to go at large again.

If the injustice is part of the necessary friction of the machine of government, let it go, let it go: perchance it will wear smooth, — certainly the machine will wear out. If the injustice has a spring, or a pulley, or a rope, or a crank, exclusively for itself, then perhaps you may consider whether the remedy will not be worse than the evil; but if it is of such a nature that it requires you to be the agent of injustice to another, then, I say, break the law. Let your life be a counter friction to stop the machine. What I have to do is to see, at any rate, that I do not lend myself to the wrong which I condemn.

As for adopting the ways which the state has provided for remedying the evil, I know not of such ways. They take too much time, and a man's life will be gone. I have other affairs to attend to. I came into this world, not chiefly to make this a good place to live in, but to live in it, be it good or bad. A man has not everything to do, but something; and because he cannot do *everything,* it is not necessary that he should do *something* wrong. It is not my business to be petitioning the Governor or the Legislature any more than it is theirs to petition me; and if they should not hear my petition, what should I do then? But in this case the state has provided no way: its very Constitution is the evil. This may seem to be harsh and stubborn and unconciliatory; but it is to treat with the utmost kindness and consideration the only spirit that can appreciate or deserve it. So is all change for the better, like birth and death, which convulse the body.

I do not hesitate to say, that those who call themselves Abolitionists   20 should at once effectually withdraw their support, both in person and property, from the government of Massachusetts, and not wait till they constitute a majority of one, before they suffer the right to prevail through them. I think that it is enough if they have God on their side, without waiting for that other one. Moreover, any man more right than his neighbors constitutes a majority of one already.

I meet this American government, or its representative, the state government, directly, and face to face, once a year — no more — in the person of its tax-gatherer; this is the only mode in which a man situated as I am necessarily meets it; and it then says distinctly, Recognize me; and the simplest, the most effectual, and, in the present posture of affairs, the indispensablest mode of treating with it on this head, of expressing your little satisfaction with and love for it, is to deny it then. My civil neighbor, the tax-gatherer, is the very man I have to deal with, — for it is, after all, with men and not with parchment that I quarrel, — and he has voluntarily chosen to be an agent of the government. How shall he ever know well what he is and does as an officer of the government, or as a man, until he is obliged to consider whether he shall treat me, his neighbor, for whom he has respect, as a neighbor and well-disposed man, or as a maniac and disturber of the peace, and see if he can get over this obstruction to his neighborliness without a ruder and more impetuous thought or speech corresponding with his action. I know this well, that if one thousand, if one hundred, if ten men whom I could name, — if ten *honest* men only, — say if *one* HONEST man, in this State of Massachusetts, *ceasing to hold slaves,* were actually to withdraw from this copartnership, and be locked up in the county jail therefor, it would be the abolition of slavery in America. For it matters not how small the beginning may seem to be: What is once well done is done forever. But we love better to talk about it: That we say is our mission. Reform keeps many scores of newspapers in its service, but not one man. If my esteemed neighbor, the State's ambassador, who will devote his days to the settlement of the question of human rights in the Council Chamber, instead of being threatened with the prisons of Carolina, were to sit down the prisoner of Massachusetts, that State which is so anxious to foist the sin of slavery upon her sister, — though at present she can discover only an act of inhospitality to be the ground of a quarrel with her, — the Legislature would not wholly waive the subject the following winter.

Under a government which imprisons any unjustly, the true place for a just man is also a prison. The proper place to-day, the only place which Massachusetts has provided for her freer and less desponding spirits, is in her prisons, to be put out and locked out of the State by her own act, as they have already put themselves out by their principles. It is there that the fugitive slave, and the Mexican prisoner on parole, and the Indian come to plead the wrongs of his race should find them; on that separate, but more free and honorable ground, where the State places those who are not *with* her, but *against* her, — the only house in a slave State in which a free man can abide with honor. If any think that their influence would be lost there, and their voices no longer afflict the ear of the State, that they would not be as an enemy within its walls, they do not know by how much truth is stronger than error, nor how much more eloquently and effectively he can combat injustice who has experienced a little in his own person. Cast your whole vote, not a strip of paper merely, but your whole influence. A minority is powerless while it conforms to the majority; it is not even a minority then; but it is irresistible when it clogs by its whole weight. If the alternative is to keep all just men in prison, or give up war and slavery, the State will not hesitate which to choose. If a thousand men were not to pay their tax-bills this year, that would not be a violent and bloody measure, as it would be to pay them, and enable the State to commit violence and shed innocent blood. This is, in fact, the definition of a peaceable revolution, if any such is possible. If the tax- gatherer, or any other public officer, asks me, as one has done, "But what shall I do?" my answer is, "If you really wish to do anything, resign your office." When the subject has refused allegiance, and the officer has resigned his office, then the revolution is accomplished. But even suppose blood should flow. Is there not a sort of blood shed when the conscience is wounded? Through this wound a man's real manhood and immortality flow out, and he bleeds to an everlasting death. I see this blood flowing now.

I have contemplated the imprisonment of the offender, rather than the seizure of his goods, — though both will serve the same purpose, — because they who assert the purest right, and consequently are most dangerous to a corrupt State, commonly have not spent much time in accumulating property. To such the State renders comparatively small service, and a slight tax is wont to appear exorbitant, particularly if they are obliged to earn it by special labor with their hands. If there were one who lived wholly without the use of money, the State itself would hesitate to demand it of him. But the rich man — not to make any invidious comparison — is always sold to the institution which makes him rich. Absolutely speaking, the more money, the less virtue; for money comes between a man and his objects, and obtains them for him; and it was certainly no great virtue to obtain it. It puts to rest many questions which he would otherwise be taxed to answer; while the only new question which it puts is the hard but superfluous one, how to spend it. Thus his moral ground is taken from under his feet. The opportunities of living are diminished in proportion as what are called the "means" are increased. The best thing a man can do for his culture when he is rich is to endeavor to carry out those schemes which he entertained when he was poor. Christ answered the Herodians according to their condition. "Show me the tribute-money," said he; — and one took a penny out of his pocket; — if you use money which has the image of Caesar on it, which he has made current and valuable, that is, *if you are men of the State,* and gladly enjoy the advantages of Caesar's government, then pay him back some of his own when he demands it. "Render therefore to Caesar that which is Caesar's, and to God those things which are God's," — leaving them no wiser than before as to which was which; for they did not wish to know.

When I converse with the freest of my neighbors, I perceive that, whatever they may say about the magnitude and seriousness of the question, and their regard for the public tranquillity, the long and the short of the matter is, that they cannot spare the protection of the existing government, and they dread the consequences to their property and families of disobedience to it. For my own part, I should not like to think that I ever rely on the protection of the State. But, if I deny the authority of the State when it presents its tax-bill, it will soon take and waste all my property, and so harass me and my children without end. This is hard. This makes it impossible for a man to live honestly, and at the same time comfortably, in outward respects. It will not be worth the while to accumulate property; that would be sure to go again. You must hire or squat somewhere, and raise but a small crop, and eat that soon. You must live within yourself, and depend upon yourself always tucked up and ready for a start, and not have many affairs. A man may grow rich in Turkey even, if he will be in all respects a good subject of the Turkish government. Confucius said: "If a state is governed by the principles of reason, poverty and misery are subjects of shame; if a state is not governed by the principles of reason, riches and honors are the subjects of shame." No: Until I want the protection of Massachusetts to be extended to me in some distant Southern port, where my liberty is endangered, or until I am bent solely on building up an estate at home by peaceful enterprise, I can afford to refuse allegiance to Massachusetts, and her right to my property and life. It costs me less in every sense to incur the penalty of disobedience to the State than it would to obey. I should feel as if I were worth less in that case.

Some years ago, the State met me in behalf of the Church, and commanded me to pay a certain sum toward the support of a clergyman whose preaching my father attended, but never I myself. "Pay," it said, "or be locked up in the jail." I declined to pay. But, unfortunately, another man   25 saw fit to pay it. I did not see why the schoolmaster should be taxed to support the priest, and not the priest the schoolmaster; for I was not the State's schoolmaster, but I supported myself by voluntary subscription. I did not see why the lyceum should not present its tax-bill, and have the State to back its demand, as well as the Church. However, at the request of the selectmen, I condescended to make some such statement as this in writing: — "Know all men by these presents, that I, Henry Thoreau, do not wish to be regarded as a member of any incorporated society which I have not joined." This I gave to the town clerk; and he has it. The State, having thus learned that I did not wish to be regarded as a member of that church, has never made a like demand on me since; though it said that it must adhere to its original presumption that time. If I had known how to name them, I should then have signed off in detail from all the societies which I never signed on to; but I did not know where to find a complete list.

I have paid no poll-tax for six years. I was put into a jail once on this account, for one night; and, as I stood considering the walls of solid stone, two or three feet thick, the door of wood and iron, a foot thick, and the iron grating which strained the light, I could not help being struck with the foolishness of that institution which treated me as if I were mere flesh and blood and bones, to be locked up. I wondered that it should have concluded at length that this was the best use it could put me to, and had never thought to avail itself of my services in some way. I saw that, if there was a wall of stone between me and my townsmen, there was a still more difficult one to climb or break through before they could get to be as free as I was. I did not for a moment feel confined, and the walls seemed a great waste of stone and mortar. I felt as if I alone of all my townsmen had paid my tax. They plainly did not know how to treat me, but behaved like persons who are underbred. In every threat and in every compliment there was a blunder; for they thought that my chief desire was to stand the other side of that stone wall. I could not but smile to see how industriously they locked the door on my meditations, which followed them out again without let or hindrance, and *they* were really all that was dangerous. As they could not reach me, they had resolved to punish my body; just as boys, if they cannot come at some person against whom they have a spite, will abuse his dog. I saw that the State was half-witted, that it was timid as a lone woman with her silver spoons, and that it did not know its friends from its foes, and I lost all my remaining respect for it, and pitied it.

Thus the State never intentionally confronts a man's sense, intellectual or moral, but only his body, his senses. It is not armed with superior wit or honesty, but with superior physical strength. I was not born to be forced. I will breathe after my own fashion. Let us see who is the strongest. What force has a multitude? They only can force me who obey a higher law than I. They force me to become like themselves. I do not hear of *men* being *forced* to live this way or that by masses of men. What sort of life were that to live? When I meet a government which says to me, "Your money or your life," why should I be in haste to give it my money? It may be in a great strait, and not know what to do: I cannot help that. It must help itself; do as I do. It is not worth the while to snivel about it. I am not responsible for the successful working of the machinery of society. I am not the son of the engineer. I perceive that, when an acorn and a chestnut fall side by side, the one does not remain inert to make way for the other, but both obey their own laws, and spring and grow and flourish as best they can, till one, perchance, overshadows and destroys the other. If a plant cannot live according to its nature, it dies; and so a man.

The night in prison was novel and interesting enough. The prisoners in their shirt-sleeves were enjoying a chat and the evening air in the doorway, when I entered. But the jailer said, "Come, boys, it is time to lock up;" and so they dispersed, and I heard the sound of their steps returning into the hollow apartments. My room-mate was introduced to me by the jailer as "a first-rate fellow and a clever man." When the door was locked, he showed me where to hang my hat, and how he managed matters there. The rooms were whitewashed once a month; and this one, at least, was the whitest, most simply furnished, and probably the neatest apartment in the town. He naturally wanted to know where I came from, and what brought me there; and, when I had told him, I asked him in my turn how he came there, presuming him to be an honest man, of course; and, as the world goes, I believe he was. "Why," said he, "they accuse me of burning a barn; but I never did it." As near as I could discover, he had probably gone to bed in a barn when drunk, and smoked his pipe there; and so a barn was burnt. He had the reputation of being a clever man, had been there some three months waiting for his trail to come on, and would have to wait as much longer, but he was quite domesticated and contented, since he got his board for nothing, and thought that he was well treated.

He occupied one window, and I the other; and I saw that if one stayed there long, his principal business would be to look out the window. I had soon read all the tracts that were left there, and examined where former prisoners had broken out, and where a grate had been sawed off, and heard the history of the various occupants of that room; for I found that even here there was a history and a gossip which never circulated beyond the walls of the jail. Probably this is the only house in the town where verses are composed, which are afterward printed in a circular form, but not published. I was shown quite a long list of verses which were composed by some young men who had been detected in an attempt to escape, who avenged themselves by signing them.

I pumped my fellow-prisoner as dry as I could, for fear I should never   30 see him again; but at length he showed me which was my bed, and left me to blow out the lamp.

It was like traveling into a far country, such as I had never expected to behold, to lie there for one night. It seemed to me that I never had heard the town-clock strike before, nor the evening sounds of the village; for we slept with the windows open, which were inside the grating. It was to see my native village in the light of the Middle Ages, and our Concord was turned into a Rhine stream, and visions of knights and castles passed before me. They were the voices of old burghers that I heard in the streets. I was an involuntary spectator and auditor of whatever was done and said in the kitchen of the adjacent village-inn, — a wholly new and rare experience to me. It was a closer view of my native town. I was fairly inside of it. I never had seen its institutions before. This is one of its peculiar institutions; for it is a shire town. I began to comprehend what its inhabitants were about.

In the morning, our breakfasts were put through the hole in the door, in small oblong-square tin pans, made to fit, and holding a pint of chocolate, with brown bread, and an iron spoon. When they called for the vessels again, I was green enough to return what bread I had left; but my comrade seized it, and said that I should lay that up for lunch or dinner. Soon after he was let out to work at haying in a neighboring field, whither he went every day, and would not be back till noon; so he bade me good-day, saying that he doubted if he should see me again.

When I came out of prison, — for some one interfered, and paid that tax, — I did not perceive that great changes had taken place on the common, such as he observed who went in a youth and emerged a tottering and gray-headed man; and yet a change had to my eyes come over the scene, — the town, and State, and country, — greater than any that mere time could effect. I saw yet more distinctly the State in which I lived. I saw to what extent the people among whom I lived could be trusted as good neighbors and friends; that their friendship was for summer weather only; that they did not greatly propose to do right; that they were a distinct race from me by their prejudices and superstitions, as the Chinamen and Malays are; that in their sacrifices to humanity they ran no risks, not even to their property; that after all they were not so noble but they treated the thief as he had treated them, and hoped, by a certain outward observance and a few prayers, and by walking in a particular straight though useless path from time to time, to save their souls. This may be to judge my neighbors harshly; for I believe that many of them are not aware that they have such an institution as the jail in their village.

It was formerly the custom in our village, when a poor debtor came out of jail, for his acquaintances to salute him, looking through their fingers, which were crossed to represent the grating of a jail window, "How do ye do?" My neighbors did not thus salute me, but first looked at me, and then at one another, as if I had returned from a long journey. I was put into jail as I was going to the shoemaker's to get a shoe which was mended. When I was let out the next morning, I proceeded to finish my errand, and, having put on my mended shoe, joined a huckleberry party, who were impatient to put themselves under my conduct; and in half an hour, — for the horse was soon tackled, — was in the midst of a huckleberry field, on one of our highest hills, two miles off, and then the State was nowhere to be seen.

This is the whole history of "My Prisons."   35

I have never declined paying the highway tax, because I am as desirous of being a good neighbor as I am of being a bad subject; and as for supporting schools, I am doing my part to educate my fellow-countrymen now. It is for no particular item in the tax-bill that I refuse to pay it. I simply wish to refuse allegiance to the State, to withdraw and stand aloof from it effectually. I do not care to trace the course of my dollar, if I could, till it buys a man or a musket to shoot one with, — the dollar is innocent, — but I am concerned to trace the effects of my allegiance. In fact, I quietly declare war with the State, after my fashion, though I will still make what use and get what advantage of her I can, as is usual in such cases.

If others pay the tax which is demanded of me, from a sympathy with the State, they do but what they have already done in their own case, or rather they abet injustice to a greater extent than the State requires. If they pay the tax from a mistaken interest in the individual taxed, to save his property, or prevent his going to jail, it is because they have not considered wisely how far they let their private feelings interfere with the public good.

This, then, is my position at present. But one cannot be too much on his guard in such a case, lest his action be biased by obstinacy or an undue regard for the opinions of men. Let him see that he does only what belongs to himself and to the hour.

I think sometimes, Why, this people mean well, they are only ignorant; they would do better if they knew how: why give your neighbors this pain to treat you as they are not inclined to? But I think again, This is no reason why I should do as they do, or permit others to suffer much greater pain of a different kind. Again, I sometimes say to myself, When many millions of men, without heat, without ill will, without personal feeling of any kind, demand of you a few shillings only, without the possibility, such is their constitution, of retracting or altering their present demand, and without the possibility, on your side, of appeal to any other millions, why expose yourself to this overwhelming brute force? You do not resist cold and hunger, the winds and the waves, thus obstinately; you quietly submit to a thousand similar necessities. You do not put your head into the fire. But just in proportion as I regard this as not wholly a brute force, but partly a human force, and consider that I have relations to those millions as to so many millions of men, and not of mere brute or inanimate things, I see that appeal is possible, first and instantaneously, from them to the Maker of them, and, secondly, from them to themselves. But if I put my head deliberately into the fire, there is no appeal to fire or to the Maker of fire, and I have only myself to blame. If I could convince myself that I have any right to be satisfied with men as they are, and to treat them accordingly, and not accordingly, in some respects, to my requisitions and expectations of what they and I ought to be, then, like a good Mussulman and fatalist, I should endeavor to be satisfied with things as they are, and say it is the will of God. And, above all, there is this difference between resisting this and a purely brute or natural force that I can resist this with some effect; but I cannot expect, like Orpheus,[6] to change the nature of the rocks and trees and beasts.

I do not wish to quarrel with any man or nation. I do not wish to split 40 hairs, to make fine distinctions, or set myself up as better than my neighbors. I seek rather, I may say, even an excuse for conforming to the laws of the land. I am but too ready to conform to them. Indeed, I have reason to suspect myself on this head; and each year, as the tax-gatherer comes round, I find myself disposed to review the acts and position of the general and State governments, and the spirit of the people, to discover a pretext for conformity.

> "We must affect our county as our parents,
> And if at any time we alienate
> Our love or industry from doing it honor,
> We must respect effects and teach the soul
> Matter of conscience and religion,
> And not desire of rule or benefit."[7]

I believe that the State will soon be able to take all my work of this sort out of my hands, and then I shall be no better a patriot than my fellow-countrymen. Seen from a lower point of view, the Constitution, with all its faults, is very good; the law and the courts are very respectable; even this State and this American government are, in many respects, very admirable, and rare things, to be thankful for, such as a great many have described them; but seen from a point of view a little higher, they are what I have described them; seen from a higher still, and the highest, who shall say what they are, or that they are worth looking at or thinking of at all?

However, the government does not concern me much, and I shall bestow the fewest possible thoughts on it. It is not many moments that I live under a government, even in this world. If a man is thought-free, fancy-free, imagination-free, that which *is not* never for a long time appearing *to be* to him, unwise rulers or reformers cannot fatally interrupt him.

I know that most men think differently from myself; but those whose lives are by profession devoted to the study of these or kindred subjects content me as little as any. Statesmen and legislators, standing so completely within the institution, never distinctly and nakedly behold it. They speak of moving society, but have no resting-place without it. They may be men of a certain experience and discrimination, and have no doubt invented ingenious and even useful systems, for which we sincerely thank them; but all their wit and usefulness lie within certain not very wide limits.

---

[6]*Orpheus:* A legendary Greek poet and musician whose music had the power to move inanimate objects and tame wild animals. — EDS.

[7]*"We must affect. . . . ":* See *The Battle of Alcazar,* a play by George Peele (c. 1558–1598). — EDS.

They are wont to forget that the world is not governed by policy and expediency. Webster[8] never goes behind government, and so cannot speak with authority about it. His words are wisdom to those legislators who contemplate no essential reform in the existing government; but for thinkers, and those who legislate for all time, he never once glances at the subject. I know of those whose serene and wise speculations on this theme would soon reveal the limits of his mind's range and hospitality. Yet, compared with the cheap professions of most reformers, and the still cheaper wisdom and eloquence of politicians in general, his are almost the only sensible and valuable words, and we thank Heaven for him. Comparatively, he is always strong, original, and, above all, practical. Still, his quality is not wisdom, but prudence. The lawyer's truth is not Truth, but consistency or a consistent expediency. Truth is always in harmony with herself, and is not concerned chiefly to reveal the justice that may consist with wrong-doing. He well deserves to be called, as he has been called, the Defender of the Constitution. There are really no blows to be given by him but defensive ones. He is not a leader, but a follower. His leaders are the men of '87. "I have never made an effort," he says, "and never propose to make an effort; I have never countenanced an effort, and never mean to countenance an effort, to disturb the arrangement as originally made, by which the various States came into the Union." Still thinking of the sanction which the Constitution gives to slavery, he says, "Because it was a part of the original compact, — let it stand." Notwithstanding his special acuteness and ability, he is unable to take a fact out of its merely political relations, and behold it as it lies absolutely to be disposed of by the intellect, — what, for instance, it behooves a man to do here in America to-day with regard to slavery, — but ventures, or is driven, to make some such desperate answer as the following, while professing to speak absolutely, and as a private man, — from which what new and singular code of social duties might be inferred? "The manner," says he, "in which the governments of those States where slavery exists are to regulate it is for their own consideration, under their responsibility to their constituents, to the general laws of propriety, humanity, and justice, and to God. Associations formed elsewhere, springing from a feeling of humanity, or any other cause, have nothing whatever to do with it. They have never received any encouragement from me, and they never will."

They who know of no purer sources of truth, who have traced up its stream no higher, stand, and wisely stand, by the Bible and the Constitution, and drink at it there with reverence and humility; but they who behold where it comes trickling into this lake or that pool, gird up their loins once more, and continue their pilgrimage toward its fountain-head.

No man with a genius for legislation has appeared in America. They

---

[8]*Daniel Webster:* Daniel Webster (1782–1852), a distinguished American lawyer, politician, and orator. — Eds.

are rare in the history of the world. There are orators, politicians, and eloquent men, by the thousand; but the speaker has not yet opened his mouth to speak who is capable of settling the much-vexed questions of the day. We love eloquence for its own sake, and not for any truth which it may utter, or any heroism it may inspire. Our legislators have not yet learned the comparative value of free-trade and of freedom, of union, and of rectitude, to a nation. They have no genius or talent for comparatively humble questions of taxation and finance, commerce and manufactures and agriculture. If we were left solely to the wordy wit of legislators in Congress for our guidance, uncorrected by the seasonable experience and the effectual complaints of the people, America would not long retain her rank among the nations. For eighteen hundred years, though perchance I have no right to say it, the New Testament has been written; yet where is the legislator who has wisdom and practical talent enough to avail himself of the light which it sheds on the science of legislation?

The authority of government, even such as I am willing to submit   45
to, — for I will cheerfully obey those who know and can do better than I, and in many things even those who neither know nor can do so well, — is still an impure one: to be strictly just, it must have the sanction and consent of the governed. It can have no pure right over my person and property but what I concede to it. The progress from an absolute to a limited monarchy, from a limited monarchy to a democracy, is a progress toward a true respect for the individual. Even the Chinese philosopher was wise enough to regard the individual as the basis of the empire. Is a democracy, such as we know it, the last improvement possible in government? Is it not possible to take a further step towards recognizing and organizing the rights of man? There will never be a really free and enlightened State until the State comes to recognize the individual as a higher and independent power, from which all its own power and authority are derived, and treats him accordingly. I please myself with imagining a State at last which can afford to be just to all men, and to treat the individual with respect as a neighbor; which even would not think it inconsistent with its own repose if a few were to live aloof from it, not meddling with it, nor embraced by it, who fulfilled all the duties of neighbors and fellow-men. A State which bore this kind of fruit, and suffered it to drop off as fast as it ripened, would prepare the way for a still more perfect and glorious State, which also I have imagined, but not yet anywhere seen.

1849

The Reader's Presence

1. Thoreau originally delivered these remarks as a lecture entitled "The Relation of the Individual to the State," and first printed them under the title "Resistance to Civil Government." (The Title "Civil Disobedience" first appeared in posthumous printings.)

Compare and contrast these titles. Which do you think best expresses the overall purpose of his essay? Why? Where in the text does Thoreau most directly state his purpose? To whom are his remarks addressed? Point to specific words and phrases to verify your response.

2. Thoreau builds his argument on two assertions: "That government is best which governs not at all" and that "Government is at best but an expedient." Prepare a list of the examples he presents to clarify and support these assertions. Comment on the effectiveness of these examples. What does he establish as the moral arbiter of his actions? Summarize his argument against paying taxes. What does he mean when he says that an "honest man" must "withdraw from this co-partnership?" How would Thoreau respond to the allegation that his remarks are a recipe for anarchy? In this respect, pay special attention to the final few paragraphs. What argument does he mount there to resist such notions?

3. Thoreau's remarks have had a far-reaching impact on twentieth-century political thought and action, and especially on the principles and practices of such prominent voices in the struggle for freedom as Mahatma Gandhi and the Reverend Martin Luther King, Jr. What is there about Thoreau's fierce individualism that has influenced so many later social and moral activists?

4. In addition to the substantive points he makes, what features can you identify as the hallmarks of Thoreau's individualistic prose style? What evidence might you point to in "Civil Disobedience" to illustrate Thoreau's definition of the art of writing (articulated in his journal entry for August 22, 1851): "Sentences which suggest far more than they say, which have an atmosphere about them, which do not merely report an old, but make a new impression, sentences which suggest as many things and are as durable as a Roman aqueduct: to frame these, that is the *art* of writing."

77 ────────────────────

Cornel West

Race Matters

> Since the beginning of the nation, white Americans have suffered
> from a deep inner uncertainty as to who they really are. One of the
> ways that has been used to simplify the answer has been to seize
> upon the presence of black Americans and use them as a marker, a
> symbol of limits, a metaphor for the "outsider." Many whites could
> look at the social position of blacks and feel that color formed an
> easy and reliable gauge for determining to what extent one was or
> was not American. Perhaps that is why one of the first epithets that
> many European immigrants learned when they got off the boat was
> the term "nigger" — it made them feel instantly American. But this is
> tricky magic. Despite his racial difference and social status, some-
> thing indisputably American about Negroes not only raised doubts
> about the white man's value system but aroused the troubling suspi-
> cion that whatever else the true American is, he is also somehow
> black.
>
>   – *RALPH ELLISON,* "What America Would
>   Be Like without Blacks" (1970)

What happened in Los Angeles in April of 1992 was neither a race riot
nor a class rebellion. Rather, this monumental upheaval was a multiracial,
trans-class, and largely male display of justified social rage. For all its ugly,
xenophobic resentment, its air of adolescent carnival, and its downright
barbaric behavior, it signified the sense of powerlessness in American society. Glib attempts to reduce its meaning to the pathologies of the black
underclass, the criminal actions of hoodlums, or the political revolt of the
oppressed urban masses miss the mark. Of those arrested, only 36 percent
were black, more than a third had full-time jobs, and most claimed to shun
political affiliation. What we witnessed in Los Angeles was the consequence of a lethal linkage of economic decline, cultural decay, and political

For biographical information on Cornel West, see p. 667.

lethargy in American life. Race was the visible catalyst, not the underlying cause.

The meaning of the earthshaking events in Los Angeles is difficult to grasp because most of us remain trapped in the narrow framework of the dominant liberal and conservative views of race in America, which with its worn-out vocabulary leaves us intellectually debilitated, morally disempowered, and personally depressed. The astonishing disappearance of the event from public dialogue is testimony to just how painful and distressing a serious engagement with race is. Our truncated public discussions of race suppress the best of who and what we are as a people because they fail to confront the complexity of the issue in a candid and critical manner. The predictable pitting of liberals against conservatives, Great Society Democrats against self-help Republicans, reinforces intellectual parochialism and political paralysis.

The liberal notion that more government programs can solve racial problems is simplistic — precisely because it focuses *solely* on the economic dimension. And the conservative idea that what is needed is a change in the moral behavior of poor black urban dwellers (especially poor black men, who, they say, should stay married, support their children, and stop committing so much crime) highlights immoral actions while ignoring public responsibility for the immoral circumstances that haunt our fellow citizens.

The common denominator of these views of race is that each still sees black people as a "problem people," in the words of Dorothy I. Height, president of the National Council of Negro Women, rather than as fellow American citizens with problems. Her words echo the poignant "unasked question" of W. E. B. Du Bois, who, in *The Souls of Black Folk* (1903), wrote:

> They approach me in a half-hesitant sort of way, eye me curiously or compassionately, and then instead of saying directly, How does it feel to be a problem? they say, I know an excellent colored man in my town. . . . Do not these Southern outrages make your blood boil? At these I smile, or am interested, or reduce the boiling to a simmer, as the occasion may require. To the real question, How does it feel to be a problem? I answer seldom a word.

Nearly a century later, we confine discussions about race in America to the "problems" black people pose for whites rather than consider what this way of viewing black people reveals about us as a nation.

This paralyzing framework encourages liberals to relieve their guilty 5 consciences by supporting public funds directed at "the problems"; but at the same time, reluctant to exercise principled criticism of black people, liberals deny them the freedom to err. Similarly, conservatives blame the "problems" on black people themselves — and thereby render black social misery invisible or unworthy of public attention.

Hence, for liberals, black people are to be "included" and "integrated" into "our" society and culture, while for conservatives they are to be "well behaved" and "worthy of acceptance" by "our" way of life. Both fail to see that the presence and predicaments of black people are neither additions to nor defections from American life, but rather *constitutive elements of that life*.

To engage in a serious discussion of race in America, we must begin not with the problems of black people but with the flaws of American society — flaws rooted in historic inequalities and longstanding cultural stereotypes. How we set up the terms for discussing racial issues shapes our perception and response to these issues. As long as black people are viewed as a "them," the burden falls on blacks to do all the "cultural" and "moral" work necessary for healthy race relations. The implication is that only certain Americans can define what it means to be American — and the rest must simply "fit in."

The emergence of strong black-nationalist sentiments among blacks, especially among young people, is a revolt against this sense of having to "fit in." The variety of black-nationalist ideologies, from the moderate views of Supreme Court Justice Clarence Thomas in his youth to those of Louis Farrakhan today, rest upon a fundamental truth: White America has been historically weak-willed in ensuring racial justice and has continued to resist fully accepting the humanity of blacks. As long as double standards and differential treatment abound — as long as the rap performer Ice-T is harshly condemned while former Los Angeles Police Chief Daryl F. Gates's antiblack comments are received in polite silence, as long as Dr. Leonard Jeffries's anti-Semitic statements are met with vitriolic outrage while presidential candidate Patrick J. Buchanan's anti-Semitism receives a genteel response — black nationalisms will thrive.

Afrocentrism, a contemporary species of black nationalism, is a gallant yet misguided attempt to define an African identity in a white society perceived to be hostile. It is gallant because it puts black doings and sufferings, not white anxieties and fears, at the center of discussion. It is misguided because — out of fear of cultural hybridization and through silence on the issue of class, retrograde views on black women, gay men, and lesbians, and a reluctance to link race to the common good — it reinforces the narrow discussions about race.

To establish a new framework, we need to begin with a frank acknowl- 10 edgment of the basic humanness and Americanness of each of us. And we must acknowledge that as a people — *E Pluribus Unum* — we are on a slippery slope toward economic strife, social turmoil, and cultural chaos. If we go down, we go down together. The Los Angeles upheaval forced us to see not only that we are not connected in ways we would like to be but also, in a more profound sense, that this failure to connect binds us even more tightly together. The paradox of race in America is that our common destiny is more pronounced and imperiled precisely when our divisions are deeper. The Civil War and its legacy speak loudly here. And our divisions are growing deeper. Today, eighty-six percent of white suburban Americans live in neighborhoods that are less than one percent black, meaning that the prospects for the country depend largely on how its cities fare in the hands of a suburban electorate. There is no escape from our interracial interdependence, yet enforced racial hierarchy dooms us as a nation to collective paranoia and hysteria — the unmaking of any democratic order.

The verdict in the Rodney King case which sparked the incidents in Los Angeles was perceived to be wrong by the vast majority of Americans. But whites have often failed to acknowledge the widespread mistreatment of black people, especially black men, by law enforcement agencies, which helped ignite the spark. The verdict was merely the occasion for deep-seated rage to come to the surface. This rage is fed by the "silent" depression ravaging the country — in which real weekly wages of all American workers since 1973 have declined nearly twenty percent, while at the same time wealth has been upwardly distributed.

The exodus of stable industrial jobs from urban centers to cheaper labor markets here and abroad, housing policies that have created "chocolate cities and vanilla suburbs" (to use the popular musical artist George Clinton's memorable phrase), white fear of black crime, and the urban influx of poor Spanish-speaking and Asian immigrants — all have helped erode the tax base of American cities just as the federal government has cut its supports and programs. The result is unemployment, hunger, homelessness, and sickness for millions.

And a pervasive spiritual impoverishment grows. The collapse of meaning in life — the eclipse of hope and absence of love of self and others, the breakdown of family and neighborhood bonds — leads to the social deracination and cultural denudement of urban dwellers, especially children. We have created rootless, dangling people with little link to the supportive networks — family, friends, school — that sustain some sense of purpose in life. We have witnessed the collapse of the spiritual communities that in the past helped Americans face despair, disease, and death and that transmit through the generations dignity and decency, excellence and elegance.

The result is lives of what we might call "random nows," of fortuitous and fleeting moments preoccupied with "getting over" — with acquiring pleasure, property, and power by any means necessary. (This is not what Malcolm X meant by this famous phrase.) Post-modern culture is more and more a market culture dominated by gangster mentalities and self-destructive wantonness. This culture engulfs all of us — yet its impact on the disadvantaged is devastating, resulting in extreme violence in everyday life. Sexual violence against women and homicidal assaults by young black men on one another are only the most obvious signs of this empty quest for pleasure, property, and power.

Last, this rage is fueled by a political atmosphere in which images, not 15 ideas, dominate, where politicians spend more time raising money than debating issues. The functions of parties have been displaced by public polls, and politicians behave less as thermostats that determine the climate of opinion than as thermometers registering the public mood. American politics has been rocked by an unleashing of greed among opportunistic public officials — who have followed the lead of their counterparts in the private sphere, where, as of 1989, one percent of the population owned thirty-seven percent of the wealth and ten percent of the population owned eighty-six percent of the wealth — leading to a profound cynicism and pessimism among the citizenry.

And given the way in which the Republican Party since 1968 has appealed to popular xenophobic images — playing the black, female, and homophobic cards to realign the electorate along race, sex, and sexual-orientation lines — it is no surprise that the notion that we are all part of one garment of destiny is discredited. Appeals to special interests rather than to public interests reinforce this polarization. The Los Angeles upheaval was an expression of utter fragmentation by a powerless citizenry that includes not just the poor but all of us.

What is to be done? How do we capture a new spirit and vision to meet the challenges of the post-industrial city, post-modern culture, and post-party politics?

First, we must admit that the most valuable sources for help, hope, and power consist of ourselves and our common history. As in the ages of Lincoln, Roosevelt, and King, we must look to new frameworks and languages to understand our multilayered crisis and overcome our deep malaise.

Second, we must focus our attention on the public square — the common good that undergirds our national and global destinies. The vitality of any public square ultimately depends on how much we *care* about the quality of our lives together. The neglect of our public infrastructure, for example — our water and sewage systems, bridges, tunnels, highways, subways, and streets — reflects not only our myopic economic policies, which impede productivity, but also the low priority we place on our common life.

The tragic plight of our children clearly reveals our deep disregard for   20
public well-being. About one out of every five children in this country lives in poverty, including one out of every two black children and two out of every five Hispanic children. Most of our children — neglected by overburdened parents and bombarded by the market values of profit-hungry corporations — are ill-equipped to live lives of spiritual and cultural quality. Faced with these facts, how do we expect ever to constitute a vibrant society?

One essential step is some form of large-scale public intervention to ensure access to basic social goods — housing, food, health care, education, child care, and jobs. We must invigorate the common good with a mixture of government, business, and labor that does not follow any existing blueprint. After a period in which the private sphere has been sacralized and the public square gutted, the temptation is to make a fetish of the public square. We need to resist such dogmatic swings.

Last, the major challenge is to meet the need to generate new leadership. The paucity of courageous leaders — so apparent in the response to the events in Los Angeles — requires that we look beyond the same elites and voices that recycle the older frameworks. We need leaders — neither saints nor sparkling television personalities — who can situate themselves within a larger historical narrative of this country and our world, who can grasp the complex dynamics of our peoplehood and imagine a future grounded in the best of our past, yet who are attuned to the frightening obstacles that now perplex us. Our ideals of freedom, democracy, and equality must be invoked to invigorate all of us, especially the landless, propertyless, and luckless. Only a visionary leadership that can motivate "the better angels of our nature," as Lincoln said, and activate possibilities for a freer, more efficient, and stable America — only that leadership deserves cultivation and support.

This new leadership must be grounded in grass-roots organizing that highlights democratic accountability. Whoever *our* leaders will be as we approach the twenty-first century, their challenge will be to help Americans determine whether a genuine multiracial democracy can be created and sustained in an era of global economy and a moment of xenophobic frenzy.

Let us hope and pray that the vast intelligence, imagination, humor, and courage of Americans will not fail us. Either we learn a new language of empathy and compassion, or the fire this time will consume us all.

1993

The Reader's Presence

1. Toward what end has Cornel West written this essay? What is the thesis upon which he builds his argument? Characterize the structure of his essay. Outline the movement from one section to the next. Comment on the effectiveness of his decision to frame his essay with a discussion of what he calls "the earthshaking events" in Los Angeles in April 1992. Summarize briefly the major steps that he proposes that Americans ought to take in creating "a genuine multiracial democracy." What role, for example, does he envision for "liberals" and "conservatives" to play in the reconstitution of American equality?

2. West's essay is, in many respects, about the limitations of specific frames of reference and points of view in dealing with contemporary American experience, and especially in responding to the issue of race. When — and how — does he demonstrate the narrowness of the frameworks of "the dominant liberal and conserva-

tive views of race in America"? What explanation does he offer for why these discussions of race are "truncated"? What is the "common denominator" of these views of race? What specific strategies does he present for transcending the limits of such points of view?

3. Identify West's own point of view and characterize his presence in this essay. Consider, for example, the first two sentences of his essay, where he declares: "What happened in Los Angeles in April of 1992 was neither a race riot nor a class rebellion. Rather, this monumental upheaval was a multiracial, trans-class, and largely male display of justified social rage." How does he clarify and support his assertion that the events there were "justified"? To what extent does he anticipate opposing points of view in building his case for why such actions were justified? How successfully does he respond to each of those arguments? What does he see as "the paradox of race in America"? How would you describe the vision of society that West constructs? What models and sources does he draw on in articulating a clear sense of that vision?

78

Joy Williams

The Killing Game

Death and suffering are a big part of hunting. A big part. Not that you'd ever know it by hearing hunters talk. They tend to downplay the killing part. To kill is to put to death, extinguish, nullify, cancel, destroy. But from the hunter's point of view, it's just a tiny part of the experience. *The kill is the least important part of the hunt*, they often say, or, *Killing involves only a split second of the innumerable hours we spend surrounded by and observing nature* . . . For the animal, of course, the killing part is of considerably more importance. José Ortega y Gasset, in *Meditations on Hunting*, wrote, *Death is a sign of reality in hunting. One does not hunt in order to kill; on the contrary, one kills in order to have hunted.* This is the sort of intellectual blather that the "thinking" hunter holds dear. The conservation editor of *Field & Stream*, George Reiger, recently paraphrased this sentiment by saying, *We kill to hunt, and not the other way around*, thereby making it truly fatuous. A hunter in West Virginia, one Mr. Bill

For biographical information on Joy Williams, see p. 668.

Neal, blazed through this philosophical fog by explaining why he blows the toes off tree raccoons so that they will fall down and be torn apart by his dogs. *That's the best part of it. It's not any fun just shooting them.*

Instead of monitoring animals — many animals in managed areas are tagged, tattooed, and wear radio transmitters — wildlife managers should start hanging telemetry gear around hunters' necks to study their attitudes and listen to their conversations. It would be grisly listening, but it would tune out for good the *suffering as sacrament* and *spiritual experience* blather that some hunting apologists employ. *The unease with which the good hunter inflicts death is an unease not merely with his conscience but with affirming his animality in the midst of his struggles toward humanity and clarity,* Holmes Rolston III drones on in his book *Environmental Ethics.*

There is a formula to this in literature — someone the protagonist loves has just died, so he goes out and kills an animal. This makes him feel better. But it's kind of a sad feeling-better. He gets to relate to Death and Nature in this way. Somewhat. But not really. Death is still a mystery. Well, it's hard to explain. It's sort of a semireligious thing . . . Killing and affirming, affirming and killing, it's just the cross the "good" hunter must bear. The bad hunter just has to deal with postkill letdown.

Many are the hunter's specious arguments. Less semireligious but a long-standing favorite with them is the vegetarian approach: You eat meat, don't you? If you say no, they feel they've got you — you're just a vegetarian attempting to impose your weird views on others. If you say yes, they accuse you of being hypocritical, of allowing your genial A&P butcher to stand between you and reality. The fact is, the chief attraction of hunting is the pursuit and murder of animals — the meat-eating aspect of it is trivial. If the hunter chooses to be *ethical* about it, he might cook his kill, but the meat of most animals is discarded. Dead bear can even be dangerous! A bear's heavy hide must be skinned at once to prevent meat spoilage. With effort, a hunter can make okay chili, *something to keep in mind,* a sports rag says, *if you take two skinny spring bears.*

As for subsistence hunting, please . . . Granted that there might be one   5 "good" hunter out there who conducts the kill as spiritual exercise and two others who are atavistic enough to want to supplement their Chicken Mc-Nuggets with venison, most hunters hunt for the hell of it.

For hunters, hunting is fun. Recreation is play. Hunting is recreation. Hunters kill for play, for entertainment. They kill for the thrill of it, to make an animal "theirs." (The Gandhian doctrine of nonpossession has never been a big hit with hunters.) The animal becomes the property of the hunter by its death. Alive, the beast belongs only to itself. This is unacceptable to the hunter. *He's yours . . . He's mine . . . I decided to . . . I decided not to . . . I debated shooting it, then I decided to let it live . . .* Hunters like beautiful creatures. A "beautiful" deer, elk, bear, cougar, bighorn sheep. A "beautiful" goose or mallard. Of course, they don't stay "beautiful" for long, particularly the birds. Many birds become rags in the air, shredded, blown to bits. *Keep shooting till they drop!* Hunters get a thrill out of see-ing a plummeting bird, out of seeing it crumple and fall. *The big pheasant folded in classic fashion.* They get a kick out of "collecting" new species. *Why not add a unique harlequin duck to your collection?* Swan hunting is satisfying. *I let loose a three-inch Magnum. The large bird only flinched with my first shot and began to gain altitude. I frantically ejected the round, chambered another, and dropped the swan with my second shot. After retrieving the bird I was amazed by its size. The swan's six-foot wing-span, huge body, and long neck made it an impressive trophy.* Hunters like big animals, trophy animals. A "trophy" usually means that the hunter doesn't deign to eat it. Maybe he skins it or mounts it. Maybe he takes a picture. *We took pictures, we took pictures.* Maybe he just looks at it for a while. The disposition of the "experience" is up to the hunter. He's entitled to do whatever he wishes with the damn thing. It's dead.

Hunters like categories they can tailor to their needs. There are the "good" animals — deer, elk, bear, moose — which are allowed to exist for the hunter's pleasure. Then there are the "bad" animals, the vermin, var-mints, and "nuisance" animals, the rabbits and raccoons and coyotes and beavers and badgers, which are disencouraged to exist. The hunter can have fun killing them, but the pleasure is diminished because the animals aren't "magnificent."

Then there are the predators. These can be killed any time, because, hunters argue, they 're predators, for godsakes.

Many people in South Dakota want to exterminate the red fox because it preys upon some of the ducks and pheasant they want to hunt and kill each year. They found that after they killed the wolves and coyotes, they had more foxes than they wanted. The ring-necked pheasant is South Dakota's state bird. No matter that it was imported from Asia specifically to be "harvested" for sport, it's South Dakota's state bird and they're proud of it. A group called Pheasants Unlimited gave some tips on how to hunt foxes. *Place a small amount of larvicide* [a grain fumigant] *on a rag and chuck it down the hole . . . The first pup generally comes out in fifteen minutes . . . Use a .22 to dispatch him . . . Remove each pup shot from the hole. Following gassing, set traps for the old fox who will return later in the evening . . .* Poisoning, shooting, trapping — they make up a sort of sportsman's triathlon.

In the hunting magazines, hunters freely admit the pleasure of killing to one another. *Undeniable pleasure radiated from her smile. The excite-ment of shooting the bear had Barb talking a mile a minute.* But in public, most hunters are becoming a little wary about raving on as to how much fun it is to kill things. Hunters have a tendency to call large animals by cute names — "bruins" and "muleys," "berry-fed blackies" and "handsome cusses" and "big guys," thereby implying a balanced jolly game of mutual satisfaction between the hunter and the hunted — *Bam, bam, bam, I get to shoot you and you get to be dead.* More often, though, when dealing with

10

the nonhunting public, a drier, businesslike tone is employed. Animals become a "resource" that must be "utilized." Hunting becomes "a legitimate use of the resource." Animals become a product like wool or lumber or a crop like fruit or corn that must be "collected" or "taken" or "harvested." Hunters love to use the word *legitimate*. (Oddly, Tolstoy referred to hunting as "evil legitimized.") *A legitimate use, a legitimate form of recreation, a legitimate escape, a legitimate pursuit.* It's a word they trust will slam the door on discourse. Hunters are increasingly relying upon their spokesmen and supporters, state and federal game managers and wildlife officials, to employ the drone of a solemn bureaucratic language and toss around a lot of questionable statistics to assure the nonhunting public (93 percent!) that there's nothing to worry about. The pogrom is under control. The mass murder and manipulation of wild animals is just another business. Hunters are a tiny minority, and it's crucial to them that the millions of people who don't hunt not be awakened from their long sleep and become antihunting. Nonhunters are okay. Dweeby, probably, but okay. A hunter *can respect the rights* of a nonhunter. It's the "antis" he despises, those *misguided, emotional, not-in-possession-of-the-facts, uninformed zealots who don't understand nature . . . Those dime-store ecologists cloaked in ignorance and spurred by emotion . . . Those doggy-woggy types, who under the guise of being environmentalists and conservationists are working to deprive him of his precious right to kill.* (Sometimes it's just a *right;* sometimes it's a *God-given* right.) Antis can be scorned, but nonhunters must be pacified, and this is where the number crunching of wildlife biologists and the scripts of *professional resource managers* come in. Leave it to the professionals. They know what numbers are the good numbers. Utah determined that there were six hundred sandhill cranes in the state, so permits were issued to shoot one hundred of them. Don't want to have too many sandhill cranes. California wildlife officials reported "sufficient numbers" of mountain lions to "justify" renewed hunting, even though it doesn't take a rocket scientist to know the animal is extremely rare. (It's always a dark day for hunters when an animal is adjudged *rare*. How can its numbers be "controlled" through hunting if it scarcely exists?) A recent citizens' referendum prohibits the hunting of the mountain lion in perpetuity — not that the lions aren't killed anyway, in California and all over the West, hundreds of them annually by the government as part of the scandalous Animal Damage Control Program. Oh, to be the lucky hunter who gets to be an official government hunter and can legitimately kill animals his buddies aren't supposed to! Montana officials, led by K. L. Cool, that state's wildlife director, have definite ideas on the number of buffalo they feel can be tolerated. Zero is the number. Yellowstone National Park is the only place in America where bison exist, having been annihilated everywhere else. In the winter of 1988, nearly six hundred buffalo wandered out of the north boundary of the park and into Montana, where they were immediately shot at point-blank range by lottery-winning hunters. It was easy. And it was obvious from a video taken on one of the blow-away-the-bison days that the hunters had a heck of a good time. The buffalo, Cool says, threaten ranchers' livelihoods by doing damage to property — by which he means, I guess, that they eat the grass. Montana wants zero buffalo; it also wants zero wolves.

Large predators — including grizzlies, cougars, and wolves — are often the most "beautiful," the smartest and wildest animals of all. The gray wolf is both a supreme predator and an endangered species, and since the Supreme Court recently affirmed that ranchers have no constitutional right to kill endangered predators — apparently some God-given rights are not constitutional ones — this makes the wolf a more or less lucky dog. But not for long. A small population of gray wolves has recently established itself in northwestern Montana, primarily in Glacier National Park, and there is a plan, long a dream of conservationists, to "reintroduce" the wolf to Yellowstone. But to please ranchers and hunters, part of the plan would involve immediately removing the wolf from the endangered-species list. Beyond the park's boundaries, he could be hunted as a "game animal" or exterminated as a "pest." (Hunters kill to hunt, remember, except when they're hunting to kill.) The area of Yellowstone where the wolf would be restored is the same mountain and high-plateau country that is abandoned in winter by most animals, including the aforementioned luckless bison. Part of the plan, too, is compensation to ranchers if any of their far-ranging livestock is killed by a wolf. It's a real industry out there, apparently, killing and controlling and getting compensated for losing something under the Big Sky.

Wolves gotta eat — a fact that disturbs hunters. Jack Atcheson, an outfitter in Butte, said, *Some wolves are fine if there is control. But there never will be control. The wolf-control plan provided by the Fish and Wildlife Service speaks only of protecting domestic livestock. There is no plan to protect wildlife . . . There are no surplus deer or elk in Montana . . . There numbers are carefully managed. With uncontrolled wolf populations, a lot of people will have to give up hunting just to feed wolves. Will you give up your elk permit for a wolf?*

It won't be long before hunters start demanding compensation for animals they aren't able to shoot.

Hunters believe that wild animals exist only to satisfy their wish to kill them. And it's so easy to kill them! The weaponry available is staggering, and the equipment and gear limitless. *The demand for big boomers has never been greater than right now,* Outdoor Life *crows, and the makers of rifles and cartridges are responding to the craze with a variety of light artillery that is virtually unprecedented in the history of sporting arms . . .* Hunters use grossly overpowered shotguns and rifles and compound bows. They rely on four-wheel-drive vehicles and three-wheel ATVs and airplanes . . . *He was interesting, the only moving, living creature on that limitless white expanse. I slipped a cartridge into the barrel of my rifle and threw the safety off . . .* They use snowmobiles to run down elk, and dogs to run down and tree cougars. It's easy to shoot an animal out of a tree. It's virtually impossible to miss a moose, a conspicuous and placid animal of steady habits ... *I took a deep breath and pulled the trigger. The bull dropped. I looked at my watch: 8:22. The big guy was early. Mike started whooping and hollering and I joined him. I never realized how big a moose was until this one was on the ground. We took pictures* ... Hunters shoot animals when they're resting ... *Mike selected a deer, settled down to a steady rest, and fired. The buck was his when he squeezed the trigger. John decided to take the other buck, which had jumped up to its feet. The deer hadn't seen us and was confused by the shot echoing about in the valley. John took careful aim, fired, and took the buck. The hunt was over* ... And they shoot them when they're eating ... *The bruin ambled up the stream, checking gravel bars and backwaters for fish. Finally he plopped down on the bank to eat. Quickly, I tiptoed into range* ... They use decoys and calls ... *The six point gave me a cold-eyed glare from ninety steps away. I hit him with a 130-grain Sierra boat-tail handload. The bull went down hard. Our hunt was over* ... They use sex lures ... *The big buck raised its nose to the air, curled back its lips, and tested the scent of the doe's urine. I held my breath, fought back the shivers, and jerked off a shot. The 180-grain spire-point bullet caught the buck high on the back behind the shoulder and put it down. It didn't get up* ... They use walkie-talkies, binoculars, scopes ... *With my 308 Browning BLR, I steadied the 9X cross hairs on the front of the bear's massive shoulders and squeezed. The bear cartwheeled backward for fifty yards* ... *The second Federal Premium 165-grain bullet found its mark. Another shot anchored the bear for good* ... They bait deer with corn. They spread popcorn on golf courses for Canada geese and they douse meat baits with fry grease and honey for bears ... *Make the baiting site redolent of inner-city doughnut shops.* They use blinds and tree stands and mobile stands. They go out in groups, in gangs, and employ "pushes" and "drives." So many methods are effective. So few rules apply. It's fun! ... *We kept on repelling the swarms of birds as they came in looking for shelter from that big ocean wind, emptying our shell belts* ... A species can, in the vernacular, be *pressured by hunting* (which means that killing them has decimated them), but that just increases the fun, the *challenge.* There is practically no criticism of conduct within the ranks ... *It's mostly a matter of opinion and how hunters have been brought up to hunt* ... Although a recent editorial in *Ducks Unlimited* magazine did venture to primly suggest that one should *not fall victim to greed-induced stress through piggish competition with others.*

But hunters are piggy. They just can't seem to help it. They're over- 15 equipped ... insatiable, malevolent, and vain. They maim and mutilate and despoil. And for the most part, they're inept. Grossly inept.

Camouflaged toilet paper is a must for the modern hunter, along with his Bronco and his beer. Too many hunters taking a dump in the woods with their roll of Charmin beside them were mistaken for white-tailed deer and shot. Hunters get excited. They'll shoot anything — the pallid ass of another sportsman or even themselves. A Long Island man died last year when his shotgun went off as he clubbed a wounded deer with the butt. Hunters get mad. They get restless and want to fire! They want to use those assault rifles and see foamy blood on the ferns. Wounded animals can travel for miles in fear and pain before they collapse. Countless gut-shot deer — *if you hear a sudden, squashy thump, the animal has probably been hit in the abdomen* — are "lost" each year. "Poorly placed shots" are frequent, and injured animals are seldom tracked, because most hunters never learned how to track. The majority of hunters will shoot at anything with four legs during deer season and anything with wings during duck season. Hunters try to nail running animals and distant birds. They become so overeager, so *aroused*, that they misidentify and misjudge, spraying their "game" with shots but failing to bring it down.

The fact is, hunters' lack of skill is a big, big problem. And nowhere is the problem worse than in the new glamour recreation, bow hunting. These guys are elitists. They doll themselves up in camouflage, paint their faces black, and climb up into tree stands from which they attempt the penetration of deer, elk, and turkeys with modern, multiblade, broadhead arrows shot from sophisticated, easy-to-draw compound bows. This "primitive" way of hunting appeals to many, and even the nonhunter may feel that it's a "fairer" method, requiring more strength and skill, but bow hunting is the cruelest, most wanton form of wildlife disposal of all. Studies conducted by state fish and wildlife departments repeatedly show that bow hunters wound and fail to retrieve as many animals as they kill. An animal that flees, wounded by an arrow, will most assuredly die of the wound, but it will be days before he does. Even with a "good" hit, the time elapsed between the strike and death is exceedingly long. *The rule of thumb has long been that we should wait thirty to forty-five minutes on heart and lung hits, an hour or more on a suspected liver hit, eight to twelve hours on paunch hits, and that we should follow immediately on hindquarter and other muscle-only hits, to keep the wound open and bleeding,* is the advice in the magazine *Fins and Feathers*. What the hunter does as he hangs around waiting for his animal to finish with its terrified running and dying hasn't been studied — maybe he puts on more makeup, maybe he has a highball.

Wildlife agencies promote and encourage bow hunting by permitting earlier and longer seasons, even though they are well aware that, in their words, *crippling is a by-product of the sport*, making archers pretty sloppy for elitists. The broadhead arrow is a very inefficient killing tool. Bow hunters are trying to deal with this problem with the suggestion that they use poison pods. These poisoned arrows are illegal in all states except Mississippi (*Ah'm gonna get ma deer even if ah just nick the little bastard*), but they're widely used anyway. You wouldn't want that deer to suffer, would you?

The mystique of the efficacy and decency of the bow hunter is as much an illusion as the perception that a waterfowler is a refined and thoughtful fellow, a *romantic aesthete,* as Vance Bourjaily put it, equipped with his faithful Labs and a love for solitude and wild places. More sentimental drivel has been written about bird shooting than any other type of hunting. It's a soul-wrenching pursuit, apparently, the execution of birds in flight. Ducks Unlimited — an organization that has managed to put a spin on the word *conservation* for years — works hard to project the idea that duck hunters are blue bloods and that duck stamps with their pretty pictures are responsible for saving all the saved puddles in North America. *Sportsman's conservation* is a contradiction in terms (We protect things now so that we can kill them later) and is broadly interpreted (Don't kill them all, just kill most of them). A hunter is a conservationist in the same way a farmer or a rancher is: He's not. Like the rancher who kills everything that's not stock on his (and the public's) land, and the farmer who scorns wildlife because "they don't pay their freight," the hunter uses nature by destroying its parts, mastering it by simplifying it through death.

George ("We kill to hunt and not the other way around") Reiger, the   20
conservationist-hunter's spokesman (he's the best they've got, apparently), said that the "dedicated" waterfowler will shoot other game "of course," but *we do so much in the same spirit of the lyrics, that when we're not near the girl we love, we love the girl we're near.* (Duck hunters practice tough love.) The fact is, far from being a "romantic aesthete," the waterfowler is the most avaricious of all hunters ... *That's when Scott suggested the friendly wager on who would take the most birds ...* and the most resistant to minimum ecological decency. Millions of birds that managed to elude shotgun blasts were dying each year from ingesting the lead shot that rained down in the wetlands. Year after year, birds perished from feeding on spent lead, but hunters were "reluctant" to switch to steel. They worried that it would impair their shooting, and ammunition manufacturers said a changeover would be "expensive." State and federal officials had to weigh the poisoning against these considerations. It took forever, this weighing, but now steel-shot loads are required almost everywhere, having been judged "more than adequate" to bring down the birds. This is not to say, of course, that most duck hunters use steel shot almost everywhere. They're traditionalists and don't care for all the new, pesky rules. Oh, for the golden age of waterfowling, when a man could measure a good day's shooting by the pickup load. But those days are gone. Fall is a melancholy time, all right.

Spectacular abuses occur wherever geese congregate, Shooting Sports-man notes quietly, something that the more cultivated Ducks Unlimited would hesitate to admit. Waterfowl populations are plummeting and waterfowl hunters are out of control. "Supervised" hunts are hardly distinguished from unsupervised ones. A biologist with the Department of the Interior who observed a hunt at Sand Lake in South Dakota said, *Hunters repeatedly shot over the line at incoming flights where there was no possible chance of retrieving. Time and time again I was shocked at the behavior of hunters. I heard them laugh at the plight of dazed cripples that stumbled about. I saw them striking the heads of retrieved cripples against fence posts.* In the South, wood ducks return to their roosts after sunset when shooting hours are closed. Hunters find this an excellent time to shoot them. Dennis Anderson, an outdoors writer, said, *Roost shooters just fire at the birds as fast as they can, trying to drop as many as they can. Then they grab what birds they can find. The birds they can't find in the dark, they leave behind.*

Carnage and waste are the rules in bird hunting, even during legal seasons and open hours. Thousands of wounded ducks and geese are not retrieved, left to rot in the marshes and fields . . . *When I asked Wanda where hers had fallen, she wasn't sure.* Cripples, and there are many cripples made in this pastime, are still able to run and hide, eluding the hunter even if he's willing to spend time searching for them, which he usually isn't . . . *It's one thing to run down a cripple in a picked bean field or a pasture, and quite another to watch a wing-tipped bird drop into a huge block of switch grass.* Oh nasty, nasty switch grass. A downed bird becomes invisible on the ground and is practically unfindable without a good dog, and few "waterfowlers" have them these days. They're hard to train — usually a professional has to do it — and most hunters can't be bothered. Birds are easy to tumble . . . *Canada geese — blues and snows — can all take a good amount of shot. Brant are easily called and decoyed and come down easily. Ruffed grouse are hard to hit but easy to kill. Sharptails are harder to kill but easier to hit* . . . It's just a nuisance to recover them. But it's fun, fun, fun swatting them down . . . *There's distinct pleasure in watching a flock work to a good friend's gun* . . .

Teal, the smallest of common ducks, are really easy to kill. Hunters in the South used to *practice* on teal in September, prior to the "serious" waterfowl season. But the birds were so diminutive and the limit so low (four a day) that many hunters felt it hardly worth going out and getting bit by mosquitoes to kill them. Enough did, however, brave the bugs and manage to "harvest" 165,000 of the little migrating birds in Louisiana in 1987 alone. *Shooting is usually best on opening day. By the second day you can sometimes detect a decline in local teal numbers. Areas may deteriorate to virtually no action by the third day* . . . The area *deteriorates.* When a flock is wiped out, the skies are empty. *No action.*

Teal declined more sharply than any duck species except mallard last year; this baffles hunters. Hunters and their procurers — wildlife agencies — will *never* admit that hunting is responsible for the decimation of a species. John Turner, head of the federal Fish and Wildlife Service, delivers the familiar and litanic line. Hunting is not the problem. *Pollution* is the problem. *Pesticides, urbanization, deforestation, hazardous waste,* and *wetlands destruction* are the problem. And drought! There's been a big drought! Antis should devote their energies to solving these problems if they care about wildlife, and leave the hunters alone. While the Fish and Wildlife Service is busily conducting experiments in cause and effect, like releasing mallard ducklings on a wetland sprayed with the insecticide ethyl parathion (they died — it was known they would, but you can never have enough studies that show guns aren't a duck's only problem), hunters are killing some 200 million birds and animals each year. But these deaths are incidental to the problem, according to Turner. A factor, perhaps, but a *minor* one. Ducks Unlimited says the problem isn't hunting, it's *low recruitment* on the part of the birds. To the hunter, *birth* in the animal kingdom is *recruitment*. They wouldn't want to use an emotional, sentimental word like *birth*. The black duck, a very "popular" duck in the Northeast, so "popular," in fact, that game agencies felt that hunters couldn't be asked to refrain from shooting it, is scarce and getting scarcer. Nevertheless, it's still being hunted. *A number of studies are currently under way in an attempt to discover why black ducks are disappearing, Sports Afield* reports. Black ducks are disappearing because they've been shot out, their elimination being a dreadful example of game management, and managers who are loath to "displease" hunters. The skies — *flyways* — of America have been divided into four administrative regions, and the states, advised by a federal government coordinator, have to agree on policies.

There's always a lot of squabbling that goes on in flyway meetings — 25 lots of complaints about short-stopping, for example. Short-stopping is the deliberate holding of birds in a state, often by feeding them in wildlife refuges, so that their southern migration is slowed or stopped. Hunters in the North get to kill more than hunters in the South. This isn't fair. Hunters demand equity in opportunities to kill.

Wildlife managers hate closing the season on anything. Closing the season on a species would indicate a certain amount of *mis*management and misjudgment at the very least — a certain reliance on overly optimistic winter counts, a certain overappeasement of hunters who would be "upset" if they couldn't kill their favorite thing. And worse, closing a season would be considered victory for the antis. Bird-hunting "rules" are very complicated, but they all encourage killing. There are shortened seasons and split seasons and special seasons for "underutilized" birds. (Teal were very recently considered "underutilized.") The limit on coots is fifteen a day — shooting them, it's easy! They don't fly high — giving the hunter something to do while he waits in the blind. Some species are "protected," but bear in mind that hunters begin blasting away one half hour before sunrise and that most hunters can't identify a bird in the air even in broad daylight. Some of them can't identify birds in hand either, and even if they can (#% *!I got me a canvasback, that duck's frigging protected . . .*), they are likely to bury unpopular or "trash" ducks so that they can continue to hunt the ones they "love."

Game "professionals," in thrall to hunters' "needs," will not stop managing bird populations until they've doled out the final duck (*I didn't get my limit but I bagged the last one, by golly . . .*). The Fish and Wildlife Service services legal hunters as busily as any madam, but it is powerless in tempering the lusts of the illegal ones. Illegal kill is a monumental problem in the not-so-wonderful world of waterfowl. Excesses have always pervaded the "sport," and bird shooters have historically been the slobs and profligates of hunting. *Doing away with hunting would do away with a vital cultural and historical aspect of American life,* John Turner claims. So, do away with it. Do away with those who have already done away with so much. Do away with them before the birds they have pursued so relentlessly and for so long drop into extinction, sink, in the poet Wallace Steven's words, "downward to darkness on extended wings."

"Quality" hunting is as rare as the Florida panther. What you've got is a bunch of guys driving over the plains, up the mountains, and through the woods with their stupid tag that cost them a couple of bucks and immense coolers full of beer and body parts. There's a price tag on the right to destroy living creatures for play, but it's not much. *A big-game hunting license is the greatest deal going since the Homestead Act,* Ted Kerasote writes in *Sports Afield. In many states residents can hunt big game for more than a month for about $20.* It's cheaper than taking the little woman out to lunch. It's cheap all right, and it's because killing animals is considered *recreation* and is underwritten by state and federal funds. In Florida, state moneys are routinely spent on "youth hunts," in which kids are guided to shoot deer from stands in wildlife-management areas. The organizers of these events say that these staged hunts *help youth to understand man's role in the ecosystem.* (Drop a doe and take your place in the ecological community, son . . .)

Hunters claim (they don't actually believe it but they've learned to say it) that they're doing nonhunters a favor — for if they didn't *use* wild animals, wild animals would be useless. They believe that they're just *helping Mother Nature control populations (you wouldn't want those deer to die of starvation, would you? . . .).* They claim that their tiny fees provide *all* Americans with wild lands and animals. (People who don't hunt get to enjoy animals all year round while hunters get to enjoy them only during hunting season . . .) Ducks Unlimited feels that it, in particular, is a selfless provider and environmental champion. Although members spend most of their money lobbying for hunters and raising ducks in pens to release later over shooting fields, they do save some wetlands, mostly by persuading farmers not to fill them in. *See that little pothole there the ducks like? Well, I'm gonna plant more soybeans there if you don't pay me not to . . .* . Hunters claim many nonsensical things, but the most nonsensical of all is that they *pay their own way.* They do not pay their own way. They *do* pay into a perverse wildlife-management system that manipulates "stocks" and "herds" and "flocks" for hunters' killing pleasure, but these fees in no way cover the cost of highly questionable ecological practices. For some spare change . . . *the greatest deal going* . . . hunters can hunt on public lands — national parks, state forests — preserves for hunters! — which the nonhunting and antihunting public pay for. (Access to private lands is becoming increasingly difficult for them, as experience has taught people that hunters are obnoxious.) Hunters kill on millions of acres of land all over America that are maintained with general taxpayer revenue, but the most shocking, really twisted subsidization takes place on national wildlife refuges. Nowhere is the arrogance and the insidiousness of this small, aggressive minority more clearly demonstrated. Nowhere is the murder of animals, the manipulation of language, and the distortion of public intent more flagrant. The public perceives national wildlife refuges as safe havens, as sanctuaries for animals. And why wouldn't they? The word *refuge* of course *means* shelter from danger and distress. But the dweeby nonhunting public — they tend to be so literal. The word has been reinterpreted by management over time and now hunters are invited into more than half of the country's more than 440 wildlife "sanctuaries" each year to bang them up and kill more than half a million animals. This is called *wildlife-oriented recreation*. Hunters think of this as being no less than their due, claiming that refuge lands were purchased with duck stamps (. . . *our duck stamps paid for it . . . our duck stamps paid for it . . .*). Hunters equate those stupid stamps with the mystic, multiplying power of the Lord's loaves and fishes, but of 90 million acres in the Wildlife Refuge System, only 3 million were bought with hunting-stamp revenue. Most wildlife "restoration" programs in the states are translated into clearing land to increase deer habitats (so that too many deer will require hunting . . . you wouldn't want them to die of starvation, would you?) and trapping animals for restocking and study (so hunters can shoot more of them). Fish and game agencies hustle hunting — instead of conserving wildlife, they're killing it. It's time for them to get in the business of protecting and preserving wildlife and creating balanced ecological systems instead of pimping for hunters who want their deer/duck/pheasant/turkey — animals stocked to be shot.

Hunters' self-serving arguments and lies are becoming more preposterous as nonhunters awake from their long, albeit troubled, sleep. Sport hunting is immoral; it should be made illegal. Hunters are persecutors of nature who should be prosecuted. They wield a disruptive power out of all proportion to their numbers, and pandering to their interests — the special interests of a group that just wants to kill things — is mad. It's preposterous that every year less than 7 percent of the population turns the skies into shooting galleries and the woods and fields into abattoirs. It's time to stop actively supporting and passively allowing hunting, and time to stigmatize it. It's time to stop being conned and cowed by hunters, time to stop pampering and coddling them, time to get them off the government's duck-and-deer dole, time to stop thinking of wild animals as "resources" and "game," and start thinking of them as sentient beings that deserve our wonder and respect, time to stop allowing hunting to be creditable by calling it "sport" and "recreation." Hunters make wildlife *dead, dead, dead*. It's time to wake up to this indisputable fact. As for the hunters, it's long past check-out time.

1992

The Reader's Presence

1. Characterize the principal strategies Williams employs in attempting to persuade her readers that "Sport hunting is immoral" and that "it should be made illegal." Is the overall appeal in this essay to her readers' emotions? to their ethics? to their sense of reason? to some combination of these appeals? to something else? Consider, for example, her treatment of bird hunting in paragraphs 20 and following. She announces that "More sentimental drivel has been written about bird shooting than any other type of hunting." Does she rely principally on logic, ethics, or emotion to make her case about the "carnage and waste" of bird hunting?

2. What is the cumulative effect of the information Williams presents? What differences do you notice between the way Williams writes and the ways hunters talk about their "sport"? What can you learn about writing from either? Comment on the effectiveness of her decision to intersperse the language of hunters into her critique. Show how she counters this language by unmasking the reality of the consequences of their actions. How does she summarize — and characterize — the arguments of the prohunting forces? Choose two of these arguments, and show how she demolishes each of the points the "hunting apologists" raise. Comment on the effectiveness of Williams's final paragraph. Why is (or isn't) it persuasive? How does she recapitulate her appeal to her readers' sense of morality and justice there? How does her selection of examples earlier in the essay contribute to the effectiveness of the final paragraph?

3. Review Williams's own presence in the essay. Show how she reveals her attitude toward hunters — as well as the language and values of hunting — in the first paragraph. Select paragraphs from the middle and final sections of her essay and demonstrate that her attitude remains consistent. Given your analysis, what more generally can you infer about the compositional strategies she relies on to make her points? In this respect, pay particular attention to her use of irony. At what points does irony slide into sarcasm? into humor? With what effects? Show how her use of these devices affects the persuasiveness of her appeal.

The Writers

Ackerman, Diane (b. 1948)

"Not to write about Nature in its widest sense...," as Diane Ackerman has asserted, "...is not only irresponsible and philistine, it bankrupts the experience of living, it ignores much of life's fascination and variety." Her writing fully literalizes this belief, as her essay "The Grandeur of the Grand Canyon" exemplifies. First published in *Harvard Magazine*, this piece displays what she calls her "affectionate curiosity" regarding "the full sum of Creation" that characterizes her nonfiction writing as well as her verse. Ackerman's works of prose include *Twilight of the Tenderfoot: A Western Memoir* (1980), *On Extended Wings: An Adventure in Flight* (1985), *A Natural History of the Senses* (1990), and *The Moon by Whale Light: And Other Adventures Among Bats, Penguins, Crocodilians, and Whales* (1991). She has also written a play, *Reverse Thunder* (1988), and several volumes of poetry, *The Planets: A Cosmic Pastoral* (1976), *Wife of Light* (1978), *Lady Faustus* (1985), and *Jaguar of Sweet Laughter* (1990). Ackerman has received numerous awards for her writing; her more significant honors include fellowships from the National Endowment for the Arts (1976, 1986) and the Creative Artists Public Service Program (1980); the *Black Warrior Review* poetry prize (1981); Pushcart Prize VIII (1984); and the Peter I. B. Lavan Younger Poet Award from the Academy of American Poets (1985). A semifinalist in the Journalist-in-Space Project, Ackerman is also an avocational pilot with a strong interest in astronomy. She has been visiting writer at William and Mary College (1983), Ohio State University (1983), Columbia University (1986), New York University (1986), and Cornell University (1987). Ackerman also served as writer-in-residence and director of the writing program at Washington University, St. Louis (1984–1986) and was an assistant professor of English at the University of Pittsburgh (1980–1983). She has been a member of the Planetary Society since 1980, and a staff writer for *The New Yorker* since 1988.

Angelou, Maya (b. 1928)

Maya Angelou is perhaps best known for the first installment of her autobiography, *I Know Why the Caged Bird Sings* (1970), but her talents also include dancing, singing, composing, and theater arts. She has acted in Genet's *The*

Blacks and in the television series *Roots,* and she has written, directed, and acted in several other TV, film, and stage productions. In addition to the several volumes of her autobiography, she is the author of articles, short stories, and poetry. Maya Angelou grew up in St. Louis and in Stamps, Arkansas, a victim of poverty, discrimination, and abuse. Angelou courageously confronts the pain and injustice of her childhood in *I Know Why the Caged Bird Sings,* from which the selection "What's Your Name, Girl?" is taken. James Baldwin praised this book as the mark of the "beginning of a new era in the minds and hearts of all black men and women." Maya Angelou is currently Reynolds Professor of American Studies at Wake Forest University. Most recently, Angelou wrote and performed the poem "On the Pulse of Morning" for President Clinton's Inauguration in 1993.

Baldwin, James (1924–1987)

James Baldwin grew up in New York City but left for France in 1948 because he felt artistically stifled as a black, gay man in America. His first novels, *Go Tell It on the Mountain* (1953) and *Giovanni's Room* (1956), and his first collection of essays, *Notes of a Native Son* (1955), were written during Baldwin's first stay abroad, where he felt able to write critically about race, sexual identity, and social injustice in America. The essay "Stranger in the Village" appears in *Notes of a Native Son.* After nearly a decade in France, he returned to New York and became a national figure in the civil rights movement. Henry Louis Gates, Jr., eulogized Baldwin as the conscience of the nation, for he "educated an entire generation of Americans about the civil-rights struggle and the sensibility of Afro-Americans as we faced and conquered the final barriers in our long quest for civil rights." Baldwin continues to educate through his essays, collected in *Nobody Knows My Name* (1961), *The Fire Next Time* (1963), *No Name in the Street* (1971), and *The Devil Finds Work* (1976). Langston Hughes wrote of these works, "Few American writers handle words more effectively in the essay form than James Baldwin."

Berry, Wendell (b. 1934)

Wendell Berry lives and farms in Kentucky. His novels, short stories, poems, and essays present his love for nature and his concerns with agriculture, the environment, and the maladies of modern industrial society. During the 1960s and 1970s he taught at New York University and the University of Kentucky; he left academia in 1977 to devote himself full time to farming and writing, but since 1987 has resumed part-time teaching. Berry's writing has been published in numerous journals, including *The Nation, New World Writing, Prairie Schooner, Contract, Chelsea Review,* and the *Quarterly Review of Literature.* His essay "The Journey's End" appears in *Recollected Essays* (1981). Berry's other works of nonfiction include *The Unsettling of America: Culture and Agriculture* (1977), *The Gift of Good Land* (1981), *Standing by Words* (1985), *Home Economics: Fourteen Essays* (1987), *Harlan Hubbard: Life and Work* (1990), *What Are People For?* (1990), and *Standing on Earth: Selected Essays* (1991). *Fidelity:*

Five Stories was published in 1992, and his *Collected Poems* was published in 1985. Wendell Berry was a Wallace Stegner Fellow in 1957–1958 and has received grants from the Guggenheim and Rockefeller foundations. He received the Bess Hokin Prize for poetry in 1967 and a National Institute of Arts and Letters Literary Award in 1971.

Bok, Sissela (b. 1934)

Born in Sweden and educated in Switzerland, France, and the United States, philosopher and teacher Sissela Bok is a member of a new generation of thinkers who have moved philosophy away from abstraction toward the consideration of concrete moral issues. Bok has been a lecturer on philosophy and medical ethics at Simmons College and Harvard University, and she has been a professor of philosophy at Brandeis University since 1989. She has served on numerous committees and advisory boards, including the Amnesty International Medical Committee (1975 to present), the U.S. Department of Health, Education, and Welfare (1977–1980), the Pulitzer Prize Board (1988 to present), and the American Philosophical Association and Soviet Academy of Sciences exchange on nuclear weapons policy (1989). Bok has applied her profoundly humanist ethics to a variety of issues ranging from euthanasia, debated in *The Dilemmas of Euthanasia,* coedited with John A. Behnke (1975), to international politics, addressed in *A Strategy for Peace: Human Values and the Threat of War* (1989). In her book *Secrets: On the Ethics of Concealment and Revelation* (1983), from which this selection is taken, Bok

continues to explore the moral questions raised by her earlier book, *Lying: Moral Choice in Public and Private Life* (1978). Bok observes that secrecy and lying "intertwine and overlap." "Lies are part of the arsenal used to guard and to invade secrecy; and secrecy allows lies to go undiscovered and to build up." Bok's most recent publication is about her mother, Alva Myrdal, a diplomat who won a Nobel Peace Prize in 1982. Originally published in Swedish in 1987, *Alva Myrdal: A Daughter's Memoir* was issued in English in 1991. In 1978 Bok received the George Orwell Award from the National Council of Teachers of English as well as the Frederic G. Melcher Book Award from the Unitarian Universalist Association for *Lying.* Bok was awarded the Abram L. Sachar Silver Medallion from Brandeis University in 1985, and she has received honorary degrees from Mount Holyoke College (1985), George Washington University (1986), and Clark University (1988). A mother of three children, Bok has been married to former Harvard University president Derek Bok since 1955.

Bosmajian, Haig A. (b. 1928)

Born in Fresno, California, Haig Bosmajian received his bachelor's degree from the University of California in 1949 and his master's degree from the University of the Pacific in 1951. After completing his doctorate at Stanford University in 1960, Haig Bosmajian was an assistant professor of speech at the University of Connecticut, Storrs. Since 1973 he has been a professor in the Department of Speech Communication at the University of Washington, Seattle.

Professor Bosmajian focuses on dissent, language and behavior, and the language of social movements. He has edited numerous books, including *Readings in Parliamentary Procedure* (1968), *The Principles and Practice of Freedom of Speech* (1971), and *Freedom of Religion* (1987). He has collaborated with his wife, Hamida Bosmajian, on *The Rhetoric of the Civil Rights Movement* (1969) and *This Great Argument: The Rights of Women* (1972), and he is coauthor of *Sexism and Language* (1977). Bosmajian is editor of the *First Amendment in the Classroom* series, and his other publications include *The Rhetoric of Nonverbal Communication* (1971), *Dissent: Symbolic Behavior and Rhetorical Strategies* (1972), *Obscenity and Freedom of Expression* (1974), *Justice Douglas and Freedom of Speech* (1980), and *Censorship, Libraries, and the Law* (1982). Bosmajian is a member of the Speech Association of America, the American Association of University Professors, and the Western Speech Association. The essay reprinted in this volume originally appeared as the introduction to *The Language of Oppression* (1974).

Brownmiller, Susan (b. 1935)

Susan Brownmiller has made a long and successful career in journalism, starting as an editor for *Albany Report,* working as a researcher for *Newsweek,* and writing on the staff of the *Village Voice* and ABC-TV. Since 1968 she has been a free-lance journalist and writer and has contributed to many national magazines, including *Newsweek, Esquire,* and the *New York Times Magazine.* She created a national sensation with her 1975 book *Against Our Will: Men, Women, and Rape.* Exploring the history and politics of rape, this book made Brownmiller famous throughout the country, and *Time* magazine elected her one of the twelve Women of the Year for 1975. She is the founder of Women Against Pornography. "Let's Put Pornography Back in the Closet" is taken from *Take Back the Night* (1980). Brownmiller has been honored with grants from the Alicia Patterson Foundation and the Louis M. Rabinowitz Foundation. Her most recent publications are *Femininity* (1984) and *Waverly Place* (1989).

Carver, Raymond (1938–1988)

Son of a laborer and a homemaker in Clatskanie, Oregon, Raymond Carver resembles the characters in the short stories for which he is widely acclaimed. Once a manual laborer, a gas station attendant, and a janitor himself, Carver acquired his vision of the working class and the desperate lives of ordinary folk through direct experience. The Pacific Northwest of Carver's writing is peopled with types such as "the waitress, the bus driver, the mechanic, the hotel keeper" — people who Carver feels are "good people." "God, the country is filled with these people." Carver describes his characters as "people doing the best they could." First published in *Esquire,* "My Father's Life," Carver's account of his father's hardships during the Great Depression, puts a biographical spin on these "good people." Carver attended the Writers' Workshop at the University of Iowa after graduating from California State University at Humboldt. He taught writing at the University of California at Santa

Cruz, University of California, Berkeley, Syracuse University, the University of Texas at El Paso, and the Writers' Workshop at the University of Iowa. Although Carver's short stories have brought him many honors — including the Joseph Henry Jackson Award for fiction (1971), the Wallace Stegner Creative Writing Fellowship at Stanford University (1972–1973), a Guggenheim Fellowship (1977–1978), a National Endowment for the Arts Award in Fiction (1979), and the Mildred and Harold Strauss Living Award from the American Academy and Institute of Arts and Letters (1983) — his poetry has also received much critical acclaim. Carver won the National Endowment for the Arts Discovery Award for poetry in 1970 and the Levinson Prize for Poetry in 1985. Carver's short-story collections, *Will You Please Be Quiet, Please?* (1976), *Cathedral* (1984), and *Where I'm Calling From* (1988), were all nominated for the National Book Critics Circle Award. The latter two collections were also nominated for the Pulitzer Prize for fiction in 1985 and 1989 respectively. Carver's verse is collected in *Where Water Comes Together with Other Water* (1985), recipient of the 1986 Los Angeles Times Book Prize; *Ultramarine* (1986); and *A New Path to the Waterfall* (posthumously published in 1989). Carver divorced his wife of twenty-six years in 1983. He married poet Tess Gallagher in 1988, shortly before he died of lung cancer.

Chan, Sucheng (b. 1941)

Sucheng Chan received her Ph.D. from the University of California, Berkeley, where she also taught for ten years. Her publications include *Asian Americans: An Interpretive History* (1991) and the critically acclaimed *This Bittersweet Soil: The Chinese in California Agriculture, 1860–1910* (1986). Chan's essay, "You're Short, Besides!" is a candid account of being physically handicapped as well as Asian American. Rather than feeling triply marginalized as "nonwhite, female, and handicapped," Chan analyzes her situation with humor and toughness, revealing an indomitable spirit that shrugs off the limitations of labels. "You're Short, Besides!" originally appeared in *Making Waves: An Anthology of Writings by and About Asian American Women* (1989). Chan is currently a professor at the University of California, Santa Barbara, where she teaches history.

Cofer, Judy Ortiz (b. 1952)

Born in Puerto Rico, Judy Ortiz Cofer moved to the United States in 1960. She challenged herself to learn English well enough not only to teach it, but to write poetry in it, and has been very successful in both. Her poetry has appeared in *Prairie Schooner, New Letters, Southern Poetry Review,* and *Poetry Miscellany,* among other literary magazines. Collections of her poems have also been published: *The Native Dancer* (1981), *Peregrina* (1986), *Reaching for the Mainland* (1987), and *Terms of Survival* (1987). Her first novel, *The Line of the Sun* (1989), was nominated for the Pulitzer Prize. "Silent Dancing" is from Cofer's 1990 essay collection, *Silent Dancing: A Partial Remembrance of a Puerto Rican Childhood.* Her latest book, *The Latin Deli: Prose & Poetry,* was published in 1993.

Cofer has taught at Broward Community College, the University of Georgia, and the University of Miami. In 1981 she was a fellow of the Fine Arts Council of Florida, and in 1977 studied at Oxford University as a scholar of the English Speaking Union.

Cooper, Bernard (b. 1951)

Born, raised, and still residing in Los Angeles, Bernard Cooper received his B.F.A. (1973) and M.F.A. (1975) from the California Institute of the Arts. He has been a creative writing instructor at the Otis/Parsons Institute of Art and Design in Los Angeles since 1978, and he has taught at the Southern California Institute of Architecture, Los Angeles, since 1987. His collection of essays, *Maps to Anywhere* (1990), covers a wide range of topics as varying as the aging of his father, the extinction of the dinosaur, and what life might be like in the future. Cooper's work is represented in *The Best American Essays 1988*, edited by Annie Dillard and Robert Atwan. He contributes to various periodicals such as *Harper's*, where "A Clack of Tiny Sparks: Remembrances of a Gay Boyhood" first appeared in January 1991. His first novel, *A Year of Rhymes*, was published in 1993.

Cunningham, Amy (b. 1955)

Amy Cunningham has been writing on psychological issues and modern life for magazines like *Mademoiselle, Glamour, McCall's, Washington Post Magazine,* and *Lear's* since she graduated from the University of Virginia in 1977 with a bachelor's degree in English. Cunningham says that the essay grew out of her own experience as an "easy to get along with

person" who was raised by Southerners in the suburbs of Chicago. She is currently studying psychoanalytic psychotherapy at the Washington Psychoanalytic Institute. "Why Women Smile" originally appeared in *Lear's* in 1993.

Didion, Joan (b. 1934)

The author of novels, short stories, and essays, Joan Didion began her career in 1956 as a staff writer at *Vogue* magazine in New York. In 1963 she published her first novel, *Run River,* and the following year returned to her native California, where she lives today. Didion's essays have appeared in periodicals ranging from *Mademoiselle* and *Life* to the *American Scholar* and the *National Review.* Her essay "On Keeping a Notebook" can be found in her collection of essays, *Slouching Towards Bethlehem* (1968). The critic Alfred Kazin remarks that in Didion's work "silence as a form and fear of imminent breakdown is a significant element . . . She refers often to her fragility in *Slouching Towards Bethlehem,* and she writes about her panics with a deliberation that is not merely disarming but that always makes a point, in perfect style, about something other than herself." Didion's other nonfiction publications include *The White Album* (1979), *Salvador* (1983), *Miami* (1987), and *After Henry* (1992). Her fourth novel is *Democracy* (1984).

Dillard, Annie (b. 1945)

In 1974 Annie Dillard was awarded the Pulitzer Prize for general nonfiction for her book *Pilgrim at Tinker Creek,* from which "Seeing" is excerpted. Dillard describes this book through reference to Henry David Thoreau, calling it "a meteorological journal of the mind." Eudora Welty writes of Dillard that "A reader's heart must go out to a young writer with a sense of wonder so fearless and unbridled. It is this intensity of experience that she seems to live in order to declare." Annie Dillard has also published poems in *Tickets for a Prayer Wheel* (1975), literary theory in *Living by Fiction* (1982), essays in *Teaching a Stone to Talk* (1982), and autobiography in *An American Childhood* (1987). Her book *The Writing Life* (1989) contains reflections on the writing process. Dillard published her first novel, *The Living*, in 1992. From 1973 to 1982 she served as contributing editor to *Harper's* magazine, and since 1979 she has taught creative writing at Wesleyan University.

Douglass, Frederick (1817?–1895)

Born into slavery, Frederick Douglass was taken from his mother as an infant and denied knowledge of his father's identity. He escaped to the north at the age of twenty-one and created a new identity for himself as a free man. He educated himself and went on to become one of the most eloquent orators and persuasive writers of the nineteenth century. He was a national leader in the abolition movement and, among other activities, founded and edited the *North Star* and *Douglass' Monthly*. His public service included appointments as United States marshall and consul general to the Republic of Haiti. His most lasting literary accomplishment was his memoirs, which he revised several times before they were published as the *Life and Times of Frederick Douglass* (1881 and 1892).

"Learning to Read and Write" is taken from these memoirs.

Early, Gerald (b. 1952)

Gerald Early is the author of *Tuxedo Junction: Essays on American Culture* (1989), which he wrote as a postdoctoral fellow at the University of Kansas. Currently, Early is professor of English and Afro-American studies at Washington University. He has received awards from the Whiting Foundation and CCLM-General Electric, and contributed to such journals as *Antaeus, The Antioch Review, Callaloo, Cimarron Review, The Hudson Review, The Kenyon Review,* and *Obsidian II.* Recently Early edited the essay collections *Speech and Power: The Afro-American Essay and Its Cultural Content from Polemics to Pulpit* (1992) and *Lure and Loathing: Essays on Race, Identity, and the Ambivalence of Assimilation* (1993). "Life with Daughters" originally appeared in *The Kenyon Review* in fall 1990.

Eighner, Lars (b. 1948)

Lars Eighner was born in Texas and attended the University of Texas at Austin. An essayist and fiction writer, he contributes regularly to *The Threepenny Review, Advocate Men, The Guide,* and *Inches.* He has published a volume of stories, *Bayou Boys and Other Stories* (1985), and a book on gay erotica, *Lavender Blue: How to Write and Sell Gay Men's Erotica* (1987). Eighner became homeless in 1988, when he left his job of ten years as a mental-hospital attendant. "On Dumpster Diving" is Eighner's prize-winning essay based on this experience. It originally appeared in the fall 1991 issue of *The Threepenny Review.*

Eighner is currently living in an apartment in Austin with his dog Lizbeth and is working on a memoir on homelessness and wandering.

Ephron, Nora (b. 1941)

Nora Ephron started her writing career as a reporter for the *New York Post* and also worked as a free-lance reporter before joining the staff of *Esquire,* where she wrote the "Women" column in 1972 and 1973. In 1973 she became a contributing editor of *New York* magazine, and in 1974 returned as senior editor to *Esquire.* Her work has also appeared in *Oui, McCall's,* and *Cosmopolitan.* Ephron has published four collections of essays on popular culture, *Wallflower at the Orgy* (1970), *Crazy Salad* (1975), from which the essay "A Few Words about Breasts" is taken, *Crazy Salad Plus Nine* (1984), and *Nora Ephron Collected* (1991). She has also published *Scribble, Scribble: Notes on the Media* (1979) and *Heartburn* (1983), and written the screenplays *Silkwood* (with Alice Arden) and *When Harry Met Sally.* In 1992 she directed her first movie, *This Is My Life,* written with her sister Delia Ephron. Recently she wrote the screenplay for *Sleepless in Seattle.*

Epstein, Leslie (b. 1938)

Novelist, essayist, and short-story writer, Leslie Epstein presently directs the creative writing program at Boston University. He previously taught at the Queens College of the City University of New York, where he became a professor of English in 1976. He has received a Rhodes scholarship (1960–1962), a grant from the National Endowment for the Arts (1972), a Ful-

bright Fellowship (1972–1973), a CAPS grant (1976–1977), and a Guggenheim Fellowship (1977–1978). His novel *King of the Jews: A Novel of the Holocaust* (1979) was nominated by the National Book Critics Circle for Most Distinguished Work of Fiction and received a Notable book citation from the American Library Association. His other novels are *P. D. Kimerakov* (1975), *Regina* (1982), and *Pinto and Sons* (1990). Epstein's short stories are collected in *The Steinway Quintet Plus Four* (1976) and *Goldkorn Tales* (1985). He contributes regularly to various periodicals such as *The Atlantic, Esquire,* and *The Nation.* "Civility and Its Discontents" originally appeared in *The American Prospect.*

Faludi, Susan (b. 1959)

Susan Faludi's best-selling book *Backlash: The Undeclared War Against American Women* (1991) became a cause célèbre because of her controversial assertion that the social, economic, and political advances of women and feminism were subtly being attacked throughout the 1980s by media armed with skewed statistics and a conservative ideology. Praised as "feminism's new manifesto" by Eleanor Smeal of the National Organization for Women and denounced as a "conspiracy theory" in a *New Republic* review, the highly publicized, hotly debated *Backlash* turned Faludi into what she self-deprecatingly referred to as the "feminist du jour." Formerly a journalist for the *Boston Globe,* the *New York Times,* and the *Miami Herald,* Susan Faludi had shown talent as a cultural watchdog as early as 1985, when she won first prize for news and feature reporting from the Georgia Associated Press. After she moved to the West Coast, she contributed regularly to *Mother Jones, Ms.,* and *California West,* while serving as a staff writer for *West,* the Sunday magazine of the *San Jose Mercury News.* During this time (1985–1989) she was honored by Women in Communications, the California Newspaper Publishers Association, and the Association Press of California and Nevada. She was also awarded a Robert F. Kennedy Memorial Journalism Award citation. While a staff writer for the San Francisco bureau of the *Wall Street Journal* from 1990 through 1992, Faludi won a John Hancock Award for Excellence in Business and Financial Journalism (1992) and a Pulitzer Prize for "The Reckoning" (1991), an investigative piece on the human costs of Safeway stores' leveraged buyout. The essay reprinted here, "Blame It on Feminism," appeared in *Mother Jones* shortly after Faludi received these honors and immediately before Crown Publishers rushed *Backlash* to bookstores in October 1991 — a moment when, Faludi observed, "women were ready to wake up." The book arrived as abortion rights were being threatened and Americans were watching the Clarence Thomas hearings and the William Kennedy Smith rape case trial. Susan Faludi currently lives in the Haight Ashbury district of San Francisco. Her next project, tentatively titled *The Man Question,* is scheduled to be published by William Morrow and Avon in 1994.

Fussell, Paul (b. 1924)
A well-established English professor who taught at Rutgers before accepting tenure at the University of Pennsylvania in 1983, Paul Fussell did not successfully break with academic prose until he tired of writing what he was "supposed to write." After twenty years of writing critical works such as *Poetic Meter and Poetic Form* (1965) and *The Rhetorical World of Augustan Humanism* (1965), Fussell published his first work of nonfiction for a general audience. *The Great War and Modern Memory* (1975) won the National Book Award and the National Book Critics Circle Award and received wide critical acclaim for its examination of how World War I changed what Frank Kermode called "the texture of our culture." Fussell continued to touch upon the subject of war in his subsequent books, *Abroad: British Literary Traveling Between the Wars* (1980), which was nominated for a National Book Critics Circle Award, and *The Boy Scout Handbook and Other Observations* (1982). Fussell then wrote *Class: A Guide Through the American Status System* (1983; published in England as *Caste Marks: Style and Status in the USA*) and edited *The Norton Book of Travel* (1987). Fussell returned to his favorite subject in his collection of essays *Thank God for the Atom Bomb and Other Essays* (1988), from which this selection is taken. Fussell's most recent publications are *Wartime: Understanding and Behavior in the Second World War* (1989) and *The Norton Book of Modern War* (1991). In addition to other honors, Fussell has received a senior fellowship from the National Endowment for the Humanities (1973–1974), a Guggenheim Fellowship (1977–1978), an award for

excellence in literature from the American Academy and Institute of Arts and Letters (1980), and a Rockefeller Fellowship (1983–1984). He contributes to numerous periodicals and has served as contributing editor to both *Harper's* and *The New Republic*.

Gordon, Mary (b. 1949)

From 1974 to 1978 Mary Gordon taught English at Dutchess Community College in Poughkeepsie, New York. Since that time she has published several novels, including *Final Payments* (1978), *The Company of Women* (1981), *Men and Angels* (1985), and *The Other Side* (1989); a collection of stories, *Temporary Shelter* (1987); and the essay collection *Good Boys and Dead Girls and Other Essays* (1991). Her latest, *The Rest of Life: Three Novellas,* was published in 1993. Gordon frequently contributes articles and reviews to the *New York Times,* in which the essay "More Than Just a Shrine" originally appeared. Francine du Plessix Gray observes of Gordon that "at a time when many of her contemporaries have capitulated to the chic anomie of postmodernism, she continues to grapple with some of the vast issues that have given the novel form much of its grandeur. What is redemption? What is charity? What is our specific gravity of grace? Who else, among her peers, is asking such searing questions?"

Gould, Stephen Jay (b. 1941)

Stephen Jay Gould is professor of geology and zoology at Harvard and curator of invertebrate paleontology at Harvard's Museum of Comparative Zoology. He has published widely on evolution and other topics and has earned a rep-

utation for making technical subjects readily comprehensible to lay readers without trivializing the material. His *The Panda's Thumb* (1980) won the American Book Award, and *The Mismeasure of Man* (1981) won the National Book Critics Circle Award. Gould has published over one hundred articles in scientific journals, and contributes to national magazines as well. "Sex, Drugs, Disasters, and the Extinction of Dinosaurs" appeared in *Discover* magazine in 1984. More recently, Gould has written *An Urchin in the Storm* (1987), *Time's Arrow, Time's Cycle* (1987), *Bully for Brontosaurus* (1991), and *Eight Little Piggies* (1993). Among many other honors and awards, he has been a fellow of the National Science Foundation and the MacArthur Foundation. John Updike comments that "Gould, in his scrupulous explication of [other scientists'] carefully wrought half-truths, abolishes the unnecessary distinction between the humanities and science, and honors the latter as a branch of humanistic thought, fallible and poetic."

Gray, Francine du Plessix (b. 1930)

Born in France, Francine du Plessix Gray came to the United States when she was eleven years old. She has been a free-lance writer for many years, contributing to *Vogue, The New Yorker, The New Republic, Saturday Review, The New York Review of Books,* and the *New York Times Book Review,* in which "I Write for Revenge Against Reality" appeared in 1982. She has also taught at Yale University and Columbia University, and in the 1974 served as judge of the National Book Award in philosophy and religion. Gray won the National Catholic Book Award for *Divine Disobedience: Profiles in Catholic Radicalism* (1970) and the Front Page Award for *Hawaii: The Sugar-Coated Fortress* (1972). Gray has written the novels *Lovers and Tyrants* (1976), *World Without End* (1981), and *October Blood* (1985). In 1987 she published a collection of essays called *Adam and Eve in the City.* Her newest book, *Soviet Women,* came out in 1990.

Greenfield, Jeff (b. 1943)

Former CBS-TV sportswriter, humorist, and media commentator Jeff Greenfield graduated from the University of Wisconsin and Yale University School of Law. Earlier in his career, he served as a staff aide and writer of speeches for both John V. Lindsay, former mayor of New York City, and the late attorney general Robert F. Kennedy. Greenfield presently works as a political and media analyst for ABC-TV news programs, regularly guest anchors the news show *Nightline,* and writes a syndicated column. His books include *A Populist Manifesto* (1972), *Where Have You Gone, Joe DiMaggio?* (1973), *The World's Greatest Team* (a history of the Boston Celtics, 1976), *Television: The First 50 Years* (1977), *Playing to Win: An Insider's Guide to Politics* (1980), and *The Real Campaign* (1982). The essay reprinted here, "The Black and White Truth about Basketball," is subtitled "A Skin-Deep Theory of Style" and was first published in *Esquire* in 1975.

Hamill, Pete (b. 1935)

Pete Hamill began his career in journalism as a reporter for the *New York Post,* and also wrote for *The Saturday Evening Post* before becoming a war correspondent in Vietnam in 1966. In the past two decades he has written columns for *Newsday,* the *New York Daily News,* the *Village Voice,* and *Esquire.* Hamill's journalism has earned awards from the Columbia University Graduate School of Journalism and the Newspaper Reporters Association. His newspaper columns have been collected in *Irrational Ravings* (1971) and *The Invisible City: A New York Sketchbook* (1980). Hamill also writes short stories (including the 1992 collection *Tokyo Sketches*), screenplays, and novels. His more recent novels include *Dirty Laundry* (1978), *The Deadly Piece* (1979), *The Guns of Heaven* (1983), and *Loving Women* (1989). He contributes to many national magazines including *Cosmopolitan, Life,* the *New York Times Magazine,* and *Playboy;* "Crack and the Box" appeared in *Esquire* in 1990. Hamill is currently editor-in-chief of the *New York Post.*

Harris, Daniel R. (b. 1957)

An essayist and book reviewer, Daniel Harris lives in Platteville, Wisconsin. His work has appeared in *Harper's, The Nation,* the *Washington Post, Salmagundi, The Antioch Review,* and elsewhere. "Effeminacy" originally appeared as a two-part essay in the winter 1991 issue of *Michigan Quarterly Review.* His work has been published in *The Best American Essays.*

Hasselstrom, Linda M. (b. 1943)

Linda Hasselstrom is a rancher and writer who lives in western South Dakota. She has written about her experiences as a rancher in *Windbreak: A Woman Rancher* on the Northern Plains (1987) and Going Over East: Reflections of a Woman Rancher (1987). Hasselstrom has also written a volume of poetry, Caught by One Wing (1990), and a collection of poems and essays, Land Circle: Writings Collected from the Land (1991), from which this selection is taken.

hooks, bell (b. 1952)

Gloria Watkins, who writes under the pseudonym "bell hooks," teaches at Oberlin College. She contributes regularly to Zeta Magazine and has written several books including And There We Slept: Poems (1978), Ain't I a Woman: Black Women and Feminism (1981), Feminist Theory from Margin to Center (1984), Talking Back: Thinking Feminist, Thinking Black (1989), in which "Feminism: a Transformational Politic" is found, Breaking Bread: Insurgent Black Intellectual Life (1991), and Black Looks: Race and Representation (1992).

Hughes, Langston (1902–1967)

One of the leading figures of the Harlem Renaissance, Langston Hughes was a prolific writer. He started his career as a poet, but also wrote fiction, autobiography, biography, history, and plays, as well as working at various times as a journalist. One of his most famous poems, "The Negro Speaks of Rivers," was written while he was a high school student. Although Langston Hughes traveled widely, most of his writings are concerned with the lives of urban working-class African Americans. Hughes used the rhythms of blues and jazz to bring to his writing a distinctive expression of black culture and experience. His work continues to be popular today, es-

pecially such collections of short stories as The Ways of White Folks (1934), such volumes of poetry as Montage of a Dream Deferred (1951), and his series of vignettes on the character Jesse B. Simple, collected and published from 1950 to 1965. Hughes published two volumes of autobiography; "Salvation" is taken from the first of these, The Big Sea (1940).

Hurston, Zora Neale (1901?–1960)

Born in Eatonville, Florida, in a year that she never remembered the same way twice, Zora Neale Hurston started writing when she was at Howard University, which she entered in 1923. In 1926 she won a scholarship to Barnard College, where she was the first black woman to be admitted. There Hurston developed an interest in anthropology, which was cultivated by Columbia University's distinguished anthropologist Frank Boas, Hurston's intermittent mentor for over ten years. From 1928 to 1931 she collected voodoo folklore in the South and published her findings in Mules and Men (1935). Two successive Guggenheim Fellowships (1937–1939) allowed Hurston to do field work in Jamaica, Haiti, and Bermuda, which resulted in another anthropological study, Tell My Horse (1938). During this time she also collected folklore about Florida for the Works Progress Administration and published the two novels for which she is justly famous, Jonah's Gourd Vine (1934) and Their Eyes Were Watching God (1937). Langston Hughes said that "she was always getting scholarships and things from wealthy white people." But when the economy collapsed and brought the famous Harlem Renaissance down with it, Hurston's patrons all but disappeared. She managed to publish two more books, *Moses, Man of the Mountain* (1939) and *Seraph on the Suwanee* (1948), and her autobiography, *Dust Tracks on a Road* (1942), before her reputation suffered a serious decline during the 1950s. After working as a librarian, part-time teacher, and maid near the end of her life, Hurston died in a county welfare home in Florida in virtual obscurity. The rediscovery of her work is largely attributed to Alice Walker, who edited a collection of Hurston's writings, *I Love Myself When I'm Laughing* (1975). "How It Feels to Be Colored Me" was reprinted in Walker's anthology and originally appeared in *The World Tomorrow* in 1928.

Iwata, Edward (b. 1957)

Edward Iwata is a business writer for the *Orange County Register* in Los Angeles and a former reporter and editor for the *San Francisco Chronicle*. He has also worked as a freelance journalist, writing extensively about the media, literature, racial issues, Asian American culture, and the Pacific Rim for the *Los Angeles Times, Editor & Publisher* magazine, *Newsweek Japan, San Francisco Focus* (where "Race without Face" first appeared), and other publications. He and his wife are former residential educators at Stanford University's Okada House, a residence hall and community center for students interested in Asian American, Asian, and cross-cultural topics.

Jordan, June (b. 1936)

June Jordan taught at the City College of the City University of New York, Sarah Lawrence College, and the State University of New York at Stony Brook before going to the University of California at Berkeley, where she is professor of Afro-American studies and women's studies. She is the author of novels, short stories, poetry, children's fiction, and biography. Her essays can be found in such collections as *Civil Wars* (1981), *On Call* (1986), *Moving Toward Home: Political Essays* (1989), and *Technical Difficulties: African American Notes on the State of the Union* (1992). The essay "Nobody Mean More to Me than You and the Future Life of Willie Jordan" is found in *On Call*. She has also published stories and poems in numerous national magazines, including *Esquire, Black World, The Nation,* the *Partisan Review, Essence,* and the *Village Voice*. Her numerous honors include fellowships from the National Endowment for the Arts and the New York Foundation for the Arts. Toni Cade Bambara remarks that "as a poet, novelist, journalist, scenarist, urban designer, and teacher— June Jordan has always worked hard to keep before us the essential questions of life, death, choice, and honor. She has done it *not* from the relatively safe vantage point the writer's desk affords, but always from the danger zone, in the heated thick of things."

Kamata, Satoshi (b. 1938)

A 1964 graduate of Waseda University in Japan, Satoshi Kamata worked briefly for a trade paper in the steel industry and as an editor for a popular general magazine before becoming a full-time, freelance reporter specializing in Japanese industry and labor. "Six

Months at Toyota" is excerpted from Kamata's 1973 book, *Japan in the Passing Lane,* which was updated in 1980 and published in the United States in 1982. The book's translator, Tatsuru Akimoto, writes that the impetus for Kamata's third book came from "conversations with a friend who had been a seasonal worker for several years at Honda manufacturing plants." Wanting "to experience the situation firsthand," Kamata signed a six-month contract with Toyota, which he chose because "he had heard that the working conditions there were much harsher than at other automobile plants in Japan." *Japan in the Passing Lane* resulted from the diary Kamata kept while he worked there.

Kincaid, Jamaica (b. 1949)

Jamaica Kincaid was born in Antigua and immigrated to the United States. She has been a contributor and staff writer for *The New Yorker* since 1976. Her collection of stories *At the Bottom of the River* (1983) won the Morton Dauwen Zabel Award from the American Academy and Institute of Arts and Letters. She has also published *Annie John* (1985), *A Small Place* (1988), and the novel *Lucy* (1990). Commenting on her stories, David Leavitt says that "Kincaid's particular skill lies in her ability to articulate the internal workings of a potent imagination without sacrificing the rich details of the external world on which that imagination thrives." "On Seeing England for the First Time" first appeared in *Transition* in 1991.

King, Martin Luther, Jr. (1929–1968)

Martin Luther King, Jr., was born

in Atlanta, Georgia, and after training for the ministry became pastor of the Dexler Avenue Baptist Church in Montgomery, Alabama. He became active in the civil rights movement in 1956 when he was elected president of the Montgomery Improvement Association, the group which organized a transportation boycott in response to the arrest of Rosa Parks. King later became president of the Southern Christian Leadership Conference, and under his philosophy of nonviolent direct action he led marches and protests throughout the South, to Chicago, and to Washington, D.C. In 1963 King delivered his most famous speech, "I Have a Dream," before 200,000 people in front of the Lincoln Memorial in Washington, D.C., and in 1964 he was awarded the Nobel Peace Prize. King was assassinated on April 3, 1968, in Memphis, Tennessee. Martin Luther King was a masterful orator and a powerful writer. As well as his many speeches, King wrote several books, including *Why We Can't Wait* (1963), *Where Do We Go From Here: Chaos or Community?* (1967), *The Measure of a Man* (1968), and *Trumpet of Conscience* (1968). "Letter from Birmingham Jail" appeared in *Why We Can't Wait.*

Kingston, Maxine Hong (b. 1940)

"No Name Woman" comes from Maxine Hong Kingston's first book, *The Woman Warrior: Memoirs of a Girlhood Among Ghosts* (1976), which won the National Book Critics Circle Award for nonfiction. *Time* magazine named this book one of the top ten nonfiction works of the 1970s. In 1981 Kingston won the American Book Award for *China*

Men (1980), and she has also received acclaim for her most recent book, *Tripmaster Monkey* (1989). Kingston is the recipient of the *Mademoiselle* award (1977), an NEA writing fellowship (1980), and a Guggenheim Fellowship (1981). Her poems, short stories, and articles have appeared in numerous national magazines, including the *New York Times Magazine, New West, Ms., The New Yorker,* and *Iowa Review.* Kingston has taught at high schools in California and Hawaii and at the University of Hawaii, Eastern Michigan University and, most recently, the University of California at Berkeley.

Kozol, Jonathan (b. 1936)

Jonathan Kozol is a writer and social critic who has worked extensively in education, especially the education of underprivileged children. He won the National Book Award in 1967 for *Death at an Early Age.* Other publications include *Alternative Schools: A Guide for Educators and Parents* (1982), *Prisoners of Silence: Breaking the Bonds of Adult Illiteracy in the United States* (1980), *Rachel and Her Children: Homeless Families in America* (1988), *Illiterate America* (1985), *The Night Is Dark and I Am Far from Home* (1990), and *Savage Inequalities: Children in America's Schools* (1991). The essay "Distancing the Homeless" is adapted from *Rachel and Her Children* and appeared in *The Yale Review* in its present form. Kozol has been a Saxton Fellow in creative writing, and has received other fellowships from the Guggenheim, Field, Ford, and Rockefeller foundations.

Lopez, Barry (b. 1945)

Barry Lopez writes on nature and the environment, using both fiction and nonfiction to convey the mystery and beauty of, for example, arctic wolves. A frequent contributor to such newspapers and periodicals as the *New York Times,* the *Washington Post, National Geographic,* and *Antaeus,* Lopez is also the author of several books. He is currently a contributing editor to *Harper's* and *North American Review.* "The Stone Horse" appeared in *Antaeus* in 1986. In 1979 he received the John Burroughs Medal, in 1982 he was recognized by the Friends of American Writers with an award for fiction, and in 1986 he received an award in literature from the American Academy and Institute of Arts and Letters. His publications include *Of Wolves and Men* (1978), *Winter Count* (1981), *Arctic Dreams* (1986), *Crossing Open Ground* (1988), *Coyote Love* (1989), and *The Rediscovery of North America* (1990).

Lorde, Audre (1934–1992)

Self-styled "black, lesbian, feminist, warrior poet, mother," Audre Lorde was the daughter of Caribbean immigrants who eventually settled in Harlem. Also known by her adopted African name, Gamba Adisa, Lorde published her first book, *The First Cities,* in 1968. Sixteen others followed, including *Cables to Rage* (1970), *Coal* (1976), *The Black Unicorn* (1978), the "biomythography" *Zami: A New Spelling of My Name* (1983), *Sister Outsider: Essays and Speeches* (1984), and *Undersong: Chosen Poems Old and New* (1992). Lorde's most famous work is *The Cancer Jour-*

nals, a powerful chronicle of the first stages of the breast cancer that was discovered in her in the late 1970s. A monumental influence on women's literature, Lorde was unabashed about her lesbianism as well as her conviction that she spoke for "the oppressed, the disenfranchised silent people." Designated Poet Laureate of New York in 1991, Lorde was awarded many other high honors. In 1973 her collection of poetry *From a Land Where Other People Live* was nominated for a National Book Award. *A Burst of Light,* a collection of essays, won the National Book Award in 1989. She also received honorary doctorates from Hunter, Oberlin, and Haverford colleges. After a fourteen-year battle with the disease, Lorde died in Christiansted, St. Croix, of liver cancer. Her last collection of poems, *The Marvellous Arithmetics of Distance,* was published posthumously in 1993. The essay reprinted here was originally delivered as a series of comments at a Second Sex Conference session entitled "The Personal and the Political Panel" that was held in New York on September 29, 1979.

Mairs, Nancy (b. 1943)

Nancy Mairs has contributed poetry, short stories, articles, and essays to numerous journals. The collection of her essays from which "A Letter to Matthew" comes, *Plaintext,* was published in 1986. More recent publications include *Remembering the Bone House: An Erotics of Time and Space* (1989), *Carnal Acts: Essays* (1990), and *Ordinary Time: Cycles in Marriage, Faith, and Renewal* (1993). From 1983–1985 she served as assistant director of the Southwest Institute for Re-

search on Women in Tucson, and has also taught at the University of Arizona and at UCLA. Nancy Mairs was a William P. Sloan Fellow in nonfiction (1984) and received the Western States Book Award in 1984.

Marshall, Paule (b. 1929)

Paule Marshall's family immigrated to New York from Barbados shortly before she was born, and the themes and language of her work are influenced by her Caribbean heritage. Author of novels and short stories, Paule Marshall's books include *Brown Girl, Brownstones* (1959), *Soul Clap Hands and Sing* (1961), *The Chosen Place, The Timeless People* (1969), *Reena and Other Stories* (1983), *Praisesong for the Widow* (1983), *Daughters* (1991), and *Merle, A Novella and Other Stories* (1985). She also contributes to the *New York Times Book Review,* in which "From the Poets in the Kitchen" appeared in 1983. Marshall has lectured on creative writing and black literature at many universities, including Yale, Oxford, Columbia, Michigan State, and Cornell. Her honors include a Guggenheim Fellowship (1960), a Rosenthal Award from the National Institute of Arts and Letters (1962), a Ford Foundation grant (1964–1965), a National Endowment for the Arts grant (1967–1968), a Before Columbus Foundation American Book Award (1984), and a MacArthur Fellowship in 1992.

Martin, Judith (b. 1938)

Judith Martin, or "Miss Manners," as she is known to the readers of her widely syndicated column of the same name, has set herself the task of improving the etiquette of Americans, "because people cannot stand the abrasiveness level of this society anymore." A 1959 graduate of Wellesley College, Martin has published several collections of her columns as well as etiquette books, including *The Name on the White House Floor* (1973), *Miss Manners' Guide to Excruciatingly Correct Behavior* (1981), *Miss Manners' Guide to Rearing Perfect Children* (1984), and *Common Courtesy: In which Miss Manners Solves the Problem that Baffled Mr. Jefferson* (1985). She has also written two comedies of manners, *Gilbert* (1982) and *Style and Substance* (1986). Martin's latest book is *Miss Manners' Guide for the Turn-of-the-Millennium* (1989). "The Pursuit of Politeness" was originally delivered as a lecture at Harvard University before it was published in *The New Republic*.

McPhee, John (b. 1931)

Before becoming one of the most revered staff writers of *The New Yorker,* John McPhee had sent the magazine more than one hundred "pieces of writing" that were rejected. By the time the magazine finally accepted a piece from him in 1963, McPhee had worked as a playwright for the television show *Robert Montgomery Presents* and submitted pieces to *Time*. McPhee still lives in his native Princeton, where he has been the Ferris Professor of Journalism at Princeton University since 1975. Author of scores of articles and more than twenty critically acclaimed books, McPhee has written about topics ranging from pinball to plate tectonics, with numerous forays into art, sports, cooking, and medicine. "Ideas are a dime a dozen. They just stream by," he explains. Books such as McPhee's early effort *Oranges* (1967), his own favorite *The Survival of the Bark Canoe* (1975), and his biographical pieces *Rising from the Plains* (1986) and *Encounters with the Archdruid* (1972) have tempted some to label McPhee an "environmental writer." But he has written so compellingly on the hard sciences that the Geological Society of America nominated him a fellow in 1986 and then awarded him the U.S. Geological Survey's John Wesley Powell Award in 1988. Later that year, McPhee was also elected to the American Academy and Institute of Arts and Letters. McPhee's best-known work is *Coming into the Country* (1977), and a sample of his writings can be found in *The John McPhee Reader* (1977), *Table of Contents* (1985), and *Pieces of the Frame* (1975), in which this essay originally appeared. His most current publications are *Outcroppings* (1988), *The Control of Nature* (1989), *Looking for a Ship* (1990), and *Assembling California* (1993).

Momaday, N. Scott (b. 1934)

N. Scott Momaday was born on a Kiowa Indian reservation in Oklahoma and grew up surrounded by the cultural traditions of the Kiowa people. He earned his B.A. from the University of New Mexico in 1958 and his Ph.D. from Stanford University in 1963. Momaday has taught at the University of California at Santa Barbara and at Berkeley, and at Stanford University. Since 1982, he has been professor of English at the University of Arizona. His first novel, *House Made of Dawn* (1968), won a Pulitzer Prize,

Momaday is also the author of poetry and autobiography, and has edited a collection of Kiowa oral literature. His most recent publications are *Ancestral Voice: Conversations with N. Scott Momaday* (1989), *The Ancient Child* (1989), and *In the Presence of the Sun: Stories and Poems* (1991). He contributes regularly to the *New York Times Book Review* and other national periodicals; "A First American Views His Land" was published in *National Geographic* in 1976. Wallace Stegner observes that "Momaday has not invented himself, as many Americans have tried to do. He has let the blood speak, looked for tracks, listened and remembered. . . . He has pieced together a tradition and created his ancestors . . . They empty like feeder streams into the river of his sensibility and awareness. He comes out of them." Among other honors, Momaday has been awarded an Academy of American Poets Prize (1962), a Guggenheim Fellowship (1966–1967), and a National Institute of Arts and Letters grant (1970).

Naylor, Gloria (b. 1950)

Gloria Naylor's first novel, *The Women of Brewster Place* (1982), won an American Book Award. Her other works of fiction include *Linden Hills* (1985), *Mama Day* (1988), and *Bailey's Café* (1992), and her nonfiction has been published in *Centennial* (1986). In addition to these books, Naylor contributes essays and articles to many periodicals, including *Southern Review, Essence, Ms., Life, Callaloo,* and *The Ontario Review.* Also, she recently founded One Way Productions, an independent film company which she established to bring the novel *Mama Day* to the screen. Naylor holds an M.A. in Afro-American studies from Yale University. She has worked as the "Hers" columnist for the *New York Times* and as a visiting professor and writer at Princeton University, New York University, the University of Pennsylvania, Boston University, and Brandeis University. In addition, Naylor was a cultural exchange lecturer in India in 1985 and a senior fellow at the Society for the Humanities, Cornell University, in 1988. The article "A Question of Language" first appeared in the *New York Times* in 1986.

Njeri, Itabari

Itabari Njeri won the American Book Award for her 1990 book *Every Good-bye Ain't Gone: Family Portraits and Personal Escapades.* Before she became a writer, Njeri was a singer, and was named best new pop vocalist of 1969 by MGM Records. Her political commitments led Njeri to become a journalist in the 1970s, and she earned degrees in communications and journalism from Boston University and Columbia University. Njeri has published articles and essays in *Harper's, Essence,* and other national magazines; currently, she writes for the *Los Angeles Times,* where she specializes in immigration issues and cultural diversity. Her numerous awards include an Associated Press Award, two UNITY Awards, and the Los Angeles Press Club Certificate of Excellence. "Who Is Black?" originally appeared in *Essence* in September 1991.

Noda, Kesaya E. (b. 1950)

Kesaya Noda was born in California and raised in New Hampshire.

She began to study Japanese after graduating from high school, and spent eighteen months living and studying in Japan. After finishing college, Noda wrote her first book, *The Yamato Colony* (1981), a history of the community in California where her grandparents settled and where her parents grew up. "Growing Up Asian in America" is found in *Making Waves,* an anthology of Asian-American writing. Noda holds a master's degree from Harvard Divinity School and is currently working toward her doctorate in religious studies at Harvard University.

Oppenheim, Irene (b. 1939)

Irene Oppenheim began her writing career as a dance and theater critic. She has been a correspondent for *Dance Magazine* and has had essays, articles, and reviews published in *New West,* the *Village Voice,* the *New York Times,* and the *Los Angeles Times.* In addition to her work as an essayist and journalist, Oppenheim began writing plays in 1980. Since then, she has won several national competitions, a number of her works for stage and radio have been produced, and she has been awarded grants by the National Endowment for the Arts and the California Arts Council. In her teens Oppenheim landed an after-school job walking a deaf Doberman pinscher. Since then her long and still increasing list of jobs (many of which she has written about) include stints as a waitress, interviewer for a mental health survey, receptionist, and editor of a children's book about tooth fairies. "On Waitressing" originally appeared in *The Threepenny Review.* Beyond serving "as a guide into a world that to many is as

unfamiliar as a foreign country," Oppenheim feels the essay also demonstrates that writers are lucky people. After all, she maintains, for those who write, "even the dreariest of life's activities may reemerge as good subject matter."

Orwell, George (1903–1950)

George Orwell was born Eric Arthur Blair in Bengal, India, the son of a colonial administrator. He was sent to England for his education, and attended Eton on a scholarship, but rather than go on to university in 1922 he returned to the East and served with the Indian Imperial Police in Burma. Orwell hated his work and the colonial system; published posthumously, the essay "Shooting an Elephant" was based on his experience in Burma. The essay "Politics and the English Language," although first published in 1946, is found in the same collection, *Shooting an Elephant and Other Essays* (1950). In 1927 Orwell returned to England and began a career as a professional writer. He served briefly in the Spanish Civil War until he was wounded, then settled in Hertfordshire. Best remembered for his novels *Animal Farm* (1945) and *Nineteen Eighty-Four* (1949), Orwell also wrote articles, essays, and reviews, usually with a political point in mind. In 1969 Irving Howe honored Orwell as "the best English essayist since Hazlitt, perhaps since Dr. Johnson. He was the greatest moral force in English letters during the last several decades: craggy, fiercely polemical, sometimes mistaken, but an utterly free man."

Percy, Walker (1916–1990)

Walker Percy received his M.D. in 1941 and began a career practicing and teaching medicine shortly thereafter. However, as a resident physician he contracted tuberculosis, and the disease changed the course of his life. During his recovery he read extensively in literature, philosophy, and theology, and this reading program became the basis for a new career of reading and writing. His first novel, *The Moviegoer* (1961), won a National Book Award. He wrote a number of other novels, including *The Thanatos Syndrome* (1987), as well as works of nonfiction such as *Lost in the Cosmos* (1983) and *The Message in the Bottle* (1975). The latter work contains the essay "The Loss of the Creature." The critic Alfred Kazin called Percy a "philosopher among novelists," and commented that there "is a singularity to his life, to his manifest search for a new religious humanism, there is a closeness to pain and extreme situations, that makes him extraordinarily 'sensitive' — to the existentialist theme of life as shipwreck — without suggesting weakness."

Reed, Ishmael (b. 1938)

Ishmael Reed is a prolific writer who also finds time to support and encourage other writers; he has helped establish and manage the Yardbird Publishing Company, Reed, Cannon & Johnson (a publishing and video production company), and the Before Columbus Foundation, which supports the work of ethnic writers. He has also taught at Yale, Dartmouth, Columbia, and Harvard, and currently teaches at the University of California at Berkeley. Reed's work has been nominated for National Book Awards in both fiction (*Mumbo Jumbo*, 1972) and poetry (*Conjure: Selected Poems*,

1972). His essays are collected in *Shrovetide in Old New Orleans* (1978), and *God Made Alaska for the Indians* (1982). His poems are collected in the 1988 *New and Collected Poems*. His essay "America: The Multinational Society" appears in *The Graywolf Annual Five: Multicultural Literacy* (1988).

Little Rock Reed

Little Rock Reed is a mixed-blood Lakota who has been behind bars in an Ohio correctional facility for many years. When he is released from prison, Reed will be working as director of the Native American Prisoners' Rehabilitation Research Project in Villa Hills, Kentucky. "Broken Treaties, Broken Promises" is adapted from a book he has coauthored called *The American Indian in the White Man's Prisons: A Story of Genocide*, forthcoming from Snowbird Publishing Company.

Rich, Adrienne (b. 1929)

Adrienne Rich's work has appeared in numerous volumes of poetry and in several anthologies. She received her first award for poetry, a Yale Series of Younger Poets Award, while a student at Radcliffe College in 1951. Since then Adrienne Rich has received many other professional honors, including a National Institute of Arts and Letters Award (1961), a National Book Award (1974), a Fund for Human Dignity Award from the National Gay Task Force (1981), and the Lenore Marshall *Nation* Poetry Prize for her 1991 book, *An Atlas of the Difficult World*. Adrienne Rich's poetics are informed by her political work against the oppression of women and against homophobia, and her critics charge her with being overly polemical. As Margaret Atwood points out, however, Rich's politics do not limit her artistry for she "is not just one of America's best feminist poets or one of America's best woman poets, she is one of America's best poets . . . she is eloquent, she convinces, and inspires." Besides poetry, Rich's publications include *Of Women Born: Motherhood as Experience and Institution* (1976), *On Lies, Secrets and Silence: Selected Prose, 1966–1978* (1979), and *Blood, Bread and Poetry: Selected Prose* (1986), from which "Split at the Root" is excerpted. She has taught at many colleges and universities and since 1986 has been professor of English and Feminist Studies at Stanford University.

Rodriguez, Richard (b. 1944)

Richard Rodriguez earned his B.A. from Stanford University and did graduate work at Columbia University, the Warburg Institute in London, and the University of California at Berkeley, where he completed his Ph.D. in English Renaissance literature. Rodriguez has contributed articles to many magazines and newspapers, including *Harper's, Saturday Review, Neustro, American Scholar,* the *Los Angeles Times,* and the *New York Times,* in which "Toward an American Language" (published under a different title) appeared in 1989. His most sensational literary accomplishment, however, is his autobiography, *Hunger of Memory: The Education of Richard Rodriguez* (1987). In it, Rodriguez outlines his positions on such issues as bilingualism, affirmative action, and assimilation, and concludes that current policies in

these areas are misguided and only serve to reinforce current social inequalities. Rodriguez has been honored with a Fulbright Fellowship (1972–1973) and a National Endowment for the Humanities Fellowship (1976–1977). Currently, he works as an educational consultant, lecturer, and freelance writer. His most recent book is *Days of Obligation: An Argument with My Mexican Father* (1992).

Rose, Phyllis (b. 1942)

Phyllis Rose is perhaps best known by the reading public for her book reviews and essays, which appear in *The Nation, The Atlantic,* the *Washington Post,* and the *New York Times;* "Shopping and Other Spiritual Adventures" appeared in the *Times* in 1984. Rose is also the author of biographies of Virginia Woolf and Josephine Baker and of *Parallel Lives* (1983). Her essays are collected in *Never Say Goodbye* (1990). She has taught at Harvard, Yale, and Berkeley, and since 1976 has been professor of English at Wesleyan University. Phyllis Rose was an NEH fellow in 1973 and 1974, a Rockefeller Fellow in 1984 and 1985, and a Guggenheim Fellow in 1985.

Ruiz, Judy (b. 1944)

Judy Ruiz teaches writing at Southwest Missouri State University in Springfield, Missouri. Her poems have been widely published in various literary journals and have been collected in her book, *Talking Razzmatazz* (1991). Another collection of poems will be published soon. "Oranges and Sweet Sister Boy," which originally appeared in *Iowa Woman* in

1988, was selected for *The Best American Essays 1989.*

Sanders, Scott Russell (b. 1945)

Scott Russell Sanders writes in a variety of genres: science fiction, realistic fiction, folktales, children's stories, essays, and historical novels. In all his work, however, he is concerned with the ways in which people live in communities. Some of his more recent books include *Stone Country* (1986), *Bad Man Ballad* (1986), *The Paradise of Bombs* (1987), from which "The Men We Carry in Our Minds" is excerpted, *Secrets of the Universe: Scenes from the Journey Home* (1991), and *Staying Put: Making a Home in a Restless World* (1993). Sanders also contributes to both literary and popular magazines such as *North American Review, Georgia Review, Omni, Transatlantic Review,* and *New Dimensions.* For many years he wrote a column for the *Chicago-Sun Times.* Professor of English at Indiana University, Sanders has been honored as a Woodrow Wilson Fellow (1976–1978), a Marshall Scholar (1967–1971), a Bennett Fellow in creative writing (1974–1975), and a National Endowment for the Arts Fellow (1983–1984).

Schwartz, Lynne Sharon (b. 1939)

Lynne Sharon Schwartz attended Barnard College, Bryn Mawr College, and New York University. She has served as an associate editor of *The Writer* magazine, worked as a civil rights housing activist in New York City, and taught at Hunter College and New York University. Her first novel, *Rough Strife* (1980), was nominated for the American Book Award. She has also received the James Henle Award from

Vanguard Press (1974) and the Lamport Award from the Lamport Foundation (1977). Her translation from the Italian of Liana Millu's *Smoke over Birkenau* received the 1991 PEN Renato Poggioli Award. Her stories have been represented in many anthologies, including *The Best American Short Stories* (1978, 1979), *Banquet* (1979), and *O. Henry Prize Stories* (1979). Her other books include *Balancing Acts* (1981), *Disturbance in the Field* (1983), *Acquainted with the Night and Other Stories* (1984), *We Are Talking About Homes: A Great University Against Its Neighbors* (1985), *The Melting Pot and Other Subversive Stories* (1987), and *Leaving Brooklyn* (1989). Schwartz's work is collected in *The Lynne Sharon Schwartz Reader* (1992). "Beggaring Our Better Selves" originally appeared in *Harper's* in 1991.

Selzer, Richard (b. 1928)

Selzer, like Anton Chekhov, W. Somerset Maugham, and William Carlos Williams, is that rare breed of doctor who is also a writer. Both careers cross-pollinated each other for a long time, and Selzer has said that "A doctor walks in and out of a dozen stories a day. It is irresistible to write them down." Before leaving medicine to write full-time, Richard Selzer spent fifteen years teaching surgery at the Yale School of Medicine and running a private surgical practice. Selzer has published several books, including *Confessions of a Knife* (1979), *Letters to a Young Doctor* (1982), *Taking the World in for Repairs* (1986), *Imagine a Woman and Other Tales* (1990), *Down from Troy: A Doctor*

Comes of Age (1992), and *Raising the Dead* (Selzer's 1993 account of his near-death experience from Legionnaires' disease and his slow recovery). His essays have appeared in *Harper's, Esquire,* (where "What I Saw at the Abortion" first appeared in 1976), *Antaeus,* and many other magazines. He holds honorary degrees from the University of Pennsylvania Medical College, Georgetown Medical School, Union College, and Albany Medical College. He won the Pushcart Award for fiction in 1982, the American Medical Writers' Award in 1983, and a Guggenheim Fellowship in 1985. He has been a resident of Yaddo as well as the Rockefeller Foundation's Bellagio Study Center in Italy. He lives in New Haven, Connecticut.

Shilts, Randy (b. 1951)

Author and journalist Randy Shilts is widely regarded as the leading reporter on the AIDS epidemic. The nation's first openly gay journalist, Shilts has reported full-time since his graduation from the University of Oregon School of Journalism. After writing for *The Advocate,* Shilts worked as a reporter for KQED, San Francisco, and KTVU, Oakland. He is currently national correspondent for the *San Francisco Chronicle,* where he has worked since 1982. Shilts's familiarity with covering the AIDS epidemic resulted in his highly acclaimed best-seller, *And the Band Played On: Politics, People, and the AIDS Epidemic* (1987), which has been translated into six languages and released in fourteen nations. The book earned him the designation of Author of the Year in 1988 by the American Society of Journalists and Au-

thors. Shilts's first book, *The Mayor of Castro Street: The Life and Times of Harvey Milk* (1982), is currently being made into a feature film by director Oliver Stone. Shilts's syndicated stories have appeared in the *Washington Post,* the *Chicago Tribune,* the *New York Times,* and the *Village Voice,* among others. He was awarded the Media Alliance Award for outstanding nonfiction author and the Gay Academic Union Award for outstanding journalist in 1982. He has also received special citations from the San Francisco Board of Supervisors (1982, 1987), a Silver Medal from the Commonwealth Club for best nonfiction author of 1987, and the Outstanding Communicator award from the Association for Education in Journalism and Mass Communication (1988). Shilts's latest book is *Conduct Unbecoming: Gays and Lesbians in the U.S. Military* (1993). "Talking AIDS to Death" originally appeared in *Esquire.*

Soto, Gary (b. 1952)

Gary Soto was born and raised in Fresno, California. He attended Cal State Fresno and the University of California, Irvine. He has published eight collections of poetry, including *Black Hair* (1985), *Home Course in Religion* (1991), *Neighborhood Odes* (1992), and *The Elements of San Joaquin* (1977), which won the United States Award from the International Poetry Forum. Two more collections of verse, *Canto Familiar/Familiar Song* and *New and Selected Poems,* are forthcoming in 1994. Soto has also written and edited several collections of essays and short stories, the most recent of which are *Pieces of the Heart:*

New Chicano Fiction (editor; 1993), *Local News* (1993), and *Jesse* (1994). "Looking for Work" is from his autobiographical collection *Living Up the Street* (1985), which won the American Book Award. Soto has been awarded the Bess Hokin Prize and the Levinson Award from *Poetry*. He has also received the Andrew Carnegie Medal, the Discovery/the Nation Prize, and the California Library Association's John and Patricia Beatty Award, in addition to fellowships from the Guggenheim Foundation, the National Endowment for the Arts (twice), and the California Arts Council. Soto writes fiction for children as well, and he recently produced two films for public television. He lives in Berkeley, California, where he is senior lecturer in the English Department at the University of California, Berkeley.

Staples, Brent (b. 1951)

Brent Staples earned his B.A. from Widener University in 1973 and his Ph.D. in psychology from the University of Chicago in 1982, and has made his career in journalism. When he lived in Chicago, Staples wrote for *Chicago Magazine, The Chicago Reader,* and *Down Beat Magazine.* He also contributes to *Harper's, New York Woman,* the *New York Times Magazine,* and *Ms.,* in which "Just Walk on By" appeared in 1986. Since 1990 he has been on the editorial board of the *New York Times,* and currently he is writing his autobiography.

Steele, Shelby (b. 1946)

Shelby Steele earned his Ph.D. from the University of Utah in 1974, and is currently professor of English at San Jose State Univer-

sity. He has contributed articles and reviews to such periodicals as *Confrontation, Black World, Harper's,* and the *Western Humanities Review.* Steele's writings on race relations in the United States have placed him in the center of the national debate on affirmative action and other issues. "On Being Black and Middle Class" appeared in *Commentary* in 1988. Recently, Steele published his first book, *The Content of Our Character: A New Vision of Race in America* (1990).

Steinem, Gloria (b. 1934)

One of America's most prominent activists for women's rights, Gloria Steinem is the founding editor of *Ms.* magazine and has worked for many political organizations, including the National Women's Political Caucus, the Women's Action Alliance, and the Student Non-Violent Coordinating Committee. Steinem's writing career began before she became involved in politics, with *The Thousand Indians* (1957), based on two years spent living in India. Since 1958 Steinem's writing has focused on women's issues. She has written several books as well as scripts for TV and film, and has published articles in many magazines including *Esquire, Show, Vogue, Life,* and *Cosmopolitan.* The selection "Erotica vs. Pornography" comes from her collection of essays, *Outrageous Acts and Everyday Rebellions* (1983). Steinem's most recent publications are *Marilyn* (1986) and *Revolution from Within: A Book of Self-Esteem* (1992).

Swift, Jonathan (1667–1745)

Jonathan Swift was born and raised in Ireland, son of English parents. He was ordained an Anglican priest, and although as a young man he lived a literary life in London, he was appointed against his wishes to be dean of St. Patrick's Cathedral in Dublin. Swift wrote some poetry, but is remembered principally for his essays and political pamphlets, most of which were published under pseudonyms. Swift received payment for only one work in his entire life, *Gulliver's Travels* (1726), for which he earned £200. Swift's political pamphlets were very influential in his day; among other issues, he spoke out against English exploitation of the Irish. Some of Swift's more important publications include *A Tale of a Tub* (1704), *The Importance of the Guardian Considered* (1713), *The Public Spirit of the Whigs* (1714), and *A Modest Proposal* (1729).

Tan, Amy (b. 1952)

Amy Tan was born in California shortly after her parents immigrated to the United States from China. She started writing as a child and won a writing contest at age eight. As an adult, Tan made her living as a freelance business writer for many years, but started to write fiction in 1985. In 1987 Tan traveled to China for the first time, an experience that helped shape her consciousness of both her American and Chinese identities. In 1989 Tan published her best-selling first novel, *The Joy Luck Club,* followed by *The Kitchen God's Wife* (1991) and the children's book *The Moon Lady* (1992). "Mother Tongue" originally appeared in *The Threepenny Review* in 1990.

Thomas, Lewis (b. 1913)

Lewis Thomas was trained as a pathologist at Harvard Medical School and has pursued a distinguished career as a researcher and administrator at Tulane University, Bellevue Medical Center, and Yale University Medical School. He served as president and chancellor of Memorial Sloan-Kettering Cancer Center, and more recently as professor of pathology and medicine at Cornell University Medical School. Aside from a few poems, Thomas published mainly scientific articles and books until 1971, when he became a regular communist for the *New England Journal of Medicine* (in which "The World's Biggest Membrane" originally appeared). In 1974 his columns were collected in *The Lives of a Cell,* which became a best-seller and won an American Book Award. In a review of *The Lives of a Cell* Joyce Carol Oates commented that the book "anticipates the kind of writing that will appear more and more frequently, as scientists take on the language of poetry in order to communicate human truths too mysterious for old-fashioned common sense." Thomas continues to write about medical and biological issues for a general audience, and has published *The Medusa and the Snail* (1979), *Late Night Thoughts on Listening to Mahler's Ninth Symphony* (1983), *The Youngest Science* (1983), *The Lasker Awards: Four Decades of Scientific Medical Progress* (1986), *Et cetera, Et cetera: Notes of a Word-Watcher* (1990), and *The Fragile Species* (1992).

Thoreau, Henry David (1817–1862)

Regarded today as one of the central literary figures of the nineteenth century, in his lifetime Thoreau was for the most part viewed as a talented but largely unsuccessful disciple of Ralph Waldo Emerson. In fact, although the two men held many beliefs in common, Thoreau possessed a fiercely independent intellect together with political convictions that sometimes alienated Emerson. Thoreau articulates his thoughts on political activism in the essay "Civil Disobedience" (1849), which influenced the nonviolent strategies of both Mahatma Gandhi and Martin Luther King, Jr. Despite the considerable impact of his writing on contemporary thought, it was not until the 1930s that Thoreau's masterpiece, *Walden* (1845), began to be studied widely, and only more recently that the value of his other writings has been recognized. As Emerson observed, "One would say that, as Webster could never speak without an antagonist, so Henry [David Thoreau] does not feel himself except in opposition. He wants a fallacy to expose, a blunder to pillory, requires a little sense of victory, a roll of the drums, to call his powers into full exercise." In addition to philosophical and biographical essays, Thoreau wrote poetry, speeches, and natural history. Halfway through his two-year stay on Walden Pond, Thoreau took a backwoods vacation in Maine. He wrote an account of his journey in *The Maine Woods,* which was published serially in *Sartain's Union Magazine* in 1848.

Tisdale, Sallie (b. 1957)

A writer and part-time nurse, Sallie Tisdale has written two books on the nursing profession, *The Sorcerer's Apprentice* (1986) and *Harvest Moon* (1987). She also contributes articles to *Harper's,* in which "A Weight that Women

Carry" appeared in 1993. Her most recent books are *Lot's Wife: Salt and the Human Condition* (1988) and *Stepping Westward: The Long Search for Home in the Pacific Northwest* (1991).

Twain, Mark (1835–1910)

Mark Twain, the pseudonym of Samuel Clemens, was a master satirist, journalist, novelist, orator, and steamboat pilot. He grew up in Hannibal, Missouri, a frontier setting which appears in different forms in several of his novels, most notably in his masterpiece *Adventures of Huckleberry Finn* (1869). His satirical eye spared very few American political or social institutions including slavery, and for this reason, as well as because it violated conventional standards of taste, *Huckleberry Finn* created a minor scandal when it was published. Nonetheless, with such books as *The Innocents Abroad* (1869), *Roughing It* (1872), *Old Times on the Mississippi* (1875), *The Adventures of Tom Sawyer* (1876), and *The Prince and the Pauper* (1882), Twain secured himself a position as one of the most popular authors in American history. "The Damned Human Race" comes from *Letters from the Earth* (1938). Twain built his career upon his experiences in the western states and his travels in Europe and the Middle East, but he eventually settled in Hartford, Connecticut. His last years were spent as one of the most celebrated public speakers and social figures in the United States.

Walker, Alice (b. 1944)

Alice Walker was awarded the Pulitzer Prize and the American Book Award for her second novel, *The Color Purple* (1982), which has subsequently been made into a popular film. This novel helped establish Walker's reputation as one of America's most important contemporary writers. In both her fiction and nonfiction she shares her compassion for the black women of America whose lives have long been largely excluded from or distorted in literary representation. Walker is also the author of other novels, short stories, several volumes of poetry, a children's biography of Langston Hughes, essays, and criticism. Her work has been recognized with a Lillian Smith Award (1979), a Rosenthal Award (1973), and a Guggenheim Foundation Award (1979). Her most recent books are *The Temple of My Familiar* (1989), and *Possessing the Secret of Joy* (1992). The essay reprinted here comes from her 1983 collection, *In Search of Our Mothers' Gardens*. In addition to writing, Alice Walker has been a civil rights activist and has taught at numerous universities including Wellesley, Yale, Brandeis, and the University of California at Berkeley. Currently, she runs a publishing company, Wild Trees Press.

West, Cornel (b. 1953)

Grandson of a Baptist preacher in Tulsa, Oklahoma, Cornel West decided that he would attend Harvard College after reading a biography of Theodore Roosevelt and learning that the former president had also suffered from an asthma problem. After receiving degrees from Harvard as well as Princeton, West went on to teach at Union Theological Seminary and then at the Divinity School at Yale University, where he had a joint appointment with the American Studies department. In addition,

West has taught at Harvard University and at the University of Paris, and since 1988 he has directed the Afro-American Studies department at Princeton University, where he also teaches religion. West, who is hailed as a "black Jeremiah" by literary critic Henry Louis Gates, Jr., describes his particular brand of philosophy as "a rapprochement between the best of liberalism, populism, and democratic socialism that takes race, class, and gender seriously." This "prophetic pragmatism" informs his most recent book, *Race Matters* (1993), in which this essay appeared as the introduction. West's previous publications include *Prophecy Deliverance! An Afro-American Revolutionary Christianity* (1982), *Prophetic Fragments* (1988), *The American Evasion of Philosophy* (1989), *The Ethical Dimensions of Marxist Thought* (1991), and *Breaking Bread: Insurgent Black Intellectual Life* (1991). He also coedited *Post-Analytic Philosophy* (1985) and *Out There: Marginalization and Contemporary Cultures* (1990).

White, E. B. (1899–1985)

Elwyn Brooks White started contributing to *The New Yorker* soon after the magazine began publication in 1925, and in the "Talk of the Town" and other columns helped establish the magazine's reputation for precise and brilliant prose. Collections of his contributions can be found in *Every Day Is Saturday* (1934), *Quo Vadimus?* (1939), and *The Wild Flag* (1946). He also wrote essays for *Harper's* on a regular basis; these essays include "Once More to the Lake" and are collected in *One Man's Meat* (1941). In his comments on this work, the critic Jonathan

Yardley observed that White is "one of the few writers of this or any century who has succeeded in transforming the ephemera of journalism into something that demands to be called literature." Capable of brilliant satire, White could also be sad and serious, as in his compilation of forty years of writing, *Essays* (1977). Among his numerous awards and honors, White received the American Academy of Arts and Letters Gold Medal (1960), a Presidential Medal of Freedom (1963), and a National Medal for Literature (1971). He made a lasting contribution to children's literature with *Stuart Little* (1945), *Charlotte's Web* (1952), and *The Trumpet of the Swan* (1970).

Williams, Joy (b. 1944)

A 1965 graduate of the University of Iowa Writers' Workshop, Joy Williams grew up in Cape Elizabeth, Maine. She still considers herself a New Englander, despite the fact that she now lives in Key West, Florida, the setting that inspired her to write *The Florida Keys: A History and Guide* (1987). Williams's first novel, *State of Grace* (1973), was received with wide critical acclaim. She subsequently published two more novels, *The Changeling* (1978) and *Breaking and Entering* (1988), and two collections of short stories, *Taking Care* (1982) and *Escapes* (1989). She has received a National Endowment for the Arts grant (1973), a Guggenheim Fellowship (1974), and a Strauss Living Award from the American Academy of Arts and Letters (1993). Williams's fiction has been extensively anthologized, appearing in such collections as *The O. Henry Prize Story*

Collection, The Best American Short Stories, and *American Short Story Masterpieces.* Her nonfiction includes articles on sharks, James Dean, the electric chair, and the environment. "The Killing Game" originally appeared in *Esquire* and was reprinted in *The Best American Essays 1992.* Williams has taught at the University of Houston; the University of Florida, the University of California, Irvine; the University of Iowa, and the University of Arizona.

Woolf, Virginia (1882–1941)

One of the most important writers of the twentieth century, Woolf's innovations in indirect narration and the impressionistic use of language are now considered hallmarks of the modern novel and continue to influence novelists on both sides of the Atlantic. Together with her husband Leonard Woolf she founded the Hogarth Press, which published many experimental works that have now become classics, including her own. A central figure in the Bloomsbury group of writers, Woolf established her reputation with the novels *Mrs. Dalloway* (1925), *To the Lighthouse* (1927), and *The Waves* (1931). The feminist movement has helped to focus attention on her work, and Woolf's nonfiction has provided the basis for several important lines of argument in contemporary feminist theory. *A Room of One's Own* (1929), *Three Guineas (1938), and The Common Reader* (1938) are the major works of nonfiction published in Woolf's lifetime; posthumously, her essays have been gathered together in *The Death of the Moth* (where the essay reprinted here appears) and in the four-volume *Collected Essays.*

Acknowledgments (Continued from page iv)

James Baldwin, "Stranger in the Village." From *Notes of a Native Son* by James Baldwin. Copyright © 1955, renewed 1983 by James Baldwin. Reprinted by permission of Beacon Press.

Wendell Berry, "The Journey's End." From *Recollected Essays 1965–1980* by Wendell Berry. Copyright © 1981 by Wendell Berry. Reprinted by permission of North Point Press, a division of Farrar, Straus & Giroux, Inc.

Sissela Bok, "Gossip." From *Secrets: On the Ethics of Concealment and Revelation* by Sissela Bok. Copyright © 1982 by Sissela Bok. Reprinted by permission of Pantheon Books, a division of Random House, Inc.

Haig A. Bosmajian, "The Language of Oppression." Reprinted by permission of the University Press of America.

Susan Brownmiller, "Let's Put Pornography Back in the Closet." Copyright © 1979 by Susan Brownmiller. This article originally appeared in *Newsday*.

Raymond Carver, "My Father's Life." Reprinted by permission of Tess Gallagher. Copyright © 1984 by Tess Gallagher.

Sucheng Chan, "You're Short, Besides!" From *Making Waves* by Asian Women United. Copyright © 1989 by Asian Women United. Reprinted by permission of Beacon Press.

Judith Ortiz Cofer, "Silent Dancing." Reprinted with permission from the publisher of *Silent Dancing: A Partial Remembrance of a Puerto Rican Childhood* (Houston: Arte Publico Press—University of Houston, 1990).

Bernard Cooper, "A Clack of Tiny Sparks: Remembrances of a Gay Boyhood." Copyright © 1990 by *Harper's Magazine*. All rights reserved. Reprinted from the January 1991 issue by special permission.

Amy Cunningham, "Why Women Smile." Reprinted by permission of the author.

Joan Didion, "On Keeping a Notebook." From *Slouching Towards Bethlehem* by Joan Didion. Copyright © 1966, 1968 by Joan Didion. Reprinted by permission of Farrar, Straus & Giroux, Inc.

Annie Dillard, "Seeing." From *Pilgrim at Tinker Creek* by Annie Dillard. Copyright © 1974 by Annie Dillard. Reprinted by permission of HarperCollins Publishers Inc.

Gerald Early, "Life with Daughters: Watching the Miss America Pageant." First published in *The Kenyon Review* — New Series, Fall 1992, Vol. XIV, No. 4. Copyright © 1992 by Kenyon College. Reprinted by permission of the author and *The Kenyon Review*.

Lars Eighner, "On Dumpster Diving." Copyright © 1991 by Lars Eighner. From the book *Travels with Lizbeth* and reprinted with permission from St. Martin's Press, Inc., New York, NY.

Nora Ephron, "A Few Words about Breasts." Reprinted by permission of International Creative Management, Inc. Copyright © 1972 by Nora Ephron.

Leslie Epstein, "Civility and Its Discontents." Copyright © 1991, New Prospect Inc. Reprinted by permission from *The American Prospect*, Summer 1991.

Susan Faludi, "Blame It on Feminism." From *Backlash* by Susan Faludi. Copyright © 1991 by Susan Faludi. Reprinted by permission of Crown Publishers, Inc.

Paul Fussell, "A Well-Regulated Militia." Copyright © 1988 by Paul Fussell. Originally appeared in *The New Republic*. Reprinted by permission of Simon & Schuster, Inc.

Mary Gordon, "More than Just a Shrine: Paying Homage to the Ghosts of Ellis Island." Copyright © 1985 by The New York Times Company. Reprinted by permission.

Stephen Jay Gould, "Sex, Drugs, Disasters, and the Extinction of Dinosaurs." Reprinted from *The Flamingo's Smile: Reflections in Natural History* by Stephen Jay Gould, by permission of W. W. Norton & Company, Inc. Copyright © 1985 by Stephen Jay Gould.

Francine du Plessix Gray, "I Write for Revenge against Reality." Reprinted by permission of Georges Borchardt, Inc. for the author.

Jeff Greenfield, "The Black and White Truth about Basketball." Reprinted by permission of the Sterling Lord Literistic, Inc. Copyright © 1975, 1993 by Jeff Greenfield.

Pete Hamill, "Crack and the Box." Reprinted by permission of International Creative Management, Inc. Copyright © 1990 by Pete Hamill.

Daniel R. Harris, "Effeminacy." Reprinted by permission of the author.

Linda M. Hasselstrom, "Why One Peaceful Woman Carries a Pistol." From *Land Circle: Writings Collected from the Land,* by Linda M. Hasselstrom, Fulcrum Publishing, Inc., 350 Indiana St., #350, Golden, CO 80401 (303) 277–1623.

bell hooks, "Feminism: A Transformational Politic." Reprinted by permission of South End Press and between the lines.

Langston Hughes, "Salvation." From *The Big Sea* by Langston Hughes. Copyright © 1940 by Langston Hughes, renewed in 1968 by Arna Bontemps and George Houston Bass. Reprinted by permission of Hill and Wang, a division of Farrar, Straus & Giroux, Inc.

Zora Neale Hurston, "How It Feels to Be Colored Me." Reprinted by permission of Clifford J. Hurston, Jr.

Edward Iwata, "Race without Face." Reprinted by permission of the author.

June Jordan, "Nobody Mean More to Me than You and the Future Life of Willie Jordan." Reprinted by permission of the author.

Satoshi Kamata, "Six Months at Toyota." From *Japan in the Passing Lane* by Satoshi Kamata, trans. by Tatsuru Akimoto. Translation copyright © 1982 by Tatsuru Akimoto. Reprinted by permission of Pantheon Books, a division of Random House, Inc.

Jamaica Kincaid, "On Seeing England for the First Time." Copyright © 1991 by Jamaica Kincaid, reprinted with the permission of Wylie, Aitken & Stone, Inc. First appeared in *Transition.*

Martin Luther King, Jr., "Letter from Birmingham Jail." Reprinted by arrangement with The Heirs to the Estate of Martin Luther King, Jr., c/o Joan Daves Agency as agent for the proprietor. Copyright © 1963 by Martin Luther King, Jr., copyright renewed 1991 by Coretta Scott King.

Maxine Hong Kingston, "No Name Woman." From *The Woman Warrior* by Maxine Hong Kingston. Copyright © 1975, 1976 by Maxine Hong Kingston. Reprinted by permission of Alfred A. Knopf, Inc.

Jonathan Kozol, "Distancing the Homeless." From *Rachel and Her Children: Homeless Families in America,* Crown 1988, copyright © by Jonathan Kozol.

Barry Lopez, "The Stone Horse." Reprinted by permission of Charles Scribner's Sons, an imprint of Macmillan Publishing Company, from *Crossing Open Ground* by Barry Lopez. Copyright © 1988 by Barry Holstun Lopez. (First appeared in *Antaeus* magazine Autumn, 1986).

Audre Lorde, "The Master's Tools Will Never Dismantle the Master's House." Copyright © 1984 by Audre Lorde, excerpted from *Sister Outsider,* The Crossing Press, Freedom, CA.

Nancy Mairs, "A Letter to Matthew." Reprinted from *Plaintext,* by Nancy Mairs, by permission of the University of Arizona Press, copyright © 1986.

Paule Marshall, "From the Poets in the Kitchen." First appeared in *The New York Times Book Review.* Copyright © by Paule Marshall. Reprinted by permission of the author.

Judith Martin, "The Pursuit of Politeness." Reprinted by permission of *The New Republic,* copyright © 1984, The New Republic, Inc.

John McPhee, "Pieces of the Frame." From *Pieces of the Frame* by John McPhee. Copyright © 1970, 1975 by John McPhee. Reprinted by permission of Farrar, Straus & Giroux, Inc. Published in Canada by Macfarlane, Walter & Ross, Toronto.

N. Scott Momaday, "A First American Views His Land." Reprinted by permission of the author.

Gloria Naylor, "A Question of Language." Copyright © 1986 by Gloria Naylor. Reprinted by permission of Sterling Lord Literistic, Inc.

Itabari Njeri, "Who Is Black?" *Essence,* September 1991.

Kesaya E. Noda, "Growing Up Asian in America." From *Making Waves* by Asian Women United. Copyright © 1989 by Asian Women United. Reprinted by permission of Beacon Press.

Irene Oppenheim, "On Waitressing." Reprinted by permission of the author.

George Orwell, "Politics and the English Language." Copyright © 1946 by Sonia Brownell Orwell and renewed 1974 by Sonia Orwell, reprinted from his volume *Shooting an Elephant and Other Essays* by permission of Harcourt Brace & Company, the estate of the late Sonia Brownell Orwell, and Martin Secker & Warburg Ltd.

George Orwell, "Shooting an Elephant." From *Shooting an Elephant and Other Essays* by George Orwell, copyright © 1950 by Sonia Brownell Orwell and renewed 1978 by Sonia Pitt-Rivers, reprinted by permission of Harcourt Brace & Company.

Walker Percy, "The Loss of the Creature." From *The Message in the Bottle* by Walker Percy. Copyright © 1975 by Walker Percy. Reprinted by permission of Farrar, Straus & Giroux, Inc.

Ishmael Reed, "America: The Multinational Society." Reprinted with the permission of Atheneum Publishers, an imprint of Macmillan Publishing Company from *Writin' Is Fightin'* by Ishmael Reed. Originally in *San Francisco Focus,* December 1983. Copyright © 1983 by Ishmael Reed.

Little Rock Reed, "Broken Treaties, Broken Promises." Reprinted with permission from *The Other Side,* 300 West Apsley, Philadelphia, PA 19144. This article is extracted from a chapter of the soon-to-be-published essay collection, *The American Indian in White Man's Prisons: A Story of Genocide.*

Adrienne Rich, "Split at the Root: An Essay on Jewish Identity." Abridged, from *Blood, Bread, and Poetry: Selected Prose 1979–1985,* by Adrienne Rich, with the permission of the publisher, W. W. Norton & Company, Inc. Copyright © 1986 by Adrienne Rich.

Richard Rodriguez, "Toward an American Language." Copyright © 1989 by Richard Rodriguez. Reprinted by permission of Georges Borchardt, Inc., for the author.

Phyllis Rose, "Shopping and Other Spiritual Adventures in America Today." From *Never Say Good-bye* by Phyllis Rose. Copyright © 1991 by Phyllis Rose. Used by permission of Doubleday, a division of Bantam Doubleday Dell Publishing Group, Inc.

Judy Ruiz, "Oranges and Sweet Sister Boy." First published in the Summer 1988 *Iowa Woman* magazine. Reprinted by permission of the author.

Scott Russell Sanders, "The Men We Carry in Our Minds." Copyright © 1984 by Scott Russell Sanders; first appeared in *Milkweed Chronicle*; reprinted by permission of the author and Virginia Kidd, Literary Agent.

Lynne Sharon Schwartz, "Beggaring Our Better Selves." Reprinted by permission of International Creative Management, Inc. Copyright © 1991 by Lynne Sharon Schwartz.

Richard Selzer, "What I Saw at the Abortion." Copyright © 1976 by Richard Selzer. Reprinted by permission of Georges Borchardt, Inc., for the author.

Randy Shilts, "Talking AIDS to Death." Copyright © Randy Shilts. Reprinted by permission.

Gary Soto, "Looking for Work." From *Living Up the Street,* by Gary Soto. Copyright © 1985 by Gary Soto. Used by permission of Strawberry Hill Press, Portland, Oregon.

Brent Staples, "Just Walk on By: A Black Man Ponders His Power to Alter Public Space." Reprinted by permission of the author.

Shelby Steele, "On Being Black and Middle Class." Reprinted from *Commentary,* January 1988, by permission; all rights reserved.

Gloria Steinem, "Erotica vs. Pornography." From *Outrageous Acts and Everyday Rebellions* by Gloria Steinem. Copyright © 1983 by Gloria Steinem. Copyright © 1984 by East Toledo Productions, Inc. Reprinted by permission of Henry Holt and Company, Inc.

Amy Tan, "Mother Tongue." First published in *The Threepenny Review.* Copyright © 1990 by Amy Tan. Reprinted by permission of the author.

Lewis Thomas, "The World's Biggest Membrane." Copyright © 1971, 1972, 1973 by The Massachusetts Medical Society, from *The Lives of a Cell* by Lewis Thomas. Used by permission of Viking Penguin, a division of Penguin Books USA Inc.

Sallie Tisdale, "A Weight that Women Carry." Copyright © 1993 by *Harper's Magazine.* All rights reserved. Reprinted from the March issue by special permission.

Mark Twain, "The Damned Human Race." From *Letters from the Earth* by Mark Twain.

Index
of Authors and Titles